THE WAYS OF THINGS

A PHILOSOPHY OF
KNOWLEDGE, NATURE, AND VALUE

PRENTICE-HALL PHILOSOPHY SERIES

ARTHUR E. MURPHY, PH. D., EDITOR

PERCEPTION AND AESTHETIC VALUE, *by* Harold Newton Lee.

FORMAL LOGIC, *by* Albert A. Bennett *and* Charles A. Baylis.

PROBLEMS OF ETHICS, *by* Moritz Schlick. *Translated by* David Rynin.

THE WAYS OF THINGS, *by* Wm. Pepperell Montague.

A PHILOSOPHY OF RELIGION, *by* Edgar S. Brightman.

THE WAYS OF THINGS

A PHILOSOPHY OF KNOWLEDGE, NATURE, AND VALUE

BY

WM. PEPPERELL MONTAGUE

PROFESSOR OF PHILOSOPHY, BARNARD COLLEGE, COLUMBIA UNIVERSITY; AUTHOR OF "THE WAYS OF KNOWING," "BELIEF UNBOUND," AND "THE CHANCES OF SURVIVING DEATH"; CO-AUTHOR OF "THE NEW REALISM."

NEW YORK : PRENTICE-HALL, INC.

1940

PRINTED IN THE UNITED STATES OF AMERICA

TO

JOHN HENRY MUIRHEAD

WITH AFFECTION AND RESPECT

PREFACE

MY BOOK is an experimental undertaking in that it seeks to introduce philosophy to the reader by two quite different procedures. First, in Part One, I have given a very condensed but comprehensive survey of the whole field of philosophy, its typical theories and schools of thought, its general problems, and my own tentative solutions of those problems. Second, in Part Two, I have dealt with special problems of many kinds in the domains of Knowledge, Nature, and Value. The justification for appending to a systematic survey of philosophy a series of essays published at various times and for various occasions is that the latter specifically illustrate and develop the more general ideas of the former. And the disadvantage of the diversity of subject matter in the second part is offset by the opportunity it offers for different types of readers, or for the same readers in different moods, to pursue their varied interests. For the convenience of those reading the book, the essays are classified in two groups. Those marked with an asterisk (*) require for their understanding no previous knowledge of philosophy. Those not so marked presuppose some acquaintance either with philosophy or with science.

Most of the articles in Part Two, and especially those on Relativity, the Quantum, and the Fourth Dimension, are experiments in speculation. I have taken the risk of suggesting possible solutions of problems for which science has as yet no actual solutions. Philosophers oft rush in where scientists fear to tread, and all philosophizings are in a broad sense experiments, or, in Whitehead's phrase, "adventures in ideas." But philosophy can be likened not only to an experiment and an adventure, but also to a game in which, as in that other royal and ancient game, the veriest duffer may make some perfect shots. It is, however, a game in which one plays not just for fun, but in earnest too. The stakes are high and the players should be warned that heartbreak or confusion may be their lot when once they leave the shelter of some authoritarian creed and venture out alone to face the universe. Despite these risks of tragic failure, I think that we should hold the faith that Socrates proclaimed and in defense of which he gave his life—the faith that freedom of thought is not only a privilege but a right, and not only a right but a duty. Anyone who regards himself as a rational being is under a sacred obligation to submit his beliefs about nature and human duty to a critical examination, and, in the light of all the evidence available, work out, however tentatively, a philosophy of thought and action. Everyone should do this, and everyone *can* do this. And if the philosophy which I present in this volume serves in some measure to arouse its readers to construct a philosophy for themselves, one of my aims will be achieved.

But in addition to the desire to make others philosophize, I have a more personal desire to win consideration for my own philosophy, its logic, and its ethics, and, even more, for those postulates on which its metaphysical hypotheses depend. These postulates are three:

I. That consciousness is neither separate from material motion nor just an aspect of it, but is itself a high and special form of that same energy which manifests itself in matter and in life.

II. That nature is not only running down but also running up, and, in its long ascent from protons and electrons to the souls within our brains, displays the same strange type of power that we experience as mind.

III. That, therefore, there is more than mere analogy between what is highest in our inner selves and deepest in reality.

On these three postulates (and just a touch of mystical experience) my system of philosophy is based.

Acknowledgments

For advice and assistance in the organization of the material of this book, and for preparation of the questions contained in the Appendix, I am deeply indebted to my friend and former student, Dr. Pasquale Romanelli, of the department of philosophy in Brooklyn College. I am also grateful to my two colleagues at Barnard, Dr. Gertrude V. Rich, who helped in preparing the manuscript and made some important suggestions, and Professor Helen H. Parkhurst, who has given me continuous counsel and performed the arduous labor of making the Index.

There are two other friends and colleagues, both of them mathematicians, from whose wisdom I have been enlightened: Professor Cassius Jackson Keyser and Professor Edward Kasner. From the one I gained a new appreciation of the beauty and objective reality of mathematical forms; from the other, a realization of the gay and varied uses to which a creative mathematical imagination can be put. And in this context it would be appropriate to thank two other mathematicians: Professor W. M. Whyburn, of the University of California, for his valuable technical comments on my article on the Rainbow Series, and Professor Jekuthiel Ginsberg, of Yeshiva College, for systematizing those comments.

For permission to reprint articles that have appeared under their auspices, I have to thank the editors of *Religious Realism, Philosophy, Scripta Mathematica, The Philo-*

sophical Review, *The International Journal of Ethics*, *The Proceedings of the Aristotelian Society*, *The Journal of Philosophy*, *The New Republic*, and *The Saturday Review of Literature*, and lastly, my old friend, Dr. J. McKeen Cattell, Editor of *The Scientific Monthly*. For similar courtesies I am indebted to the following publishers: The Macmillan Company, Henry Holt, Longmans, Green, The Columbia University Press, The University of California Press, The Oxford University Press, Hermann et Cie and Félix Alcan of Paris, and Allen and Unwin of London. Specific acknowledgments are noted at the beginning of each of the essays that are reprinted.

W. P. M.

Barnard College
Columbia University
February 20, 1940

CONTENTS

PAGE

PREFACE vii

PART ONE

AN INTRODUCTION TO PHILOSOPHY

FOREWORD. PHILOSOPHY: ITS MEANING, AFFILIATIONS, AND DIVISIONS 3

Chapter I. Knowledge and the Ways of Knowing: Formal Logic 18

Chapter II. Knowledge and the Ways of Knowing (*Continued*): Material Logic 38

Chapter III. Knowledge in Relation to Nature: Epistemology 52

Chapter IV. Nature and the Ways of Being: Metaphysics of the Macrocosm . 77

Chapter V. Nature and the Ways of Being (*Continued*): Metaphysics of the Microcosm 93

Chapter VI. Nature in Relation to Value: Theology 110

Chapter VII. Value and the Ways of Liking: Esthetics 124

Chapter VIII. Value and the Ways of Liking (*Continued*): Ethics, Individual and Social 140

Part Two

EXPERIMENTS IN PHILOSOPHY

PAGE

Prologue. The Vision of Philosophy 171

Section I. Formal Logic 173

*1. On the Nature of Induction 173

A new analysis of Mill's canons or methods of induction by the use of which uniform or causal correlations of phenomena are disentangled and isolated from those that are temporary or casual. It presupposes some knowledge of formal logic.

*2. A Defense of Causality 182

An argument to establish, as the basis of inductive inference, the hypothesis that causal tendencies are really operative in nature. It is shown that the alternative to that hypothesis is infinitely improbable and would entail a world of perpetual miracle and incredible runs of luck.

3. The Rainbow Series and the Logarithm of Aleph Null 189

An illustrative example of the way in which induction, deduction, and imagination were employed in the discovery of a new infinite series and a new series of infinites. It presupposes some knowledge of algebra.

Section II. Material Logic 203

*4. The Antinomy and Its Implications for Logical Theory 203

An analysis of "antinomic" situations such as those presented in Zeno's famous puzzles about motion where Sense and Reason, the major cri-

PAGE

*4. The Antinomy and Its Implications for Logical Theory (*Continued*)

teria of belief, appear to be in irreconcilable conflict. The paper reveals the need for a Material Logic consisting in the enumeration and comparative evaluation of the methods of attaining knowledge.

SECTION III. EPISTEMOLOGY 230

*5. The Story of American Realism 230

An informal history and criticism of epistemological tendencies in recent philosophy in the United States. It presupposes some knowledge of philosophy.

6. Truth Subsistential and Existential . . . 262

An analysis and comparison of the Platonic realm of abstract forms and the physical realm of particular events in space and time. It presupposes a knowledge of philosophy.

SECTIONS IV AND V. METAPHYSICS 281

*7. Beyond Physics 281

An untechnical and impressionistic sketch of the novelties of present-day physics and their philosophic implications.

8. The Einstein Theory and a Possible Alternative 295

A comparatively untechnical summary of the theory of Relativity, its philosophical implications, and its picturesque paradoxes, followed by the description of an alternative hypothesis and a possible experiment for testing it. It presupposes some knowledge of physics.

PAGE

9. A Possible Interpretation of the Quantum . 327

A comparatively untechnical and impressionistic sketch of the Quantum theory combined with suggested hypotheses for the solution of its three outstanding problems: (1) the greater energy of shorter light waves; (2) the photon as wave or particle; (3) the structure of the atoms from which photons are emitted. It presupposes some knowledge of physics.

10. A Theory of Time Perception 363

An attempt to explain the paradox of the "specious present," that is, the appearance at each present instant in time of a segment of the past, by the hypothesis of a limiting differential ratio of the velocity of change of the field of consciousness as a whole to the velocity of change of its several components. Some implications and applications of this hypothesis are developed. Some knowledge of psychology and mathematics is presupposed.

11. Time and the Fourth Dimension 382

The Howison Lecture for 1925. An exposition and defense of a hypothesis, partly similar to and partly different from Einstein's, in which time is regarded as a fourth dimension of space. From this hypothesis is derived (1) a conception of electrons and protons as four-dimensional "hills" and "hollows," and (2) a conception of the memory-system or soul as a four-dimensional magnitude developed in the brain but not dependent upon it.

12. Substance, Potentiality, and Cause: A Positivistic Theory of Rationalistic Categories 408

In the present essay is developed a theory designed to serve as a reconciliation of Positivism and Rationalism. According to this theory the

PAGE

12. Substance, Potentiality, and Cause: (*Cont.*) rationalistic or extra-experiential categories are accepted as valid; but it is shown how they can be interpreted in positivistic or intra-experiential terms. It is proposed: I. To offer a definition of the rationalistic category of Substance and of its derivatives, Potentiality and Cause. II. To analyze and appraise the attitudes of rationalists and of positivists toward these categories. III. To establish a compromise theory and to explain its affiliations with the metaphysical systems of Bergson and Descartes.

*13. A Materialistic Theory of Emergent Evolution 418

A quantitative interpretation of the various qualitative levels of life that successively emerge in the course of evolution. The whole process of development from the simplest protoplasm to the highest forms of spiritual life is depicted as a transformation of mechanical or externally determined systems in which kinetic energy is dominant into teleological or self-determining systems in which potential energy is dominant. It presupposes a little knowledge of biology.

14. Variation, Heredity, and Consciousness . 441

An analysis of the mechanistic and vitalistic interpretations of variation, heredity, and consciousness, combined with an exposition and defense of the theory that these three basic aspects of life are expressions of protoplasm's capacity to accumulate within itself intensive hierarchies of potential energy. It presupposes some knowledge of biology and psychology.

*15. Consciousness a Form of Energy 482

A systematic account of the analogies between a field of consciousness as experienced from

PAGE

*15. Consciousness a Form of Energy (*Cont.*)
within and a field of potential energies as experienced from without, followed by a demonstration of the probable identity of the two fields. It presupposes some knowledge of psychology.

SECTION VI. THEOLOGY 511

*16. The Promethean Challenge to Religion . 511
A plea for a new orientation in religion in which the life-affirming and rationalistic attitudes of the anticlerical opponents of the church can be combined with a belief in God and in the possibility of a mystic communion with Him.

17. The Trinity—A Speculation 531
An exposition and defense of a trinitarian theory of the world-ground, somewhat similar to the Christian theory, but providing for a different conception of the origin of evil. An attempt to reconcile the idea of a God limited in power with the idea of a God infinite and all-embracing. It presupposes some knowledge of philosophy and theology.

*18. The Two Immortalities 540
A brief argument in support of personal immortality and an appeal for a more effective commemoration of the less known members of universities and other great social organizations.

SECTION VII. ESTHETICS 550

*19. The True, the Good, and the Beautiful from a Pragmatic Standpoint 550
Truth, goodness, and beauty are depicted as sharply contrasting species of one and the same genus.

PAGE

*20. Beauty Is Not All: An Appeal for Esthetic Pluralism 560

An appeal to artists to supplement their creations of beauty or objectified joy with creations in which any emotion, even the most painful and terrible, is objectified, to the end that art may cease to be a sophisticated affair of the studios and become once more a power in the life of the people.

SECTION VIII. ETHICS 564

*21. The Philosophy of Friedrich Nietzsche . . 564

A comparison of the strong and weak points in the philosophy of Nietzsche with the strong and weak points of the Christian philosophy.

22. The Missing Link in the Case for Utilitarianism 584

An attempt to provide a basis for the higher and lower qualities of pleasure, recognized by John Stuart Mill, without departing from the conception essential to utilitarianism that all differences in value are quantitative.

*23. The Geometry of the Good Life . . . 600

The account of a new law of values—the "law of increasing returns"—in accordance with which values are strengthened by concentration and weakened by diffusion, resulting in an "ethical dualism" calling for one tactic for enhancing good and an opposite tactic for diminishing evil.

*24. Democracy at the Crossroads 612

An analysis of Liberalism, Parliamentarianism, and Capitalism as the three components of Democracy, in the light of the challenge of Total-

PAGE

*24. Democracy at the Crossroads (*Continued*)
itarianism, followed by a plan of ECONOMIC DUALISM, by means of which the essentials of democracy could be saved.

POSTSCRIPT. CONFESSIONS OF AN ANIMISTIC MATERIALIST 648
One of a series of intellectual autobiographies in which American teachers of philosophy were asked to explain for the benefit of their students how they arrived at their conclusions.

APPENDIX 679
Questions on Part I 679
Questions on Part II 685

INDEX 697

PART ONE

AN INTRODUCTION TO PHILOSOPHY

FOREWORD

PHILOSOPHY: ITS MEANING, AFFILIATIONS, AND DIVISIONS

PHILOSOPHY, meaning literally "the love of wisdom," is the vaguest, oldest, and most comprehensive of all organized inquiries. It is the attempt to gain a reasoned conception of the universe and man's place in it. How and what can we learn about reality? What should we value in it? And what may we hope from it?

I. Philosophy and Religion

Philosophy resembles religion in its subject matter but differs from it in its spirit and method. Every great religion embodies a vision of the world and of man's place in it, and in that respect resembles a system of philosophy. But a religion is in general accepted by its followers on the basis of authority. It is viewed as a revelation of divine truth to be taken on faith and with a spirit of humility. A philosophy, on the other hand, is a work of the human mind, attained by a union of intellectual analysis and creative imagination. As such, its conclusions call for criticism and doubt rather than for loyal submission. From the predominantly rational character of philosophy there results a further difference between it and religion. A religion is, in general, something to be emotionally experienced and given a practical realization in life. It is mainly a matter of feeling and action, while philosophy is mainly a matter of thought. If we wished to condense into a single phrase both the likeness and the difference of the two disciplines, we could characterize religion as a philosophy of the heart and the will, and philosophy as a religion of the mind. Finally, there is a difference between philosophy and religion that is secondary rather than primary, yet one that has had important historical consequences. Feeling and practice are largely social in character; they are embodied in ritual and custom, and pertain to a group. Thinking, and especially imagining and questioning, are affairs not of a group but of an individual; and Professor Whitehead's characterization of religion as what a man does with his solitude would seem to apply better to philosophy. The philosopher goes alone to his study to ponder and speculate. The religionist goes with his neighbors to the church of his fathers to celebrate in prayers and hymns their common faith. A religion is a philosophy only to its founder; to its followers it is not something to be personally thought about and questioned, but something to be socially accepted and followed. Once a philosophy has become a religion by being accepted by a group and made incarnate in its social tissues, it often develops an antagonism to the enterprise of philosophy itself because, to the latter, suspension of judgment and freedom of thought are vital necessities. For these reasons conflicts between the religionists who have already accepted a creed and the philosophers who are still seeking one have been many and momentous, and they will probably continue.

II. Philosophy and Art

The relation of philosophy to art is not so deep as its relation to religion, but it deserves to be noted.

The essence of art is to present an imaginative synthesis (fraught with emotion and meeting the needs of emotion) of some concrete matter of sensory experience—shapes, colors, tones, or even words and their meanings. The philosopher takes for the object of his synthesis not some specific sensory experiences, but the broader and deeper possibilities of Being that are disclosed to his intellectual vision, and his aim is the satisfaction of reason rather than of emotion. But, granting this difference of theme and aim, the procedure of the philosopher is more like that of the artist than the philosopher himself often cares to admit. All inquiry is a compound of experiential facts, with an imaginative synthesis and supplementation of them formulated in a theory. But the relative proportions of the two components greatly vary, and in general the broader and deeper the problem to which the inquiry is addressed, the less the component of assured facts and the greater the component of creative imagination. The maker of a vast system of philosophy may appear in his own eyes to be a scientist on a grand scale, but to his observers and critics he will seem more like an artist who has supplemented a small body of facts with a large body of fancy. Such merit as the product may possess will then be due not to its actual truth but to the novelty, unity, and symmetry imposed by the philosopher's own temperament, which he has in some sense projected and objectified in his portrait of the cosmos.

This resemblance of a philosophy to art is good as well as bad, for it means that philosophy at its best will be a vision of the possible and probable rather than a certainty of the actual, while even at its worst and furthest from scientific truth it will have at least something of the unity and beauty of an artistic creation.

III. Philosophy and Science

The relation of philosophy to science is in a way the reverse of its relation to religion. Instead of being similar in aim and contrasting in method and spirit, philosophy and science are similar in temper and attitude but different, though not opposite, in their goals. Science aims at retail or specific truth, philosophy at wholesale or generic truth. But the procedure of both is that of free intellectual inquiry in a spirit of sceptical and critical seeking for the new rather than of submissive loyalty to ancient authority and dogma.

From the standpoint of our diagram, philosophy, especially metaphysics, has been called *scientia scientiarum*. But we must realize that many scientists would repudiate their kinship to philosophers, and would maintain that there was more difference than similarity between the imaginative visions of philosophy and the empirically verified conclusions of science. Yet, even if this be admitted, it must also be admitted that the philosophic theories of one age have sometimes become the scientific truths of a later age, as witness the hypotheses of atoms and of evolution. And, as William James pointed out, so soon as a philosophic problem is definitely solved, it is automatically claimed as a part of science, with the result that philosophy is, as it were, left "holding the bag," and restricted to questions that have not yet been answered. The philosopher can, however, console himself with the realization that the problems which have not been solved and which are still matters for speculation are the deepest, broadest, and most momentous of all the problems that the mind can contemplate.

IV. The Divisions of Philosophy

The field of philosophy can be roughly but not inaccurately divided into three primary topics of inquiry and two that are secondary.

The three primary or elementary divisions are:

The Logical inquiry into Knowledge and the *Ways of Knowing*, subdivided into Formal and Material Logic.

The Metaphysical inquiry into Nature and the *Ways of Being*, subdivided into the Metaphysics of the Universe or Macrocosm and of the Individual or Microcosm.

The "Kalological" inquiry into Value and the *Ways of Liking*, subdivided into Esthetics and Ethics.

The two secondary or composite topics are:

The Epistemological inquiry into the Relation of Knowledge to Nature, which belongs between Logic and Metaphysics.

The Theological inquiry into the Relation of Nature to Value, which belongs between Metaphysics and Kalology.

This series of themes adequately covers the main subject matter of philosophy not only as we shall treat it in this book, but as it has been treated in the past. Though there is a certain novelty in the arrangement which we have adopted and in some of the names which we have used, most of the topics to which the captions refer are those of traditional philosophy. The full meaning of the formidable words in the classification can be made plain only in the chapters to follow, where each of the eight final divisions of philosophy—Formal Logic, Material Logic, Epistemology, Metaphysics of the Macrocosm, Metaphysics of the Microcosm, Theology, Esthetics, and Ethics—will be taken up in the order in which they are listed, and the typical problems and theories connected with them briefly set forth and explained.

But prior to that more detailed treatment, something in the way of general elucidation would seem to be in order.

Knowledge and the Ways of Knowing: Logic. The logical inquiry as to the ways of knowing is concerned with the question of *how our beliefs are derived and justified.* Take, for example, our belief that Socrates is mortal. I can *deductively* justify that belief by referring it to and inferring it from two other beliefs: that Socrates is a man and that man is mortal. Or again, I can *inductively* justify the belief that women in general could use the suffrage advantageously on the ground that the women of Sweden, of Finland, of New Zealand, and other communities have done so. Now the ways in which beliefs that are always expressible as propositions can be justified or proved by being referred to other beliefs or propositions constitutes the domain of Formal Logic, Deductive and Inductive. But formal logic is *relative* logic. It derives propositions from other propositions, which in turn are derived from still others, and so on. Such a process cannot keep on indefinitely. Sooner or later there must be propositions or beliefs that are accepted at first hand or on grounds more fundamental than that of being implied by other propositions of the same sort. The problem of what we have called "Material Logic," the second subdivision of Logic, is the problem of discovering these first principles or ultimate grounds for beliefs which are the sources of the material and of the validity of all knowledge. And the sense in which formal logic is relative is the sense in which material logic is absolute. But in spite of, or rather because of, its aim at absoluteness, material logic lacks the precision and the certainty of the less pretentious discipline of formal logic.

Nature and the Ways of Being: Metaphysics. The nature of the second of the three primary divisions of philosophy and its two aspects can be conveniently shown by means of a small classificatory diagram which I like to call the "Wheel of Knowledge."

We shall represent the sciences, or rather the great groups of sciences, as the spokes of a wheel, and we shall follow the principle of Auguste Comte in arranging them in the order that begins with the most abstract and generic and that ends with the most concrete and specific. In such a scheme *mathematics* has a claim to first place because it deals with that whole network of abstract and formal relationships (those of space and number being only the most familiar) which no possibly existent universe can violate. We can, for example, imagine the existence of a world without minds and of a world without apples, but we cannot imagine a world in which either 31 apples or 31 minds, if they did exist, could fail to be equal to $20 + 11$ or $47 - 16$. Abstract forms and relations do not *enjoin* the existence of *anything*, but they *prohibit* the existence of everything that violates them.

Next in generality to mathematics we might put *physics*, which deals with the "laws" or invariant relations common to all forms of matter and energy. And next to physics could come *chemistry*, where the emphasis is on the differences of substances and the laws pertaining to them rather than upon the qualities common to all. The laws of chemistry presuppose the more general laws of physics, as the latter presuppose the still more general laws of mathematics.

Of all the physico-chemical compounds, the most interesting is that called *protoplasm*, which has the peculiar capacity to grow and reproduce—in short, to "live." And it is *biology*, the science or group of sciences dealing with physical life, that comes next in the series. Its laws presuppose the laws of chemistry, but they supplement those more general laws with a specific content of their own.

Now, as living is the most interesting and peculiar of chemical processes, so thinking or even just being *conscious* is the most interesting and peculiar of living processes. An organism that not only can grow and reproduce, but that can somehow mirror or represent in its internal states and processes the external things and relations of the environment and then react to the *here and now* in the light of the *there and then*, guiding its immediate response to objects by their relation to what is past and future in time and distant in space—such an organism is "minded," or, as we say, "has a mind." It is not just *in* the world; it is "aware of" or "conscious of" the world. This most important and peculiar function, which some, if not all, living beings can exercise, deserves a special organized inquiry. *Psychology* is the name for that inquiry, and its more special laws presuppose and supplement the more generic laws of biology.

And now lastly, a most important (some would say the most important) thing that beings with minds can also do, is to *huddle together* in many different ways, and by their collective or "social" activity create that peculiar product known as *culture*. This variegated outcome of interrelated minds, especially of the human type, is studied by the *social sciences* or—if a single word can cover so vast and heterogeneous a field—by *sociology*, which makes the last of the sciences or science-groups upon our list. And the laws of sociology or of the social sciences, pertaining as they do to the behavior of minds in groups, presuppose the psychological laws, which are primarily concerned with the mental behavior of individuals.

We now have the six fundamental branches of science: Mathematics, Physics, Chemistry, Biology, Psychology, and Sociology, each of them (except, of course, the first) logically dependent on its predecessor. And all of them are to be represented as the successive spokes of a wheel. This is the "Wheel of Knowledge," but so far there is nothing to bind the spokes together. It is this binding or unifying function which *metaphysics* aspires to perform. There are many who will feel that such a function is as gratuitous as it is grandiose. Who knows whether there is any unity in the field of science? And are not the professional scientists themselves better qualified to discover whatever there may be of deep-lying and far-flung relations between their special domains than meddlesome amateurs calling themselves metaphysicians, ontologists, and cosmologists? Perhaps. And yet even if the rebukes implied in these questions be deserved, there is to them an unanswerable retort. Metaphysics, whether a good or a bad thing, is at least a necessary thing in the sense that the urge to it is irresistible. Accepting humbly and gratefully from the sciences their verified discoveries of the truth of this and this and that and that, we must still ask, *What is it all about?* What is the nature of things, and where do we come in? To most of the people some of the time and to some of the people most of the time, such queries make an appeal that will not down. And not until the noble capacity for *wonder* has deserted the human soul will metaphysics cease. And after all, what is there to be afraid of? A metaphysician has nothing to lose but his claims, and a world to gain—a world in which there is the certainty of that solemn joy which comes only from meeting and grappling face to face and hand to hand with the greatest problems of existence; a world, furthermore, in which there is always the possibility of extracting from the products of creative imagination some nuggets of deep and precious truth.

So now, with no further apologies, let us bind together the spokes of our wheel of science in the two ways in which spokes are usually bound—at the hub and at the rim. And we will let the hub symbolize ontology, which is the analytic aspect of metaphysics concerned with the presuppositions of science—the basic concepts and categories which the scientists take for granted as defining their special fields. Like good workmen who are so busy using their tools that they have little time or inclination to criticize and compare them and must leave that task to someone else, so the workers in science seeking to discover the laws that operate in the domains of categories such as space, time, energy, life, minds, and so forth, can leave to the metaphysical ontologists the business of comparing, analyzing and systematizing those categories themselves. But this inquiry into the fundamental aspects of what Aristotle called "Being as such" is only a part (and the least profitable part) of the metaphysical enterprise. Besides the roots of science, there are its fruits to be considered. And it is the latter that provide the subject matter of cosmology, which is the synthetic half of metaphysics. *The metaphysician as cosmologist interests himself in the far-flung conclusions of the sciences rather than in their deep-lying assumptions.*

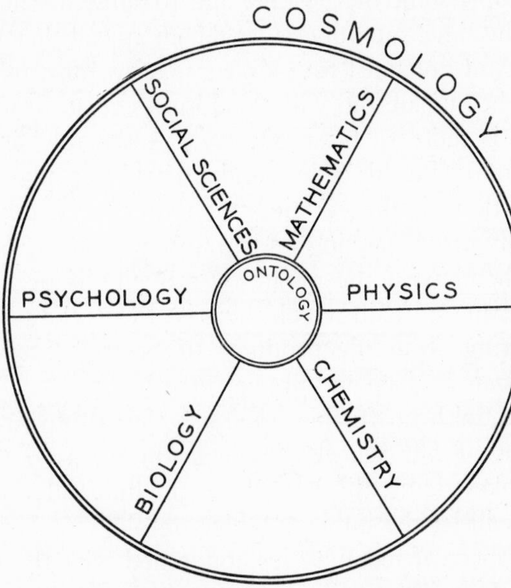

FIG. 1. THE WHEEL OF KNOWLEDGE.

Accepting these conclusions with humble gratitude, he seeks to piece them together as the parts of a picture-puzzle and gain from their synthesis a bird's-eye view of the universe as a whole. Cosmology as thus conceived is really the more interesting of the two aspects of metaphysics, and, as you will have guessed, its place in our diagram will be at the *rim* of the "Wheel of Knowledge." The wheel as now completed includes the generalized, or metaphysical, as well as the scientific, or specialized, inquiries into the nature of existence. And what it has taken many words to describe can now be seen at a glance in a rough but not inaccurate diagram of man's actual and potential knowledge of the world in which he lives. (See Figure 1.)

Although it is important to understand, as exhibited on the "Wheel of Knowledge," the distinction between ontology and cosmology, which are, respectively, the analytic and the synthetic aspects of metaphysics, it is hardly practicable to carry out the distinction in an elementary exposition of metaphysics such as is undertaken in Chapters IV and V. For that purpose it seemed better to depart from the diagram and to divide the metaphysical problems into those that concern the universe as a whole (metaphysics of the macrocosm) and those that concern the individual (metaphysics of the microcosm).

Value and the Ways of Liking: Kalology. "Value" is the somewhat commercial-sounding name which is used in philosophy to characterize any object, situation, process, or quality, real or imaginary, that elicits from anyone a favorable response, that is, an attitude of enjoying, desiring, approving, or liking. To *like* anything is to accord it *value.* Raspberries and cream, a warm bath, the works of Titian and Beethoven, courage, kindness and justice, strength and fame, saints and heroes, friends, parents, children, animals, and flowers—all of these are "values" or "have value" to the extent that they or the ideas of them are, in one way or another, regarded with favor or *liked.* The ways of valuing are, in short, the ways of liking, and they are as various as the kinds of things that are liked; but there are at least two quite general types of division or classification which are especially significant: there are intrinsic and instrumental values and there are sensory and non-sensory values. The first of these divisions is self-explanatory. Some things are liked in and for themselves, while others are liked because they are a means to the intrinsic values which result from them or are associated with them. These two groups do not necessarily exclude each other, for there are, of course, things that are valued both for themselves and for what they will bring. The second division of values into the sensory and the non-sensory is less obvious and more important, for on it is based the traditional distinction between Esthetics and Ethics. Esthetics as generally understood is concerned with value or likableness as embodied in sensory qualities and their relational patterns, notably the visual qualities of size, shape, and color, and the auditory qualities of tone, timbre, and rhythm.

Value of this sensory or esthetic type is usually called "beauty." The other type of value is not embodied in sensory objects, but in the conduct or character of persons. Such qualities, for example, as generosity, honesty, and loyalty elicit an attitude of liking of the kind that we call approval, respect, or admiration. These invisible and inaudible values constitute "goodness" or "virtue," and the branch of inquiry concerning them is called "ethics."

It is convenient to have a single name to cover both these branches of the theory of value. And I have chosen *Kalology* because the Greek word *kalos* was used to designate the invisible beauties of character as well as the beauties of sensible objects. Other words that have been suggested, such as *axiology* and *agathology*, are, by their etymology, more definitely restricted to the ethical types of value. And then, too, even if *kalos* and its derivative should suggest to us more of an emphasis on the beautiful than on the moral, I should regard that as in itself a good fault. *Ethics* and *morals* are singularly inappropriate names for that nobility of character which we ought to strive to produce in ourselves and in those we love. The words are derived from the Greek *ta ethika*, and the Latin *mores*, both meaning "customs." And customs, when made explicit and backed up by force, become "laws."

Hence, the notion has been ingrained that goodness, righteousness, or virtue is a matter of conformity to law, and obedience to authority. But there is no worth in obedience or conformity merely as such. If a law or custom is itself evil, and works for suffering and injustice, it is disobedience rather than obedience that is called for.

Let the word *kalology*, awkward and unfamiliar though it be, serve to remind us that as the arts aim at beauty in the objects of sense, so the art of life, or what by a poisoned etymology we call "morality," should aim at beauty of the spirit such as is exemplified in sympathy, justice and courage.

Now that the three primary divisions of philosophy—Logic or the Ways of Knowing, Metaphysics or the Ways of Being, and Kalology or the Ways of Liking—have been defined and briefly explained, it will be in order to consider the two secondary or composite divisions of our subject: Epistemology, which is concerned with Knowledge in relation to Nature, and Theology, which is concerned with Nature in relation to Value.

Knowledge in relation to Nature: Epistemology. There are things that *appear* as objects of sense or of thought to an individual at each instant of his waking life, and there are things that are *real* whether or not they appear as perceptual or conceptual objects. What is the relation of this world of *appearance* which each of us *experiences* to the world of *reality* in which each of us *believes?* This is the theme of what is called "epistemology."

From the naïve viewpoint of a little child anything and everything that appears is believed to be real; but as the child grows older, he learns to make a distinction between appearance and reality. He finds, for example, that what appears on the other side of the looking glass is really not in front of him at all but behind him, and that what he takes to be a friend at a distance turns out on a nearer view to be a stranger or perhaps not a person at all. Then, again, the happenings of his dreams, which seem real enough at the time, cannot be fitted into the world of his waking experience; and he is forced to regard them as "unreal." Nor is the child's growing disillusionment limited to the domain of sensory appearances. He will learn that not only his senses but his thought also may be in error. At the time when he is punished by his parent he may think of the latter as an enemy actuated by hatred for him. But later when he comes to realize the sin or danger involved in the deed for which he was punished, he will discover that his chastiser was not an enemy but a friend, and that his earlier judgment was false because what it asserted was not a reality. Thus does the child quickly gain the view that things are not always what they seem, and that the world of seeming or of appearance somehow depends upon and is to be explained by the world of reality.

How are these two worlds related? Are they partly identical or overlapping? Is the world of appearance a copy, sometimes good and sometimes bad, of the world of reality? And, if that is so and all that can appear or that can be directly apprehended at any moment is but a copy of the real, how can we know reality itself at all? May it be that *reality* is merely a pretentious and misleading name for a later and more adequate appearance? In the light of what I believe at present or what seems now to be real, the objects of any earlier belief or experience will be regarded as mere appearance to whatever extent they disagree with the beliefs experienced at this moment; but what if that which I now call reality should at some still later moment be rejected as false and thus in its turn be relegated to the realm of mere appearance?

All questions such as these concern the relation of knowing to being—or of what seems to be real to what really is real, and in the third chapter of our first Part we shall have to consider more carefully the problems themselves and give some account of the principal epistemological theories that have been advanced as solutions.

But let us pass now to the second of the composite branches of philosophy in which the connection between metaphysics and kalology constitutes the theme of discussion.

Nature in relation to Value: Theology. Is there, in addition to the specific values exemplified in parts of the world, any general or basic value pertaining to the world as a whole or embodied in its core? Those who answer this question in the affirmative may be said to have a "theology." For they believe in a *Theos* or *God,* which is goodness incarnate in nature, an ideal realized in existence, a power that is at once stronger and higher than ourselves. A deity is, thus, always an object with two aspects, a *metaphysical* or existential aspect and a *kalological* aspect, of worth or value.

There are various theological theories as to the kind of value that is embodied in the universe as a whole and as to the manner in which it is made manifest. And there is also the atheological or atheistic theory of those who can find no evidence of other than special and finite values in nature. What these theories are, what arguments are used in their support, and what problems they involve will be taken up in Chapter VI.

Our Foreword is now completed, and we turn from the survey of philosophy as a whole to a more detailed treatment of its eight principal parts.

CHAPTER I

KNOWLEDGE AND THE WAYS OF KNOWING: FORMAL LOGIC

FORMAL LOGIC is, by long tradition and custom, regarded as a philosophic discipline, but it has been systematized with such completeness and precision that it has more resemblance to a branch of mathematical science than to the vague and general themes of philosophy.

Aristotle, the real creator of logic, makes two great assumptions which constitute the foundation for his entire doctrine. The first of these assumptions is to the effect that all of the judgments or propositions by which beliefs are expressed can be regarded, irrespective of their particular subject matter, as *relations between classes.* *Class* means any collection of things which possess a character or group of characters in common, and the word or group of words designating a class is called a *term.* A class may have any number of members from one to infinity. Relations between classes are of many kinds. Concerning two classes, *A* and *B*, *A* may be larger or smaller than *B*, loved or hated by *B*, near to or remote from *B*, ancestor or descendant of *B*, and so forth. But the second great assumption of Aristotle was that underlying and presupposed by all other relations between classes are *four* primary relations, one or the other of which must always hold between any two classes whatever. These four primary or fundamental relations are such that if *S* is any class and *P* is any other class, it will always be true that *S* is either totally included in *P* or at least partially included in *P*, or that it is totally excluded from *P* or at least partially excluded from *P*. Any belief put into words or symbols is a proposition, and any proposition, however much else it may express, *must* express at least one of these four relations. The four kinds of proposition, with their symbols, are usually written:

A All *S* is *P*.
I Some *S* is *P*.
E No *S* is *P*.
O Some *S* is not *P*.

The symbols *A*, *I*, *E*, and *O* are taken, not from the Greek used by the founder of logic, but from the Latin, which was used by later philosophers in the elaboration and interpretation of Aristotle's thought. *A* and *I*, the first and second vowels of the verb *affirmo*, symbolize, respectively, the two affirmative relations of total and partial inclusion of the subject class *S* within the predicate class *P*. *E* and *O*, the first and second vowels of the verb *nego*, symbolize, respectively, the two negative relations of total and partial exclusion of the subject class *S* from the predicate class *P*.

Now the real business of formal logic, as we have already said, is reasoning or proof, that is, the substantiation of a proposition which is questioned or challenged, by tying it up to propositions that are already accepted. But in view of Aristotle's preliminary assumptions as to classes and their relations, concerning which we have just been speaking, there is a preliminary or introductory part of logic that consists in (1) the analysis by way of Definition and Division of the terms or *classes* which are related in propositions; (2) the Reduction of the complex statements of ordinary speech to one or the other of the four highly formalized types of proposition symbolized by *A*, *I*, *E*, and *O*; (3) the "Immediate Inferences" from each of the four types of proposition to the other three, and to the propositions involving the same two terms *S* and *P* but derived from them primarily by change in the order of the terms and in their positive or negative qualities.

Once the preliminaries are over, the logician is ready for his main task, the investigation and evaluation of the methods by which propositions can be proved "formally" (that is, irrespective of their specific subject matter) by reference to other propositions. The two principal ways in which such proof is accomplished are "deduction" and "induction."

Induction is much the more important branch of proof, but it has not been elaborated and systematized with anything like the thoroughness that has been achieved in deduction.

Now, deduction assumes the truth of universal propositions as premises for its demonstrations, while induction, starting from the bottom, as it were, seeks to derive and justify those universals. I shall therefore follow the wise though novel plan adopted by my late friend and colleague, Professor Adam Leroy Jones, of letting induction precede deduction.

Inductive logic is the art or science of proving universal conclusions by appealing to particular premises. The universal proposition will usually express a causal law or invariant relation of coexistence or sequence in nature, such as, "Water always quenches fire"; or "The quantity of mass is always conserved unchanged through every chemical reaction or qualitative alteration." To prove conclusions like these we have to take for our premises the particular cases presented in experience. Thus, we have perceived that water quenches fire at this, that, and the other time and place and under this, that, and the other set of circumstances; and from these particular observations we infer that water will always quench fire. And again, in the same way we infer that mass is always conserved, from the many cases in which, under greatly varied conditions, the alteration in appearance that occurs to a body undergoing a chemical reaction (for example, the change of wood into smoke and ashes by combustion) is followed—if we are careful to take account of all the components in their new form—by no change in weight or mass.

The particular experiences which are our data are expressible as particular propositions, and the problem of induction is the problem of how, when, and why we can prove that all *S* is *P* from premises that tell us only that some *S* is *P*. We can diagram the inductive inferences as follows:

$$\begin{array}{l} s_1 \text{ is } P \\ s_2 \text{ is } P \\ s_3 \text{ is } P \\ \quad\cdot \\ \quad\cdot \\ \quad\cdot \\ \hline \therefore \text{ Any } s \text{ or all } S \text{ is } P. \end{array}$$

Aristotle himself, though he recognized induction, wrote little about it that was of value. The nineteenth-century British philosopher, John Stuart Mill, has given what is generally regarded as the classic presentation of the subject, and his methods or canons of induction, especially those which he called "agreement," "difference," and "concomitant variation," are undoubtedly valid ways of distinguishing the causal and essential relations between phenomena from the casual and irrelevant connections with which they are entangled in experience.

In the essay entitled "On the Nature of Induction,"[1] I have given a summary and attempted an interpretation of Mill's methods. But despite the efforts of Mill and his many later followers, the formal logic of induction is not

[1] Pages 173–181.

very satisfactory for the reason that the nature of inductive procedure is determined almost entirely by the specific nature of the subject matter. Hence, it is the scientists themselves who will devise their own methods of investigation; and the little that the logician can add as to the general form apart from any particular matter is apt to be rather empty and trite.

The great philosophical problem involved in the logic of induction is the problem of justifying the fundamental postulate required for any universal inference from the particular facts presented in experience. This postulate is usually called, after Mill, the "Uniformity of Nature," meaning that what has happened in the past will happen in the future if the conditions are the same. Thus, when by Mill's methods, or in any other way, we have discovered an invariant relation like that between water and the quenching of fire or between the respective masses of a body before and after it has undergone a chemical change, we are faced with a question as to our right to infer that *what has been uniformly the case in the past will continue to be uniformly the case in the future.* We *assume* that it will be, but is this assumption upon which all inductive science proceeds anything more than an *act of blind faith?* To this crucial question logic has found no really satisfactory answer, and it remains one of the many unsolved problems of philosophy. I will not speak further of it here because I have analyzed and dealt with it as best I could in the essay entitled "A Defense of Causality," which is the second of the studies comprising Part II of this volume.

Let us now pass on to the deductive branch of formal logic, which accepts and employs as its premise at least one of the universal propositions that induction is assumed to have justified.

The conclusion proved by a simple deductive argument

or syllogism is a proposition expressing one or the other of the four primary relations between two classes: a subject class *S* and a predicate class *P*. These four relations are, as we have already noted: *A*, all *S* is *P*; *I*, some *S* is *P*; *E*, no *S* is *P*; *O*, some *S* is not *P*. The proposition thus constituting the "conclusion" of a syllogism is proved by reference to two other propositions constituting the "premises" of the syllogism. The subject *S* of the conclusion is called the "minor" term because its extension or scope is usually less than that of the predicate term *P*, which is therefore called the "major" term. Each of the two premises expresses a relation of inclusion or exclusion between one term of the conclusion and a third or middle term, *M*, which thus serves as a connecting link or bridge between the subject *S* and the predicate *P* of the conclusion. The premise connecting the middle term with the predicate, or major term, of the conclusion is called the "major premise" and is usually put first. The premise connecting the middle term with the subject, or minor term, of the conclusion is called the "minor premise" and is usually put second. The conclusion itself is usually put third or last, and is said to "follow from" or to be "implied by" the premises. We see, then, that any deductive argument, when reduced to the form of an Aristotelian syllogism, consists of three terms (each term designating a class) and three propositions (each proposition expressing a relation of total inclusion *A*, or of partial inclusion, *I*, or of total exclusion *E*, or of partial exclusion *O*). The order in which the propositions are put does not, of course, affect the validity of the argument, but for purposes of identifying and classifying the syllogism some fixed order is agreed upon and adhered to, and that order is, as we have said:

Major Premise
Minor Premise
Conclusion

Here are some of the many possible syllogisms expressed in symbolic form, and each of them is illustrated by a concrete example.

FIGURE I

A	All *M* is *P*.	*A*	All animals are mortal.
A	All *S* is *M*.	*A*	All men are animals.
∴	(*A*) All *S* is *P*.		Therefore, (*A*) all men are mortal.

FIGURE II

A	All *P* is *M*.	*A*	All metals are elements.
E	No *S* is *M*.	*E*	Brass is not an element.
∴	(*E*) No *S* is *P*.		Therefore, (*E*) brass is not a metal.

FIGURE III

A	All *M* is *P*.	*A*	Arabs are warlike.
A	All *M* is *S*.	*A*	Arabs are Semites.
∴	(*I*) Some *S* is *P*.		Therefore, (*I*) some Semites are warlike.

FIGURE IV

A	All *P* is *M*.	*A*	All gods are immortal.
E	No *M* is *S*.	*E*	No immortals are men.
∴	(*E*) No *S* is *P*.		Therefore, (*E*) no men are gods.

We have divided these syllogisms into four kinds, according to the four positions of the middle term as subject or as predicate in the premises. The position in which the terms occur in the premises determines the "figure" of the syllogism, while the quantities and qualities of the three propositions taken in succession and each symbolized by *A*, *I*, *E*, or *O*, determines the "mood" of the syllogism. To identify a syllogism, one must state both its mood and its figure. Thus:

FIGURE I

E No *M* is *P*.
I Some *S* is *M*.

∴ (*O*) Some *S* is not *P*.

is the mood *E I O* in Figure I.

FIGURE II

E No *P* is *M*.
I Some *S* is *M*.

∴ (*O*) Some *S* is not *P*.

is the same mood *E I O* but in Figure II. In the following syllogisms,

FIGURE III		FIGURE III
A All *M* is *P*.		*O* Some *M* is not *P*.
A All *M* is *S*.	and	*A* All *M* is *S*.
∴ (*I*) Some *S* is *P*.		∴ (*O*) Some *S* is not *P*.

we have different moods but in the same figure. Finally, in the following pair,

FIGURE I		FIGURE IV
A All *M* is *P*.		*E* No *P* is *M*.
A All *S* is *M*.	and	*A* All *M* is *S*.
∴ (*A*) All *S* is *P*.		∴ (*O*) Some *S* is not *P*.

we have syllogisms differing both in mood and in figure. Each of the figures has an axiom or self-evident principle which applies to it as its canon and is exemplified by each of its valid moods. Thus:

For Figure I:

Whatever class includes or excludes a middle class, *M*, will include or exclude, respectively, whatever is included in *M*.

For Figure II:

Any two classes that are respectively included in and excluded from the same middle class, *M*, will be excluded from each other.

For Figure III:

Any two classes that include the same middle class, *M*, will be partly included in each other.

For Figure IV also an axiom can be devised, but it is very complicated and the figure itself is so unnatural that it is practically never used.

Figure I is by far the simplest and most natural and is used in about nine out of ten arguments. It is capable of proving conclusions of all four kinds, *A*, *I*, *E*, and *O*, and it is the *only* figure capable of proving the universal affirmative *A*, which is the most valuable of the four. Figure II is well adapted to proving *negative* conclusions, and those are the only ones that it can prove. Figure III is well adapted to proving *particular* conclusions, and those are the only ones that it can prove. Figure IV is, as we have said, not well adapted to proving any sort of conclusion.

Aristotle seems to have hated the fourth figure so much that he did not even include it in his doctrine; but he loved the first figure supremely and regarded it as the only one that was truly axiomatic. The second and third figures in his opinion owed their validity to the fact that they could be reduced to or verified by the first figure.

The number of valid syllogisms is only 19: four in the first figure, four in the second, six in the third, and five in the fourth. They can be listed as follows:

Figure I: AAA, EAE, AII, EIO.
Figure II: EAE, AEE, EIO, AOO.
Figure III: AAI, AII, IAI, EAO, OAO, EIO.
Figure IV: AAI, AEE, IAI, EAO, EIO.

The medieval logicians devised an amusing set of hexameter lines, incorporating each of the 19 valid moods in an artificial name, the first three vowels of the name being the propositional symbols for the mood in question. The rest of the lines consisted of regular Latin words which indicated the figures to which the moods severally belonged. And then, as a final touch of cryptogrammatic elegance, the artificial syllogistic names contained significant consonants, *s*, *p*, and *m*, indicating the way in which each syllogism in the second, third, and fourth figures could, without change in meaning, be reduced to (or validated by) the syllogism with the same initial letter in the first, or perfect, figure. Here are the famous lines:

Barbara, *Celarent*, Darii, *Ferio*que prioris;
Cesare, *Camestres*, *Festino*, *Baroko*, secundae;
Tertia *Darapti*, *Datisi*, *Disamis*, *Felapton*,
Bokardo, *Ferison*, habet; quarta insuper addit
Bramantip, *Camenes*, *Dimaris*, *Fesapo*, *Fresison*.

The total number of formally possible syllogisms can be found by combining (by multiplying) the four possible conclusions *A*, *I*, *E*, and *O*, all of which by definition must have *S* as their subject with the eight possible minor premises having either *S* or *M* as subject and the eight possible major premises having either *M* or *P* as their subject, $4 \times 8 \times 8 = 256$. All but 19 of these moods are invalid. We can derive the valid 19 from the total possible in two ways: first, *directly* by applying the special canon of each figure; second, *indirectly*, by making each of the 256 moods run the gauntlet of certain general rules which list the conditions that must be fulfilled if a syllogism is to be valid. The 237 worthless syllogisms will be eliminated by this procedure and 19 valid ones will survive.

The syllogistic rules can be stated as follows:

There must be three terms and three propositions.
From two negative premises no conclusion can be drawn.

If (and only if) one of the premises is negative, the conclusion will be negative.

The middle term must be "distributed" (universal) at least once.

Neither term in the conclusion should be "distributed" (universal) unless it was "distributed" in its premise.

(The word *distributed* as applied to a term means that the class designated by that term is referred to universally or in its entirety. Thus, the subject of a universal proposition, *A* or *E*, and the predicate of a negative proposition, *E* or *O*, are distributed.)

The rules really boil down to two demands:

1. That the middle term be so related to the minor and major terms in the premises as to establish a definite rather than an indefinite connection between them.
2. That what is inferred about the minor and major terms in the conclusion shall not go beyond what we were told about each of them in the premises.

We must, however, refrain from further discussion of the syllogism, regardless of how fascinating such discussion may be to those who enjoy purely formal analysis, and proceed to consider whether the thumbnail sketch of deduction which we have given suggests any basic philosophic problem comparable to the great problem as to a foundation for induction. There are, I think, two such problems, and the one that will concern us least I will state first.

How are the four primary relations between classes to be integrated with other formal relations such as are dealt with in mathematics? This problem was, I believe, first raised by George Boole nearly a hundred years ago in what he called *The Algebra of Logic.* In that work Boole succeeded in reformulating each of the four Aristotelian propositions as a kind of algebraic equation. The quantified classes that figured as the terms of these equations could be combined according to special rules which were partly the same as and partly different from the rules of ordinary algebra.

The new algebraic logic of Boole was not quite so convenient for practical use as the older Aristotelian logic, but it was interesting in itself and still more interesting in the results to which it contributed. For what began as a reduction of logic to algebra developed into something like a reduction of all mathematics to logic, or at least to an integration of the two. And partly as a consequence of Boole's work, mathematicians were led to take a new interest in the foundations of their science and to seek such a unified systematization of its various branches as was finally achieved in the great *Principia Mathematica* of Russell and Whitehead.

But the problem or problems involved in this unification of all abstract science, though in a sense arising from the ancient philosophic discipline of logic, have now passed properly enough from the hands of the philosophers to the hands of the mathematicians; and this branch of mathematics is called "Symbolic Logic" or "Logistics." We shall leave it now and pass to the second of the fundamental philosophic problems involved in the logic of deduction.

Our new problem arises from a long-standing indictment brought against the Aristotelian deductive syllogism on the ground that it is guilty of the fallacy of *petitio principii*, or *begging the question*, and that as such it is empty and futile and completely ineffective as a form of proof. When the learned doctor in Molière's *Malade Imaginaire* proves that opium will put people to sleep because it possesses a dormitive virtue, we laugh because we realize that to say that a thing possesses a dormitive virtue is just a stilted way of saying that it puts people to sleep. The doctor is arguing in a circle. What he adduces as a premise for the conclusion is really a repetition of the conclusion itself. He has assumed and begs his audience to grant him the very point that is at issue and that requires proof.

Now, when we argue as in the ancient syllogism that has been used as a paradigm for two thousand years in courses in logic,

> All men are mortal.
> Socrates is a man.
>
> ———
>
> Therefore, Socrates is mortal.

are we not guilty of the very same fallacy? For how could we believe that all men were mortal unless we already believed that each being whom we regarded as a man was mortal? And if he whom we call Socrates is known to be or believed to be a man, why then, of course, his mortality is presupposed by the statement that all men are mortal. Hence, the conclusion that Socrates is mortal is not proved by the premises but simply assumed in them, which is what we call "begging the question." Of course, if this indictment is valid, it is "just too bad," for it means that the syllogism with its elaborate doctrine has no real function in human thinking and exists only for the purpose of giving professors of logic a dishonest means of earning a living.

I am, however, convinced that the indictment is not valid, and for the following reasons:

First, we never, or almost never, base our beliefs about what is true of a whole class upon an examination of each member of the class. Such a method is not only unnecessary, it is impossible; for, usually, the number of members in a class is infinite—if not actually, at least potentially; and the number of cases that we can observe as the basis for an induction constitutes not only a small fraction but an infinitesimal fraction of the class about the totality of which we speak in stating a universal proposition such as "All men are mortal," or "All Euclidean plane triangles have the sum of their angles equal to 180°." Whether we have a *right* to make these inductive generalizations is the philosophic problem pertaining to the logic of induction which we have already considered; but that, rightly or wrongly, we *do* make them there is no question. Consequently, my holding the belief that all men are mortal does not mean that I have examined all individual men, including the man Socrates, and found each of them to be mortal. I have derived my belief about the mortality of men by a method which, whether good or bad, is at least quite different from the absurd and impossible enterprise of looking at each individual.

And second, let us note that *finite minds can have beliefs without ever having put them together*. We keep many of our beliefs in water-tight, or rather "thought-tight," compartments, and the function of proof in general and of the Aristotelian syllogism in particular is to *make* us join together what the imperfect nature of our brain has kept asunder. For example, you may have known all your life that women were taxpayers; and, as a good American, you may also have known that "taxation without representation is tyranny," or, in other words, that taxpayers should have the right to vote. Yet, despite these two bits of knowledge, it may come to you (as I remember it came to me) as a distinct surprise to hear someone who is arguing for votes for women enjoin you that if you believe that taxpayers should vote and that women are taxpayers, then you ought to believe that women should vote. This simple syllogism in "Barbara," the mood *AAA* in the first figure, will have made you put two and two together, and by thus *connecting* your old beliefs it will force you to accept as a new belief a proposition which you had hitherto regarded as untenable and absurd but which the syllogism now reveals to your reluctant gaze as absolutely necessitated by what you have always known to be true.

Of course, a prerequisite for the effectiveness of a syllogism is that the premises invoked by the speaker be accepted as true or at least as probable or plausible by the audience. The premises of a syllogism must be free from (1) ambiguity; (2) irrelevance; (3) question-begging; and (4) must conform to the other rules of the syllogism by conveying *adequate* information about the minor and major terms and about the middle term which bridges the gap between them. But even when these four general conditions for formal validity are satisfied, the syllogism will be hollow and without power to convince unless it fulfills the fifth and final condition of the truth or supposed truth of its premises. Logicians in their treatment of the syllogism usually leave out this fifth prerequisite as not germane to logic as such or in itself. But the elementary student is always puzzled to know why the long list of syllogistic fallacies fails to include a "fallacy of false premise." In this matter the instinct of the student is sound, and the technique of the professor is at fault; for unless a debater offers you premises that you are *willing* to accept, he cannot *force* you to accept his conclusion.

It follows as a corollary of the above statements that the principle of disproof as exemplified in what is called the *reductio ad absurdum* has for its prerequisite a belief in the falsity of a syllogism's conclusion. One or both of the premises of a valid syllogism can be proved to be false if they can be shown to imply a conclusion that is already known to be false. If the truth of a hypothesis would lead us to a conclusion that is false or absurd, the hypothesis itself must be false. This procedure of disproof or refutation is used not only as a direct end in itself, but even more often as an indirect means of proving something else. If I can disprove the contradictory or the only alternative to a certain proposition, then I have by so doing established the truth of that proposition as effectively as if I had proved it directly from premises that were admitted to be true.

And now that we have vindicated the syllogism against the objection that it begs the question by assuming in the premises the very proposition that it pretends to deduce as a conclusion, there remains a final objection advanced not so much by technical philosophers as by students and practical people. The objection I refer to is directed against the seeming artificiality of syllogisms, at least in the form in which they appear in textbooks on logic: "All men are mortal, Socrates is a man, therefore Socrates is mortal." Would any ordinary human being ever really give utterance to these famous sentences? I think we must admit that the syllogism as thus traditionally formulated does sound pretty pedantic and unnatural.

Now Aristotle, the founder of logic, was a formalist if not a pedant; and with all his greatness he made what seems to me to have been a mistake, the mistake of putting the premises of his beloved syllogism *before* instead of *after* the conclusion, thereby loading down his new science with a quite unnecessary weight of artificialities. Logic is not, as I see it (though here I must disagree with John Dewey and Susan Stebbing), the art and science of thinking or inquiry. It is not concerned with all stages of an inquiry, but only with the second stage, in which proof and disproof enter on the scene. The first stage in solving a problem or getting out of a predicament is concocting a plan or hypothesis. It is not *reason* but *imagination*, which, working on the data of the situation and on the memories of similar situations in the past, *concocts* or *creates* or *discovers* by intuition a hypothesis, a plan, a possible way out. Then and only then does reasoning in the proper sense of the word really begin. That activity consists in evaluating, sifting, rejecting, and confirming the possibilities which have been imagined. In short, we may say that imagination proposes and reason disposes. For to reason is to give reasons for (or against) a proposition already before the mind; and to give reasons for (or against) it is to prove (or disprove) it. Thus, reasoning is *proving* (in the negative as well as the positive sense), and *logic* is neither more nor less than the *theory of proof*. If this is so, it follows that the "conclusion" of a syllogism or unit process of proof is always a "thesis" to be justified by "premises" which follow rather than precede the proposition or belief in whose behalf they are invoked. "*S* is *P* *because* *S* is *M* and *M* is *P*." "Socrates, yes, even the divine Socrates, must be mortal because we know that he is a man, and, alas, we have to remember that whoever is man is also mortal." Thus, we see that even the hackneyed old paradigm can be "pepped up" into a semblance of life by being put in its natural and proper order rather than in the unnecessarily artificial order sanctioned by tradition. The proper conjunction for reasoning or proof is not the word *therefore* (∴) but the inverse or upside-down of *therefore*, that is, the word *because* (∵). Viewed in this light, the Aristotelian syllogism is as natural as breathing. And to discover that we have been speaking in syllogisms for the greater part of our lives is like discovering that we have always been speaking prose. Ordinary conversation is, of course, highly elliptical, and our syllogisms more often than not omit one of the premises as being too well understood to require explicit statement. Thus: "Even poets are mortal because they are human"; "Even the lightest gasses must be subject to gravitation because they are material"; "Laws should usually be obeyed even when they are unjust because they are prerequisites for social order"; "He won't sleep in this room because it is number thirteen"; "Take this coffee back for it has got too cold"; "I hit Baby Sister 'cause she hit me" and so forth. These are all perfectly good formal syllogisms in "Barbara," though in each case the major premise is implied rather than expressed; and probably one out of every three statements that a person utters from the time he is two years old until he dies (or goes insane) is of the same sort.

So, far from being artificial or outmoded, the Aristotelian syllogisms are the blood and flesh, or at least the connective tissue, of all human discourse; and indifference to the logical laws which they exemplify is intellectual triviality, for it means indifference to the laws of any possible universe that the intellect can apprehend.

Note: There is a further objection that has been urged against the Aristotelian logic which, though rather technical, is so far-reaching in its implications that it should not be passed by without mention.

Aristotle regarded it as self-evident that the truth of a universal proposition entailed the truth of its corresponding particular proposition, or what is called its subaltern. Thus, if we know that the whole class *S* is (or is not) *P*, he thought that we could infer that at least some of the class *S* is (or is not) *P*. To make such an inference would be merely an application of Aristotle's great axiom on which all reasoning was founded: what can be affirmed or denied of a class can be affirmed or denied of any species or members of that class. The objectors to this Aristotelian *dictum de omne et nullo* claim that the universal proposition does not imply the existence of any members of the subject class, whereas a particular proposition introduced by the word *some* does imply the existence of the individuals of which the predicate is affirmed or denied. Hence, to infer the truth of a particular proposition from the truth of its corresponding universal would, so they claim, be to infer something about existence from a premise that told us nothing about existence.

Let us consider two examples of the kind that the objectors have in mind:

All mermaids have fishes' tails.
All mermaids have women's heads.
Therefore,
Some beings with women's heads have fishes' tails.

And again:

> All round squares are round.
> All round squares are square.
> Therefore,
> There are some squares that are round.

But, say the objectors, although the premises of these syllogisms are perfectly true, being mere explications of the meaning of a mermaid and of a round-square, the conclusions are not true, for there are not in existence any round things that are square or any fishy-tailed beings that have women's heads. Because of this, the objectors claim that each of these Aristotelian syllogisms is invalid in that it makes an existential particular follow from one or more non-existential universals.

If, however, we understand the meaning of "existence," we shall see that it is not Aristotle but the objectors who are in error. To say that an object "exists" means that it has membership or place in an ordered system or "universe."[2] The kind of system in which the terms of a proposition have membership is determined by the nature of the things about which we are discoursing; hence, the system itself is called the "Universe of Discourse." When we say, "All mermaids have women's heads," and "All mermaids have fishes' tails," it is the fairy-tale universe of imaginary objects such as mermaids to which our discourse refers. In that universe of discourse, though not necessarily in any other, all the mermaids of which we speak in each of our universal premises "exist" or have membership. And in that same universe, though not necessarily in any other, there do exist objects that have both fishes' tails and women's heads. If we shift from the universe of merely imaginary objects such as mermaids to the universe of actually impossible objects such as round-squares, we find the same situation: in that universe in which all round-squares are square and all round squares are round there will exist some round things that are square. In short, put more briefly and formally, when we infer the conclusion "Some *S* is *P*" from the

[2] The term *existence* as used in logic is relative, not absolute. It applies to any one of the possible universes of discourse. But *existence* in a physical or metaphysical sense designates membership in that absolute universe of discourse consisting of the total *zusammenhang* of space-time. (See pages 262–280.)

premise "All *S* is *P*," the *somes* of the conclusion enjoy existence in the same universe of discourse as the *alls* of the premise.

References to Part Two

* 1. "On the Nature of Induction," page 173.
* 2. "A Defense of Causality," page 182.
3. "The Rainbow Series and the Logarithm of Aleph Null," page 189.

CHAPTER II

KNOWLEDGE AND THE WAYS OF KNOWING (CONTINUED): MATERIAL LOGIC

We can see how beliefs can be derived from other beliefs which, in turn, are derived from still others, and so on; but this business of borrowing one belief from another cannot continue forever, and sooner or later we must come to primary beliefs that have for their sources certain absolute and ultimate principles. Let us ask, then: What are these ultimate sources of our knowledge? And what are the comparative merits of these sources as methods of validating our beliefs? These are the problems of what we are calling Material or Absolute Logic to distinguish it from the Formal or Relative Logic which we have surveyed.

The first question (as to the *source* of beliefs) is, however, a mere psychological preliminary to the second question, which concerns the *ground* of beliefs, or the basis and criterion of their validity. The actual sources of beliefs are five in number: (1) the testimony of others; (2) instinctive feeling or intuition; (3) the self-evident insights of reason; (4) what appears in sense perception; (5) the practical results of action.

Let us illustrate these five sources by five successive examples: (1) That Napoleon Bonaparte existed—I believe because of the *testimony* of others. (2) That certain of the people that I am meeting for the first time would make good and congenial friends, and that certain others would prove disagreeable and untrustworthy—I believe because of an inner feeling or *intuition.* (3) That two things equal to a third thing are equal to each other—I believe because to my *reason* it appears self-evident. (4) That water when greatly heated changes into steam and when greatly chilled into ice—I believe on the evidence of my *senses.* (5) That certain optimistic conceptions of life are sound (often despite appearances to the contrary)—I believe because the holding of those conceptions has led me to successful results in *practice.*

Each of the beliefs that I have used as illustrations seems to be derived primarily, if not exclusively, from some one of the five sources listed. But there are many that are derived from two or more, and quite a few that originate from all five. Each of the five sources can be and has been defended as the ultimate ground for validating beliefs. Consequently, there are five methods or methodological schools which severally ascribe a preferential, if not exclusive, validity to some one of the five sources. These schools may be defined as follows:

1. Those preferring the testimony of others in whom they have complete trust or faith are "Authoritarians."

2. Those preferring inner feeling or intuition are the "Intuitionists" or "Mystics."

3. Those preferring the principles which seem self-evident to reason are the "Rationalists."

4. Those preferring the evidence of sense perception or experience are the "Empiricists."

5. Those preferring the successful consequence of applying a belief in practice as a criterion of its validity are the "Pragmatists."

6. Those who regard none of these criteria either when taken separately or when combined with others as adequate to justify our beliefs are the "Skeptics." Thus, Skepticism

(or "Agnosticism," which is skepticism restricted to ultimate questions of metaphysics) is the negative member of the logical sisterhood.

There is much that can be said, and that has been said, in favor of each of the great logics. In a book entitled *The Ways of Knowing, or the Methods of Philosophy*, I separated as far as possible these problems of Material Logic (and also of epistemology) from the metaphysical and ethical problems with which they are entangled. And then by way of solving the problems thus separated, I essayed an analysis and comparative evaluation of Authoritarianism, Intuitionism or Mysticism, Rationalism, Empiricism, Pragmatism, and Skepticism considered in turn. Also, in the article entitled *The Antinomy and Its Implications for Logical Theory*, in Part II of the present volume, I undertake, in a rough preliminary fashion, the same task, but with especial reference to the interesting situation that arises when reason and sense perception, which are the two major criteria of our knowledge, come into sharp conflict with one another, giving rise to what I term a "major antinomy." Because of these two rather elaborate treatments of the problems of "Material Logic," one of them included within these covers, I shall add in this place only a paragraph or so of summary and appraisal of each of the methods.

1. *Authoritarianism.* Man is an imitative and suggestible animal. When Simon says "Thumbs up!" or "Thumbs down!", our thumbs obediently go up or down. We have a natural and well-nigh irresistible tendency to believe the words we hear and see. "Barker's Bread is the Best Bread"; "Whiffy's Cigarettes are actually *good* for the nerves." The dinning of our ears and the smearing of our landscapes with stuff like this, attained at a cost of billions of dollars of human skill and effort, give ample testimony to the effectiveness of the Authoritarian method of induc-

ing beliefs. But, of course, this is only half the story. Who am I that I should pit some little guesses that I call a "philosophy" against the great creed of great men who assert that they in turn accept it on the authority of the Almighty? If my betters had faith, doesn't it behoove me to have it too? "What is good enough for father is good enough for me." My wit and my opportunities are so limited that I have, in any event, to take nine-tenths of what I believe on the say-so of others. Why should I hesitate, then, in matters of eternal moment to surrender my private intellect and private conscience to authority and "toe the party line" (theologically speaking, of course)? Perhaps this kind of talk may seem all right when it is a case of Authoritarianism against the field. But when it is a case not of authority versus the other methods, but of authority versus authority, what then? Buddha or Mohammed? Old Testament or New Testament? Calvin or St. Thomas? Granted that I am willing to surrender, to whom shall I surrender? Shall I go by the blackmail principle of Pascal's Wager and yield to the one that promises the most reward for my acceptance and threatens me with the worst punishment if I reject? Shall I take the oldest faith or the one with the most numerous adherents? Or shall I yield to the creed that came to me earliest as a child at my mother's knee, on the principle of "First come, first served"? Or how about flipping a coin?

These are difficulties, but in spite of them Authoritarianism will probably always remain the refuge of humble and puzzled minds and of minds that are tired. And whatever its limitations, it must always remain the great and primary source of our information about other men's thoughts and about the past.

2. *Intuitionism or Mysticism.* The "intuitions" favored as the supreme source and criterion of philosophic truth by those who are called "Mystics" spring from the

whole inner nature of the individual—his past experiences funded in memory, his inherited instincts, and (maybe) the inspirations of an immanent God. Why are they not more trustworthy as a source and criterion of belief than the comparatively external and superficial guides of sense and reason, or those of practical success or the testimony of others?

Heaven is filled with the saints and prophets who used their inner light to illuminate the world. Also, the secular pantheons of painting, poetry, and music are made up of those whose deep internal dreams have been externalized in beauty. And even in the galleries of philosophy we find hanging cosmic portraits which are the work not only of systematic thinking but of imaginative vision. In fact, *intuition* may be defined as *imagination touched with conviction.*

Yet, on the other side, we must remember that insane asylums no less than pantheons contain the work of "Mystics," or at least of those who tragically mistook their mad fancies for intuitions of great truth. How to tell the self-authenticating revelation of the Deep from the no less seemingly self-authenticating voice of some subconscious love or hope or hate—that is for the mystic the great problem. And all the counsel I can offer is to take all your intuitions with gratitude, of course, but take each one *cum grano salis.* And, above all, put it to the test of other nonintuitive methods of attaining truth. Then, if your vision is indeed a valid mystic revelation, it probably will withstand those tests (Bruno's did, and so did Joan of Arc's); and if not, you may, by this prosaic checking up, have saved yourself from trouble and even perhaps from madness.

3 and 4. *Rationalism and Empiricism.* These methods go together and, at least for science, are the most important sources of our knowledge. Empiricism through percep-

tion provides the food or raw material of truth. Rationalism through the intellect digests and organizes what the senses bring. Some sciences are infantile and some are mature. The former are mostly empirical and only a little rational—like botany. But the well-developed sciences—like physics—are mostly or largely mathematical and rational and not so dominantly empirical. The scientists, like the sciences themselves, are different in this matter. There are those like Einstein and Archimedes who spend much time alone making deductions and little time in the laboratory making observations and inductions. Others, like Francis Galton and Francis Bacon, are strong for observations and experiments and cautious in making inductions from them. It is said that when all the world of science was in a dither of excitement over the photographs of the 1919 eclipse of the sun, resulting, as they did, in an empirical confirmation of Einstein's theory, that Einstein himself was indifferent and almost bored. He was so sure (as a rationalist) that his deduction was right that if the facts had not confirmed it, it would have been simply too bad—not for him but for them! Empiricism and Rationalism are each of them *self-correcting* (in a way that the other methods are not); and, moreover, each of them can and does derive confirmation from the other.

5. *Pragmatism.* To realize the strength of Pragmatism it is necessary to remember that man is an animal and that, as in other animals, his organs, functions, and faculties have been evolved as useful instruments in the struggle for existence.

The mind and its thinking, so we are told, are in this respect no different from other biological powers and functions. Thought is an instrument for action, and the criterion of its value or validity is its success in action and for action. The good thought is the thought that "delivers the goods," that gets you to wherever it is you want to go.

Consequently, all other criteria are in a sense subordinate to the criterion of practical success or satisfactory working. But what sort of successful working is relevant as a measure of a thought's validity or truth? The answers to this question are ambiguous and have aroused controversy. We cannot go into them here, and I will only express a private opinion that Pragmatism as a method of Material Logic is strongest when it is applied to questions of practical and ethical evaluation.

6. *Skepticism.* The function of this negation of all the methods is to show up our logical weakness and inject a leaven of modesty into the dogmatic certainties to which we are all of us too prone—especially in philosophy. In claiming that no truth is by any method or to any extent attainable, I think Skepticism goes too far. But it can and should teach us that no human belief, however certain it seems, can really be any more than probable.

I have said that the Pragmatic method is especially applicable to questions of practice and ethical evaluation. In the same way each of the other logical methods is especially applicable to some one of the domains into which the objects of experience and investigation may be divided.

These objects are usually classified on the basis of their intrinsic properties. Our present interest is, however, not in things as they are in themselves, but as they are related to a mind that would know them. From this purely methodological standpoint we may divide knowable objects into the following five classes or domains: (I) the domain of objects and events that can be experienced only by minds other than our own; (II) the dual domain of (A) ultimate and non-instrumental values, and (B) a supposed ultimate and ineffable truth; (III) the domain of commensurable and abstract relations; (IV) the domain of particular facts and concrete relations; (V) the domain of individual and social conduct.

All of the logical methods are applicable in some measure to the investigation of each of the above-mentioned domains of reality. But it is to the first domain that the method of *authoritarianism* is peculiarly applicable; to the second, *intuitionism* or *mysticism;* to the third, *rationalism;* to the fourth, *empiricism;* and to the fifth, *pragmatism.*

(I) *Authoritarianism and the first domain.* It is necessary for an individual to trust other individuals in matters which he cannot investigate for himself; and unless there is reason to suppose that the witnesses are biased or incompetent, their testimony should be put on a par with his own. The major part of the first domain consists of the past, and in that field the method of authoritarianism must hold a dominant position. It will, to be sure, usually be possible to confirm or refute by the methods of rationalism and empiricism the direct testimony of witnesses—even in the matter of things past and gone—by the indirect evidences contained in facts that are accessible to present observation. The great monuments of historical scholarship could never have been erected without the use of the strictest scientific procedure. The ultimate premises of the historian must nevertheless rest upon the testimony of other minds than his own, and it is both justifiable and inevitable that we should give at least provisional credence to all disinterested authorities. Viewed in this manner, the method of authoritarianism can be assigned a permanent and honorable place in the federation of logical methods.

(II) *Intuitionism or Mysticism and the second domain.* The second domain, as we have said, comprises two quite distinct regions—the first consisting of the objects of those evaluative interests and judgments which are elemental as distinguished from those which are composite. In this region, intuition in the sense of immediate feeling would seem to be not merely the most appropriate faculty, but the only faculty for affording information. We might take as an example of an elemental interest romantic love and the judgment of faith on which it is based. It would surely be a vain and preposterous undertaking to discover one's true sweetheart by accepting the authority of others, by using deductive reasoning and calculation, or by considering the extent to which she might be a practical utility. In other words, the lover as such is and must always remain a mystic. Also, in forming the belief on which one bases his choice of a friend, intuition is almost as indispensable as in choosing a mate. True friendship is certainly not based upon either calculation or utility, but upon the direct appeal to our sympathies and affections. The same might be said of objects of art, the primary enjoyment of which is not based upon considerations that are rationally analyzable.

The other region of this domain is far more problematic than the one just considered. We described it as the hypothetical realm consisting of the ineffable realities which are regarded as both super-sensuous and super-rational. Mystics claim that their intuitions of the higher truth possess at least as much clearness and certainty as the revelations of reason and sense. But is such a feeling of immediate certainty to be trusted? This at least we may say: that so long as mystical revelations are confined to things which have no bearing upon the world of experience and practical life, they are in any case harmless; but when they are made to yield theoretical deductions and practical consequences which conflict with our ordinary knowledge of life and nature, they may prove exceedingly dangerous checks to intellectual and ethical progress.

Intuitionism is and must be pre-eminent in the dual domain of elemental interests and of super-sensuous revelation, but the fact that it is the only method primarily applicable to these realms must not be taken to imply that the results attained by it are always valid. Evaluations based upon sympathy and intuition are often proved to be mistaken, and revelations of the supernatural are by no means a guarantee of their own validity. The gravest danger of intuitionism is its tendency to transcend the limits of the domain proper to it, and thereby to place itself in competition with the other methods in matters in which they should have a predominant, if not an exclusive, sway. If, however, these qualifications are borne in mind, intuitionism may legitimately be assigned a place in the methodological federation.

(III) *Rationalism and the third domain.* Some relations, notably those of quantity, are capable of being combined in such a way as to yield new relations of the same general type. These chains and systems of relations comprise the science of mathematics, a science whose procedure is governed primarily by rationalistic deduction. The method of rationalism is applicable not only to abstract relationships in isolation, but also to bodies of particular facts in so far as commensurable relations hold between them. In other words, deductive reasoning is of use in applied mathematics and in all concrete sciences to the extent that the material under investigation is susceptible of quantitative treatment.

Yet, like the other methods, rationalism can prove dangerous to the cause of truth when it is applied beyond its own domain—and for that matter even within its own domain when it refuses the corroborations of empiricism. The chief abuse of this method, as manifested in the history of thought, has consisted in the attempt to substitute a priori reasoning for empirical observation, as when it was argued that the orbits of the planets must be circular rather than elliptical because planetary motions are heavenly motions, and heavenly motions are perfect motions, and perfect motions are circular. The search for *explanations* is praiseworthy and should be encouraged, but it should never be allowed to stand in the way of the search for *descrip-*

tions. With these provisos, the rationalistic method may be assigned its permanent place in the federation of methods.

(IV) *Empiricism and the fourth domain.* The method of empiricism may rightly be regarded as the most widely applicable and reliable of all the methods. It is the only suitable method for the domain of particular facts and relations, and it is usually susceptible of being applied at least indirectly and as a check in the other domains. The authoritarian, the mystic, the pragmatist, and, above all, the rationalist can well afford to permit their somewhat precarious procedures to be reinforced and corroborated by the superior tests of sense-perception. To empiricism, therefore, belongs the honor of the highest place in the federation.

(V) *Pragmatism and the fifth domain.*[1] Pragmatism, when applied to the domain of human action, is both valid and pre-eminently valuable. It is of doubtful validity when applied to inquiries into the nature of the objective facts and relations of the material environment. This dual verdict is justified by the contrasting natures of the search for the good and the search for the true. In the search for the true, we are concerned with the adjustment and subordination of our ideas and beliefs to the structure of physical nature. To permit our decisions of scientific problems to be controlled by our practical interests or by our emotional fears and aspirations would be fundamentally subversive of scientific truth. But when we are interested not in the theoretical search for the truth but in the practical achievement of the good, our personal interests are no longer distorting and irrelevant factors, but controlling and essential guides. For the "Good" means that

[1] For further elucidation of this topic, consult the essay in Part II on "The True, the Good, and the Beautiful from a Pragmatic Standpoint," page 550.

which fulfills any tendency, desire, or capacity; and its attainment means an aggressive alteration of the environment which should continue until the extra-individual reality has been completely adapted to intra-individual needs. The attitude of the truth-seeker is and should be cosmocentric, but the attitude of the seeker for good is and should be bio-centric. The realization of either truth or goodness means the attainment of an equilibrium between the individual and his environment, but that equilibrium in the case of truth is attained by subordination of the individual to the environment, while in the case of the good it is attained in the converse manner—by the subordination of the environment to individuals. And the fixed laws of nature, knowledge of which from the point of view of theoretical inquiry constitutes an end in itself, are from the point of view of moral and practical endeavor to be regarded as instruments to be used by us for the achievement of human good.

The pragmatic method, then, is justifiable only in so far as it expresses the attitude of ethical utilitarianism—that attitude which looks upon all moral codes from the standpoint of pure expediency, and which recognizes only one unchanging moral law, the law that every person should strive at every moment of his life so to act as to produce an intensive and extensive maximum of well-being for all. This is the categorical imperative of ethical pragmatism. It applies, of course, not only to the control of individual living but also to the control of the social customs and institutions—political, economic, educational, and religious—which make up the conditions under which our individual lives must be passed. When thus restricted to its own domain, pragmatism may claim a high and permanent place in the final federation of logical methods.

(VI) *Skepticism in relation to the other methods.* The function of the skeptic is to make us realize that no knowledge attainable by the human mind is absolutely certain. Systems of belief in all of the five domains which we have considered are and must always be open to revision. Even if one and the same judgment could claim the support of the five positive methods, it would acquire thereby not certainty, but only a high degree of probability.

To retain toward all problems a measure of open-mindedness is as difficult as it is important. We have an almost unconquerable temptation to shun uncertainty and to commit ourselves definitely either for or against a given proposition. Yet it shows at least as much wisdom to suspend judgment when the evidence is insufficient as to hold a definite conclusion when the evidence justifies it. And suspension of judgment does not, as is erroneously supposed, mean suspension of action. It is often better to run the risk of acting wrongly than not to act at all. It is possible to act upon a hypothesis while clearly realizing that the probabilities against its truth are even stronger than those in its favor.

Skepticism, wholesome for everyone, is especially wholesome for the philosopher. Philosophy is the most uncertain and least successful of all the sciences. That is the price it must pay for its lofty and comprehensive ideal. And philosophy in the past has often exhibited an unwillingness to admit the tentative character of its conclusions, and has attempted to conceal its shortcomings by making the most extravagant claims for the superiority of its procedure over the procedure of science. Skepticism is most needed in philosophy just because philosophers have often shown themselves willing to court absurdity by boasting of their strength on the very point in which they are weakest —the point, namely, of the certainty of their conclusions. "A priori validity" and "transcendental necessity" are eulogistic descriptions which philosophers are fond of applying to their own methods. The obvious discrepancy between their claim and their accomplishment has resulted in making the layman even more distrustful of the philosopher than the circumstances need warrant. If for the "revealed dogmas" of the theologian, and the "transcendental certainties" of the philosopher we could substitute the modest phrase "working hypotheses," a great deal of needless criticism would be obviated and even the more extravagant conclusions of those who speculate about the universe would receive a patient and sympathetic hearing.

The negative method of skepticism should have a place in the federation along with the five positive methods as a necessary prophylactic for each of them, and as a constant reminder of the limitations of human faculty and the need of tolerance and open-mindedness, especially on the part of philosophers.[2]

Reference to Part Two

* 4. "The Antinomy and Its Implications for Logical Theory," page 203.

[2] The preceding paragraphs are in part a borrowing from Chapter VII of Part I of my book *The Ways of Knowing, or The Methods of Philosophy*. (George Allen and Unwin, London, and The Macmillan Company, New York, 1925.)

CHAPTER III

KNOWLEDGE IN RELATION TO NATURE: EPISTEMOLOGY

How is appearance related to reality? Or, how are the things that come before your mind, the things that you are aware of and *apprehend*, either by perception or by conception, related to the things you *believe* in and which, as believed in, you call real or true? This is the primary question or problem of that branch of philosophy which is called—or which we, at any rate, shall call—"epistemology." There are four types of epistemological theory: Objectivism, Subjectivism, Dualism and Relativism. We shall consider the first three at some length and the fourth more briefly.

The usual approach to the problem is to limit the meaning of the term *appearance* to sensory appearance, that is, to the things that are perceptually apprehended as visual, auditory, tactual, and so forth, and then proceed to *work up* from a discussion of these perceptually apprehended objects in their relation to reality to a discussion of the relation to reality of conceptually apprehended objects such as our remote ancestors, the other side of the moon, and the age of dinosaurs. I shall take the liberty of reversing this procedure and extending the term *appearance* to include all the things that are apprehended at a given moment, conceptual as well as perceptual. I shall begin with the conceptual and *work down* to the perceptual. I ask you, then, to consider, for purposes of illustrating and focusing the problem, your paternal grandfather's father, whom I will assume you have never seen. Take this great-grandfather as an object of your thought. He is now one of the objects before your mind, a *conceptual appearance*. I am sure I am not assuming too much if I assume that this great-grandfather of yours is not only an object that is conceptually apprehended but also an object you believe to be real, as real as you yourself. Here the apprehended and the real are identical. You here and now can know or apprehend a reality that existed there and then. Your thought can bridge any gap in space and time that separates you as thinker from the object of your thought. Now, when you realize that your ancestor lived before you ever thought of him, you may be tempted to say that he himself could not be the object within your thoughts, which are occurring here and now, and that it must be only some image more or less like him that you are apprehending. If you are tempted to say this, please resist the temptation, for it will involve you in self-contradiction. You cannot compare to its disparagement one object (here, a mental image of your great-grandfather) with another object (your great-grandfather himself) without having both as objects which you are comparing, considering, or thinking of. To deny that you can conceptually apprehend or think of a real (or unreal) object is by that very act of denying it to affirm it as an object of thought, which is self-contradictory. Thought can never exclude any object from its reach or scope. A real object can be apprehended, but its reality in no way depends on the fact that it is or is not apprehended. Neither does an unreal object depend for its unreality upon whether or not it is apprehended. But because we can never be quite certain when we are apprehending an object whether it is real or not, a foolish notion has arisen that the mind can know only its own states, and that the objects known or apprehended belong in a sort of limbo of neither real nor unreal things but just "ideas." An uncertain apprehension, or even a false apprehension, in no way reduces the objects thus apprehended to an exclusively subjective realm. All thinkable objects possess some sort of Being or "istence."

But only a tiny minority of the totality of "istence" have *ex*istence or reality. The rest have merely "sub-istence," or sub(s)istence. The aristocratic minority that enjoy the status of reality or existence are the events that have position in the *zusammenhang* of space-time together with the relations and attributes of such events. The real is that which is the explanation and ground of all that *appears*, whether real or unreal. To be nonexistent is to be nowhere and "no when." Consequently, unreal things lacking a locus and a date produce no primary effects in their own right, but only secondary effects through the agency of those who apprehend them. Real or existent things, on the other hand, produce not only secondary effects by grace of being apprehended, but also primary effects of their own by right of occupying positions in the causal *zusammenhang* of space-time.

This view which I have been expounding and defending is "Epistemological Objectivism." It maintains that everything apprehended is independent of the apprehender. It is one of the four possible solutions of the epistemological problem.

I turn now to the opposite type of theory, which I shall call "Epistemological Subjectivism." According to this theory, every object that is apprehended is created or constructed by or is a function of the apprehender or of his states and processes. Take your great-grandfather again. Why did you, a few minutes ago, think of him or make him an object of your conceptual apprehension? I'll answer: Your eyes, and through them your brain centers, were affected in a definite, complicated fashion by the light waves reflected from the printed words of this book. This direct sensory effect was further complicated and modified by your understanding of printed English words and by your memories of what you had been told about your great-grandfather. These processes occurring in your brain—or in your soul, if you have one—determined completely and adequately what you thought of, in this case, your great-grandfather. For further details, consult the psychologists. Anything and everything else, real or unreal, past or present, near or remote, that you in any way apprehend or are conscious of, is due to the same sort of intra-organic activities. If I were endowed with the technique of the physiologist a thousand years in the future, I could, I dare say, lay bare your cerebral cortex and, by tickling it with the right kind of electrical stimulation, cause to come before your mind any one of a great variety of objects. But whether or not such stimulation by an outsider can ever do the trick, I say again that there is no slightest doubt that the processes in your brain at any moment are the proximate determiners of what objects you apprehend at that moment. Doesn't this mean that all the objects of your thought, even such previously existing objects as your ancestors, are created by you, their descendant?

But how can the past be created—the very past itself, mind you—and not any mere replica of it? For have we not seen that it was your great-grandfather *himself* and *as such*, rather than any present image of him, that was the object or content of your thought? To answer this question and untangle this tangle is to solve the central problem of epistemology. Let us put it in the form of a conundrum: "When is a creation not a creation, or less than a creation?" I answer, "When it is a 're-creation.'" To re-create is to create something that already exists or has existed. An ordinary *created* thing depends on its creator and cannot antedate the creative act. But a re-created thing is not affected by and does not depend upon its re-creator, yet it is a quite definite function of the re-creating states and processes. It is, indeed, more truly and more intimately a function of them than an ordinary creature is of its creator. The cause is a function of its effects, and the states and processes in the brain which are the proximate determiners of what is apprehended are themselves the ultimate effects of the things that are apprehended.

Your great-grandfather, for example, was the cause of the long series of effects modified by many other things, including the words of this book, which finally terminated in the processes occurring in your brain a few minutes ago. And these ultimate effects of your ancestor were the re-creators, or revealers, of him, their cause as an object of your thought. Under certain peculiar conditions effects can reinstate or re-create their causes. These conditions are the conditions for what we call consciousness or awareness or apprehension. It is quite ordinary for causes to produce their effects. Past causes create present effects. Why doesn't it occur to us that this process can be reversed and that present effects can "re-create" past causes? For two reasons: first, the thing is too close to us, it *is* us, or our minds, and we don't see it, for the same reason that we don't see our eyes; second, our own lives and everything that we observe in nature go forward from the past into the present and future. This is the characteristic of kinetic energy or motion. But, as we shall see later in our section on metaphysics, when kinetic energy is changed into potential energy in the brain, the externally observable stimulus becomes the not externally but internally visible sensation. When *doing* ceases, *sensing* and *thinking* begin. Doing creates the future; thinking and even sensing "re-create" the past. We live forward, but we think backward. All consciousness is retrospective, a perception of what already was, a fact, a *factum*, a *fait accompli*, something done and past. In short, the same hypothesis that explains invisible mind in relation to visible brain also explains the capacity of that mind to apprehend or "re-create" by means of its present states objects that are outside it and even remote from it in space and time.

If you have understood and assented to what I have said, you will now agree that Epistemological Objectivism, according to which all objects are independent of and unaffected by being apprehended, and Epistemological Subjectivism, according to which all objects are functions of and "re-created" by anyone who apprehends them, are two theories which, despite their seeming contradiction, are both of them true and each of them compatible with the other.

But now there is a third theory called "Epistemological Dualism" which we must consider. It is also called the "representative theory" and the "copy theory" for reasons soon to be made plain. Let us go back again to your great-grandfather and note that he is a member of two kinds of societies. He was a man who had his family and his cronies and who produced and received all kinds of effects; and that whole society or system to which he belonged was a nineteenth-century affair and, I dare say, far away in space from where you are now. But your great-grandfather has also become, thanks to our colloquy, a member of a quite different society, namely, that of your thoughts and feelings. You can discover, and the psychologists can help you to understand, the way in which he, your ancestor, as an object of your present thought, is causing all sorts of associations and various new thoughts and feelings, perhaps of curiosity, which may in turn lead to action, such as your looking up the family album. In this way, even long after he was dead, your ancestor, as a member of the society of your thoughts, may have proved himself to be pretty active and effective. Reflecting on this peculiar situation in which your great-grandfather bestrides the centuries and functions in two systems a hundred years apart, you may be tempted to *double him up*, and think of the man who is now interacting with your thoughts as a representative, or copy, or idea, of the man of long ago. You can do this *now*, without self-contradiction, because you are not extruding anything from the reach of your thought. Your ancestor himself is still an object of your thought all right, but he is an object that functions in two such spatially, temporally, and causally different contexts that it is convenient to think him as two, one a sort of copy of the other and in maybe a one-to-one correspondence with the other. And, of course, what you can do with this example, you can do with all other objects of knowledge. This is Epistemological Dualism. When your thoughts agree with reality, they are true; when they are bad copies and don't correspond to it, they are false. For example, the Desdemona who was the object of Othello's jealous thought had become unfaithful; but the Desdemona who was real had all the while been loving and true. Later—and too late—the Moor was to discover that the one Desdemona was not a good copy of, and did not correspond to, the other. This dualistic or copy theory *can*, then, be applied, no less than the two monistic theories of objectivism and subjectivism, to the domain of conceptual knowledge or thought. But in this domain the Dualistic Epistemology is a little bit strained, as I dare say you realized when I asked you to split your great-grandfather in two: one who interacted with his nineteenth-century contemporaries and one who interacted with the twentieth-century thoughts and feelings of your mind.

Dualism won't get its real innings until we leave conceptual and come to perceptual knowledge. We shall have to face this more traditional epistemological set-up in a minute, but before doing so let us ask, What *is* a "copy"? And just *how* is a *picture*, or a *map*, or a *representative* related to the reality to which it is said to "correspond"?

I have before me a picture in which the mountains, hills, houses, fields, clouds, and sky look much as such things do look. I have also a map of the North Atlantic Ocean with something of the lands on each side of it. The picture is an artistically realistic copy; the map is a scientifically realistic copy. The picture resembles nature in the *qualities* of its several elements. The map resembles nature in its internal *relational* structure. For physical science, and especially for the science of physics, terms are almost nothing, while relations are almost everything. The qualities —visual, auditory, olfactory, and so forth, but mostly visual—that are perceptually apprehended as attributes of bodies matter only as identification tags. They are like proper names, such as "Cinders" and "Jock," which are the names of my dogs. Neither for me nor for the dogs themselves have these names any resemblance to the beings which they quite adequately denote. Just so, the quality of greenness which the man with normal eyes perceives as a character of yonder grass, is for the physicist a mere denotative tag or sensory symbol for the some hundreds of trillions per second of electromagnetic oscillations emanating from the surface of the grass and which constitute its reflected light as "green" in the physical sense of that word. Now, the epistemologists are more scientific than artistic in their aims, so let us credit the Epistemological Dualists, when they say that things apprehended are copies of things that are real, with meaning the map kind rather than the picture kind of copying.

If the relational structures of the map and of the reality that is mapped are the same, and if the sameness or difference of their corresponding terms is unimportant, in what relevant respect do they differ? Why are they not one identical thing? Answer: because, of course, they have different *external relations,* which means different *positions* in the total system of things. The black circle that represents London on my map is distant a few feet west of the paper on which I am writing. London itself is many miles distant and lies to the east rather than to the west of my manuscript. This difference of external relations is the essential difference between even the best copy and the thing it copies; and it would remain even if the map were life-size or full-scale. But this means, if the Epistemological Dualist is right, that no object of thought can be identical in position with the real object of which it is a copy. And this, in its turn, means that no real object, such as your nineteenth-century great-grandfather, can ever be thought of. But this view of the matter is, as we have seen, self-contradictory, because in the very act of denying that you can think of the man as he "really was," you *are* thinking of him as he "really was." What shall we do in this impasse? Let us do what we did before. When we found that everything of which we could think was in a sense a creation of the thinker, and yet at the same time existing prior to the thinker and independent of him and his creative acts, we put to ourselves the conundrum, "When is a creation less than a creation?" And we answered, "When it is a *re-creation,* that is, a function of the 'creator' but not dependent on him." In the same way, a cause is a function of its effect and implied by it, but still not dependent upon it. Let us now, moved by the success of this previous device, pose to ourselves another conundrum: "When is a copy *more* than a copy?" We answer, "When it partly *intersects* or *coincides* with that which it copies." This does the trick. For, consider my map of the Atlantic and its coastal regions on which New York, like London, is represented by a dot. Here within this dot (though, of course, so small as to need an enormously powerful magnifying glass to see it) is represented my house, my table, and this paper. And by putting the map properly down I can make the copy coincide with the reality that it copies. It then becomes "a copy that is more than a copy." This is the kind of thing that happens when the things that are thought of happen also to be the things that are real. The situation can be diagrammed by two lines, L (objects real) and l (objects thought of), with their respective sets of points,

$$P_1 \; P_2 \; P_3 \; \ldots\ldots\ldots \; P_{c'} \; \ldots\ldots \; P_{c''} \; \ldots\ldots \; P_{c'''} \; \ldots\ldots \text{ and}$$

$$p_1 \; p_2 \; p_3 \; \ldots\ldots\ldots \; p_{c'} \; \ldots\ldots \; p_{c''} \; \ldots\ldots \; p_{c'''} \; \ldots\ldots$$

The respective point-sets are determined by the respective equations E and e, E symbolizing the physical laws determining the things concerned, and e symbolizing the psychological laws determining the thoughts of those things. But while $P_{1,\,2,\,3}$—and $p_{1,\,2,\,3}$—are *separate* and merely correspond to one another (as exemplified by Othello's *false* conception of Desdemona), $P_{c',\,c'',\,c'''}$—and $p_{c',\,c'',\,c'''}$—are points *common* to the two lines, and not only correspond to but are identical with one another (as exemplified by your *true* conception of your great-grandfather).

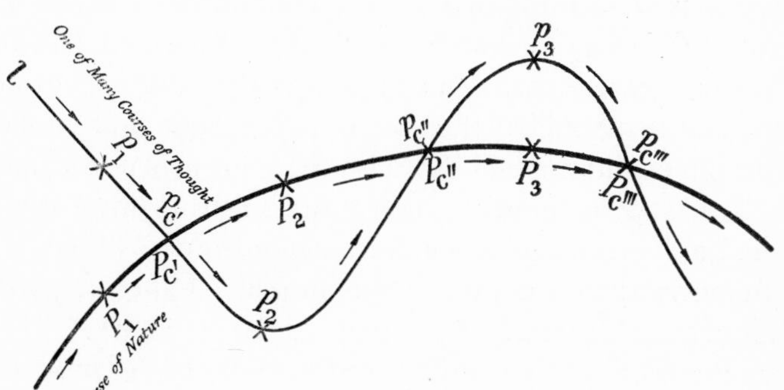

FIG. 2

And now that we have shown that the first three types of epistemology can be formulated in a fashion to make each of them true and each of them compatible with the other two in the realm of conceptual apprehension, or *thought*, we must turn to that other realm—perceptual apprehension, or *sense*, and see how the matter lies.

Perception differs from conception in two ways. In the first place, it is direct and specific or sensory knowledge—what William James called "knowledge by acquaintance"—in contrast to conception, which is indirect and schematic, or rational—what William James called "knowledge about." In the second place, it is what we may call positional; that is to say, an object or event that is perceived is apprehended as located in a time and space continuous with that of the perceiver himself, while in conception there is no consciousness of a bridge or space-time medium extending from the thinker to his object. It is this feature of perception that gives the feeling of—or the immediate belief in—the *reality* of the perceived object and causes motor reactions to it, such as focusing the eyes, pricking up the ears, and contracting the muscles.

The other feature of perception which we listed first means, as was said, that the object appears in itself rather than as a function of something else. It is perceived as possessing primarily the qualities appropriate to the sense organ through which the stimulus has come, and secondarily the qualities associated with these in the past and now elicited from memory to constitute what William James called a "fringe," which gives *meaning* to the object and differentiates it from a mere sensation. Thus, while the baby visually perceived the knife as just a blob of color, shape, and size, the man visually perceives it not only as a colored shape but as *sharp* and *dangerous*. To us, because of past associations, the ice "looks" smooth and hard and cold as well as gray and flat. When you conceive of your great-grandfather or of mankind or of justice or courage, you have before your mind a vast, vague fringe of relations sensuously focused, if at all, only by the visual or auditory image of the *name* of the thing conceived. This, in James's phrase, is "knowledge about." To illustrate, consider Helen Keller's knowledge of the color *green*. It is conceptual rather than perceptual. It is "knowledge about" rather than "knowledge by acquaintance." Being educated, Miss Keller knows green to be a something as qualitatively specific as an odor or flavor but unimaginably different from them. She probably also knows it to be an attribute of grass and young leaves, to be "between" what she has "heard" called "yellow" and "blue," and capable of being perceived by means of the normal human eye when that organ is stimulated by some 600 trillions per second of light waves. Contrast this way of knowing green with the way in which a normal child knows it. He can sense it directly and as such. He has the "knowledge by acquaintance" that Miss Keller lacks. But he has none of the "knowledge about" green that Miss Keller shares with the scientists. Another illustration: The planet Neptune and some of the recently discovered chemical elements were conceptually known in terms of their relations to other things before they were visually perceived.

Does sense perception ever deceive us? Or is it only the judgments or beliefs associated with it that deceive us? This is a purely verbal question. Are we to follow ordinary usage, and include as part of the meaning of the word *perception* the affirmation of the independent existence of the perceived object, which is as clearly present in the experience as the sensory qualities themselves? Or are we to follow the usage of some psychologists and philosophers and employ the word *perception* to designate the appearance of the perceived object minus its reality-feel? I myself prefer what I think is the common-sense usage. Taken in this sense, perception often deceives us, as, for example, when I see two feet behind the mirror a face exactly like my own. The object that I perceive there is not there, and the apparent object does not coincide with reality.

There are two kinds of apprehension that are neither conception nor sense perception. I can apprehend an object with specific sensory qualities but not continous with me in space or time. This is *imaging*. For example, I can call up the visual image of the front door of my house, or the auditory image of the tune of *Yankee Doodle*. Images of this sort are for some faint and schematic, and for others detailed and vivid. People differ a great deal in this respect; but whether the images are faint or vivid, they are not located or dated with reference to the person imaging them. They are like objects in a picture or events in a novel.

The other kind of apprehension that is neither conception nor sense perception is something which has no name. I am going to call it "non-sensory perception." It is the opposite of imaging; for imaging had the sensory content of a perceived object but lacked the consciousness of a space-time bridge connecting it with the perceiver, and non-sensory perception has the bridge but lacks the sensory content. I am immediately or directly aware of the space beyond the surface of an opaque wall, and of the time that is before and after the sense-filled patch of duration that is termed my "specious present." I do not perceive what fills this trans-sensory time and space. But I have a perceptual assurance of the space and time being there whether filled or empty. I think that it was this characteristic of space and time as experienced by us that made Kant call them neither concepts nor sense data but "a priori perceptions." For reasons which I cannot go into here, I feel that they guarantee their own authenticity or validity and that they are concrete and singular or individual rather than abstract and universal. All spaces and times are parts of one space and one time.

Is perceptual cognition *true* with respect to the sensory qualities of its objects, or are those specific and so-called secondary qualities purely subjective, or at least relative to our consciousness and *not* present out there? In other words, is blood really red in itself and is grass really green in itself? Or are these qualities like the pleasantness of a delicacy—merely effects produced in us?

There are several answers to this question:

(I) The naïve or common-sense answer that the colors and other secondary qualities that appear in objects are thereby guaranteed with certainty to be actually in them independently of their relation to us who perceive them. I do not accept this guarantee as sufficient for the simple reason that the appearance of a thing can change as we change our relation to it, though the thing itself remains unchanged. The same mountain looks blue from a distance, green from nearer by, and mottled with all sorts of shades and hues from close by. It could not have these contradictory colors absolutely and in itself.

(II) There is the answer that is opposite to the common-sense one that we have just examined. It is the theory held by Galileo and Descartes and by most of the later physicists. We shall call it the Cartesian theory. It is the view that bodies in themselves have no secondary qualities at all, neither those which they appear to have nor any others. They possess, it is claimed, only the quantitative or so-called "primary" qualities such as shape, size, number, mobility, velocity, acceleration, solidity, and inertia. The secondary qualities are merely the effects which the primary qualities produce upon our minds; and we spontaneously and inevitably, but falsely, *ascribe* the characters of these internal mental effects to their external physical causes. The real reason for the wide prevalence of this view was the progressive discovery that more and more and finally apparently all of the physical changes that a body goes through can be adequately explained in terms of its primary qualities, together with those of neighboring bodies and the quantitative relations between them. The secondary qualities which bodies appear to have were not needed (except as identification tags) to explain their behavior and were consequently denied to have physical existence.

I do not think we can deny the uselessness of the secondary qualities to explain the motions of "dead" matter. And, as we shall see later, it is this fact that gives enduring strength to the metaphysics of materialism, according to which masses and their mechanically determined motions are the primary reality. I refuse, however, to accept the conclusion that the secondary qualities of bodies are unreal because they are useless from the point of view of physics. The brains whose states and processes determine the appearance of secondary qualities and of those other still more internal things such as feelings and thoughts—"tertiary qualities," as they have been called—are composed of the same chemical atoms as other material bodies. The brain's organization is, of course, infinitely more complex; but that material organization might well have for its function not the determination of simple qualitative elements, but the mental organization of those elements; which would mean that the latter could perfectly well be the correlates of such simple energies as are found in dead matter. I do myself believe that Bergson and Jean Jaurez before him are more likely to be right than Descartes in holding, as they do, that Nature is not poorer but richer in qualities than she appears to us to be. In that case, the function of the sensory nervous system would not be to *create* (like the miracle-working Cartesian soul) qualitative sensations out of merely quantitative stimuli, but to *select* from the vast welter of energies *already qualified* the few kinds needed by the organism. These energies, transmitted to the brain and stored there as an intensive hierarchy of memory traces, could then be built up into the far-flung relational systems that constitute even the simplest mind.

(III) This conception of the matter makes the third of the possible answers to the question as to the external reality of the secondary qualities. It stands between the impossible dogmatism of common sense and the unnecessary negativism of Descartes. Must it remain only a metaphysical speculation? I think not. There is a possible experiment which, if it were performed, would give a scientific answer to the question as to whether grass is really green in itself and not merely in its effect upon our senses. The experiment would consist in making physical estimates first of the pattern of energies on the surface of the grass, and second of the pattern of energies in the visual cerebral centers of a man who reported a perception of green. If the two energy patterns turned out to be the same, the probability would be overwhelming that in that case the green of the grass was not merely a subjective appearance but an objective reality. It may be a long time before the technique of physiology makes possible the performance of this experiment, but there have already been at least two approaches to it. First, there are the experiments on the flatfish reported by Sumner nearly thirty years ago and properly exploited for their epistemological significance by Pitkin in his essay in *The New Realism.* Those experiments showed that the fish transmitted through his central nervous system and reproduced on his skin without essential alteration, not the actual pattern with which his skin was in contact, but the peculiar distortion of that pattern which he *saw* through the distorting glasses fitted on him. More recent experiments have shown that the vibration pattern of a tone changed into radio waves could be transmitted (again without essential alteration) through the auditory nerve of a cat. Both experiments indicate that the labyrinth of the nervous system is not the distorting medium that it has been supposed to be, and that the brain energies that determine sensation qualities may be the duplicates—and, hence, *their* qualities true copies of—the energies and qualities of extra-organic bodies.

Our next question is concerned not with a comparison of the *qualities* of perceived objects and real objects, but with a comparison of their respective *locations and dates.*

As to the dates, we can answer at once, definitely and without fear of dispute, that the perceived events and the real events to which they refer are never identical in temporal position. For an event to be perceived, a stimulus must, as sound waves, light waves, and so forth, traverse the distance from the locus of the event to the locus of the brain of the perceiver. And as no stimulus that we know of travels at an infinite speed, there must always be a time-lag and a consequent aberration of the event as perceived with respect to the event as it really occurred. *Nor does perception itself indicate by any sign its own out-of-dateness.* The astronomer perceives the explosion of a star as contemporaneous with his adjustment of his telescope, though he may know that the explosion itself occurred thousands of years ago, and that the star as such is possibly no longer in existence. The movements of sun spots that are seen at any moment have taken place eight minutes before that moment. The bell in the church 1200 feet distant began to sound there more than a second before it is *heard* to sound there. Listen to an airplane, and notice that the sound is perceived to come from some distance behind the place where the airplane is seen, and so on. This ever-present temporal aberration brings with it a spatial aberration whenever the source of the stimulus is moving in relation to the observer, as in the case of the sound of the airplane and the sight of the sun spots. And while both vision and hearing give some clues to the distance of the source of the stimulus, no form of sense perception gives any clue as to what has happened to that source after the stimulus had left it. In short, perceived events appear falsely but incorrigibly contemporaneous with the present.

Because of these differences in position between the real event and the perceived event, the dualistic or copy theory would seem the only one of the three theories so far considered that is applicable to perceptual apprehension. For (it will be remembered) the essence of a copy is a sameness of the internal terms or relational patterns of the two systems combined with a difference in their respective external relations or *positions*. In the case of thought or conceptual apprehension, this condition was ameliorated by the fact that the map and the things mapped intersected in the case of spots where thoughts were true. Then the real and the conceived object became identical. Thus was "a copy more than a copy." In perception this intersection of the real and the perceived constituting identity of position can never happen, for the reasons that we have stated. There is, however, a peculiar aspect of the situation in perceptual apprehension which I wish to commend to your consideration. In perception the sensory picture of the world is a moving picture not only of the world external to our bodies, but of our bodies themselves and of their movements and actions. As between things outside the self and their perceptual appearance, there is an aberration or dislocation of position; but as between the real self and the perceived self, there is a positional identity. The self with its actions has membership in both the real and the perceptual systems. To this common central point the remaining members of each system are externally related and related in the same way, by which means they too acquire a kind of identity of position. It is not an identity of position in time or space; it is a positional identity wth respect to practical action. I perceive in the telephone receiver an auditory copy of my friend's voice. The friend's voice itself is miles distant in space and a fraction of a second removed in time from its telephonic copy. But my friend and I react to each other's words and ideas exactly as if we were not separated by these space and time intervals. And because the auditory copies have in relation to ourselves and our actions the same external relations as the real voices, we should feel it to be a sort of artificial understatement of some bystander if he were to say to us, "Please remember that you are not listening to one another's voices but only to their copies in two far-separated telephone receivers." We could answer him by posing our former conundrum, "When is a copy more than a copy?" and answer, "When, though having membership in a different causal system, it nevertheless enjoys either an identity of position in a space and time frame of reference, as in conception, or an identity of position in a *functional and actional frame of reference*, as in perception." Then, too, we should realize (because of the continuity and comparative completeness of the one-to-one correspondence between our existing environment and the moving picture we have of it in sense and perception) that there is, if not a deeper, at least a far wider communal identity than in thought between the reality and its copy in perceptual knowledge.

And, finally, let us note that just as the objects of conceptual knowledge could be regarded as located in the mind of the knower, interacting with his other cerebral processes, and also as located in the world external in space and time to the knower, so too can the objects of perceptual knowledge be located both inside and outside of the self that knows them. It is this duality of location of objects in perception no less than in conception that justifies the copy theory and at the same time transcends it, thus making possible in each realm of knowledge both Epistemological Objectivism and Epistemological Subjectivism as well as Epistemological Dualism.

Relativism

There is a fourth theory of epistemology which must now, by way of conclusion, be briefly considered.

Different names, emphasizing slightly different aspects, have been used to designate it, such as "Relativistic Objectivism," "Objective Relativism," and "Logical Positivism." We shall call it simply *Relativism.* It is the view held by those who would deny the legitimacy of the epistemological problem. So, too, Positivism in general is the view of those who would deny the legitimacy of the metaphysical problem.

For the Relativist, there is no propriety in our talk about the relation of Knowing to Being, or of things perceptually and conceptually apprehended to things believed to exist, or, in general, of appearance to reality. Reality *is* appearance, and appearance is as real as anything that we can get. The Monistic Objectivist, or "realist," as he is often called, must give up his doctrine that there are things real in themselves which have absolute position in the causal *zusammenhang* of space and time and which constitute the ground or explanation of the totality of actual and possible appearances. And the Monistic Subjectivist, or "idealist," as he is often called, must give up his doctrine that things real in themselves are things as they would appear to a possible absolute self who could have the totality of whatever is actual and possible with all their relations in a single, infinite unity of experience. And above all (according to the Relativist), the Epistemological Dualist must give up his doctrine that real things are external to and independent of the appearances which copy them. Nothing really exists apart from some experiential context, and everything that appears to exist does exist in some experiential context. Your cane partly immersed in water appears to be bent. Well, in that particular visual context it *is* bent, as truly as in other contexts it is straight. The railroad tracks over which you are traveling appear to be convergent when you look back upon them from the observation platform of your train; therefore, in that context they *are* convergent just as truly as they are not convergent but parallel when viewed from directly above. Desdemona actually was unfaithful to Othello, in the context of Iago's slanders and her husband's belief in them—and so on and so on. All appearances are equally true and real, though it is admitted by the relativist that some are more "convenient" than others.

To this view (very popular with certain technical philosophers at the moment), I shall present here two objections.

First, that which is perceived at a moment of consciousness bears unmistakable witness to its alien origin. Sensations in particular come with all the insolent irrelevance of a sneeze, butting into the quiet course of our meditations. Intrusions call for explanation. That is what we demand and that is what we get in our immediately formed conceptions of a something other than ourselves, a something out there, an external world of physical objects as the cause and explanation of the sensory bombardment to which, during all our waking lives, we are continuously subjected. In other words, the perceived is always more than what is actually present. It implies both for perception and for thought something other than itself with which it is continuous. It is as though we were prisoners in an ivory tower through the windows of which long poles could be thrust. We can see and touch only the hither ends of these poles, but neither for sense nor for conception can there be a pole with only one end, a body with only one side, a hither without a thither, an internal to which there is no corresponding external. The sensory perception of the here and now as given involves in its very nature the non-sensory perception of a there and then as a presupposition and necessary complement or supplement of the sense datum itself.

My second objection to Relativism has been touched on at the beginning of this chapter and developed at length in "The Story of American Realism" (see pages 230–261), and I will repeat it here only very briefly. The Relativist's notion that appearances are all on a dead level of *ontological equality* and differentiated only by *practical convenience* is demonstrably untenable. The one set of appearances vulgarly regarded as unreal and false can be explained by the other set of appearances vulgarly regarded as real and true. We cannot, however, turn this around and express the true in terms of the false. Thus, the straight stick taken as real can explain the appearance of that stick becoming bent by being partly immersed in water, but not conversely. The parallel railroad tracks, if taken as real, can explain both the passage of the train over them and their false appearance of convergence when viewed from the rear platform. But if the apparent convergence were taken as real, it could explain neither the passage of the train nor the appearance of parallelism when viewed from above. If Desdemona's faithfulness is taken as "real," Othello's dreadful delusion can be explained as a result of Iago's lies; but if the objects of Othello's deluded fancy are taken as real, then nothing can be explained. In short, *real objects can appear and also explain, while unreal objects can only appear.* The difference between the two sets of appearances is decidedly more than a difference of "practical convenience."

If my refutation is accepted as valid, does it mean that there is no element of truth in the epistemological theory of Relativism? Not at all. Relativism in a chastened form, purged of its arrogant negativisms (a subconscious awareness of which is probably the explanation for its amusing fondness for calling itself "Positivism" and so achieving a kind of linguistic compensation), contains a unique and valuable contribution to truth. That everything can appear and not merely exist or subsist in lordly independence; and that Reality itself can appear as a series of humble, finite, momentary experiences and not merely as an ultimate resultant of the totality of all things experienced "coherently" by an Absolute Mind—these are insights worth having. Reality and truth may be more than experience, but they certainly are not less; and we can gratefully learn from the Relativist that they can be procured piecemeal and at retail in the stores of sense data and not merely at wholesale from the universe in its entirety. And, finally, we must credit the Relativist with having given to the errors and unrealities of the world a new and significant status. For just as "every man was some mother's baby," so every unreality and error, no matter how glaring or how crazy, is a possible object of belief in some experiential context. The faithlessness of the faithful wife, the bentness of the straight stick, the mechanically impossible convergent rails over which the train has gone, the bed-post acting like a serpent in the nightmare world of the sufferer from delirium tremens—all of such objects of perceptual illusion and conceptual delusion can function as if they were realities and truths within the experiential contexts that are requisite for their appearance.

And now, by way of conclusion, let us represent the

four theories as the four cardinal points of the epistemologist's compass:

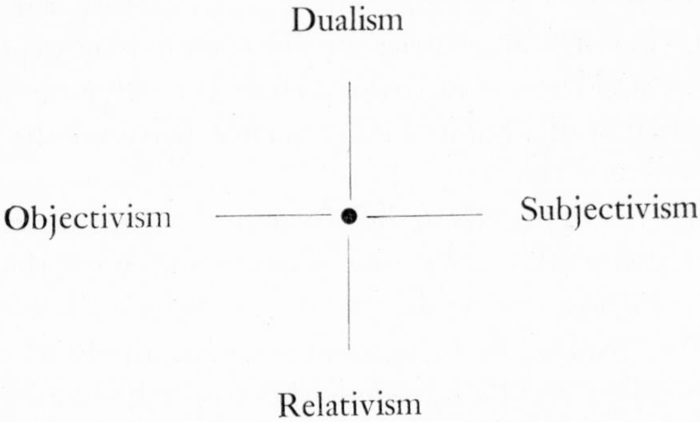

And let us remember that in each of these theories we found an element of weakness and an element of strength. Taken as they stood, they were incompatible with one another and incompatible with the facts. By our critical analysis we deprived them of their false and negative claims. Thus:

I. We deprived *objectivism* of its negative claim that objects, because they were independent of the knowing subject, were therefore not a (re-created) function of the knower.

II. We deprived *subjectivism* of its negative claim that objects because they were (re-creative) functions of the knowing subject were therefore not independent of being known for their existential status.

III. We deprived *dualism* of its negative claim that because objects as known were determined by a system of causes separate from the causal system of the real objects of which they were copies, therefore the members of the two systems could never be truly identical either by intersection or by functioning identically in relation to the body and its actions.

IV. We deprived *Relativism* of its negative claim that because both real and unreal objects could figure as appearances in finite experiential contexts, therefore there was nothing beyond an experience by which that experience could be validated, and consequently no difference except in the matter of practical convenience between the "real" or "true" and the "unreal" or "false."

When thus purged of their negations, the four theories became compatible with one another and with the facts. I believe that my fourfold analysis and synthesis constitute an adequate solution of the problem concerning the relation of Knowing to Being, and therefore I name it the "Epistemological Eirenicon." [1]

References to Part Two

* 5. "The Story of American Realism," page 230.
6. "Truth Subsistential and Existential," page 262.

[1] In the second part of my book *The Ways of Knowing* I followed the same line of thought but applied it only to the first three theories, Relativism being omitted.

CHAPTER IV

NATURE AND THE WAYS OF BEING: METAPHYSICS OF THE MACROCOSM

THE FIRST of the two primary problems of metaphysics is the problem of the relative importance of mind and matter in the general scheme of the universe or macrocosm.

Quite early in the life of the child there dawns on him a realization of two pretty different kinds of things in the world: (1) public, outside things that he and others can *see* and *touch;* (2) private, inside things that he alone can *feel.* As the child grows up and as the race grows up, this vague duality becomes sharper and clearer until at last the universe comes to be regarded as made up of two kinds of substances completely different, if not opposite, in their nature: the one, body, material and not mental, the other, spirit, mental and not material. But long before the primitive duality develops to this radical antithesis of body and spirit, there are stages of belief in which the two components are thought of as blended in various ways. There is an early stage in which all bodies are conceived to be animated by a kind of life and spirit of their own. Along with this idea that body is to some degree mental, there usually goes the correlative belief that spirit is to some degree material. But as culture develops and men become more and more able to control the bodies around them and to predict their future situations by discovering regular routines or uniformities in their behavior—unvarying relations of sequence and coexistence that are called "laws" —there seems less and less point in thinking that rivers and seas and mountains and clouds are animated and directed by spirits as our own bodies are. So matter gets deader and deader, as it were, and its movements and other changes become more and more explicable in terms of the external or spatial relations of bodies to one another. The systems of bodies in which such external determination prevails are called *mechanical* or *mechanistic*, the words being used, as such words often are, to designate both the theory or explanation and the things explained. As this view of material nature develops and becomes fixed, there is substituted for the idea of many directing spirits one great spirit, or God. But belief in this God as a creator and sustainer of nature is not permitted to interfere very much with the notion of a world of dead matter behaving in accordance with mechanical laws. As the concept of matter becomes purged of its spiritual nature, the concept of spirit becomes purged of its irrelevant accompaniments of vague materiality, such as extension, color, vaporousness, and so forth; and along with this dematerializing of mind there comes a clearer recognition of the sort of process or law that is characteristic of mind. This kind of law is the opposite of material law or mechanism. It is essentially *purposive*. As spirits or minds, we can and do form plans and set before ourselves *ideals*, *goods*, or *ends*, to be attained in the future. Our behavior is directed and controlled by our present consciousness of these future possibilities and our desire or will to make them into actual facts, or, as we say, to "realize" them. The Greek word for "end" is *telos*, and the Latin word for it is *finis;* hence, the purposive laws and processes that are characteristic of spirit or mind are called "teleological" and sometimes "final" or "finalistic." "Teleological" or "final" causation is internal or *ab intra* causation, as mechanistic causation was external or *ab extra* causation. And matter as determined from without is inert, passive; while spirit as determined from within is self-determined, spontaneous, active, and free.

Thus, very roughly, we have tried to show how from the vague childhood recognition of a duality of inner states that can be *felt* and outer objects that can be *seen,* there has developed the metaphysics of *dualism,* a vision of the world as composed of two more or less sharply contrasted *things* directed, respectively, by two more or less sharply contrasted kinds of *laws: matter and mechanism* on the one hand, *mind and teleology* on the other.

This dualistic metaphysics in a somewhat modified form is widespread and popular. It is the metaphysics of common sense, and it is ingrained in our whole system of language. It was elaborated (though in its modified or moderate form) with magnificent clarity and completeness by St. Thomas Aquinas at the climax of the medieval period. It was again elaborated also with great clarity, but in a much more extreme form and with the contrast of matter and spirit much sharper, by René Descartes, the founder of modern philosophy.

In both its Thomistic and its Cartesian forms there is a great deal to be said in support of metaphysical dualism. But the human mind in all its inquiries, whether physical or metaphysical, proceeds like a wave in alternating phases. And as the trough of a wave is followed by the crest and that in turn by another trough and crest, so is inquiry an alternation of analysis—synthesis, analysis—synthesis, and so forth. In a vague and general chaos (M), two contrasting aspects, P and Q, are analyzed out; but the intellect cannot rest with this achievement. It must go on to unite what it has put asunder and reduce the plurality or duality by expressing P as f_a (Q), or Q as f_b (P), or P and Q as, respectively, f_1 (M) and f_2 (M). So it is that as the metaphysical separation between matter and mind grows sharper, the urge to reunite them grows stronger. And from this urge there issue three further types of metaphysical theory. First, and on the Left, there is *materialism*, according to which mind and all its teleological processes are reducible to functions or by-products or aspects of matter and its mechanistic processes. Second, and on the Right, there is *idealism*, according to which matter and its mechanistic processes are reducible to mind and its teleological processes. And, finally, in the Center, but opposite to *dualism*, there is *positivism*, according to which both mind and matter are reducible to functions (or constructs) of the immediate data of sensory experience. Let us present the four theories in a diagram analogous to the diagram of the preceding chapter. And as we called that earlier tetradic diagram the "Epistemological Compass," we will call this one the "Metaphysical Compass."

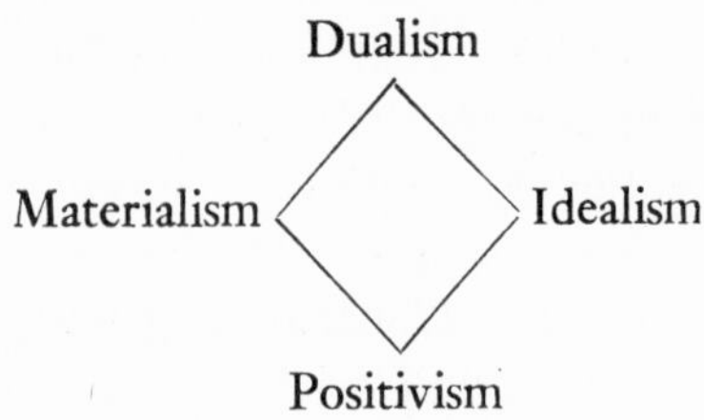

My metaphor or simile of the compass may seem a bit artificial, but I think it exemplifies at least two lessons that are useful both for the philosopher and for the student of philosophy. The navigator wants the four cardinal points of North, South, East, and West to stand out with prominence on his chart and compass, not because any given voyage will lie in some one of these principal directions, but because the infinitely more numerous intermediate directions can be perceived with exactness by being referred to the primary four. And if the course of the voyager must change from time to time, as it usually does, it is all the more important to be able to have a reference frame of fixed directions against which, or in terms of which, he can chart his deviations.

Now, neither in metaphysics nor in epistemology will you find any actual philosophy which could be located on the chart at the exact "North" or "South" or "East" or "West." Take, for example, the metaphysics of ordinary theistic religion. We can best locate it about halfway between dualism and idealism. For religious orthodoxy, the world consists of bodies and spirits, but the Divine Spirit is its author and guide. Again, I should regard both Dewey and James as positivists in the sense in which we have used the term, but I should put Dewey and his "naturalism" halfway between positivism and materialism; while James, with his "Rightist" religious tendencies, I should put midway between positivism and idealism. It would be neither possible nor desirable to carry this business too far or to seek a specific place in the chart for each of the world's great metaphysicians; but I do think that this compass, and also the one for epistemology, are useful both for our own philosophizing and for traversing the history of philosophic thought. The two compasses, though made on the same tetradic model—a black, a white (the two opposing views), a gray, and a striped (the two types of compromise)—should be carefully distinguished. It is true that the metaphysics of positivism, especially in its modern form, is almost identical with the epistemology of relativism. And between the idealism that interprets the world as a manifestation of mind and the subjectivism that would reduce known objects to the self that knows them there is, indeed, a strong affinity. It is no mere accident that modern "idealism" is a union of both doctrines. But the remaining pair of theories have no necessary connection. To hold with *epistemological* dualism that what is known is a copy of what is real does not commit you at all on the question of *metaphysical* dualism. In metaphysics Hobbes was a materialist and Descartes a dualist. But in epistemology they both advocated, and on much the same grounds, the dualistic or copy theory of knowledge. And lastly, to be an objectivist in epistemology does not mean that you must be a materialist in metaphysics. The independently real objects in which you believe needn't of necessity be wholly or even partly comprised of material bodies. They could also be other souls, or Platonic Ideas, or a combination of these and still other objects which might or might not include bodies among their number.

And now that we have gained a glimpse of the four types of theory that apply to the "metaphysics of the macrocosm," we must undertake the preposterously gigantic task of indicating in the brief remainder of this chapter some of the strong points and weak points of each of the four theories.

1. *Dualism.* To dwell on the strength of this view would be to elaborate the obvious. It would also be both to repeat in large measure what we have said already and to anticipate what will be said in the succeeding chapter, where dualism is applied to the *microcosm* or conscious individual, rather than, as here, to the *macrocosm* or world as a whole. Let us, then, merely remind ourselves that any metaphysics, both in its ontological and in its cosmological aspects, must provide, in its scheme, for a definite measure of real duality as between the kind of existence called mental and the more or less contrasting kind of existence called material. This duality cannot be "*explained away*," and therein consists the strength of dualism. But that it must be *explained*, and by dualism itself is not explained, constitutes the theory's weakness. No self-respecting intellect can rest in peace so long as heterogeneous things are left dangling with no thread of homogeneity to bind them together. A world like that of Descartes, consisting of

two quite disparate substances communicating intimately and constantly (but only God knows how), would be unbearable even if true.

2. *Positivism.* Metaphysical positivism, like the epistemological relativism, to which it is closely akin, has its strength in the claim that whatever else the real may be, it is at least *experienceable.* The table before me may be, as common sense believes, a body that in itself and independently is very much like what it appears to be. Or, again, it may be an aggregate of nineteenth-century atoms or of twentieth-century electronic particles and waves. Or, still again, it may be an infinity of Leibnizian *monads*, or a thought in the mind of Berkeley's God. But quite regardless of the truth of any or of none of these metaphysical hypotheses, the table "in itself" is at least a something that can be *experienced by us* as the kind of thing we call a table.

So much, then, for the strength of the metaphysics of positivism. What are its weaknesses?

First of all, there is the unconquerable artificiality of the doctrine. The founder of modern positivism was David Hume, whose theory combined the negative parts of the philosophies of two of his predecessors, Thomas Hobbes, the materialist, and George Berkeley, the idealist. Hobbes had believed that there were material substances or bodies but no mental substances. Berkeley believed that there were mental substances or spirits, but no material substances. Hume denied both kinds of substances. He believed that what we call minds should be regarded as bundles of perceptions constituted of two kinds—"impressions" and "ideas." In this he was like Hobbes. But he also believed that what we call bodies should be regarded as groups of sensory qualities, such as hardness, size, and shape, and so forth. In this he was like Berkeley. I don't myself think that Hume really believed these theories to be true. Like most skeptics, his denials were rejections of the possibility of *proving* beliefs and not rejections of the beliefs themselves. However this may be, the world that Hume and the Positivists who came afterward offer us for our consideration is a world of attributes without substances. And attributes without substances are very much like adjectives without substantives. Note the curious change from naturalness to artificiality when you translate from the language of common sense into the language of positivism the two following propositions: "The table *has* its qualities" and "I *have* my perceptions." They become, respectively, "The table *is* its qualities" and "I *am* my perceptions." Are not the second pair of statements curiously artificial? And if you substitute for *perception* the arch-weasel word *experience*, so much in vogue with positivists today, is the matter any better? *Experience* is originally a transitive verb that requires both a subject that does the experienc*ing* and an object that is experienc*ed*. "An experience," "a hate," and "a love" are elliptical for "an experiencing," "a hating," and "a loving"—of some object by some subject. It is only in the recent academic language of positivists and idealists that "an experience" is used to mean "an experienc*ed* object." If you asked an ordinary man if a table, a chair, a star, or this molten earth before there existed any conscious beings were "experiences," he would think you just didn't know how to talk. A world consisting only of adjectives and verbs is a very queer, floaty sort of world—especially when one applies it to his own mind and tries to think of himself as a "bundle" or "stream" of experiences. I don't know anything that expresses more penetratingly the floatiness and artificiality of Hume's positivistic world than the jolly jingle of some years ago. I forget who was its author or where it was published, but it ran, I think, as follows:

Little Miss Muffet sat on a tuffet,
Studying Hume for "exam."
And she said, "I can't see
If ideas are *me*,
Just exactly where all of me *am*."

A second objection to positivism is its inability to keep the *meanings* of an experience from transcending the experience itself. Suppose we waive altogether our first objection and agree to think of every mind and every body as a bundle of experiences. Then consider such questions as these: Does my Tuesday morning's waking-up experience come after my Monday night's going-to-sleep experience? Is your toothache as bad as mine? Or worse? And is it before or after or contemporary with mine? A *relation between* experiences may itself be experienced, at least intellectually, but its meaning cannot possibly be exhausted by being experienced. If the laws of nature are to be positivistically conceived as "invariant relations of sequence and coexistence" between experiences, then those laws by their very meaning as *inter*-experiential relations are more than and independent of any *intra*-experiential relations. But if we must go beyond experience with respect to *relations*, why not go on to *things*, substantives and substances, and so get back once more to a regular world? But to continue with this objection would be to repeat what was said in our criticism of *epistemological relativism.*

It was not Hume, the originator, or Auguste Comte, the systematizer, but John Stuart Mill, the rationalizer of positivism, who was the first to make it conform to the proprieties of our thought and our language. And he bridged the gap between self-contradictory nonsense and sound good sense by his injection of a single blessed word—*possibility*. For, when with Mill you call the tables or stars or other material bodies not "experiences" but "*per-*

manent possibilities of experience," you are intelligible, and you are also safe against the contingencies of any metaphysical reality or of none. If *possibility* means not "mere possibility" but "possibility at least," then when you call the table a permanent possibility of certain familiar experiences you are not committing yourself to any one of the theories of what it is in itself or even as to whether it is *anything* "in itself." You have a device that enables you to "carry on" while you are waiting for whatever ultimate truth may turn up. Finally (and here we arrive at the real strength of positivism), you can use your perceptual experience not as an impossible container of the world that so obviously contains it, but as the *terminus a quo* and *terminus ad quem* of all verifiable knowledge about that world.

3. *Idealism.* The metaphysics of idealism is usually supported by two rather different lines of argument. There is, in the first place, the undeniable claim to a status of primary reality for one's own mind. *Cogito ergo sum.* And it seems natural to assume that other minds testify to their primary reality with as much certainty as does one's own. Supplement these considerations with what we found to be the truth in *epistemological subjectivism:* (1) that reality, whatever else it may be, is certainly a function of the subject, "a re-creation" of the objective world out of the subject's own states and activities; and (2) that the *meaning* of any object or event increases not only in amount but in accuracy with the increase of the number and systematicity of the experiences to which it is related. The consequence is that the full and complete *meaning* of a thing would consist in its relation to and membership in a unitary experience of the totality of things (both real and unreal) by an Absolute Mind. Take, for example, the actual event of Caesar's crossing the Rubicon. To men like Brutus and Mazzini, the event *meant* the sad begin-

ning of the fall of the noble Roman Republic. To men like Bismarck and Mussolini the same event meant the glad beginning of the glorious Roman Empire. The real and complete meaning of such an event will not be known till "the end of time." Then it could be seen in the light of its bearings on all events and in the light of its various appraisals in all systems of valuations—democratic, communistic, Fascistic, Tolstoyan, and so forth. To the extent that the meaning of a thing is at least one aspect of its reality, that aspect in its completeness would seem to imply an Absolute Mind. But, granting this, are the idealists justified in claiming that such a mind is an actuality that is existent rather than a possibility that is merely subsistent? I am afraid not. The full meaning of what you and I actually are involves a reference to the ideal beings that we might have been. But we can hardly infer from that that these ideally perfected editions of our mediocre selves are actually in existence. And yet, despite this objection that I have just made, I feel that the idealistic doctrine of an absolute mind has a certain degree of validity.

A second and quite different line of argument for idealism is the ancient one found in the great religions. There is so much of meaning and of beauty in the cosmos and in the human spirit at its best and highest that it seems reasonable, if not necessary, to believe that the Cause of all things cannot be less in these respects than its own effects, and that it is in all probability much more. An infinitely great and good mind is thus indicated as the ground for the universe and as the nature of ultimate reality. We shall examine this argument later in our chapter on theology; and I will only say here that the theory that the cause must always be higher than its effects is far from being the self-evident axiom that so many religious people take it to be. If not a better case, at least a very good case can be made for the opposite principle, that causality involves growth, and that, therefore, the effects are higher rather than lower than that from which they spring.

There is a third line of argument which for some reason is spurned by the idealists as tending to belittle their metaphysics and expose it to ridicule. This is the argument from *dreams*. Dreams seem to me increasingly wonderful; and if I were ever to become an idealist, I should go in for them in a big way. Consider, for a moment, any one of such fairly long and elaborate dreams as most of us on occasion have enjoyed. Here is presented a world of time and space richly and variously filled with objects and processes that may conform to regular laws. Persons are in that world—ourselves and our friends and complete strangers—some natural, some grotesque. And often in the most surprising manner they will speak "in character" —make novel remarks that at the moment bewilder us and at a later moment make us realize that, of course, they *would* say just that. And when we go from our sleeping dreams to the daydreams set forth in literature, we find the miracle repeated in a new and larger manner. "Sentimental Tommy" in the sequel to the book that bears his name grows up in a way that is terrifyingly real; and the charming weaknesses of his childhood become, as we know they would become, a something not at all charming in his manhood. Could Nature do a better or more consistent job with any of her real Tommies than Barry has done with his own dream-creature? Yet surely the personages of a dream cannot be more than mere appearances. They are not (as *real* things were) "*re-creations*" of the mind; they are its outright *creations*, dependent on the mind and incapable of existing before it or apart from it. Where, then, does their semblance of independent realness come from? If they are nothing but appearances, is it sense or nonsense to discuss whether Hamlet is *really* mad or *really* had an "Oedipus complex"? Nor can we belittle a work of imagination by calling it "just a new combination of old and pre-existing sensory material"—for it is the combination, not the material, that matters. A Shakespearean sonnet and a jumble of letters; a Gothic cathedral and a heap of stones—does the identity of material in each case detract from the significance of the difference in the way it is combined?

So I say again that if I were an idealist, I would found my metaphysics upon dreams, and would argue that, if the world of fancy can be created by and contained within our finite minds, why might not *the* world be the creation of an infinite mind and have its entire being within that mind?

4. *Materialism.* There are many today who will say that materialism as a theory of substances and mechanism as a theory of change or process are outmoded. Matter or mass has been reduced to energy; and *mechanism* as a synonym for *mechanics* in the old, simple sense is quite overshadowed by the sciences pertaining to electricity in its various branches. Now, such distinctions are of great importance for physics; but for metaphysics they are mischievous, misleading, and artificial, and the theologians who today are building fresh hopes upon them and rejoicing over the death of "materialism," their ancient enemy, are due for a very sad awakening. I am using, and, I think, justifiably using, the name *materialism* for the belief that the primary elements of reality are space-occupying things whose processes are determined *mechanistically*, that is, by their spatial relations to what is outside them rather than teleologically by a something more or less like mind that is inside them. That being the case, it is of no relevance whatever whether the space-occupying elements are small, solid, spherical atoms, sneeringly compared to billiard balls (by those who, I suppose, are haters of billiards), or whether they are unit electric charges or clusters, *à la* De Broglie, of electromagnetic waves. Personally, I

like billiards, and I cannot forget that Sir Isaac Newton, with his vulgar billiard-ball atoms, was a theistic dualist, while Einstein, whose physical elements are something very fancy indeed, is a Spinozist and what I should call a materialist or materialistic positivist. But, be the atomic elements what they may, it is not their *stuff* that matters, but their *laws;* and materialism, from Leucippus and Democritus to Einstein and Heisenberg, is the doctrine that all processes, including those of our own minds, are reducible to or correlated with movements of particles which are mechanistic (1) in the positive sense of being describable in terms of external spatial relations and (2) in the negative sense of lacking purposiveness or foresight, and so being, as we say, governed by "blind forces." What is the strength of materialism as we have defined it, and what is its weakness? [1]

The strength of materialism lies, as I see it, in two advantages which the method of mechanistic procedure possesses and which other methods of procedure are devoid of.

First, any mechanistic hypothesis can be verified or refuted by experiment. If a body's behavior is alleged to be determined by an external relation to another body, say, by a force of gravity varying inversely as the square of its distance from that other body, it will be easy to confirm such a hypothesis by observation and experiment. And if, instead of the inverse square, it had been the inverse third power or inverse fourth power that the hypothesis had

[1] Many scientists and philosophers today prefer to call their doctrine "naturalism" rather than "materialism." Naturalism does not explicitly stress the materiality of natural elements or the quantitatively mechanistic character of natural processes. It contents itself with denying that mind ever attains sufficient independence of matter to interact causally with it, either in the macrocosm or in the microcosm. I cannot myself see how this vaguer and softer-sounding theory of "naturalism" differs from materialism in its bearing upon the metaphysical questions that we are discussing.

asserted, we should still have found it easy to make the experimental test, though in the latter cases it would be the falsity of the hypothesis rather than its truth that would have been established. *The supreme preliminary qualification for a scientific theory is not truth, but verifiability.* Now, *teleological* explanation of a process does not lend itself to this sort of testing because its postulated cause is hidden and internal rather than, as in mechanism, exposed to view as external. In the light of what we have just said, we can understand why materialists are usually atomists and why atomism is, as it were, the handmaid of materialism. The behavior of such bodies as a stick of dynamite or a kettle of boiling water cannot be explained by their external relations to other bodies. They seem, rather, to be determined by occult or hidden and possibly purposive causes. Now, it is the function of *atomism* to externalize the internal. By conceiving of a body as a system of atomic particles, we can in terms of *their* external relations account mechanistically for what seemed at first to be the bodies' definitely internal and antimechanistic spontaneity. Thus does atomism fulfill the function of materialistic explanation.

The second element of strength in mechanistic materialism lies in the fact that the external relations that it uses are not only experimentally verifiable, but mathematically calculable. Mechanistic laws of nature can be expressed as equations, and then combined with other equations, permitting far-reaching deductions to be made. As modern science really dates from the union of the experimental and the mathematical methods of procedure, we can understand the sense in which the philosophy of materialism is really the life and soul of physical science.

And now, what is the weakness of materialism? It is, I believe, the same sort of weakness that infects each of the other three primary metaphysical theories—the weakness of omission rather than of commission. In short, it is good as far as it goes, but no further. In the world of dead matter, each body, at least if interpreted in terms of its atomic components, does seem capable of being regarded as a puppet of its external relations. And materialism has won, and fairly won, a long succession of victories in one domain after another of the cosmos by replacing with its own clear and cold and fertile formulae the sentimental and pleasingly anthropomorphic but utterly sterile formulae of a pre-scientific teleology of nature. But when we pass from dead matter to living matter, and from the merely poetic ascriptions of teleology to such things as stars, planets, liquids, and gases to the directly verifiable teleology of our own selves, the situation is changed. Not only are the victories of mechanism slowed up, if not stopped, but even the possibility of explaining life and life's values and meanings in mechanistic terms seems to recede.

In short, the materialistic philosophy has the "defects of its qualities"; and while very successful in dealing with the physical universe at large, it is met by a sharp challenge when applied to the conscious individual. Let us turn, then, from the metaphysics of the macrocosm to that of the microcosm.

References to Part Two

* 7. "Beyond Physics," page 281.
8. "The Einstein Theory and a Possible Alternative," page 295.
9. "A Possible Interpretation of the Quantum," page 327.
10. "A Theory of Time Perception," page 363.
11. "Time and the Fourth Dimension," page 382.
12. "Substance, Potentiality, and Cause," page 408.
* 13. "A Materialistic Theory of Emergent Evolution," page 418.
14. "Variation, Heredity, and Consciousness," page 441.

CHAPTER V

NATURE AND THE WAYS OF BEING (CONTINUED): METAPHYSICS OF THE MICROCOSM

THE UNIVERSE is all very well, but to ourselves it is we ourselves that matter most. And sooner or later the four high-flown theories of the cosmos come home, as it were, to roost, and gain, by their application to the problem of what we as individuals really are, a strange and crucial poignancy. The first thing we notice when we take up this new enterprise is that the tetradic question, with its four possible answers, becomes contracted into a dyadic question with but two possible answers: materialism and dualism. The problem as to which of these theories is true is the only problem that has central importance and pertinence for the "metaphysics of the microcosm." Sooner or later Death will call all hands; and on that final showdown each player at the game of life will win or lose. Are we, our minds and personalities, mere adjectives of our indubitably perishable bodies and therefore bound to perish with them? If so, we lose. Materialism is true. Or are our minds not adjectives of brain and nerves, or inner aspects of their motions, but real substantives, or souls, in some sense independent of the bodies from whose soil they grow and in whose soil they bloom and fade? If so, we win. Materialism is false and dualism true. That it must be either dualism or materialism for the individual irrespective of which of the other theories is true of reality in general can easily be made plain. Assume for a moment that positivism is valid for the macrocosm. Would it not be true that the "group of experiences" constituting the mind of a person was distinct from the "group of experiences" constituting his body? And would it not remain a question as to whether the first group was or was not dependent upon the second group? No philosophy can alter the fact that at death the body (whatever it may ultimately be) continues in the form of a corpse as an observable fact while the mind (whatever it may ultimately be) ceases to be an observable fact. The positivist could in no way dodge the question as to whether the mind, as he conceives it, is or is not *bound up with and dependent upon* the (living) body, as he conceives that to be. If he answers the question in the affirmative, he sides with the materialist in making the mind a function or aspect of a material organization. If he answers in the negative and denies the mind's dependence on the body, he sides with the dualist.

Now, if we change from positivism to idealism, the situation is the same and the dilemma is the same. Instead of conceiving of mind and body as two "groups of experiences," or two "bundles of perceptions," we are now to conceive of them as two "fragmentary phases of an Absolute Self" or two kinds of "thoughts in a divine mind." And the same question or dilemma presents itself. Is that which we call a person's mind dependent, as the materialist believes, on that which we call his body? Or is it, as the dualist believes, rooted in something other than the body's organization and hence capable of surviving the body's death?

The question cannot be dodged or verbalized away. Both positivists and idealists believe in funerals, which means that they recognize at least a *distinction* between the body and the personality of the dead friend. The body may be, in Mrs. Eddy's phrase, only "an error of mortal mind," but it has to be buried just the same. And the self may be, in Hume's phrase, only "a bundle of perceptions," but it has vanished just the same. And whether it has vanished from existence or merely vanished from our sight remains as much of a question for Hume (or for an idealist) as for the man in the street. As a matter of fact, on this question most of the positivists take the materialistic position of psychophysical monism, while most of the idealists take the position of psychophysical dualism. There are, however, exceptions. William James, despite his *radical empiricism* or positivism, inclined, after his sittings with Mrs. Piper the medium, to dualism. And G. F. Stout, the great idealist, inclines (if I am not mistaken) to psychophysical monism.

What are the strong and weak points of these rival theories, materialism and dualism, when applied to the individual or microcosm?

The strong points of materialism are those we have named in the preceding chapter, together with the tremendous prestige that goes with them. The parts of the world that are most clearly explained are the parts dealt with by physics; and there materialism (in the sense in which we have been taking it) reigns supreme. Shall we, then, shrink from taking our own medicine and be afraid to apply to organic beings, including our very selves, the same formulae that have proved successful in the realm of inorganic matter?

To this general argument for surrendering our lives and minds to the materialistic metaphysics, we must add a second and much more specific argument. *As varies the body, so varies the mind.* There is a vast and diversified mass of facts that testify to this correlation. Ordinary observation and scientific experiment, psychological and physiological, ontogenetic and phylogenetic, reveal the great dependence of mind on body and of vital processes on the physical and chemical properties of matter. Drug the brain, and the mind is dulled. Injure the brain, and the mind is injured. And as we ascend the ladder of successively higher degrees of cerebral organization ontogenetically in the growing individual and phylogenetically in the evolution of species, we find the mentalities correlated with those organizations becoming successively higher too. And then, also, quite apart from the business of mind, one after another of the functions and functional products formerly supposed to be the exclusive prerogative of a "vital force" have been explained and sometimes (as in the case of urea) actually duplicated by chemical or physico-chemical processes.

So much, then, for a bare indication of the strength of materialism. What shall we say of its weakness and of the consequent strength of the dualism that is its rival and which in this context is often called "vitalism"?

First of all, there is the argument already stated in the preceding chapter. Dualism is testified to at first hand by each man's own consciousness. Each of us feels himself to be, I will not say a "captain of his soul," which would imply a mastery over all errant and evil impulses—and only a few of us could boast of that—but at least a *captain of his body*. Despite diseases and injuries which are the body's minor mutinies, and despite the great and final mutiny of death, in which the captain is cast overboard to sink or swim in strange waters—despite these limitations of our power, each of us does truly pilot his body for the normal duration of the voyage, urging, checking, and guiding it according to his plans.

Associated with the naturalness of dualism for direct experience is the unnaturalness of its rival for reflective experience. For now consider the situation which as materialists we should have to accept. Every physical effect must have a physical cause. Therefore, any motion in the brain and nerves and muscles must be completely determined by a preceding motion or physical occurrence. But this means that the physical series is a closed series with no place for the mind or for any state or function of the mind to enter in as a cause of our actions. Consciousness, thus deprived of causal efficacy, is reduced to an "epiphenomenon"—a mere shadow or series of shadows that come tagging along as passive inner aspects of the real causes which are mechanistically determined by electronic attractions and repulsions. A Judas betraying a friend, a saint befriending an enemy, a mathematician solving a problem, are nothing but the ineffective adjectives of particles in a brain moving blindly. Each and every one of us is, then, like Chanticleer in Rostand's play, who boasted that by his crowing he had caused the sun to rise. All that had really happened to the poor fowl was that he had been carried by the revolving planet into a place to which the sun's rays had access. So we, like Chanticleer, and like the equally vainglorious fly who thought that he was causing the rotation of the coach wheel on which he had alighted, accomplish nothing at all by our desires, our will, or our conscious effort. Our minds are dragged around and around by the cerebral mechanisms on which they ride, and the notion that we make those mechanisms go or make anything else go is a pathetic delusion. It is, of course, hard to believe in such a situation even in the interest of a great theory. But perhaps that is just our fault. Chanticleer, too, would have found it hard to believe in what we know to have been the reality.

But now, quite apart from what our feelings say about the naturalness of dualism and about the impossible artificiality of mechanistic materialism as applicable to minds, is there anything that Reason can say on the subject? I think that there is; and I put the comment in the form of the following questions: What is the probability that the atoms of the central nervous system, if left to their own mechanical devices undirected by anything analogous to mind, would hit upon all or even any of the purposeful processes of conscious activity? To me the probability seems infinitesimal. If there were only the single fact of memory, which is, indeed, the very essence of the mental, that in itself would be sufficient. For no configuration of material particles could be an adequate basis for what Bergson calls *durée réelle,* the presence in each present moment of a long enduring past.

Turn from the realm of mind to the origin and growth of an individual organism, and ask a similar question: What is the probability that with only mere chemical and physical forces a fertilized germ from which an animal develops could recapitulate in its ontogeny the age-old series of ancestral forms and finally issue forth from egg or womb fully equipped, not only with organs of alimentation, respiration, and reproduction, but with sense organs and a nervous system for dealing effectively with a variegated environment? Again I answer that the probability of such a process taking place without a directive factor analogous to mind is infinitesimal.

Third, turn from ontogeny to phylogeny and ask a question similar to the two preceding questions as to the probability that without some more than mechanistic factor the proportion of useful variations from which evolve new species would be anything like as high as we find it to have been. I must answer again: the chance is infinitesimal. In phylogeny, in ontogeny, and, above all, in the realm of mind, an aggregate, no matter how complex, of blindly moving particles, each one in good mechanistic fashion determined by its space relations to those outside it, would have no least chance of doing what we know is done in these three fields of purposeful activities. At the game of chance, dualism wins hands down. *Some agency other than the attractions, repulsions, and impacts of atomic particles* MUST *be present.*

But if my argument is sound, how can the dualist defend himself against the great mass of evidence for a concomitant variation of mind and body, with its alleged implication of a dependence of the latter on the former? I think that there is an answer that can be given. In the first place, the concomitant variation of body and mind is by no means as one-sided as the materialist would have it. The mind takes the initiative at least as often as the body in bringing about the co-variance. A sick and injured body can, to be sure, cause a sick and injured mind—at least when the affected part of the body is the brain or nerves. But it is also true that a cheerful and confident mind can initiate corresponding increases in the health of the body. As to how far what is called *psychotherapy* can go, there is no complete agreement among physicians and physiologists. Some, like Alexis Carrel, would hold it capable of going very far and would feel that many of the miraculous cures by faith alleged to occur at Lourdes were quite authentic. Others would ascribe very little power of this kind to the mind and its attitudes. An equally disputed domain of the same sort relates to the powers over their bodies that Hindu ascetics are said to attain. Yet, notwithstanding all these true and allegedly true instances of the influence of mind over matter, I feel that in the realm of general therapy the materialist has, on the whole, the stronger case.

But when we change from the autonomic and sympathetic to the sensorimotor and voluntary nervous system, I think that it is dualism that has the stronger case. This is the realm in which, as we have already said, the mind steers the body. And we can scarcely conceive that its behavior could be what it is unless directed by ideas and acts of will. I am often tempted to illustrate the situation by the case in which music issues from an instrument which we can accurately observe and even subject to experiment. As we vary its structure and perhaps injure it by injecting fluids into it or by cutting away some of its parts, we hear corresponding variations in the music. But the instrument is so situated that no one can look behind it to find out whether there is a musician operating it or whether it plays itself; hence, the audience divides into two groups—"dualists" and "materialistic monists." Now, materialists will probably claim that this, like so many illustrations and analogies, is unfair to their side and really begs the question against them. For we all know that musical instruments are made by men to be operated directly (or indirectly, by phonographic devices) by men. This is true; but, on the other hand, it is also true that the dualist could complain that the illustration was unfair to *his* side because, in the case of the brain (from which intelligent actions emanate like the music from the instrument), there is in each case one person: the owner of the brain, who can testify as to what is concealed from the audience. Let us, then, be careful to let the illustration serve only for clarification and not for proof. Even so, it does make clear that the concomitant variation of two factors *C* and *B* can never decide between the possibility that *C* is a function of *B* alone and the rival dualistic possibility that *C* is a function of *B* co-operating with *S*, that is, consciousness (*C*), a function of the body (*B*) co-operating with a soul (*S*).

Although, as I have said, dualism seems to me to have the better of the controversy, yet, if I stopped there, I should feel a great unhappiness on the general ground that any duality clamors for some underlying unity to bridge the gap between the two components. On this point, however, the reader should be warned that Sheldon, of Yale, the most radical dualist alive today, holds an opinion contrary to mine. He is contented and unashamed in his dualism, and feels that duality is not only an ultimate but a fruitful and productive principle. Whichever of us may be right as to dualism in general, I feel even more certain that I am right in being discontented with dualism as applied to body and mind. The special reason for discontent here is that, whatever its defects may be, materialism is the life of science. It is just because a scientist never gives up the search for physical causes for all physical effects that science has progressed so tremendously. Now, if we abandon this materialistic procedure and invoke a non-physical "spirit" or "vital force" or "psychoid" or "entelechy" to help us out whenever we are stuck, we are giving up the scientific game and opening the gates to a perfect flood of concepts or pseudo-concepts that lead us nowhere. What would other players think of a man who became frightened at his opponent's attack on him in a chess game and avoided defeat by upsetting the table and spilling the pieces? And what would other workers think of a man in a physiological laboratory who, after succeeding in finding a series of physical causes one after another, finally got stuck and, instead of searching further, exclaimed with triumph: "Here's where the soul comes in, and it must be the 'vital force' that is the cause of this motion, because I simply can't find any regular force or motion that will fill the bill." Such a worker would, I am sure, be ejected from the laboratory by his fellows. And yet he might be right, at that. The point is that, in introducing a spirit or soul into the orderly system of physical processes, he would have introduced an unfruitful concept incommensurate and discontinuous with the other concepts, like an alien that could not be naturalized or a food that could not be assimilated. This is why I feel *ashamed*, as it were, of the dualism that I am forced to accept. Unlike my friend Sheldon, I cannot take my dualism straight. I must mitigate it by seeking for some underlying unity in terms of which and as functions of which both mind and body can be expressed. Until that saving concept can be found, we are in an absolute impasse: the fruitful falsity of *materialism* versus the sterile truth of *dualism.*

Conclusion

The account of my struggles to escape from this quandary and the way out that I found are set forth with detail in Essays 13, 14, 15, and 16 and the Postscript of Part Two. But by way of concluding the introductory survey of the types or schools of metaphysical theory as outlined in this chapter and the one preceding it, it may be worth while to give here, in brief and summary fashion, the hypothesis for a solution of the central problem of metaphysics, that is, the problem of the nature of matter and the nature of mind, and the manner in which those two contrasting natures are related.

Accepting the theory of contemporary physics that not only motion but matter, or mass itself, is a form of energy, let us supplement that generally accepted theory with a theory not generally accepted: *that mind also is a form of energy, but a form that is opposite to, though homogeneously continuous with, the forms of energy exemplified by matter in motion.*

The ultimate particles of matter—protons and electrons, neutrons, mesotrons, positrons, and whatever else physics may accept—are regarded as the more or less permanent and relatively self-contained units of energy. They occupy small regions of space and move from one region to another. However wave-like their structures may be, and however much kinetic energy they may acquire by their motions from place to place, the energy of which they themselves are composed is essentially stored up, or "potential." Mass is potential energy, or potentiality of motion, in the sense that under certain circumstances masses may disappear and be converted into, or be replaced by, the motion or kinetic energy of electromagnetic waves which radiate out through space with the velocity of light. In addition to these two kinds of energy: (1) the pure or primary potential energy of mass itself; and (2) the pure or primary kinetic energy of electromagnetic waves, there is, of course, the familiar kind of energy that consists of matter in motion. Let us call it "secondary kinetic energy," and remind ourselves that it is measured by $\frac{1}{2}\,mv^2$ or one-half of the product of the units of mass-energy and the square of the velocity with which they move.

The corpuscles or ultimate units of mass become aggregated (but how or why is not known) into fairly permanent systems called "atoms" of some 92 different kinds. Each of these atoms consists of a close-packed "nucleus" of protons, electrons, and neutrons. The protons, each of which has a unit of positive electric charge, outnumber the electrons, each of which has a unit of negative electric charge, so that the nucleus as a whole is positively charged; but its deficit in the number of electrons is balanced by an equal number of outlying or "planetary" electrons, varying from one to 92. These atoms, each with its "nucleus" and "planets," are further aggregated into persistent, though less permanent, systems called "molecules," of a vast number of kinds, which in turn combine into the gaseous, liquid, and solid bodies that are manifested to our senses. In the compounding of smaller systems into larger systems there usually occurs a transformation of the kinetic energies exemplified in the motions of the smaller systems into potential or stored-up and suspended energy in the larger system. This transformation takes place at each stage in the hierarchy of systems or aggregates. Thus, when two masses are moved away from one another against any attractive force such as gravity, the kinetic energies of their motions are transformed into potential energy of position;

and when two bodies are moved toward one another against a repulsive force such as the resistance of a coiled spring to compression, or, for that matter, of any body, to compression by any other, the kinetic energies of their motions are transformed into potential energy of elasticity. Again, when chemical atoms are compounded into molecules such as those of petroleum or dynamite, the kinetic energies of their motions are transformed into chemical potential energy within the molecules thus formed. When, as in combustion, such molecules are broken down, the potential energy can be transformed back into the motions of pistons, wheels, or projectiles. And when, in their turn, corpuscles are compounded to form atoms, the kinetic energies of their motions are transformed into potential energy within the atomic nucleus which may be transformed back into motions of sub-atomic masses, either by artificial bombardment of the nucleus with neutrons and protons or by the natural processes of breakdown exemplified in uranium and radium.

The four types of energy that we have mentioned up to now are (1) the pure or primary potential energy of the corpuscles or units of mass; (2) the pure or primary kinetic energy of electromagnetic waves or radiation; (3) the secondary kinetic energy of masses (molar, molecular, atomic, and corpuscular) in motion; and (4) the secondary potential energy acquired by the compounding of smaller material systems into larger. All of these examples of energy are predominantly mechanistic in the sense that their changes are mainly determined by their external relations rather than by any self-directive power within themselves. I say "mainly" rather than "completely" determined because, of course, their own masses and velocities enter in as determiners, together with their relations to what is external to them.

A significant departure from this seemingly pure mechanism takes place when certain molecules compounded principally of hydrogen, oxygen, nitrogen, and especially carbon become, for some reason, compounded into units or "cells" of what we call "protoplasm." These new systems have a capacity not present, or at least not clearly noted, in the other systems, of transmitting their specific patterns of energies to other material in which such patterns are lacking. The first phase of this transmission is the assimilation or *anabolism*, in virtue of which the relatively non-specific food material carried into the cell is built up or synthesized into the highly specific substance of which the cell in question (lung cell, liver cell, or what not) is composed. The second phase of the process is *reproduction*, a duplication of the cell's entire energy pattern, with the result that two daughter cells take the place of the original single cell. In the case of unicellular life, the daughter cells go their separate ways. But in the case of multicellular organisms, they stick together in a more or less close-knit association in which each cell embodies, in addition to the energy pattern of its parent cell, something of the energy pattern of the whole colony of which the parent cell was a member. It follows that in the lower, and more loosely organized, multicellular systems every cell is capable not only of reproducing itself but of generating, by a chain of reproductions, the entire organism. As the organization becomes more complex, however, its constituent cells become more specialized and lose their original capacity to regenerate the whole collection. The latter power is then reserved to a particular segregated group of germ cells, such as spores, seeds, ova, and spermatozoa. Of the vast and increasingly complicated and variegated business of organic life whose salient characteristics I have attempted to summarize in a few sentences, the point to which I desire to call particular attention is that with the advent of protoplasm on this planet a type of energy-system which, so far as we know, was not previously existent made its appearance. In vital systems the invisible form of energy which, for lack of a better name, we call "potential" does not merely maintain itself unchanged, as in the protonic and electronic particles of mass; nor does it break down and diffuse itself in kinetic energy or motion; but it grows, increases, and accumulates into deeper and richer systems, reproducing itself or transmitting its hidden pattern from one place to another by induction rather than by conduction. Here, for the first time, we find a natural system in which the inner self-determination, which is teleological, predominates over the determination from without, which is mechanistic. All potential energy is a stored-up resultant of past motion. And in a living cell, particularly a germ cell, we can, and must, explain its power to reproduce in its ontogeny the phylogeny or sequence of its ancestral types as due to an intensively superposed hierarchy of specific forms of potential energy stored up in the chromosomes. In the case of kinetic energy, each present configuration is *replaced* by another configuration. Only in the case of potential energy can a past succession be *retained* as a present duration—what Bergson calls a *durée réelle*. Thus, time, rather than space, is the primary milieu of organic or living matter as distinguished from matter that is inorganic or dead.

Something akin to life may be present, though in a form that we do not recognize, in all that exists in space. And something akin to mind may be present, though again without our recognition, in all that possesses life. However that may be, we find, at least in the higher animal organisms, a seemingly new and different manner in which the past is stored up as potential energy in the present. For in those animals there is a brain to which energies in the form of stimuli are conveyed from all parts of the body, and from the world outside the body through such organs as eyes and ears. In the brain the stimuli are co-ordinated with one another and with the traces of past stimuli, and are then returned along motor or efferent nerves as reactions. Some, if not all, of the incoming energies produce private, or not externally observable, effects which we call sensations. Each sensation fades rapidly as the energy causing it departs from the brain, but it leaves in the brain a trace of itself which we call a memory, with the result that, as we have just said, the new stimuli are co-ordinated, not only with one another, but with the traces of previous stimuli, so that each present reaction is guided by the individual's past experience. To react to the present in the light of the past, and with reference to an imagined future based on that past, is purposiveness or teleology. The system of memory-traces in the form of an intensive hierarchy of forms of potential energy bears all the hall marks of mind. It has unity, organicity, privacy, and above all duration, or extension in time. It is a past which is present, and which deepens or lengthens in proportion to the lengthening of the individual's life. In the main it resembles the intensive hierarchy of energy forms which constitutes the mosaic of hereditary tendencies in the chromosomes of the germ cell. But the system of potential energies accumulated in the brain differs from that of the chromosomes in two important respects. First, it is the past record of the individual and of his encounters with the environment, rather than a record of the bodily forms of his ancestors; and because of this, the cerebral memory expresses itself in action or behavior, whereas the "memory" or heredity in the germ-cell expresses itself in a sequence of bodily forms. Second, while we have no direct knowledge of the actual nature of the potential energies stored in the germ, we do have a direct knowledge of the sensations and memories stored up in the brain. And it is my claim that what we know so directly from within as our own mental states are nothing but that which from the standpoint of an external observer would be classed as the forms of potential energy into which the currents of kinetic energy or stimuli are transformed when they are obstructed and redirected in their passage through the brain.

At first hearing it seems foolish to identify consciousness with anything physical. Even a thorough-going materialist will not, unless he is muddled, identify consciousness with *motion*, but only with an "inner aspect" of motion. For a sensation is *sui generis*, and to identify it with an external object of experience is like identifying sound with color. But when I identify sensation with potential energy I am not identifying it with an object of outer experience. When visible kinetic energy passes into potential energy it does not change into another visible entity, it changes into *nothing*—that is, nothing that is externally observable. We name it "potential" in reference to the motion that it was and the motion that it will be. But in itself at the time that we call it potential, what is it? What we know is that at the moment it ceases to be an externally observable reality there begins to be an internally observable reality which we call "sensation." Isn't it a good bet that the sensation that appears from within *is* the energy that has disappeared from without? Our mind or system of memories would then be identical with the system of traces or residues of potential energy that remain—after most of the energy of the stimuli has lapsed back into motor reaction—stored up in an intensive hierarchy, the later strata being superimposed on the earlier and each retaining its specific character, yet forming an organic unity with the others. This invisible mental organism within the visible bodily organism would be a veritable soul—not an adjective of the nervous system, but a mind that was substantive in its own right. And as ordinary matter itself consists of mass particles of relatively permanent and self-maintaining potential energy, so also would the mind consist of potential energy and as such possess a kind of attenuated mass. But instead of being extensive and divisible like a material aggregate, it would be intensive and indivisible. And instead of its substance remaining constant, it would be continuously increasing with the successive deposits of experience. Finally, and most important of all, it would be self-determining instead of mechanical and blind.

I beg the reader to consider the theory, the bare outline of which I have here so hastily sketched. The arguments for it and some of its broader implications are to be found in the essays referred to earlier in this chapter and also in the little book entitled *The Chances of Surviving Death.*[1]

If the hypothesis is indeed true,[2] it bridges the gap between materialistic monism and spiritualistic dualism or vitalism. By exhibiting consciousness as a form of energy it brings mind and its purposive laws into physical and causal continuity with matter and its mechanical laws, while preserving to the full the distinctive and contrasting natures of each. And finally, to close with a truth that may sound like a paradox: if mind is itself substantive and reducible to a special kind of matter or energy, it is freed from the odium of being an adjective of the ordinary matter or energy of which our perishable bodies are composed.

References to Part Two

11. "Time and the Fourth Dimension," page 382.
* 13. "A Materialistic Theory of Emergent Evolution," page 418.
14. "Variation, Heredity, and Consciousness," page 441.
* 15. "Consciousness a Form of Energy," page 482.

[1] Montague, Wm. Pepperell, *The Chances of Surviving Death*, Cambridge, Harvard University Press, 1934.

[2] See the note on page 510.

CHAPTER VI

NATURE IN RELATION TO VALUE: THEOLOGY

Is there, at the heart of Nature, something somehow good? Or are the only values those that finite beings attain to when successful, with Nature in the large or at the core indifferent to the things we like? To answer this great question would be to solve that basic problem of theology from which all high religions get their meaning. For, as we have seen, religion is generally the expression in organized and institutional forms of man's experience (whether illusory or true) of standing in significant relation to a Being greater than himself both in power and in value. A *Divinity* or *God* means just such a Being, and nothing else. And what is felt and practiced by religion is by theology (at least, as we shall use that term) set forth in terms of thought and reason. Taking theology in this broad sense, rather than in the traditional and more restricted sense of sacrosanct principles or dogmas allegedly revealed by God and to be unquestioningly believed on pain of the deadly sin of heresy, we find ourselves confronted with four possible solutions of the central theological problem of the relation of Nature to Value. These four solutions are: (1) Atheism, (2) Pantheism, (3) Polytheism, and (4) Theism.[1]

[1] Theism is of two kinds, which might be called transcendent and immanental. The first kind regards God as something apart from the world. In its more extreme form it becomes Deism. The second type of Theism regards God as indwelling or "immanent" in the world. The

(1) Atheism is the completely negative theory that there is no God, or that Nature as such has no essential relation to value, that is, no relation other than the casual production of finite living animals like ourselves.

(2) Pantheism is the semi-negative theory that Nature is a unified system or unitary Being, embodying an esthetic value or sublimity of its own but lacking ethical value or personality, and hence indifferent to the weal or woe of living individuals.

(3) Polytheism is the semi-positive theory that Nature, though not itself a unitary Being, yet does contain immortal gods far higher and more powerful than ourselves who take an active interest in our welfare and with whom we may communicate to our enduring profit.

(4) Theism is the completely positive theory that Nature embodies the creative activity of a personal Being physically infinite in extent and duration and morally infinite in goodness, closer to us than hands and feet, to whom we can and should relate ourselves without reserve, and so attain not only added strength and joy but an ultimate completion of our incomplete and fragmentary souls.

Pantheism and Polytheism, though for different reasons, are comparatively unimportant. Pantheism on its positive side is pretty much a truism and quite compatible with the other three conceptions. For who would deny that the great whole of Nature does possess at least sublimity? Even if the universe is no such closely integrated unity as that believed in by Spinoza, it has in any event such poor and empty majesty as allness and infinity confer. Even an atheist might indulge himself at moments with the vision of a totality which was his universe and to which he in turn belonged. Nor would a polytheist, and still less a

divinity asserted by Pantheists is also, of course, immanent, but lacking in personality and therefore in the ethical values bound up with personality.

theist, begrudge to anyone such vague thrills of cosmic emotion. The more specific personal values that they believe to operate in Nature would not exclude but merely supplement the cold esthetic value in which Pantheism believes. It is not what the pantheist affirms that matters, but only his denial of anything more or better that alienates from him all but outright atheists.

Polytheism's unimportance, at least for us, rests on a quite different reason. It fails to meet that double need which all religion, whether true or false, at least aspires to meet. I mean the need for metaphysically ultimate reality in union with perfection. There may, of course, quite possibly exist innumerable finite beings far greater than ourselves in power and in goodness. Ordinary angels, guardian angels, and archangels, not to mention saints and other helpful intermediaries, are talked of in traditional religions. But all such gentle quasi-polytheism derives whatever significance it has from monotheism as a background. And whatever truths and values the older outright Polytheism possessed have been absorbed by that same monotheism. And while it may well be that Fechner was right in his hypothesis that something like a personal consciousness may be associated with galaxies, solar systems, and even the earth on which we live, yet all such secular equivalents of ancient gods are bound to leave us cold, not only because there is a lack of any cogent reason for believing in them, but still more because they seem at best to stand in no relation to us that is either clear or comforting. And so we see that, of the four possible and classical solutions of the theological problem, only two, Theism and Atheism, remain as of sufficient significance to merit discussion.

As I view the matter, theology in relation to the theistic hypothesis swings like a pendulum between two opposite extremes, each of them impossible of acceptance. There is too much evil in Nature for Theism in its traditional form to be true; and there is too much good in the world for Theism in some form not to be true.

From time immemorial what is called the "Problem of Evil" has been the mainstay of all atheists and a thorn in the flesh of all Theists. The problem has been stated as follows: *If God were all good, He would wish to abolish evil; and if He were all-powerful He would be able to abolish evil. Therefore, since He doesn't abolish evil, it must be either because He won't or because He can't.* From this it follows that we are obliged to conclude that the orthodox beliefs in a God who is both all-powerful and all-good are definitely proved to be false by the undeniable existence of evil in the world.

The struggle of Theism to escape from either horn of this dilemma without becoming impaled upon the other are both comic and tragic. The vast majority of orthodox theists seem to care more about God's power than His goodness. And to anyone who understands even a little of the history of culture and of the all-important part played by the principle of authority, the prevalence of the worship of power is quite understandable. Might can never make right in the eyes of reason. But in practice might does make right most of the time. "The King can do no wrong," and those who are above us *de facto* usually succeed in convincing us that their superiority is not merely *de facto* but *de jure*. The interests of the ruling class become the duties of the subject class. And the innate greed of the former is fed by the innate slavishness of the latter.

But whatever the reason may be, the orthodox, religious authoritarian will preserve God's power at any price, even at the price of sacrificing His goodness as judged by the human conscience. There are two slightly different ways of choosing this horn of the dilemma. We may say that God's standards are not our standards, and who are we that we should pass moral judgments on His acts. "God works in a mysterious way His wonders to perform." "Evil is good in disguise," and so forth. The other variant of this view is the theory that evil is really nothing in itself. It is "subjective," "mere appearance," "pure illusion," "mâyâ," or "error of mortal mind."

There are two objections that apply with the same force to each form of the view that the evils of the world can be justified or explained away and thus made compatible with the infinite goodness and power of God. The first of these objections is expressed in the question, "If evil is good in disguise, or if it is pure illusion, why the disguise and why the illusion?" When an evil that appears in an illusion or as a disguise is not recognized as an illusion or as a disguise, it is just as evil as if it were "real." The vivid illusion of an agonizing pain is an agonizing pain. And if the miseries suffered here below are means to heavenly bliss for some Absolute Being or even for ourselves, that happy sequel cannot wipe out the evil by means of which it was attained.

The second objection to the view under discussion is practical and ethical; and it is even more devastating than the theoretical and metaphysical objection just considered. If evil is either pure illusion or a mere disguise for good, why should we fight against it? Surely what satisfies God should satisfy us; and if God wills the pains and failures of our lives, should we not will them, too? In short, we are bereft by this philosophy of any motive for making the world a better place. If "God's in His Heaven and all's right with the world," there is no improvement possible. These considerations, if they were to be consistently applied, would soon lead to an intolerable passivism. Consequently, they never are applied with consistency. The actual upshot of the orthodox attempt to reconcile the existence of evil with divine omnipotence is a sort of half-admitted "double standard of morals," a higher one for us and a lower, or at least a quite different one, for God. God sends his rain equally on the just and the unjust. He sends earthquakes, famines, and pestilence that cripple and kill with fine impartiality both the innocent and the guilty. He creates a "Nature red with tooth and claw" in which those who live live only by killing and devouring their brethren in the struggle for existence—each life demanding ten thousand deaths as the price of its own continuance. And finally, while we, on the one hand, are exhorted to eschew vengeance and to love our enemies, God, on the other hand, is permitted by the Jews to visit His vengeance upon the children to the third and fourth generation, and by the Christians He is actually praised for vindicating His justice by torturing in Hell for all eternity the majority of those who have trespassed against Him. Surely it would indeed seem that "His ways are not our ways." Now, the great trouble with Pantheism was its refusal to ascribe to God any of the ethical virtues that would endear Him to us. And orthodox Theism, when confronted with the Problem of Evil, is driven by its insistence upon omnipotence to oscillate between sheer inconsistency on the one side and something very like Pantheism with its non-moral God on the other.

Now let us turn to the other horn of the dilemma, and listen to those who say frankly that it is not the power but the *goodness* of God that must be preserved at any price. Better right than might. Better the pure conscience of Job than the arrogance of a Jehovah determined to break the spirit of his honestly questioning creature. Better, infinitely better, the sublime Prometheus undauntedly bearing his tortures than the tyrant Zeus who could not bear that the eternal ideal of right for which Prometheus stood should challenge His own omnipotent might. From this standpoint the reason that in spite of God's existence evil also exists is painfully simple. He doesn't abolish it because He can't abolish it. Being Himself the actuality of perfect goodness, He would naturally wish that there were no evil, but He is prevented by some external agency from fulfilling His wish. According to Zoroastrianism, which is the only one of the great traditional religions sufficiently courageous and generous to solve the problem of evil by sacrificing divine omnipotence to divine goodness, the agency believed to be external to God was another God, or rather, a Devil who created evil and worked to increase it. But this is, of course, Polytheism, though in its dualistic and all but minimum form, and hence it suffers from the mild defects (metaphysical rather than ethical) which, as we saw, pertained to Polytheism. Moreover, Zoroastrianism, despite its nobility, suffers from an additional specific defect of its own. Evil, unlike its opposite, good, hardly requires a single positive cause. Though far from being itself negative or illusory, it can be sufficiently accounted for by the indifference or inertia of the general run of things other than God. Evil is the *failure* of good to be achieved, or the triumph of a lesser over a greater good. Sin or "moral evil" does not consist in the seeking out of the bad for the sake of its badness, but rather for the sake of the element of good associated with it. The most vile and cruel murderer who kills deliberately for greed or lust or vanity or vengeful hate is seeking a pleasure for himself which could be in itself a good if it were not for the tragic evil it involved for the victim and for society in general.

Let us turn, then, from Zoroastrianism to the second form of that Theism which would preserve God's unlimited goodness at the cost of limiting His power by some external agency. And it is in Plato's *Timaeus* that we find the classic and beautiful alternative to the dyadic Polytheism of Zoroaster. Here we have not an active Satanic spirit, but an inert and imperfect *matter* eternal and coeval with the God who, as a Demiurge or mighty sculptor, molded a cosmos from it. The world as thus created would, then, be expected to show just what it does show—a mixture of good and evil, the latter resulting from the imperfect clay with which the all-perfect Creator was obliged to work. We spoke of the two Gods of the Zoroastrian religion as affording us an "all but minimum" Polytheism. Here in the *Timaeus* we reach the true and absolute minimum—nothing external to God except mere matter. Yet even *that* is too much if we are to satisfy the deep religious longing for an infinite value that is intrinsically related to reality by being incarnate in the heart of Nature. As long as matter lurks outside of God, how can even He be safe from who knows what incalculable vicissitude? In short, we find that, as the more orthodox form of Theism verges upon Pantheism with its infinite but nonmoral God, so does the less orthodox form of Theism, with its good but quite finite God, verge upon Polytheism. Before pursuing the question further, suppose we turn from Theism and the objections that afflict both of its rival forms, to Atheism, which is quite untroubled by the Problem of Evil. If there is no all-good and all-powerful God in the universe, there is no more need to explain the existence of evil than there is to explain the existence of redness or roundness or anything else.

Atheists are almost always materialists; and materialists, as we have seen, regard all values and even life and consciousness themselves as incidental by-products of the mechanically determined atoms of matter. The theistic hypothesis is for them a carry-over from the pre-scientific culture in which conceptions of Nature and its laws were based on fancies rather than facts. At best it is today a pathetic example of wishful thinking, and at worst a mischievous device for sanctioning ancient tyrannies and escaping present duties. As long as men believe in God and trust Him to make everything right in the end (rectifying the evils of this world by the rewards of another more real and better world), there will be little interest in making the earth a better place. The "Fatherhood of God" thus becomes not a supplement to, but a noxious substitute for, the "brotherhood of man." So speak the "atheists plus"—atheists, that is, who are more than atheists and are called "anti-clericals" because they believe that Theism and the claims of its priests or clerics are not only false but wicked. Old Lucretius was the first and greatest of them, and Karl Marx is, if not the greatest, at least the most influential of the modern anti-clericals. Lucretius, after recounting a dreadful story of a priest who sacrificed his own daughter under the compulsion of one of those religious beliefs that so shock the secular conscience by their blend of the false and trivial with the cruel, gives his appraisal of the affair in his famous sentence, "To such damned deeds, religion urges men." Karl Marx gives his appraisal in the even more famous phrase, "Religion is the opium of the people." From Lucretius to Marx, and from Marx through the comparatively mild anti-clericalism of late nineteenth-century France to the fierce and cruel persecutions in recent Russia and Radical Spain, there have been thousands of bitter Left Wing crusaders who have regarded religion in any form as the enemy of all scientific and social progress. That there is strong ground for these anti-clerical indictments seems to me obvious. All too often the preoccupation with a supernatural Other World has led to neglect and worse than neglect of this world and of the power of secular intelligence to change it for the better. Yet this is only part of the story. Think of the thousands and even millions of deeply religious people who have used their faith in God and in a supernatural world not as a means of escape from this world, but rather as an added stimulus for transforming it. Father Damien and Father Gapon, the Catholics; Evangeline Booth and Dr. Grenfell, the Protestants; and Mahatma Gandhi and Tagore, the Hindus, exemplify the possibility of employing a religion of other-worldliness as a means of making God's "Kingdom come on Earth as it is in Heaven."

When we turn from the atheists' ethical indictment of religion to their metaphysical indictment, we are brought back to the controversy that we have already considered in our discussion of the metaphysics of materialism. On the one hand, idealistic theists, seeing the beauty and meaningfulness and slowly increasing goodness of life on this planet, infer that at the heart of things there must be an omnipotent Being, beautiful, meaningful, and good. On the other hand, materialistic atheists, seeing the ugliness and the evil of the vast jungle of organic life and the lack of purpose and of any meaning except mechanistic in the infinite wilderness of inorganic matter, infer that nowhere in Nature can there be that "Power not ourselves that makes for righteousness" which men call "God."

But corresponding to the "Problem of Evil" which Theism was unable to solve without lapsing into the *amoralism* of the Pantheists or the *finitism* of the Polytheists, there is for Atheism an analogous problem which (if I may be pardoned a slight grammatical impropriety) I shall call the "Problem of Good." For the reasons stated in our criticism of materialism, Atheism simply cannot account for the amount of good in the world. It cannot explain that any more than Theism can explain the evil in the world. The truth must lie somewhere between. And so, as we said at the beginning of this chapter, theology swings like a pendulum between an untenable Theism and an untenable Atheism. Too much evil to be compatible with an omnipotent God; too much good to be compatible with mere blindly moving atoms.

The pure mechanistic forces or processes which constitute both the glory and the weakness of materialism seem to apply primarily to the "dissipation" or "katabolism," or *running down*, of energy. When once the organism is formed, we can explain mechanistically many of the separate functions and functional products in and through which it gives back to the environment the energies accumulated from it. Such expenditure of energy is "katabolism." It is, however, difficult if not impossible to explain mechanistically how the organism accumulates energies from the environment and with them builds up its organs and tissues and maintains its vital equilibrium. The latter process is "anabolism." Now, all through nature there runs a tendency of energy to pass from more intensive and concentrated forms to more extensive and dissipated forms. And an aspect or corollary of this tendency is the passage from a differentiated to a uniform distribution of energies. Drop a stone in the pool, and watch how the high waves in a small area become low waves diffused over a large area. The hot stove, instead of sucking into itself the lesser heat of the air around it, diffuses its own more intense heat until stove and room have become equal in temperature, and so forth. This law is called variously the "Dissipation of Energy," the "Second Law of Thermodynamics," or, more generically, the "Second Law of Energy," to distinguish it from the Conservation of Energy, which is the First Law. A further and more recent name for this Second Law is the "Increase of Entropy," where "entropy" is the form of energy that by reason of its uniformity of distribution and lack of differentiation is unavailable for use. In the light of this dread law, it would seem that the universe was running down and would come to an end, not by a loss of its quantity or substance, but by an increase in the unavailability of its quality or form. This, in turn, would seem to imply either an original infinite amount of counter-entropic distribution of energy or a miraculous beginning of the world at some finite time in the past. Now, as neither of these possibilities is exactly attractive from the standpoint of physical science, one can hardly help wondering whether there may not be in the universe some counter-entropic tendency for energy under certain conditions to concentrate and become more intensive and differentiated. Before there can be spending there must have been saving, and before there can be diffusion there must have been concentration of energy. Before the organism's katabolism there must have been the anabolism expressed in its ontogeny or development from germ to maturity, and that ontogeny itself implies a phylogeny or prior evolution of the higher from the very lowest species of life. Before the molecules can give out energy by breaking down into their constituent chemical atoms or sub-molecular particles, as in combustion, there must have been an accumulating of energy in the organization of the atoms into molecules. Before the atoms themselves can give out energy by breaking down into their constituent sub-atomic corpuscles, as in the radioactivity of such substances as uranium and radium, there must have been an accumulating of energy in the organization of the corpuscles into atoms; and finally before the protons, electrons, positrons, mesatrons, or other sub-atomic corpuscles can exist as units of mass, there must have been a concentration or accumulation in relatively stable and self-contained form of that energy of which mass or matter itself is now known to consist. In short, throughout the entire hierarchy from the protoplasmic organisms embodying life and mind in forms sufficiently like our own to be recognized for what they are, down through molecules and atoms to the very electrons themselves, we find the implications of an accumulative, anabolic, or counter-entropic activity. But though *indirect* evidences of this ascending trend are present everywhere, there is only one place in which each can find *direct* evidence of it. In one's own mind, with its *durée réelle*, or preservation of the past in the present, its steadily deepening store of memories and the creative imagining of things to come, far-flung plans and possibilities abstract and concrete, grotesque, beautiful, and terrible, including ideals of absolute and infinite perfection—here we get a first-hand revelation of what anabolism in its inner nature really means and is. In view of this, it does not seem a groundless speculation to assume that the chaos everywhere is permeated with a leaven of creative power, intrinsic and essential to the very being of Nature. And yet this vital urge is everywhere pressed in by death, destruction, wasteful conflict, and confusion. It is a will to good, a will, that is, to more harmonious and more abundant lives, cosmic in its extent and depth, yet finite.

Now let us take another line and ask ourselves the question: Is it probable than any single compound substance such as protoplasm should have an absolute monopoly of such primordial things as life and mind? To me, at least, it seems not probable. And quite regardless of whether intermediate material systems, larger than our organisms but smaller than the world, possess in themselves sufficient organicity to be vehicles of individual minds, I feel quite certain that the universe as a whole must have a unity more articulate and complete, and, hence, a higher organicity, than any of its parts. And if, as I believe, the "sentient" or "psychical" is energy in potential form and "mind" is that same sentiency organized into a system, why then the organized totality of things should be a Cosmic Mind containing all that is, and consequently not only good but evil and indifferent things as well. Such things would constitute what the great mystic Boehme called "that in God which is not God." Could such a Cosmic Mind be "personal"? It seems to me it could, despite the pantheist's conviction that "personal" and "infinite" are not compatible. For, as I see it, personality is only consciousness more unified, articulate, and self-reflective than what unpersonal sentiency could be.

This, then, is my solution, tentative and highly speculative, to be sure, of the general problem of theology. Not no God at all, as Atheism thinks; not a God omnipotent, willing all things, including those quite opposite to good as human conscience understands it; nor yet a merely finite God, good, indeed, but only a part, and hence a precarious part, of the world in which He is. The God that I believe to be most probable is infinite and eternal like the universe which is His body, all-perfect in Himself and in His will to good, but limited in power by that totality of possible and actual beings which is within Himself yet not Himself, and which in what we may call evolution is undergoing the endless leavening and perfecting that such an infinite chaos would require.

References to Part Two

* 16. "The Promethean Challenge to Religion," page 511.
17. "The Trinity—A Speculation," page 531.
* 18. "The Two Immortalities," page 540.
* 21. "The Philosophy of Friedrich Nietzsche," page 564.

CHAPTER VII

VALUE AND THE WAYS OF LIKING: ESTHETICS

ESTHETIC EXPERIENCE seems to involve a blend of two kinds of valuing—a subjective, hedonic, or pleasure value, and something more objective and rational. Consequently, theories of esthetics range from the subjective or hedonistic to the objective or rationalistic. Let us turn first to the rationalistic theory.

Now reason, as we have already noted, proceeds by alternating steps of analysis and synthesis. An original vague chaotic mess will be clarifyingly analyzed into sharply distinct and even antithetic elements $a, b, c, \ldots,$ and then the plurality will be clarifyingly synthesized by a reduction, making $a = f_1(m)$, $b = f_2(m)$, $c = f_3(m)$, and so on. Identity will be found in difference, unity will be found in variety, and the heterogeneous and discontinuous will be revealed as reducible to variants of a common denominator or homogeneous and continuous medium. That is what the spirit of reason craves; and in the satisfaction of that craving there is a joy not exactly sensuous yet very intense and bright.

I am not sure to what extent usage would justify the application of the word *beauty* to schematic harmonies in which there are no relevant elements of a sensory kind. Music is beautiful, and it is a sort of incarnation, in the sensory material of sounds, of mathematical relations. Perhaps mathematics can be in turn regarded as desensualized or disembodied music. And instead of starting with actual music and discovering a posteriori its mathematical pattern, it would be interesting to reverse the procedure, and, starting with some simple algebraic formula, try to "set it to music." Could the Binomial Theorem, for example, either in its generalized form or better, perhaps, in its application to the square or cube, be given a musical incarnation possibly comparable, let us say, to the *Doxology?* I must leave it to those who combine a knowledge of music with a knowledge of mathematics to say whether such a question is sense or nonsense.

The unification of which we have just given a symbolic representation may be of different kinds. There can be a purely arithmetical unification, as in the Fibonacci series:

$$0, 1, 1, 2, 3, 5, 8, 13, 21, \ldots\ldots$$

where each successive pair of numbers sums up to the number following, thus conferring a simple rational unity upon a sequence of what would otherwise appear as an intolerably heterogeneous aggregate of members. Or the unification can be of the type used in physics to correlate the series of colors from red to violet with successively shorter electromagnetic waves. Or, again, there is the kind of unity found in analogy and metaphor, where diverse materials are brought together in a word or phrase by an identity of functional meaning or of relational pattern. Then there are poetry and music, which get their unity in diversity through the identities of various kinds of rhythm. And last, we may mention the living organism and the work of art, treated together by Immanuel Kant in his *Critique of Judgment* because in each case there is a material diversified into functional and structural elements, all of which in turn are reunited by their service to the common whole.

Moved by considerations like the above, we may be tempted to say that esthetic value is grounded entirely in the nature of the object, and that the beauty of a thing, like its truth and its reality, is quite independent of whether it is liked by anybody or not.

As opposed to these objectivistic interpretations of esthetic value, we have the subjectivistic esthetics according to which the adjective *beautiful* is nothing but a somewhat solemn and decorative synonym for the adjective *pleasant;* and the substantive *beauty* designates the more or less permanent possibility of a thing to produce pleasure in us. Thus, I say, "Blue and red are lovely colors. They are *beautiful,* far more beautiful, indeed, than green and yellow. Raspberries and cream are really delicious, and so, too, is a properly broiled steak with fried onions. They are examples of a gustatory beauty just as roses and lilies of the valley exemplify supreme beauty in the field of smell. And if you cannot enjoy these savors and odors, I feel for you a mixture of sorrow and contempt. Furthermore, let me tell you frankly and with no false modesty that a gay seascape by Maxfield Parrish is far lovelier than Rembrandt's tiresome *Old Woman Paring her Nails,* and that jolly stirring songs like *Fair Harvard* and *The Marseillaise* (which a fellow can recognize with almost no effort) are incomparably superior to a dreary hour-long piano solo from something in Beethoven!" But now it is your turn, and if you deign to say anything at all, you will express a contempt so intense as to be untinged by pity for my esthetic evaluations, at least in the fields of painting and music. If I am such a hopeless Philistine as to derive greater pleasure from the paltry than from the classics of esthetic value, might I not at least have the grace to call my judgments merely *hedonic* rather than to use profanely such a term as *beauty?* Suppose I defend myself by saying, with Santayana, that *beauty is simply objectified or externalized pleasure;* and that to me, constituted as I am, anything that gives me pleasure merits the term *beauty* as much as do the objects that give you pleasure. "Some like shad, others like custard." *De gustibus non disputandum.* Will you accept such a defense as sufficient to put my silly and untutored judgments on the same plane as your own cultured and expert appraisals? I am afraid not. But if you appeal, as is sometimes done, to the authoritarian criteria of age and number, and claim that that which has pleased the most people through the longest time should be esthetically preferred, I can reply that there are many instances in which things that you will admit to be ugly and vulgar have given pleasure to the majority. Cockfights, dog fights, bullfights, the baiting of bears or badgers, the torturing of captives, criminals, and heretics, gladiatorial shows, and, in short, any spectacle involving the infliction of death and agony upon some living beings by other living beings, human or animal, have given intense pleasure to millions of people for thousands of years. Probably you do not admire spectacles of this sort; and since you must admit that the vast majority do now admire or in the past have admired them, you may abandon your appeal to democracy and invoke an aristocratic criterion. Not what pleases the most people, but what pleases the best people, winning praise from a "consensus of the competent"—there is the real test of esthetic value. But who are the "competent" or "best" people in such matters? By what criterion shall we discover them? The history of art is full of revolutions. "New" schools of "Independents" opening their galleries in defiance of stuffy old "Academicians." Romanticists rebelling against classicists, and so on. Is the *Nude Descending a Staircase* a greater work of art than a Raphael *Madonna?*

I can see only one way to answer such questions and to determine from the subjective standpoint in esthetics which of two rival appraisals of beauty is the more reliable. In general, and other things equal, the judgment that is based on the more inclusive experience is superior to one based on only a fragment of that experience. If that criterion is applied to the illustrations used above of my own preferences in painting and in music (which I chose deliberately as "horrible examples" of what would be generally regarded as gross incompetency of taste), I shall bow my head in humility and acknowledge my error. Thus, when an expert in music and in painting convinces me that he can get the same kind and degree of enjoyment that I, with my almost complete lack of an "ear" for music and of an "eye" for painting, can get from simple songs and pretty little pictures; and if he then goes on to explain and elucidate, with illustrations suited to my limited powers, how the music of Beethoven and the painting of Rembrandt resemble my childish favorites in the same way that a great poem resembles a witty limerick—then I do get at least a dim realization that I was bored by the masterpieces because of a sensory stupidity that prevented my perceiving what was really *there.* After such a sobering lesson I can no longer take refuge in *De gustibus non disputandum* and exclaim with my former pettish arrogance, "You like classical music and *I don't*, and *so what!*"

But it is necessary that the simple as well as the complex be experienced to the full and by the same person before the criterion can be successfully applied. The mere fact that classical music is more complex and that I had failed to detect the patterns of it would not have sufficed to make me revise my appraisal. Simple beauties are often superior to those that are elaborate. Compare, for example, most of the long and complicated poems that have been esthetically canonized with Shelley's "Life like a dome of many-colored glass stains the white radiance of eternity," and who is there that would dare not to give the palm to the latter, despite its simplicity and brevity?

There are, of course, many cases in which the application of our criterion gives conflicting results. Just as there are some who like custard best and others who prefer shad, even among those who have tasted both, so there will always be classicists and romanticists even among those who have experienced both kinds of beauty.

To Schopenhauer, as to Aristotle and most of the ancients, the Type, the Norm, the Idea, the Golden Mean, should be concretely exemplified and made incarnate in the perfect work of art. This is the static beauty of classicism. The beauty of romanticism, on the other hand, is dynamic, and embodies change, novelty, variation, deviation, evolution, and adventure. The glory of nature consists, for the romanticist, not in an eternal preservation of fixed species, but in an unending advance from lower to higher forms. To an intellectualistic conservative like Aristotle, a Darwinian or a Bergsonian world would have been unseemly and distasteful and a crazy departure from reality. To a congenital Buddhistic passivist like Schopenhauer, evolution was a horror that was all too real. Hence, for him art was a mechanism of escape from life and existence in space and time. And in its depiction of eternal types or ideas it yielded us while still alive a foretaste of Nirvana and the peace of absolute death.

Before leaving this phase of our topic, in which we have been considering the attempts to arrive at a criterion for esthetic value from the subjectivistic position in which beauty is regarded merely as pleasure objectified, there is one very interesting classification of hedonic satisfactions according to their places in the series, reaching from the most generic and extensive to the most specific and intensive. This is an arrangement of the kind discussed and illustrated by Professor Parkhurst in her book *Beauty: An Interpretation of Art and the Imaginative Life.*[1]

There are, first of all, the satisfactions based upon the characters which we share in common with almost all animals—pleasures pertaining to the instincts of hunger and sex. Slightly less extensive would be the gratifications relative to parental, filial, conjugal, and fraternal affections. Then would come those values that are rooted in our upright bipedal posture and the needs growing from it. Consider, for example, how different our architecture would be if we could swim like fishes or fly like birds or even walk as quadrupeds, while retaining our status as rational animals. Following in such a series would come in succession the pleasures peculiar to our racial, national, local, and family culture and traditions; and, finally, those peculiar to the special set-up of interests, sympathies, and antipathies which we as individuals in various moods and in various situations and at various moments would possess. Certain foods, certain costumes, certain poems, certain friends, may be exquisitely adapted to certain occasions and ill adapted and out of tune with others. The Rabelaisian tales and songs that go well with one's cronies in the tavern and so possess genuine esthetic value would be esthetically terrible in the nursery or the drawing-room, and so on. I do not think, however, that we can ascribe more or less value in proportion to the breadth or narrowness of the context. A poem that might suit only a single mood or occasion; a word that a Flaubert might find after days of search to be perfectly fitted to one particular piece of prose, might conceivably be (though, again, it might not be) as beautiful as something that would please any man under any circumstances. But the series from extensive to intensive, though by no means correlated with ascending or descend-

[1] Parkhurst, Helen Huss, *Beauty: An Interpretation of Art and the Imaginative Life.* New York, Harcourt, Brace and Company, 1930.

ing degrees of esthetic value, is nevertheless an interesting and important classification to keep in mind.

As we said at the beginning of this chapter, theories of esthetic value have varied from an objectivism in which beauty is identified with a structure or pattern possessed by a thing independently of its relation to a percipient, to a subjectivism in which the pleasure produced in the percipient, regardless of the nature of the object producing it, is the sole determinant of beauty. These two trends of theory in esthetics are derived from two opposite aspects of the experiential fact of the kind called *esthetic:* an objective *apprehension* and a subjective *thrill.* The two factors—the one cognitive, the other emotive or affective—can be distinguished in retrospection, but while the esthetic experience is going on they are perfectly blended. We can cognize objects with little or no emotion, and we can have emotions and feelings, throbs and thrills of joy, misery, anger, terror, melancholy, and so forth, with little or no cognition of an object. But the esthetic experience is a blend of *feeling* and *cognition.* It is an *emotive perception.* And that is why the private and inner attitude of subjective liking or disliking is by a kind of psychological paradox externalized and projected into the object, which thereby attains an immediate or "consummatory" "value." The two-facedness of the esthetic experience leads one to make claims that are contradictory and that seem contradictory even to the one who makes them. Beauty is an attribute of a perceived object, and as such it *ought* to be perceived by everybody, for it is out *there* in the object, as much as roundness or squareness; and if you can't see it, it is your *fault,* and you are blind to a reality. On the other hand, the beautiful object is something that pleases me. And there is no reason at all to believe or still less to demand that what pleases me, constituted as I am, should please you, constituted as you are. Hence it is that both in concrete practice and in abstract theory we alternate between an attitude of arrogance, in which we claim universal validity for our esthetic judgments in the conviction that beauty is something that can be defined objectively, and the other quite different attitude of modesty, in which we admit that beauty is subjective and relative. Some like one thing and so call it beautiful; others like and find beautiful something quite different—each to his taste.

It seems to me that Immanuel Kant, in his theory of esthetics set forth in *The Critique of Judgment,* dealt more justly and more penetratingly with the two aspects of beauty than any other philosopher. Moreover, Kant combines with his treatment of beauty an equally adequate treatment of the two other primary esthetic values, the Sublime and the Comic, which stand on either side of Beauty, half-sisters, as it were, the one graver, the other more frivolous than the queen herself. Because of these excellences of the Kantian theory, I offer here a brief analysis and appraisal of it.

For Kant, Beauty is that character of an object in virtue of which it appeals to the sensuous and to the rational aspects of our nature and appeals in such a way as to put them in harmony with each other. It must be a case of a rational structure, pattern, or meaning incarnate in a specific sensory fact or group of facts. This blend of the meaningful and factual must not be deliberate or in any way labored; it must occur spontaneously as an incident or happy accident of the natural or factual order, operating externally in physical nature, as in the production of a violet, or internally in human nature, as in the production of a picture or a lyric through the imagination of an artist. *Zwecklicheit ohne zweck*, "purposiveness without purpose," is Kant's own incisive and clarifying phrase by which he seeks to distinguish beauty on the one hand from mere *pleasure*, and on the other hand from the *teleological* or *deliberately* purposeful creation of something—a tool, for example—as a means to an end.

I have often wished that by some benign anachronism Kant could be made to comment on Santayana's definition of beauty as "pleasure objectified." My guess is that he would immediately qualify his approval by a statement to the effect that we never *would* objectify our pleasures unless our rational as well as our sensory faculties were aroused by something like a rational or meaningful pattern in the object itself. It is because of this vaguely "rational" quality that is for Kant a necessary prerequisite for the esthetic as distinguished from the merely hedonic, that he insists that esthetic experience depends on the "form" of the object rather than on its "matter" (existential content), and that consequently esthetic enjoyment is "disinterested" rather than selfish and that the esthetic judgment claims to be of universal validity rather than just an individual preference. My only objection to the long and elaborate Kantian analysis of beauty which I am trying to summarize in a few sentences that are very inadequate but not, I trust, essentially misleading, is that the distinctions made by Kant, though of fundamental importance, are less absolute and more a matter of relative emphasis and degree than Kant himself was willing to admit. For example, is my pleasure in the visual beauty of a painting "disinterested" and based on its "form," which is "universal," rather than on its existential "content" or particular substance in relation to me? And do these characteristics differentiate the "esthetic" evaluation of a painting from the merely *hedonic* evaluation of a beefsteak? To enjoy the steak I have to consume its substance. My attitude toward it would seem to be not disinterested but monopolistic. And if I were told that the steak did not exist or that it would never be mine, I should lose my interest in it. The picture, on the other hand, I can enjoy without possessing; and if

I were told that it was a mere hallucination and lacked material existence, my enjoyment would not be dimmed. These illustrations would seem to confirm Kant's distinction between the hedonic and the esthetic. But I am afraid that our analysis has not been fair, and that it has involved an unwitting and misleading emphasis on the physiological accidents that differentiate visual from gustatory perception. A group of *gourmets* sampling little bits of the steak and smacking their lips with dreamy, contemplative approval are, to be sure, dependent for their experience upon the molecules that impinge on their gustatory (and olfactory) nerve-endings. But so, too, are a group of connoisseurs of visual art taking little peeps at a picture dependent for *their* experiences on the waves of radiant energy that impinge upon the visual nerve-endings in their retinas. I don't see that the "form" or "disinterestedness" or "universality" of the pleasure or beauty is essentially different in the two cases.

The term *rational*, which is one of Kant's key words, is itself, if not ambiguous, at least extremely relative. And in a course on Kantian philosophy given by William James, I well remember our teacher's delighted snorts of affectionate derision for the category of "charm" intermediate between the merely hedonic and the properly esthetic which Kant was obliged to invent as applicable to certain simple but indubitably lovely things, such as pure tones and colors, in which pleasure was externalized in the object with full esthetic assurance, but in the absence of any relational pattern that could be regarded as "rational." And so because of the non-configurational simplicity of their nature such objects must be said to possess "charm" rather than "beauty." It seems to me that intermediate cases of this kind show the correctness of my colleague H. L. Hollingworth's claim that between the so-called "lower" senses, at one extreme, in which the specific sensory contents and the values pertaining to them have a minimum of rational or relational patterns and hence are less likely to be externalized and objectified and given definite names, and the so-called "higher" senses, at the other extreme, concerning which the opposite is true, there is something like a continuum of degrees of objectification.

But even though the great Kantian distinctions are relative rather than absolute distinctions, they are, as we have already said, of fundamental importance. And this importance is crucially exemplified in Kant's treatment of the Sublime and the Comic in relation to the Beautiful. In the experience of the sublime, as in the experience of the beautiful, our rational and sensory faculties are jointly aroused, but instead of being activated in harmony they are put into a curious sort of discord, the sensory being cast down in defeat while the rational is exalted in triumph. Kant's favorite illustration of this variant of esthetic value is the observation of a storm at sea (from a secure position on shore). The spectacle of Nature's mighty powers raging unrestrained makes us painfully and fearfully conscious of our own littleness and our insignificance as physical beings. Yet all the while our rational self, or spirit, soars high with the gods of the storm and shares vicariously in their triumph. Thus does Kant seek to explain in terms of our sensory-rational duality of nature the feeling of awe blended of fear and exaltation, which when objectified we call "sublime."

From the sublime to the ridiculous is proverbially only a step, but in Kant's conception of the situation it is two steps. For if we go back to Beauty and make a step in the direction opposite to that which took us to the sublime, we shall find the Comic. In this third member of the trinity of primary esthetic values, as in the other two, the rational and the sensory faculties are aroused together; but instead of the two being harmoniously gratified, as in beauty, or the rational dominating over the sensory, as in the sublime, it is now the turn of the sensory and lower side of our nature to triumph over the higher and rational side—and that is the "comical." The domination takes the form of brute fact upsetting expectation. What we expect is the normal, the proper, the appropriate. When the unexpected turns up and congruity is defeated by incongruity, it is to laugh. In short, for Kant *the humorous is the incongruous*. Other theories of the comic (as, for example, Bergson's view that it consists in a living being acting like a mere mechanism), seizing upon some *species* of incongruity and making it all in all, pay unconscious tribute to the Kantian theory that sees in incongruity *as such* the basis of the comic. The truth of a theory is often brought home to us more vividly by the corollaries that follow from it than by the direct arguments advanced in its support. And this is the case with the two corollaries that Kant appends to his theory of the comic.

First Corollary: *The incongruity must burst upon us suddenly and take us by surprise.* For if we know and expect the climax, it will be in accord with the set of our minds and so attain a subjective reasonableness that will lessen or destroy that triumph of the sensuous over the rational, which constitutes the incongruity that is vital to the comic. That is why in telling a funny story we must be careful not to spoil it by giving the point away prematurely and why we say, "Stop me if you've heard this one." Jokes will not bear repetition to the same audience. They grow stale and lose their amusing quality. Note that this is not at all the case with the other two esthetic modalities. The values of the sublime and the beautiful are not lessened and may even be increased by familiarity and repetition.

Second Corollary: *The incongruity that constitutes the comical must be trivial.* We cannot, or at least we should not, enjoy the triumph of the lower and sensuous over the higher and rational side of our being except in the realm of what does not really matter. When the brute facts of nature defeat the cherished hopes and longings of ourselves or others and bring pain or humiliation, it is tragic rather than comic. If an overdressed and pompous person parading majestically slips on a banana peel and falls in the mud, we may laugh. But if the poor fop in falling had really hurt himself instead of his clothes, only a boor would derive humorous enjoyment from the situation.

This is true both in the physical and in the social and verbal domains. Practical jokes and witty and humorous talk can be comical in their different ways, and they can also involve pain. But the joke, whether practical or linguistic, that without justification really hurts is made and enjoyed only by those who are cruel.

There is a third principle which might be regarded as a corollary to the Kantian theory of the comic, or as a combination of that theory with Thomas Hobbes's delightful conception of laughter. The case of the comic in which the rational and expected is defeated by brute fact is only one among several possible cases in which what Kant calls the "sensuous" gains what Hobbes calls a "sudden glory." The feeling of exuberant health and happiness is expressed by the laugh of *glee;* a feeling of one's victory already achieved or to come is expressed in the harsh laughter of battle and conquest; the feeling of another's discomfiture is expressed in the mean and sneering laugh of malice; the feeling of one's own discomfiture or bewilderment at something novel, as when the yokel sees the unfamiliar dress of the visiting foreigner, is expressed in the self-defensive nervous, giggling laughter of embarrassment; the feeling of kicking over the traces of propriety and getting free from the restraints of decency is expressed by the leering grin or lustful laughter of obscenity (which need not be *humorous* at all). All of these and especially the last are cases of the flesh militant. The "Old Adam" in us or the life-generating power of Pan gets the upper hand and gives us in many widely differing forms that feeling of a sudden burst of sensuous power which expresses itself mainly through the sympathetic rather than the cerebrospinal nervous system in the convulsive quaking cachinnation of belly, chest, and larynx that constitutes *laughter*.

I should like to conclude this chapter with a few words as to the relation of positive esthetic values such as beauty to the function of art. On this point I am in hearty agreement with Ducasse, of Brown University, who was, I believe, the first to claim that a work of art need not be or seek to be a thing of beauty. In the essay in Part II, entitled "Beauty Is Not All—An Appeal for Esthetic Pluralism," I have given my version of this claim—a claim which to many may seem paradoxical. Beauty and the somewhat different modalities of the sublime and the comic are the three positive esthetic values. As such they are defined by Santayana's illuminating phrase "pleasure objectified." But there are many emotions other than pleasure or joy that are objectified in the things of nature and that can be objectified in the things of art. Using the word *value* in its generic rather than in its restricted and eulogistic meaning, we can speak of values that are negative and mixed and indifferent as well as of values that are positive. In this sense a thing can be said to have esthetic significance or "value" which exemplifies the objectification of any emotion whatever. Pain, sorrow, terror, horror, anger, cruelty, and even loathing and disgust, if they are adequately externalized or objectified, become things of esthetic value. How should we regard such objectifications of negative, distressing, and evil emotions? I think we should regard them not only as exciting and thrilling but as wholesomely, if terrifying, instructive. By creating *all* esthetic values rather than by creating beauty alone, the artist can reveal in his works with a flaming clarity that science can never attain the whole nature of the human soul, the depths of shame to which it may sink as well as the heights of glory to which it may rise. That is why "beauty is not all" that art should seek.

References to Part Two

* 19. "The True, the Good, and the Beautiful from a Pragmatic Standpoint," page 550.

* 20. "Beauty Is Not All: An Appeal for Esthetic Pluralism," page 560.

CHAPTER VIII

VALUE AND THE WAYS OF LIKING (CONTINUED): ETHICS, INDIVIDUAL AND SOCIAL

I. INDIVIDUAL ETHICS

WE HAVE SAID that anything has "value" to the extent that it is *liked*. The value of a thing is its likableness; and as both objects and actions elicit the attitude of liking, so both objects and actions—together with the permanent habits and possibilities of action which we call "character"—possess value. And with regard to the ethical values ascribed to actions no less than with regard to the esthetic values ascribed to objects, theories of value vary from the subjective or sensory to the objective or rational.

According to the extreme subjective theory of ethical value, no action is good unless one has a sensory or immediate inclination to perform it. To do whatever you like is right. This view is fallacious because it leads to a kind of self-contradiction. The infant likes to touch the pretty fire, but he very much dislikes the painful burn that follows. To like (at one moment) a situation which (at the next moment) you will dislike is a self-contradiction, provided you feel, as most of us do, that our self of one moment is identical with our self of later moments. It follows that very early in the life of children and animals there is acquired a secondary set of likes and dislikes that supervene upon and control the primary likes and dislikes of their sensory nature. In the case of animals we call the acquirement "conditioning." In the case of human beings we call it "conscience." This body of secondary values is composed of three distinct parts. The first is *prudence*, which we illustrate by the burnt child's dread of fire. It is the capacity to like and dislike possible actions not in terms of their present sensory appeal, but in terms of their consequences to me as imagined for the future on the basis of being remembered in the past. I have a sensory shrinking from the pain of the dentist's ministrations, but I overcome my fear, or at least I feel that I "ought" to overcome it, by the expectation of the pleasant freedom from the toothache that has tormented me. And as I can endure present pain for the sake of gaining future pleasure, so too I can forego a present pleasure for the sake of avoiding future pain, as when I resist my impulse to eat or drink too much. The second ingredient of conscience is *sympathy*, the capacity to be concerned for the likes and dislikes of others. I love my neighbor (at least to some extent) as myself, or I feel that I ought to so love him. And my own likes and dislikes both sensory and prudential are controlled by this sympathy or "*altruism*."

The third and final component of conscience is *suggestion*. Man in common with most animals is not only *prudent* and *sympathetic*, but *suggestible*. He tends to do what he is told to do, and he tends to imitate the actions and to conform to the customs and laws of those about him. We tell a child to do this and not to do that; or we let him observe and thus assimilate the manners and morals of a chosen group in which we place him. Whether the suggestion comes by precept or by example, consciously administered through commands and exhortations or through unconscious imitation of what he observes—he will quickly and surely acquire in this way the third and by far the largest set of secondary and non-sensory controls. Sometimes these authoritarian controls will repeat or harmoniously supplement the other controls of sympathy and of prudence. At other times they will contradict them; and quite often they will have no bearing either favorable or unfavorable upon the needs of one's self or of one's neighbors. Thus, the body of rules prescribed and proscribed by a religion other than one's own (that of the ancient Aztecs, for example) usually seems to contain a large amount both of downright evil and of futility and obscurity.

The authoritarian or non-rational component of conscience, which is based on human suggestibility and imitativeness, is the most important and distinctive though not the most valuable of the three constituents. Before considering the ultimate question of its worth in comparison with prudence and sympathy, we should take note of two significant truths. First, for every mandate of the authoritarian part of conscience, no matter how outrageous and fantastic, some rational justification in terms of prudence or sympathy can be concocted. Second, the rational justifications thus concocted are of no psychological importance in determining our feeling of obligation to obey the mandates in question. For example, the human sacrifices of the Aztecs could be rationalized on the belief that the world is controlled by demonic powers who would destroy the entire tribe unless certain members of it were offered to propitiate them. The sacrifice would then be a duty of prudence. And, in general, obedience to the will of "the powers that be," regardless of the apparent cruelty or silliness entailed by such obedience, will be to the interest of one's self or of one's neighbors. In addition to this blanket type of theological justification, there are more specific reasons that can be imagined. The Mosaic Law, for example, might be justified in forbidding the eating of pork and shellfish because such foods (especially in a warm climate) may easily become dangerously indigestible. The Puritan code might be justified in frowning upon such innocent pleasures as dancing, card-playing, play-going, and so forth, on the ground that, being of this world, they would distract the mind from meditation on that other world in which the soul's destiny is determined. In short, "rational" justifications of all sorts can obviously be found for any set of civil and religious rules of conduct. And, like the rules themselves, the rationalizations will be sometimes good and sometimes bad. But our second and more important point in this connection is that such reasons, whether good or bad, do not enter at all into the fabric of conscience. The mandates of the third or authoritarian component of conscience are unconditional; they are felt as absolute and without need of justification, in terms of the consequences to which they lead. Immanuel Kant divided commands or injunctions into two kinds, which he called hypothetical imperatives and categorical imperatives. You ought to get up early if you want to see the sun rise. You ought to save your money if you want financial comfort in your old age. These are hypothetical imperatives. But if you don't happen to want to see the sun rise or to have financial comfort in your old age, then the obligation to get up early or to save your money simply vanishes. The *ought* depends on an *if*, hence Kant called it *hypothetical.* But now consider such injunctions as "You ought to tell the truth," "You ought not to commit suicide." Here the *ought* does not depend on an *if*. It is unconditional or *categorical.* No matter what the consequences may be of conforming to these obligations, and no matter whether you like or dislike those consequences, you ought to conform anyhow, absolutely and unconditionally. Now, there is no disputing the psychological correctness of Kant's analysis or description of at least one kind of "ought." Whether or not from the standpoint of a perfected system of ethics I ought ever to disregard consequences, I certainly *feel* that I ought to when conscience issues certain of its commands. These feelings of unconditional obligation come especially from the third or authoritarian part of conscience. Rules of conduct, positive and negative, prescriptions and proscriptions that have been enjoined upon me as a child, have become part of that secondary system of controls that we call *conscience*. Some of them will have good reasons, others bad reasons, still others just foolish and irrelevant reasons or no reasons at all; but be the reasons for the maxims of authoritarian conscience good, bad, or irrelevant, they will not figure in my experience of a moral obligation to obey those rules. That experience will be what Kant called *categorical*. It will be "reasonless" in the sense that any reason given on the basis of the moral sentiment itself will be purely verbal, a repetition in other terms of the obligation itself. I ought to obey my conscience because to obey it is *right* and not to obey it is *wrong*. But in this case "right" and "wrong" only mean what "ought" and what "ought not" to be done. "I ought because it is right," is just "I ought because I ought." For example, I badly want my neighbor's money, and I now have a chance to take it without fear of ever being detected, but I feel that I ought not to steal. Ethical philosophers can easily explain to me that stealing brings disastrous consequences to the victim, the community, and ultimately to the thief himself. The arguments are convincing, and in this case the authoritarian command is not an arbitrary or mischievous taboo, but is justified by the criterion of consequences. But no such criterion enters into my conscience. I feel that I ought not to steal the much-needed money because stealing is wrong—something, that is, which I ought not to do.

This curious feeling of unconditional obligation usually comes into the focus of attention when a person has a sensory impulse to do something that would conflict with it.

Such an impulse may be (1) to avoid a pain or attain a pleasure at the present moment; or (2) to avoid a pain or attain a pleasure for those with whom we sympathize; or (3) for our own self in the future for whose well-being we are prudently concerned. But to each of the three kinds of consequences authoritarian conscience may be equally opposed. Regardless of any consequences immediate or remote, to ourselves or our neighbors, we may feel that we ought to act in a certain way, no matter how much unhappiness to any or all of us will ensue as a consequence.

Now, one of the two great opposing types of ethical theory is based upon this experience of *categorical* obligation. It is the one that is the antithesis of the purely sensory and subjective theory that we mentioned at the beginning of this chapter. According to this view, moral value, that is, value as embodied in conduct and character, consists in doing or willing the *Right*. "Let justice be done though the heavens fall." "Duty is independent of consequences," except, of course, to the extent that the consequences resulting from the application of a rule may be needed to clarify its meaning. But it will always be in the act itself rather than in its consequences that moral value resides. We should practise virtue for virtue's sake as an end in itself and not as a means to any so-called "good."

This basic conception of ethical value as consisting in the *right* rather than in the *good* has had a long history and a variety of forms, the most significant of which are asceticism, authoritarianism, Stoicism, British intuitionism, Kantian rigorism, and the "Contractualism" of certain contemporary Oxonians.

Asceticism is the view that momentary sensory satisfactions are evil and should be resisted, not because they are sometimes incompatible with the greater sensory satisfaction of others or of ourselves at future times, but because they are always and intrinsically incompatible with such non-sensory satisfactions of the spirit as come from obeying the will of God, or, as the mystics believe, from attaining an intimate union with God. The view is based on a conviction that the flesh and the spirit are at war, and that between them there can be no peace with honor. It derives its strength from the fact that morality begins with self-control. We quickly come to realize that resistance to the impulse of the moment is of value as a means to a greater satisfaction, and from this it is psychologically a short and easy step to the position that resistance is an end in itself. Just as a miser begins by saving in order that he may spend to better advantage and then goes on to regard saving as an end in itself and all spending as bad, so the ascetic, who can be regarded as the miser of morals, convinces himself that self-denial is an absolute good and that it is his duty to forego the pleasures of eating and drinking, of sexual love and comradeship, and all the physical and esthetic comforts, which he lumps together as pertaining to "the world, the flesh, and the Devil." It cannot be denied that the strenuous self-discipline of the ascetic has sometimes been followed by the joys of a real or supposed union with God; but it is at least a question whether such raptures were attained because of or in spite of the life-negating practices. All too often the hatred of worldly and sensuous pleasures has led to masochistic insanity in the individual and to squalor and cultural stagnation in the society in which ascetic attitudes are encouraged.

Authoritarianism, especially in the ethics of religion, makes logically explicit the authoritarian principle, which, as we have seen, operates psychologically to generate the conviction that the *rightness* of an action is a value independent of the good that may or may not follow as its consequence. Without question each of us does feel an unconditional obligation or duty to conform our actions to the customs, laws, and commands (especially religious commands) to which we have been subjected. Authoritarian ethics translates this psychological fact into a deliberate doctrine to the effect that conformity or obedience is revealed by intuition as the essence of all value in the field of conduct. Duty is obedience to society or its governmental rulers, to one's own guild or class, to one's ancestors or elders or teachers, to God the supreme commander or, in default of God, then at least to Nature and the ways of things as they are. This is the oldest, most deeply rooted, and most widespread of all ethical philosophies. In each of its many varieties it exemplifies the principle that *might makes right.* The doctrine cannot stand up under criticism, as is easily seen by considering an authoritarian code other than our own. If a devotee of some primitive religion were to justify human sacrifice by saying that it was a sacred command and sanctioned by law and custom, we would assuredly reply that that in itself, so far from making the action righteous, only showed that the laws and customs were themselves unrighteous. As it was with the logic of authoritarianism, so it is with the ethics of authoritarianism. When authorities conflict, some rationalistic or non-authoritarian principle must of necessity be invoked. There is, indeed, only one element of validity in the authoritarian ethics. *Almost any code of rules is better than no code at all.* To have stood the test of time means that the code must have met the needs of some members of society, and to that extent must have possessed some degree of good. Consequently, the customs embodied in the mandates of conscience should, as it were, be given the right of way and be presumed innocent until proven guilty.

The other forms of "Rightism" in ethics we have listed as Stoicism, British intuitionism, Kantianism, and "Contractualism." We must for lack of space pass them by with the blanket comment that they each single out one or more rules of conduct and attitudes of will which appear to their respective defenders to possess an unconditional obligatoriness. Each group feels that its chosen principle is revealed in an immediate intuition as self-evident in the same way that the validity of the proposition "Things equal to the same thing are equal to each other" is intuited as self-evident. This reliance on intuition is found not only in the group of English moralists who called themselves "Intuitionists" and arranged the virtues in a sort of hierarchy based on their differing degrees of dignity or beauty, but in the Stoics, who emphasized the supreme value of a courageous indifference to pleasure and pain. Intuitionism is also exemplified by the Kantians, who emphasized the logical self-consistency of the moral law as exhibited in the possibility of universalizing its maxims without producing self-contradiction. Finally, the most recent instance of intuitionism or "Rightism" is to be found in the group led by Prichard and Ross, of Oxford, who, if I am not mistaken, emphasize our feeling of the sacredness of contracts or promises as proof of the impossibility of reducing the moral value of an action to the value of the consequences to which it leads.

Let us now turn from the Ethics of the Right, all forms of which by a slight extension of the traditional meaning of a term can be called Intuitionism, to the Ethics of the Good, all forms of which—again by a slight extension of the traditional meaning of a term—can be called *Utilitarianism.* In making this transition from the *right* to the *good*, we must turn from a consideration of the third component of conscience, which because it is built up by *suggestion* gives us unreasoned duties or "categorical imperatives," to the first and second components of conscience, which because they are built up by *prudence* and *sympathy* give us reasoned duties or "hypothetical imperatives."

Of prudence and its duties not much needs to be said because of their obviousness to all. To guide our reactions to the present by a vision of our future good is the beginning if not the end of moral action. To see this is easy, but to do it is often difficult. My desires and fears of the moment have about them a vivid sensory urgency. I may realize quite clearly that I shall gain by resisting them, but the image or picture of the greater good to come is pale and weak in comparison with the strength of the present impulse. Ideals, even the most purely selfish, seldom realize themselves automatically. We must, as William James so truly said, throw into the balance the weight of our whole self in what is called voluntary moral effort if we are to tip the scales of action in favor of the higher but weaker alternative. The tension of the moral crisis in such a case is expressed in the feeling that I *ought* to do *that* though I *want* to do *this*. Conscience is here the voice of the larger (but future) self-satisfaction in conflict with the lesser (but present) self-satisfaction.

There is today a widespread but fallacious opinion that duty is exclusively *social*, and that no one can owe a moral obligation to himself. That such an opinion is an absurdity is revealed not only by direct experience but by rational reflection. I feel my obligation to conquer my fear of the painful operation for the sake of being free from still greater pain in the future. If I fail to muster sufficient strength to make a successful effort, I suffer shame and remorse and look upon myself as a cowardly fool. To say that Robinson Crusoe had no moral duties because he had no neighbors is to forget that one's nearest neighbor is one's own future self. Crusoe could have yielded to despair and let himself come as near death as his physical appetites would have permitted, or he could have "bucked himself up" (as he actually did) and carved out of his solitude a courageous and intelligent life.

Sympathy, the second of the components of conscience, is, I think, the most important of all, for the good that it discloses is unlimited. Prudence, which can be thought of as a "sympathy" for one's future self, has for the object of its devotion just that one individual. But sympathy proper has as objects of its devotion the totality of sentient individuals. To feel the values of other beings as your values is to enrich and enlarge your own being and to make your life vicariously, but quite genuinely, more abundant. Man's distinctive glory lies not in the extent of his knowledge, but in the extent of his sympathy and in the vast cooperative life which is thereby made possible. But it is no less true that man's distinctive shame lies in the fact that the extent of his sympathy, vast though it is, is so much less than it might be. For, while a Christ will possess a flame of active sympathy for all humanity and a Buddha a passive sympathy for all sentient beings, most of us restrict our sympathies to those bound up with us by ties of propinquity or homogeneity. Neighborhood, nation or class, family, and race or species in varying degrees afford a basis for altruistic regard. But all too often it seems impossible to make people's sympathies extend to more than a fraction of one or a few of these cultural domains. There are so many who limit in some cruel and arbitrary way their concern for others. Consider the attitudes of the orthodox to the heterodox, of the white to the colored, of the nationalist to the alien, of the greedy exploiter to his tenants or hirelings, of the Nazi "Aryan" to Jews and liberals, of the Bolshevik proletarian to members of another class or even of another revolutionary party, and last, but by no means least, the incredible lack of feeling on the part of the majority of human beings for the animals whose mental inferiority and helplessness at our hands should elicit from us a very special and chivalric pity. It is curious as well as sad that this sympathy, which is the loveliest of the virtues and which in some of us shines brightly in some directions, can be so easily deadened or dimmed in other directions by the blindness of prejudice.

It should not be counted as a detraction that sympathy has a sensuous and instinctive basis. Unless there were a modicum of inborn feeling for others, an inherited liking by an animal mother for her offspring and later for her mate, her kin, and the fellow members of her pack or herd or tribe, there could have been neither evolution nor even survival of any of the higher species. There may have been tigresses who devoured their kittens, but such complete egoism, like complete sterility, could never have been transmitted by inheritance.

The sensory or instinctive basis of sympathy in human conscience expands rapidly into a rational recognition of the fact that, as the Hebrew proverb has it, "our brother's blood is as red as our own," and that the pains and pleasures of any other member of our group demand at least as much attention as our own. To think otherwise would be to assume that I had in my own little self a monopoly of all values, which would be as groundless as to assume with the solipsist that I had within myself a monopoly of all truth and reality.

The *good*, at least in one of its forms, appears quite clearly as "the greatest happiness of the greatest number," or as that which is the most valued by the most people. In the light of this ideal of the good, conscience no longer enjoins me to behave in certain ways rather than in others, "categorically" or without regard to consequences. I still have the feeling of absolute duty or obligation, but now it is the duty or obligation so to act as to bring about the best consequences, or the highest good. This change from neglect of all consequences to a selection of the best consequences is the change from an intuitionist conception of moral value as consisting in the *right* to a utilitarian conception of moral value as consisting in the *good*. It would be a great mistake to assume that the change from a blind or unreasoning conscience to a conscience that sees the goal as reason for the actions it enjoins involved any lessening of the sense of obligation. The call to realize greater and more manifold good rather than the good of the present moment is a clarion call, even more stern and compelling than the call of a taboo (or categorical imperative) informing us that we ought just because we ought, or because it is *right*.

Another element of strength in Utilitarianism or the ethics of the *good* is its unification of the primary or sensuous values of the moment with the derivative or moral values of conscience. Those who defend the ethics of the *right* are confronted with a puzzling dualism of primary and secondary values. To deny that pleasure is a value would be absurd. But if virtue with no reference to pleasure is also a value, what quality can they have in common to justify our classing them as species of a single genus designated by the term "value"?

So much by way of a rough statement of the strength of Utilitarianism; now I would point out a certain weakness in the theory. Some forms of happiness seem to us incommensurably greater than others. We feel that a happiness which consisted in the satisfaction of the aspiration and in the attainment of the ideals of a saint or hero would have infinitely more value than any possible number of momentary throbs of sensuous pleasure. And with respect to disvalue or negative value, do we not also feel that a sense of spiritual shame, such, for example, as would come from breaking a promise to a dead friend, could never be balanced by thrills of pleasure however numerous? Let us suppose that it is a word-of-honor pledge solemnly and tenderly made, with full knowledge by both parties of the difficulties involved in carrying it out, and with an assured belief by the one who promises that there is no continuance after death, no God to witness the bargain, and finally no possible chance of anyone, human or divine, now or ever, discovering whether or not the pledge was fulfilled. Yet would we not in such circumstances feel bound in decency and honor to make our word good? And would not the complete security with which we could break the promise make it seem all the more binding and ourselves all the more contemptible if we did break it? It is such cases, actual or hypothetical (it matters not which) that make up the real strength of Intuitionism and the real weakness of Utilitarianism. I have tried at some length to solve the problem in the essay on "The Missing Link in the Case for Utilitarianism" contained in Part II of this book. I will only say here that I believe that the true nature of moral value consists in an *increase of the substance of a life or a self*, and that an integral component and infinitely the most important component of the self is that rational or spiritual nature of which conscience itself is an expression. Pleasure is good because it satisfies a finite need and so adds a finite increment of psychic substance. But honor too is good and infinitely more good, because to act in accordance with it, is to satisfy an infinite need, and thus add an increment of *higher dimension* to one's psychic substance. And as with honor, so too, of course, with love and courage, for they are parts of the eternal tree whose fruit and *raison d'être* is happiness.

One of my friends, Professor T. V. Smith, in his book *Beyond Conscience*,[1] has attacked the moral value of that faculty. Another of my friends, Professor Arthur Murphy, has written in its defense. With each of these writers I am in partial agreement. The conscience composed of taboos that gives us the feeling that we ought to do something regardless of consequences and for no reason is, in-

[1] Smith, T. V., *Beyond Conscience*, New York, McGraw-Hill Book Company.

deed, as Smith so truly claims, a nuisance and a menace which calls for correction. But the conscience that bids us work for the greater good in the face of a sensory urge toward the lesser, is, as Murphy so truly claims, the highest and deepest part of man's self. Everybody's conscience is a mixture of these two kinds of moral compulsions. They *feel* the same in that both have the "imperative" quality of "oughtness." But we have a moral obligation to rationalize and clarify our sense of moral obligation itself. Following the Socratic teaching of more than two thousand years ago, we should strive to construct for ourselves a *free man's ethic*, by submitting our code of rules for the conduct of life to a critical examination that will enable us to discard the worthless and even mischievous junk of mere suggestions and imitation, in order the better to devote ourselves to the attainment of the highest good. But in pursuing this enterprise we must not forget that an infinitely important part of the end or good is the preservation and strengthening of the virtues that lead to it; they constitute the tree that bears the fruit, and just because they are *permanent possibilities* of happiness they should take precedence over any transitory *actual* happiness which would corrupt them.

The doctrine that *the end justifies the means*, in the sense in which it is usually taken, is not only ugly and false but actually self-contradictory. For to suppose that there is any end or good, however high, that would justify any means however vile is to forget that the high good itself must include as its most essential part the preservation of spiritual integrity. The reason why "It does not profit a man to gain the whole world and lose his own soul" is that any world really worth the gaining would include that soul as an essential part.

In accordance with the views just expressed in an attempt to reconcile the ethics of the Right with the ethics of the

Good, my own theory should, I suppose, be characterized as a form of what has been called "Perfectionism" rather than what has been called "Hedonism." Both Perfectionism and Hedonism place the value of an action in the *goodness* of the end rather than in the *rightness* of the means; but Hedonism, in defining the good exclusively in terms of pleasure (*hedoné*), takes insufficient account of the dignity and beauty of *virtue*, to which we cannot help ascribing a value greater than that of anything that can properly be called pleasure. Perfectionism, on the other hand, by including virtue and its satisfaction as intrinsic constituents of the *good* for which we strive, is able to do justice to the element of validity in the ethics of the *Right* without abandoning the ultilitarian emphasis on *consequences* as affording the ultimate criterion of moral value.

I have made this introductory sketch of the problems of ethics turn upon the antithesis of the Right and the Good because that division of the subject seems to me the most important, but there are, of course, other classifications which have their advantages. Laird, of Aberdeen, has recently given a threefold division of ethical theories into the deontological (axiological), emphasizing rightness, the aretological, emphasizing virtue, and the agathopoeic (agathological), emphasizing good consequences. This is a novel and interesting treatment of the problem, from the reading of which I have profited; but I still prefer the dualistic division of the Right and the Good which I have adopted.

An older division, which is also a threefold one, is that of Henry Sidgwick—into Egoistic Hedonism, Altruistic Hedonism, and Intuitionism. As in the tripartite division of Laird, so also in this one of Sidgwick, it seems to me that the difference between the first and the second members of the divisions is quite subordinate in importance to the difference between either or both of them and the third.

But while in Laird's treatment it is the two varieties of "Rightism" that are elevated into primary divisions, in Sidgwick's treatment it is the two varieties of "Goodism" that are elevated into primary divisions. However, despite my conviction of the relative unimportance of the difference between egoism and altruism, their alleged opposition has figured so prominently not only in Sidgwick's book but in the whole history of Ethics that some excuse for my having relegated it to a minor position seems called for. My reasons for so doing are as follows:

If we restrict our conception of the good to the number, duration, and intensity of sensory or worldly pleasures, there will assuredly be many irreconcilable conflicts between my own good and the good of my neighbors. From such a standpoint the old saying "Honesty is the best policy" is valid only for one who is too stupid in his dishonesty to avoid detection and punishment. If I am a clever knave rather than a stupid one, I shall seek to live by plunder and do quite ruthlessly anything in accordance with the slogan so popular among the criminals of today: "Only suckers really work." Suppose, however, that I realize the truth of what my former colleague, Professor Herbert G. Lord, was wont to emphasize, that *one's ego is itself an indeterminate entity*. Granted that I want to serve my ego, but what kind of ego shall I seek to be? A large ego or a small ego? In my own case, or in the case of a child whom I loved and for whose upbringing I was responsible, would I prefer to build up a self that was vicariously broadened and deepened by sympathy for others, approaching in its spiritual dimension the stature of a hero or saint? Or would I, on the contrary, prefer to picture my future self or the future self of the child I loved as that of a successful rogue who would have gained by effective chicanery every imaginable worldly advantage? When put in that form, the question carries its own answer. The real quantity of a satisfaction depends not only and not mainly on the intensity of the pleasure that accompanies it, but essentially upon the size or volume of the ego that is satisfied. Sensuous satisfaction is good because it adds an increment of psychic substance to the sensory self of the moment. But that sensory self of the moment is only a temporal phase, a cross section, a single dimension of the multidimensional magnitude of the whole self. Between the egoistic service of this latter larger self and the altruistic service of other selves there can be no possible conflict, for the larger self owes its very largeness to the other selves with whom through sympathy it is genuinely, though vicariously, identified.

II. Social Ethics

Individual ethics is at once the prelude and the prerequisite for the much vaster subject of social ethics. To inquire as to what society and its institutions ought to be, or as to which of the possible forms of social organization have the greater and which the lesser value, would be a meaningless undertaking unless we had already in mind some conception of the nature of individual value. Society and its institutions have no values of their own because they have no life or consciousness of their own. And even if there were a collective consciousness, and if society were itself not metaphorically but quite literally an organism with a life of its own, over and above the lives of the individuals composing it, such a life could have no significant relation to our scheme of duties. We could have no knowledge of what its "needs" were or whether its "ideals" were similar or dissimilar to ours or higher or lower than ours. The pseudo-mystical conception of a *social mind* is as irrelevant for ethics as it is improbable for psychology and metaphysics. Individuals are the ultimate consumers of all joys and sorrows; and society and its forms of organization have moral value only insofar as they contribute to the values of individual life. But because these institutional values are instrumental and secondary rather than intrinsic and primary, it does not follow that they are unimportant. On the contrary, they may be and usually are of more importance than the happiness of single individuals, because they are the basic conditions for the development of whole groups of individuals. It is right to die for one's country, not because one's country is itself a living being, but because it is or may be indispensable to the lives of one's fellow countrymen.

The problems of social ethics are, then, the problems of what *institutions*—meaning the basic forms of social organization—are most conducive to the greatest good of the greatest number of individuals.

The principal institutions of human society are six in number. They are those pertaining to (1) property, (2) government, (3) the family, (4) education, (5) religion, and (6) the relation of diverse and potentially conflicting *groups*—racial, national, or factional. With regard to the enormous mass of questions that are here involved, we shall limit ourselves in the remaining pages of this chapter to a mere mention of one or two problems characteristic of each of the last five institutions and to a slightly longer consideration of the problem of *property* with a hint as to its possible solution.

Government is the institution for enforcing the will of some on the will of others. In any society short of an anarchistic Utopia such an institution is a necessary evil, because the conscience and intelligence of most men are far from being developed to a level where justice and efficiency could be secured by voluntary co-operation and without the threat of force by either a minority or a majority of the community.

Three main problems pertaining to government should

be distinguished, though they usually are not. First, as to the *extent* of governmental power: should it cover all the activities of individuals, and control their speech and thought, their education and religion, their eating and drinking and sexual relations; or should it control only the more essential aspects of individual conduct, or perhaps only those actions of an individual which have direct effects upon other individuals? Second, as to the *concentration* or diffusion of governmental power: should sovereignty be vested in one individual, a dictator or absolute monarch, or in a small group, an oligarchy or aristocracy, or, lastly, in the majority of all the citizens? Third, as to the *qualification* for holding governmental power: should we have government by the wisest, which is "sophocracy"? Or by the most valorous, which is "timocracy"? Or by the richest, which is plutocracy? Or by the most popular as determined by the suffrage, which is democracy? Or by whoever is strong enough through force or cunning to seize the power, which is "kratocracy"?

The *family* is the institution for the breeding and rearing of offspring. Because of the sexual way in which the offspring of man and of all but the lowest animals are produced, the ethics of the family includes as one of its two principal problems the comparative evaluation of the various patterns of sexual association, polygamy, polyandry, monogamy (with and without divorce), together with the various combinations of the above and the two opposite extremes of celibacy and promiscuity. And second, because of the major share of the female in the creation and tending of offspring, the ethics of the family has for the other of its two principal problems the social status of women. Should women be restricted wholly or in the main to the maternal function and to the domestic duties connected with it, or should they be accorded equal rights with men and given the liberty and opportunity to regulate their lives as they please and to embrace any career that their talents and inclinations may dictate?

Education, which is the institution concerned mainly with transmitting to the child the cultural heritage of his elders, yields as many problems as there are types of children and types of subjects to be taught. But the principal problem connected with the school, at least in our own country and at the present time, seems to center on the comparative merits, on the one hand, of a traditional program of prescribed subjects administered with formal discipline, and, on the other hand, of a "progressive" program of elective subjects in which the interest of the pupil rather than the authority of the teacher is relied upon to achieve the result.

Religion, taken not as a system of theological doctrine but as a social institution, is an organization for the maintenance of communion with the Divine. The chief ethical problem pertaining to the institution turns on the question as to whether the allegations of the generally retrogressive effects of the churches upon social and intellectual progress are true, and as to whether, even if true, the bad effect upon society is not more than balanced by the consolations and spiritual enrichment which religion confers upon the individuals who believe and practise it.

Group relationships engender the many-sided problem of how to harmonize or at least to mitigate the conflicts which arise and which threaten to injure or destroy not only one or the other of two warring groups but the larger group or society within which the conflict arises. Whether the quarrel is between employers and employees, two political parties, two races, two churches, or two nations at war, the problems of social ethics that are involved pertain not to an institution already established, but to the means by which some institution or even some general principle for the settlement of the discord can be discovered and brought into operation. In short, the institution of the "inter-group" is an institution that for the most part is still in the making. It is true that for disputes between political parties there is, at least in democratic countries, the institution of the *vote* by means of which the conflict can be settled. And when the dispute is between individuals, there is the *law*. In industrial disputes there are partially established mechanisms for arbitration, mediation, and direct negotiation as alternatives to the destructive but relatively bloodless war called a *strike*. And even for the conflicts between countries there is the ancient institution of diplomacy supplemented by embryonic World Courts and Leagues of Nations. But when direct negotiations fail and when arbitration and mediation are either unavailable or undesired, then comes the basic and dreadful problem of when to surrender a principle or interest that seems of vital importance, and when to resort to physical force on its behalf. To this problem there is as yet no general solution. Both of nations and of individuals it is true that some fight and some don't; and that of those that do, some fight aggressively for greed and others defensively for justice. Yet a war, however just, has always about it a kind of ethical irrelevance; it decides, incidentally and not always, on which side lies the greater right, but, primarily and in every case, on which side lies the greater might. Let us cherish the hope that in more and more of the domains of social life methods for settling conflicts without force will be organized, and that a time will come when it will not be necessary for any parties to a conflict on vital issues to choose between the dread alternatives of surrender of principle and of resort to war.

The relation of a nation to other nations may be the most important of the external problems of a country, involving as it does the issues of war and peace; but the most important of its internal problems, at least in this day and age, is the problem of *property*. How shall property (or, more specifically, that kind of property which is used for the production of other property and which as such is called *capital*) be owned and used? The problem of property has always been important, but it has assumed a new and greater importance as a result of the "industrial revolution" by which the machine tools of applied science that are too large and costly to be owned by the workers who must use them have replaced the pre-scientific hand tools which could be owned by the workers. Capital property consists of the means and instruments of production, including the land and its natural resources as well as such artificial resources as machinery and its products. How and by whom shall this capital be owned or controlled? And how and to whom shall its products be distributed for consumption? The principal solutions of the problem are three in number. And though they are naturally susceptible of variations and blends of all sorts, they stand out from one another with sufficient distinctiveness to make possible and profitable a fairly definite comparison of their respective meanings and values. The first solution is that of *economic individualism* or *laissez faire*. It is the theory accepted by the capitalistic democracies of Western Europe and the Americas. *Give each man liberty and equality of opportunity to use as he likes whatever wealth he can honestly get by his earnings, his profits, and his inheritance.* This plan has worked marvelously in increasing to a vast amount the total wealth of the societies in which it operates. The freedom that makes possible individual initiative and that necessitates individual responsibility, together with the competition that stimulates hard work, thrift, originality, and invention, all contribute to the survival of the economically fittest. But the forms of industry and finance grow more complex; the external markets are more and more absorbed and pre-empted; the increase of technological efficiency decreases the number of men needed to produce a given quantity of goods; and, as a result of all this, the capitalistic system is developing signs of grave trouble. There occur crises and depressions in business that cause widespread and distressing unemployment and a still more widespread sense of insecurity, not only for the workers who still have jobs but for small capitalists whose investments are endangered. These depressions, in which people suffer for lack of the goods they need, are not only tragic: they are absurd, because they come from an "overproduction" (in the form of an unsalable surplus) of the very goods that are needed, and needed by the very people who have produced them. The only way under capitalism by which goods can be distributed is by being bought. The workers are the buyers; and when they are unemployed, they lack the money to buy what they need of the surplus they have produced. The result is *starvation in the midst of plenty*, which is the cancer of capitalism. This paradox of economic self-contradiction does not, of course, last indefinitely. The depression passes, business and industrial enterprise increase, the unemployed are gradually re-employed, and the community enters the prosperity phase of the manic-depressive cycle of business. In the democracies the majority both of economists and of ordinary citizens still feel that these tragically recurrent depressions will somehow get less tragic and less frequent as time goes on, and that in any event the good points of the system far outweigh its evils. In Italy, Germany, and the Soviet Union there prevails a quite opposite view. For social and political as well as for economic reasons, it is felt there that democratic individualism has failed, and that not only social, political and economic *justice* but social, political, and economic *efficiency* can be given a tremendous improvement by a revolutionary substitution in all domains of cultural life of *strict governmental control through a single party and its bureaucratic leaders* for the loose democratic control by the many divergent and competing groups of men and women. These opponents of democratic individualism and capitalism are called "Totalitarians." They divide sharply into two schools: the Fascists and National Socialists on the one hand, and the Soviet Communists on the other. The former emphasize militaristic nationalism and anti-Semitic racialism, and content themselves with a governmental *regulation* of property. The Communists, on the other hand, go further in the matter of economic control and advocate full governmental *ownership* of capital; but they repudiate racialism altogether, and claim that their nationalistic militarism and anti-democratic dictatorship are only temporary means to a world-wide proletarian society in which true democracy will for the first time be realized. Each group of totalitarians regards its difference from the other group as fundamental and its similarity as superficial. To most believers in democratic individualism, however, it seems the other way around; and while some would regard Communism as the lesser evil and others Fascism, most would agree that in their ruthless opposition to individual liberty, economic, political, and cultural, the two forms of totalitarianism are pretty much alike. But let us not forget, democrats though we be, that the dictatorships are alike not only in their bad points but also in their good points. And certainly in one point, the matter of unemployment, we must admit that totalitarianism in each of its rival forms has found a cure that capitalistic democracy has failed to find. The cure may be worse than the disease, but it is at least a cure. When goods are produced for use rather than for profits, there can be no such thing as "overproduction" and its accompanying unemployment. So long as there are goods that are needed and workers that can produce them, those goods will be produced. Their distribution to the consumer will no longer depend on his ability to buy, but on his ability and willingness to work.

Wherever there are two opposed ways of controlling an institution like property, there will always exist a third or middle way. Hence, in addition to the advocates of the new forms of totalitarianism and the old forms of economic individualism, we find a series of schools of thought in which an intermediate or compromise solution is urged. These compromises range from the Fabian socialism or democratically administered collectivism upheld by men like Norman Thomas to the mild policies of the New Deal, in which our present capitalism is to be continued but restricted and tempered in certain phases by a *Fabian fascism* designed to raise gradually the economic level of farmers and wage earners by an increase in governmental spending made possible by an increase in the taxation of the rich. These compromises, like all compromises, combine the defects as well as the merits of the two extremes between which they would mediate.

There is, however, a fourth way of treating the problem of property. It is neither Red, White, nor Pink; neither totalitarian, capitalistic, nor in between. I call it "Economic Dualism," or *communism within capitalism*—communism for those who need it and are willing to accept security at the price of discipline, and capitalism for those who can afford it and who are willing to accept risk as the price of economic liberty. Each man is to be free to choose the one regime or the other and to change as often as he likes from the one to the other. In the essay in Part Two entitled "Democracy at the Crossroads" the plan is explained and defended. I will only say here that it exemplifies in a specific theory of economics a much more general theory which is applicable to the whole field of ethics both social and individual, and which in its abstract form is set forth in the essay in Part Two entitled "The Geometry of the Good

Life." In the latter paper I point out that there is in the domain of *values* a "Law of Increasing Returns" in accordance with which all values, both those that are positive or good and also those that are negative or evil, tend (within certain obvious limits) to *increase* with *concentration* and to *decrease* with *diffusion.* Inasmuch as the aim of applied ethics is not only to increase the good but to decrease the evil of life, it follows that if our Law of Increasing Returns is valid, we should seek to concentrate and therefore strengthen our positive values by distributing them in what of necessity will be irregularly apportioned lumps, and at the same time to diffuse and therefore weaken our negative values by distributing them as widely and uniformly as possible. This means that we should use one tactic for *achieving good* and an opposite tactic for *avoiding evil.* Now, the various patterns of life that have found favor in the past can be divided into what we may term the "classic" and the "romantic," together, of course, with the many intermediate forms. The classic ideal is the balanced, orderly, and temperate life—"Safety first" and "Nothing too much." The romanticists, on the other hand, extol the taking of risks and the enthusiastic plunging for great rewards even at the cost of great penalties; not "Safety first," but "Live dangerously" is their motto. It is obvious to see and trite to say that each of these designs for living has its advantages and its disadvantages. What, so far as I know, has not been seen or said is that the reasonable way to live may be to adopt *the romantic tactic in coping with the problem of maximizing the positive values of individual and social life*, but to adopt *the classic tactic of temperance and security in dealing with the quite different problem of minimizing life's evils.* With the hope that the reader will consent to ponder this thought for whatever it may be worth as elaborated in the two essays to which I have just referred, I conclude my attempt to present an introductory survey of the main problems of philosophy.

References to Part Two

* * 16. "The Promethean Challenge to Religion," page 511.
* * 19. "The True, the Good, and the Beautiful from a Pragmatic Standpoint," page 550.
* * 21. "The Philosophy of Friedrich Nietzsche," page 564.
* 22. "The Missing Link in the Case for Utilitarianism," page 584.
* * 23. "The Geometry of the Good Life," page 600.
* * 24. "Democracy at the Crossroads," page 612.

PART TWO

EXPERIMENTS IN PHILOSOPHY

PROLOGUE

THE VISION OF PHILOSOPHY[1]

PHILOSOPHY is a vision as religion is a faith. The faith of religion is that values are immortal in the realm of existence. The vision of philosophy is of values that are eternal in the life of the spirit. This, I believe, is the Platonic revelation. The forms of religion are many, but through all that are in any wise significant there runs the ancient and pathetic hope that existence is in reality better than it appears in our experience. And through the even more numerous forms of philosophy there is present in one sense or another the vision of a realm of values whose validity is independent of whether they are realized in existence or not. But, while independent of the changes of history, these Platonic ideals are the unmoved movers of whatever of goodness or beauty a history may achieve.

Existing situations do, of course, determine which values are relevant to their time and place, but success or failure in realizing the appropriate ideal neither creates nor destroys the validity of that ideal.

Of what use to the world is this Platonic theory of values —a theory that is implicit in every genuine philosophy from the most *right* of the idealisms to the most *left* of the pragmatisms? Its use, as I see it, is to prevent man from committing the sin against his own spirit, the unforgivable sin of subordinating the ideal to the real and accepting whatever is as therefore right.

[1] *Proceedings of the Sixth International Congress of Philosophy*, Longmans, Green and Company, 1927, pages 707–708.

The religious hypothesis that the world at heart is somehow good has had and will have great fluctuations in its probable truth. In some ages the body of natural knowledge seems to indicate its almost certain truth; in others, the reverse. The vision of philosophy is not poignant, sweet, and consoling, as is the faith of religion. It is thin, cool, and steadfast, like the light from the stars. But the eternity of values is certain, while their existential immortality can never be more than probable.

In all our lands today the spirit of Thrasymachos is rife. Discouraged at the failure to realize our ideals, there are those who deny that there *are* any ideals *to* realize. And we are proffered the old and shameful doctrine that conscience should bow down to the forces of Nature and to those of government, either "red" or "white." Philosophy and the spirit of philosophy are, then, profoundly relevant to the present scene, for at no time have the peoples of the earth been so in danger of losing that vision without which they perish—the Platonic vision of an eternal good, multiple in its aspects and applications, but single in its validity, subsisting quietly through all the vicissitudes of existence.

I

* ON THE NATURE OF INDUCTION[1]

A new analysis of Mill's canons or methods of induction by the use of which uniform or causal correlations of phenomena are disentangled and isolated from those that are temporary or casual. It presupposes some knowledge of formal logic.

ANY proposition is susceptible to two sorts of proof. We can adduce premises that directly imply it, or we can adduce premises that indirectly imply it because they imply the falsity of its contradictory alternatives. In inductive reasoning we prove universal propositions by adducing as premises the particular propositions furnished by experience. Formal logic tells us that the value of a particular proposition consists in its power to disprove its contradictory universal rather than to prove its subalternate universal. We might naturally suppose that the evidential function of experience, as a knowledge of particulars, was to disprove universal statements rather than to prove them, and that if a universal conclusion was proved true by appeal to experience, the proof would be based upon the disproof or elimination of alternatives. That induction is actually and always of this indirect type of inference, and that as such it is properly expressed by a disjunctive syllogism in

[1] Read at the annual meeting of the American Philosophical Association, at Cambridge, December, 1905. Reprinted from *The Journal of Philosophy, Psychology and Scientific Methods*, Vol. III, No. 11, May 24, 1906, pp. 281–286.

the negative mood (*modus tollendo ponens*), is what I wish to show.

There is, of course, no novelty in the conception of induction as a process of elimination. Mill's canons are efficacious because they embody implicitly the eliminative principle. In Hobhouse and Aikins, to mention only two of the modern logicians, the principle is explicitly recognized, and the chief problems of induction are treated, especially by Hobhouse, from that point of view. Yet, so far as I am aware, there has been nowhere an attempt to identify induction in all its phases with the kind of indirect inference known as the *reductio ad absurdum*, and it has seemed to me worth while to make that attempt for two reasons: first, because the several inductive methods, when viewed from this standpoint, appear not as a group of disconnected principles, but as an organic system and hierarchy which is applicable in its entirety to every inductive problem and in which each principle has its own function and virtue by which it supplements the defects of the principles that precede it; second, on account of the new light thrown by the indirect theory of induction upon the general epistemological problem of deriving universals from particulars.

And now, by way of introduction to the more positive treatment of the subject, let us consider some of the difficulties involved in what is still, I think, the usual conception of induction. Induction, when treated as a mode of direct inference, is divided into two kinds—perfect and imperfect. In perfect induction, we reason that as these *A's* are *B's* and as these *A's* are all the *A's*, it must follow that all *A's* are *B's*. It is clear that what is called perfect induction is only possible when the total number of individuals making the class is limited. Thus, we can prove by this method that all the months in the year have less than thirty-two days, or that all the flowers in the garden are fragrant, but not that all bodies gravitate or that all men are mortal. In the latter propositions, which are genuine universals, the classes contain an unlimited number of members, and experience can never supply us with more than an insignificant fraction of them. In imperfect induction, which is supposed to be a degenerate form of perfect induction, we boldly conclude that because an infinitesimal portion of a class has been observed to possess a certain property, the whole class will have that property. The methods or canons of induction are the principles that inform us when we can and when we cannot take the inductive leap.

Now there is one circumstance in particular which might lead us to suspect that there was something radically wrong with the notion that induction is a degenerate form of perfect induction. Neither the actual number of positive instances observed nor the ratio of that to the total number has anything whatever to do with the degree of validity possessed by the induction. Perfect induction is essentially quantitative, depending, as it does, upon observation of all the members of a given class. The canons that guide us in making the so-called imperfect induction are, on the other hand, essentially qualitative, and not, as we might suppose, imperfectly quantitative. That is to say, it is never a question of observing almost all, a bare majority, or even an appreciable fraction of the whole number of material bodies, for example, as evidence for the inductive generalization that all bodies gravitate. We contrive in the few cases under our control to eliminate by the methods of difference and especially of agreement all the characteristics of bodies that could possibly cause their gravitation except those of extension and inertia, and on the strength of this elimination we unhesitatingly conclude that a material body, merely as such (and, hence, all material bodies), will gravitate.

And now that we have briefly considered the contradiction between inductive theory as exemplified in the supposedly archetypal syllogism of perfect induction, and inductive practice as exemplified in Mill's canons, we may look to see how this contradiction can be removed by treating induction as belonging essentially and exclusively to the indirect type of inference.

Every inductive problem indirectly, and the usual inductive problem directly, concerns the determination of a causal relation. A phenomenon occurs in which we are for some reason interested, and we at once seek among its antecedents and consequents for phenomena which are related to it as cause and as effect. Defining a causal relation as the relation of universal concomitant presence, absence, and variation of two phenomena, we must assume as the basal postulates of all induction (1) that every event has an antecedent and a consequent with which it is causally or universally related, and (2) that we can enumerate these possible causal relations, by the aid of perception and previous knowledge. Now let *M* be a phenomenon whose causal relations we are seeking to discover, and let *A* be an antecedent or consequent phenomenon which we suspect, or provisionally assume, to be, and which in reality is, causally related to *M;* we can then classify the possible causal relations of *M* with respect to *A* under five heads. This division may be briefly stated in the form of a disjunctive proposition which will constitute the major premise of a typical inductive syllogism. Thus, we can say that:

The cause or effect of *M* is either (1) a phenomenon, symbolized by *X*, that is related to *A* only casually or by chance; or (2) a phenomenon symbolized by *B*, *C*, or *D*, which is collocated with *A* but not indissolubly; or (3) a complex phenomenon, symbolized by *A B*, *A C*, or *A D*, of which *A* is an indispensable part; or (4) a phenomenon, symbolized by *a*, which is an aspect, phase, or degree of *A;*

or (5) *A* itself. The four inductive methods of simple enumeration, difference, agreement, and concomitant variation express the types of particular negative propositions furnished by experience, and as such they constitute the complex minor premises of the syllogism and serve to contradict or eliminate all but one of the alternatives set forth in the major premise. The conclusion is, of course, the categorical affirmation of the only alternative not eliminated. I shall now try to show how each of the inductive methods is especially suited to eliminate one of these alternatives, and that the eliminative function is the only function that they could or do perform. First, then, to remove the possibility that *A* and *M* are connected merely by chance, we use the method of simple enumeration. We observe the frequency with which *M* occurs in conjunction with *A*, and compare this with the frequency with which *M* might be expected to occur with *A* if they were quite independent. If the former frequency greatly exceeds the latter, we consider the conjunction to be something more than casual. The *number* of observations required to eliminate the hypothesis of chance is, thus, strictly determined by the joint independent probability of the events in question.

Having eliminated chance by the method of simple enumeration, we next eliminate by the method of difference the possibility that *M* is causally related, not to *A*, but to the antecedents and consequents with which *A* is collocated. We find, let us say, cases in which *B*, *C*, and *D* are simultaneously or successively present when the event *M* is absent. The results of such observations may be stated in the form of a particular negative proposition, as follows: some cases of *B*, *C*, and *D* are not cases of *M*, which means that the universal affirmative proposition: all cases of *B*, *C*, or *D* are cases of *M*—which expresses a possible causal relation—is eliminated.

Supposing, now, that the phenomenon *A* has not been found present in the absence of *M*, and consequently has not been eliminated, it becomes necessary to apply the method of agreement in order to decide whether *M* is not causally related to a complex phenomenon such as *AB*, *AC*, or *AD*, of which *A* is only a part, for the weak point in the method of difference lies in the fact that it can only prove that *A* is at least a part of the cause or effect of *M*, not that it is the whole. We observe by the method of agreement that *B*, *C*, and *D* can be simultaneously or successively absent when *M* and *A* are both present. This again eliminates *B*, *C*, and *D*, but it also eliminates the possibility that *A* needs to co-operate with *B*, *C*, and *D* in order to be causally related to *M*.

We have now proved that *M* is causally related either to *A* or to some phase of *A* which we called *a*. And to secure the elimination of this fourth alternative, we use the last and most powerful of the inductive canons, that of concomitant variation. If we find that *M* and *A* vary in perfect concomitance, we know that every phase or degree of *A*, rather than some particular phase such as *a*, is causally related to every phase or degree of *M*. If, on the other hand, we had discovered that *A* did not vary with *M* in any manner, we should have proved that the true cause or effect of *M* was *a* and not *A*, as such. Or, again, if we had found that *M* did not vary directly with *A*, but with some function of *A*, we should conclude that the cause or effect of *M* was *A* in conjunction with *a*.

The universal affirmative conclusion of an inductive syllogism is, thus, in any case the result of successive eliminations—in the form of the particular negative propositions furnished by experience—of all but one of the alternative universals set forth in the disjunctive major premise as hypotheses. And each of the inductive methods is, as we have seen, adapted to the elimination of a certain type of alternative.

And now a word must be said in regard to the two methods which we have not mentioned—the method of residues and the joint method of agreement and difference. The method of residues is confessedly a method of elimination; it is, however, hardly worthy of being ranked with the other methods, for it is applicable only when both the antecedents and consequents are quantities of matter or energy, for in no other case can we apply the conception of a cause exhausting its causality in the production of a given effect. As for the joint method, its continued existence in logical textbooks affords a good illustration (1) of the fact that logicians have failed to recognize the exclusively eliminative nature of induction and (2) of the results of that failure. The joint method bids us supplement the method of agreement, by the collection of as many different instances as possible of the absence of a phenomenon along with the absence of its supposed cause. Now, it can easily be shown that these cases of concurrent absence are, as such, quite worthless as evidence of causal connection. If we are considering whether a protective tariff causes national prosperity, we do not adduce as evidence the generation of Roentgen rays or the constructing of a sonnet; and yet these are different cases of the concurrent absence of protection and prosperity, and as such perfectly conform to the requirements of the joint method as worded by Mill and as symbolized by Jevons. What we actually seek to find in such an investigation is always cases in which not merely the supposed cause is absent, but in which *the alternatives to the supposed cause are present* along with the absence of the effect, and hence are eliminated. In the method of difference as usually schematized, this is done in a single pair of instances in which *ABC* followed by *M* is compared with *BC* followed by the absence of *M;* but it can equally well be done piecemeal or by a succession of instances, one showing simply the presence of *B*, a second the presence of *C*, a third the presence of *D*, and so forth, along with the absence of *M*. Now, as the so-called joint method is, when rightly understood, nothing whatever but a combination of the method of agreement and the method of difference where each is applied successively in several instances, rather than simultaneously in a single pair, it does not deserve to be classed as a separate canon.[2]

The claim was made, at the beginning of the paper, that the identification of induction with the indirect type of argument, or *reductio ad absurdum*, possessed two advantages: (1) the unification of the inductive methods, and (2) the exhibition in a new light of the general epistemological problem of deriving universals from particulars. I have said what I could in regard to the first of these advantages, but I should like in conclusion to speak further as to the second.

The attacks upon the possibility of reasoning from particulars, which have been made by the skeptics on the one hand and by the extreme apriorists on the other, are based in the main upon a quite proper realization of the

[2] By way of illustration I subjoin (1) the incorrect and meaningless symbolization of the joint method given by Jevons, *Lessons in Logic*, p. 247; (2) the correct symbolization substantially as given by Aikins, *The Principles of Logic*, p. 275; (3) the symbolization in a single pair of instances of the method of agreement and of the method of difference. The substantial identity of (2) and (3) is obvious.

(1)	(2)	(3)
ABC — abc	*ABCD — abcd*	*ABC — abc*
ADE — ade	*ABGH — abgh*	*ADE — ade*
AFG — afg	*ACGK — acgk*	
AHK — ahk		
PQ — pq	*BDE — bde*	*ABC — abc*
RS — rs	*CDG — cdg*	*BC — bc*
TV — tv	*BEF — bef*	
XY — xy		

gulf between a subaltern proposition and its subalternates. The number of cases exemplifying a genuine universal or law of nature is, as we have said, always infinite, and hence the direct inference from some to all is not only uncertain (which would be admitted by inductive logicians), but would seem to be not even probable—to be, in fact, infinitely improbable. For we can, of course, never observe even an appreciable fraction, to say nothing of a majority, of the members of an infinite series. Now, when we give up this attempt at direct inference and exorcise from inductive theory the specter of a so-called perfect induction as an ideal to be approximated, the whole problem appears in a less paradoxical and more hopeful light. For the experiential evidence in the form of particular propositions, which was worthless as a means of direct proof of the subalternate, is perfectly capable of disproving the contradictory and thus indirectly establishing a hypothesis as a survival of the fittest. Of course, this does not mean that we have merely, by the substitution of the intensive for the extensive view of the subject, removed uncertainty from generalizations from experience, but only that from our point of view we may more clearly see why it is that the degree of probability of any inductive conclusion is measured by the number of antecedently possible alternative conclusions and by the ease with which they can be isolated, enumerated, and eliminated, rather than by the mere number of instances observed.

2

* A DEFENSE OF CAUSALITY [1]

An argument to establish, as the basis of inductive inference, the hypothesis that causal tendencies are really operative in nature. It is shown that the alternative to that hypothesis is infinitely improbable and would entail a world of perpetual miracle and incredible runs of luck.

WHENEVER *two phenomena occur together much more frequently than would be expected from their separate frequencies, we infer a causal relation between them.* Thus, if I were to draw a card from a pack and you were to make a guess as to what the card was, there would be one chance in 52 that your guess would be correct. If you were to guess correctly not once out of every 52 trials, but once out of every 10, we should probably regard it as an amusing coincidence and possibly indicative of a causal relationship. While if you guessed correctly three out of every four trials, we should certainly infer a causal connection of some kind between the two events. It is not the mere frequency of conjunction of two events but the extent to which that frequency exceeds what would be the independent joint frequencies that justifies the inference of causal relationship.

Within the world of actual and possible data we thus recognize two kinds of concurrence—casual concurrences in which the frequency does not differ greatly from the

[1] Reprinted from *Proceedings of the Seventh International Congress of Philosophy*, Oxford University Press, 1931, pages 198–202.

product of the separate frequencies of the concurrent phenomena, and a second class of concurrences the frequency of which does differ greatly from the product of the separate frequencies or probabilities of the events that concur.

As to the question of whether we should or should not go beyond the objective data and postulate a transcendent causal power to explain such concurrences of events as greatly exceed in frequency the product of their separate frequencies, I advocate making the transcendent postulate for the two following reasons:

First, we have the quality of *enforcement* as itself a datum, though of a peculiar and internal kind. We have the feeling of one experience generating another. The relational essence thus presented may have no existence apart from the moment in which it is presented, but we experience it as we experience our own activity. It is not, for example, like a four-dimensional space or like what color is to a man born blind. It is a character of which we have "knowledge by acquaintance." Consequently, when we postulate a property of enforcement we know what it is that we mean, in the same sense in which we know what it is that we mean when we postulate a mermaid. We may, to be sure, be as much mistaken in inferring the reality of causal enforcement as in inferring the reality of mermaids. But we have no right to exclude a priori as false or meaningless either the hypothesis that mermaids are real or that causality is real. Whether they are real in any other sense than as data of our subjective experience can be determined only indirectly and according to probability by appeal to many different experiential situations.

This, then, is my first reason for refusing to accept the positivistic claim that causal enforcement is an illegitimate category. Before going on to give my second reason, I wish to consider briefly the attempt to discredit our experience of the quality of causal enforcement by calling it a merely muscular or kinesthetic sensation. Such derogatory appellations leave me cold because, even if we accept the somewhat dubious psychological theory that all sensations of enforcement are muscular, they would not be disgraced by that fact or in any way disqualified as candidates for independent existence in the world of physics. Colors and even shapes may conceivably have no existence except as data in human experience, but you could not prove this merely by calling them retinal sensations. The fact that sensory or relational data are revealed by one or the other of the bodily organs and mechanisms in no sense militates against their claim to objective reality apart from relation to the body. The muscles are not unworthy organs, and if it is by their aid that I get experiences of the qualities of force and power, I am the more grateful to them. Like the telescope, they can reveal truth without constituting it.

My second reason for believing in the objective existence of causality in nature is the extreme improbability of the alternative to that belief.

Once grant me my first claim that real causality is a possibility, then my second claim that it is an overwhelming probability follows easily. There will now be two possible worlds—one causal, the other non-causal—with which we are confronted and between which we must choose. In external appearance the two worlds would be exactly the same. In each world there will be conjunctions of phenomena repeated with enormously greater frequencies than would be indicated by the product of their separate frequencies. But in the world in which the events were independent and lacking in any real causal bonds, these repeated concurrences would be outrageous runs of luck; while in the alternative type of world in which the data, instead of being self-sufficient and independent, are endowed with real though non-observable causal power, the repetitions of concurrence would be the simple expression of such power. They would be normal and to be expected.

Let us take Hume's famous example of the billiard balls as a typical case of a concurrence of events that is repeated with a frequency that would be out of all proportion to the probabilities in a world lacking causal powers. Billiard ball *a* rolls with a certain velocity up to billiard ball *b*. And at the moment of contact *b* starts off with a velocity which in direction and intensity is the same as that of *a*. That this should happen once is no reason for wonder from any standpoint because it is no more peculiar or specific than any other event that would have filled the ensuing moment. But the chance that in the absence of any internal causal determination the concurrence of *b's* motion with *a's* contact will happen not only once but twice, thrice, and a million million times in succession is almost zero. While if, on the other hand, there *is* internal causal determination, the continued concurrence is just what would be expected. The repeated concurrences must be either casual or causal. If the chance that they would occur in a universe in which all concurrence is casual is measured by a fraction that is almost zero, the chance that they are occurring in a universe in which there is causality is measured by one minus that fraction, which is itself a fraction almost equal to unity. The first alternative is all but impossible, while the second alternative is all but certain. Add to the case of the billiard balls all the cases of routines or repeated concurrences of phenomena in nature, and compare for yourselves the relative probabilities of these ubiquitous successions being, on the one hand, amazing runs of luck in a universe whose data are self-contained and independent of one another, or, on the other hand, normal manifestations of a universe whose data enjoy a real though invisible power to determine one another.

Now, against the argument just stated, the following objections may be urged:

First, there is the old doubt about the principle of probability itself. Is it merely an expression of our ignorance, and in that case how can we base upon it any claim to new knowledge? Or is it only a measure of subjective belief, in which case its significance would be psychological rather than logical? Or is it perhaps merely a statement of past frequencies, objective, indeed, and empirically grounded, but hopelessly retrospective and incapable of being used as a legitimate basis for predicting the future except by being supplemented with some such principle as the Uniformity of Nature? I cannot enter into the complexities of the philosophy of probability which are raised by these questions and must content myself with stating that conception of probability which seems to me the simplest and best.

The probability that an event e will occur is expressed by the fraction $\frac{E}{E+\overline{E}}$, where E is the number of ways in which (to our best knowledge) e can occur and $\overline{E}$ the number of ways in which it can fail to occur. This probability fraction applied to a prospective event is a measure neither of pure knowledge nor of pure ignorance, but of the combination of *disjunctive knowledge of what* the possibilities are with *ignorance as to which* of them will be actualized. Our ignorance of the actuality is minimized by being blended with a knowledge of the possibilities. Thus, if I toss up two pennies a and b, the probability of my getting one head and one tail is $\frac{E}{E+\overline{E}} = \frac{2}{2+2} = \frac{1}{2}$. $E = 2$ because there are two ways in which the event e can happen (a can be head and b tail, or b can be head and a can be tail), and $\overline{E} = 2$ because there are two ways in which the event can fail (both pennies can be heads and both can be tails). There would be no sufficient reason for saying that the event in question was certain or even that it was more likely than not. Nor would there be any sufficient reason for saying that the event was impossible or even that it was less likely than not. Any judgment that departed in either direction from the ratio of the number of possibilities of the event happening to the total number of possibilities comprising both happenings and failures to happen would be arbitrary, and the more it departed the more arbitrary it would be. While, if I were to refuse to say anything about the prospective event on the ground that everything in nature is definite and neither probable nor improbable, and that instead of projecting my uncertainty into the objective world it would be better to keep silent, that would be arbitrary also, because it would wantonly and gratuitously leave out of account my knowledge of the possibilities exemplified in our illustration by the two-sided structure of the pennies. Consequently, whoever refuses to abide by the principle of probability and to apply his knowledge of the possibilities for and against a prospective occurrence, is guilty of conduct which cannot be justified without making more arbitrary assumptions than are made by the one who bases his inferences on probability. *The principle of probability is the principle of least action (least arbitrary action) in logic.* It is the grand device by which ignorant mortals can minimize their ignorance when they cannot remove it.

The universe may be one in which all the laws, routines, or uniformities of nature will hold up to noon of next Thursday or Friday or Saturday. Or it may be one in which a trillionth, a millionth, a third, a half, or any other of the infinity of fractions of those laws will hold up to the above-mentioned times or up to any one of the infinity of other times in the future. That all the laws will hold for all future moments is at best only one out of an infinity of possibilities. We must grant that its chance is as good as any other of the same specificity, just as we must grant the chance that from now on every dealer at a bridge game will deal himself 13 spades. That is highly improbable, but no more improbable than the precise series of hands which will as a matter of fact be dealt. It is always the improbable that happens. But what is the reason for picking out one horse from an infinity of other perfectly similar horses and backing him to win not just against some other horse but against the whole field? There would be no conceivable reason for such a proceeding except that he was your horse and that you loved him very much. And so it is with the postulate of the Uniformity of Nature in a non-causal universe. There is only a great wish and a great hope that nature's routines will continue and that we may be justified in making our wills and in preparing for the breakfasts of next morning and the eclipses of next summer. But note that if there is but the least chance that causality is real, then the Uniformity of Nature is transformed from a paradox of improbability to a virtual certainty. And in place of the shameless impudence of animal faith and hope masquerading in the garb of a logical postulate, we have the firmly grounded inference that nature's repetitions are no longer runs of luck but expressions of causal forces pertaining to each event in its own right irrespective of place and date as such. The crux of my case is the assumption that there is at least the possibility of causal power in nature. If there is even that bare possibility, be it as antecedently improbable as you like, then the fact of nature's routines transforms it into an overwhelming probability. For the chance that those routines are causal is one minus the chance that they are casual. The only alternative to the hypothesis that causal power exists is the hypothesis that nature's laws are stupendous runs of luck.

⁂ 3 ⁂

THE RAINBOW SERIES AND THE LOGARITHM OF ALEPH NULL [1]

An illustrative example of the way in which induction, deduction, and imagination were employed in the discovery of a new infinite series and a new series of infinites. It presupposes some knowledge of algebra.

THIS paper has three parts. Part I contains a description and proof of a curious equality relation pertaining to the simple harmonic series $1 + \frac{1}{2} + \frac{1}{3} + \frac{1}{4} + + + \cdots$ and the series derived from it by merely alternating the signs of the terms thus, $1 - \frac{1}{2} + \frac{1}{3} - \frac{1}{4} + - + - \cdots$.

Part II contains a description (deduced from Part I), of a new type of series that I call the "Rainbow" which has a definite summation value but which lacks both a first term and a last term.

Part III contains the proof (deduced from Part II) of a new Cantorian (or "sub-Cantorian") *transfinite* which is the logarithm of Aleph Null and the first of an endless series of logarithmic transfinites intervening between Aleph Null and the finite numbers.

PART I. A CURIOUS EQUALITY RELATION PERTAINING TO TWO SERIES

With respect to the following pair of series, Series I, $1 + \frac{1}{2} + \frac{1}{3} + \frac{1}{4} + \cdots + \frac{1}{n} + \frac{1}{n+1} + \frac{1}{n+2} + \cdots + \frac{1}{2n}$, and Series II, $1 - \frac{1}{2} + \frac{1}{3} - \frac{1}{4} + \cdots - \frac{1}{2n}$, we shall

[1] Reprinted from *Scripta Mathematica Library*, Volume V.

prove that the sum of the terms in the second half of Series I (namely, those from $\frac{1}{n+1}$ to $\frac{1}{2n}$ inclusive) is always equal to the sum of both halves of the terms in Series II (namely, those from 1 to $-\frac{1}{2n}$ inclusive).

When we take $2n$ as equal in turn to 2, 4, and 6, we can see by inspection that the equality relation pertaining to the two series holds true, thus:

When $2n = 2$, Series I is $1 + \frac{1}{2}$, Series II is $1 - \frac{1}{2}$, and $\frac{1}{2} = 1 - \frac{1}{2}$

When $2n = 4$, Series I is $1 + \frac{1}{2} + \frac{1}{3} + \frac{1}{4}$, Series II is $1 - \frac{1}{2} + \frac{1}{3} - \frac{1}{4}$, and $\frac{1}{3} + \frac{1}{4} = 1 - \frac{1}{2} + \frac{1}{3} - \frac{1}{4}$

When $2n = 6$, Series I is $1 + \frac{1}{2} + \frac{1}{3} + \frac{1}{4} + \frac{1}{5} + \frac{1}{6}$, Series II is $1 - \frac{1}{2} + \frac{1}{3} - \frac{1}{4} + \frac{1}{5} - \frac{1}{6}$, and $\frac{1}{4} + \frac{1}{5} + \frac{1}{6} = 1 - \frac{1}{2} + \frac{1}{3} - \frac{1}{4} + \frac{1}{5} - \frac{1}{6}$

Now that we have found that the equality relation pertaining to our two series does actually hold true when $2n$, the number of terms in each series, is equal to either 2, or 4, or 6, we shall show that when the equality relation holds for any given even number of terms, it will also hold for the next greater even number of terms. In other words, if it can ever be *assumed* to hold when the number of terms is $2n$, it can be *proved* to hold when the number of terms is increased from $2n$ to $2n + 2$.

When $2n$ is the number of terms in each of the two series, they can be written thus:

Series I, $1 + \frac{1}{2} + \frac{1}{3} + \frac{1}{4} + \cdots + \frac{1}{n} + \frac{1}{n+1} + \frac{1}{n+2} + + + \cdots + \frac{1}{2n}$

Series II, $1 - \frac{1}{2} + \frac{1}{3} - \frac{1}{4} + \cdots\cdots\cdots - \frac{1}{2n}$

And our assumption of an equality between the sum of the second half of the terms in Series I and the sum of all the terms in Series II can be written thus:

$$\frac{1}{n+1} + \frac{1}{n+2} + \cdots + \frac{1}{2n} = 1 - \frac{1}{2} + \frac{1}{3} - \frac{1}{4} + \cdots - \frac{1}{2n} \quad (1)$$

When the number of terms in each series is increased from $2n$ to $2n + 2$, they can be written thus:

$$\text{Series I,}\ 1 + \tfrac{1}{2} + \tfrac{1}{3} + \tfrac{1}{4} + + + \cdots + \tfrac{1}{n} + \frac{1}{n+1} + \frac{1}{n+2} + \frac{1}{n+3} + + + \tfrac{1}{2n} + \frac{1}{2n+1} + \frac{1}{2n+2}$$

$$\text{Series II,}\ 1 - \tfrac{1}{2} + \tfrac{1}{3} - \tfrac{1}{4} + - \cdots - \tfrac{1}{2n} + \frac{1}{2n+1} - \frac{1}{2n+2}$$

And the equality between the sum of the terms in the second half of Series I and the sum of all the terms in Series II can be written thus:

$$\frac{1}{n+2} + \frac{1}{n+3} + + + \cdots + \tfrac{1}{2n} + \frac{1}{2n+1} + \frac{1}{2n+2} = 1 - \tfrac{1}{2} + \tfrac{1}{3} - \tfrac{1}{4} + - + - \cdots - \tfrac{1}{2n} + \frac{1}{2n+1} - \frac{1}{2n+2} \qquad (2)$$

Comparing equation (2) with equation (1), we see in the first place that the left-hand member of equation (2) has been derived from the left-hand member of equation (1) by adding $\frac{1}{2n+1} + \frac{1}{2n+2}$ and subtracting $\frac{1}{n+1}$; and we see in the second place that the right-hand member of equation (2) has been derived from the right-hand member of equation (1) by adding $\frac{1}{2n+1}$ and subtracting $\frac{1}{2n+2}$. But the changes made in each member are equal because

$$\frac{1}{2n+1} + \frac{1}{2n+2} - \frac{1}{n+1} = \frac{1}{2n+1} - \frac{1}{2n+2} \qquad (3)$$

And inasmuch as when equals are added to equals the sums are equal, it follows that if equation (1) is true, equation (2) must also be true. In other words, if the equality relation pertaining to Series I and Series II holds true when the number of terms in each series is any even number ($2n$), it must also hold true for each and all the succeeding even numbers of terms $(2n) + 2$, $(2n + 2) + 2$, $(2n + 2 + 2) + 2$, *etc.* And since we have already found by empirical inspection that the equality relation pertaining to the two series (when the number of their terms is the same) holds true when that number ($2n$) is substituted in turn for 2, for 4, and for 6, it follows that the sum of the terms in the second half of Series I is always and for any even number whatever equal to the sum of all the terms in Series II.

Q. E. D.

Part II. The Rainbow Series

The series which we have referred to as Series II, namely, $1 - \frac{1}{2} + \frac{1}{3} - \frac{1}{4} + - + \cdots - \frac{1}{2n}$, is convergent; and as the number of its terms is increased, the limiting value of the sum of the terms is the logarithm of 2 to the base e, the so-called "natural logarithm" of 2, symbolized by $ln2$. Now, the series which we have referred to as Series I, namely, $1 + \frac{1}{2} + \frac{1}{3} + \frac{1}{4} + + + \cdots \frac{1}{2n}$, is divergent; but, inasmuch as the sum of the second half of its terms has just been proved to be equal to the sum of all the terms in Series I (this latter being convergent and when n is infinite equal to $ln2$), it follows that though Series I as a whole is *divergent*, yet the "second half" of it is *convergent* and (when n is infinite) is itself equal to the natural logarithm of 2. The limiting form of the "equality relation" pertaining to Series I and Series II can then be represented by the following equation:

$$\lim_{n \to \infty}\left[\frac{1}{(n+1)} + \frac{1}{(n+2)} + + + \cdots + \frac{1}{(2n)}\right] = \lim_{n \to \infty}\left[1 - \frac{1}{2} + \frac{1}{3} - \frac{1}{4} + - + - \cdots - \frac{1}{(2n)}\right] = ln\,2 \quad (1')$$

This equation (1′) is simply the limiting form of the equation (1) which was proved true in Part I. But the series $\lim_{n \to \infty}\left[\frac{1}{(n+1)} + \frac{1}{(n+2)} + \cdots + \frac{1}{(2n)}\right]$ is a most peculiar thing, for it is a series which has no proper first term and no proper last term, yet which does nevertheless possess a definite finite value because it is equal to the limiting value of Series II, which in its turn is equal to the natural logarithm of 2.

The expression $\frac{1}{(n+1)}$, though we have written it as a "first" term, is really no proper term at all; nor has it any proper or definite position in the whole array of terms in Series I. The same is true of the expression $\lim_{n \to \infty} [\frac{1}{2n}]$ (which we have written as the "last" term), and also, of course, of each and all of the infinity of terms that lies between the pseudo boundaries of the series. But what is most remarkable is that though the series $\frac{1}{n+1} + \frac{1}{n+2} + \cdots + \frac{1}{2n}$ in its limiting form has boundaries that vanish into vagueness and indeterminacy, yet it is just in that limiting form and when the *boundaries* become indefinite that the *sum of the terms* becomes *definite* and equal to the natural logarithm of 2.

Now, the horizon on the left in which a rainbow may be said to begin and the horizon on the right in which it may be said to end are no proper or definite places, yet the rainbow itself and as a whole possesses a perfectly definite length. Though extending from "nowhere" to "nowhere," its linear value has a definiteness that is untainted by the indefiniteness of its terminals.

Thus it is with the limiting form of my series $\frac{1}{n+1} + \frac{1}{n+2} + + + \cdots \frac{1}{2n}$, and for this reason and in the hope of conveying by a metaphor some hint of its strange beauty, I have named it the "Rainbow Series."

Part III. The Logarithm of Aleph Null and the Infinite Series of Logarithmic Transfinites

It is a property, and from the modern standpoint it is a definitive property, of any aggregate called infinite that it possesses parts with which it can be put in one-to-one correspondence. This does not mean that an infinite can be put in one-to-one correspondence with every one of its parts, nor does it mean that infinite assemblages can always be put in one-to-one correspondence with each other. In fact, those infinites which differ so greatly in magnitude that they cannot be put in one-to-one correspondence with one another, form the series of infinites discovered by Cantor and named by him the "Transfinites." The first or lowest of these transfinites is Aleph Null, exemplified by the number of all rational numbers, or, more simply, by the number of all integers. The second transfinite called Gamma is exemplified by the aggregate of all the combinations of all the integers contained in Aleph, or by the number of all real numbers both rational and irrational, or by the number of points in a line or in any other continuum of higher order so long as the number of its dimensions remains finite. The transfinite Gamma can be attained by raising any finite number or Aleph itself to the Aleph power. And, analogously, a third transfinite can be attained by raising any finite number, or Aleph, or Gamma, to the Gamma power. And, in general, an endless series of successively higher transfinites can be generated by taking each in turn as an exponent, thus making it the logarithm of the next higher transfinite. Symbolizing Aleph Null by $T_{(0)}$, Gamma by $T_{(1)}$, and the others correspondingly, we get the sequence:

$$T_{(0)}, T_{(1)}, T_{(2)}, T_{(3)} \cdots,$$

in which each member will be the logarithm of its successor. And apart from any other exemplifications which may be found for it, any one of these higher transfinites, $T_{(n)}$, will exemplify the totality of combinations, $2^{T(n-1)}$, of the members of its predecessor, $T_{(n-1)}$. Aleph Null, as the first member of this sequence, has no predecessor, and hence, of course, can have no logarithm.

I wish now to prove that, contrary to the accepted belief, Aleph Null does have a logarithm, and that this logarithm is not only a true transfinite predecessor of Aleph Null, but the first of an endless descending series of logarithmic transfinites which intervene between Aleph and the domain of finite numbers.

Let us write the simple harmonic series which we have

referred to above as Series I as a series of "segments," the number of terms in the successive segments increasing with the successive powers of two; thus:

$$1 + (\tfrac{1}{2}) + (\tfrac{1}{3} + \tfrac{1}{4}) + (\tfrac{1}{5} + \tfrac{1}{6} + \tfrac{1}{7} + \tfrac{1}{8}) + \cdots + (\tfrac{1}{n+1} + \tfrac{1}{n+2} + \cdots + \tfrac{1}{2n})$$

Now let us note, first, that the number of terms in this Series I is the number of the totality of integers, inasmuch as the successive terms of the series have the successive integers as their denominators, their numerators being, of course, always unity.

Let us note, second, that the number of terms in our series is not only Aleph Null, but, when considered as arranged in m successive segments, it is equal to $1 + 2^m - 1$. For the number of terms in any succession of m segments beginning with the first segment containing only the single term $(\frac{1}{2})$ can be represented as $2^0 + 2^1 + 2^2 + 2^3 + \cdots + 2^{m-1} = 2^m - 1$. And when the number of terms in Series I is infinite and equal to the totality of integers or to Aleph Null, the number of segments which we denoted by m must also be infinite, but an infinite logarithmically or transfinitely lower than the other, and we can write $\lim_{n \to \infty} [1 + 2^m - 1 = 2^m]$ = Aleph Null. And m becomes the logarithm of Aleph Null, whose "existence" we are seeking to prove.

Let us pause here for a moment to consider the meaning of the term "existence" in a mathematical context such as the one before us. Obviously, the existence of the logarithm of Aleph is not to be proved merely by our ability to write the symbols "2^m = Aleph." If m is to be proved to *exist*, it must be shown to be something more than a "symbol *ad hoc*" having only a prima facie meaningfulness. The problem of establishing a mathematical existence is indeed significantly analogous to the problem of legitimatizing a scientific hypothesis. Each must be demonstrated to be a *vera causa*, that is, an entity capable of specific exemplification in a context other than the one for which it is invoked.

If at this point we are challenged as to our right to express the simple harmonic series when expanded to infinity as composed of *m* segments, and hence as containing 2^m terms, we can reply that any number will differ from some integral power of 2 by a number less than itself. So, even if Aleph were provisionally assumed not to be expressible as an integral power of 2, it would differ from some other transfinite that *was* expressible as an integral power of 2 by a number less than itself. And, as Aleph plus or minus any number less than Aleph is nothing but Aleph, the supposed "other" transfinite would be Aleph itself.

We may say, then, that Aleph is equal to 2^m, where Aleph is the number of terms in the harmonic series. And we may say further that *m*, the logarithm of that number, can be exemplified in the number of segments of which the series can be regarded as compounded.

In a sense, then, the number of segments of our series does already provide the existentiality of the logarithm of Aleph, for which we have been seeking.

If it should be said that these *segments* are artificial and abstract and hence do not furnish the degree of concretely specific exemplification demanded by "existence," I might reply that they are no more abstract and artificial than the *combinations* of the elements of an Aleph assemblage which in their totality undoubtedly exemplify the transfinite Gamma. Such a reply on my part would, however, savor too much of a *tu quoque* retort; and, even at that, it would leave untouched those who would refuse to admit that the existentiality of Gamma was established by using it *merely* as the number of Aleph's combinations. Fortunately, it is possible to go further in the direction of specific exemplification and to use the "segments," not as in themselves establishing the existentiality of the logarithm of Aleph, but as a valid stepping-stone to that goal.

To show how this advance can be made, we turn from a consideration of the segments merely in themselves to a consideration of the actual sum of the terms of the harmonic series when viewed in the light of those segments. And writing the series again,

1st segment, 2nd segment, 3rd segment, · · · *m*th segment:

$$\lim_{n \to \infty} [1 + (\tfrac{1}{2}) + (\tfrac{1}{3} + \tfrac{1}{4}) + (\tfrac{1}{5} + \tfrac{1}{6} + \tfrac{1}{7} + \tfrac{1}{8}) + \cdots (\tfrac{1}{(n+2)} + + + \cdots \tfrac{1}{(2n)})]$$

we observe that the *sum of the terms* in each one of the segments is a finite quantity that increases from $\frac{1}{2}$, which is the minimum sum in the first segment, to $(\frac{1}{n+1} + \frac{1}{n+2} + \cdots \frac{1}{2n})$, which is the maximum sum of the terms in the *m*th segment. But when n is infinite, this maximum sum, which is also the limiting sum, becomes the sum of the terms in the Rainbow Series, which, as we proved above in Part I and Part II, is equal to the natural logarithm of 2. If the sums of the terms in the successive segments were all equal, we could get the sum of the terms in the whole series by multiplying the sum in each segment by m, which is the number of segments, and adding one to this product. As it is, we can only say that the sum of the terms in the whole series is a quantity greater than $m \cdot (\frac{1}{2}) + 1$ and less than $m \cdot (ln2) + 1$. When n, the number of terms in the series, is infinite and equal to Aleph Null, m, the number of the segments of the series, is also infinite, but it is the infinite of next lower potency and is therefore, at least in a formal sense, the logarithm of Aleph. And this "formal" logarithm of Aleph, multiplied by $\frac{1}{2}$ or by $ln2$ or by any intermediate finite quantity, is not changed in its "*potency*" or even in its "order," and thus remains simply the logarithm of Aleph. But this logarithm of Aleph, when taken as lying between $m \cdot (\frac{1}{2})$ and $m \cdot (ln2)$, truly and concretely expresses the sum of the simple harmonic series,

$$\lim_{n \to \infty} [1 + \tfrac{1}{2} + \tfrac{1}{3} + \tfrac{1}{4} + \cdots + \tfrac{1}{(2n)}]$$

and thereby loses its merely formal character and acquires that "specific exemplification" or "existentiality" which we have sought to establish.

It remains now for us to prove that the existence of the logarithm of Aleph entails the existence of a further transfinite of next lower potency, which would be the logarithm of the logarithm of Aleph; and that the latter entails a third logarithmic transfinite which in its turn entails by the same process a fourth, and so on without end.

To achieve this demonstration, we shall replace Aleph by its own logarithm, m, as the infinite number of terms in an infinite section of the harmonic series. We shall now let $m = 2^r$, with the same justification that we let Aleph $= 2^m$, and divide this new and still infinite section of the series into segments, the number of terms in each of these successive segments to be equal, as before, to the successive powers of 2. Since the number of terms in the new series is to be $m = 2^r$, the number of its segments will be r, which is the logarithm of m. Taking this new logarithm in the same formal sense that we took m itself, we multiply it as we multiplied m by the natural logarithm of 2 (or by any other finite quantity between $ln2$ and $\frac{1}{2}$), and thus get in a new form the sum of the harmonic series. But the number of terms of the series as we are now taking it is no longer Aleph, but rather m or the logarithm of Aleph. And, consequently, the sum of the series is no longer equal to m or to $m \cdot (ln2)$, but rather to $r = \log m = \log \log$ Aleph. This is still infinite, but it is an infinite of next lower potency to m, even as m itself was the infinite of next lower potency to Aleph. Thus, by using r first in a quasi-formal sense as the number of *segments* in the harmonic series of m

= log Aleph *terms*, we have been able to go further and give it specific exemplification or existentiality by the same procedure that we had already used with *m*. This procedure is obviously perfectly uniform and general, and could be repeated with *r*, thus entailing as a lower transfinite predecessor the logarithm of *r:* which could in turn be shown to entail a further still lower predecessor, and so on without end. Substituting the symbols $T_{(-1)}$ for *m*, the logarithm of Aleph, and $T_{(-2)}$ for *r*, the logarithm of *m*, we can write the series of new or logarithmic transfinites below Aleph (whose existence we claim to have established) in conjunction with the series of old transfinites above Aleph (whose existence was already established) in the following form $\cdots T_{(-3)}, T_{(-2)}, T_{(-1)}, T_{(0)}, T_{(1)}, T_{(2)}, T_{(3)}, \cdots$. Here $T_{(0)}$, symbolizing Aleph Null, stands in the middle with $T_{(1)}$, symbolizing Gamma, and $T_{(2)}$, $T_{(3)}$, and so forth, symbolizing the higher successors of Gamma. The *T's* with the succession of negative subscripts stretch persistently and hopelessly down toward the domain of the finite numbers as their unattainable limit. An analogous "hopeless persistence" is shown by the series of proper fractions stretching down from unity to their unattainable limit of zero. And as the proper fractions in getting ever closer to zero get ever closer to one another, so, too, do the logarithmic transfinites get ever closer to one another in approaching as their "zero" the Nirvana of finitude. In the light of the infinite, the finite is as nothing. Yet that "nothing" is the actuality to which even the infinite aspires.

In conclusion, let us remember that the new transfinites, pygmy members of a giant race, and so at once both huge and squat, are true Children of the Rainbow. For they owe their existence (in a technical sense) to the Rainbow Series, which thus proves itself to be as good and as useful as it was valid and beautiful. Indeed, it was only by exhibiting the harmonic series as itself composed of an infinity of series, each of the rainbow type, that our "logarithms of infinity" could pass from the shadow status of mere formal symbols to the solid status of specific and therefore existential exemplification.

Notes

1. A gentleman who heard this paper when read wrote me a letter in which he claimed that another and in some ways a simpler proof of the "Equality Relation" between the two series set forth in the first section of this paper had been published about ten years ago. Unfortunately, the letter was lost, and a careful search for the article referred to has been unsuccessful.

2. *Deduction of the Rainbow Series from Euler's Constant by Professor W. M. Whyburn, Head of Department of Mathematics, University of California:*

Euler's constant is defined as

$$\lim_{n \to \infty} [H_n - \log n] = c = .577{,}215{,}664{,}901 \ldots$$

where

$$H_n = 1 + \tfrac{1}{2} + \ldots\ldots + \frac{1}{n}$$

Now

$$\lim_{n \to \infty} [H_{2n} - \log 2n] = c$$

$\therefore$

$$\lim_{n \to \infty} [H_{2n} - \log n] = c + \log 2$$

The Rainbow Series

$$\frac{1}{n+1} + \cdots\cdots \frac{1}{2n} = H_{2n} - H_n =$$
$$= [H_{2n} - \log n] - [H_n - \log n]$$

Hence

$$\lim [H_{2n} - H_n] = \lim [H_{2n} - \log n] -$$
$$- \lim [H_n - \log n] = c + \log 2 - c = \log 2$$

This may be generalized in the following way:

Let

$$H_{jn} - H_{kn} = \frac{1}{jn} + \frac{1}{jn+1} + \cdots \frac{1}{kn} \; (j < k)$$

We shall have then

$$\lim H - \log kn = c$$

or

$$\lim_{n \to \infty} [H_{jn} - \log j - \log n] = c$$

$$\lim_{n \to \infty} [H_{kn} - \log k - \log n] = c$$

Hence

$$\lim_{n \to \infty} [H_{jn} - \log n] = c + \log j$$

$$\lim_{n \to \infty} [H_{kn} - \log n] = c + \log k$$

$\therefore$

$$\lim_{n \to 8} [H_{kn} - H_{jn} = \lim [H_{kn} - \log n] -$$

$$- \lim [H_{jn} - \log n] = (c + \log k) -$$

$$- (c + \log j) = \log k - \log j = log \frac{k}{j}$$

3. The transfinites are defined or conceived by Cantor, their discoverer, in two ways: (1) *positively* as a series of infinites each of which is the logarithm of its successor thus, $2^{T(n)} = T_{(n+1)}$; (2) *negatively* as a series of infinites separated by abysses which no relation of one-to-one correspondence can bridge.

I have taken the transfinites in the first or positive sense, as I had a right to do; but, as Professor Whyburn and others have already observed, in the course of my proof, by means of the Rainbow Series, that a logarithm of Aleph Null existed and that there was consequently no first or lowest transfinite, there emerged as an incident of the argument a kind of one-to-one correspondence between the successive transfinites. This would appear to indicate, if my demonstration is valid, that between the negative and the positive definitions of the transfinites there is a contradiction. Not knowing what else to do, I shall deposit this baby on the doorsteps of the mathematicians and proceed to run away as fast as my legs will carry me.

4

* THE ANTINOMY AND ITS IMPLICATIONS FOR LOGICAL THEORY[1]

An analysis of "antinomic" situations such as those presented in Zeno's famous puzzles about motion where Sense and Reason, the major criteria of belief appear to be in irreconcilable conflict. The paper reveals the need for a Material Logic consisting in the enumeration and comparative evaluation of the methods of attaining knowledge.

Introductory

1. *The Plurality of Logics as the Source of Antinomies.* Our ideas and beliefs can be traced to one or more of the following origins: (1) testimony of others; (2) instinctive feeling or "intuition"; (3) abstract reasoning from universal principles; (4) sensory experience; and (5) practical activity and successful consequences.

Each of these sources may be, and actually has been, accepted as a primary criterion for determining philosophic truth; and thus to the five sources of belief there correspond the following five types of logical theory: (1) Authoritarianism; (2) Intuitionism or Mysticism; (3) Rationalism; (4) Empiricism; and (5) Pragmatism.

Each of these types of logical theory has a type of belief for the evaluation of which it appears to be especially suited. For example, the following beliefs: (1) that Napoleon existed; (2) that certain acquaintances would be congenial as friends; (3) that a billion and seven is not divisible

[1] Reprinted from *Studies in the History of Ideas*, Vol. I, pp. 223–248, by permission of Columbia University Press.

by two; (4) that grass is green; (5) that it pays to advertise —would correspond in the order of their listing to the five criteria.

In addition to these special types of belief, there is a large class of judgments which lend themselves with almost equal ease to evaluation by all of the five criteria. For example, the belief that eight and four make twelve is supported by the authority of others, by its congruity with our feelings, by deductive reasoning, by empirical observation, and by the successful consequences which usually result from action based on that assumption. By far the greater number of our beliefs are of this second class; and even those which are primarily suggested and primarily tested by but one of the five logical grounds are usually felt to be at least potentially capable of being confirmed by some or all of the other criteria. Despite this general trust in the inter-confirmatory character of the five principles of logical evaluation, there does remain a class of beliefs which appears to be definitely established by some of the criteria and as definitely refuted by others. To this class of beliefs or judgments belong what are called "antinomies," and it is with the antinomy and its logical implications that we are to be concerned in this paper.

2. *The Major and Minor Antinomies.* In general, an antinomy may be said to arise whenever there is a conflict of logical criteria in regard to one and the same judgment. The following are examples:

a. Our intuition tells us that heavenly bodies must move in heavenly curves. The circle is the heavenly or perfect curve; therefore, the planets must move in circular orbits. Perception and calculation, however, prove that their orbits are elliptical. The conflict here is between intuition on the one side and sense and reason on the other.

b. Othello's instinctive feeling tells him that Desdemona is true. But this lover's intuition conflicts with the testimony of Iago, whose authority he accepts.

c. Many physicists found what they regard as contradictory attributes of the hypothetical ether, which from the standpoint of reason should disprove its existence; yet, because of the useful consequences which proceed from the assumption, they accepted its reality on pragmatic grounds.

These are all examples of what may be called "minor antinomies." The conflicting situations which they illustrate are not such as to array reason against sense; and it is only to conflicts of the latter kind that the name "major antinomies" is fully applicable. For the logics of Rationalism and Empiricism are almost universally recognized as superior in importance to those of authority, intuition, and practical success. The Authoritarians, for example, can usually be forced to admit that those whose testimony should be accepted by us did not themselves derive their information from the testimony of others (which would involve an endless regress), but from direct revelations of their superior sense or reason. The Intuitionists or Mystics, too, are apt to restrict the exclusive use of their criterion of intuition to a rather special class of cases in which reason and direct experience are either silent or ambiguous; and when, as in the question of the inhabitability of the antipodes, our intuitive certainty that men could not walk head downward on the under side of the earth comes into conflict with our explicit sensory observations of people in China, we swallow our intuitional repugnance and bow to the evidence of fact. As for the Pragmatists, it is pretty certain that most of them would resent being classed as opponents of experimental evidence, and would claim, on the contrary, that their criterion of successful practical consequences was no more than an important extension and adaptation of the logic of empiricism to the needs of an evolving world.

It is on these grounds that we regard the antinomic conflicts of sense and reason as incomparably more serious in their import for logic than the clashings of the minor criteria of truth. The major antinomy is, moreover, of infrequent occurrence. In all ordinary matters, direct perception and intellectual deduction go hand in hand and give to one another loyal and continuous corroboration; and in the rare cases of explicit conflict between them, we experience the helpless distress which is felt by an affectionate child in the presence of a quarrel between his parents. It is only the apathetic and soggy-minded who can view with indifference or boredom the spectacle of a first-class antinomy in action. The person really interested in philosophy will find the situation intolerable, and will be unable to attain peace of mind until he has dealt with it in one way or another. In dealing with a major antinomy, in which an immovable body of sensory evidence appears to be contradicted by the irresistible force of clear reasoning, there are three general attitudes or methods, of a somewhat extreme character, and three specific theories, having the character of compromise, which logically may be, and which historically have been, employed by philosophers. I shall treat them in order and under the following captions: I, The Method of Skepticism; II, The Method of Ultra-Rationalism; III, The Method of Ultra-Empiricism; IV, The Relational Theory; V, The Punctiform Theory; VI, The Double Aspect Theory.

I. The Method of Skepticism

It may be held that the antinomic conflict is irreconcilable and that the nature of reality is thereby proved unknowable. Skepticism (which is a type of logical theory in the same sense in which anarchism is a type of political theory and atheism a kind of theology) is thus established; for any problem in which the two primary criteria of truth are regarded as ultimately refuting one another would be essentially insoluble.

This attitude was probably taken by Gorgias in dealing

with the antinomies of Zeno; and in modern times it has been explicitly defended by Sir William Hamilton and Mr. Herbert Spencer in regard to such supposedly antinomic questions as the finitude or infinitude of the world.

The general arguments for and against the Skeptical position make a long story into which we cannot now enter. The dialectical argument from antinomies is only one of several ways in which the discrediting of human knowledge has been attempted. We are the more justified here in passing over it with scant treatment in that what it offers is not so much a solution of the antinomy, but rather a denial of all solutions. Its purely negative doctrine could be established only by the successful refutation of the entire group of positive types of logic. And if accepted, it would get us nowhere. Moreover, even though the Skeptic succeeded in demonstrating a complete *ignoramus* in regard to the antinomies, it would be difficult to see how he would be justified in deriving from it the arrogant pessimism of *ignorabimus*.

II. The Method of Ultra-Rationalism

It may be held that, when confronted by the antinomic situation in which reason and sense appear to conflict, sense must be discarded. For a world of *non-sense* is preferable to a world of *unreason*.

Now reason, when forced to triumph in the face of all sense, assumes many of the earmarks of Intuition; and the Rationalist, in divorcing himself permanently from Empiricism, becomes something very like an Intuitionist or Mystic. It was this ultra-Rationalist attitude that Zeno took toward his own puzzles in which the unreasonableness of motion was supposed to have been demonstrated. Not only motion itself, but the whole world of sense (because it is hopelessly tainted with motion), he condemned as unreal; and the way was thus cleared for accepting the

Mystic world of Parmenides, in which was contained nothing but pure and changeless being. There have been many since Zeno who have followed him in taking the ultra-Rationalist method of solving antinomies. Kant relegates space and time to the realm of the subjective on the ground that they contain antinomies. Mr. F. H. Bradley deals likewise and for like reasons not only with space, time, and motion, but with qualities and relations and all of the other characters of our finite experience. The ancient Hindus and the contemporary Christian Scientists, actuated doubtless by a vaguer and more religious form of the same logic, condemn evil and with it the whole world of matter as unreal. The main difference between Zeno and his various followers is linguistic. For Zeno, the world of sense experience is "non-being"; for Kant, "subjective"; for Mr. Bradley, "appearance"; for the Buddhists, "mâya," or illusion; for the Eddyites, "error of mortal mind."

Now, those of us who are at all empirically minded and who retain allegiance to sense will, of course, reject this ultra-Rationalist solution of the antinomies as false. But the Zenonian attitude has been charged with a more deadly defect than falsity, namely, futility—and it is that charge especially which I wish to consider.

Suppose we admit, for the sake of argument, that the claim of unreality for the sensory world is true; what use can we make of such a truth? Does it allay the hunger for peace between the reasonable and the sensible to be told that the latter is illusory?

We will let Zeno convince us that in order for Achilles to catch a tortoise he would have to complete an infinite series of steps in a finite time, and that it is difficult to understand how this is possible in a world of "being." But is it much easier to understand how it is possible in a world of "non-being"? The difficulties charged against tortoise-catching are not based on an analysis of "being," but on an analysis of space and time, and why these difficulties should vanish when the hunting ground is shifted to the realm of "non-being" is not very clear. Of this at least we may be sure: that no tortoise that ever crawled, not even the tortoise of Elea, would regard himself as any safer when assured by Zeno that he and the place in which Achilles was to catch him had been changed from being to non-being. If the mighty shift in metaphysical status was felt at all by a tortoise, it would be felt so gently as to seem almost verbal.

So also with Kant—we allow him to convince us of the difficulty of understanding how the divisibility of space is to be reconciled to the demand for indivisible elements of matter. But it does not become any easier to meet the difficulty if the space is made subjective and not objective, for the difficulty, such as it was, arose from the nature of space, not from the nature of "objective." The same comfortless conclusion comes to us from Mr. Bradley. The qualities and relations revealed in our experience cannot, so he tells us, be reconciled with reason; for, if a relation is to relate, it must make a difference to its terms, that is, make them other than the terms which we apprehended as related. It is too bad that there is this difficulty (if it is a difficulty). But how does it help to deny that the world of sense is "real" and to assign it a status of "appearance"? The twin concepts of reality and appearance may be valid and fruitful or they may not. Whether good or bad, they are not in question. The answer involved in the quality-relation situation did not depend on the nature of "reality" or the nature of "appearance," but simply on the nature of qualities and relations. Are the contradictions or the tragedies of our experience mitigated by assuming or even proving that beyond our experience there is another experience in which they do not occur? The intellectual and moral evils in our world of appearance are one thing. Why, then, should we suddenly change the subject (unless, of course, it proves embarrassing) and begin talking about an absolute reality?

And, finally, as to the Buddhists, Christian Scientists, and such, they tell us that "evil is good in disguise," or out and out "illusion," or "error of mortal mind." So be it, but what of it? Why the disguise? Why the illusion or error? An evil disguise is as evil as anything else. An agonizing toothache may be assigned an illusory status, but between having a vivid hallucination of a toothache and having a "real" toothache it would be hard to choose. In every case in which we seek to cure an intellectual discord, such as an antinomy, or a moral discord, such as a sin or pain, by changing the metaphysical status of the experience in which it occurs from real to unreal, we are committing the fallacy of irrelevant conclusion. For it is the actual nature of the experience and not the metaphysical status of "subjective" or "objective" with which we should concern ourselves.

In the foregoing discussion, I have tried to show that the Zenonian or ultra-Rationalist method of dealing with antinomies applies not merely to intellectual discords, but to moral discords as well, and that the method is as futile and irrelevant in the one sphere as in the other. I should like, in conclusion to this section, to make a further application of the reasons already advanced, and at the same time to remove a possible misapprehension based on the erroneous supposition that I would bar altogether the use of trans-Empirical concepts.

Transcendental is for the sophisticated philosopher the equivalent of *supernatural* for the plain man. Simple folk invent or discover paradises to help explain the puzzles and the miseries of earthly life, and gods to help explain the mystery and the cruelty of natural forces. For exactly the same reasons, the intellectual gentility invent or discover "realms" of pure being and of eternal ideas, and transcendental egos and absolutes. Simple or gentle—from the crudest supernatural paradise to the most subtle transcendental absolute—there is the same twofold motive at work: a dissatisfaction both intellectual and moral with the world of actual experience. And for gentle and simple alike, the same danger attends the procedure—the danger, namely, that the trans-Empirical, which should at most and in either of its two forms be used as a causally explanatory *supplement* to the world of experience, will be misused as a *substitute* for that world. The result of such misuse has ever been a sinister passivism in ethics and religion and a futile irrelevancy in logic and metaphysics.

Zeno's solution of his antinomies is not to be condemned because he believed with Parmenides in a sphere of pure and changeless being—for aught we know, there may exist not only an Eleatic, but also a Bradleyan, absolute, or even several of each. The real error of the method lay in supposing that the internal harmonies of any such innocently hypothetical worlds could of themselves furnish relevant answers to the antinomies of the world in which we live.

III. The Method of Ultra-Empiricism

It may be held that when confronted by the antinomic situation in which reason and sense appear to conflict, reason must be discarded; for a world of unreason is preferable to a world of nonsense. And just as Rationalism, when pushed to the extreme of opposing (and not merely subordinating) the evidence of sense and the facts of experience, became something very like Intuitionism or Mysticism, so Empiricism, when pushed to the extreme of opposing (and not merely subordinating) the evidence of reason and the laws of logic, becomes something very like Pragmatism. The two forms of what may be called "intellectualism" are (1) Rationalism, in which sense is regarded as secondary to reason but in ultimate harmony with it, and (2) Empiricism, in which reason is regarded as secondary to sense but in ultimate harmony with it. If these definitions are accepted, both Mysticism and Pragmatism can be classed as the equal and opposite forms of "anti-intellectualism." In matters of this sort, analytic definitions may give the impression of dialectical quibbling or question-begging; illustrations are better. Hence, as examples of what I mean by the ultra-Empirical attitude, I cite the following instances:

(1) There is John Stuart Mill's admission of the possibility that on some remote planet the laws of arithmetic might be such as to permit of two and two making five. (2) There is Henri Bergson's doctrine that reason is an instrument evolved by the life force for the purpose of controlling the relatively inanimate and static aspect of nature; that, in so far as it is used for this purpose, it is admirable, but that when we attempt by its means to express the nature of life itself, or even of the dynamic side of "dead" matter, it proves inadequate. Motion can be experienced, but it defies and transcends logical analysis, and the fact that it does so is proof of its ultimate and irreducible reality. (3) There is William James's contention that some sort of fusion or identity between consciousnesses, though opposed to the laws of ordinary logic, must none the less be accepted as real.[2]

The ultra-Empirical method of dealing with antinomies has developed partly as a natural reaction to the barren-

[2] The following passages from *The Pluralistic Universe* are admirably illustrative of the way in which an antinomy is dealt with by this ultra-empirical or anti-intellectualistic form of pragmatism—"That secret of a continuous life which the universe knows by heart and acts on every instant can not be a contradiction incarnate. If logic says it is one, so much the worse for logic. Logic, being the lesser thing, the static incomplete abstraction, must succumb to reality not reality to logic" (p. 207). "What must we do in this tragic predicament? For my own part I have finally found myself compelled to *give up the logic*, fairly, squarely, and irrevocably. It has an imperishable use in human life, but

ness and artificialities of ultra-Rationalism as exemplified in some forms of modern idealism, and partly as a not unnatural attempt to apply to logic itself the evolutionary theories which have so completely transformed the sciences of biology, psychology, and sociology.

The argument seems to run somewhat as follows: the structures and functions of our bodies have developed into what they are because of their utility in the struggle for existence; and the same is true of our minds. Memory and imagination and the power to form concepts and combine them have evolved to their present form because they are useful adaptations to environment and answer to the needs of life. The rules according to which we reason are conditioned by the ends which we pursue and by the material means upon which the attainment of those ends depends. As life and its environment are in a process of change, the rules by which the intellect must proceed will change also and the supposedly abstract and eternal laws of logic must share the same fate as the unchanging species and genera of pre-evolutionary days.

This argument from biology is strengthened by what we now know of the development of sociology and ethics. From the vantage ground of the present, the historian looking out over the past discovers a bewildering variety of moral codes and of political and economic institutions. He sees how those forms of social organization arose and developed in response to the needs of some particular community at some particular time and place. He sees further

that use is not to make us theoretically acquainted with the essence of reality—just what it is I can perhaps suggest to you a little later. Reality, life, experience, concreteness, immediacy, use what word you will, exceeds our logic, overflows and surrounds it" (p. 212). "If I had not read Bergson I should probably still be blackening endless pages of paper privately in the hope of making ends meet that were never meant to meet and trying to discover some mode of conceiving the behaviour of reality which should leave no discrepancy between it and the accepted laws of the logic of identity" (pp. 214–215).

that, when the interests of that community or the demands of its environment had so changed as to make desirable a new code, the cry for a change was answered by the claim that the code of the fathers was sacrosanct, ordained of God, transcendentally valid, eternally and universally applicable. Confronted as he is by the same spectacle recurring time after time and under circumstances the most varied, can we blame the social historian for smiling cynically at all claims for the changeless validity of anything, even of logic itself? "Sacred," "eternal," "universal"—are they aught but the gaudy trappings which senile inertia and wolfish privilege have ever donned when threatened by revolutionary progress?

The biological and social-historical arguments for the ultra-Empirical attitude toward logic are rounded out by the contribution of modern psychological analysis. No longer are we permitted to conceive of a faculty of pure intellect, functioning abstractly and actuated by the impersonal and luminous love of truth. Our concepts, judgments, and syllogisms are framed and uttered in response to concrete needs, and change with their change. Personal motives, temperamental preferences, can always be found as the real empirical causes of logical processes. To separate logic from psychology and ascribe to it a changeless validity that would exempt it from the universal flux and make it an end in itself, would be as absurd as to consider the laws of agriculture apart from the crops to be produced.

In concluding our dialectical defense of the neo-Protagorean doctrine, it must be remembered that no dialectical defense can possibly do it justice. The strength of the position is derived from the mass of concrete facts which have generated it. And ultra-Empiricists are perhaps justified in viewing distrustfully even the most friendly attempts to try to label the wealth of evidence which they have accumulated. The massiveness of the three lines of argument is such as to make it difficult to feel anything but pity for the old-fashioned pedant who would pick some pet aspect of experience, such as logic, and try to preserve it alone from the onrushing, all-engulfing flood of evolutionary change.

Despite the seeming hopelessness of any attempt to withstand the arguments for ultra-Empiricism, such attempts have been made, and the oldest of them is perhaps the most instructive. When Heraclitus proclaimed his doctrine of universal flux, he made no exception of any single thing in the world; everything changed. Heraclitus did not, to be sure, conceive of this omnivorous change as uniformly progressive or upward in direction, as do our Darwinian logicians of the present day; but he sang the primacy of motion over rest, of energy over substance, of the dynamic over the static, of the functional over the structural, at least as earnestly and emphatically as any of his modern successors. But the first and greatest of Dynamists did not hesitate to set a certain kind of limit to his universal flux. πάντα ῥεῖ. All *things* change, but the *laws* according to which all things changed were themselves changeless. They were changeless because they were the measure and condition of the change in things. Their changelessness was required as the presupposition of the changing things. Without their changelessness, the change in things would not only lack measure, it would lack any sort of meaning; it would vanish into nothingness. Let me exhibit the position of the founder of Dynamism in its relation to that of the evolutionary logicians in the form of an allegory.

A race is taking place. The horses run faster and faster. The excitement grows, becomes frenzied. The contagion of motion sweeps all before it. Men on foot join in the race; they are followed by dogs and birds and everything that can fly or crawl or swim; the spectators, too, are running, and even the judges have left their stand and are racing with the others. The purpose of the race has been forgotten, but the joy in motion for its own sake is universal. The Master of the Race, whose urgings all have now obeyed, observes the spectacle, and his brow clouds slightly. He is evidently still unsatisfied. At last he arises, his face alight with a final vision, the vision of the super-race. He cries in thunderous tones, "I have bidden all to run, yet is there one who disobeys. How dares the course on which ye run remain at rest and spoil my race? *Let the race-track race with the racers!* Then, indeed, will motion reign supreme." And as the poor race-track tries to obey and with dull amaze and infinite giddiness seeks for feet or wings with which to get into the running, something snaps, and the mad scene vanishes into the limbo of the utterly meaningless. What was to have become a super-race has become nothing at all.

The master of the race represents our Darwinian logicians who would bring Heraclitus up to date and make Dynamism universally consistent by relegating all logic, their own included, to the status of a concrete being. The thing cannot be done. The race-track itself cannot run with the runners, and no more can the laws by which evolutionary change is to be defined and determined themselves change or evolve.

Many who failed to see the concrete flux of Heraclitus have seen in one form or another his fluxless Logos. Parmenides saw only its shadow, the mere generic character of abstract being and permanence, projected into the abyss as a dark and homogeneous sphere. For the gorgeous mind of Plato, the Logos was reflected above the sky as a rainbow of moral beauties and creative mystic powers. To Aquinas and Leibniz it seemed as the omnipresent intellect of an eternal God. By the transcendental Germans it was taken for the presupposition of the sensible world, which it was, and then mistaken for the grandiose structure of their egos, which it certainly was not. The realistic or anti-Darwinian logicians of today perceive it less picturesquely, and more, perhaps, as Heraclitus himself. To them it is an objective and self-subsistent loom of invariant law, on which the ever-changing fabrics of evolving nature are perpetually woven.

To the Darwinian logicians we may cheerfully grant that apes have evolved into men. We refuse, however, to grant that, therefore, the meaning of an ape has evolved into the meaning of a man. We admit likewise that not only our motor and sensory organs, but also our higher functions of imagination and intellect have developed by natural selection on account of their utility for adaptation, but we refuse to admit that this in any way implies that the more recondite facts and laws which these newly evolved powers reveal to us have themselves undergone any corresponding evolution. The laws of space and number and of matter and energy have not changed from the times of Euclid and Pythagoras and Archimedes; the laws of gasoline engines were just the same in the days of the ancient Athenians as now. *We* know them and *they* did not. Not physics, but man's knowledge of physics, has changed. We may reply in the same vein to the anti-intellectualist who bases his arguments for a changing and psychologistic logic upon the recognition of the concrete and personal motives which actuate men when they claim to be reasoning from a pure love of truth. We might even admit that no discovery even in logic or mathematics had ever been made except to satisfy some human interest of the person making it. If, for example, Pythagoras discovered the Pythagorean theorem, the cause of his intellectual process may have been (1) a sentimental desire to please his disciples, or (2) an economic desire to receive pay, or (3) a theological desire to glorify the gods. It is conceivable that sentimentalists, economists, and theologians might be interested in learning which, if any, of these personal motives functioned psychologically in the concrete situation in which such a law of logic or mathematics was discovered. It is not conceivable, however, that any mathematician or logician should regard such psychological or historical information as of the slightest relevancy to the Pythagorean theorem itself.

The ultra-Empiricist who would solve an antinomy by discarding logic on the ground that its laws are the mere instrument of the life force is guilty of a fallacy of irrelevancy in which the changeless laws discovered by men are confused with the changing processes by which they are discovered. Now, it was also a fallacy of irrelevancy which we charged against the ultra-Rationalist, and I should like to conclude this part of the discussion by a comparison of the two opposite positions.

The Zenonian and ultra-Rationalist way of dealing with an antinomic conflict of reason and sense was to relegate the world of sense to a status of non-being or appearance, and to put in its place a new world of pure reason from which all change and inconsistency were barred. And we pointed out that, however beautiful these abstract and harmonious absolutes might be, their beauties were none the less irrelevant to the world of experience, which remained with all its contradictions and evils just where it was before, no matter how often you called it by abusive names such as "non-being" or "mere appearance." And on the ethical and social side, we noted the harm which these ultra-Rationalist philosophers worked when they selected some particular favorite human institution which had outlived its usefulness, and, by giving it the status of god-given or transcendental law, succeeded in fastening it on later generations. In short, the main fault with ultra-Rationalism is that it irrelevantly ascribes the unchanging character of abstract law to the changing character of concrete things, or rather to the changing character of the particular concrete things and customs which happen to be preferred, condemning the rest to the status of unreality or of evil, according as they are logical or ethical.

The Bergsonian or ultra-Empiricist way of dealing with the antinomic conflict of sense and reason was to relegate logic to the status of a relative and changing thing, and the irrelevancy in the process consisted in mistaking changeless laws for the things and processes through which men discover them.

In short, when dealing with a conflict of sense and reason, the ultra-Rationalist identifies things with laws, while the ultra-Empiricist identifies laws with things. The first course is the way of non-sense; the second, the way of unreason. If you follow the ultra-Rationalist, you are in danger of promoting a fallible opinion or custom to the status of an unchangeable verity and thereby impeding progress. If you follow the ultra-Empiricist, you are in danger of degrading objective truth to the status of shifting human opinion, and thereby rendering progress blind and meaningless.

In playing chess one does not make the ultra-Rationalist mistake of regarding the changelessness of the rules as an obstacle to the succession of moves; nor does one make the ultra-Empiricist mistake of changing or discarding the rules when confronted with a puzzling situation. *The confusion of the things that change with the laws that do not is the great mother of all confusions, and its two opposite forms are equally bad.*

We have now completed our account of the extreme methods of dealing with antinomies. The first of these methods, and the one most briefly treated, was that of the skeptic. This doctrine was treated briefly, because, as was stated, its negative attitude toward the antinomy hardly entitles it to rank as a solution. The two remaining methods of procedure were more carefully examined, and we are now free to leave the intransigeant parties by whom sense and reason are in turn sacrificed, and to attend to the theories of those who believe that antinomies can be solved by an honorable compromise.

Most, if not all, of the great antinomies of history appear to turn on a situation in which the finite as *given* in perception clashes with the infinite as *demanded* by conception. This is certainly the case with the four famous puzzles about motion which were formulated by Zeno, the Eleatic. These puzzles are not only of great intrinsic and historical interest, but they are typical of the antinomy at its best or worst; and from them we select as a basis for our discussion of the three compromise theories the one which is, perhaps, the clearest and most picturesque. It is known as "The Arrow," and may be stated as follows:

A flying arrow, as typical of all moving bodies, appears to our senses to go from one place to another. Yet reason proves this to be impossible, and all motion, together with the world that contains it, to be unreal; for at any one instant the arrow can occupy but one position (obviously a body cannot be in two places at once), hence at each and every instant of the entire time of its apparent flight the arrow will be busy occupying positions, *and there will be no time left in which it could move* FROM *one position* TO *another.*

The puzzle reveals clearly the two opposite characters that any continuum such as motion must possess. The one character is perceptual, empirical; the other, conceptual and rational. In the first character, the continuum appears as a finite, fluid unity of dynamic relations; in its second character, it appears as an infinite granular plurality of static points or terms. The three compromise theories all agree in the belief that these opposing characters can be reconciled, but they differ in that they respectively select the first, or the second, or both, as of fundamental reality.

The third theory, in which the two characters are regarded as equal and ultimate, can be named the "empirico-rational," or better, the "double-aspect," theory. The first and second theories might be called, respectively: (1) the moderate empirical and the moderate rational, or (2) the finitist and the infinitist, or (3) after Kant, the thetic and the antithetic, or (4) the fluid and the granular, or (5) after Bergson, the slide and the cinema, or (6) the dynamic and the static, or (7) the relational and the punctiform. While feeling free to use these names interchangeably, we shall adopt the last pair as, on the whole, best suited to our purpose. We have dwelt on the possibilities of terminology in order that by iteration of the opposition in its several phases we might make the understanding of the question at issue less cold and abstract and more warmly *anschaulich*. And with this preamble on the relations of the theories to one another, we may now proceed to the discussion of the theories themselves, considered separately and in order.

IV. The Relational Theory

The supporters of the relational solution of the puzzle argue that Zeno's division of time and space into durationless instants and extensionless points is unjustifiable. Duration and extension are fundamental and irreducible; instants and points are only artificial constructs which we make for certain purposes; they cannot be regarded as objective constituents of the continua to which we apply them any more than shadows can be regarded as constituents of the bodies that cast them. The boundary or intersection of two lines is in no sense a part of the lines, and points and instants are at best nothing more than cuts or boundaries. Hence, Zeno commits a fallacy of logical analysis when he infers that, because a moving body traverses a great space in a great time and a small space in a small time, therefore, it "occupies" a series of spaceless points in a series of timeless instants. If points and instants are only subjective constructs of ours with no objective existence, Zeno's moving arrow can never get stuck in them, and we shall never have to ask whether it moves from one point to the next.

This solution is nearer to the ultra-Empiricism of Bergson than to the ultra-Rationalism of Zeno, because it preserves the reality of motion, as testified to in perception. But it differs from the ultra-Empirical position in that it claims to reconcile the fact of motion with the laws of logic. The paradox is removed, not by abandoning logic, but by substituting good logic for bad. The strong feature of the relational theory is, in our opinion, its recognition that space and time contain relational constituents which cannot be resolved into points and instants. The weak part of the theory consists in its assertion that space and time are exclusively relational and that the points and instants are not genuine constituents of their continua. We can certainly find points without limit on a line, and we could not find them unless they were there to be found. And with instants it is the same. These punctiform elements of time and space are as undeniably given in perception as are the relations of succession and linearity which unite them.

The upholders of the relational theory are much given to the use of the word *abstraction* as a term of abuse. An abstraction is a feature of a situation which is distinguishable, but not separable, from other features. Color, for example, is clearly distinguishable from extension, but we cannot conceive it as separate or apart from it. In the same sense, a point is an abstraction, because we cannot separate it from other points and from lines. But why should an abstraction be regarded as "unreal," or "subjective," or "constructed by the mind"? Features of a situation would not be distinguishable unless they were there to be distinguished; and the fact that a thing like a point is only real *in situ* does not prove it unreal. There is no obvious reason why an indissoluble relationship should be prejudicial or derogatory to a thing's objectivity. The relationists seem to feel that for an element to be real *in itself*, it must be real *all by itself*.

Then, too, there is an incongruity in the way in which the real relational elements of continua are made by this theory to combine with their "abstract" or "subjective" terms. How, for an example, could an unreal point serve as the middle of a real line? How can the space filled by the earth be real and the axis and central point be unreal? Terms and relations are correlative, and they must be either real *together* or unreal *together*.

But before criticizing this theory further, let us turn to its rival, the punctiform theory, where also we shall discover both a merit and a defect.

V. The Punctiform Theory [3]

Motion is nothing but the occupancy by a body of a continuous series of spatial points in a continuous series of temporal instants. At the initial instant of its motion, a body occupies its initial position; at each succeeding instant it occupies a succeeding position; and this joint occupancy of a one-to-one series of points and instants is all that motion consists in. Thus, Zeno's question as to when does an arrow move from one position to the next position on its path is seen to owe its difficulty to a false assumption as to the nature of motion. The arrow never does move *from* one position *to* another. It *is at* one position at one instant and it *is at* another position at a later instant, and that

[3] This theory, as I understand it, was developed first by the German mathematician Weierstrass and then independently by Mr. Bertrand Russell. It is fully expounded by the latter in his references to Zeno, both in his *Principles of Mathematics* and in his *Scientific Method in Philosophy*. I trust that in my brief sketch I have made no serious misrepresentation.

is all there is to its motion. This view puts exclusive emphasis on the "at-at" character of motion, just as the preceding view emphasized the "from-to" character. And as that theory resembles Bergson's solution, so this theory resembles that of Zeno, for it admits the illusoriness of one aspect of perceived motion. We certainly do perceive motion as being *from* one place *to* another, but this aspect of "from-to" is treated by Russell as an illusion. The apparently unitary motion is, in reality, an "at-at" succession of occupied positions, and nature plays on our senses the same trick that is played by the cinema, the only difference being that in the cinematograph the successive photographs are separated from one another by small but finite intervals of time and distance; while in nature's "movie" the successive pictures form the same perfect continuum as the points of a line. To the punctiform theory there are two objections which must now be considered.

First, it may be charged that the solution is paradoxical because it resolves *moving* into a series of *restings*. But to this it is answered that the occupancy of one point for one instant is not true rest. Rest is the occupancy of one point for *more* than one instant. In short, the conception provides a certain basis, whether adequate or not, for the differentiation of rest and motion.

Second, it may be urged that the cinema theory, although it does not make motion into rest, does reduce it to a series of occurrences whose multiplex character provides no ground for the unity of motion and for the identity of the moving body. If a body merely occupies or occurs at a given instant in a given position and is then annihilated, a new body just like the old being created in the next (?) position, what is there to justify our calling the second body identical with the first? This creation and annihilation is exactly what happens in a moving picture. To this objection, it could, I suppose, be answered that the unity and identity of motion was done full justice to by permitting no gaps to separate the successive occupancies, so that an exact description of all that is real in movement is furnished by the one-to-one correlation of a mathematically continuous series of points and instants effected by the moving body. Yet, this seems to me as though we were bidden to imagine a necklace of beads without any underlying connecting thread on which the beads are strung, and told that if the beads are only sufficiently numerous to form a mathematical continuum, we shall have no need for a thread to hold them together.

What I have called the "double-aspect" theory appears to me to combine the strong points of the relational and punctiform solutions of the Zenonian puzzle and to omit the points in which they are weak.

VI. The Double-Aspect Theory

Every continuum, such as space, or time, or motion, is composed of two kinds of elements—the punctiform and the relational. A spatial line truly contains an actual infinity of points, but by themselves these points could never compose the line. They can compose it only when they are ordered or united by a certain type of relation. That is to say, all points in the series, if they are to constitute a line, must stand to one another in the relation of "besideness" or "to-the-right-and-left-of." Without this relation, they might just as well constitute a two-dimensional *patch* or a three-dimensional *lump*. Without the points, the line could not exist; without the relations between the points, they could never constitute a line. Neither the relational nor the terminal elements can be reduced to the other, though there is a certain reciprocity between them, such that we not only can regard the relational elements as relating the points, but we can equally well treat the relational elements as terms and regard the points as merely the relations (boundaries) between them. The points could not exist apart from such relations as "to-the-right-of" or "in-front-of," any more than these relations could exist without the points which they related. If one should still ask for the absolute elements which simply in and of themselves, without anything further, compose a line, we should have to answer that each such element would be a thing of double aspect—not a point, but a "point-to-the-right-of." It is important to realize that the situation is in no way changed by considering the points as constituting a mathematically continuous series, such that there would be no point on the line not included in it. No matter how densely or continuously the points are conceived as being packed together, there would still be the relational elements between them which could never be squeezed out.[4]

Now, as it is with space, so it is with time. Instants are temporal points, and, like those of space, they are perfectly objective and real—not created, but actually discovered or waiting to be discovered. But they are not the whole of time. In and of themselves they would be powerless to constitute the temporal continuum. Just as the points of space must be related by being beside one another, so the instants of time must be before and after one another. Relations of succession are as truly elements as the instants themselves. And the succession of instants is not itself an instant any more than the relation of besideness between points is itself a point. In short, time consists of instants succeeding one another, just as space consists of points be-

[4] One further reason for assuming that these relational elements can never be "squeezed out" by the continuum of points is the following: The mathematicians are insistent in warning us that there are never any *next* points, either in the continuum or anywhere else. Any pair of points not next one another constitutes the terms of a line or distance. Therefore, the *non-nextness* that holds of every point-pair on the continuum implies that everywhere on that continuum there are distance-relations which are as numerous and as omnipresent as the points themselves.

side one another. Now, motion is a secondary continuum, constituted by the combination or correlation of the two primary continua of space and of time. The punctiform theory is correct in holding that a moving body is a body that occupies a continuous series of spatial points in a continuous series of temporal instants, but it is incorrect in holding that that is the whole story. A moving body, besides involving a series of point-instant correlations, involves equally a series of "beside-succession" correlations. The first correlations exhibit motion as a series of *occupancies* of a continuum of points through a continuum of instants. The second correlation exhibits motion as a series not of occupancies but of *slips* (or from-to relations of transition) which together constitute an uninterrupted and unitary *slide*. The one aspect is as real and as essential as the other, and the whole analysis of motion exhibits it as a continuous series of occupancies in the from-to relation.

We are now in a position to give an answer to Zeno's puzzling question, which will satisfy, it seems to me, the claims of conceptual analysis, and also of perceptual experience.

Question: "If a body at each instant of the time of its motion is in one and only one position in space, when can it move *from* one position *to* another?"

Answer: "The body can move from one position to another when one instant *succeeds* to another."

Should someone object that the times when instants succeed one another must be instants, and that, therefore, at such times the body would have to be busy holding down its positions rather than moving from one position to another, I could only reply, in view of the analysis already given, that the time when one instant succeeds another is a perfectly real time, though it is not itself any instant, just as the "space where" one point is beside another is a perfectly real space, though it is not itself any point. No more is a relation between two brothers itself a brother (not even an infinitesimally small brother), though it is as real a constituent of the brotherhood as are the brothers related. Common sense recognizes that time is made up both of instants that succeed one another and of the succeeding of those instants, and, consequently, it finds no difficulty in admitting that, though a moving body is at each instant in some one place, it is also throughout the whole time changing from one place to another. Our solution claims to have justified this common-sense view of motion from the standpoint of logical analysis.

To sum up our account of the six ways of solving the antinomy: The first way, that of the Skeptic, would have us accept the unknowable as our only solvent. The second way, the ultra-Rationalism of Kant and Zeno, would have us abandon the testimony of experience and treat motion and the whole sensible world as unreal, because it appears to conflict with logic. The third solution, the ultra-Empiricism of Bergson and James, would have us abandon the validity of logic because of its conflict with the reality of experience. The fourth solution, which we named the "relational" theory, would have us deny the conceptual validity of points and instants on the ground that they are not perceived apart from the relations of besideness and succession. The fifth solution, the "punctiform" or "cinema" theory of Mr. Russell, would have us deny the perceptual reality of the from-to aspect of motion, and would bid us conceive of it as only a series of occupancies of points of space in instants of time. In our sixth solution, by showing that logical analysis not only permits but demands that the punctiform elements of the continua of space and time be supplemented by the irreducible relational constituents of "besideness" and "succession," we have avoided the paradox of regarding the motions of nature as the illusions of a cosmic cinema, and yet have retained the invaluable conception of motion as a one-one correlation of spatial and temporal elements.

In conclusion, should the reader feel equally dissatisfied with the punctiform and the relational theories, and at the same time regard my "double-aspect" compromise as merely a verbal and question-begging reconciliation of irreconcilable characters, let him still not feel compelled to revert to one of the three extreme methods of solving the antinomy which were examined in the early part of our paper. Let him rather seek for himself some as yet undiscovered solution; for such solution there somewhere surely is; and the hope of finding it should not be abandoned until time ends. A world in which so many things are known through both reason and sense cannot itself be either unknowable, unreasonable, or nonsensical.

5

* THE STORY OF AMERICAN REALISM [1]

An informal history and criticism of epistemological tendencies in recent philosophy in the United States. It presupposes some knowledge of philosophy.

I. The Pre-Realistic Background

In American philosophy, at the end of the nineteenth century, there was small interest in Empiricism and almost no interest in Realism.

The great Thomistic realism of the Catholics was unfortunately regarded by the non-Catholics as too closely bound up with theological dogmas to be of any significance for secular thought. The realistic doctrines of the Scottish school, at one time rather widely current in the country and expressed with vigor by McCosh at Princeton, had passed away. The agnostic realism of Spencer and Hamilton had not affected to any extent the teaching in the universities. The traces of realism, both Platonic and particularistic, in the philosophy of C. S. Peirce had not attracted attention, and the same may be said of the kind of realism which Hyslop, a reader of the valuable but little-known work of Thomas Case, combined with his spiritistic beliefs. Paul Carus, whose blend of Buddhism and psycho-physical monism contained realistic elements, exerted little influence on academic philosophy, and he himself never received from the universities the recognition which his

[1] Reprinted from *Philosophy*, Vol. XII. No. 46, April 1937, pages 140–161.

valuable services to philosophic journalism should have elicited.

In contrast to these fragmentary realistic tendencies, Idealism, both epistemological and ontological, was everywhere rampant. Even before the Transcendentalism of Emerson and Alcott had quite died away in New England, Dr. W. T. Harris, the much respected United States Commissioner of Education, had organized a group in St. Louis for the study of Hegelianism, and had founded the *Journal of Speculative Philosophy*. The Idealism thus started in the Middle West was further continued by Wenley at Michigan and by many others. G. H. Howison at the University of California had developed a very original though not thoroughly worked out system of pluralistic idealism in which the monadism of Leibniz and the subjectivism of Fichte were combined in a new synthesis. And by the force of his personality and the ardor of his convictions, he created on the Pacific Coast an enthusiasm for philosophy that still endures. So much for the West. In the East, Thomas Davidson at his "Bread-Winners' College" in New York was preaching a form of pluralistic idealism similar to that of Howison but more voluntaristic and strongly colored by the thought of Rosmini. At the universities, there were Creighton at Cornell, Ormond at Princeton, Fullerton at Pennsylvania, Miss Calkins at Wellesley, Butler at Columbia, Ladd and Duncan at Yale (more Lotzian than Hegelian), and at Boston University Borden P. Bowne, whose "Personalism" is being vigorously continued today by Brightman and Flewelling. Finally, at Harvard there were Everett, Palmer, Muensterberg, and Royce. (I have listed merely the names that come to mind, and many others should doubtless be added.[2])

Most of these idealists were "Right Wing" rather than

[2] There are, for example, Hocking, of Harvard; Bakewell and Urban, of Yale; Leighton, of Ohio; Rieber, of Los Angeles; Adams, of Berkeley;

"Left." From the Orthodox Christian Theism of Bowne to the Personalistic Absolutism of Royce there was little of the Spinozistic or pantheistic tendency of Bradleyan idealism. Howison, Fullerton, and Davidson were, however, in successively increasing degree aloof from the position of traditional religion; and Muensterberg with considerable originality used Fichtean transcendentalism as a façade for the thoroughgoing mechanistic naturalism which he applied to the existential world of phenomena.

II. The Revolt of the Pragmatists

The first decade of the present century was a time of change and insurgency in American philosophy. The pragmatism of William James foreshadowed in his great *Psychology* and explicitly proclaimed in his California address in 1898 was systematically expounded in the books entitled *Pragmatism* and *The Meaning of Truth.* During the same years John Dewey, first at Chicago and later at Columbia, had developed independently of James but in close sympathy with him the form of pragmatic philosophy known as "Instrumentalism." Though the pragmatism of James and the instrumentalism of Dewey were alike in opposing the monism and intellectualism of the dominant forms of idealism, it is my impression that it was the metaphysical and psychological faults of those doctrines that aroused James to revolt, while for Dewey it was rather the sociological and methodological weaknesses of idealism that merited attack. As a result of this difference in emphasis, the philosophy of James developed into a metaphysical pluralism stressing the free will and independence of the individual as opposed to the idea of what he termed the "block universe" of the absolutists. This personalistic pluralism was later extended to the even more complete

Stace, Green, and Barrett, of Princeton; Sabine and Cunningham and Smart, of Cornell; Blanshard, of Swarthmore; and the Swabeys, of New York University.

pluralism of *Radical Empiricism.* On the other hand, Dewey's instrumentalism, true to its name, developed from its first theoretical expression in his *Essays on Experimental Logic* into increasingly practicalistic treatises on education and social questions, in which the problems of traditional metaphysics were less and less stressed and finally abandoned as outmoded and artificial. In short, the instrumentalism of Dewey, both in its practicalistic motivation and in its anti-metaphysical outcome, has proved itself to be for better or for worse more purely pragmatic than pragmatism itself.

III. The New Realists and their Program

It was, I think, in the spring of 1910 that six teachers of philosophy formed a group for the purpose of expounding and defending a new kind of realistic philosophy. The group consisted of Perry and Holt from Harvard, Marvin and Spaulding from Princeton, and Pitkin and myself from Columbia. After a few meetings we published in *The Journal of Philosophy* "A Program and First Platform of Six Realists." This co-operative article was followed in a year and a half by a co-operative book entitled *The New Realism.*

Although the impressions of American realism that are to be sketched in this paper are almost exclusively concerned with the organized groups calling themselves "New Realists" and "Critical Realists," it is appropriate to mention at least the names of six American philosophers who, though they were not officially members of either group, have during the past 30 years in various ways and in varying degree expounded a realistic philosophy. These "unofficial" realists are: first and most important of the series, Woodbridge of Columbia (who was invited but refused to join the New Realists), McGilvary of Wisconsin, Boodin (now) of the University of California at Los Angeles, Cohen of the College of the City of New York, Loewenberg of the University of California, and Macintosh of Yale.

We had all been realists prior to our forming the group, and each of us had written papers in which realism was implicitly or explicitly defended. I think that Perry and I wrote the first two of the explicitly realistic articles, and these were each inspired by the bitter attack on the realistic standpoint contained in the first volume of his *Gifford Lectures* by our teacher, Professor Royce. My article in *The Philosophical Review* for March 1901 was entitled "Professor Royce's Refutation of Realism"; and Perry's article entitled "Professor Royce's Refutation of Realism and Pluralism" was printed in *The Monist* for October of the same year. Though the members of our new group differed widely in their metaphysical views, there were certain methodological and epistemological postulates which we shared in common. I may summarize them as follows:

1. Philosophers should follow the example of scientists and co-operate rather than work alone. The co-operation which we were to practise consisted in each man showing his essay to the others, taking account of their suggestions, and securing, not unanimous agreement with every proposition, but general assent to the essay as a whole.

I am not sure that this precept was put into practice to any very significant extent. We read one another's papers and listened conscientiously to one another's criticisms, and we did for the most part make the revisions or at least the omissions that were requested, but I am afraid that especially on matters about which we felt strongly there tended to develop among us a tacit and, I hope, an unconscious understanding which if made explicit could have been expressed as, "I'll pass your stuff if you'll pass mine."

2. Philosophers should follow the example of scientists in isolating their problems and tackling them one by one.

We were to follow this precept by isolating the epistemological problem and studying the cognitive relation obtaining between any knower or apprehender and any object that he knows or apprehends without prejudging or even raising the question as to the ultimate nature of the apprehending subjects or of the apprehended objects.

I think that we stuck to this precept fairly consistently. If a certain amount of ontology and cosmology was included in each of the essays in our book, it was by way of supplementation and clarification of the central issue, which was the question of whether the cognitive relation was or was not a necessary condition for the reality of the objects cognized. The point was of especial importance to me because I had a metaphysics less naturalistic and more dualistic than that of the others—with the possible exception of Pitkin—and I wanted to be quite sure that our agreement on the realistic theory that *knowledge as such makes no difference to the objects known* was not going to commit us to any theory as to the nature of those objects or of man's place among them.

3. Some, at least, of the *particulars* of which we are conscious exist when we are not conscious of them.

This was the ordinary particularistic or *existential* realism of common use.

4. Some, at least, of the *essences or universals* of which we are conscious subsist when we are not conscious of them.

This was Platonic or *subsistential* realism.

5. Some, at least, of the particulars as well as the universals that are real are apprehended directly rather than indirectly through copies or mental images.

This was the *presentative realism* of Reid, as contrasted with the representative realism or epistemological dualism of Descartes and Locke.

It will be seen from the last three of our five postulates that we planned to revive and defend ordinary realism by adding to it Platonism and by subtracting from it the dualistic or copy theory of knowledge.

IV. The Argument for Existential Realism

The general argument for our new realism as applied to particular things in space and time was itself not new but old. It consisted in the attempt to show by empirical examination and inference that the things that are believed to be real do not seem to depend on the fact that they can figure as objects of perceptual and conceptual experience. To prove this independence directly by Mill's Method of Difference is, of course, impossible; and to demand it of the realist is both unfair and absurd. We can bring a dog into the presence of a cat and observe that he growls, then take him away and note that the growling ceases, and thereupon infer with high probability that the dog's growling depended upon his being in the presence of the cat. Or, substituting a chair and a book for the cat, we can introduce a dog to their presence and by the same Method of Difference infer that his behavior is not affected by and hence not dependent upon his being in the presence of those objects. But we cannot look at a thing before we see it or after we have seen it and note whether our seeing it has changed its appearance. Yet, as Perry so conclusively showed in his classic paper *The Egocentric Predicament*, it does not follow because an object's independence of our experiencing it cannot be proved by the Method of Difference that, therefore, it cannot be proved by some other method. Still less does it follow that the idealist's hypothesis of the dependence of objects upon consciousness is implied by the fact that when objects are observed, consciousness is always present.

The presence of consciousness together with the objects of which we are conscious is merely a tautology which leaves the dependence or independence of the objects an open question to be decided by inference from their behavior *while under observation.*

The situation is analogous to the one in which we find the stars always present together with human affairs. If we wish to refute the astrologer's claim that human affairs depend upon the presence of the stars, we cannot do it by removing the stars and taking note of what then happens. So far as the Method of Difference is concerned, we are, to be sure, in a "predicament." But despite our predicament, we seek confidently to show that there are no constant or causally significant correlations between the behavior (conjunctions) of the heavenly bodies and the episodes of men's lives. In the same way and with at least as much success, we as realists can seek to show that the behavior of objects when co-present with consciousness reveals no constant or causally significant correlations with that consciousness. Even the astrologer, whatever his other fallacies, does not rest his case merely upon the irremediable co-presence of the course of the stars and the course of human affairs. But the idealist, whatever his other virtues, does incline to rest *his* case on the mere co-presence of the two terms in the situation whose dependence or independence is at issue. *He entrenches himself behind a tautology in the belief that it is an axiom.* And as Dr. G. E. Moore has remarked, if only the idealist can once be made to entertain even as a bare possibility the hypothesis that the objects of which we are aware may nevertheless be independent of that awareness, half the battle for realism is won. For whether we consider the objects of ordinary perception or the more recondite objects of science, it is somewhat pathetically obvious that in neither case does their behavior show any signs of being affected by their presence in consciousness. They come and go as they list, and while our experience and its changes depend largely upon them and upon their changes, the converse is not true. Of all the invariant relations or "laws" of physical nature, I know of no single one that depends for its reality upon the mere fact that it is or can be experienced.

V. The Argument for Subsistential Realism

The method of proving the independent reality of the universals or essences that *subsist* is the same as the method of proving the independent reality of the particular things or events that *exist*. That $7 + 5 = 12$ is entirely explained by the natures of seven, of five, and of twelve, and not in the least by the nature of consciousness. The "egocentric predicament" applies as much and means as little for our knowledge of forms as for our knowledge of particular facts. Whether the forms are numbers, or non-quantitative qualities like blue and yellow, their relations and configurations exhibit a complete indifference to the fact that we are conscious of them. It is, of course, true that *which* of the forms or *which* of the events a man will experience at any moment will be determined by the condition of his organism and even by his memories and interests at that moment. But the function of these subjective factors is *selective* rather than *constitutive*, and the objects themselves are to be explained in terms of their relations to one another and not in terms of their relations to the process of selecting them.

VI. The Argument for a Presentative rather than a Representative or Copy Theory of Knowledge

For an object to be perceived it is necessary either that it should stimulate the percipient organism, as with waves of light or sound, or else that an effect similar to that of a stimulus should in some other way be produced in the organism. Thus, we shall normally perceive a sphere in front of us if there actually is such a sphere and if it sends to our eyes light waves, and by that means ultimately produces a certain specific effect in our brain. But if the same specific effect is produced by two flat disks acting through the mechanism of a stereoscope, we shall perceive a sphere as clearly as in the other case. Everybody admits such facts as these; and there are many who have argued that, because an effect in the organism must precede the perception of an object, it must follow that the perceived object is itself identical with the effect produced in the organism. The truth of such a conclusion would mean that the whole perceptual world is inside the percipient and that it is at best no more than a copy of the external world of physical entities.

Now, we New Realists believed that this epistemological dualism was not implied by the premises invoked in its support. We argued that Descartes, Locke, and their followers were guilty of a sheer *non sequitur* in concluding that the object perceived must be identical with the intra-organic means by which it was perceived, and that as the latter was internal the former would have to be equally internal.

The arguments for our position in this matter were not, I think, as clear and consistent as they should have been. We were perhaps all in agreement that the fact that perceived objects at least *appear* to be external created a presumption that they were really external and that the burden of proof rested upon those who would deny that presumption. I think we were also agreed that the space and time of perceptual experience, despite specific aberrations that might call for correction, took up, so to speak, "all the room there was," and that consequently there was no room left for a conceptual or inferred space and time that were to be real beyond and behind the realm of perceived and perceivable objects. These seemed to be as external as possible; and if *they* were not really outside us, there was nothing else that could be.

To the extent that we attempted to supplement these rather vague feelings by explicit arguments we fell into disagreement, and of those disagreements I shall speak later.

VII. New Realism in Relation to Idealism

The fallacies of idealism as they appeared to us can be briefly stated, and such a statement may help to clarify our own position.

The first and cardinal fallacy of idealists was their ascription of self-evidence to the proposition that the relation of the knower to the object known is an "internal relation," that is, a relation such that the terms related are dependent upon the existence of the relation.

This first dogma, asserting the axiomaticity of idealism, has been held by idealists from Berkeley to Bradley. The realist, of course, denies that the relation of the knower to the object known is self-evidently revealed as "internal." He makes no counter claim for the self-evidence of the "externality" of the cognitive relation, but he does hold that the latter can be proved inductively.

Now, when the idealist has once committed himself to the postulate that no object can exist apart from consciousness or experience, he finds himself in a predicament. The universe is obviously too large and long-enduring for him to regard it as dependent upon the finite experience of himself and his neighbors; hence, there must be postulated an infinite and absolute experience in which it is contained and on which it does depend. The second postulate of Absolutism is thus made necessary to repair the havoc wrought by the first postulate of Subjectivism. If, however, we refuse as realists to take the first step, we are under no compulsion to take the second. If events can exist in their own right without the need of depending on consciousness, the hypothesis of an absolute consciousness is no longer demanded by the situation. The Absolute may, of course, be inferable on other grounds, but not on the grounds of epistemology.

VIII. New Realism in Relation to Pragmatism

From the standpoint of most realistic observers, the essential doctrine of pragmatism consists of two postulates, which we may term, respectively, the *methodological* postulate of Practicalism (which states a theory as to the *criterion* of truth), and the *epistemological* postulate of Relativism (which states a theory as to the *meaning* of truth). The methodological postulate is very ambiguous and appears to be variously interpreted even by the pragmatists themselves. When one says that a proposition can be believed to be true if it works well in practice or if it leads to successful consequences, one may mean either (1) that accepting the proposition brings happiness or (2) that it brings a sensory experience of which the proposition in question was an anticipation. A religious creed, for example, may be held to be true on the ground that it enables its adherents to function efficiently and to meet the crises of life with serenity and courage. In this sense it works well and leads to successful results in practice. But I think that most realists would regard the correlation between the truth of a proposition and its "working well" in this sense as very imperfect and unreliable. There are many false beliefs that have worked well over long periods of time for many people, and, again, there are many true propositions that can bring despair and even paralysis of action to some of the persons who believe them. If, on the other hand, we take "working well" or "successful consequence in practice" to mean *sensory fulfilment of anticipation*, then, indeed, we have a reliable criterion of truth—which is, however, nothing but old-fashioned empiricism under a new name.

But it was not the methodological postulate of pragmatism (even when interpreted "humanistically" rather than empirically) to which realists as such were mainly opposed, but rather the epistemological postulate which grew out of it. To regard the successful experiences that ensue from a belief as a criterion of its truth is one thing—and a thing that is sometimes bad and sometimes good—but to assume that *truth itself consists in the process by which it is verified* is a different thing and always bad. It makes truth a psychological affair and, as such, an affair of individual experience and relative to each individual who has the experience. I may experience successful consequences from believing that the proposition "*A* is *B*" is true; you may experience consequences that are equally successful, and successful in the same sense, from believing that it is false. Shall we, then, say that the same proposition is at once both true and false? True for me and false for you? This relativistic epistemology of the pragmatists was rejected by the realists. The truth (or falsity) of a proposition *antedates* the process by which it is verified (or refuted). The proposition "Mars is inhabited by intelligent beings" is either true or false; but it may be a long time before we discover which. When and if we do discover whether the proposition is true, it will occur to nobody except a philosophic pragmatist in the privacy of his study to imagine that the proposition waited until that moment to *become* true or to *become* false. The facts about Mars, like other facts in the world, will be regarded as having been what they were prior to the events of their discovery or verification.

To this realistic attitude the pragmatists replied by saying that we were making a fetish of "Truth in the abstract" or "Truth with a capital *T*" which could never be experienced and which consequently had no use or meaning. And they would add the comment that while it was all very well for us to say that truth was the relation of "agreement between judgments and realities," we ought at the same time to admit that such agreement could be found only in individual experiences, to which, therefore, it was relative and on which it was dependent.

It seems to me that we have here a recurrence of the "*egocentric predicament*," but in an interestingly altered form. In the original form of the "predicament" we were challenged by the *idealists* to point to a case of *reality* apart from experience. In the new form of the "predicament" we are challenged by the *pragmatists* to point to a case of *truth* (that is, the agreement relation of judgments with reality), apart from experience. We answered the idealist by pointing out that, though quite obviously facts could never be observed in the absence of experiencing them, yet when they were observed in the presence of experience they gave every sign of being independent of that experience with which they were co-present. And as it was with *facts*, so also is it with *truth*, which is the special relation of agreement or correspondence obtaining between facts and the judgments about them. The agreements can never be discovered when absent from the experience that verifies them; but, when discovered in that experience, they give every sign of not depending upon it. When Columbus verifies his hypothesis that there is land to the westward of Europe; when Newton verifies his gravitational hypothesis; when Pythagoras verifies his geometrical hypothesis —in each and every case the truth that is verified reveals a structure that could not have depended upon or have had to "wait for" the verifying experience in order to be what it is. The whole nature and behavior of things testifies to the realists' conclusion that the function of experience in general and of verification in particular is not to create in themselves the things and the agreements that are experienced and verified, but rather to reveal or discover them to us. It is we, the perceiving subjects, and not they, the perceived objects, that profit and are changed by that strangest of all relations between an individual and his environment, the relation which we variously denominate "awareness of," "consciousness of," or "experiencing."

There was a final charge that was sometimes brought by the pragmatists which made us peculiarly and justifiably indignant. This was the charge that, because we held that facts and truths do not depend upon being experienced, we should also hold that experience is *otiose* and makes no difference to the world in which it occurs. In rejecting this imputation of epiphenomenalism (at least as a necessary consequence of his epistemological theory), the realist may point out that consciousness, though not affecting objects in the act of revealing them, can and does change them through the actions of the being to whom they are revealed. Seeing an object enables the seer to adapt himself to it and to its laws, or even to adapt it to himself and to his needs. The light of a lantern does not directly affect the obstacles in the path of the traveller, but it does affect them indirectly by enabling the traveller to remove them. Thus, and thus only, are objects affected by our experience of them.

From this Section (and the one preceding) it will be seen that the epistemological controversy was triangular: Idealism, Pragmatism, Realism—each one against the other two. From our realistic viewpoint, the idealists were right in holding to the ordinary conception of truth as something absolute and not relative to finite minds, but wrong in their insistence that facts exist ultimately only as items of a single, all-embracing experience; while, on the other hand, the pragmatists were right in holding to a pluralistic world of facts, but wrong in supposing that truths about those facts were relative to and dependent upon the changing and conflicting experiences of verification. In matters of ethics, however, the pragmatists were usually on the side of the angels. And as we were all utilitarians, we approved of their making *value* relative to the needs and satisfactions of individuals while regretting that they should fail to see the contrast in this respect between value and truth. When the same proposition seems true to one man and false to another, *one* of the men must be *wrong;* but when one and the same thing is felt as a good to one man and as an evil to another, *both* of the men can be *right.* One man's meat can be another man's poison.

IX. Disagreements of the New Realists

The six members of the organized group of New Realists had come to the movement for differing reasons and with differing interests. And our views on metaphysics and even on some aspects of epistemology were by no means always in agreement. Which of these differences were the most important and how they should be formulated would themselves, I am afraid, be questions about which we should differ. As I am the one who is at present telling the story, I must of necessity formulate the points at issue between us in my own way and select as the most important those that seem most important to me. If in this matter or elsewhere in the article I inadvertently misrepresent the position of friends (or opponents), I here and now apologize.

From my standpoint, the differences that were most important both in themselves and in their influence on the later development of the neo-realistic movement centered first on the question as to the "*Behavioristic*" *nature of consciousness* and second on the question as to the "*relativistic*" *but existential status of the objects of illusion and error.* On these two questions Perry and Holt held views which I believed to be false. As to the positions of Pitkin, Marvin, and Spaulding on these points, I was never quite clear.

X. The Fallacies of Neo-Realism: Behaviorism

As to the nature of consciousness: Perry and Holt believed that an individual's awareness of an object consisted in a "specific response" of that individual's organism to the object. Now, an organism's response ("specific" or otherwise) to an object must be a *motion*, simple or complex, of some or all of the material particles composing the organism. Any motion must be up or down, east or west, north or south, or in some intermediate spatial direction. How can such a motion constitute what we experience as the "consciousness of" an object? (1) It does not resemble it in any way, unless in the small proportion of cases in which the object is itself a motion of material particles. (2) It cannot be directed toward it except in those cases in which the object of our consciousness is a spatial event contemporary with the organism's motion. (3) It affords no clue to our ability to apprehend secondary qualities, abstract ideas, other minds, or events of the past and the future. (4) Worst of all, the organism's specific response or directed motion fails to provide for the *duration* or "specious present" that characterizes every experience and significantly differentiates it from all other events and relations. Each phase or momentary cross-section of a *motion* must be over and gone before a later one can come. But with *consciousness*, it is just the reverse: each phase or momentary cross-section is not over and gone when the successor appears, but endures along with it.

These objections, which applied with sufficient strength to the older forms of materialism, are even stronger against this new materialism or Behaviorism, which would identify the awareness of an object outside the body with a "specific response," that is, a hypothetical motion of the body or its parts toward that object. The peculiar self-transcending thing called *awareness* puts an individual in relation to objects that are either in other places and times or not in space and time at all. If it is to be identified with something in the organism, that something should be anything rather than motion.

XI. The Fallacies of Neo-Realism: Objective Relativism

The second of my differences with my colleagues concerned the existential status of the objects of perceptual illusions and of other erroneous experiences. Unless I have grossly misunderstood them in this matter, they held the theory of "Relativistic Objectivism," or (as re-christened by Lovejoy) "Objective Relativism." This is the view that every object that *appears* to be in space *is* in space, and, because different and mutually incompatible objects appear (though not to the same observer at the same time) to occupy the same space, it must follow that an object at each instant has no single position and shape by its own right, but many positions and shapes, each one of which is relative to some observer.

To illustrate: The rails over which your train has travelled, when seen from the rear platform appear convergent, and when seen from directly above appear parallel. The convergent rails are apparently just as objectively existent in space as the rails that are parallel. But in each case the objective existence is not absolute but relative to an observer. Or, again, that which normally appears as two flat disks will, when viewed through a stereopticon, appear as a single solid sphere, and the latter is to the objective relativist as truly an occupant of space as is the former. Or, finally, what to a healthy man appears as a bed-post may to a man suffering from delirium appear as a serpent. Each of these objects will (it is claimed) exist objectively in space —the bed-post relative to the healthy brain, and the serpent relative to the fevered brain. In short, the things that exist objectively in space are to include along with the things ordinarily supposed to exist there the totality of actual and possible objects of perspective aberration and illusion, and even of dreams and hallucinations.

The objective relativist is, of course, careful to point out that for an objective existent to be relative to and in that sense dependent upon an actual (or possible) observer or organism does not at all mean a relativity to or a dependence upon *consciousness*. And my neo-realist colleagues would feel outraged if they were accused of having surrendered in their theory of error to that very subjectivism against which we were all pledged to revolt. And yet, despite the insistence that whatever appears can be relative to an observational context without thereby forfeiting its ontological status as a "physical" existent, it still seems to me that these relativistic objects do bear a suspicious resemblance to the sense impressions of Hume, Mill, and Avenarius; and that the New Realism in adopting them has evolved (or degenerated) into the old phenomenalism.

There are three objections to this theory of illusory perception which I feel justified in stating as a part of my story of American realism, not only because I think that they constitute a decisive refutation of objective relativism itself, but because the failure of New Realism to meet them was the cause and the justification for the coming of Critical Realism.

The first difficulty with objective relativism is its neglect of the profound *asymmetry* of the relation between the veridical and the illusory objects of perception. The asymmetry referred to consists in the fact that *the illusory perceptions can be explained by the veridical, whereas the veridical cannot be explained by the illusory*. The rails over which my train has travelled appear convergent from some viewpoints and parallel from others. If we assume that the rails *are* parallel, we can easily explain why and how and when an *appearance* of their being convergent will arise. But if we reverse this procedure and assume that they are in fact convergent, we cannot explain why the appearance of their parallelism should occur under the circumstances in which it does occur. Or, again, if the two flat disks in front of the stereoscope are in reality what they appear to be in what would usually be called veridical perception, we can then explain in terms of physical and physiological optics why these two disks when viewed stereoscopically should cause the appearance of a single sphere. But if we reverse the business and posit the solid sphere to be the physical fact, we cannot explain why or how it should ever give rise to the appearance of two flat disks.

Between the hallucinations of dreams and the experiences of waking life the same asymmetry is found. Dream worlds can be explained in terms of the waking world, but not the reverse. The dream hallucinations, like the perceptual illusions, can be as vivid and internally consistent as their veridical counterparts. Taken in themselves and by themselves, one appearance is as good as another. But when we interrelate them by that type of procedure which we call "explanation," their fatal differences in ontological status are easily discerned.

The second of the difficulties in the theory of objective relativism is a sort of generalization of the first. Real objects have two ways of producing effects; unreal or illusory objects have but one. An existent thing, be it material or mental, produces (1) direct effects, that is, effects in its own right, upon all other things; and it produces (2) indirect effects through the agency of whoever believes or even apprehends it. The thing produces this second group of effects not *by right* as existing, but *by grace* as being an object of some experience. Now, while veridical or existent things produce both classes of effects, illusory or nonexistent objects produce only those indirect effects that come through the agency of the minds whose objects they are. Consider flounders and mermaids. Flounders affect the hooks that catch them and the stomachs that digest them, and in addition as objects of contemplation they inspire fishermen and perhaps poets to do things that they would not do unless they figured in the experience of those agents. On the other hand, the mermaids, while they, too, as objects of contemplation have inspired poets and perhaps fishermen to undertake various actions, they have never in their own right affected a hook or a stomach or anything else. Or, again, compare and contrast the real God that you believe in with the unreal god believed in by your theological opponents. You, of course, know that, while the effects of the latter are restricted to the fancies and resultant actions of the unfortunates who are deluded, the effects of your God are produced not only through the minds of His followers but upon the world as a whole.

This difference holds all along the line. Unreal objects, whether they be objects of hallucination and sensory illusion, such as stereoscopic spheres and converging railway tracks, or whether they be objects of intellectual delusion and mistaken belief, such as mermaids and false gods, are characterized by their utter inability to produce any effects except on and through the victimized minds in whose experience they appear.

It is because of his failure to realize this obvious but important truth that the objective relativist is guilty of a preposterously impudent *understatement* when he says that the objects of so-called veridical perceptions are more "convenient" than the objects of so-called illusory perception. The former do not just happen to be more convenient. There is a reason; and the reason is that the veridical objects form a select aristocracy of appearances which owe their rank (1) to their ability to explain all the rest, and (2) to their ability to constitute a self-consistent and self-contained system of causally related elements. This is just another way of saying that real objects are such objects and only such objects as can produce effects directly upon one another as well as indirectly by grace of the minds that perceive them.

The last of the three weaknesses in the theory of objective relativism is based upon its unmanageable complexity. It may be possible to find room in a single spatial system for the totality of such perspective aberrations as railway tracks of various degrees of convergence and of pennies of various degrees of ellipticity; but if we add to these comparatively simple erroneous perceptions not only the stereoscopic spheres but the objects of every dream and every delirium, then not even the genius of a Russell or a Whitehead could devise a space or a space-time that would be adequate to serve as a bed, no matter how procrustean, in which such so-called and miscalled "physical existents" could all be placed and duly ordered. Yet each and all of these objects would be *physical* if by "physical" one is to mean whatever appears as spatial. Indeed, "Pan-physicalism" should be the awkward but accurately descriptive term to designate this phase of objective relativism in which the phobia against a "bifurcation" or division of spatial phenomena into subjective and objective has been indulged to such an extent as to confer the same ontological status upon everything that appears to have shape, size, and position. But if, in order at any price to avoid "bifurcation," we must practice this metaphysical egalitarianism, I for one would prefer the idealistic form of it. It is less difficult, even if not less gratuitous, to think of the totality of actual and possible appearances as being somehow synthesized and harmonized in one absolute consciousness than in any milieu of a spatial or physical kind.

Of course, the objective relativism which I have been attacking was not the only way out. Without lapsing into either dualism or idealism, it would have been quite possible for the New Realists to have dealt with the problem of error by the simple expedient of *denying any locus of any kind to the nonexistent things that figure in all erroneous experience*, as objects either of perceptual illusion or of conceptual delusion. For a thing not to exist is for it to exist nowhere. Any possible or subsistent object *can* appear in consciousness, and a few of them *do* appear there; but only a minority of such objects enjoy membership in the great society of interacting existents as well as in the little societies of objects for conscious minds. Just as one and the same point can be a member of two or more intersecting curves, so, as William James pointed out (for the first time, I believe, in a college class which I attended in 1898), can one and the same object be a member of the independent order of existence and at the same time and with no disruption of identity be also an object of experience. By accepting such a view of the matter, coupled with a refusal to accord any physical locus to the unreal objects of illusion and delusion, we can escape bifurcation or epistemological dualism without falling into either idealism or pan-physicalism.

I wish I could think of the theory just stated, which was my own solution of the epistemological problem, as the "Right Wing of New Realism"; but, alas, it takes more than one feather to make a wing, and as I was quite unable to stem the drift to the Left—that is, to Behaviorism and Objective Relativism—I fear it is historically correct to regard those movements as constituting the essence of American New Realism, at least in its later stage of development.

XII. Critical Realism

In or about the year 1920 a second group of American philosophers decided to write a co-operative book in the interest of a realistic epistemology. The group was composed of George Santayana, formerly at Harvard, C. A. Strong, formerly at Columbia, A. K. Rogers, formerly at Yale, A. O. Lovejoy at Johns Hopkins, R. W. Sellars at Michigan, J. B. Pratt at Williams, and Durant Drake at Vassar. They called themselves "Critical Realists" and entitled their book *Essays in Critical Realism.* They regarded our New Realism, with its attempt to interpret existent objects as directly presented to the mind (rather than as indirectly represented through images or copies), as a form of Naïve Realism—(which indeed it was) and they choose the word *critical* as suitably antithetic to the *naïveness* of which we, their predecessors, had been guilty.

As in the earlier group of six, so also in this later group of seven, the members combined agreement in epistemology with disagreement in metaphysics. Rogers was a skeptic, though with naturalistic tendencies. He had, however, been trained in idealism, and his realism was mellowed by a rich historical scholarship and an unusual tolerance of mind. Strong, Drake, and Sellars were all definitely naturalistic, though Strong supplemented his naturalism with a kind of pan-psychism in which Drake followed him, while Sellars supplemented his with an enthusiasm for Emergent Evolution. Lovejoy and Pratt were dualists in psychophysics as well as in epistemology, and constituted the Right Wing of the movement. Lovejoy put especial emphasis on the significance of *time* as affecting all aspects of nature and mind, and christened his philosophy "Temporalism." His pet aversions were Behaviorism and Objective Relativism, and against them he waged unremitting dialectical war, always urbane but devastatingly effective. Even further to the Right than Lovejoy and nearer than any of the others to a metaphysical spiritualism was Pratt, who combined a first-hand knowledge of the mystical idealisms of India with a strong sympathy for Christian theism. As for Santayana, his rich and many-sided philosophy is known to everybody. At least as naturalistic as Sellars, Strong, and Drake, he combined with his naturalism and materialistic epiphenomenalism a Platonic realism more completely and consistently worked out than in any previous philosophy. This blend of a materialistic conception of the realm of *existence* with a Platonic conception of the realm of *essence* from which all things derive their meanings and their values, but not their destiny, has always seemed to me (second only to Bergson's) the most challenging and instructive of modern visions. Even to one who, like the writer, is unable to share Santayana's pessimistic belief in the *causal impotence* of Platonic forms, it is a great thing to have that vast, encompassing realm of essence or subsistence depicted in its purity and completeness and freed from irrelevant entanglements with the subjectivistic theories of knowledge and the teleological theories of nature which have traditionally obscured both its meaning and its beauty.

When one turns from the original and richly varying metaphysical affiliations of the Critical Realists to the bare nucleus of epistemological doctrine on which they were all agreed and which constitutes the definition of Critical Realism itself, I am myself unable to see anything that is either rich or original. The theory may be true, but it certainly is not new. It is, indeed, nothing but a restatement of the Epistemological Dualism which is explicit in Locke and Descartes and implicit in Hobbes, Spinoza, and the other modern philosophers prior to Berkeley.

This dualistic epistemology is very simple and clear. Its tenets are the following:

1. The world is composed of at least two sets of entities. (*a*) material things; and (*b*) mental states or ideas.

2. The ideas alone are given or presented as objects in consciousness, and in that sense are *immediately* known,

while the material things are only *mediately* known, being inferred as the direct or indirect causes of the ideas.

3. The inferred material objects are always numerically or existentially non-identical with the immediately presented objects or ideas from which they are inferred; and they are, furthermore, at least partially different in kind or nature from the latter.

From this point on, epistemological dualists differ from one another. Some of them, for example, Descartes and Locke, hold that the ideas inhere in a mental substance or spirit; others, for example, Hobbes and Spinoza, hold that the ideas do not inhere in a non-material substance, but that they are phantasms or inner aspects of the body or of the substance of which the body is the outer aspect. But it is important to realize that the question of whether the mind is numerically identical or numerically non-identical with the brain is a psychophysical or metaphysical question that has no direct bearing upon the epistemological question of the relation of ideas to the material objects that are inferred as their causes. In other words, the alleged epistemological duality of internal ideas and external objects is not aggravated by supplementing it with the psychophysical dualism of Descartes, nor is it mitigated by supplementing it with the psychophysical monism of Hobbes or of Spinoza.

On the epistemological dualism which has just been summarily expounded, there are two preliminary comments which can be made without prejudgment of the question of its ultimate validity or invalidity. First, the theory seems to account simply and clearly for the illusions and aberrations of sensory experience, and for what is generally assumed as to the physical and physiological processes that condition our awareness of events distant from us in space and time. Second, the theory seems to be as weak in accounting for truth as it is strong in accounting for error.

If our experience affords direct access only to the internal realm of one's own mental states, by what magic can we jump out of our skins and infer or construct that external realm of material objects in which we undoubtedly do believe? If we emphasize the inaccessibility of an external world, we are led to skepticism, for we must doubt the extent to which that world which we can never experience can be proved to resemble the world that we can experience. In fact, we must be doubtful not only as to the nature of the external world, but even as to whether it can be shown to exist at all. On the other hand, if instead of concentrating on the numerical otherness of the external world, the epistemological dualist attends to the assumed qualitative likeness of that world to the world of his experience, then he is led not to skepticism but to idealism; for the world that he believes in and that he has alleged to be external now turns out to be an extension and elaboration of his world of ideas.

These two comments that I have just made briefly have been made at length and in detail by the whole history of philosophy subsequent to Locke.

Now what, if anything, have the Critical Realists done to mitigate the two sad dialectical sequels to epistemological dualism with which our philosophic tradition has made us familiar?

So far as I can see, their contributions to epistemology are mainly confined to a refutation of the *monistic objectivism* of the New Realists and to a restatement in slightly different form of the dualistic or representative theory of perception. In the matter of refutation, the most effective work, in my opinion, was done (1) by Drake in his arguments against any form of simple or absolute objectivism; and (2) by Lovejoy in his careful and extensive analysis of the fallacies of the relativistic objectivism of Whitehead, Russell, and the "Logical Positivists."

In the matter of restating the theory of dualistic realism, Santayana is the only member of the group whose thought makes any claim to an advance beyond the position of Locke and Descartes. Yet even in the case of Santayana, whose work in metaphysics is of such enduring value, I can find nothing of real novelty for the epistemological problem. To say that the object of awareness is always an "essence," and that one and the same essence can be exemplified both in subjective experience and in objective nature, does at first sight appear to bridge the traditional gulf between the internal realm of mental states and the external realm of material things. But this appearance of novelty in thought is, I fear, due entirely to a novelty in language—the language of Platonism being employed to describe a situation that is ordinarily described in the language of Nominalism.

To illustrate the way in which the two languages can be used with equal propriety to describe one and the same situation, let us take the classic example of Tweedledum and Tweedledee. Here are two numerically or existentially separate individuals who are, however, in quality, kind, or essence, exactly the same. If we are in a nominalistic mood and desire to emphasize their existential duality rather than their qualitative sameness, we shall characterize them as "two different individuals, Dum and Dee, who happen to be perfectly similar in respect to their *Tweedleness*." If, on the other hand, we are in a Platonic mood and desire to emphasize their qualitative sameness at the expense of their existential duality, we can characterize them as "a case in which one identical essence of *Tweedleness* happens to be exemplified or actualized twice, once in *Dum* and once in *Dee*." But it is easy to see that the two characterizations are merely different verbal formulae equally applicable to one and the same situation. For suppose that only one of the twins were given in experience; then the other could not be inferred with any more validity by calling him "a second exemplification of the very essence that is experienced" than by calling him "a second individual exactly similar to the one that is experienced." Now, if for Tweedledum and Tweedledee we substitute, respectively, *ideas that are internal and given as mental states* and *physical objects that are external and inferred as being similar to the ideas in all or some of their properties,* we don't bridge the gap between the given and the inferred by replacing the Lockian *similarity of mental and physical things* with the Santayanian *mental and physical exemplifications of the same essence.*

I should regard the analysis just given as too obvious to call for statement, were it not for the fact that I believe that the Critical Realists labor under the delusion that, quite apart from Santayana's Platonic *ontology,* the description of the exclusively internal objects of consciousness as "essences" works in a mysterious way to bridge the epistemological gap between mental states and the material things inferred from them, and thus constitutes a real advance beyond the traditional dualistic epistemology of Locke and Descartes. That such is not the case is (ironically enough) nowhere more clearly brought out than by Santayana himself, who quite frankly deduces a conclusion of pure skepticism from his own epistemology. For he tells us that the hypothesis that external things as the causes and correspondents of our ideas do exist cannot at all be proved even with probability. We *believe* that they exist on the basis of "animal faith," which is the completely nonrational but biologically necessary instinct to regard our private mental states as symbolic of a public material nature. No actual skeptic, so far as I know, has claimed to disbelieve in an objective world. Skepticism is not a denial of belief, but rather a denial of rational grounds for belief. Santayana's picturesque name of "animal faith" does not in any way differentiate his position from that of Hume or other skeptics who have bowed to the inevitable fact that our basic practical attitudes toward the world are psychologically founded upon instinct rather than logically grounded on reason.

XIII. The Influence of American Realism on American Philosophy

My story of Realism in America, sketchy and inadequate though it be, is already far too long. I shall conclude it with two comments of a nature and temper more cheerful than my mainly destructive analyses of the arguments of both the New and the Critical Realists might seem to warrant.

First, then, for our comfort let us remember that *unproven is not disproven.* Grant that I have been right in arguing that New Realism, in its eagerness to *bridge the gap* between the mind and its physical world, has by its theory of Objective Relativism degraded the pure members of that world to an unseemly parity with the objects of error and fantasy, while at the same time, by its theory of Behaviorism, it has degraded the mind itself to a mass of "specific responses." Grant also that I have been right in arguing that Critical Realism has revived an old puzzle rather than contributed a new solution of it, and that in its eagerness to *preserve the gap* between the undisciplined hordes of mutually incompatible ideas and the single self-consistent system of univalent material entities it has made that gap as hopelessly unbridgeable as it was in the earlier dualistic realisms of Locke and Descartes. Grant me both of these negative appraisals of the two schools of American Realism, and I can still say that the object of their joint devotion: a physical world existing independently of the minds that inhabit it and use it, remains inviolate at least as an object of faith if not as an object of proof. And that "faith," which, as Santayana has said, is necessary to the life of animals, may be also necessary to the growth and health of philosophy.

Certain it is that both of the recent movements of realism, whatever the validity of their arguments, have brought a new and more invigorating atmosphere to American philosophy—and this is the second and last of my concluding comments.

Prior to the advent of the New Realism, academic philosophy was curiously out of touch with common sense, with science, and even with religion. The usual tenor of a course in "Introduction to Philosophy" was to convince the students, in the first place, that Berkeley's conception of the physical world was essential to philosophic truth; and, in the second place, that it was a kind of truth which, when accepted, made no essential difference to any particular belief. The net result of such teaching was the impression that philosophy was a combination of the paradoxical and the unimportant. As for science, its working categories and great discoveries were all too often belittled as "vicious abstractions from the organic unity of experience." Philosophers as such (with the notable exception of Josiah Royce) regarded themselves as under no obligation to acquaint themselves with what experts in various departments were finding out about the universe. Finally, as to religion, the attitude of the professors alternated between a condescending neglect of it as a crude embryonic form of real philosophy and an idealistic defense of it that gave an all too easy assurance of God, Freedom, and Immortality based, not on a study of the universe and its history, but on a dialectical analysis of the problem of epistemology.

Thanks to Realism and also to Pragmatism, these thin manners of philosophy in the colleges have changed to something thicker and better. The teaching of metaphysics and ethics today is much more relevantly related to the natural and social sciences. And finally, the basic beliefs of religion are analyzed more often in terms of their connection with what is known about physical nature and human history than in terms of idealistic platitudes, with the result that on the one hand the values and the dangers of the church as a social institution are better understood, and on the other hand Theism itself is seen as an exciting and momentous hypothesis rather than as either a dialectical truism or a mere dogma of faith.

In short, to some extent, at least, there has come into our speculative thinking a revival of the ancient Ionian attitudes of curiosity as to the specific features of the universe and of wonder as to its central mystery. And for this restoration of health to American philosophy, the two movements of New and Critical Realism have, I believe, been largely responsible.

⋙ 6 ⋘

TRUTH SUBSISTENTIAL AND EXISTENTIAL[1]

An analysis and comparison of the Platonic realm of abstract forms and the physical realm of particular events in space and time. It presupposes a knowledge of philosophy.

Introduction

With the possible exception of the Pythagoreans, all philosophers prior to Plato were Aristotelian in their attitude toward universals. The only substantive entities in the universe were thought of as particular existences—bodies, souls, or what not. Universals were real, but their status was adjectival rather than substantival. They existed naturally as attributes of concrete things and they might also exist as thoughts or conceptions in a mind. But apart from the substances of which they were predicates and of the minds for which they were objects, they had no reality.

Plato seems to have been the first to formulate the extraordinary hypothesis that the qualities or characters of things were not adjectives but substantives, and that as such they enjoyed a double independence. First, they were independent of the particular things in space and time which exemplified them as instances; and, second, they

[1] Reprinted from *University of California Publications in Philosophy*, Vol. X, October, 1928, pages 243–263.

were independent of the minds which were privileged to contemplate them. They constituted in and of themselves a domain of Being which was not only independent of the world of existence, but superior to it in both logical and moral dignity. There are various names by which this strange new domain of abstract substantives may be called. If we think of them, as did their great discoverer, in the light of the method by which the mind attains to them, we may call them "ideas"—a dangerous name, because they are ideas or intellections only in the sense that a bird brought down by skillful shooting can be called "a good shot." The bird is not itself a shot; but if it has been attained by my shot, then by a kind of metonymy it may be called "my shot." Or, if we wish to think of each of these Ideas in relation to the indefinite number of particular things or instances in which they may be exemplified, we may call them "universals." If we wish to stress their character to the extent that it can figure in propositions, we may follow Meinong and call them "objectives." Or, again, if we wish to designate them by a neutral word which will not suggest any special relation to mind or objects, we may with Mr. Santayana name them "essences." Finally, if we wish to characterize them with reference to their ontological status as possessing as much of independent objectivity as particular things but an objectivity of a different kind, we may call them "subsistents."

In this discussion of "Truth Subsistential and Existential," I shall consider in succession the following questions:

I. The Formal Problem of Truth.
   1. The meaning of *true* and *false*.
   2. The relational aspects of truth as shown in "correspondence" and "coherence," and the resulting criteria for testing judgments.

II. The Components of Subsistence.

III. The Union of Subsistence with Existence.

IV. The Structure of Subsistence and Its Effect upon Existence.
V. The Significance of Subsistence.

I. The Formal Problem of Truth

There are various ways of defining and dividing the Truth-Problem. From the opening paper by Professor Muirhead to the one just preceding by Professor Loewenberg, we have had a series of impressive and significantly different analyses of the topic. Because of its relevancy to my particular needs, I shall divide the problem into a formal part and a material part. The formal question I shall treat in this first section of my paper, and the material or metaphysical questions I shall discuss in the remaining sections. Furthermore, I subdivide the formal problem of truth into a discussion, first of the Meaning of Truth, and second of the Relations of Truth.

1. *The meaning of truth.* The definition of a concept consists in the analysis of its connotation into simpler and more generic components. With terms like *truth*, that are themselves highly generic and logically simple, a direct analysis is very difficult to give. We may perhaps accomplish something by way of elucidation if we compare the category in question with other categories related to it and perhaps equally ultimate. "Reality" or "fact" is such a category, and the meaning of the *true*, though not exactly defined, is at least made clearer by recognizing its relation to the *real*. Comparing the two concepts, we discover at once that the adjective *true*, although applied to judgments or beliefs, is applied to them not because of anything in their intrinsic nature, but only and entirely because of *what* they assert. Every judgment consists of two parts or aspects, the judgment-utterance and the judgment-content —the act of asserting, and the thing that is asserted or judged. Now, if we ask the question, "What is the char-

acteristic of a judgment-content that justifies our calling the judgment itself *true?*", there is only one answer possible. Any judgment is true when the content asserted by it is a fact or a reality; and, reciprocally, any judgment is false when the content asserted by it is an unreality or non-fact. I am myself unable to find or even to imagine a single exception to this statement. On the assumption of its validity, we may define the "true" as *the "real" considered as the object of a possible judgment.* Truth is reality viewed from a certain angle, the angle of actual or possible judgment. Now, every true judgment has its contradictory which is false; thus, corresponding to every reality that can be made the object of a true judgment, there is an unreality that can be made the object of a false judgment. The realm of the unreal is exactly as rich in content and exactly as objective as the realm of the real. No judgment depends for its truth upon whether somebody actually states it or believes it. And by the same token, the false judgment owes its falsity to the unreality of what it states, and not to whether it is actually uttered or believed.

In order to mitigate any opposition to this view, I hasten to say that it does not get us very far or commit us to any special view of the universe. It merely transforms the problem of truth into the problem of reality. What it means to be real, and what are the proper criteria for determining which of the objects of possible judgment are real and which are unreal, are questions still remaining to be answered. But a certain gain has been made if we can translate the mixed and somewhat confused category of truth into the simpler and less ambiguous category of reality.

2. *The relational aspects of truth as shown in "correspondence" and "coherence" and the correlated criteria for testing judgments.* The content of every judgment is in

some sense present in the perspective, or context, or experience of the one who judges. Now, if a judgment-content of the form *A R B* is present not only in the limited context of the asserter's experience, but also in the unlimited context of the universe, then that content *A R B* is a reality, and the judgment asserting it is true. The contexts in which a judgment-content may appear vary from the very narrow to the very broad. Take the statement, "Squares are round." We have here a supposal contrary to self-evident facts within the asserter's own present experience. Such a judgment-content is present only in the extremely narrow context in which "square" and "round" are realized only dimly as distinguishable elements and not clearly as incompatible or reciprocally exclusive characters. The latter broader and clearer context containing the other context at once excludes the complex object, "round-square." As candidates for facthood, self-contradictory *asserta* are defeated as soon as they start to run—as soon, that is, as their vague natures are made explicit. A slightly less degree of unreality pertains to supposals not negated by their own explicit meaning but by other contemporary contents of the asserter's experience, as when I utter the judgment, "John is in New York," at the moment when John is appearing before my eyes in Berkeley. The judgment-content, "John in New York," is not self-contradictory, as in the case of the "round-square." The constituent essences do not exclude each other even when made explicit, but their unity is excluded by the simultaneous experience of "John present here." The candidate for facthood is not impossible, but incompossible. A still less degree of unreality pertains to such a supposal as "John is in New York" if I remembered having seen him in Berkeley a few hours ago. Here the falsity of the judgment and the corresponding unreality of what it asserts would be due to its incompatibility, not with present experience, but with my own and my neighbor's past experience of the time required to travel to New York. We might easily continue to illustrate the further steps in the series of judgment-contents which decrease in their degree of incompatibility with the asserter's total experience, passing through the neutral or as-like-as-not stage, in which compatibility and incompatibility appear equal, to the positive phase of the series, in which the compossibility of a judgment-content exceeds its incompossibility, and the system of confirming experience increases to the point where it is the contradictory of the judgment in question that figures as self-contradictory. I should agree with Professor Adams in this sense, but in this sense only: that the degree of belief in a judgment being true is measured by the multiplicity and weight of the experience-system supporting it compared with the weight and multiplicity of the experience-system opposing it. But, while belief is susceptible of degrees and measurable as just stated, I should not hold that there were any degrees of truth or reality. Reality or truth appears to me like straightness. You can, of course, have two bundles of lines, one containing a greater number of straights than another, and you can have curves approximating in various degrees to straight lines. But "straight" itself is positive and has no comparative or superlative.

Each and every judgment-content that is real must be compossible with the totality of experienceable contents. But, while every reality is compossible and every incompossible is unreal, I am not sure whether or not we may add to these equivalent statements their converses and maintain that all that is compossible is real, and all that is unreal is incompossible. Or, what amounts to the same thing: whether we may say that all that is real is implied by the totality of the possible.

Now, to test the reality of the judgment-contents which figure in our experience, we must extend the context and see whether the relation-structure *A R B* can maintain itself in that extended context. We can do this in two ways: (1) internally, retrospectively, and rationalistically; (2) externally, prospectively, and empirically. According to the first method, we test the assertion by its "coherence" with a system of old experience; according to the second method, we test the assertion by its "correspondence" with new experiences. But, though there is a genuine and important difference in the two methods, both "coherence" and "correspondence" are involved in each. For in each case I test by seeing whether a structure that appears in the small context of the moment's experience will also maintain itself in a broader context. If I think primarily of the nature of the broader context, then I stress the aspect of truth as *coherence with a system.* If I think primarily of the duality of the contexts, I stress the aspect of truth as *correspondence with fact.* Let me illustrate by a case in which we could use both methods. A man comes to me with what he claims to be a perpetual-motion machine. I distrust his claim and make the judgment, "The machine runs by energy derived now or in the past from an external source." He asks me to prove my judgment. I can answer by citing the laws of physics based on past experience and showing that the content of my judgment maintains itself in that larger context. The content *A R B* in the narrow context of my assertion coheres with the larger context of scientific theory. But I can also examine his machine and discover the external source of its motion; then the content of my judgment is found to correspond to the new datum. But because the truth of a judgment always involves both coherence and correspondence, whether tested empirically or rationalistically, I do not wish to minimize the difference between the methods of empiricism and rationalism, nor even the fact that in the one method the aspect of truth as correspondence with reality is prominent, while in the other its primary aspect is coherence with a system. For in the empirical method, we broaden the context by adding a new separate bit of experience which corresponds to what was asserted; whereas in the rationalistic method, we get the broader context by adding the whole system of experience previously attained. In the one case, the duality of the content as judged and the content as found in the newly attained experience is in the forefront of attention; in the other, it is the fitting of the judgment-content to the previously attained system. But in each case truth is that which coheres with the context and which thus involves a correspondence or agreement between the narrower context of the proposal and the broader context of the verification.

There are three points which, in closing this section of the discussion, may be noted briefly:

First, "coherence," if misrepresented to mean a system not containing previously given experience, would be empty and would test not the truth, but only the formal consistency of a judgment: "Correspondence," if misrepresented as a relation between experience contents on the one hand and totally alien and unexperienceable things-in-themselves on the other, would be blind and unworkable. Remove these misrepresentations of coherence and correspondence as the two aspects of truth, and they appear as reciprocally supplementary rather than as opposed.

Second, although the two primary methods of testing the truth of a judgment or the reality of what it asserts are on the one hand the Empiricist's retail method of adding new bits of experience, and on the other hand the Rationalist's wholesale appeal to the already attained, yet these fundamental methods are, of course, in no sense inconsistent with the various secondary methods based on the several postulates that the conformity of a belief (1) with the beliefs of respected authorities (Authoritarianism); or (2) with one's intuitions (Mysticism); or (3) with useful practical results (Pragmatism)—would be indirect indications that the content of the belief would maintain itself unscathed in the broadest possible context.

Third, let us note that the question as to whether perception can ever be false or illusory is an artificial question, in the sense that there is no disagreement or dispute of any kind as to the facts involved. Everybody admits that a straight stick partly immersed in water will appear bent, and everybody admits that in contexts other than the visual experience of the observer it will behave as straight. Everybody further admits that concomitant with the visual appearance of its bentness there is a naïve expectation or supposal that, if the visual experience were broadened to include tactual experience, the latter would confirm the former, and that the stick would feel as it looked, namely, bent. And nobody denies that this expectation or judgment would be and would be found to be false. These are all agreed to, and the only disagreement is as to whether the word *perception* should mean the appearance together with the false judgment that accompanies the appearance, or just the appearance alone. If you use the word in the first sense, "perception" can be false. If you use the word in the second sense, "perception" cannot be false. We can make this peaceful adjudication of the question without deciding that other question which is real and not merely verbal: the question, namely, as to whether the various private and momentary perspectives actual and possible are all on a level and together exhaust nature, or whether they do not imply a fixed system of events not necessarily alien in character to their perspectives, but functioning as the cause or ground of the latter, in the same way that each of us (at least in our own opinion) functions as the cause and ground of the perceptions and opinions that others have of us. Of course, we may be mistaken in thinking that we are something more than systems of experiences in the minds of our friends; and, analogously, we may be mistaken in thinking that a round penny is something more than a system of appearances to its friends, if, indeed, round pennies have any friends left. We may be mistaken in these beliefs; but then, again, we may not. This question, however, is not germane to our present discussion, and while I admit that it is real rather than artificial, I take leave of it here.

And now that we have hastily considered the problem of truth in its formal or epistemological aspect, let us pass to a consideration of the material or metaphysical part of the problem, where we shall be concerned with the nature and relations of the subsistential and existential domains of reality.

II. The Components of Subsistence

America was not confined within the limits assumed by its discoverer. And no more is the domain of subsistence confined to those logically generic and ethically eulogistic abstractions which Plato seems to have had mostly in mind as components of his world of Ideas.

Not only the good and the beautiful, but all conceivable specific phases and mixtures of goodness and badness, of beauty and ugliness; not only humanity, but Socraticity, Xanthippity, and each and every specific ensemble of characters possessed by any conceivable Tom, Dick, or Harry—of all such is the domain of subsistence composed. In short, the subsistent includes everything that can be made an object or topic of discourse, and that can be exemplified in more than a single instance. It is the sum-total of all qualities, relations, and natures. It includes all predicates except the pseudo-predicate of existence; all connotations except that pseudo-connotation which is denotation; all essences except the pseudo-essence of substance. Only that which differentiates 30 real dollars from 30 imaginary dollars is excluded from the meaning of subsistence as we are here using the term. And now, before we can inquire further as to the nature and possible structure of this subsistential domain, we must consider as best we can its relations to that other phase of Being referred to as "Existence."

III. The Union of Subsistence with Existence

In the first flush of enthusiasm for a world of Ideas independent of the existent things which exemplified them, it was natural to characterize that independence by myths, illustrations, and epithets which pictured them as though they were another set of existences spatially removed from ordinary reality, persisting unchanged through history and guiding its course. But to treat the category of subsistence in such fashion is to frustrate its meaning. And yet, if we refuse to endow our abstract essences with existence, how are we to preserve on the one hand their objectivity regardless of whether they are either exemplified or contemplated, and on the other hand account for the fact that they are to some extent exemplified in things and contemplated by minds? By what transcendent miracle would the things and minds of this world be capable of participating in an absolutely alien realm? And how explain the extraordinary *complaisance* of a material flux in submitting without causal urgings to a mastery by pure form?

We have here a sample of the problem that besets any dualism, the problem of explaining the *de facto* union in concrete experience of attributes which *de jure*, or for abstract reason, are totally sundered. Does this duality of subsistent and existent defy unification, and must we follow Aristotle in abandoning Plato's theory of forms as possessing the right to a substantive and transcendent status and bring them down to earth as adjectives of existing things?

Before adopting this Aristotelian theory so congenial to common sense, I should like to suggest trying another alternative, a theory or hypothesis that will permit us to retain the Platonic priority and substantiveness of essences and at the same time to exhibit their union with the world of existence.

What I suggest is that, instead of bringing the Ideas down to earth, we bring the things of earth up into the realm of the Ideas; not, however, by explaining away the category of existence, by interpreting it as itself an essence, but by exhibiting it as an *inter-essential relational structure*.

In order to illustrate my meaning, let us imagine a little world composed of only four simple or elementary essences, which we will call *a*, *b*, *c*, and *d*. There will also be compound essences comprising the pairs and trios of these. These secondary or compound essences will be similar to and different from each other in virtue of their possession or non-possession of the same elements. But, in addition to the various *combinations*, there will be *permutations*, such as *abc*, *acb*, *bca*, and so forth. Of the combinations, none short of the totality will be induplicable or unique; for a triadic combination like *abc* will be exemplified by being taken either alone or in conjunction with *d*, and in the same way dyadic combinations like *ab* can figure alone or in conjunction with any one or two of the remaining elements. And the same is true, and for the same reason, of permutations that involve less than all the elements; but when all the elements are involved, then each of these permutations is unique and induplicable. Each such permutation would be a microcosm containing all the connotations or essences that there were. They would differ from one another not as species from genus, or species from species, but as individual from individual. Their relations to one another would constitute a *positional or denotational order*. If we liken the primary essences to Herbartian "Reals," then we can liken each total permutation to an Anaxagorean "Homoiomeron"; and if we go a step further and consider that each of these unique substances will stand as the first term in a system of permutations of permutations, then we shall have a Leibnizian Universe, each member of which is not only a unique embodiment of all essences, but also a reflector of all other such embodiments—in short, a "Monad." To such a series of permutations of permutations there is no last term.

If we are permitted to postulate the original permutation of the totality of essences, the individual substances thus constituted will be, as it were, oriented with respect to one another coexistentially and will compose something analogous to a *spatial* configuration. No two such *coexistential configurations of the totality of* INDIVIDUALS *can coexist with one another*. For each is a unique cross section of the universe. Their coexistence would involve contradiction. There is, however, nothing contradictory in considering these coexistential permutational configurations as themselves unit members of a permutational series of a higher order; and this higher order of permutations would be analogous to the *temporal* order.

Now, the foregoing is, of course, not to be taken as an actual deduction of the categories of Space, Time, and Existence, but only as an irresponsible and tentative prolegomenon to such a deduction. It is a loose and hastily constructed fable in schematism—a groping attempt on my part to indicate the general direction in which we should seek to understand the unity of the realm of subsisting essences with the realm of existing substances or things. The latter are to be considered as in some way analogous to permutations or perspectives of the totality of essences. As such they would have position or denotation and would compose a relational order of their own different from the logical order and analogous to the spatio-temporal relations obtaining between the events of our experienced world. I should hold with Leibniz and against Spinoza that not all the possible is actual, and that there is a principle analogous to the Principle of Sufficient Reason that would partly account for the incarnation of the present world rather than of any other. But I should expect that such a principle would turn out to be a principle of *maximum compossibility*, and that, as in the "tychistic" universe of Charles Peirce, it would figure only as one tendency among many, stronger than any other single one but not stronger than all the others together. The result would be a universe of far less than maximum compossibility, but with an indeterminate, unending evolutionary trend toward more and more harmony or perfection. In such a Leibnizo-Peircian universe, the evolution of cosmos from chaos would consist of a struggle for existence between permutations or perspectives having every degree of compossibility but with an indeterminate bias in favor of the survival and gradual progressive ascendancy of the more compossible or inclusive among them.

IV. The Structure of Subsistence and its Effect upon Existence

We have now to inquire as to whether the domain of subsistence or, as Mr. Santayana terms it, the "realm of essence" possesses any structure of its own; or whether such structures as have been imputed to it are all traceable to the spatio-temporal relations of existing objects and to the pragmatic interests of the human animal in coping with those objects.

A child in his early explorations of the realm of numbers forms such expectations as that seven times eight should equal seventy-eight; or that because $3^2 + 4^2 = 5^2$, therefore $4^2 + 5^2 = 6^2$; or that because $\sqrt{4}$ is a rational number, therefore $\sqrt{2}$ is a rational number. He finds these expectations disappointed. Why? Is it because of anything pertaining to the material of the marks or beads with which he may exemplify his number-essences? Such a hypothesis can be refuted almost as soon as it is formed. But even if the results are not due to the material natures of things, may they not be due to the pragmatic interest which makes a person select one set of arithmetical postulates rather than another? If I select Euclidean postulates, it will be possible for me to find passing through any given point outside a given straight or geodesic line another geodesic that will never meet the first line. But if I select Riemannian postulates, it will be impossible to get two geodesics that will not intersect at a finite distance. Now, might I not, by selecting some queer and special postulate system in arithmetic, be able to make such expectations as $4^2 + 5^2 = 6^2$ come true without contradiction? I dare say. But what I could never do would be to make distinctively Euclidean postulates consistent with distinctively Riemannian theorems. And in the same way, no system of postulates that would prove that $\sqrt{2}$ was a rational fraction or that $4^2 + 5^2 = 6^2$ could at the same time be consistent with the theorems of ordinary arithmetic. All of which means that, while subsistence, with admirable generosity, permits us to choose from its infinite storehouse any system or pattern no matter how alien to common sense or to the procrustean beds of existence, yet when as logisticians we have exercised our freedom and selected our set of postulates, then we are confronted with a structure consisting of the stern and unalterable implications of just that particular set of postulates. And such structures are absolutely indifferent to the pragmatic interests or wishes that select them.

I believe that the granite-like structures of the world of subsistence would be more generally recognized were it not for the comparative novelty of the game of logistics and for a certain natural misinterpretation of our freedom to choose diverse rules of discourse. We are like children who have been for a long time riding on a train, restricted in their exercise to running forward and backward in the train corridors. When the train stops and they are permitted to get out to rest and play, they find a new freedom to choose among any number of delightful paths curving about in all directions. It is only later that they discover that each and any of the paths that they select has as definite a grain and structure as the train corridor itself. We have for such a long time imagined ourselves confined to the train of existence, and have devoted our endeavors so continuously to exploring its narrow corridors—in other words, to seeking only such postulates as will explain the existing facts of nature—that now when we find ourselves free to escape into the wide world of essence and to choose postulates quite without regard to their applicability to fact, we fail to realize that freedom to select is not freedom to create, and that the new world of pure forms and their relations is even less plastic and amenable to our wills than existence itself.

Suppose, then, it is granted that the domain of subsistence contains structures; we have now to ask if in its totality it exhibits a structure, or whether though an assemblage of forms it is itself formless and sprawling in logical disarray over the flat bosom of Brahma. For my part, I believe that the whole of subsistence no less than its parts possesses a structure. What that structure is may be some day discovered by phenomenology and logistic working together. Phenomenology will yield us a system of the essences that are directly intuited, such as the structural relationships of colors, tones, and the other sensory modalities, while logistic, or rather hyper-logistic, through its own discursive procedure will reveal to us the interrelationships of the various postulate systems. That there is such a complete and single structure, whatever it may turn out to be, can be seen, I think, by observing the "internality" of the relations that bind all essences together.

Take any two characters you choose, be they like or unlike, homogeneous or heterogeneous, and you will observe first that relations of many kinds obtain between them, and second, that every one of these relations is internal in the sense that it is implied by the nature of its terms. Indeed, so intimate is the union of essences with their relations that each essence in a certain sense determines all the others. It is of the very nature of whiteness to be related not only to blackness as its opposite but also to middle C and to the odor of cedar by the many specific types of indirect or mediated connection which phenomenological analysis can reveal.

And now, finally, let us consider the question as to what effect, if any, the world of subsistent forms exerts upon the world of existent events. Here, I can but state my belief without even the loose sort of demonstration that I have attempted heretofore. Subsistence is indispensable, but not sufficient to existence. As such, it possesses a veto power ensuring the *nonexistence* of all subsistential incompatibles, but not ensuring the existence of one compatible rather than another. We can be certain on essential or subsistential grounds that there will never exist a round-square, or a dozen of apples that is not composed of seven apples and five apples. We have, however, no subsistential warrant for believing that either squares or apples will exist at all. Mathematics is more than a nonexistential science, for it is also a science of the nonexistable. The structures of subsistence are the beds and banks of the river of existence. They furnish no flow of water, but as unmoved movers they control within limits the flow that is furnished.

V. The Significance of Subsistence

And now, in conclusion, we come to the question of the significance of the domain of subsistence for actual living. Supposing that you were willing to give a tentative and provisional acceptance to the theoretical arguments that I have so inadequately presented, you might properly enough demand to be informed as to whether the doctrine of subsistence implies consequences for action. I believe that there are important practical implications of the doctrine of subsistence, and in another place I have, in collaboration with a colleague, set them forth at some length.[2] I can give only a brief summary of them here.

Traditional morality has been religious, and traditional religion has been authoritarian, with the result that almost the whole of human ethics has been poisoned by the subordination of right to might, and of the ideal to the materially real. To do the will of God and to interpret righteousness as conformity to supernatural power, has been the cardinal principle of religious ethics. It has given us a morality of commands instead of a morality of ideals. It has stressed obedience rather than adventure, custom rather than innovation, the inhibition of our impulses rather than their creative fulfillment. It has, in short, preached the negation rather than the affirmation of life. At the heart of religious morality has been this evil thing—an inversion of the ideal of "making life more abundant." Now, Subsistential or Platonic Realism is the doctrine that ideals are real in their own right, that they require not the will of God, nor the might of nature, nor the edicts of society to make them better than they are. They demand of us to actualize whichever of them is pragmatically relevant to a given situation. But demands are not commands, and the appeal of

[2] W. P. Montague and Helen H. Parkhurst, "The Ethical and Esthetic Implications of Realism," *Mind*, Vol. XIX, No. 39.

an ideal to be realized on its merits is as different as possible from the threats of nature, God, or government. The ethics of subsistence is a free man's ethics. It does not preclude a faith that there are natural or even supernatural powers working for the good, but neither does it require such a faith.

It gives an assurance that nothing can take away. For, let the course of existence be what it will, ideals remain unshaken because their nature and validity are eternal. And, as it is with the ethics, so is it with whatever religion an honest knowledge of the structure of existence can permit. Should there turn out to be demons in control of nature, at least they will not be worshipped. The God of a Platonist will be a Prometheus, to be loved because he is good, rather than a Zeus to be reverenced because he is powerful. The present is a time not only of religious disillusionment, but of moral disillusionment as well. Those who have been brought up in an authoritarian religion believe that ideals have no intrinsic validity, and that their claims upon conscience depend upon supernatural power; when they lose faith in the existence of such a power, they lose interest in the appeal of ideals. They may seek to enthrone nature in place of their dead God, or to make the force of the state, either Fascist or Bolshevist, fill the role of commander of conscience. Both substitutes are hopeless, because both are subordinations of right to might and of subsistent ideals to existent forces.

The cure for the situation is to recover the vision of Plato—the vision of a realm of eternal ideals independent in their nature and validity of anything in existence, but revealing through their light the goals which existence may attain.

7

* BEYOND PHYSICS [1]

An untechnical and impressionistic sketch of the novelties of present-day physics and their philosophic implications.

"ENOUGH OF THIS TALK about monkeys and species; let us get down to fundamentals, to things that really matter." It was with some such words as these that in 1865 the Scotchman Hutcheson Sterling, a fundamentalist in philosophy, prefaced his book, *The Secret of Hegel.* The work was designed to stem the rising tide of evolutionary materialism; and it succeeded to the extent that it introduced German idealism into the universities of Scotland and England and afforded a rallying point against Darwinism for philosophers and theologians.

And now, nearly two-thirds of a century later, we are confronted with a somewhat analogous situation. Huxley and the bishops are dead, but John Watson and the parsons of Tennessee and Arkansas are living and lively; and in place of the solemn followers of Herbert Spencer's synthetic philosophy there are the hordes of Behaviorists, Pragmatists, Freudians, and Marxians, who, rejecting the kingdom of God, are actuated by an ardent faith that it can come on earth as it is not in Heaven. Behind these not always harmonious groups of anti-intellectual revolution-

[1] Reprinted from *The Saturday Review of Literature,* March 23, 1929, Vol. V, No. 35, pp. 800–801.

aries there are the well-organized armies of biological, psychological, and social science who lend the benevolent but non-partisan support of their expert knowledge to the new attempts to humanize the world on the basis of a philosophy of mechanistic evolution. In all countries, but more particularly in our own, cultural trends have been organized with respect to the Darwinian revolution of two generations ago. Directly or indirectly, serious talk has been motivated by monkeys and species and the plebeian past of man and his works.

But now there are signs that a new era is coming, an era of counterrevolution, in which theology gains a new handmaid and returns to power. In this new era, if the signs are not mistaken, there will be a radical reorientation of cultural interests, and the center of the stage on which human concerns are enacted will be occupied neither by the idealistic philosophy of eighteenth-century Germany nor by the materialistic biology of nineteenth-century England, but by the mathematical physics of the whole world of today and tomorrow.

Why physics, of all sciences, should be destined to displace from the focus of human interest the more humanistic inquiries into the nature of life and mind is a long story. It is, fortunately, a story that has been told, and told with as much beauty as one could wish and with more clearness than one could hope for, in *The Nature of the Physical World*, by A. S. Eddington, Plumian Professor of Astronomy in the University of Cambridge and Gifford Lecturer on Philosophy for the year 1927.

When a scientist of the first rank stoops to expound for the benefit of the lay reader the most recent and recondite theories in his own field, it is an event. And when the author is, as in this case, not only a scientist and expounder of science, but a Christian mystic who interprets the philosophic significance and defends the religious implications of his austere formulas, things may be expected to happen; and they do. The book is really gorgeous.

. . . . . .

The new physics is not the science of dead matter; for "dead matter" is dead, and something that is much too lively for comfort, at least for intellectual comfort, has taken its place. The ancient physics of the nineteenth century described a world of hard little particles moving separately and in clusters varying in size all the way from molecules to stars. The motions of these particles were regulated by simple forces of attraction and repulsion which varied inversely as the square of the distance, and which they exerted on one another. The space in which the particles carried on was of the homely variety known as Euclidean. It was infinite in all directions; but its appalling bigness was offset by its simplicity. Moreover, it was filled with an invisible, continuous, motionless substance called "ether," which carried the waves of light from star to star and atom to atom. Through this quiet ocean all material bodies swam like fishes. And by clever experiments, such as that of Michelson and Morley with light waves, the direction and speed with which our planet and the whole solar system were really moving with respect to the motionless ether could be discovered. In this universe there was, of course, not only space and matter and energy, but also infinite time, which was independent of space and even simpler in its nature. In fact, this old-fashioned time was so very simple and obvious that it did not need to be talked about.

Matter and energy were distinct entities and each remained constant in its quantity through all changes of quality. And, in addition to this first great law of the conservation of matter and energy, there was a second law that described an irreversible, or one-way, tendency in all processes. According to this law, named variously the "Dissipation of Energy," the "Second Law of Thermodynamics," and the "Increase of Entropy," matter always tended to concentrate itself and energy to scatter itself. Thus, when two bodies were attracted toward each other and collided, they would bounce away; but they did not bounce away quite as fast as they came together. Some of their motion or energy was imparted first to the particles composing them and later to the ether surrounding them, where, in the form of waves of light or radiant heat, it scattered ever outward. The ultimate result to be expected was a dénouement in which all the matter should be concentrated in a lifeless lump and all the energy degraded to the form of radiation, expanding forever over the shoreless sea of empty ether. The old world thus seemed to be running down. And if it had had all eternity in which to run down, it was (and still is) something of a problem as to why its dismal end had not yet been attained.

. . . . . .

This nineteenth-century universe was an intelligible universe, but the things that have happened to it in the last thirty years are terrible. First came the Theory of Relativity, which has disrupted the old world as a whole, changing its size and basic structure beyond all recognition; second, the Quantum Theory which has not only disrupted the atomic parts of the universe, but threatens to destroy the law of causality itself within those tiny regions, and to substitute for it a scheme of primary anarchy and indeterminism, not incompatible with certain secondary and statistical regularities in the world at large.

We may begin with Relativity as the better known, though less devastating, of the revolutions. First Michelson and Morley failed to discover that motion of the earth through a fixed ether which there was every reason to suppose they could find. Their apparatus was so perfect and their methods so sound that their failure was taken to mean that velocity through the ether was not only undiscovered but undiscoverable. And it is one of the rules of science, or at least of present-day science, that a thing physically undiscoverable is a thing that does not physically exist. The ether through which bodies move with a definite velocity was, then, to be regarded as nonexistent.

More followed when Einstein propounded an idea that was perhaps the most extraordinary in the whole history of science. "Let us pretend," he said, "that a light flash, which always moves at 186,000 miles a second, will always pass every other thing at the same speed, whether the other things are themselves moving toward its source, or away from it, or just standing still." If this new postulate about light does not seem queer, try to imagine the mayor's automobile traveling in such a way that when it was going either north or south on Main Street it passed at the same relative speed all the other unequally moving and oppositely moving cars, as well as those parked by the sidewalk. This would seem absurd. And if it should be discovered that the people in the other cars reported that the mayor's car had passed them at the standard rate of speed, this would arouse your curiosity and make you suspect that something was wrong with the new speedometers installed in each car and specially designed for measuring its speed relative to other cars instead of the speed relative to the road, as in the old-fashioned speedometers.

Your suspicion would be quickly confirmed, for if from your own car you could examine with a kind of spy-glass the clocks and measuring rods comprising these new instruments, you would find that their measures of time and space went slower and faster and contracted and expanded in a uniform but ridiculous fashion, so that it was no wonder they always reported that the mayor's car passed them at the same speed. Your new comfort would be of only brief duration, however, because you would find on comparing notes that each driver claimed to have discovered that all other cars, including your own, were wrong as to their speedometers, excepting only those that were at rest with him or running at the same rate beside him. In this situation someone might come to the rescue with the suggestion that you should assume that there is no fixed road and no absolute space or time with respect to which all instruments except one's own are wrong, but that space and time are nothing but the records of the instruments. So that, instead of the drivers contradicting one another as to their speeds with respect to a road which, being undiscoverable (like the ether), could be assumed not to exist, they ought all to agree to take the mayor's speed in place of the road as the standard for measuring one another's speeds. At first it would all seem queer and complicated, but after a little while the rules for estimating the deviations of the instruments in the different cars and correlating them would become familiar and simple, and then new things would be discovered.

This little fable illustrates the Special Theory of Relativity. First, postulate that the velocity of light shall be always the same with respect to any moving system. Then, in order to make the implications of this postulate self-consistent, make a second postulate, to the effect that space distances and time intervals in differently moving systems increase and decrease according to how they move. Believe, in short, not that space and time are absolute and velocity variable, but that one velocity, the velocity of light, is absolute, and space and time variable and measurable with reference to it. Then, third, in order to make this second postulate intelligible, adopt a third postulate to the effect that space and time intervals are not real apart from the instruments that record them, so that when you describe them as lengthening or shortening, curving or kinking, you are only referring to certain comparisons between the readings of rulers and clocks on one system with similar, but different, readings on another system.

. . . . . .

This Special Theory of Relativity was, as we know, extended or generalized by Einstein so as to apply not only to relative *uniform* motions, but to relative *accelerated* motions. The results have been amazing. Space and time are not only relative to the bodies and motions by which they are measured, they are relative to one another; so that, instead of a three-dimensional *space* in which matter is contained, and a one-dimensional *time* in which changes are contained, we have a single four-dimensional continuum of "space-time." This space-time is an inseparable aspect of mass and energy, which are themselves interdependent aspects of the same thing. While the *time* aspect continues to be regarded as infinite, the *space* aspect is finite though boundless. It is as if the material world were curved in a fourth dimension around into itself after the manner in which a plane is curved in a third dimension around into itself to make the surface of a sphere. The new physicists, however, warn us, sometimes sternly and sometimes querulously, not to take this analogy too literally. If we did take it literally, we should naturally ask what interesting mysteries (psychic or even theistic) lay inside our four-dimensional hypersphere and what other possible universes might lie outside of it. And to raise any such questions in polite scientific circles is regarded as the height of bad form.

Thus, we may tentatively imagine our universe as the three-dimensional curved "surface" of a hypersphere whose distance around is perhaps not much more than a billion trillion miles. If you travelled in a straight line due north, never deviating up or down or east or west, you would finally return home. This will remind us that the new universe is neo-Ptolemaic, larger in size but even more hopelessly finite than the world of pre-Copernican days. But we must subtract from this image any thought of inside or outside and conceive of it merely as a skin, finite in extent, yet with *nothing*—not even empty space—either within or without. I suppose that the reason for this harsh limitation is that no measuring rod could be directed toward the inside or outside of the three-dimensional "skin." And according to the new physics, what cannot be measured cannot physically exist.

A particularly interesting feature of this queer new world is that the velocity of light is not only an absolute, but a maximum velocity, even though finite, of 186,000 miles a second. Any body moving at that velocity would acquire an infinite mass, while at the same time shrinking to the thickness of a shadow. If it could move faster than light, we do not know what would happen to its infinitesimal thickness and its infinite mass; but we do know what would happen to its dates, for if a body could so move (only, of course, it couldn't) it would get back into the world of last Thursday. This situation is immortalized in a little limerick told to the writer by Miss May Sinclair, but whether her own or not I do not know:

> There was a young lady named Bright
> Whose speed was much faster than light;
> She eloped one fine day,
> In a *Relative way*,
> And got back on the previous night.

Fortunately for us, the question raised is not even an academic issue, since the scientists who are responsible for this sort of thing will warn us that to say that an ordinary body like Miss Bright would move into the past if it went faster than light is merely a rather dangerous and misleading way of saying that it won't and can't move faster than light, or even, for that matter, as fast. Speeds greater than that of light and their consequences are in the same category as the inside and outside of the Einsteinian hypersphere. It is simply not polite to talk about them.

A more serious phase of the new theory in its generalized form is that it enables us to conceive the three-dimensional "skin" of the nonexistent hypersphere as not only curved into itself, but as covered more or less thickly with hummocks and slopes, which appear to us as matter and fields of force. The old world of flat Euclidean space, full of ungeometrical things like bodies and forces, has been transformed into a purely geometrical world in which non-Euclidean kinks and curvatures replace the alien intruders. As Descartes, by a great feat of mathematical genius, translated the concepts of Euclidean geometry into those of algebra and gave us analytic geometry, Einstein, inspired perhaps by a suggestion of Clifford, has translated the categories of mechanics into the categories of a non-Euclidean geometry.

. . . . . .

Eddington has told at length and with great beauty the story that I have here briefly, though not, I hope, inaccurately, summarized. It was the first of the great revolutions in modern physics, and it is by now so welcome and familiar to the great majority of scientists that, by contrast with the Quantum Theory, it seems almost commonplace, a mere appendix to the so-called "classical" physics of the nineteenth century.

So far as I can discover, Eddington draws no theological conclusions from the Theory of Relativity, except the following: The peculiar transformation of space and time from the great forms and frames within which things exist to the interrelated network of pointer-readings on our measuring-rods and clocks gives to the world of the new science a symbolic and shadowy character which the old world lacked. And the more shadowy the material universe becomes, the more the need for inferring a reality beyond it.

It is the formal perfection of the Relativity Theory, rather than any information afforded by it about nature, that opens the gates to theological hopes. The laws of physics appear as truisms rather than truths—that is, logical implications of postulates already adopted. The physicist is compared by Eddington to an old college bursar who is entirely occupied with his accounts and has no intercourse with the outside world save to accept the reports of financial transactions and systematize them. Studying carefully his beloved ledgers, he discovers one day the great law of nature, *that the debits just equal the credits.*

I cannot leave the subject without making a confession that is of no importance except to myself: *I do not believe that the fundamental postulate of Relativity is true.* I do not believe that a light flash or anything else that moves with a finite and constant velocity can pass differently and oppositely moving bodies at the same relative speed. But I can entertain the belief that the instruments at our disposal are so constituted that they will record a constant speed for light passing through our system, no matter how that system may move with respect to the source of light. If we wish to *pretend*, or postulate, that the limitation of our measuring ability is a limitation of nature and then reinterpret the meanings of space and time to make them consistent with this postulate, we can do it and so derive the Special Theory of Relativity.

The Quantum Theory, which is the second of the great revolutions in physics, is quite different from, and in a sense opposite to, that of Relativity. It is not a case of our thrusting upon nature the peculiar behavior of our metric instruments, but of nature thrusting upon us, in the form of concrete experience, data which seem impossible to reduce to any rational scheme.

. . . . . .

In his earlier book, *Space, Time, and Gravitation*, Eddington referred to the Quantum affair as being, just because of its anti-rational character, the only case in which we were confronted with an objective law of nature rather than a subjective form or necessity of our own minds—an attitude that reminds us of the *Credo quia absurdum* of Tertullian.

I think it was in 1900 that Professor Max Planck of Berlin discovered that waves of radiant energy do not vary continuously and so take on all possible values. Of the infinity of possible frequencies, only a comparatively small number actually occur. Thus, an atom receiving and emitting light waves is like a man who refuses to receive or to spend any money except dimes or integral multiples of dimes. Curiously enough, it turns out that, while the different kinds of atoms give out different amounts of energy, the *product* of the energy emitted and the *frequency* or vibration period of that energy is the same for all atoms. This constant quantity which comes from multiplying energy by time is the "quantum of action." Its symbol is *h* and its value is .00,000,000,000,000,000,000,-000,000,655, or 6.55×10^{-27}, which we can pronounce in American terminology "six hundred and fifty-five nonillionths of an erg-second," where an "erg" is the amount of energy possessed by a mass of only one gram moving at the velocity of only one centimeter a second. This Lilliputian absolute is the smallest thing in the world, and it has made the biggest trouble in all history. For it has not only defied the laws of classical physics and shattered to bits the seemingly satisfactory conception of the atom as a minute solar system composed of units of positive and negative electricity, which was invented by Bohr in the first quarter of the twentieth century, but, what is much worse, in its later developments it has brought science face to face with the astounding possibility of abandoning the very principle of causality itself and admitting that the ultimate realities of the physical world are unimaginable "somewhats" which do what they do without rhyme or reason. *In short, at the heart of nature, in the inmost recesses of the tiny spaces once occupied by atoms, there are indeterminate happenings, events that have no cause.* As Eddington puts it, after stating his theory about the network of observable and measurable results of the unimaginable mystery—

"*Something unknown is doing we don't know what*—that is what our theory amounts to. It does not sound a particularly illuminating theory. I have read something like it elsewhere—

> *The slithy toves*
> *Did gyre and gimble in the wabe.*

"There is the same suggestion of activity. There is the same indefiniteness as to the nature of the activity and of what it is that is acting. And yet, from so unpromising a beginning we really do get somewhere. The reason—the sole reason—for this progress is that *numbers* are scattered freely in the description. Eight slithy toves gyre and gimble in the oxygen wabe, seven in nitrogen. By admitting a few numbers, even Jabberwocky may become scientific."

Suppose we grant that physics has got itself into a jam, the very worst in its whole long career from Archimedes to Einstein. Does that mean anything to theology?

There are two ways in which theologians can use science to support their faith: They can appeal to its *successes*, or they can appeal to its *failures*. Eddington makes a curious and characteristically original use of both methods. Relativity is so successful that it gives a shadowy world of mere metrical symbols, whose truths are truisms which cry out to be supplemented by a reality richer than themselves. On the other hand, the Quantum leads us to the brink of a baffling mystery within which we can dimly descry an indeterminate spontaneity congruent with that freedom of the will demanded by conscience and attested by inner experience. Old Epicurus declared that the atoms occasionally *swerved* indeterminately from their mechanically ordered paths, and thus furnished the basis for human free will. Generations of philosophers have smiled patronizingly at his crudity, but at last, perhaps, the tables are turned and his day has come. For in the Schroedinger waves which now occupy the tiny spaces so recently filled by the Bohr atoms, the Epicurean "swerve" has returned with a vengeance, and chance reigns in place of law.

Whether you take the successes of science or its as yet unsolved puzzles as your point of departure for the realm of religion, there is one high road over which you will be likely to travel. It is the high road of what is technically called "Pan-psychism." *As our physical brains are to the conscious minds that throb within them, so is any material structure or particle to the "mind-stuff" that must constitute its real and inner nature.* It is this philosophic theory, held in very diverse forms by Spinoza and Leibniz, and by Schopenhauer, Fechner, and Clifford, to which Eddington subscribes and which he uses as a philosophic bridge to span the gap between his physical science and his mystical religion. The theory in itself does not take us very far. For, even if we admit that stones and stars have an inner psychic nature, yet, to judge by their apparently dumb and mechanical behavior, the mind-stuff that we are ascribing to them is no more morally edifying than their outer or bodily aspects. But when this Pan-psychist theory is supplemented, as it is by Eddington, with a religious experience of spiritual reality that is as vivid and direct as his experience of beauty or of humor, the hypothesis takes on a richer significance. The philosophy of a former day could bake no bread, though it could, so we were told, give us God, Freedom, and Immortality. The philosophy of today has, in general, more in common with our bakeries than with our temples, for it is founded on the materialistic sciences of yesterday. It will be strange if Eddington turns out to be right, and if the new physics with its concepts of Entropy, Relativity, and Quanta is destined not only to increase our mastery of earth, but also to restore the old and dangerous hope for something beyond.

⋙ 8 ⋘

THE EINSTEIN THEORY AND A POSSIBLE ALTERNATIVE [1]

A comparatively untechnical summary of the theory of Relativity, its philosophical implications, and its picturesque paradoxes, followed by the description of an alternative hypothesis and a possible experiment for testing it. It presupposes some knowledge of physics.

THAT ABSTRACT and specialized form of the love of wisdom, which arrogates to itself the generic name of *philosophy*, has throughout its history been sustained by two great intellectual interests, the interest in nature and the interest in man. Now the one and now the other has predominated in the product of their union, but the greatest systems of philosophy have contributed richly and almost equally to physical theory and humane interpretation.

The nineteenth century was noted for an unprecedented progress in the knowledge of nature; and, unlike the previous periods of such progress, the gains made were due not so much to generalized deduction as to specialized and diversified experimentation. For perhaps the first time in history, the sciences got completely out of hand and established their independence of philosophy. The great syntheses of Comte and of Spencer, designed by their

[1] Presidential Address, Eastern Division of the American Philosophical Association, Brown University, Providence, R. I., Dec. 28, 1923. Reprinted from *The Philosophical Review*, Vol. XXXIII, No. 2, March 1924, pp. 143–170.

authors to incorporate the new bodies of knowledge into a unified world view, were, on the whole, failures. They were not sufficiently specific to win back into any real union the various groups of scientists, and they were too naturalistic and mechanistic to appeal strongly to the professional philosophers. The latter had not forgotten the failure of the German Transcendentalists in their *naturphilosophie;* and to compensate for the trauma which that failure inflicted, they had built up a defense mechanism consisting of a well-simulated contempt for the works of nature. As a result of all this, philosophy in the past hundred years has become definitely introverted; and its former healthy interest in cosmology has been replaced by a morbid concern for its own processes and an antiquarian curiosity as to its own past.

This somewhat arid preoccupation with matters of history and of method has, indeed, been supplemented during the last few years by a new and wholesome concern for the humanistic problems of psychology and sociology. But humanistic philosophy is at best only one half of philosophy. And at a time like the present, when the science of physics in its theories of Relativity and of Quanta is approaching what may be a great climax in the intellectual life of the race, it is indescribably humiliating that we who claim to represent the tradition of Plato and Democritus, of Descartes, Leibniz, and Kant, should have allowed ourselves to become so indifferent to the physical world and so ignorant of the new discoveries concerning it that we are unable even to appreciate the situation with which science is confronted.

In full realization of my ignorance of the mathematical technique of the Theory of Relativity, I have nevertheless chosen it as the topic of this address, and for three reasons. First, because I hope that my discussion may help in some small way to renew our ancient interest in cosmology.

Second, because the errors and misinterpretations of which I may be guilty, and which some of you may share, will perhaps tempt our scientific brethren to come to the rescue with clearer and simpler explanations. And third, because there is always a chance, however slender, that even a layman's criticisms and comments may contain something of value and of truth.

I shall confine my discussion mainly to the Special Theory of Relativity, and shall consider: *I*, its chief characteristics; *II*, the nature of its premises; *III*, the possibly fatal paradoxes to which it leads; *IV*, the crucial assumption contained in its premises; *V*, an experiment designed to test the crucial assumption; and *VI*, the nature of the alternative to that assumption. In conclusion I shall offer some comments on the meaning of the General Theory of Relativity and on the prospect which it seems to offer of explaining the physical world with a clarity and completeness that none but the great metaphysical rationalists have dared to hope for.

I. The Chief Characteristics of the Special Theory of Relativity

The earlier or Special Theory of Relativity may be described as a new and peculiar theory of the nature and connection of space and time and of the methods which we must use in measuring them.

I think that the principal points of the theory may, for our purposes, be summarily stated under five headings.

1. Space and time have no existence apart from the rods and clocks by which they are measured. Of each of them we may say: *esse est mensurari*.

2. The events whose relations constitute the spatio-temporal order of nature are identical with the sense data of individual fields of experience. They are not to be conceived as internal effects of an external world; but rather

are they to be conceived as overlapping and interpenetrating perspectives. In place of a world of extra-individual causes, we are to substitute a system of inter-individual laws as the norm or standard for measuring and comparing our experiences. We are to adopt a relativistic form of epistemological monism rather than the epistemological dualism of traditional science.

3. Space and time do not vary independently, as Newton believed. They are as dependent upon one another as upon the experiences by which they are measured. *When* events are observed to happen has no meaning apart from *where* they are observed to happen. Two events are intrinsically simultaneous only when they occur in the same place. Otherwise, they will be simultaneous for some but successive for others.

4. Time is a fourth dimension of the one world whose other three dimensions are those of space. But this does not mean that time *is* space, nor does it even mean that the time dimension is related to the other dimensions as they are to one another. In measuring the interval, ds, between two events in space-time, the squares of the subsidiary space-differences, dx^2, dy^2, and dz^2, are positive, while dt^2, the square of the time-lapse, is negative. This is expressed by the equation

$$ds^2 = dx^2 + dy^2 + dz^2 - dt^2.$$

The four-dimensional world of space-time is thus "hyperbolic," "Lobachewskian," or of "negative curvature" as regards the dimension of time; though, when free of gravitational or other forces, it is "parabolic," "Euclidean," or of "zero curvature" as regards the three dimensions of space.

5. Einstein's "light" is the most wonderful thing in the world. Its velocity is a definite, finite quantity, about 186,000 miles a second. But, though finite, it behaves in one respect like zero and in another like infinity. It be-

haves like zero because the squares of space and time enter equally, but with opposite signs, into its measure, so that when dx^2, the space factor, equals dt^2, the time factor, then $dx^2 - dt^2$, which determines the interval between any two events on the path of a light ray, is zero. The movement of light in space combined with its movement in time cause it, as it were, to stand still. All events on any one light ray happen at the same point-instant in the space-time of the world. Notwithstanding this resemblance to zero, the velocity of light also resembles infinity, because it is not altered by the addition or subtraction of any other velocity, such as that of an observer moving toward the light or away from it. Light is, for Einstein, the new and only absolute in a world where all else is relative.

II. The Premises of the Special Theory

And now that we have stated in summary fashion what appear to be the five main points of the Special Theory of Relativity, let us turn to a consideration of the evidence by which the theory is supported and by which Einstein was led to adopt it. We shall find this evidence to consist partly of an assumption and partly of concrete facts. The assumption is that the velocity of light waves is not affected by the velocity of the source from which the light waves emanate. The facts are those revealed by the great experiment conducted by Michelson and Morley in America in the year 1887.

I shall try to persuade you that, although there is no reason for doubting the alleged facts of the Michelson-Morley experiment, there is reason for doubting the assumption that the velocity of light is independent of the velocity of its source; and later I shall try to prove to you that if that assumption is false, there is a perfectly clear alternative to the Einstein Theory which must be accepted in its place.

I will begin by recalling very briefly to you the nature and consequences of the Michelson-Morley experiment. Let us suppose ourselves on a train, very broad and without walls at either the ends or sides. We have reason to believe that our train is moving silently and with uniform velocity through the motionless atmosphere, though for some reason we are not able to feel or measure the pressure of the air as it rushes by. In order to find out whether we really are moving and with what velocity and direction, we make the following experiment. A tuning fork is set vibrating, and from it there proceed in all directions sound waves moving relative to the air and regardless of our motion at a constant velocity of 1,090 feet a second. One of these sound waves we split into two halves; the first half goes forward for a thousand feet to a reflecting mirror on the front of the train and is reflected back to the ear of an observer, and the other half of the sound wave goes out to the side for the same distance and is reflected back to the same observer. It is admitted by everybody that, if our train is moving and if the two waves move at equal velocities with respect to the air which is their medium, it will take longer for one wave to go and return than for the other. And by observing which wave takes longer and how much longer it takes, we can determine the direction and magnitude of our velocity through the air. This can easily be seen if we suppose that we are moving almost as fast as sound itself and in the direction of the wave that goes forward toward the engine. If our train was moving forward at the velocity of 990 feet a second, the wave going forward at its regular rate of 1,090 feet a second would gain only a hundred feet a second over the train, so that it would take it 10 seconds to reach the reflecting mirror which is 1,000 feet ahead; and although its return trip would take only about half a second, it would still be far behind the wave that had gone off to the side and back. It takes longer for a swimmer to swim down the current of a river and back than to swim at the same rate and for the same distance relatively to the river across the current and back. The difference in the durations of the two trips measures the speed of the current or of the train, as the case may be.

Now substitute our earth for the train, and waves of light in the ether for waves of sound in the air, and we have the Michelson-Morley experiment which was designed to test the motion or drift of the earth through the ether. To the surprise of everybody, the results were negative. The two rays of light reunited on the return from their journeys without showing the interference bands which would certainly have been caused had the one ray taken longer to go and come than the other.

How were the negative results of this epoch-making experiment to be interpreted?

By Lorentz and Fitzgerald, independently, it was suggested that if the unit measuring rods decreased in length in the direction of their motion through the ether in the ratio of $1 : \sqrt{1 - v^2/c^2}$, where v is the velocity of the earth and c is the velocity of light, the failure of the experiment to disclose such a motion could be explained in the following way. The distance measured out in the direction of the earth's motion would have been measured in smaller units than the distance out to the side; hence, the path which the forward-going ray would have to travel would be enough shorter to make up for the greater duration of its journey.

This ingenious hypothesis of Lorentz and Fitzgerald has not, so far as I am aware, ever been disproved; but it possesses a kind of methodological disadvantage because it assumes an action of ether on matter which is inferred *ad hoc* to meet this single difficulty and which is in comparative isolation from the general system of physical theories.

Einstein's way of accounting for the negative results of the Michelson-Morley experiment is quite different and involves a radical break with the intuitions or prejudices of common sense. *To the old assumption that the velocity of light is independent of the velocity of its source he adds his own new hypothesis that the velocity of light relatively to any observer is independent of the velocity of that observer.* This means that whether an observer goes toward a ray of light or away from it, he will pass it at the same rate. This is the essence of the Special Theory of Relativity. However true it may prove to be, it is in appearance paradoxical in the extreme. Any finite velocity previously imagined will give unequal results when unequal velocities are added to it. The velocity of light is like an infinite quantity in that any other velocity added to or subtracted from it leaves it unchanged. Denoting this new absolute by c, we must believe that $c - 10 = c - 5$, that $c + 100{,}000 = c - 100{,}000$. In short, $c \pm$ anything is still equal to c. If c were infinite, we might not balk, but c is finite and measurable, equal to 186,000 miles a second. We are asked to believe that, though finite, it can claim the privileges of the infinite.

The rest of the theory consists of the supplementary assumptions which must be made in order to keep the primary assumption from conflicting with the facts of observation. These assumptions, as we have seen, include the belief that not only measuring rods but clocks also change their units as they change their velocities, and that the velocities which cause these changes are not absolute with reference to a fixed ether but relative to anything whatever. We must not belittle these assumptions by interpreting them merely as a new set of metrical conventions. They are partly methodological or subjective rules and partly (alleged) physical facts.

III. The Apparent Paradoxes of the Special Theory

Now that we have seen something of the nature of the Special Theory and of the evidence that led Einstein to formulate it, let us inquire as to whether the theory is self-consistent and in agreement with fact, or whether it leads to contradiction and to error. I shall try to show you that there are at least three possible situations in which the implications of the theory appear to contradict either its own peculiar assumptions or the assumptions which it shares with common sense. For reasons which will appear, these situations might be respectively entitled: (1) Two Friends, a Radio, and an Eskimo; (2) The Land of the Mad Dictator; (3) When the Traveler Returns.

1. A New Yorker and a Californian agree that if the Einstein theory is true, it should be possible by the exchange of radio messages to discover whether or not the cloud-covered earth on which they live is rotating on its axis. They choose their respective positions 3,000 miles apart and on the same parallel of latitude. They then undertake to synchronize their clocks. This procedure is, in general, repulsive to the Einsteinian because he wishes to abandon the assumption of simultaneity at a distance and to substitute for it only such temporal correlations of clocks as can be got by exchanging light signals. Our friends, however, may plead that even on a revolving platform or globe, the Special Theory admits that clocks at the same latitude or distance from the center go at the same rate. There is, indeed, no sufficient reason for them not to do so, as their positions are perfectly symmetrical. Moreover, our friends agree to observe the Einsteinian etiquette to the extent of setting their clocks by light signals. They do, however, insist on abandoning the question-begging method of a merely *tête-a-tête* exchange. They are going

to establish a triadic rather than a dyadic chronometric standard. To this end they employ a trained Eskimo who lives at the North Pole and revolves on his axis or not according to whether the earth revolves on its axis or not. In either case, he is equidistant from the two friends and his state of rest or motion is symmetrically related to theirs. They regulate their clocks by his clock, and if, when thus regulated, their clocks go slower than they otherwise would, it is no matter, for at least they go at the same rate. It is agreed between the experimenters that when through their radio-telephones they hear the Eskimo say *Go!* they are to radio the same word to each other, and each is to note with a stop-watch the time that elapses between his giving his own signal and receiving that of his friend. Now if, as may be true, the earth really does revolve from west to east, the Californian will get the New Yorker's signal in a shorter time than if the earth was standing still, for he will be going to meet it, and even Einsteinian light travels a shorter distance in less time than it does a longer distance. The New Yorker will be moving away from his friend, and hence will get the signal in a slightly longer time than if the earth had been at rest. The difference between the times as measured by the friends will discover to them the rotation of their globe; and the sense and degree of this difference will reveal the direction and the velocity of the rotation. We can imagine that on completing their experiment the participants will hasten to congratulate each other. And well they may; for they will have done something which, though it may not be heinous, in itself is at least forbidden by the Einsteinian laws. *They will have proved absolute rotation from the internal evidence of their own system.* And they will have proved it kinematically and not dynamically as Newton did by appealing to a centrifugal force which some follower of Ernst Mach can later attack by postulating suitably attractive fixed stars. Our investigators will, moreover, have played the game according to the Einstein rules—just giving and receiving signals. Of the stars that may lie beyond their cloud-covered planet they know nothing and care less, and any attempt to drag in these bodies and ascribe to them mysterious pseudo-gravitational equivalents of centrifugal forces will be even more offensively gratuitous than usual.[2]

2. I pass now to a second consequence of the Special Theory, which, like the one just given, appears to contradict the premises from which it follows. We will put the case in the form of an allegory, and compare the world of Einstein to a country ruled by a Mad Dictator. The Dictator, besides being mad, is passionately fond of motoring. He drives everywhere, and always at the tremendous speed of 186,000 miles a second. He has two curious whims which he has imposed upon the country by edicts. The first of these whims is that without changing his own speed

[2] The technique of radio-telegraphy and of chronometry is probably not sufficiently developed at present to make the experiment just described more than imaginary or hypothetical. But none the less, its implications have a theoretical significance much more far-reaching than that of forcing the Einsteinian to what he (though not we) would regard as a *reductio ad absurdum*, a proof of absolute rotation.

The experiment would, in the first place, be a crucial test of the generally accepted belief that the velocity of light is not affected by the velocity of the source from which the light comes. For if this assumption, which is held equally by the older and the newer physics and by both Einstein and Lorentz, is valid, the results of the experiment would certainly be *positive*, and just as described in my story. While if, on the contrary (as I myself believe, and attempt later to prove), that assumption is *not* valid, then the results of the experiment would be *negative*, because the radio waves from the Californian (moving eastward) would go enough faster than the waves that issued from the receding New Yorker to compensate for the increased length of their journey. In this respect the experiment would serve the same purpose as the one which I shall in a few minutes seriously propose that we perform.

But now, in the second place, suppose that the results were positive, as recounted in the episode of the two friends; then it *would be possible by an extension of the experiment to decide between the theory of Lorentz and the theory of Einstein.* This could be done in the following way: Our two friends would abandon California and New York in favor

he shall always be able to pass every citizen at the same speed, so that whether a citizen is at rest or is moving fast or slow, north or south, the Dictator must always pass him at the same speed. The second whim of the Dictator is that no two objects shall ever pass each other at a speed greater than that of the Dictator himself. The people love their ruler and gladly obey his laws; and being skilled in mathematics they have their motors equipped with clocks and speedometers which are cunningly adjusted so as to register not only the speed relative to the road but also the speed relative to every moving object which they may pass. When diverse velocities are compared with the velocity of the Dictator, the people accept the axiom that when unequals are added to equals the results are equal. If any speedometer fails to record the Dictator's speed as constant relative to the citizen's own speed, no matter what that may be, it is known to be wrong and is immediately confiscated.

of Europe and South Africa, and take their positions not on the same parallel of latitude, but on the same meridian of longitude. These positions would be 3,000 miles apart as before, the one north of the equator, the other an equal distance south of it. To synchronize their clocks they would use not an Eskimo at the Pole, but, let us say, a Pygmy at the equator. They would then proceed as before with an interchange of radio signals. Now, on *any* theory, the north-going and south-going signals would take equal times; but if Einstein is right, these times would also be equal to the *mean* of the west-going and east-going times of the earlier experiments, while if Lorentz is right, the longitudinal times would be slightly greater than the mean of the latitudinal times. The reason for this discrepancy would lie in the fact that on the Lorentzian theory the latitudinal (but not the longitudinal) units of space-measurement would have undergone the Lorentz-Fitzgerald contraction because of the earth's rotation; and thus the signals would really have traversed a shorter distance through the ether over the 3,000 miles measured east and west than over the same distance measured north and south.

I have thought it worth while to state this at some length because, so far as I know, there has never been suggested the possibility of even a hypothetical decision by experiment between the Lorentzian and the Einsteinian interpretations of the Michelson-Morley results. The preference for Einstein seems to be based only on the methodological ground that the Einsteinian formulae are simpler and more uniformly applicable than the purely Lorentzian.

As to the second great law that no two bodies shall ever pass each other at a velocity greater than 186,000 miles a second, it happened that in the early days of the dictatorship a traffic policeman who had just been appointed caught sight of two motors approaching his crossing from opposite directions. He recognized the drivers as the Beta brothers, nephews of the Dictator and famous or rather infamous for the furious speeds at which they drove. On this occasion he noted that they were each travelling at $\frac{7}{8}$ the velocity of the Dictator himself. The policeman was an honest loyal fellow but a bit dull in arithmetic. Hence he reasoned that if the young men passed him in opposite directions going at $\frac{7}{8}$ the speed of their uncle, they would pass each other at almost twice that speed. Figure it as he would, he always came back to the absurd conclusion that $\frac{7}{8} + \frac{7}{8}$ would make 14/8. So he ordered the speeders to stop, and politely handed them the customary summons. When their case was called, the judge of the traffic court asked each of them to state the readings of his speedometer. They testified that their speedometers had been constructed in the manner approved by the Dictator and that the records showed that they were indeed moving toward one another, and that relative to the officer their velocities were $\frac{7}{8}$ of 186,000 miles a second, but that with reference to each other their velocity, as measured, was only about 15/16 that of the limit allowed by law. The judge realized that everything was correct, discharged the defendants with an apology for the inconvenience to which they had been put, and sternly reprimanded the officer who had caused the arrest. The poor cop, greatly humiliated, muttered something about his calculation that $\frac{7}{8}$ and $\frac{7}{8}$ would make 14/8; whereupon the judge, after threatening to punish him for contempt of court, delivered himself of the following weighty pronouncement: "In all measurements of relative velocities the method shall be dyadic and never triadic.

That is to say, every person when in motion shall measure the speeds of other persons relative to one another separately and in terms of his own clocks and measuring-rods. He shall not commit the error of the traffic officer and calculate the speed of bodies relative to one another by adding their speeds relative to him. If two and two were put together in such a manner, they might make four, even though the law called for only three. The relative speeds of two bodies must," he repeated, "always be measured directly and dyadically from the point of view of one of them and never calculated triadically or indirectly from the point of view of a third. The triadic system would lead straight to Bolshevism, and even the discussion of its implications is henceforth prohibited." The policeman, however, having by this time recovered his self-possession, begged so earnestly for one more chance to speak that the judge gave his consent. The officer began by repeating reverently the motto which the country had adopted when the dictatorship was established: "Let us set the clocks of the universe, and we care not who makes its laws." He was, he said, as loyal to those great words as anyone in the courtroom, but he felt that it was not only a right but a duty to point out that his complaint that the Beta brothers had exceeded the speed limit relatively to one another was supported not merely by the calculation which he had already put in evidence but by the testimony which the brothers themselves would have been willing to give had they been asked. For both before they had started from the opposite ends of the Boulevard and also after they had been halted by him, they would have been willing to admit that the distance separating them was such that they could only have come together when they did by travelling relatively to one another at a speed of 14/8 the velocity of the Dictator. "And is it fair," asked the policeman in conclusion, "that the space and time measurements taken while a journey is in progress should entirely supplant measurements which were made at the beginning and end of the journey, especially when it is the latter set of measurements which agree with one another as well as with those of a neutral third party?"

To this final plea the judge made no reply except to adjourn the court. But at least one spectator was convinced that the officer's point was a valid one and revealed a contradiction between the time and space measurements made while travelling and the permanent and self-consistent results of measurement which must be deduced or inferred after the travel was over.

3. The third illustration of an apparent conflict between the implications of the Special Theory and the assumptions which it shares with common sense results from applying the change of time which all moving bodies undergo to the special case of a living body or organism. If two events are separated by a certain length of time on our system, it is possible by using a formula derived from that applied to measuring-rods by Lorentz and Fitzgerald for us to calculate the quite different time-lapse between those events as experienced or lived through on another system moving relatively to us. And just as the space-distance always grows less the faster a body moves relatively to us, so the time-distances always grow longer; in other words, the clocks run slower as the rods get shorter. Now, one might suppose that these apparent differences in the space and time magnitudes of systems, moving relatively to one another would be merely apparent; in which case it would be quite understandable that my inches might look to you shorter than yours and that your inches might look to me shorter than mine. From which we should conclude that the relative motion of two persons produced a sort of perspective aberration in the appearance of each to the other. My inches wouldn't *be* shorter than yours, while yours *were* also shorter than mine; they would only *look* so. In any

event, this path of escape seems to be spurned by the Relativists, at least in the case of Time. For we are told by Professor Eddington that if a person could step onto the magic carpet described in the old fairy tale and travel with almost the velocity of light to the star Arcturus, he would be, let us say, only a half-hour older when he reached his goal than he was when he set out. Yet from the point of view of us who were left behind, something like two hundred years would have elapsed. And again Professor Herman Weyl confirms this amazing application of Einstein to physiology by the more moderate supposition that if there are twin brothers one of whom stays at home while the other travels abroad for a few years at a speed approximating that of light, the latter brother, when he returns, will look perceptibly younger than the twin who remained behind. This would follow from the fact that the molecules of our bodies, whose rhythmic changes determine the aging or passing of our lives, are natural clocks, and like all clocks they must slow down when our bodies move. But if our molecular processes slow down, then the atrophying of glands and muscles and the hardening of arteries proceed more slowly—in short, we grow old more slowly.

In spite of the attractiveness of this hypothesis, I do not believe that it is true. In a Lorentzian world in which motion was absolute, we might hope that the same ether which shortens the spaces of moving bodies would also lengthen their times and slow down such of their processes as took place in the direction of their motion. In that case all very speedy travellers would appear to us not only foreshortened or flattened, but also rejuvenated in that one of their dimensions which they had chosen for the direction of their journey. But in the other two dimensions they would be as large and as old as if they had never moved. In an Einsteinian world, however, in which there is no ether and no absolute motion, I cannot see how even a linear rejuvenation could occur. To appreciate the difficulty involved, let us take a second look at Professor Weyl's twins, one of whom travels and the other does not. Suppose that the stay-at-home brother should feel piqued by the youthful appearance of the other who has returned from abroad. He would have only to remember that all motion is relative, and that consequently he had a perfect right to regard himself as the traveller and his brother as having remained stationary. In that case it would be *he* who looked and really *was* younger. Now, not even in an Einsteinian world would it be possible for two brothers, especially twins, each to be a few years younger than the other. That could happen only in a universe in which all squares were round and the *principio contradictionis* had been put to sleep.

This puzzle, it may be noted, is touched upon by Eddington, though not, so far as I have discovered, by Weyl. Eddington solves it—rather lamely, as it seems to me—by forbidding his traveller to Arcturus ever to return to earth and debate as to who really did the travelling, on the ground that the awkward situation thus created would be *asymmetrical*. But one would suppose that two people each of whom was younger than the other would suffer from an excess of symmetry rather than from a lack of it.

IV. The Crucial Assumption Contained in Einstein's Premises

Now, it may be that all of the apparently paradoxical consequences of the Special Theory of Relativity are susceptible of a self-consistent explanation; but before we accept a conclusion so revolutionary as that of Einstein, common sense would seem to dictate a most careful re-examination of the premises by which that conclusion is supported. To this examination we now proceed.

The argument, as I understand it, can be stated as follows:

If, first, we accept the old assumption that the velocity

of light *in vacuo* is unaffected by the velocity of its source, and if, second, we accept as correct the negative results of the Michelson-Morley experiment, then, third, we *must* accept as a necessary conclusion either Einstein's theory or some highly complex form of the Lorentz theory.

Now, the results of the Michelson-Morley experiment are too well attested to permit of a reasonable doubt as to their correctness. Whatever escape there may be from the conclusion depends solely on the other premise: the assumption that the velocity of light is unaffected by the velocity of its source. The evidence for the truth of this assumption is meager, at least in comparison with the tremendous weight of the conclusion which rests upon it. It is, in the first place, a kind of hold-over from the days of the ether. Ships moving through the ocean send their backward-going waves from the stern as fast as their forward-going waves from the bow. It is the same with sound-waves in the air. In general, the velocity of waves in a medium depends entirely upon the structure of the medium, its density and elasticity, and not a bit upon the velocity of the body that sends them. Consequently, if luminous bodies move through an ocean of ether, we should expect that their light waves would behave like other waves. But now that Einstein has abolished the ether, there seems no reason to saddle the new light with the disabilities of a medium that no longer exists. The situation reminds us of the anomalous procedure of David Hume, who continued to regard sensory objects as states of mind after he himself had abolished the mind whose states they were. When old postulates are abandoned, their implications are at least open to question; and if they are to be retained at all, they must be newly substantiated. Einstein's position seems to be that, though there is no motionless ether such as Lorentz and his predecessors believed in, yet light-waves must be assumed to behave in relation to the velocity of their source as if there were such a medium. What is the alternative to this crucial assumption?

We cannot suppose that light is made up of corpuscles emitted by bodies as they move, for light is in almost all respects wavelike rather than corpuscular. Nor can we suppose that the earth and all other bodies push and drag along with them a portion of the ether-ocean in which they move, for we find no trace of the whirlpools and other disturbances which would be produced by the collision of these moving ethers. To find a tenable alternative to Einstein's assumption we must, I think, look in a slightly different direction. As such an alternative I propose the theory *that the medium or carrier of light waves is not a doubtfully existent ether-substance, but the certainly existent field of force which each proton and electron carries with it.* As each of these fields extends in all directions and without limit, it inter-penetrates every other field, and thus space must be thought of as filled with infinite spheres of force, *macro-monads,* each of which contains all the others. Now, because these fields are centered in their particles, it follows that when a particle moves, its field must move with it. What will be the velocity of waves emanating from a particle under these conditions? Their velocity will be compounded of the velocity *in* the field and the velocity *of* the field. The velocity *in* the field will be constant and absolute, equal to 186,000 miles a second. The velocity *of* the field that carries the undulations will be variable and relative; for the velocity of the field will be the same as the velocity of the particle which is its nucleus and center, and the velocity of a particle is variable and can be measured relatively to any other particle.

If this alternative to Einstein's assumption is true, then the negative results of the Michelson-Morley experiment are exactly what we should expect. There is in them no mystery whatever, and there is no need to subject our traditional Newtonian mechanics either to a Lorentzian reform or to an Einsteinian revolution.

And now I wish to describe to you an experiment which, if it can be carried out, will settle the main point at issue definitely and once for all.

V. The Experiment Designed to Test the Crucial Assumption

Is the velocity of light affected by the motion of the body from which it comes, or is it, as generally supposed, quite independent of the velocity of its source? That is the question, and here is the experiment I propose.

A steel sphere one foot in diameter is mounted on a horizontal axle running through its center. (See the accompanying figure.) The sphere is wound with steel or platinum wires which are heated until they become luminous by an electric current passing through them. The

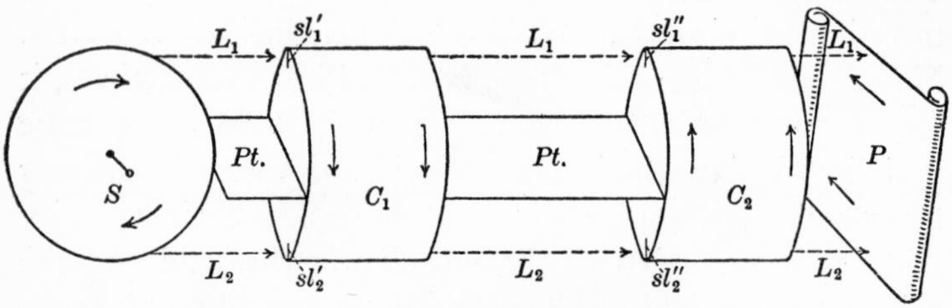

Fig. 3. Diagrammatic Model of Apparatus for Proposed Experiment

The sphere, *S*, rotating in the direction indicated by the arrows, sends out from its upper and lower halves light beams, L_1 and L_2, which, separated by the partition *Pt*, pass through, respectively, slits sl_1' and sl_2' in the first cylinder, C_1, which is rotating clockwise, and through the slits sl_1'' and sl_2'' in the second cylinder, C_2, which is rotating counterclockwise; registering separately upon the sensitive paper, *P*, which is moving in the direction indicated by the arrows.

The whole is enclosed in a tunnel.

sphere revolves on (or with) its axle 263 times a second. The points on its upper and its lower surfaces, respectively, will thus be moving with equal and opposite velocities of about 833 feet a second. From the upper and lower surfaces there will be given off two parallel sets of light rays which will be kept separate from each other by a thick horizontal partition 264 feet or one-twentieth of a mile in length and extending forward from the middle of the sphere and in the direction in which the upper half of it is moving. Directly in front of the sphere is a steel cylinder 3 feet long and 3 1/7 feet in circumference, with its end-planes perpendicular to the light coming from the sphere. In this cylinder are two slits one inch long and 1/250 of an inch in width. At the other end of the partition 264 feet away is another cylinder in line with the first and having the same dimensions. This second cylinder also has two opposite slits of the same length and width as those on the first cylinder. Just behind this further cylinder is a sheet of sensitive photographic paper slowly moving from left to right. The whole apparatus is enclosed in a tunnel and the cylinders are set rotating, the one clockwise, the other counterclockwise, and at velocities gradually increasing to that of the sphere, that is to say, 263 times a second. This means that any point on the circumference of one cylinder will have a velocity of 2 × 833 or 1,666 feet a second relative to any point on the other cylinder, so that the corresponding slits on the two cylinders will be opposite one another for 1/5,000,000 of a second. It will take the light from the sphere a little longer than this (about 1/3,720,000) to pass over the one-twentieth of a mile that separates the cylinders. Consequently, if the cylinders are gradually speeded up, there will come a time when the two sets of light rays will cease to make a record on the sensitive paper.

Now, if Einstein is right, the two sets of light rays will disappear simultaneously; but if Einstein is wrong, the lower set will disappear before the upper set. For we must remember that the lower set of light waves will be emanating from the bottom of the sphere, which has a backward velocity of 833 feet a second, while the upper light rays will be sent from the top of the sphere, which has a forward velocity of 833 feet a second. The two sources of light will thus have a difference in their velocities of 1,666 feet a second, and the experiment should tell us whether this difference in the velocities of the sources of light results in a difference in the velocities of the light itself.

For the past fifteen years I have been discussing with Professor Bergen Davis and other members of the Physics Department at Columbia an experiment like the one I have described except that disks instead of cylinders were to have been used. But until very recently there seemed to be no way to meet one of the objections which Professor Davis advanced. Why should not the light rays, after passing through the slits in the first disk spread out in such a way as always to pass through the second slits, whether or not they were directly in line? This objection, it was urged, could not be met except by placing a third disk with similar slits but fixed and not rotating, in front of the further of the two revolving disks and then synchronizing the latter so perfectly that their corresponding slits would come opposite to one another only when they were in line with the slits in the fixed disk. Now, it is very doubtful if any such degree of synchronization of bodies rotating so fast and at such a distance would be possible. To meet this objection it recently occurred to me that the two disks should be made thick, like grindstones or cylinders, so that the only light that could get through would be that which travelled perpendicularly to the planes of their ends. This does away with the need of synchronizing because the slits in the upper halves are bound to be opposite each other *somewhere* twice in each revolution; and, of course, the same applies to the lower halves. And it does not matter what the angular position of the slits when they cross each other, or how that position may vary through variation of rotational velocity. For the revolving sphere will send off rays in all planes, so that at whatever angle the slits may choose to cross, some light will be there ready to shoot through. The light from the more slowly moving regions adjacent to the poles of the horizontal axis of the sphere could safely, and should probably, be blocked off from entering the slits and the tunnel.

Whether or not the sphere and the cylinders can be sufficiently speeded up to make the two sets of light waves disappear; and whether, second, the centrifugal force resulting from such a degree of speed would not make the heat-softened wires on the sphere fly to pieces; and whether, third, the hypothetical difference in the speed of the two sets of light rays would be sufficient to produce an observable difference in the intensity of the upper and lower impressions on the sensitive paper, are questions that can best be settled by trial.[3]

The cost of the experiment might run to $20,000. Philosophers are supposed to pray only on rare occasions, and it may be that for that very reason the gods take special heed of their appeals. Perhaps some of you will be willing to pray that there be sent to me a kind-hearted rich man

[3] The last objection is, I think, far more serious than the others. The intensities of the two sets of light rays when they have scraped through their respective pairs of slits will, as I calculate it, differ only in the ratio of 200 to 199. It may well be that this difference is too small to be detected on the paper. In that case, the dimensions of the apparatus would have to be extended. The length of the tunnel might be increased tenfold, that is, from a twentieth of a mile to a half-mile. This drawback would be partly compensated for by the increase which we could then make in the width of the slits from 1/250 to 1/25th of an inch. In that case, although both sets of light waves would be fainter, we should only have to detect a difference of one part in twenty instead of one part in two hundred. But, nevertheless, I am very much worried over this difficulty. It may be fatal.

who will take a sporting chance and put up the necessary funds to try this thing out.

There are, of course, various modifications of my experiment which might be tried, if in its primary form it proved impracticable. In place of light from our luminous sphere, we might use the light from the sun at sunrise when we are rotating toward it and again at sunset when we are rotating away from it. This would, however, require an absolute and very precise measure of the velocity in each case instead of the detection of a mere difference-effect. Or, again, as suggested by two of my colleagues, we might use the light from the opposite edges of the revolving sun, in which case a mere difference-effect would suffice. There would be, however, the chance that in using extra-terrestrial rays of light, any difference in their velocities might be evened up when they entered the part of space in which the fields of earthly particles were stronger than those of the particles from which they originated.[4]

The use of mirrors would simplify these experiments and would reduce them to modifications of the Fizeau or Foucault methods of light-measurement. But there is a bare possibility that the difference in the velocities of the light impinging on the mirror might be neutralized in the process of being reflected. This danger would also militate against a suggestion made by another colleague that my revolving sphere should be illuminated by arc-lights from above and below.

VI. The Nature of the Alternative to the Special Theory of Relativity

Before closing this discussion of the Special Theory of Relativity, I should like to return to a consideration of the

[4] This possibility would also seem to detract from the conclusiveness of certain experiments similar in intent to mine made by De Sitter and others on double stars, of which a friend has just informed me.

alternative to that theory which it is possible that the experiment I have been describing might justify. The conception that the vehicle of light undulations is the field of force of which the vibrating particle is the nucleus possesses a peculiar status intermediate between the old theory of Absolute Motion in an absolute space and the new theory of Relativity.

What really counts in the motion of anything is not its change of position in a supposed absolute space, nor is it, on the other hand, its merely relative change of distance from any and every other object. The most significant thing about motion is *the relation of the moving body to its own past*, or what is much the same thing, *the relation of what moves to the source from which the motion originated.* "Auto-absolutism," or "intra-relativism" are words which might serve to express my meaning. Let me illustrate. Suppose two planets are approaching each other in otherwise empty space. You take a position on one of these bodies, and I will take mine on the other. There is, perhaps, no meaning in asking whether I am moving toward you or you toward me. We see only that we are approaching. Let us each arrange on our respective planets to have a number of marbles capable of rolling freely in level grooves parallel with the line of our motion, and let us suppose that our approach is varied by successively equal spurts of uniform acceleration, not like gravitational accelerations, which act equally on all particles, but like those which would be produced by the recoil of a cannon fixed in the ground and discharging projectiles in the direction from which the planet had moved. We should very soon be able to divide these spurts into two or three kinds: there would be the spurts in which my marbles rolled backward and yours didn't, and the other spurts in which yours rolled backward and mine didn't, and perhaps also a third case in which both sets of marbles rolled backward. The velocity with which the marbles roll in their grooves will measure the difference between the present and the past states of our motions. The change in my state when my marbles rolled would be an intrinsic and vital change, altering the relative position of objects in my system. When your marbles rolled, although my rate of approach to you would be equally accelerated, the change would not be vital or intrinsic to me. We have, then, to distinguish between accelerations that are intrinsic or intra-relative, felt as well as seen, and those that are extrinsic or relative in the ordinary sense, and which are seen but not felt. Is this difference to be explained by an appeal to an absolute velocity in absolute space? Certainly not; because, assuming for the moment that such a space exists, we can see its irrelevance by imagining that all the particles of matter on our two planets are moving together with respect to the fixed points of this absolute space in any direction, at any rate of velocity, and with any degree of acceleration. In no such case would any of the phenomena associated with the rolling of the marbles be affected.

We see, then, that what counts in acceleration is neither the change with reference to an absolute space nor the change with reference to bodies outside the system and unconnected with it. What does count in acceleration is the change of parts of a system with reference to one another; and this "intra-relative" change is at the same time "auto-absolute," that is, a register of the difference between the past and the present states of the system as a whole. When your planet was accelerated toward mine in such a way that your marbles seemed to roll backward with uniform velocities, they registered in their apparent backward motion the differentiation of your present state from your past.

But now you may object that even if this intermediate conception is intelligible at all, it applies only to acceleration and not to velocity. To which I should reply that every velocity of translation has been born at some time or other of an acceleration. And if the motion of a body has originated within the system, its rate of uniform velocity will measure the acceleration which gave it birth. And that acceleration was an intrinsic change.

Suppose we stand at the center of a circular platform, and suppose we are ignorant as to whether it is rotating or not; we can settle our doubts by rolling marbles out along a radius of the platform. If the platform is at rest, the marbles will continue to roll on the radius along which they started; but if the platform is rotating, they will undergo increasing changes of longitude as they roll. This will have nothing to do with centrifugal force, because the change of radial direction on the part of the marbles will —disregarding friction—be independent of their masses. An imponderable shadow, if there were any way to shoot it out free of us, would register the same curve as would a mass as great as our entire platform. Here, as in the case of the planets, the outward-rolling marble would register our (angular) state at the moment in the past when its movement started. And we could thus use our own past, preserved in the path of the marble, as a standard with reference to which the amount of our intrinsic change could be measured.

Now, finally, there are two difficulties, and very grave ones, with which such a conception as I am defending is confronted. There is, first, the difficulty of how to interpret the evidence from electrodynamics which points to the velocity of light as an absolute maximum. It would seem that, in maintaining that the fields of force in which light moves are themselves in motion, I had come into conflict with a body of physical doctrine much older than the Einstein Theory.

As a possible way of meeting this difficulty, I suggest that the velocity at which the mass of a particle would become infinite, and which for that reason is regarded as a maximum, might be interpreted and measured in the manner that I have called intra-relative or auto-absolute. It might well be that there is a limit to the amount to which we could increase the velocity of a body relative to the system in which the increase was caused. The effort ordinarily required to change a body's velocity increases as the square of the velocity. Thus, the energy involved in changing 2 units of mass from 4 feet a second to 5 feet a second is $\frac{1}{2}2 \times 5^2 - \frac{1}{2}2 \times 4^2 = 9$. And to change the velocity of the same mass from 9 feet a second to 10 feet a second requires $\frac{1}{2}2 \times 10^2 - \frac{1}{2}2 \times 9^2 = 19$ units of energy. But please observe that, if this formula is to be valid, the velocities must always be measured intra-relatively, that is to say, with reference to the source of the change. If a body is moving 9 feet a second, relatively, say, to the fixed stars, and if we also are moving along beside it at the same rate, then it will take only one unit of effort from us to increase its velocity from 9 to 10 feet a second. In short, the velocity imparted to a body so far as it is relevant to its energy is never to be measured relatively to the fixed stars or to absolute space or to any outside body, but must always be measured relatively to the source of the change. Now, if this elementary formula for the amount of energy required to increase a velocity is to be interpreted in this intra-relative fashion, why might not the more complex rules derived from electrodynamics be interpreted in the same way? We could then admit that an infinite effort would be required to impart to a particle a velocity equal to that of light relative to us who imparted it, and at the same time refuse to admit any limit to the velocity at which a body could move relatively to anything unconnected with its source. This would mean that an alpha particle might be discharged from a star that was itself moving in the same direction at a very high velocity, and then that a beta particle could be discharged from the alpha particle again in the same direction and with a velocity relative to its source of 99/100 the velocity of light. The beta particle would then be moving well beyond the velocity of light with reference to the *original* source. In short, a system of *rockets within rockets* could be devised which could seemingly produce by successive steps any degree of velocity whatever.

If it is asked what would happen not at the *source* but at the *terminal*, if a body moving with one of these super-velocities should crash into another system, we might counter with the question as to what would happen *now* if two beta particles moving at 9/10 the velocity of light should collide head on, lock horns, and so be prevented from getting relief through rebounding. It would seem rather a frail protection from such a cataclysm to say that the clocks on each would from the standpoint of the other be running slow.

The second of the grave difficulties with which my hypothesis is confronted is the empirical evidence which seems to confirm the Einstein Theory, a part of which its author to his everlasting credit was able by his deductions to predict. The empirical facts to which I refer are, as you know: (1) the bending of light waves by gravity to a degree double that to be expected on Newtonian assumptions; (2) the rotation of the elliptic orbits of planets, illustrated to an observable extent in the case of Mercury; (3) the lessened frequency of light waves issuing from strong gravitational fields, manifested in a shift of spectrum lines toward the red.

The first and second of these Einsteinian deductions have been sufficiently verified to satisfy most physicists, and the third, sufficiently to satisfy some.

As to the second and third, I will only point out that, on the alternative theory that I am defending, the whole field of a particle as well as the particle itself should be subject to gravity, and that the resulting slight apparent modification in the Newtonian law might be of the kind and extent needed to account for the facts in question. In the case of Mercury, the phenomenon would be due not to the falsity of the Newtonian law itself, but to the unsuspected presence between the sun and Mercury of the *quasi-matter* of the solar and Mercurial *fields*.

As to the first and most striking of Einstein's deductions, the bending of the light rays from the stars by the sun's gravitational field, the situation is perhaps a little clearer. If light travels in and with respect to the field of its source rather than in and with respect to either an empty space or stationary ether, we should expect that such light would undergo the same double gravitational deviation that was predicted and observed. For, in the first place, the field of force would be attracted by gravity and bent in toward the sun; and in the second place, the light wave themselves, constituting as they do a kind of transitory matter capable of exerting pressure, would be attracted on their own account. And *rays* that were deviated in a *field* that was also deviated would give the same double deviation that was called for by Einstein.

Conclusion

And now, at last, I will say a word as to the character of that General Theory of Relativity, for the appreciation of which some understanding of the Special Theory is essential.

It is not, I think, too inaccurate to say that while the Special Theory reduces geometry to physics and is offensively destructive and phenomenalistic in its conception of the world, the General Theory reduces physics to geometry and its tone and temper are rationalistic and constructive. The muddy prose of Hume and Mach gives place to the clear poetry of Riemann and Clifford.

The General Theory, as its name might indicate, was developed by Einstein as an extension of his formulae for calculating the conditions on one moving system from the standpoint of another. From the special case in which the systems are in uniform or unaccelerated relative motion, the formulae were generalized to include cases in which systems are moving relatively and with accelerated motions. But bodies moving with accelerated velocities are subject to forces; hence the later Einstein theory consists, first, of a new though Cliffordian conception of the nature of *force;* and, second (growing out of that), of a new though Riemannian conception of the *universe itself* as a domain at once boundless and finite. It was Clifford, working under the inspiration of the new geometry of Riemann, who, I think, first suggested that matter could be conceived as a non-Euclidean wrinkle in space. Put more generally: the same spatial medium which to a being measuring his movements according to Euclid would appear as filled with accelerative forces, would for a being who measured his motions according to Riemann be quite empty, though wavy. This means that if we replace Euclidean with non-Euclidean measures, we can substitute for the old dynamic conception of forces in a space of zero curvature the new and purely geometrical conception of just space but of many and varying curvatures. And if a field of force can be thought of as a continuously varying curve or "hill" in space, then the material particle at its center can be conceived as the unattainable peak of such a hill. It is pleasant to think that Clifford, whose mind was of such rare beauty and who in his appreciation of spiritual values possessed what the musicians call a sense for absolute pitch, should have been the first to hold a conception which now seems destined to have most far-reaching consequences.

Notwithstanding the fact that Einstein reasoned from the Special Theory to the General Theory, I do not believe that the truth of the latter logically necessitates the truth of the former. The essence of the General Theory is, I think, quite compatible with the alternative to the Special Theory which I have defended. Nor can I feel, as some interpreters of Einstein apparently do feel, that the category of *force* is disgraced or annihilated by being expressed as a curve in space. Curves themselves were not annihilated when expressed as numerical equations. And Einstein's geometry of mechanics no less than Descartes's algebra of geometry should be celebrated as the fertile marriage of two categories rather than as the funeral of one.

As to the value of the second great claim of the General Theory to give us a universe that is self-contained like a closed curve, in place of our old world that straggled so inordinately through the endless wastes of Euclidean space—opinions will be varied and emotions mixed. Some will undoubtedly feel stifled and penned in at the thought that if they were to travel in a "straight" line for only a few septillions of miles, they would find themselves on the way home without ever having turned around. Others will find the new Riemannian hypersphere large enough for all practical purposes; and they will delight in the possibility of relating in some curious way the curvature or size of the universe as a whole to the dimensions of its minimum elements. For this would take us to that climax of rationalist aspiration in which even the arbitrary and existential constants of physics would be reduced to a crystalline precipitate of purely subsistential mathematical relations.

But I have already gone too far in these hints as to the fairyland that may now be opening for science and philosophy. If anyone is stirred by the errors of my essay to say well the kind of thing I have tried to say, handicapped by ignorance, I shall be happy. For it is time that we in philosophy should go back to Nature, no matter how steep the path or how hard we fall.

⋙ 9 ⋘

A POSSIBLE INTERPRETATION OF THE QUANTUM[1]

A comparatively untechnical and impressionistic sketch of the Quantum theory combined with suggested hypotheses for the solution of its three outstanding problems: (1) the greater energy of shorter light waves; (2) the photon as wave or particle; (3) the structure of the atoms from which photons are emitted. It presupposes some knowledge of physics.

Introduction

THE THREE ASPECTS of the quantum phenomena which seem to be the most puzzling and most challenging to the imagination are:

I. The revolutionary conception of radiant energy as consisting of definite multiples of a definite unit, Planck's mysterious constant *h*.

II. The reconciliation of the new conception of radiation as discrete and quasi-corpuscular with the older but equally valid conception of radiation as continuous and undulatory.

III. The structure of the atoms and the manner in which a discretely continuous radiation is emitted from and absorbed by them.

I shall consider these three problems in turn and suggest a possible solution for each of them.

[1] Reprinted from *The Scientific Monthly*, April, 1934, Vol. XXXVIII, pages 343–360.

I. The Nature of h and the Reason for the Equation $e = h \cdot \text{nu}$

The intensity of light, like the intensity of sound and gravitation, varies inversely as the square of its distance from the source. Yet despite this undenied fact, the energy of a light wave (as measured by the energy given to an electron that is expelled from a photoelectric screen by the impact of the wave) depends not at all upon the distance of the light wave from its source, but solely upon the length of the wave. The shorter the waves, the higher the frequency or number passing a given point in a second. And the energy of light of a given wave-length is measured by the product of its frequency, symbolized by nu, and a certain very small fixed quantity. This small quantity is itself the product of energy and time, and as such is called "Action." It is the famous constant discovered by Professor Planck. Its value is $6.55 \cdot 10^{-27}$ erg-seconds, and its symbol is h. Hence, the measure of the energy, e, of a light wave or, more properly, of an electromagnetic wave of any length is expressed in the equation $e = h \cdot \text{nu}$. The baffling situation thus presented and formulated raises two fundamental and hitherto unanswered questions:

(1) Why does the energy of radiation increase with its frequency?

(2) What is the real nature of Planck's constant h?

I trust that the reader will bear with me if I first state my answer to these questions in the form of a little fable or allegory. Allegories do not usually help in matters of physics, but I think that this one will. It will help me, at any rate, to make plain the conception which I wish to submit for consideration.

When I was very young, there lived in my town a prosperous and happy but most peculiar family. There was

Henry, the father, who was thin and incredibly tall, a regular giant, in fact. He had two children, Harry, who was a sturdy, half-grown boy, and Harriet, a tiny girl but amazingly active for her size and age. There was also a nephew, Cousin Hal, as the children called him, a tall, slender youth who visited the family almost every Sunday. Last but in some ways most important of all was the mother, who was affectionately known to everybody as Mrs. H. In fact, the whole group was always called simply "the H. family," and whether they had a surname or not I do not know. The really striking thing about the family was not what they were named but what they did. They had a game that they always played when they went walking together. I suppose that all of us have played this game in boyhood, but probably only in a haphazard sort of way. You walk along the road and as you walk you kick the little stones that lie in your way, taking them in your stride and noticing how far they go. This was the game played by the H. family; but there was nothing haphazard about their method of playing. They had a definite and unvarying procedure and they observed three rather precise conditions, which were as follows: (1) They all walked at the same rate but their steps were of different lengths. Henry's step was six feet, Hal's was three feet, Harry's was two feet, and the steps of little Harriet were only one foot. Each member of the family kept to his own length of step and never varied from it. Henry set the pace, which was just six feet a second, neither more nor less. (2) They walked with a sort of limp that made them look as though they were cantering. This was due to their always taking the step in advance with the right foot, which was the one with which they kicked the pebbles, and they merely brought the left foot up even with the right instead of advancing it in turn as in a regular walk. (3) They wore rubber-toed shoes, so constructed that each pebble that was kicked absorbed all the energy of the step regardless of whether the impact occurred early or late in its progress. This necessitated a fresh initiating effort for the next step but produced the same effect on the pebble as if it had been kicked by the foot when moving at a speed equal to its average speed.

It was a delightful experience to see the H. family coming down Main Street of a Sunday morning playing their jolly game. Henry's appearance was comical in the extreme, for he wore an expression of preternatural solemnity owing to his intentness upon keeping the pace at exactly six feet a second, which happened to be the legal speed limit of the town and was never exceeded by any one. But Hal and the children were very gay and kicked all the pebbles that they could find so long as they could take them in their stride and without deviating. The funniest sight of all was Mrs. H., who, though she did not play the game herself, managed to co-operate in a most important way. She had come from a famous mathematical family, the Plancks of Berlin, I believe, and had inherited a passion for exact measurement. So with surprising agility she went scampering along in front of the rest and by the aid of a queer little contraption that she had devised she measured the mv^2 of most of the stones that were kicked. The results of these measurements were really astonishing and filled the town's population with wonder and perplexity.

In the first place, they showed that Harriet's kicks were the hardest of all. Each of her steps was only a foot in length, but her stones had twice the energy of those of Harry, whose steps were two feet long, and three times the energy of those of Hal, who took a full yard in each stride. I must remind you again that the family never varied the differing lengths of their respective steps any more than they varied their speed of progress, though that was the same for all. Now, on comparing the results of the measurements, it was found that if you multiplied the *energy* of any pebble by the *time* occupied by the step of the one who kicked it, you always got the same result, no matter whose pebble you were considering. Harriet, for example, took six steps to the second, so that the time occupied by each of her steps was one-sixth of a second. For the same reason, the time of Harry's two-foot step was one third of a second, and that of Hal's three-foot step was one-half of a second. If we represent the energy of Hal's step (as measured by the energy of the pebble which absorbed it) as $2e$ and multiply it by the one-half of a second or unit of time, t, which his step occupied, the product $\frac{1}{2}t \cdot 2e$ will equal et. Harriet's step-energy was, as we saw, three times that of Hal's, that is, $6e$. But $6e$ multiplied by $\frac{1}{6}t$ equals et. And as for Harry, the energy of his step was only half that of his sister's, that is, $\frac{1}{2} \cdot 6e = 3e$, and $3e$ multiplied by $\frac{1}{3}t$, which was the time taken by Harry for one of his steps, is again equal to et. The members of the H. family were very much pleased with this result. It gave them a new sense of solidarity that made up for the bewildering and rather distressing differences in the energies of their several kicks. They decided to call the new quantity by the family initial, *h*, uncapitalized, of course, because it did not represent the first letter of any particular person's name; it was just the family constant.

Quantities of this kind that are got by multiplying energy by time are called "Action." Now, in the year in which these happenings occurred there was much talk about Time as a sort of fourth dimension being bound up with Space in somewhat the same way that one spatial dimension is bound up with another. And many people had a queer deep feeling that the hybrid category of *Action* was more fundamental than energy itself, and that in some strange way it bore witness to the new union of space and time in a four-dimensional continuum of space-time.[2]

It was easy for all of us to see that if the energy of each step of a member of the H. family when multiplied by its time produced the quantity *h*, then, conversely, the energy itself could be expressed as the product of *h* and the reciprocal of the time, which latter will coincide with the frequency or number of steps per second, usually symbolized by the Greek letter nu.* For, if $et = h$ and $t = \frac{1}{\text{nu}}$, then $e \cdot \frac{1}{\text{nu}} = h$ and $e = h \cdot \text{nu}$. Thus, Harriet's time for a step being one-sixth of a second, the reciprocal of which is 6, her energy will be equal to $6h$. With Harry and Hal the frequencies will be 3 and 2, respectively, and the energies of their respective steps will be $3h$ and $2h$; and, in general, the energy of any such step will be expressed by the equation $e = \text{nu} \cdot h$.

But just what was the real nature of this *h*, and why did multiplying it by the frequency of the step give the energy of the step? In other words, why should the energies severally associated with the members of the H. family be the reverse of what you would naturally expect, Harriet's more than Harry's, and his more than that of his tall cousin? These questions fascinated me, and I kept thinking about them when I ought to have been doing my regular stuff. At last, I determined to get a stop-watch and check up on the various factors involved in the situation. Thus

[2] "Multiplying [energy] again by hours would seem a very odd sort of thing to do, but it does not seem quite so strange when we look at it in the absolute four-dimensional world. Quantities such as energy, which we think of as existing at an instant, belong to three-dimensional space, and they need to be multiplied by a duration to give them a thickness before they can be put into the four-dimensional world."

See Eddington: *The Nature of the Physical World*, p. 180. New York, The Macmillan Company, 1928.

* I spell out the Greek letter ν as *nu* to avoid possible confusion with our English letter *v*, the symbol for *velocity*.

equipped, I took up a good position on the sidewalk and observed very closely the steps of the family as they cantered past me. I noticed how much more quickly Harry and Harriet completed their steps than Hal and Henry; but, of course, that increased quickness of stepping didn't explain anything, because the steps of the little ones were that much shorter. Why should Harriet increase her energy by making a step six times as quickly as her father, if in that step she only went one-sixth the length of his step? But one day I got a clue. I noticed that the time taken by each step was divided into a *resting-time*, during which the foot was on the ground, and a *going-time*, during which it was moving through the air. Though each of Harriet's resting periods was actually shorter than that of the others, nevertheless there were more of them; and in proportion to the total time of her step, each of her resting periods was longer than that of the others. I worked on this aspect of the situation, with my stop-watch recording the moving-time and the resting-time for the various steps, and this was what I found. Henry's resting-time was a very small fraction of a second, which for simplicity I will designate by the letter R. His going-time was consequently $1 - R$, and the velocity of his foot while it was moving was, therefore, $\frac{6}{1-R}$ feet per second. The going-time of Hal, who took two steps per second, was $(\frac{1}{2})^2 \cdot (1-R)$ in each step, so during the entire second he was on the go $2 \cdot (\frac{1}{2})^2 \cdot (1-R) = \frac{1}{2}(1-R)$; in other words, for just half the time during which his Uncle Henry's foot was moving, so that in order to keep up with his uncle his foot had to move just twice as fast as the latter's foot. Harry, who took three steps a second, was on the go $(\frac{1}{3})^2 \cdot (1-R)$ in each step and hence $3\ (\frac{1}{3})^2 \cdot (1-R) = \frac{1}{3}(1-R)$ in each second, which meant that having exactly one-third of his father's traveling time he had to travel three times as fast. In the same way, Harriet's total traveling time was $6 \cdot (\frac{1}{6})^2 \cdot (1-R)$, or just one-sixth of Henry's traveling time, with the result that if she herself was to go as fast as her father, her foot had to go six times as fast as his foot. In short, I discovered the general law that I had been searching for. In any family of steppers like the H. family there is an *internal velocity* of each stepper which is proportionate to the frequency of his steps per unit of time, and hence can be obtained by multiplying that frequency by the *internal velocity* of a leader or standard stepper whose frequency of stepping is one per second. Let us denote the *internal velocity* of the standard stepper (whether actually existing or only potential does not matter) by $V = \frac{C}{1-R}$, where C is the length of the standard step and R is the portion of the unit of time during which the foot is at rest and therefore $(1-R)$ the time in which the foot is moving. Then, using v to denote the *internal velocity* and nu to denote the frequency of any other stepper, we have as a true equation:

$$v = \text{nu} \cdot V, \text{ or } v = \text{nu} \cdot \frac{C}{1-R}.$$

In the light of this equation, it was no longer surprising that little Harriet kicked her pebbles the hardest of all the family, for her feet moved the fastest, not *in spite* of but *because* of, her steps being the shortest. Harriet was, indeed, like an automobile which had to make an average speed of sixty miles an hour, but which had to stop for traffic lights every ten miles. You can imagine how much faster such a car would have to travel in between the stops as compared with another car making the same general average of sixty miles an hour but only obstructed by traffic lights once each sixty miles. The average "internal velocity" of the former car, by which I mean the velocity *between each of its stops*, would be six times as fast as that of the latter, and the energy which it would impart to either a pebble or a pedestrian that got in its way would be correspondingly greater and sadder.

I was feeling very happy over this analysis of the situation, knowing as I did that when a thing's velocity increased it gained in energy, when suddenly all my happiness vanished and I spent a most perplexed and disconsolate half hour. For it came over me that while the velocity of the step varied with its frequency, the energy of a moving thing varies not with the velocity itself but with the velocity squared. It was such an oversight as only a child would make, and my chagrin and humiliation were bitter indeed. And then suddenly I was all right again, for I bethought me of a perfectly obvious fact that I had completely forgotten to take account of, the fact, namely, that the *mass* of the leg and foot of the stepper varied directly with the length of his step or inversely with its frequency. The tiny leg and foot of Harriet, for example, were one-sixth the mass of her father's, Hal's were a half, and Harry's were a third of that mass; therefore, the energy mv^2 will increase with the *first* power of v because the other power of v will be neutralized, so to speak, by the decrease of the mass m. Thus, if we call Henry's energy in each step mv^2 and if we bear in mind that the mass factor in Harriet's step is $\frac{1}{6}m$, in Harry's $\frac{1}{3}m$, and in Hal's $\frac{1}{2}m$, then Harriet's energy will be symbolized by $\frac{1}{6}m\ (6v)^2 = 6mv^2$; Harry's will be $\frac{1}{3}m\ (3v)^2 = 3mv^2$; and Hal's will be $\frac{1}{2}m\ (2v)^2 = 2mv^2$; and in general the "step-energy" of any member of the family will be $\frac{1}{\text{nu}}\, m\ (\text{nu} \cdot v)^2 = \text{nu} \cdot mv^2$.

Up to now we have not spoken directly of the energy of Henry's steps. Whether from an old-fashioned conjugal piety or from some special difficulty, real or imagined, Mrs H. never measured the energy of her husband's steps as contained in the pebbles that he kicked. But, if she had, she would of course have found them in agreement with the general formula:

$$e = h\text{nu}.$$

And as in Henry's case nu = 1, his step-energy was *h* times 1, or simply *h*. In short, when *energy* is multiplied by *time*, and *time* is 1/nu, and nu is 1, then the product of *energy* and *time* is the same as—or is measured by the same number as—the energy itself. Of Henry we may say that his *energy* and his *action* were the same thing, namely *h*. Now, it is all very well to call Henry's step-energy *h* and to note that the step-energies of the members of his family were all discrete multiples of that energy, nu, the discrete multipler, being the frequency which determined the velocity which determined the energy of movement within each step. But we must also remember that Henry's energy, like all energies, can be expressed as one-half the product of a mass and the square of its velocity. Hence, we can call Henry's step-energy not only *h* but $\frac{1}{2}mv^2$; and we must ask what is the *m* and what is the v^2 which, when multiplied together and divided by 2, are equal to *h*. The mass factor is, of course, the mass of Henry's leg and foot, and we will not bother about that just yet, as it pertains too exclusively to the secondary details of our story. But the v^2 is more important because it is the square of the velocity of a step *whose internal speed is critical in any given system of measurements*, being the speed of the step of a person who takes but a single step in each unit of time.

My fable has been long, but its application can be very brief. The H. family, or rather the steps taken by its members, are of course the fictional analogue of the family of light waves which range in length and frequency from the longest of the radio waves to the shortest of the gamma waves. They all travel at the same constant velocity, which is, however, not 6 feet a second, but 300,000 km a second.

The pebbles that were kicked off the ground and that received and registered the energy of the stepper who kicked them are the electrons that are knocked off the photoelectric screen with a velocity that embodies the energy of the impinging light waves. As Mrs. H. in the fable measured the energy of the pebbles—and, hence, of the steps which caused their motion—by her "contraption," so does the physicist, by compelling the electrons to pass through his magnetic and electrostatic fields, succeed in measuring *their* energy and, hence, indirectly the energy of the light waves which caused their motion. Corresponding to Henry with his six-foot steps there is a potential light wave whose frequency would be one a second, whose length would be 300,000 km and whose energy would be the real h as the energy of Henry's step was the fictitious h. There is nothing intrinsically peculiar about this wave as such, but in our system of measurements it is most peculiar because its energy will figure as the mysterious unit of which the energy of all other waves will be discrete multiples, as expressed in the famous equation $e = \text{nu} \cdot h$.

The energy of the standard or unit wave will be $\frac{1}{2} M \left(\frac{C}{1-R}\right)^2$, where C is, of course, the velocity of light, R the resting-time of such a wave, $(1-R)$ its going-time, and consequently $\frac{C}{1-R}$ its internal velocity.

As for the mass factor, M, it would be a real but periodically intermittent condensation (186,000 miles long) of the ether that was dear to Queen Victoria and her subjects. But if anyone thinks that it would be better to describe this real but regularly intermittent mass-factor in a light wave as a periodically recurrent non-Euclidean warp in space or space-time, he is welcome to do so.

My theory can be summed up as follows: All light waves have the same *external velocity* or speed of propagation, but each of them has an *internal velocity*, and hence an internal energy, that is different for different waves, being proportionate to the frequency or shortness of the waves in question. The validity of this conception rests upon my fundamental hypothesis that a light wave is analogous to the step of a man walking in a certain manner, in that its total period is divided into a *resting-time* which intervenes between the successive steps or pulses of propagation, and a *going-time* in which the *internal velocity* of the pulse or step passes from zero to its maximum and back to zero. The greater the frequency of a wave per second, the greater the number of its resting periods *during* that second and the less the time that is left in which to do its traveling, and hence the faster it must go if it is not to drop behind. In short, if a wave of frequency nu is to keep up in the procession with all waves, and in particular with a standard wave whose frequency is one per second, its individual pulses will have to go nu times as fast as those of the standard wave. Its average *internal velocity* will thus be measured by its frequency, and its resulting energy will equal one-half the product of its *internal velocity* squared and its mass. But if the mass-factor of a wave does itself vary inversely with its frequency, which was our assumption, then its energy will be equal, not to the second power, but to the first power of its frequency multiplied by the energy of the standard wave. If Planck's mysterious constant *h* is simply the energy of the standard electromagnetic wave of unit frequency, then the energy of any other wave will be nu times *h*. My assumption that the mass-factor varies inversely with the frequency and directly with the length of a wave is not an arbitrary one, because the shorter the wave, the less the volume of spatial field that undergoes the periodic concentration or warpage that constitutes the mass-factor of a wave. Our theory suggests the curious possibility of there being a quantum, or something analogous to it, in every system of waves.

Having now stated my interpretation of the nature of *h* and the reason for the equation $e = h \cdot \mathrm{nu}$, I turn to the second of the three problems of the quantum.

II. The Reconciliation of the Undulatory and the Corpuscular Aspects of Radiation

Something happens within an atom, and immediately there is emitted from it radiant energy which travels away from its source with a velocity of 300,000 km per second. These units of radiation possess many of the characteristics of waves or periodic changes. Not only do they seem to be of different length and frequency and to travel always at the same rate, regardless of the motion of their source, but they exhibit the phenomenon of interference, counteracting and enhancing one another. Now, if a wave goes out in all directions from its source, we can think of it as spread over the surface of a sphere, a sphere that is expanding with the speed of light. One would suppose that the intensity of such a wave should vary inversely with the square of its distance from its source. Covering a larger and larger area as its distance grows, there will naturally be less and less of it for each unit of area. Sooner or later a physicist will hold up a photoelectric screen and tap this wave to test its energy. The source of the wave may be at the other end of his laboratory or at the other end of the Milky Way, but in either case the entire energy that issued from the atom will be instantly mobilized from all over the spherical surface of the advancing wave and delivered intact to the electron whose movement will record the transaction and the amount received. Now, when one tries to think of this instantaneous reconcentration of energy, imagination is challenged and reason baffled to an extent unparalleled in the history of science. Sir William Bragg has aptly compared the situation to one in which a wave is aroused by a log dropped into the water and spreads out for miles in an ever-widening circle of ever-diminishing intensity. Finally this ripple comes into contact at one point of its vast circumference with another log, and suddenly reassembling all its scattered energies, shoots it up into the air with a force as great as that possessed by the original log which far away and hours ago had started the process.

Confronted with such a paradox, we tend to abandon the conception of light or radiation as consisting of *waves* at all. The fact that distance has no effect on the energy suggests that light is composed of some kind of corpuscles. If that were so, we could understand how these corpuscular elements of radiation, being unretarded by friction, could maintain unchanged their velocity and therefore their energy throughout any distance. As to the fact that, while their energy does not depend upon their nearness to the source, it does depend upon their shortness or frequency—we might at least hope to interpret that as due to discrete differences in the mass of such corpuscles. The so-called shorter light elements might, for example, contain proportionately larger multiples of some ultimate unit of radiant mass. What we call the *intensity* of the radiation or the brightness of light would then be purely a *group-phenomenon* due to the number of corpuscles that in a unit of time impinged on a unit of surface. And this number would vary inversely as the square of the distance, as intensity or brightness should do. From such a theory it would follow as a corollary that the intensity of light would be increased either by increasing the number of radiating units at the source or by lessening the distance of the recipient from the source; and the effect of such increased intensity upon the photoelectric screen would be what as a fact we find it to be, namely, an increase in the *number* of electrons shot off and not an increase in their *velocity*.

The corpuscular theory, however, while thus capable of explaining many of the properties of radiant energy, still appears incapable of explaining such ineradicably undulatory properties as interference of radiations with one another and the continuity of their incidence upon a receiving surface such as the lens of a telescope. If light consisted of separate corpuscles, their increased distance from one another as they diverged or scattered from their center of origin (like a charge of bird shot from a gun) should become sufficiently great to make its effect appreciable in the form of gaps or discontinuities to an observer who was as far from some of the observed stars as we are. But though such an effect has been looked for, it has not been found. Light from the most distant sources preserves its continuity of frontal surface just as little waves would and just as little corpuscles wouldn't and couldn't.

There is, moreover, against this corpuscular theory another objecion, which is interesting in itself and which possesses at least an *ad hominem* force. *If light were composed of corpuscles, either the Ritz Hypothesis would be true or else the Doppler effect would be a one-way affair and would reveal to us an Absolute Motion expressed as an empirical difference between the situation in which a luminous source moves toward an observer, and the reverse situation in which the observer moves toward the luminous source.* For in the latter case, we should meet the light corpuscles with more force than if we stayed still, and thus be able to observe an increase of their energy as a Doppler shift toward the violet. But if the light-giving object was moving toward us, and if the speed of the corpuscles emitted by it was unaffected by the speed of their source, they would reach us in greater *number* per unit of time but not with greater individual *velocities*. And thus the photoelectric screen would fail to register any shift toward the violet. The only way to lay the specter of Absolute Motion would be to accept Ritz's Hypothesis that, light being corpuscular, its velocity, like the velocity of an ordinary projectile, varies with the velocity of its source. It would *then* make no difference whether we moved faster toward the corpuscles or whether they moved faster toward us. The shift toward the violet would in the two cases be equally observable in the increased energy of the individual electrons that were knocked off the photoelectric screen. But this way of restoring symmetry to the Doppler effect would be spurned by most physicists and astronomers. For, whether they are Einsteinian Relativists or Newtonian Classicists, they appear to agree in believing that De Sitter's deductions from the observations of double stars, as well as certain recent observations of the aberration of light from distant nebulae, are conclusive disproof of the assumption that the velocity of light varies with the velocity of the source. To all believers in Einstein's Special Theory of Relativity the implications of the corpuscular theory for the Doppler effect should have a fatally decisive though *ad hominem* force. For, in accepting the corpuscular theory, they would have to couple their acceptance either with a belief in the Ritz Hypothesis or with a belief in Absolute Motion.

The whole situation is, in a sense, desperate. And desperate situations call for desperate remedies. One such remedy is characterized by Sir Arthur Eddington as the Sweepstake Theory. The situation that leads to the theory and the theory itself are set forth by him in *The Nature of the Physical World*, from which I quote the following passages: [3]

[3] Eddington, Sir Arthur Stanley, *The Nature of the Physical World*, New York, The Macmillan Company, 1928, pages 185–190.

"The pursuit of the quantum leads to many surprises; but probably none is more outrageous to our preconceptions than the regathering of light and other radiant energy into *h* units, when all the classical pictures show it to be dispersing more and more. Consider the light-waves which are the result of a single emission by a single atom on the star Sirius. These bear away a certain amount of energy endowed with a certain period and the product of the two is *h*. The period is carried by the waves without change, but the energy spreads out in an ever-widening circle. Eight years and nine months after the emission, the wave-front is due to reach the earth. A few minutes before the arrival some person takes it into his head to go out and admire the glories of the heavens and—in short—to stick his eye in the way. The light-waves when they started could have had no notion what they were going to hit; for all they knew they were bound on a journey through endless space, as most of their colleagues were. Their energy would seem to be dissipated beyond recovery over a sphere of 50 billion (10^{12}) miles radius—How is it managed? Do the ripples striking the eye send a message round to the back part of the wave saying, 'We have found an eye, let's all crowd into it!'. . . . Suppose that the light-waves are of such intensity that, instead of each atom absorbing one millionth of a quantum one atom out of every million absorbs a whole quantum. That whole quanta are absorbed is shown by the photoelectric experiments already described.

"It would seem that what the light-waves were really bearing within reach of each atom was not a millionth of a quantum but a millionth chance of securing a whole quantum. The wave-theory of light pictures and describes something evenly distributed over the whole wave-front which has usually been identified with energy. Owing to well-established phenomena such as interference and diffraction it seems impossible to deny this uniformity, but we must give it another interpretation; it is a uniform *chance of energy*. Following the rather old-fashioned definition of energy as 'capacity for doing work' the waves carry over their whole front a uniform chance of doing work. It is the propagation of a chance which the wave-theory studies."

Now, there are two objections to this Sweepstake Theory. First, there is the one which Eddington himself goes on to state, but which I take the liberty of presenting in my own words. How does it happen that the first atom to touch the expanding spherical surface of probability-waves always draws the winning ticket and receives the prize of actual energy? If a conjurer on the stage threw out over the heads of his audience a scattering pack of cards, and if the member of the audience who caught the first card, regardless of where he was sitting, always found it to be the ace of spades, we should have to draw one of two conclusions. Either the conjurer had this man "planted" in the theater as a confederate and knew just where he was sitting, or else every card in the pack was an ace of spades. The latter conclusion would be barred out by making sure (as we actually do) that the conjurer had only one of the prize-winning aces in each pack that he threw out. The other conclusion as to the presence of a confederate would remain. And it would have its analogue in the fascinating but ultra-quixotic theory of Gilbert Lewis, that an atom cannot muster up courage to emit a vibration until it knows exactly where and when that vibration will be received. The recipient scientist with his eye or his photoelectric screen may be trillions of miles away in space and not due to be born for hundreds of years after the light issues from the star. But, according to the Special Theory of Relativity, in the case of a light ray, the spatial and temporal distances cancel one another, $ds^2 - dt^2 = 0$; and between the start and the finish of the ray, there is a kind of contact in space-time, a mystical *rapport,* which is the basis for Lewis' feeling that the atom must "know" where its light will land before it emits it. I do not know what Lewis would say to the case of a physicist who, having read his theory, decided to thwart destiny and instead of holding up his photoelectric screen at the time and place he had intended before reading should decide to leave the date and location to be determined by the throw of dice. I should think Lewis would have to say of such a situation that fate could not be thus circumvented, and that the prophetic insight of the atom in the distant galaxy would have been so keen that it would have forseen or seen through the reading of Lewis' book by the scientist, the casting of the dice, and their resulting configuration determining the time and place of the electronic recipient of the light—despite the fact that all these events happened "after" the light had been irrevocably started on its journey. Now, notwithstanding my friendship and high respect for Gilbert Lewis, I must really ask to be excused from believing this. If it is true, as Lewis believes, that such an absurdity is actually implied by Einstein's Special Theory, then all I can say is, "So much the worse for the Special Theory."

But even if we waive this objection to the Sweepstake analogy, we are immediately confronted with another: What is to become of all the other chances of energy that have been propagated from the atom after the winning chance has been actualized? Lottery tickets that have been declared unsuccessful are at least worth the paper they are printed on and they continue to occupy space, albeit in the scrap baskets of their unsuccessful owners. But these unsuccessful *probabilities* that have been traveling outward with the velocity of 186,000 miles a second and that are dispersed over the surface of the huge sphere have nothing to do and nothing to be. They lapse into absolute nonentity on the instant that the lucky ray conveys its freight of actual energy to the receiving electron.

In view of all this, it seems to me that the Sweepstake Theory completely fails, and that, as Sir William Bragg has so happily phrased it, we are left with the necessity of teaching the classical theory of light on Monday, Wednesday, and Friday and the Quantum Theory on Tuesday, Thursday, and Saturday. Both cannot be, and each must be, true. Such a situation is so outrageous that no one, not even the most extreme positivist or empiricist can "take it lying down." Anyone who has in the veins of his mind a single drop of the red blood of reason must demand satisfaction in the form of some conception of what it is that is really happening to produce these seemingly incompatible sets of appearances.

When doctors disagree or fail to cure, there is a chance for the quack to peddle his nostrum; and as a poor but honest quack, I want now to proffer my nostrum. At worst, it will do no harm.

Let us suppose that the mysterious entity that issues from an atom is a condensation in the ether (or a non-Euclidean warp of "space") that is shaped like a cone but with so slender an angle of divergence as to approximate a cylinder, and that it moves outward from the atom at the speed of light. The path of this movement or the volume generated by it is a conical sector of a sphere whose center is the center of the nucleus of the initiating atom and whose base or advancing frontal surface is as distant as may be. The movement outward through the volume of this expanding cone is a periodic movement. It is the movement of an advancing wave. I shall assume that this movement consists of progressively alternating "twist-thrusts" like those of a corkscrew—clockwise, then counterclockwise, then clockwise, then counterclockwise, and so on.

Perhaps I can bring my idea more clearly to your minds if I simply ask you to picture a long, slender cone cut transversely into sections of equal length but remaining *in situ*, that is: as they were before they were cut. Paint these sections alternately black and white and think of their contact surfaces as possessing a cog-like mechanism such that shortly after the right-hand or clockwise twist-thrust of one completes itself there will begin a counterclockwise twist-thrust in the next. Then imagine the series of periodic and alternating twist-thrusts to start from the apex of the cone and travel outward, and the thing that you would see advancing outward and expanding as it went along and through the whole cone would be the kind of thing that according to my hypothesis a light-wave is—a thing that would wriggle or worm or *squirm* its way through space at a velocity of 186,000 miles a second. Let us call the light wave as thus conceived a "squirm." Squirms could be of various lengths, as light-waves are; and while the speed of the procession as a whole would be the same, irrespective of the length or correlated frequencies of the constituent squirms, the *internal velocity* of each squirm (which is the measure of its energy) would vary inversely with its length and directly with its frequency. For, just as in the family of steppers in the fable with which my paper began, the total period of each squirm would be divided into a *going-time* and a *resting-time*. The shorter the squirm, the greater the number of its resting periods and, hence, the faster it would have to go during the time when it was going. And, as the mass of a squirm varies inversely with its *internal velocity*, the internal energy or mv^2 of the squirm varies directly only with the first power of that velocity, which is in turn determined by its frequency and will, therefore, be expressed by multiplying its frequency, nu, by a constant. That constant is h, which is the unit energy of the standard or critical squirm which in our system of metrical units has a length of 300,000 kilometers and a frequency of one per second. All squirms of frequencies greater than one or multiples of one will have energies that are corresponding multiples of *h*.

Now, the foregoing characteristics of the light-squirms as to mass, length, frequency, external velocity, and *internal velocity* are characteristics which they share with all waves.

First, though the mass of any squirm is a function of its length and, hence, remains unchanged no matter how far out from their source squirms of a given length (that of red light, for example) may have traveled, yet the *character* of the mass changes, its density or intensity of concentration decreasing as its volume increases, for it is obvious that the truncated sections of a cone, if they are of constant length, take up more space the further they are from the apex.

Second, a squirm of radiant energy, as I conceive it, will "vibrate" in a direction nearly but not quite perpendicular to its direction of propagation. But this so-called vibration will consist of alternating rotations or twists which will lie in the ever-varying plane of a shallow whorl to which the "ray" or longitudinal dimension of the cone is almost normal. Hence, when a squirm strikes the electron on the photoelectric screen, it will cause it to move off sideways rather than in the line of the light ray.

Third, the advancing front of the squirm will occupy the same proportion of the surface of a sphere at one distance as at another. And a group of squirms going out from a light-emitting center will always remain as adjacent to one another as they were at the start. They will not possess the fatal capacity to scatter that disqualified the corpuscular hypothesis. They will be true waves, and as such they will exhibit the requisite phenomena of undulatory interference, no matter how far from their source. But, at the same time that they preserve their continuity as a group, they will also preserve their quasi-corpuscular discreteness and integrity as individuals. The squirm is not only "big" enough to enter the astronomer's telescope in the way it does, it is also "small" enough to be sucked in by the electron on the photoelectric screen of the physicist. No matter how large its frontal cross-section and the radius of its twist may be, the twist itself will be as much of a single unit as when it was first emitted, and as such can impart all its energy to the electron almost on the instant of contact with the same ease with which a large top could impart its energy of spin to a small object with which it came into fatally intimate contact and in such a way that what was velocity of spin in the giver would become velocity of translation in the receiver.

In short, because of its seemingly harmonious combination of the undulatory characteristics of classic light with the corpuscular characteristics of quantic light, I respectfully nominate my "squirm" as a candidate for the high office of "wavicle," the felicitous name suggested by Eddington for that blend of wave and particle which is the great desideratum for light as known today. It was the reconciliation of these apparently contradictory properties of radiation that constituted the second of our three problems of the Quantum. Let us now turn to the third and last of the puzzles—the nature of the emitting atom, tiny source of all the mischief.

III. The Nature of Atoms and the Manner of Their Discrete but Continuous Emissions

I accept the hypothesis proposed by Professor Louis King and by other physicists that the electrons spin or rotate on their axes. I supplement this hypothesis with the further one that the *protons* also spin, and I propose to employ these hypotheses in a manner that, so far as I am informed, has not been suggested before.

An electric charge in rotation becomes a magnet with a north pole and a south pole. Hence, the spinning protons and electrons are related to one another by magnetic as well as by electrostatic forces. There are, of course, an infinity of angles possible between the axes of any two such spinning particles, but I wish to limit my discussion to the single case in which the axes of spin are exactly, or very nearly, in line. I adopt this limitation partly to avoid unmanageable complexities and partly because I suspect that two spinning charges, freely interacting, would arrive at this configuration sooner or later whatever might have been the initial inclination of their axes in relation to one another. Observing this limitation, we can picture our pair of spinning particles with their axes end to end or like a pair of spinning tops one above the other; and there would then appear to be four different situations to be taken account of:

(1) Two particles of dissimilar electric charge with similar magnetic poles adjacent.

(2) Two particles of dissimilar electric charge with dissimilar magnetic poles adjacent.

(3) Two particles of similar electric charge with similar magnetic poles adjacent.

(4) Two particles of similar electric charge with dissimilar magnetic poles adjacent.

These situations may be symbolized thus:

	S		N		S		S		N		N
	—		—		+		—		+		—
	N		S		N		N		S		S
1	N	2	N	3	N	or	N	4	N	or	N
	+		+		+		—		+		—
	S		S		S		S		S		S

In analyzing these four situations, there is a most important principle which we must keep before our minds: *When the dimensions of two magnets are negligibly small in comparison to the distance between them, the magnetic force, whether of attraction or repulsion, varies inversely not with the second power but with the third power of the distance of the magnets from one another.*

Inasmuch as the *electrostatic* force of attraction or repulsion varies inversely with the *square* of the distance, it follows that for our particles, which are both charges and magnets, the electrostatic force will be the dominant determiner of behavior at relatively large distances (the magnetic force diminishing more rapidly with increase of distance than the electric), while at relatively small distances the magnetic force will be the dominant determiner of behavior, for it will increase more rapidly than the electric force with the decrease of distance; and finally, *when the electric force is attractive and the magnetic force is repulsive*, there will be a critical distance at which the two forces will balance.

In the light of these facts, we can see at once that in situation number 4 the two protons or electrons, if by themselves and uncemented by a third particle of opposite charge between them, will repel one another and execute an unending reciprocal retreat; for they would ordinarily never have a chance to get near enough to have their magnetic attraction dominate their electric repulsion.

In situation number 3, where the two similarly charged particles suffer at all distances a double repulsion, both magnetic and electric, their retreat from one another will be even more obvious.

In situation number 2 we have the reverse of number 3. Instead of suffering a double repulsion, the dissimilar electric charges with their dissimilar magnetic poles adjacent will enjoy a double attraction and will cuddle close into a nuclear nest.

We now turn to situation number 1, which is by far the most interesting of the four that are listed in the diagram. Here we have two particles with dissimilar charges but with similar magnetic poles adjacent. We have already remarked that such a blend of electric attraction and magnetic repulsion means that when the distance separating the particles is great, the electric force will predominate and the particles will converge; but when the distance is small, the reverse will be true, magnetic force will predominate and the particles will diverge. Between the "great" distances and the "small" distances there will, however, be an intermediate distance at which the opposed tendencies will just balance. In the hydrogen atom, for example, with its single proton as nucleus and its single "planetary" electron, there will be a critical distance between proton and electron, at which magnetic repulsion will equal the electrostatic attraction. Representing this critical distance by D, the magnetic force by Fm, and the electrostatic force by Fe, we have:

$$\frac{Fm}{D^3} = \frac{Fe}{D^2}, Fm = D \,.\, Fe, D = \frac{Fm}{Fe}.$$

If by some external influence the distance of the electron from the nucleus is made longer, the magnetic repulsive force will decrease more rapidly than the electrostatic attractive force, and therefore the electron will tend to snap back inward. If, on the other hand, the distance is made shorter, the magnetic repulsion will increase more rapidly than the electric attraction and the electron will tend to snap back outward. The two elements of the system, united as they are by their diverse forces, will constitute a sort of coiled spring such as one finds in chairs and sofas. It will offer resistance both to compression or shortening and to expansion or lengthening. This resistance will be as gentle as you please for slight changes in either direction, and proportionately stronger for greater changes.

I wish now to pass from these deductions from my primary hypothesis and to propose certain further and secondary hypotheses. I make these subsidiary hypotheses or guesses very diffidently and in the hope that if some or even all of them should prove to be not good, they may nevertheless suggest to those more competent than myself hypotheses that will be good.

First, then, let us suppose that the proton-electron system above described can vibrate in halves, thirds, quarters, fifths, and so forth, of its length. Such vibrations we will call its "tones." And we will assume further that the system can entertain, at least for a time, several or all of them simultaneously, as a superposed hierarchy of periodic motions.

Second, let us suppose that that which in the first section of our discussion we called the "internal velocity" of the step or wave varies (when *within* the spring) *not inversely but directly* with the length of the step or wave. Thus when the spring was vibrating in thirds, the *internal velocity* of those vibrations would be as much greater than the *internal velocity* of vibrations that were fourths as one-third is greater than one-fourth, and in general that the *internal velocities* of vibrations whose lengths were $1/n$ and $1/(n+r)$ would be to one another as $1/n$ is to $1/(n+r)$. This is not so arbitrary a supposal as it might seem, for it is certainly true that the further you jam down (or stretch up) a coiled spring, the harder and faster it will fly back. The greater the length of the periodic displacement, the greater the velocity of return.

Third, let us suppose that the mass factor in these periodic movements does not vary directly with the length and inversely with the internal speed, as in the case of the light waves outside the atom, which we discussed previously, but that it is *constant.* It will be as though the mass of the whole system entered into each and all of its vibrations.

Now let us examine the implications of our supposals or postulates. We notice that if the atom be conceived as a spiral spring, its vibrations are in their lengths and velocities

$$1/1,\ 1/2,\ 1/3,\ \ldots$$

which means that the energies of these vibrations will be the products of a mass factor, M_p, characteristic of the spring itself, and the squares of the several velocities; thus:

$$E = \tfrac{1}{2} M_p \cdot \left\{(1/1)^2,\ (1/2)^2,\ (1/3)^2\right\}.$$

These energies will travel in both directions, up and down the spring, from the nucleus out to the electron, and back in from the electron to the nucleus. Now any one of these vibrations, if left to itself, would go like a shuttlecock between two battledores, peaceably outward and back through the spring forever. There would be no friction to slow it down and no way for it to *get out*. But when one vibration meets or overtakes another of a different length and rate—what then? Well, if the interference occurred within the atom, that is, between the nucleus and the electron, I suppose that they would pass right through each other as proper waves do, and be none the worse for it, their integrities remaining unscathed by their transitory union. Perhaps one of Maxwell's demons, if he lived in the atom, might hear some beats or difference-tones, but that would be all. Nothing would get to the ears of the outside world. But now suppose that their interference occurred at the electronic terminus of the trip. The vibration $1/n$ just arriving meets the vibration $1/(n+r)$ which is just starting back. The electron which constitutes the outer end of the spring cannot accommodate the two vibrations by moving in opposite directions at the same instant. The situation is serious, and, so far as I can see, the lesser vibration, whose energy was $\tfrac{1}{2} M_p \cdot \left(\frac{1}{n+r}\right)^2$, would neutralize such part of the stronger vibration as was equal to itself, leaving an unneutralized remainder whose energy would be equal to $\frac{1}{2} M_p \cdot \left\{\frac{1}{n^2} - \frac{1}{(n+r)^2}\right\}$. This remainder, a sort of "difference-tone," would have nothing to do but *slip off into space*, as a new-born squirm or light wave, and go on about its business. The energy of the young squirm, like that of any squirm, would be equal to Planck's constant, *h*, multiplied by its own frequency, nu. But as witness to the values of its parents of whose unhappy union it was the fruit, its energy would also be equal to $\frac{1}{2} M_p \cdot \left\{\frac{1}{n^2} - \frac{1}{(n+r)^2}\right\}$, where n and r are any positive integers.[4] The factor M_p would have just the value that was necessary to make $h \cdot nu$, the "difference-tone," equal to the *difference between* the two "tones," $\frac{1}{n}$ and $\frac{1}{n+r}$, from which it originated. And that value would be characteristic of the type of atom emitting the radiation. From these considerations we can see that a light wave coming from an atom is not merely a member of the general tribe of squirms, but also a member of a special family, as symbolized by the subscript letters in M_p, M_q, M_w, and so forth. That special family in the case we are considering is the group of light waves registering as lines in the spectrum of hydrogen. It is a large family, containing perhaps an infinite number of members. But the members are by no means a continuum composed of all possible values. They have only such values as are represented by the differences between pairs of *terms* in the series.

Let us glance briefly at the prospective history of a squirm such as the one whose birth we have described. It glides out into the ether and swims freely but in the direction determined by the line that joined the proton and

[4] I believe, however, that usually if not always $r = 1$.

electron at the instant of its leaving them. It squirms its way along, with alternating twist-thrusts, at the rate of 186,000 miles a second. Its volume gets larger as it occupies successively the larger and larger truncated sections of the cone which is its path and from whose apex it originated and toward whose infinitely distant base it travels. But this growth in volume is balanced by an equal diminution in density. As it grows bigger, it becomes more and more tenuous, with the result that since its length and *internal velocity* do not change, its energy and mass also remain constant.

There are two alternative destinies in store for every squirm: one, ignominious and tragic, the other happy if not glorious. The ignominious fate that may befall a squirm is to be swallowed by an electron and utilized as food to give the electron energy of translation. In having its own periodic motion thus transformed into the electron's motion of translation, its specific structural identity is permanently lost and only its quantity is conserved—destined perhaps to be measured by a scientist if the devouring electron is located on a photoelectric screen. Let us suppose, however, that the squirm escapes this death by absorption. In the course of its travels it will meet with various atoms. In some of these atoms the defining constant, M_q or M_w (differing from its own defining constant, M_p), will be such that no product of the form:

$$\frac{1}{2} M_{q}, \cdot_{w} \left\{ \frac{1}{n^2} - \frac{1}{(n+r)^2} \right\}$$

will be equal to:

$$\frac{1}{2} M_p \left\{ \frac{1}{n^2} - \frac{1}{(n+r)^2} \right\},$$

or the particular value of $h \cdot nu$, which is the energy measure of the squirm in question. Atoms of this kind will neither absorb and devour our squirm, nor will they welcome him. He will be courteously turned away, and transmitted or simply reflected by them. Some day, however, he may have the luck to meet with an atom of his own family, a hydrogen atom, one line in whose spectrum belongs to him. It will be then that he will have recourse to his birth-certificate and recall that he is not merely *h · nu* but also and equally:

$$\tfrac{1}{2} M_p \left\{ \frac{1}{n^2} - \frac{1}{(n+r)^2} \right\}.$$

As such, he will enter the atom by the same type of door as that through which he came out, and be peacefully transmuted from a "difference-tone" into two "terms" or "tones" *whose difference in energy is equal to what his energy was.*

In short, atoms *give* light of a definite wave-length and frequency represented by a definite line in the spectrum by *synthesizing* their internal and self-contained vibrations, "terms" or "tones," and emitting a "difference-tone." They *receive* light waves by *analyzing* a "difference-tone" (when it can be so analyzed) into two of their own tones. Emission is a case of

$$\tfrac{1}{2} M_{p, q, w} \cdots \left\{ \frac{1}{n^2} - \frac{1}{(n+r)^2} \right\}$$

becoming *h · nu*. Reception is a case of this process reversed.

Let us conclude with some reflections upon atoms other than hydrogen, in the light of our theory of an atom as a sort of spiral spring constituted by the balance at a critical distance of two forces, a magnetic repulsion varying inversely as the third power and an electrostatic attraction varying inversely as the second power—these forces to obtain between and to originate from a positively charged and predominantly protonic nucleus that spins one way, and an oppositely situated negatively charged and exclusively electronic "planet" (or "planets") spinning the same way. By "oppositely situated" I mean, as previously stated, that a line joining the centers of the nucleus and any "planet" would be perpendicular (or more or less nearly perpendicular) to the planes of their respective rotations. The clumsy guardedness of the above statement is necessary to make the definition fit not merely the special and limitingly simple case of the hydrogen atom, but the general class of cases exemplified by the other atoms, from helium to uranium.

With the protons and electrons acting alternately as a sort of cement for one another, various nuclear structures would be possible. The structure of the alpha-particle or helium nucleus seems to be the most stable; and for that reason it is an apparently universal element in all complex atomic nuclei. Such complex nuclei containing both electrons and protons might exemplify different directions of spin, but one of these directions would probably predominate. There would then be a critical distance for as many "planetary" electrons as were needed to make good the electronic deficit in the nucleus, which deficit defines the atomic number. The planetary electrons could not, however, all occupy the same position. They would push one another somewhat away and take their places on a shell or plane that was curved like the surface of a *parachute*. With respect to them the nuclear center would occupy a position analogous to that of the man hanging from the parachute. There might be several such shells, one beyond the other, and except in the case of hydrogen they would probably be located on both sides of the nucleus. The whole structure would thus resemble an *hourglass*. Between the nucleus and each of the outside electrons there would exist the same sort of spring-like balance of forces as we found in the hydrogen atom. "Tones" and the "difference-tones" that were emitted and absorbed would also exist in the same way. And each atom would thus have its series of spectral lines different from, but on the same generic plan as, that of hydrogen.

If the ordinary light waves, together with the infrared, the ultraviolet, and perhaps the X rays, are to be accounted for by the vibrations passing between the nucleus and the outlying or so-called planetary electrons, what provision does our hypothesis make for those very short waves such as the gamma radiation which appears to have an exclusively intranuclear origin? So little is known about the detailed structure of the nucleus that even the most tentative answer to such a question may seem hardly worth while. We do know, however, that the protons are for some reason nearly two thousand times the mass of the electrons, and we know also that there are no atoms with negative atomic numbers; in other words, every close-packed or nuclear configuration of protons and electrons contains an excess of the former. It may be that this excess of protons over electrons in the nucleus is due to the fact that the greater inertia of two protons would cause them to separate less rapidly in response to their electrostatic repulsion than a pair of equally repellent electrons, and that it would thus be easier for one electron to cement together two protons as in the newly discovered isotope of hydrogen, or two electrons to bind together four protons as in the ubiquitous alpha-particle, than for a larger number of electrons to be cemented by a smaller number of protons. In any event, on our hypothesis of the protons and electrons as spinning and as being therefore not merely electrostatic but also magnetic, there would be spring-like balances of repulsion and attraction *within* the nucleus as well as *between* the nucleus and the outlying electrons. And from the vibrations within these purely intra-nuclear "springs," there might proceed as "difference-tones" the gamma rays and possibly even the cosmic rays.

Although the exigencies of recent quantum theories have

required the abandonment of the attractively simple model of the older Rutherford-Bohr atom, yet, unless I am greatly mistaken, the relatively unpicturable conceptions of the atom today involve in some form the original notion of the separate orbits (with their resulting separate energy-levels) in which the electrons revolve, giving forth their discrete bundles of radiant energy by jumping from one orbit to another. Now, it was surely bad enough that the chemists should have been forced to abandon the static type of atom which, as chemists, they would naturally prefer, in favor of the dynamic type which physics appeared to necessitate. And when to that disadvantage there had to be added, by reason of the Quantum phenomena, the intolerably arbitrary conception of orbits, separated from one another like *grooves*, between which the electrons must choose with no possibility of intermediate paths, the burden upon belief became almost too great to be borne. Let us, then, remember that, apart from the purely sentimental analogy with the solar system (which for all its unworthy irrelevance may not have been lacking in an unconscious psychological effectiveness), the only reason for making the outlying electrons revolve around their positively charged nucleus was to keep them from falling into it. If it is possible by such a hypothesis as I have advanced to explain through a balance of magnetic repulsion and electric attraction the existence of electrons held at arm's length from their nucleus without the necessity of preserving their distance by the centrifugal force of planetary revolution—is that not an advantage? And if the static atom can then not only be revived, but be revived in such a form that its discretely quantic radiation can be accounted for as the "difference-tones" or terminal interferences of the various waves which, like the tones and overtones of a musical string, would run to and fro over the spring-like *field* connecting nucleus and electrons, is that not a further advantage of sufficient promise to extenuate the crime of a layman in venturing with amateur conceptions into regions where, until further facts are known, even experts fear to tread?

I conclude these highly speculative suggestions with four still more speculative corollaries in the form of queries.

(1) Is it not possible that the wave-like behavior of particles, not only electrons and protons, but even atoms and molecules, could be explained by their postulated spins which would undergo periodic retardation and acceleration on contact with obstructions such as screens and gratings?

(2) Is it not possible that the puzzlingly excessive radiation of the stars is caused by clashes between their intrinsically spinning corpuscles rather than (as is currently supposed) by a destruction of their mass through a suicidal proto-electronic amalgamation?

(3) Knowing, as we do, that alpha and beta particles are expelled with enormous velocities from the nuclei of radioactive atoms, is it not possible, and even probable, that these velocities have their source in a primal energy of spin on the part of the corpuscles composing the nucleus? For, when rapidly rotating particles come in contact with one another, part of their energy of rotation is changed into energy of translation. Contacts of this violently disruptive type might well be periodically recurrent and would certainly be more noticeably frequent in the massive, complicated, and therefore presumably unstable nuclei of radium and uranium.

(4) If a light wave or squirm consisting of alternating twist-thrusts were to encounter an obstacle that would neither transmit nor reflect it, but simply stopped it from going forward, absorbing the energy of its thrust without impairing the energy of its twist, would not the wave then become a particle—electron or positron, according to its direction of twist, when stopped? Such particles would

seem to differ from the waves from which they originated (and into which, when the circumstances were reversed, they could return) only in this: that a twist which loses its forward thrust must continue its twisting and become a stationary spinning particle; while, conversely, a twist that acquired a thrust must spend itself by *inducing* a counter twist or twist-thrust directly in front of where it was, and so become an advancing wave.

L'Envoi

A "stepper," a "squirm," and a "spiral spring"—
Those were the gifts he wanted to bring
And concerning their nature he wanted to sing.
(A philosopher's fancy must have its fling.)

BUT

Do they fit the facts like a truthful thing—
His STEPPER *and* SQUIRM *and* SPIRAL SPRING—
Or are they nothing but ting-a-ling-ling?

10

A THEORY OF TIME PERCEPTION[1]

An attempt to explain the paradox of the "specious present," that is, the appearance at each present instant in time of a segment of the past, by the hypothesis of a limiting differential ratio of the velocity of change of the field of consciousness as a whole to the velocity of change of its several components. Some implications and applications of this hypothesis are developed. Some knowledge of psychology and mathematics is presupposed.

I. The Specious Present

The first question to be faced in a study of time perception is the question of the "specious present"; for without the consciousness of an extended segment, or period, of past time, it would be impossible to perceive either duration or succession. This problem of the specious present is not only the most important, it is also the most perplexing of the many problems of our time consciousness. It is a case in which sense perception presents as an actuality what reason must regard as an impossibility. The present of metaphysical or conceptual time is a point, separating past and future; the present of psychological time—the specious present—is a continuous segment extending appreciably into the past. We cannot hope to solve this antinomy by violating reason; we must not accept the presence of what is no longer present as a

[1] Reprinted from *The American Journal of Psychology*, Vol. XV, No. 1, Jan. 1904, pp. 1–13.

reality. Sense must be subordinated to reason, and the specious present must be regarded as specious, as an illusion which is somehow explicable on the assumption that the real present is a point. The problem may then be stated as follows:

How is it that at any one moment there can appear to be present several moments?

II. The Measurement of Time

Time is the form of change, and the amount of change is the measure of the time which is perceived to have elapsed during the change, precisely as the size of a body is the measure of the space actually or possibly filled by the body. Taken in abstraction from all content, space and time, if not nothing, are at least quite without determinate form and size. As space and time are measured by what fills them, so, too, is the concrete filling measured by comparison with other concrete filling. A body is large or small according to the smallness or largeness of a second body selected as the standard of measure. A change is great or small according to its relation to some other change which we take as a basis of comparison. Magnitude, whether conceptual or perceptual, is intrinsically relative.

III. The Subjective and Objective Aspects of a Psychosis [2]

Every psychosis has two distinguishable but inseparable aspects, the subjective and the objective. The subjective element, or "knowing thought," is the whole system of conscious contents taken collectively and including the incoming content, while the latter is the *object* of the (normally prospective) act of attention. A content is

[2] This word *psychosis* is not used in its more recent sense to designate a diseased condition of mind, but in its earlier sense meaning any momentary state of mind or state of consciousness.

perceived as an object only in so far as it is projected upon a subjective background of pre-existing states. In Herbartian terms, we may describe every psychosis as the assimilation of an entering sensation-mass by a receiving apperception-mass.

I believe that the solution of the problem of the specious present depends on our realizing that the subjective and objective elements of a psychosis possess differing rates of change.

What is sometimes called the "Law of Relativity" is an expression of the fact that in consciousness every content is determined not only by its stimulus, but also by every other content. A change in one state is necessarily attended by a change in the other states, both individually and collectively. If we are right in regarding the knowing thought or subjective aspect of a psychosis as the totality of existing states, considered as forming a system having a single structure, or configuration, it will be clear that the changes induced in the form of that totality by a change in one of its parts will usually be less than the change in that part. In a word, a change in one conscious state produces a change (though a lesser change) in the system of states; and, other things equal, the larger the apperception-mass, the smaller the changes produced in it by the changes in any one of its sensory aspects. The perception of a change is a changing perception, but a perception that changes less rapidly than the change that is perceived.

It cannot be too strongly emphasized in this connection that the increment of change produced in a conscious state—or apperceptive system of states—while it varies directly with the stimulus causing it, also varies inversely with the content in which it is caused. Thus, if s be a conscious state and δs be its increment of change, δs will be large in proportion as s is small. In this respect, and, so far as I can see, in this respect only, do increments of *change* differ from the increments of *substance*, ordinarily considered in the calculus.

There is a second point to which I would especially call the reader's attention before proceeding further. I have spoken, and shall speak throughout, of conscious states as quantities, expressible by quantitative symbols and subject to quantitative laws; nevertheless, these quantitative expressions can be, *and perhaps should be*, interpreted as applying to the *physiological concomitants* of conscious states. The reader who is sensitive on this subject can substitute the physical for the psychical interpretation of the quantitative symbols without changing the meaning of the argument at any point.

Let Δo symbolize the amount of change or alteration in the objective content o produced in any period of time Δt, and let Δs symbolize the resulting change produced in the subjective aspect of consciousness during the same time. Then, $\frac{\Delta o}{\Delta s}$ will represent a change in the objective as compared with the change in the subjective element in the time Δt. As Δt is made to decrease without limit, Δo and Δs will correspondingly decrease; but the fraction $\frac{\Delta o}{\Delta s}$ will not necessarily decrease, but will either approach or, if the rate of change be uniform, maintain the finite value $\frac{do}{ds}$. Now, this derivative of the objective change with regard to the change of the subjective element is a finite quantity, but one that is realized at each infinitesimal moment of time. If we were right in affirming in the preceding section that perceptual space and time magnitudes are essentially relative matters, determined not by the "absolute" size of the magnitude to be measured but by the ratio of that magnitude to the unit of measure, it will be evident that the amount of objective time or change which appears to be present at any one moment will be measured by its ratio to the subjective change which accompanies it. And if the subjective unit of measure be infinitesimal, the objective change-magnitude may also be infinitesimal and yet may *appear* finite. In short, the infinitesimal time-change which occurs at the unextended metaphysical present will be appreciated as an extended psychological present, provided that it be measured in terms of an infinitesimal of different order.

That Δs, the change in the subjective totality of conscious contents, is less or "slower" than Δo, the change in that phase of the totality selected as object by the act of attention, has been shown. Consequently, the symbol $\frac{do}{ds} = \lim_{\Delta t \to o} \left[\frac{\Delta o}{\Delta s} \right] > 1$ may be accepted as properly representative of the "specious" or "extended" present; *and the latter is, from this point of view, seen to be compatible with the real or metaphysical present of conceptual time.*

IV. Duration and Succession

At the outset of our discussion it was stated that the perception of the specious present was prerequisite to the perception of duration and succession. Now, introspection assures us that the specious present never maintains the same value from moment to moment. It is always either expanding or contracting. *But an increase in the specious present means an increase in the period of past time which appears as present, that is to say, an increase in the time during which the events filling it have been perceived.* The objects or events, therefore, which occupy the expanding specious present are felt as "enduring," while, conversely, those that fill the contracting specious present are felt as "passing" or "succeeding." This alternate increase and decrease of $\frac{do}{ds}$ implies, of course, a corresponding alternation in the sign of the second derivative. When an object o is perceived as enduring, $\frac{d^2o}{ds^2}$ is positive; at the moment when o is succeeded and displaced in consciousness by some other object, $\frac{d^2o}{ds^2}$ is negative.

V. "Time Dragging" and "Time Flying"

The second derivative of the objective with regard to the subjective change not only indicates by its *sign* the enduring or passing phase of its contents, but by its *magnitude* it marks the *seeming rate of the time-flow itself.* A small or large change-rate (whether increasive or decreasive) in $\frac{do}{ds}$ means a correspondingly small or large value of $\frac{d^2o}{ds^2}$. In view of the fact previously mentioned that $\frac{s}{o}$ varies as $\frac{do}{ds}$, it is interesting to note that, as might be expected, the first and second derivatives also vary inversely. The longer an event endures, that is, the greater the value of $\frac{do}{ds}$, the less the rate of its change and the less the value of $\frac{d^2o}{ds^2}$. The further past an event seems, the more slowly does it appear to increase in pastness; while, conversely, the events of the present are those which seem to fly by most rapidly.

This would seem to afford a clue to the curious alterations which we experience in the *rate* of time-flow. For it is obvious that when new objects continuously distract the attention, the specious present is constantly being destroyed and made anew; and, as we saw, this enforced smallness of $\frac{do}{ds}$ would mean a correspondingly large value of $\frac{d^2o}{ds^2}$. The seeming rate of the time-flow is great in proportion to the number of new distractions. And, conversely, when the mind is without internal or external distractions, when there is nothing to think about and nothing to do, the specious present, with its single content of *ennui*, that is, the consciousness merely of being conscious, grows to an enormous size, with a consequent decrease in $\frac{d^2o}{ds^2}$, a decrease, that is to say, in the apparent rate of the time-flow. Time here is felt to *drag* as in the presence of distraction it is felt to *fly*.

VI. The Rhythmic Character of Consciousness

We have only to reflect upon the nature of the specious present as already described to understand the intrinsically rhythmic character of consciousness.

Let us suppose a mind to experience a series of sensations o_1, o_2, o_3, and o_4 in the moments t_1, t_2, t_3, and t_4. The specious present at t_2 has a duration of two moments and contains the image-trace of o_1 and also the sensation o_2; and the specious present at t_3 has a duration of three moments and contains, in addition to the sensation o_3, the images of o_1 and o_2. From the persistence of images, the specious present tends to increase not only in "length" but in contents. This increase is not, in a finite consciousness, unlimited, but depends upon the degree to which the accumulating contents are harmonized in a single meaning.

In consciousness as we know it, each content is to some degree a *rival* of its fellows. Of course, it is also true that different contents to some extent support and enhance one another, and the law (first formulated, I believe, by Fechner) that the intensity of attention varies inversely with its extent is only a half-truth. That is to say, it is only true for psychoses in which the "competition" of contents tends to become stronger than their "co-operation." The law is, in general, however, rather more true than false, because as the number of elements in a system increases, co-operation becomes less easy and antagonism less difficult. And as the sweetest-toned instrument will, if too loudly or too variously excited, reach a point at which the dissonance of the overtones will exceed their harmony, so with the specious present there inevitably comes a time when the manifoldness of its contents makes their unity no longer capable of transcending their variety.[3]

Returning to our example, we will suppose that in the mind which has experienced o_1, o_2, and o_3, the specious present has reached the critical point at which the further dispersal of attention demanded by a new content will result in its dissolution. The new content o_4 enters; the specious present ceases its slow expansion and begins rapidly to contract. The images of o_1, o_2, and o_3 crumble away, and the attention thus liberated is caught by the strongest bidder, which, in our case, is the present sensation o_4. On this as a foundation, a new specious present is rapidly built up, containing as a halo or "fringe" the shade of its parent. It is important to bear in mind the fact that the manner in which our specious presents are destroyed is different from the manner in which they are rebuilt. The old contents do not flow out as the new contents flow in. The events which are born singly die in cycles.

A rhythmic series of experiences affects us strongly and holds our attention because its objectively recurring periods

[3] Professor Loeb (in *Comparative Physiology of the Brain*, Chap. XIX) holds that the intensity of a mental state is diminished by the simultaneous presence of other states when, and only when, the underlying physiological processes are *aperiodic*. Simultaneous periodic processes, so far from diminishing, may actually enhance each other's intensity.

harmonize with the subjectively recurring contractions and expansions of the specious present, each series being, thus, reinforced by the other. Subjectively viewed, the rhythmic character of consciousness is due, as we have seen, to the fact that each specious present contains, in addition to the birth-seeds of new presents, the seed of its own decay. Like other live things, our time-consciousness is rhythmic, because, like them, it is born with the canker of death at its heart.

VII. Memory

So far, we have been dealing with the immediate apprehension of the just past. We have now to discuss the bearing of the theory upon the consciousness of the more remote past. Memory proper, or recall, is differentiated from the consciousness of the just past by the fact that in the latter, the event has been continuously present to consciousness since the time of its occurrence, while in recall, as the word indicates, the event remembered has been absent from consciousness between the time of its occurrence and the time of its recurrence. Every case of memory is, thus, a case of recurrence, but every case of recurrence is not a case of memory. In addition to the fact of recurrence there must be a recognition of recurrence, a recognition that something is being experienced *again*. The mere fact of recurrence is not difficult to understand. If the physiological ground or concomitant of an experience leaves as a trace of itself a specific modification of the brain structure—a "path," for example—it is natural that when that particular part of the brain is re-excited, whether by stimulus or from within, we should re-experience the content. The really curious thing about memory is not the recurrence, but the recognition of the recurrence, the consciousness of having experienced the *same* content at a more or less definitely localized moment of the past. Now, we have seen that within the scope of a single specious present the amount of time which has elapsed since the occurrence of an event is measured by the ratio of its change-rate to the change-rate induced by it in the apperceptive system upon which it is "projected." [4] This apperceptive system or apperception-mass is (when the attitude of attention is retrospective) nothing but the collective totality of contents which have been perceived since the event in question first appeared. And the change-rate of such a system is inversely proportional to its size. The specious present, then, increases with the increase of the apperception-mass; and, hence, the extent of the latter suffices to measure not only the duration of time from a point in the past up to the present, but, conversely, the felt distance of that point from the present, that is, its date. Thus, when the specious present is large, the date of its earlier events is felt to be remote; while, conversely, the earlier events of a small specious present are felt to be of recent date.

I believe that the date of a remembered object is measured in the same way. The specifically modified brain-cell, when re-excited, excites in its turn the physiological traces of the experiences intervening between its first oc-

[4] It might be objected that the experience of unequal amounts of change occurring in equal times is in flat contradiction to the statement that time is measured by its contents. When, however, we seek for the grounds on which the two unequally filled times are judged equal, we see that their estimated equality arises from our comparing them, not with an absolute time, but with other changes of content, either those of our subjective consciousness or those of a third object, such as a clock. That absolute or empty time does not enter as a factor into the perceptual estimate of time is further shown by the fact that when equal time-intervals containing unequal quantities of change are perceived separately and without relation to a third object, they are, as a matter of fact, felt to be unequal. And the estimated inequality of their times is in proportion to the perceived inequality of their contents. Notwithstanding the uselessness of absolute time as a standard of perceptual measurement, the idea has a certain validity. The absolute clock is the totality of things, viewed as a single system.

currence and the present moment, with the result that these intervening experiences vaguely and very schematically recur as an apperception-mass for the recurrence of the content which suggested them. And, precisely as in the case of the specious present, the rate of change in this apperceptive system is, in proportion to its extent, small as compared with the change in the single content. The ratio of the latter to the former, $\frac{do}{ds}$, measures and represents the date, that is, the period of time that appears to have elapsed since the event first occurred. But the remembered event is not only projected upon this large and schematic apperception-mass; it is, together with the latter, projected also upon the background of concrete experiences which fill the regular specious present of the moment. Thus, it appears to us in two contexts or aspects —as a present event in our mental life, and as an event of the past. The *againness* of the remembered event is due precisely to this duality of its apperceiving system.

The view that the date or temporal sign of a remembered happening is determined by the recurrence of the intervening experiences is borne out by the recognized facts of the memory consciousness. For, in the first place, we can recall the date of an event only when we have some memory of what has followed it. (By *date* I mean, of course, the *felt* date, not the date as abstractly known.) When the intervening experiences are numerous and interesting, the apperceptive system, *s*, in which they schematically recur, is large, and the differential fraction $\frac{do}{ds}$, which measures the lapse of time since the occurrence of *o*, is also large. Conversely, when few experiences have intervened between an event and our memory of it, the apperception-mass is small and the date appears more recent than it is.[5]

[5] The rate of time-flow is, as we know, reversed in retrospect. Periods that felt brief when passing are remembered as long, and *vice versa*.

Finally, when the activity of the perceptive faculty is completely suspended, as in trance or change of personality, and when consequently there are no intervening experiences out of which to make a memory apperception-mass, we find, as our view would lead us to expect, no appreciation of the period of time separating the remembered event from the moment at which it is remembered. In such cases, the events of months ago are regarded as those of yesterday.

In spite of the "concomitant variation" of the number of intervening experiences, and the distance of the assigned date of the remembered event, it may still seem that we have not sufficiently explained the profound difference between memory of the remote past and immediate consciousness of the just past. In order to remove any such misgivings, let us sum up the points of difference already noted between the two kinds of consciousness of the past. In the first place, in immediate apprehension the apperception-mass is the concrete complex of experiences which, having just occurred, have not yet faded from consciousness. In memory, on the other hand, the principal apperception-mass is a vast, hazy, highly schematic group of contents, the merest skeleton of the experiences of the intervening period. Second, in addition to this contrast in the backgrounds upon which the two kinds of past are, respectively, projected, there is a single background in the case of immediate apprehension while in memory there is a double background—the schematic system just mentioned and the concrete system of contents which makes up the specious present of the moment in which the act of memory takes place. And to this duality of apperceptive context is due, as we have seen, the feeling of *againness* or recurrence which is distinctive of the memory psychosis.

VIII. Familiarity

The feeling of familiarity, which is akin to memory, differs from recall proper in two ways. In the first place, the event recognized as *familiar* is normally caused by an external stimulus, and hence possesses the vividness and arbitrary "*givenness*" characteristic of a sensation as distinguished from an image. In the second place, the memory apperception-mass is so entirely subordinated to the specious present in which the familiar sensation occurs that it serves merely to give to the latter a fringe of pastness in which there is no appreciable indication of date. In short, the feeling of familiarity is the apprehension of a present event with a fringe of pastness, or "recurringness"; while in the memory judgment, the recognition of a more or less definitely dated past is primary, being only secondarily qualified by a fringe of presentness due to the act of memory itself.

IX. The Conditions Under Which Time Perception Originates

When we inquire how a specious present begins or how it can apply to a single sensation, we are confronted by a peculiar difficulty. According to our view, there must always be a pre-existing background of mental states upon which the content perceived as an object is projected. But in the first moment of a psychosis, or in the case of a single sensation, this would seem impossible. And yet, when we are awakened from a state of unconsciousness by a touch or a sound, we do not experience a sensation that is without duration. If anything, the time-form is more noticeable in the simple and approximately sensational first stage of an experience than in the later and more complex stages. The *meaning* of a sensory content is felt only when we feel its relation to other contents, but not so with its duration. As soon as it is perceived, or rather, in order that it may be perceived, we must be conscious of it as enduring. Our problem is to point out what it is that plays the part of apperception-mass in the case of a single sensation and at the first moment of an experience.

Let us begin by considering the case of a possible single sensation which has established itself in consciousness. Along with the sensation at any moment will be the consciousness of it as it was in the just preceding moments. Let o_4 represent the sensation at the fourth second of its existence, and o'_1, o'_2, and o'_3 symbolize the present image-traces of its earlier existence. It will be sensed in the light of these image-traces precisely as an incoming element in a complex psychosis is apperceived by the other elements. The "apperceptive system" for a single sensation—if such were possible—would then be nothing but the image-traces of its just-past existence. And the specious present, $\frac{do}{ds}$, of such a sensation would be expressed (at the fourth second) by the symbol $\frac{do_4}{d\,(o'_1\,o'_2\,o'_3)}$. When the apperceptive system or subjective background, composed of the image-traces o'_1, o'_2, and o'_3, became greater or more prominent for consciousness than the present sensation o_4, the rate of change of the former would become less than that of the latter, that is, $\frac{do_4}{d\,(o'_1\,o'_2\,o'_3)} > 1$, and a specious present or perceptual time-form would be realized.

So much for the time-form of a single sensation after its origin. Can we make use of this account to explain the *simultaneous* origin of an experience and its time-form? Here, as elsewhere, in explaining the origin of anything in consciousness, we are compelled to fall back upon those physiological processes which are the secondary, or it may be the proximate, conditions of sensory states. When by the action of a specific stimulus an equally specific disturbance in the cortex is produced, the latter does not, we may suppose, die out the instant the stimulus ceases, but continues for a short time, as the violin string continues to vibrate after the bow has been withdrawn. If the same stimulus be applied again, the resulting disturbance will be a complex of the pre-existing disturbance and the renewed effect of the stimulus. Now, if the stimulus act in such a manner that the disturbance in the brain-center due to past action shall become greater than the effect of its present action, *there will be produced on the physiological level a perfect counterpart of the psychological conditions of the specious present.* That is, we shall have a "subjective" or pre-existing state of disturbance greater or more vigorous than the incoming impulse. The modification in the nerve center due to the just past will dominate that due to the present. If under these conditions a sensation arise, it will arise with a time-form. Let us suppose a case in which a stimulus must act continuously for four seconds in order that a sensation may arise. We may represent the resulting disturbances of the central organ by $o_{(-4)}$, $o_{(-3)}$, $o_{(-2)}$, and $o_{(-1)}$, and their traces by the same symbols primed. We may suppose that at the moment when the sensation o_1 arises, the physiological stimulus-traces $o'_{(-4)}$, $o'_{(-3)}$, and $o'_{(-2)}$ are together equal in intensity to the impulse $o_{(-1)}$; and that, when increased by the trace of the latter, the pre-existing state will dominate the incoming state—which, if it be felt at all, will be felt in a time-form or specious present represented by

$$\frac{do}{d(o'_{(-4)}o'_{(-3)}o'_{(-2)}o'_{(-1)})} > 1.$$

Now, inasmuch as every sensation which we can imagine ourselves to experience has a time-form, we must conclude that, in defining the conditions of the origin of a specious present, we have at the same time defined one of the essential conditions for the origin of conscious states in general.

The several steps in our argument may be summed up as follows:

I. The central fact of time-consciousness is the "specious present"—the present consciousness of what is no longer present. Without this apparent projection of past moments upon each present moment, there could be no consciousness of either duration or succession.

II. Time is the form of change; and change, like every magnitude, is relative to its unit of measure. The amount of perceived change in an object is relative to the actual concomitant change in the perceiving subject.

III. Regarding the "object" as simply the objective aspect, and the "subject" as the subjective aspect, of a psychosis, we may hold that each incoming objective content is apperceived by or projected upon the entire system of pre-existing states. The psychosis considered only in its collective unity is subjective; considered only in its distributive plurality, it is an aggregate of objects; considered (as it must be) under both aspects simultaneously, it is a "subject-perceiving-objects." As the apperceptive system is larger than any of its objective contents, the constant stream of increments and decrements produces in the latter changes that are proportionately greater or faster than the change that they in turn cause in the system as a whole. *This difference in the rates of an objective change and the subjective change which reflects it, measures the amount of perceived change and perceived time.* And though Δs and Δo (the actual subjective and objective changes, respectively, produced in s and o by the environmental increment of content) would approach zero as Δt approached zero, yet the ratio $\frac{\Delta o}{\Delta s}$ would approach or maintain the finite value $\frac{do}{ds}$. And this for the same reason that the velocity of a moving body, if uniform, maintains, and if accelerated approaches, a finite value, when the space through which and the time in which it moves approach zero. By assuming the amount of perceived time to be a continuously present *differential rate*, it becomes possible to reconcile the "specious," "vicarious," or "perceptual" presence of an extended segment of the past with the real or unextended present. Finite positive portions of time and change are perceived as present when $\frac{s}{o}$, and, consequently, $\frac{do}{ds}$, are greater than unity.

IV. Time is felt as *enduring* when $\frac{do}{ds}$ is increasing in value, that is, when $\frac{d^2o}{ds^2}$ is positive; and, conversely, when the second derivative is negative, the events are felt as escaping or *passing*.

V. As the positive and negative *signs* of the second derivative, respectively, denote the enduring and the passing phases of perceptual time, so the *value* of the same ratio measures the perceived *rate* of time. Time "flies" or "drags" according as $\frac{d^2o}{ds^2}$ is large or small. And as in this case the first and second derivatives vary inversely—that is, the longer the time-span or specious present, the slower its rate of change—it follows that the events that are near to the present appear to *acquire pastness* more rapidly than those further past. (This I take to be the explanation of the apparent conformity of time-perception to Weber's Law.)

VI. A specious present tends constantly to increase, but this naturally cumulative tendency brings about automatically in every finite consciousness a counter-tendency;

for, in so far as the contents of a psychosis are not perceived in the light of a single plan, the degree to which each is attended to is inversely proportional to the number of all, and there comes a time when the content of longest duration can no longer hold the attention.[6] That activity, on being thus torn from its attachment to the keystone of the system by the dissipative force of numbers, is for the moment open to the highest bidder, which is usually the most recent sensation; and about this as a center, a new present is built up. This alternation of slow accumulation and rapid crumbling in the time-span throws light alike on the rhythmic character of consciousness and upon the pleasurableness of objective rhythm.

VII. Memory differs from the immediate consciousness of the past in two ways. In the first place, the remembered event (that is, the re-excited trace of the past experience) is projected upon a schematic and hazy apperception-mass, composed of traces of a few of the more important intervening experiences. This makes possible the felt date, while it enables us also to account for its indefiniteness and inaccuracy. In the second place, the remembered event is less noticeably projected upon the concrete apperception-mass of the specious present in which the act of memory takes place. It is, thus, seen in two contexts, and to this duality of background its "againness" may be ascribed.

VIII. The feeling of familiarity differs from memory proper in that the trace of the past event is excited sensorily

[6] There are two fundamentally distinct features of a content that attract the attention—its intrinsic intensity and its intrinsic bearing upon other contents. The latter is the conceptual or unifying factor and is usually possessed in the greatest degree by the content of longest duration, because it is the center in relation to which the rest of the system is interpreted. On the other hand, the intensive or sensory factor is peculiarly the property of the sensation of the moment—and it is the gradual but inevitable gain of the latter, or centrifugal, over the former, or centripetal, factor that brings about the periodic dissolution of each psychosis.

from without, and is projected primarily upon the specious present of the moment, and only secondarily upon the background of intervening experiences. *It is an experience of the present with a fringe of the past, while memory is an experience of the past with a fringe of the present.*

IX. The manner in which a time-form can apply to a single sensation, and the manner in which it can originate at all, present peculiar difficulties. Confining our attention to a possible single sensation, we find that in such a case the apperceiving background for the sensation, after its origin, would be composed of the image-traces of the sensation itself. The formula for the specious present becomes $\frac{do}{do'}$, where o' represents the pre-existing subjective traces due to the presence of the sensation in the preceding moments. But these quantitative symbols may with equal or, as some psychologists would hold, with greater propriety be used to denote the physiological concomitants of sensation. And the symbol $\frac{do}{do'}$, when taken physiologically, may represent a condition just *antecedent* to perception. From this point of view, we can understand how it is that the time-form of a psychosis arises simultaneously with its contents.

»» 11 ««

TIME AND THE FOURTH DIMENSION [1]

The Howison Lecture for 1925

An exposition and defense of a hypothesis, partly similar to and partly different from Einstein's, in which time is regarded as a fourth dimension of space. From this hypothesis is derived (1) a conception of electrons and protons as four-dimensional "hills" and "hollows," and (2) a conception of the memory-system or soul as a four-dimensional magnitude developed in the brain but not dependent upon it.

[George Holmes Howison, in whose honor this lectureship (Howison Lectureship in Philosophy in the University of California) was established, was to many of us not merely an inspiring philosopher, but also a friend and guide. And his guidance, like his friendship, was not restricted to those fortunate enough to be his pupils and disciples, but was generously extended to include many whose methods and conclusions in philosophy were very different from his own. It is as a member of the latter group that I wish gratefully to express my indebtedness to Professor Howison for a certain attitude toward the whole adventure of philosophy which I can trace in large part to my acquaintance with him and his writings.]

Philosophers have been wont to divide their energies between formulating their visions and formulating arguments to prove their visions true. And of all the great company

[1] Reprinted from *University of California Publications in Philosophy*, Vol. VII, December, 1925, pp. 181–207.

from Thales down, I can think of no single one who has not succeeded vastly more with his visions than with his proofs. The imaginative constructions of philosophers have, on the whole, been great and free, equal or superior to those of the poets; but the reasonings of these philosophers have usually been labored and artificial, affording a painful contrast to the arguments of scientists, with whom imagination is, properly enough, at the mercy of reason. Certainly, the philosophy of Howison has afforded a notable illustration of the degree to which the intuitions of a great seer and prophet can surpass in their intrinsic cogency the arguments so conscientiously contrived to support them. Let us, therefore, make a virtue of necessity, and do openly and confessedly what we shall probably do anyway. As philosophers, let us cease to take pride in adducing proofs for the unprovable, and instead, let us devote our principal energies to the dreaming of dreams and the building of cities in the sky. Reason must be content if she succeed in keeping our visions of the possible within the bounds of the probable and relevantly related to the problems of an actual world.

Should my readers hesitate to agree in this as a general policy for philosophy to adopt, I ask their permission to let me adopt it in the present paper. For the propositions which I desire to submit to you constitute a portrait, or rather a crude impressionistic sketch, of a possible cosmos, and if I make no claim that it must be true, you may be the more willing to entertain the claim that it may be true—and that is all I ask.

All existing things move and have their being in space and time, and to these great entities there thus pertains a peculiar metaphysical dignity. Are they primary and absolute in their reality, or are they secondary and relative to the concretions which they embrace? Are they objective and independent of the minds in whose experience they figure, or are they merely subjective forms and instruments by means of which those minds organize their perceptions? These two questions concerning, respectively, the relativity and the subjectivity of space and time, important as they are, will not bear directly on our present inquiry. Hence, I pause only to remind you that, as Russell has remarked, though the two questions are closely related, they are not interdependent. Either can be answered without prejudicing or determining the answer to the other. To Descartes, for example, space and time were objective or independent of the mind and absolute or independent of the bodies and processes that filled them; while to Leibniz they were objective but relative. To Berkeley, again, space (if not time, also) was subjective and relative; while to Kant both space and time were subjective but absolute.

Let us now turn from these old questions of the relation of space and time to the subjects that know them and to the objects that fill them, and consider the newer question of the relation of space and time to each other.

What are their similarities, and what are their differences? Are they sufficiently similar to be fruitfully combined into a single four-dimensional continuum of space-time or time-space containing and contained in all concrete realities? Are they co-dimensional attributes distinguishable in thought but as inseparable in existence as the length and breadth of a solid are inseparable from its thickness?

The independent or quasi-independent variable properties shared in common by all elements of an assemblage constitute its dimensions. Thus, the points of our space are a three-dimensional assemblage because it is necessary and sufficient to define each of them in terms of three independently variable distance relations to some one of them chosen as origin.

Now, the objects that occupy space or fill it with sensory content of some kind are differentiated from one another, irrespective of their content, in terms of the position or distance and direction of their points from a point chosen as origin. Thus, I can say that the middle point of a given object is distant from the middle point of the floor of this room one foot northward, two feet westward, and three feet upward. An object whose points were defined in this manner would be unambiguously *placed* in space; but in order to differentiate it from another similar object occupying the same points tomorrow or yesterday, it would be necessary to add a fourth independent variable, that of time. Then the object would be not only *placed* but *dated*. Now, it is obvious that this fourth or temporal dimension is very similar to the dimensions of space, but it is also obvious that it possesses very puzzling points of difference. Let us try to formulate, first, the similarities, and second, the differences, between time and a spatial dimension:

1. The series of dates or instants is continuous and infinite, like the series of one-dimensional points on a line.

2. Intervals of time are like intervals of space in that they are measured in terms of specific sensory content and in relation to some point or instant chosen as origin.

3. Spatial objects have *position* or *locus* in virtue of the relation of their points to some other point chosen as origin; and in addition to their position, they have *size* and *shape*, in virtue of the relation of their points to one another. Their size is determined by the distances between their extreme or bounding points, and their shape by the directional relations of the internal distances to one another. The size of a body is, then, an extrinsic property depending on its relation to other bodies or to units of distance chosen independently of the body itself. The shape is an

intrinsic property, because the directional relations of a body's internal distances are constant, regardless of what the unit of distance may be or how it may change. A strictly one-dimensional object would have only size, because there would be no plurality of directions to be related. With reference to the time dimension, durations are like spatial lines in that quantitatively they differ only in size, that is, in being longer or shorter.

If the foregoing similarities of time to one-dimensional space were the whole story, then, indeed, time would long ago have been recognized to be not only a fourth variable, differentiating sensory objects from one another, and vaguely *analogous* to a spatial dimension, but quite definitely and simply *as the* fourth dimension of space.

It is because of the differences, either seeming or real, between the series of instants in time and the series of points on a line that we have had to wait until recently for the conception of a four-dimensional continuum.

Let us examine the most striking of these differences, and endeavor in each case to see whether the difference in question is intrinsic to the nature of time itself, or whether it may not be due to some more or less accidental limitation of our consciousness or of the particular objects to which our consciousness is restricted.

1. Time seems to enjoy, at least occasionally, a self-sufficiency and aloofness from spatial dimensions which the latter are by no means capable of in themselves.

I can, for example, count one, two, three, four, one, two, three, four, and mark the time intervals clearly enough for my own purposes. Sounds, acts, and thoughts suffice to reveal quite unmistakably the varying quantities of duration or temporal extent. The space changes embodied in material clocks are important adjuncts to facilitate the communication and the refinement of time measurement, but they are no more necessary to time itself and to the experience of it than written or printed records are necessary to thought. But while temporal processes can exist without space, spatial bodies cannot exist without time, nor one spatial dimension without the others.

The dissimilarity just stated seems to me to be secondary rather than primary, dependent upon what might be called the accidents of our experience rather than upon the intrinsic nature of time itself. In the first place, such events as sounds and thoughts, even if they lack spatial extension, are not without spatial position. If a thing happens, it must happen somewhere. For a thing to happen nowhere would mean that it did not happen. To me, at least, it is impossible to conceive of sensations and thoughts that are not located in the space occupied by the conscious being who has them. In the second place, I believe, though with less confidence, that mental states have not merely spatial position, but spatial extent. We are too ready to assume that, because some objects of thought, such as abstract ideas, have no size or shape, therefore the experience of them is equally non-spatial. And even if this should not be so, and if there were concrete events that had only temporal extension, we cannot be sure that there might not also be real objects that possessed only one spatial dimension—true lines of force, for example, lacking any breadth or thickness; at least, I can see no contradiction involved in this idea.

2. The dimensions of a space system are, as we have said, the independent variable properties possessed jointly by each and all of its elements. The number of dimensions is the number of such variables. To define or demarcate any element it is necessary and sufficient to evaluate or measure each of its variable properties in relation to some other element taken as standard or origin. Thus, in a two-dimensional or plane space, two such independent measures

or co-ordinates, x and y, are necessary to define a position; while in a space of three dimensions, three co-ordinates, x, y, and z, are requisite. Taking the term *dimension* in this sense, an assemblage of elements, each of which possessed a temperature and a color varying independently and measurably from element to element, might be called a manifold of two dimensions. The dimensions of space are, however, something more than mere independent variables. Not only is each of them a continuum in itself, but each is continuous with the others. In a plane, for example, between the x-line measuring the horizontal distance and the y-line measuring the vertical distance from a chosen origin to any point, there can be found a continuous pencil of lines having all possible directions from the horizontal to the vertical. From the traditional standpoint, no such continuous passage from the time dimension to the other dimensions of space-time can be found. Apparently, time is not so homogeneously and continuously different from a direction in space as is the latter from a direction perpendicular to it. Between the direction of next Thursday and the direction of the North Star there would seem to be nothing in the way of an intermediate direction. Thus, even though time resembles a spatial dimension in being a continuous and independent variable, applicable to the same events to which the space dimensions are applicable, its apparent discontinuity with the latter is like the discontinuity of different sensory modalities, such as color and hotness, and unlike the homogeneity of spatial dimensions, such as length and height.

That this apparent dissimilarity between time and a spatial dimension resembles the previous ones in being secondary and apparent rather than primary and intrinsic can be shown, I think, by considering the manner in which it has for some years been customary to represent motion. If we symbolize the time direction by a vertical line and the spatial path along which a body is moving by a horizontal line, the various degrees of velocity which such a body might be supposed to have will be symbolized by the lines of various directions between the vertical and the horizontal. And the challenge to imagine any direction between next Thursday and the North Star will be answered by imagining the path traversed by a body moving from where we are now at such a rate of speed as to arrive at the place where the North Star now is by next Thursday. It follows as a corollary that as uniform rectilinear velocities will be represented by straight lines, *accelerated* or *retarded* rectilinear velocities will be represented by lines curving, respectively, toward the horizontal, or space, axis and toward the vertical, or time, axis. The precise inclination of the line which symbolizes in a diagram any given velocity will depend on the units of time and space that we choose to represent by equal lengths on the two axes.

We have now arrived at something like the four-dimensional continuum of space-time which has been familiar to us from the day of Minkowski's famous address on "Raum und Zeit" in 1908. The "world," as Minkowski calls it, consists of lines or histories whose intersections constitute *episodes* that are absolute and objective and which are separated from one another by spatio-temporal intervals, also absolute and objective.

But just as one and the same line can be the diagonal of many rectangles and thus measured in different ways, so the interval between any two intersections of world-lines will be measured by as many different combinations of the space factor and the time factor as there are different rates of motion of the observers who do the measuring. Hence, while spatial and temporal separation will be relative, the spatio-temporal *interval* between any two episodes will be constant and absolute for all observers. This relativity of space as such, and of time as such, as well as the further fact that the interval between any two intersections is measured in terms of the difference between the squares of the spaces and times rather than, as we might expect, by their sum—($ds^2 = dx^2 - dt^2$) rather than ($ds^2 = dx^2 + dt^2$)—is a consequence of Einstein's Special Theory of Relativity, according to which the velocity of a ray of light is to be regarded as constant for every observer regardless of his own motion toward it or away from it.

The peculiar postulate of Einstein makes the continuum of space-time different in some ways from an ordinary four-dimensional Euclidean continuum; but these differences are not, I think, vitally relevant to the hypothesis which I wish to put before you. Hence, I shall take the liberty of avoiding the complexities which a further consideration of them would involve.

From the result of our analysis so far, time would seem to have been successfully reduced to a fourth dimension similar to, though not identical in character with, the three dimensions of space. The world from this standpoint would be composed of events, groups of actual or potential sensory qualities, having spatial positions and temporal dates. (1) When such a group of qualities has a plurality of spatial positions associated with single dates, it is said to have extension. (2) When, on the other hand, it has a plurality of dates associated with single positions, it is said to have duration or to be at rest. (3) When its dates vary with its positions, it is said to move. (4) And when, with or without variation of its position, some of its qualities vary concomitantly with its dates, it is said to be changing its attributes.

Now, a quality group may or may not vary in its attributes or in its spatial position; but if it is a concrete existent, and not a mere abstraction, it must vary in its dates. Hence, while some things change their attributes or their positions or both, all things have to change their date. The world, therefore, consists not of events merely, but of series of events varying continuously in time. These event series are histories, and are represented as tracks in space-time. Every object is a history or series of events, but not every history is an object. An object is a special kind of history in which a sufficient nucleus of qualities remains invariant throughout the variation of dates.

The world would seem, then, to consist of the sum and system of histories or tracks and their intersections in the four-dimensional continuum of space-time.

What is wrong with this picture? I answer that it is the picture of a world that is dead. Minkowski's world-lines or world-tracks depict history that has been made, not history in the making. Yet all history is or was or will be history in the making. There is nothing in the world-lines, as such, to indicate the fact that they are *growing*. The footprints of a man are not the man. And even if man moved through a jelly-like medium infinitely receptive of all his qualities at each moment, the perfect history thus recorded would not be the man himself. What we have is the play of *Hamlet* with the Prince of Denmark left out. Yet, even so, the play is good and true as far as it goes, and we need to omit nothing from it, but only to add something to it.

Now, the aspect of reality which is not included in the four-dimensional universe of world-tracks is usually referred to as the *passage* or *flow* of time. Time not only *extends* into the past and future, but it is said to *flow* at a uniform rate and in an irreversible direction. Now, how can time both flow like a river and also extend like the bed and banks of that river? The answer is that it cannot do both of these things and does not have to. The familiar phrase "Time flows" is false and misleading. It is as though we were to look from the window of our moving train and with egocentric naïveté declare not only that the houses and the hills but the space containing them was *flying by*. It would be we who were flying through space, not space through us. And it is we, the beings of the universe, who pass through time, not time through us. Time, then, is not, as Newton thought, like a stream or river flowing at a uniform rate. Time is rather the banks and bed through which the river of existence makes its way.

If this is true, and if we consent to take the burden of "passage" upon *us,* then everything that has been said about time being a fourth dimension through which the histories of things are mapped as tracks can be kept as valid. Nay, more, it was the half-conscious thought of time as something that flowed as well as extended that made us careful to call time a fourth dimension of a complex continuum of space-time rather than a mere fourth dimension of space itself. But, now that we have decided to regard the universe as moving through time, we can boldly identify time with a fourth dimension of space perpendicular to the three that we recognize as north-south, east-west, and up-down. Nor need we be deterred from this identification by the peculiar character of the time dimension which results from Einstein's postulate as to the constancy of the speed of light for all observers. Even if that postulate is true, the new dimension, despite its peculiar relation to the other three, might still be purely spatial.

The movement or march of things through time differs in a peculiar way from all other movements—it differs in being universal and uniform. The now and then of time have many resemblances to the here and there of space. But there are two great differences. When a thing goes from here to there, the other things in the universe do not move with it; but when a thing goes from now to then, from today into tomorrow, everything else goes and must go along with it. Nothing can go faster or slower in time than anything else. You could not dash ahead into next week and wait there for the world to catch up with you. Things vary from one another in quality and position and in their rates of change; but in their uniform march through time, they display a magnificent solidarity.

In short, time is a space differing from what we call "space" not in itself, but in the fact that all things move, and move together, in it, whereas in ordinary space things can move or not, and in different and opposite directions. Ordinary movements are thus localized and differentiated from their environment. They are relative and therefore observable; but movement in time is universal and absolute, and therefore not noticed for what it is but ascribed confusedly to the flowing of time itself.

It is because of this march through time of the universe as a whole, with all things abreast, that there can be no such thing as an enclosure of empty time, though there might be of empty space. A true spatial vacuum may or may not be physically possible, but a temporal vacuum within existence is not even imaginable. It would mean that some things could pass from Tuesday to Thursday without going through Wednesday.

I wish now to consider certain objections to the conception that I have set forth.

Have I not involved myself in a logical circle in interpreting time and what is involved in it as the movement of the universe in a fourth dimension of space? For how can a thing move in a fourth dimension or anywhere else unless there is a time as well as a space for it to move in? It may seem that the concept, time, which I thought I was analyzing, has slipped through the sieve of my analysis quite intact, and that matters have been made worse rather than better. For have I not added to the old and inevitable mystery of time new and superfluous mysteries of my own willful making, such as a fourth dimension and a universe in motion through it?

To this indictment I plead guilty in part, but only in part. The time problem is really two problems. First, there is the problem of the extension or stretch of time comprising the past and the future, and the relation of this stretch to the threefold stretch of space.

Second, there is the problem usually phrased as the lapse or passage of time. Now, the stretch of time I have identified with a fourth spatial dimension. This may be false and fantastic, but it is not verbally or logically circular. It needs only to be true to be a real solution.

The second problem of the lapse or flow or passage of time, I have reduced to the problem of the flow or passage of the universe through the time stretch. This, again, is not a merely verbal or logical restatement. If true, it is important. But what I have not analyzed is the category of passage itself. To the extent that passage, merely as such, involves time, to that extent we still have our category ultimate and intact. All I can claim is that, if we accept movement of the universe in a fourth dimension, then, though we cannot explain that movement in terms of anything else, we can explain everything else pertaining to time in terms of it. The alternative to the theory that the universe passes through time is the theory that time itself flows or passes, and passes through what?—through its own extent or stretch. Does the present moment move into the future, or is it the whole future that flows into the past, and in what time does this movement or flow of time take place? My view leaves passage itself unanalyzed; but by making the universe the subject of the verb *to pass*, or *to endure*, it at least escapes such confusing circles as the foregoing.

A second very natural objection to the theory that I am

proposing is that an absolute motion of the whole universe would be incapable of being detected, if not also devoid of meaning, except from the standpoint of an observer outside the universe, with respect to whom such a motion would be relative and therefore significant. All the discussions of relative and absolute motion assume that there are only two alternatives that are even provisionally conceivable:

1. Motion relative to the points of a universal medium, ether or just space itself—which would be absolute motion, and
2. Motion relative to some body outside the system.

The first is generally regarded as undiscoverable and in a sense meaningless, and therefore all motion of objects is regarded as relative to other objects. There is, however, a third type of motion conceivable which would be the motion of a body *relative to its own past states.* Such a motion might be called "intra-relative" because it would be measured in relation to itself at a former time. Now, leaving accelerated motion out of account, we can see that the only condition, and a sufficient condition, for the discovery of a uniform motion of this intra-relative type would be the preservation of the past along with the present as an object of consciousness. Located in such a system, we could feel its motion without reference either to a fixed medium or to any external objects. Now, such a situation is by no means unfamiliar, only, instead of calling it "motion," we apply the names "growth" and "duration." But growth or duration is motion—marked off from the more plebeian kinds of motion by the fact that it is cumulative. What was in the past is retained and continually increased by each new present. The growth motion is a swelling or expansion, a circumference moving outward from a fixed center.

The motion of the universe in a fourth dimension is

absolute in the sense that it is intra-relative. It moves like a rocket, adding to its past track; or like a wave spreading out from a center and involving a continuous increase of the area which it encloses. And the motion of the universe in time, so far from being difficult to observe, is observed at each instant of our consciousness in the experience of duration, primary in the specious present, secondary in memory.

A third objection to the theory we are defending will be found to be already answered in what we have just said. It might be claimed that, in identifying time stretch with a fourth dimension of space, and time passage with a movement of the universe in this dimension, we had run counter to that *irreversibility* which has always been recognized as time's essential nature. It is of the nature of space to provide for an order or permutation that is always capable of being reversed, but to reverse time would be to contradict its essence. This can be seen by supposing *per impossibile* that a man could reverse the direction of his life and grow backwards into childhood. The childhood so attained could never be other than a second childhood coming after the first, and therefore not identical with it. We might revisit the past, but the revisiting could never be identical with the original living of it.

There is, it seems to me, only one conceivable basis for an irreversible order, and that is cumulativeness. The series of ordinal numbers, first, second, third, fourth, has an asymmetry or quasi-irreversibility that is due to the cumulative character of the cardinal numbers, 1, 2, 3, 4, on which the ordinals are based. Two includes one, as three includes two and four includes three. Each successive cardinal *is* the preceding number with something added. The later numbers contain the earlier, and therefore presuppose them as integral parts of their own meaning. In the same way, the present includes or presupposes the past.

Memory reveals the cumulative character of time, but does not constitute it. We remember the past only because the existence of the past is already implied by the existence of the present.

We see, then, that the same cumulativeness or growth which gave meaning to our conception of an absolute motion of the universe in time, serves also as the sufficient and necessary ground for time's irreversibility. Growth motion is the only kind of motion that is absolute and yet discoverable, and it is furthermore the only kind of motion that is irreversible. Time's passage is growth or increase of the universe. Time's stretch or extension is the direction perpendicular to our space in which that growth takes place.

And now, finally, there may be objection to my postulate of the existence of a fourth dimension of *space*. This conception seems to have become increasingly unpopular of late among philosophers of science. There are, I think, two main reasons for this unpopularity. The philosophers most conversant with physics and mathematics today are in an extremely positivistic mood. They wish to reduce the universe to our sense data and avoid postulating anything beyond. A special and pertinent case of this prevailing positivism or phenomenalism is the insistence that space and time not only in themselves, but even when taken together as space-time, are nothing except relations of sense data to one another. A fourth dimension of space savors too much of a realm transcending our experience; and, hence, even when the positivists of today recognize on purely empirical grounds a certain non-Euclidean character in their three-dimensional relational space, they dislike to interpret it as due to curvature in a higher dimension. For to speak of a Riemannian space as curved in a fourth dimension would imply the prior reality of an empty Euclidean space, against whose flatness the curvature of the world of sense data was measured. And that would be incompatible with the view that space was nothing but a relational aspect of concrete phenomena. A second reason for the current prejudice is due to the manner in which popular mystics, spiritualists, theosophists, and others have seized on a fourth dimension as a suitable place for ghosts and other occult entities.

It is not necessary to say much in answer to these objections. As regards the one just stated, it is sufficient to remind ourselves that no amount of misuse of a hypothesis by mystics or others can affect its logical claims upon our belief—it has to be taken on its own merits; while with regard to the positivistic objection, I can only say that if the relations of sense data can be made intelligible by postulating a space beyond them but implied by them, there is the same justification for accepting such a postulate as there is for believing in the other side of the moon or in the geological processes that occurred before there were any human or animal sense data.

Two things about a four-dimensional space are clear. First, that many mathematicians, notably the late Professor Stringham of the University of California, have worked out its geometry with the same certainty and by the same methods that have been used for the geometry of three-dimensional space, so that we know perfectly what it is like, whether it exists or not. And second, there is absolutely nothing in experience to refute the possibility of its existence. Indeed, there are even some few aspects of our experience, such as those to which I have been appealing in this discussion, which lend to the hypothesis of an existing four-dimensional space a certain degree of probability.

In view of the foregoing analysis of what might have seemed insuperable difficulties, I feel justified in asking my readers to entertain as hypotheses (1) the existence of a fourth dimension of Euclidean space, and (2) a motion of expansion or growth of our three-dimensional space system in that fourth dimension. And I feel the more justified in making this request in that I am not demanding a belief that the hypotheses in question are actually true but only that they be entertained in fancy as possibly true.

The portrait or sketch of the universe which I threatened in my introductory remarks to inflict upon you is a portrait suggested by the two hypotheses just now stated, together with certain supplementary suggestions growing out of them and bearing upon the nature of matter and of mind. Let us preface our examination of the portrait in question by two observations.

First, the proposed interpretation of the relation of time to space is not in principle bound up with any special number of space dimensions. Imagine a one-dimensional universe, whose space would consist of a single line. Were such a universe to be moving as a whole in a direction perpendicular to itself and so as to generate an expanding or growing area, such a movement would be felt by its inhabitants as the irreversible flow of time. And to us higher beings looking down upon such a moving line, the past histories of its inhabitants would be visible at each instant in their entirety, somewhat as the growing area of devastation generated by a prairie fire, or the footprints of an advancing army, are visible to spectators situated above the plane in which such motions take place. Similarly, a flatland or two-dimensional world, if it moved as a whole in a third dimension, would trace out its past history in that dimension. *In short, no matter what number of spatial dimensions a world might possess, so long as it moved as a whole in some further dimension, that motion, provided it was cumulative and therefore irreversible, would be felt as* TIME.

The second preliminary observation which I wish to make is that, so long as the motion of an *n*-dimensional universe is in an $n+$ first direction, it does not need to be precisely perpendicular to the internal dimensions of such a world in order to be felt as duration. It is necessary only that it should be in a direction not wholly included in the intrinsic or space dimensions. It is not even necessary that the temporal motion be rectilinear or uniform. If the Special Theory of Relativity as usually interpreted is true, we might have to reckon with a time movement analogous in its path and in its rate to the motion along the surface of a hyperbola the asymptotes of which made angles of 45 degrees with the three dimensions of our space. Partly for the sake of simplicity, however, and partly to conform to the current notion of a Riemannian space, boundless but finite, I shall select from the various possible kinds of fourth-dimensional motions a motion that is a spherical or, rather, hyperspherical expansion from a center. Let us, then, picture our entire space system as curved in a fourth dimension around into itself and in such a way as to constitute a hyperspherical "surface," analogous to the two-dimensional curved surface of an ordinary sphere. And then to this Einsteinian revival of a Riemannian world, let us add the conception of its expansion or growth along the lines of its radii, such uniform velocity of expansion constituting the uniform passage or flow of all things in time.

We cannot, of course, form an image of such a universe, because we cannot form an image of a fourth dimension; but the conception itself is perfectly clear and definite, and we can translate it into terms of imagery by the usual device of stepping down the dimensions one degree and picturing our universe as analogous to a spherical surface or flatland which behaves like a soap bubble that is being steadily inflated, with the result that every point of its surface moves uniformly away from the center.

Outside the sphere is the future; inside the sphere is the past; on the growing, swelling surface is the present, which is the spatial plane of possible action and reaction and of all material existence.

Now, the space of our actual world contains numerous material particles which interrupt its continuity and homogeneity. How shall we make the pure ether which pervades the smooth surface of our soap-bubble universe conform to the granular rigors of atomic existence?

Imagine any kind of being in any kind of space, and predicate of such a being a definite normal rate of effortless progress, uniform, accelerated, or retarded. As long as nothing hinders this normal rate, the being will regard himself as moving in empty space. Let him come to a place where his normal rate is modified, and he will regard himself as entering a field of force, repulsive or attractive according to whether it retards or accelerates his normal or effortless rate of velocity. If his normal progress is not only diminished but actually stopped, he will regard that portion of the medium as filled with matter. To a being capable of moving only in a plane, or in a space of definite curvature, a lump on the plane or a distortion of the curvature to which he was adapted would appear either as a field of force or as impenetrable matter.

These considerations make it possible to translate mechanical categories into geometrical categories, and, following the epoch-making suggestion of W. K. Clifford, in 1875, to regard material particles as little hills protruding in a fourth-dimensional direction and, therefore, impenetrable to beings whose free and normal motions are confined to three dimensions.

Many people seem to suppose that, in order to take advantage of what is called the curvature of space, whether with Riemann we apply it to the universe as a whole or whether with Clifford to material particles, it is necessary to abandon the conception of a flat or Euclidean space as the inevitable norm with respect to which all curvatures, macrocosmic or microcosmic, must be measured. I think that this is a mistake, and that it has operated mischievously to delay acceptance of the new notion by putting upon it undeservedly the odium of paradox.

By the "curvature of space" we need mean only the curvature of the ether in space, that is, the curvature of the medium in which motion is normal, free, and without effort. Thus, Euclidean space can and, indeed, must retain all its ancient dignity and primacy as the place in which media of varying curvatures are contained and with respect to which they are measured. As real numbers imply a real zero, so non-Euclidean curved space systems imply a Euclidean space of zero curvature.

Fortified by these considerations, let us return to our expanding soap bubble and observe the manner in which Clifford's conception of matter would apply to it.

The first thing that we notice is startling in the extreme. We can have on the surface of our expanding sphere, not only little *hills*, but also little *holes*—fourth-dimensional depressions pointing inward toward the center from which the universe has grown in the past, as well as fourth-dimensional protuberances pointing outward in the direction of the future. We seem to have on our hands not only material particles, but two opposed kinds of material particles. And if we choose to imagine that the two types of particles are generated by opposite *thrusts* accompanied by opposite *twists*, clockwise and counterclockwise, we could expect that the creation of one would by a kind of induction create the other, so that their numbers would be equal. Moreover, the twists that they had received would register as fields of curved lines of strain in the medium surrounding them; hence, as they moved through that medium, they with their fields would revolve oppositely, producing effects analogous to the magnetic fields generated by moving charges.

Between any two particles, whether protons or electrons, an attractive force would apply that would be inversely proportional to the square of their distances and directly proportional to the energies embodied in the particles as a result of the stress to which the medium would have been subjected when they were created. Between the protuberances and the depressions there would be a further tendency to come together—complete coalescence being prevented by the opposite twists of their respective fields. But between un-neutralized and similar particles, there would be a corresponding repulsion. We may notice also that the vibrations of these particles would be in the direction of the time dimension in which they extended, and hence perpendicular to all ordinary dimensions of the space in which their waves would diffuse. And the velocity of such waves would seem to be equal to the velocity with which the medium was expanding.

Lastly, the motions of the particles in the spatial medium would be as unretarded by ordinary friction as the motion of three-dimensional wrinkles in a two-dimensional sheet of steel. But, as their velocities in the spatial medium approached the velocity with which that medium was expanding, a centrifugal force would set in which would produce the same kind of strain as that which was involved in the production of the particles. They would be, so to speak, pulling against the universe, and their density or mass would increase.

In conclusion, I turn from the protons and electrons of the material world to the even more puzzling entities that we call psychical. Does the expanding spherical shell of our bubble universe offer any particular provision for the self-directing systems of sensation and memory which we find growing like invisible flowers in the visible gardens of cerebral matter?

For a long time I have cherished a theory that sensations,

which are the simplest kind of psychic being, result whenever the kinetic or externally observable currents of neural energy are converted at the synapses of the central nervous system into states of latent energy, not externally observable but inferred as the specific possibilities of future motions. The potentiality of the physical is the actuality of the psychical. I believe, further, that while most of the energies of cerebral stress and strain are changed back into currents of kinetic energy which run out through the motor nerves to the muscles and glands, there is an infinitesimal fraction of the energy of each sensation that is retained as a memory image. The brain, thus, acts as a kind of trap for the energies that pass through it, and builds up a steadily growing system of forms which embody the past and project the future possibilities of the organisms in question.

I will not attempt here to repeat the arguments which I have adduced in support of this identification of consciousness with the system of intensive or potential energies sensorially accumulated in and through the brain. I will say only that the proofs of the theory are based not on superficial analogies, but upon a complete identity in form and structure between mind as we know it from within and the kind of energy system of which I have spoken. In particular, it can be shown that that most notable characteristic of consciousness—its duration or extension in time—of which Bergson has written so eloquently is adequately represented in the transformation of kinetic into potential energy; while, conversely, there is nothing else whatever in physical nature, real or imaginable, that could provide for the possibility of a past that endures in the present.

Assuming this theory provisionally and just for the sake of the argument, observe how our present hypothesis of a three-dimensional spatial universe temporally expanding in a fourth dimension bears upon it.

Notice, first, that when the energy of motion in a universe of three dimensions is converted into potential energy of stress, the latter will constitute a displacement in the fourth dimension, in which the world as a whole is moving. The motion of a nerve current, like any other motion, will be represented, following Minkowski, as a "world-line"; and the angle made by that line with the space axis will represent the velocity of the motion in question. If the world is, as we are assuming, moving as a whole in a direction perpendicular to its space, these world-lines will themselves be growing or increasing; and when a motion is stopped and redirected, the world-line representing it will change its direction to coincide with the time axis. This rotation of the world-line can be accomplished only by pressing down and back into the direction of the past. The intensity of the sensation will thus be a certain function of the momentum of the stimulus, while its duration will be equal to the time during which the stimulus operates. Sensations, as well as the memory images which they leave as traces, will thus constitute a system of specific forms extending downward or backward into the fourth dimension, which is the domain of pastness or duration. This system of durational forms is the mind, and it will itself move on in space and time with the aggregate of cerebral particles which constitutes its matrix.

When this material matrix breaks up and its particles scatter—in other words, when death occurs—the four-dimensional system of psychic forms that is attached to it will no longer possess the ordinary means of affecting the material environment. I cannot myself see how or why this severance of the bonds attaching a four-dimensional mind to a three-dimensional material surface should involve the destruction of that mind, but whether the being thus isolated from its bodily mechanism would be able to keep up with the universe of the present as it moves on through time or whether it would be left behind in the past like a man who has lost his hold on a boat which has been pulling him through the water, are questions that will be answered for us only by the great adventure itself.

I have tried to put a metaphysical fantasy into a semblance of orderly discourse. Its main argument is simple, and may be summarized as follows:

1. The striking similarities and the more striking contrasts between space and time are harmonized and explained by conceiving of our three-dimensional space system as the surface of a four-dimensional hypersphere; and this hypersphere is, in turn, to be conceived as possessing a uniform cumulative movement of expansion, which appears to us who participate in it as simply the *flow* or *passage* of time.

2. On the smooth surface or ether of this cosmic bubble there are little hills and holes, protuberances and depressions, whose behavior in relation to one another would seem to resemble the electric, magnetic, and mechanical behavior of the protons and electrons that make up the actual world of matter.

3. Some, at least, of the material systems that move on the surface of three-dimensional space are pervaded by secondary systems composed of forms of potential energy which are created whenever motion is changed into stress. These systems extend down into the past below the three-dimensional surface of space. They are thick in the direction of the fourth dimension, but their thickness appears to us as the duration evidenced in the specious present and in memory. They have all the characteristics of minds, and they are minds, initiated by means of the body, but not dependent on the body for their continuance.

This, then, is the cosmos as I fancy it may be and as I have attempted to depict it. If the picture seems unduly materialistic, endeavor to realize that when minds themselves are shown to be purely physical, then the physical itself is shown to be purely psychical. Materialism, if sufficiently radical, will lead us to a new type of idealism in which matter is not denied but transfigured. For we must remember that there is a mighty energy that creates and pervades the expanding hypersphere of our four-dimensional universe. As the systems of energy that pervade our brains are in themselves our very souls, so, too, that cosmic energy may be *in itself* a soul, akin to our own, and in touch with our own.

⁂ 12 ⁂

SUBSTANCE, POTENTIALITY, AND CAUSE: A POSITIVISTIC THEORY OF RATIONALISTIC CATEGORIES [1]

In the present essay is developed a theory designed to serve as a reconciliation of Positivism and Rationalism. According to this theory the rationalistic or extra-experiential categories are accepted as valid; but it is shown how they can be interpreted in positivistic or intra-experiential terms. Herein it is proposed: I. To offer a definition of the rationalistic category of Substance and of its derivatives, Potentiality, and Cause. II. To analyze and appraise the attitudes of rationalists and of positivists toward these categories. III. To establish a compromise theory and to explain its affiliations with the metaphysical systems of Bergson and Descartes. Presupposes some knowledge of philosophy.

I

EXPERIENCE REVEALS to us an apparently external world of sensory objects. A sensory object is a group of many qualities sharing a single position. The objects of one moment are succeeded by the objects of the next moment, which are sometimes the same and sometimes different. Certain types of these successions leave the observer at ease and incurious. Other types move him irresistibly to postulate in the objects something beyond that which appears on the surface, an extra-sensory entity or an

[1] Reprinted from *Travaux du IXe Congrès International de Philosophie*, 1–6, Août, 1937, Paris, Hermann et Cie, pp. vii, 71–77.

extra-experiential category such as "substance," "potentiality," or "cause."

To illustrate: A chair or table persists comparatively unchanged through a succession of moments and perhaps through a succession of positions. In other words, its qualities and particularly its quality of inertia are repeated instant after instant. If it were no more than the image or phantasm that appears, why should it not vanish, to be succeeded by anything or nothing? When there are so many more things that it might be, *why* should it be what it is? This question, implicit in the attitude of common sense, is answered instinctively by ascribing to the sensory object a "substance," an extra-sensory somewhat that *stands under* the qualities which "inhere" in it as "attributes" or "accidents," holds them together, and "explains" their endurance. A second illustration: The acorn becomes the oak again and again, even when the environment varies widely. Common sense cannot help ascribing to the acorn an extra-experiential entity, called "potentiality," which is a kind of substance and postulated for the same kind of reason but employed to explain future rather than past behavior. A third illustration: Water quenches fire again and again and again. Here, as before, common sense is impelled to ascribe to the water an extra-sensory somewhat, a force or power which as a *cause* transforms mere sequence into consequence.

Substance is the first member of this trinity of more or less interchangeable rationalistic categories, and also in a sense the genus of them all; for potentiality is substance in prospect, causality is substance actualizing itself in a present process, while substance proper is substance in retrospect—that which has persisted or endured. Because of its primacy, I shall deal mostly with substance; but when occasion calls, I shall substitute one or the other of the derivative categories.

II

As a Rationalist, I shall claim that the *de facto* procedure of common sense as set forth above is also *de jure*. The case for Rationalism depends on our right to apply probability in the way in which common sense actually (though implicitly) does apply it.

I shall demand of the Positivist first that he concede that there is some chance, no matter how small, say one in a trillion, that his theory that things just happen is wrong, and that therefore his enemy, the common-sense Rationalist, is right in holding that things do not just happen, but happen for a reason, even though we cannot observe it. Now, let him estimate the probability that such routines in nature as acorns becoming oaks, water quenching fire, and so forth, would have just happened, or happened by chance. Let him then compare that probability with the miserably ungenerous one which he reluctantly accorded to the theory of his opponent, and he will see that the latter, however small it may be, is infinitely more than the alternative possibility in which he believes. For, let the probability be what it may, say $\frac{x}{x+y}$, that on a single occasion an acorn would grow to an oak, or the inertia of a closed system at one moment be followed by an equal inertia at the next moment; then the probability in either case that the sequence would be repeated n times is $\left(\frac{x}{x+y}\right)^n$. And as n representing the number of occasions when such sequences have been observed is enormously large, the fraction $\left(\frac{x}{x+y}\right)^n$ is very near to zero, regardless of the values of x and y. But it is just that infinitely small fraction that measures the probability that the rationalism of common sense is wrong and that things are merely what they seem.

I must now assume that our Positivist has been beaten into submission, and that he can but look on with sullen acquiescence while I as the victorious defender of common sense proceed to enjoy at my leisure the hard-won Rationalistic categories of substance, potentiality, and cause.

But now, alas! when I start to use my victory, I am nonplussed, for sensory experience is the *terminus a quo* and the *terminus ad quem* of all utilizable knowledge. It provides both the ultimate source and the ultimate meaning for all conceptions, no matter how Rationalistic they may be. Substance is that extra-sensory somewhat in a sensory object which enables it to persist in time with all or some of its attributes. Yes, but just what is that somewhat? What is substance in itself? What is causality in itself over and above the recurring sequences which it is supposed to explain? And what is the actuality of potentiality, the specific nature of that entelechy in the acorn in virtue of which it grows into an oak? I cannot answer—yet answer I must, and it is now the turn of my supposedly vanquished opponent, the Positivist, to gloat triumphantly in the conviction that defeat for me is victory for him. My predicament is that of a man who can draw checks but cannot cash them. I have earned the right to draw checks on the bank of reason, but I can cash them only at the bank of experience. Yet it was the inadequacy of experience to explain its own sequences that justified our resort to Rationalistic or extra-experiential categories. Here is the real strength of positivism. Any victory won by its enemies is sterile, and without sense or meaning.

In this plight I suddenly bethink me of René Descartes, who, when he found the outer world of experience not to his liking, or at least not sufficient to his logical needs, turned to the inner world of his own consciousness and there discovered *res cogitans*, a kind of experience no less empirical and specific than the experience of *res extensa*, and yet withal curiously different. For in myself I directly perceive that which in the outer world I could merely conceive and infer—a something persisting in time not fortuitously by grace of luck, but by right of preserving its past in its present. The *durée réelle* of Bergson is the "substance" of philosophic tradition. But now it is no longer an empty Rationalistic category, but a specific experience, revealed to us in empirical terms. And as with substance, so also with causality. I directly experience in myself not merely sequence, but the power to enforce sequence, to transform it into consequence. In virtue of that causal power, the regular recurrence of water quenching fire is no longer a miraculous run of luck, but rather the manifestation in the external world of the sort of thing that I find in the internal world as an immediate datum of consciousness. Even David Hume, arch-enemy of causality, did himself inadvertently admit it as an experiential fact. For in a moment of forgetfulness, he spoke of the "gentle force" exercised by our "ideas"! But surely a gentle force is just as truly a force as one that is rough and ungainly, like that which he sternly denied to his billiard balls. And finally, as to potentiality—do we not experience the future as present in the present whenever we imaginatively anticipate a plan of action?

My Positivistic theory of Rationalistic categories can now be definitely stated. It is the theory that substance, potentiality, and cause, which can be and must be conceptually inferred to explain the otherwise infinitely improbable routines of the external sensory world, are susceptible of a perceptual or Positivistic interpretation in terms of the internal sensory world.

III

I have turned to the two great philosophers, René Descartes and Henri Bergson, not because they are Frenchmen and we are in France to celebrate the memory of the one and to enjoy the presence and the presidency of the other, but simply because, as I have already indicated, I find in the *durée réelle* of Bergson the true interpretation of the *res cogitans* of Descartes; and I find in the *res cogitans* itself the true and Positivistic interpretation of the Rationalistic categories which we apply to external reality. But now, despite my deep obligations to these philosophers, I must confess to a partial dissent from each of them.

I cannot agree with the attitude of mysticism and anti-intellectualism which M. Bergson appears to take toward the realm of the mind, nor can I agree with Descartes's interpretation of the duality of *res extensa* and *res cogitans*. I find in the realm of the psychical nothing that is intrinsically unanalyzable in intellectualistic terms. On the contrary, I sympathize with Herbart's great dream of a future psychodynamics, a genuinely mathematical science of the mind and its workings. And when our psychologists become weary of the desert in which for nearly 40 years they have been wandering, and again turn their attention to the psyche itself rather than to the details of its physiological responses to the environment, I believe that they may develop among their number a scientist who will do for the mental world what Galileo and Newton did for the physical.

And the reason for my dissent from M. Bergson is also the reason for my dissent from Descartes. I do, indeed, find between *res cogitans* and *res extensa* a radical contrast, but for me it is a contrast of relations rather than the Cartesian contrast of quality or attribute. I can best express my relational Dualism by defining the physical world as a system of events ordered in *space-time*, and the psychical world as a system of the same or similar events ordered in *time-space*. In the space-time of the material order, space predominates over time, change over duration, extensity over intensity, the plurality of parts over the unity of their wholes, and, in short, *ab extra*, mechanical determination over teleological self-determination. In the mental order, all of these predominances are reversed. Matter and mind are each of them in both space and time, but space is the primary milieu of *res extensa* while time is the primary milieu of *res cogitans*.

Of all the contrasts between the two orders, the most significant is that revealed to M. Bergson in his great *aperçu*. It is that *psychic being is distinctly and pre-eminently characterized by its* DURÉE RÉELLE, *the presence of the past within the present*. The physical world as such is, as Descartes believed, a continuous series of momentary events, and the moments of physical time are mutually exclusive, for each moment must cease before another can come. In mental time, it is just the reverse. Each moment includes, not excludes, the moments preceding it; and instead of time as primarily succession, we have time as primarily duration. The ultimate elements from which matter is derived may well be no more than the waves of the De Broglies and of Schroedinger slithering endlessly from one space to another, a veritable Heracleitean Flux. But floating on this spatio-temporal ocean of change are the temporo-spatial islands that we call "substances." Unlike mere sensory phenomena, they withstand devouring time; and against the laws of probability that would demand their passing, they manage to endure. Each of us is one of these islands and can experience within himself that *durée réelle* which for the physicist is but a Rationalistic postulate. I have compared the substances within the flux to islands, but the stuff of these islands is formed, or at least is mainly formed, of what the environing ocean brings. Each substance consists of retained traces of the motions which have impinged upon it. These minute forms of what the physicist must call *potential* energy, naming them for what they were and will be as externally viewed, are, when internally observed, our psychic actualities. Superposed on one another in an intensive hierarchy, the specificity of each event and the temporal order in which it came are both preserved. This is such stuff as souls are made on. Floating on the three-dimensional surface of the *res extensa*, they have the major portion of their being in that other dimension which is *time* in the form of memories. For they reach downward into the past and upward into the future in the form of the anticipative imaginings correlated with those memories. The latter are, as it were, the shadows projected by the actualities of a single past on the skies of all possible futures.

The history of the world is the history of the forming, deepening, and heightening of substances. It is a history that runs from ancient chaos through countless ages of emerging cosmos. It is an evolution of *time-space* within *space-time*, of the growth within the *res extensa* of substances of the type *res cogitans*.

These substances perhaps begin with the congealing of the waves of radiation into protons and electrons. We know that mass is energy and capable of measurement as such in terms of Einstein's formula. This means that mass is that potential form of energy in which the motions of the past are intensively summed up and held in promise for the future. Next come the syntheses of these first corpuscles into the chemical atoms, and of these in turn into the molecules, and so, at last, the bodies within our field of observation. The stages of this emergent evolution which, in addition to the ones just mentioned, appear to us most crucial are first the storing up of energies in such a way that not mere undirected motions issue from them, but motions that result in sequences of structures as manifest in protoplasm's power to assimilate and reproduce not merely single cells, but, in the higher kinds of life, the recapitulative series of ancestral forms traversed by every embryo. And, following upon and growing up within the merely living organism, there comes that higher form of integration in which the past adventures of an individual and his relations to the world outside are all preserved and unified in what we call a "mind." Here, for the first time, we can experience directly what really always happens when extensive motion passes into that intensive form of being which in our theory constitutes true substance. On lower levels this could only be inferred; but when the kinetic energy of a sensory nerve current passes through the cerebral synapses which check or redirect its motion, then, as always in such cases of arrest, some of the kinetic energy becomes potential and disappears from possible external view. At those moments sensations manifest themselves. The probability seems overwhelming that that which, looked at from without, is called "potential" energy in token of its past and future, is, when seen from within and in its present actuality, just our mental states. And when these transitory fields of neural stress pass back into the outwardly visible or kinetic form of energy and make their exit through the efferent nerves as motor reactions, they do not quite all go. Immeasurably small, but quite specific, traces of energy in potential form remain. These traces are our memories, and, superposed successively on one another, they constitute that ever-present record of our past which is our soul. This high form of substance is the latest, though not, we hope, the last, of evolution's products. But through the age-long series up from protons to *res cogitans* itself, the essence of all substance is that same *durée réelle* which each can find within himself and find to be himself.

The emerging, growing, deepening of substances in this Bergsonian sense pervades the whole of evolution and is its single theme.

13

* A MATERIALISTIC THEORY OF EMERGENT EVOLUTION [1]

A quantitative interpretation of the various qualitative levels of life that successively emerge in the course of evolution. The whole process of development from the simplest protoplasm to the highest forms of spiritual life is depicted as a transformation of mechanical or externally determined systems in which kinetic energy is dominant into teleological or self-determining systems in which potential energy is dominant. It presupposes a little knowledge of biology.

IN THIS PAPER I shall explain and defend three propositions:

(1) That a *living being* is an individual whose reactions to the present environment are controlled primarily by its actual past history and secondarily by its potential future history.

(2) That a *person* is that higher kind of living being in whom the vital power to react to his present in the light of his past and future is not restricted to the preservation of the physical organism and its species—so that, for the first time in evolution, individuals become ends in themselves rather than means to the perpetuation of their type; and the life of the body becomes secondary and instrumental to the life of the spirit.

(3) Finally, I shall argue that "Emergent Evolution,"

[1] Reprinted from *Essays in Honor of John Dewey*, New York, Henry Holt and Company, 1929, pages 257–273.

which means the temporally continuous development of qualitatively discontinuous levels of being, can be explained by a special adaptation of physical categories, and to that extent "materialistically."

From Newton to Einstein, scientists have agreed that the behavior of inanimate bodies can be described in terms of motions, actual or potential; and that these motions are determined in their intensity, direction, and acceleration by the spatial relations between the bodies concerned. Molecular, atomic, and electronic theories serve the purpose of reducing to external or spatial relations of particles what would otherwise figure as the internal or occult nature of the wholes which those particles compose. But while scientists generally are agreed that this mechanistic conception suffices for the description, prediction, and control of inorganic nature, there is no such unanimity in the belief that mechanism applies equally well to the realm of organisms.

Wherever there is *life*, a new factor appears to be involved in the determination of behavior; and this new factor can, I think, be described as the determination of a body's movements, not only by the spatial relations of its mass and velocity to other moving masses, but also by its temporal relations to its own past and future. External neighborhood is supplemented and dominated by internal history as the controlling factor; and time replaces space as the primary *milieu* of all that lives.

This description of the nature of life in general may be given more clarity and plausibility by a consideration of the three specific types of life that are revealed in our experience—Plants, Animals, and Persons. For in an ideal definition, the *principium definitionis* should be capable of serving also as a *principium divisionis;* and if the essence of life consists, as we have stated, in duration or extension in time, the three stages in the hierarchy of life forms should be describable as the successively higher manifestations of this "temporal extension."

In vegetative or plant life, we find that the protoplasmic individual is content to objectify the history which makes up its heredity in the series of material forms that constitute its growth from the comparatively amorphous seed to the comparatively differentiated and articulated system of interacting members composing the adult organism. The typical plant seems to dedicate its individual efforts to the realization of a material structure and to the reproduction of other instances of that material structure. Such activity of *function* as it displays is secondary and instrumental to the building of its *structure*. And in keeping with this subordination of *doing* to *being*, we find its effective intercourse with the environment mainly confined to the domain of immediate contact, and its own locus usually stationary rather than mobile.

The general truth of this description of the vegetative type of life is, I think, quite compatible with the atypical and border-line cases in which plants may dispense with chlorophyll, or devour insects, or react to the presence of water or other nutrient substances not in contact with them, or even move from one part of space to another.

Now, in the animal type of life, we find most of the vegetative powers and then something different and more advanced. The chick in the egg, and the calf in the uterus express the history embodied in their heredity by transforming a comparatively amorphous germ into a comparatively differentiated organism. During gestation, the vital functions of an animal are dedicated like those of a plant to the building up of a material structure. And even in its post-embryonic life its assimilative functions, though more extended and elaborate than those of the plant, are directed largely to the growth and maintenance of a physical organism. But supervening upon these essentially vegetative activities, we find at the typically animal stage of life a power of the living being to control its reactions to the present environment, not merely by an *inherited* past, but by an *individually acquired* past. The animal uses two histories where the plant uses but one. The nervous system characteristic of the animal provides for the retention and accumulation of traces of its past reactions. And these traces of past experience, constituting what we call memory and the capacity to learn by experience, make the animal far more of an individual than the plant. It has an acquired private life over and above the inherited life common to its species. It reacts to things not merely in virtue of their general nutrient value, but in virtue of their individual bearing upon its individual history. How a dog will react to the visual stimulus of a whip or to the auditory stimulus of his master's voice will depend upon what his own past experience has been. There are, moreover, certain secondary concomitants of this primary capacity for developing an individual history which are so often found at the level of animal life that we come to think of them as in themselves definitive. I refer particularly to the capacity to be affected specifically by spatially distant objects, which we call "perception," and the affiliated capacity for selective and self-directed motions of the whole organism with reference to such distant objects, which we can call "volition."

Now, of the two kinds of vital capacities present in animal life, which is the more important, the old capacity to grow, preserve, and reproduce the material structure common to its species, or the new capacity to accumulate and utilize an individuated system of functional activities relevant to its private history? The first-named capacity it shares in common with the plant, the second differentiates it from the plant. Which is the controlling influence in its life? The two factors are, I think, of about *equal* importance. They exist reciprocally, each for the sake of the other. On the one hand, the vegetative process by which the brute's organism is built up in its ontogeny is obviously subordinate to and determined by the distinctively animal functions of his post-embryonic life. The *anabolism* primary in the fetus or in the plant is directed to the formation of organs adapted to the *katabolism* which is the primary and distinctive feature of an adult animal. Energy is accumulated in organic structures to the end that it may be expended in functional activity. But, on the other hand, while vegetative growth is determined by, and preparatory to, animal function, those animal functions are themselves, apparently, determined by, and adapted to, the preservation and reproduction of the physical organism. The animal develops a private and individual history, but he can use it only or mainly for the public good: that is, for the perpetuation of the species which he shares in common with his fellows. The animal has a mind or mirror image of the world outside him, an organism within his organism, consisting of the traces of his past by which he controls his present and anticipates his future; but his "mind," as thus constituted, is an organ of his body, and restricted in its scope to the serving of bodily needs. If we say that an animal remembers, perceives, and imagines, we must say also that these psychic activities are not emancipated from the material interests which they serve. They are not an end in themselves, but a means. The brute is not a vegetable, but he is a slave to his vegetable nature, which is the soil from which his intelligence grows and by which it is nourished and directed.

Now, when we pass from the Animal to the Person, we enter upon a level that is not only higher but easier to analyze, for our external observation of the behavior of others can be supplemented by the internal experience which we have of ourselves. On this third level of life, we discover at once that, as the brute includes most of what the plant can do, so the person includes, in his complex life, the two earlier forms from which he has evolved. In the first place, man is a plant in that his organism develops vegetally from the parental seed; and throughout his life he will be largely occupied with activities instrumental to the nourishing of his body and the procreating of his species. In the second place, man is not only a plant but an animal, in that he acquires an individual or private history, through which he learns by experience. He has perception of distant objects and the volitional power of self-directed motion. But in the third place, man is something more than either plant or animal; and it is my contention that this increment of vitality in which man differs from the lower forms of life is adequately traceable to a *reversal* of the relative potencies: first, of the physical and the psychical; second, of the public history of the species, given in heredity, and the private history acquired by the individual.

The traces of individual experience constituting the memory in an animal seem only strong enough to modify his conduct at any moment to the extent that they are relevant to the practical needs and the physical situation of his organism at that moment. It is only in man that the brain has passed the critical point and evolved in retentiveness and complexity to a stage in which memory ceases to be a mere slave of perception and attains autonomy and self-determination. Images of absent objects, which in the waking life of the brute occur only as parasites of the present situation, in man become preoccupations with reference to which the present situation is subservient or altogether disregarded. In the animal, there are no images of absent objects that occur spontaneously and apart from perceptual bidding except those dream-images which come when the senses are closed and perception itself is in abeyance. Man alone can dream without sleeping, for only in him are the images of memory and imagination strong enough to endure the rivalry of perception. Man's thoughts are waking dreams. They are like stars so steadfast and bright that not even daylight can pale them.

It is this critical *excess* in the strength of his memories that makes man capable of living more in the past and future than in the present. He is the absent-minded animal, and his thinking is lyrical and abstract in contrast with the brute, whose consciousness is so pathetically concrete and practical. Between the two types of life the difference is infinite; and the old theologians who talked of the animal and vegetable "kingdoms" apart from the "kingdom" of man were nearer the truth than we, who, having discovered the descent of man from the animal, have forgotten the abyss that that genealogy has bridged. We may put the matter in the form of a question: How can a spatio-temporally continuous process give rise to qualitatively discontinuous types of life?

The answer is to be found in recognizing, first, that one and the same pair of factors can give opposite products according to whether one or the other factor *predominates;* and, second, that *this change of one product into its opposite can be brought about by the gradual increase of one of the factors until the critical point is reached in which it just exceeds the strength of its former superior.* Consider the "evolution" of water into steam. In each of these contrasting states of matter, there are the same factors of molecular attraction and molecular repulsion. In the liquid state, the attraction exceeds the repulsion. As the application of heat is increased, the agitation among the molecules becomes greater, until the critical point is attained at which the repulsion of the molecules for one another becomes just greater than their attraction. The water *boils*, and we have the "emergent evolution" of a gas from a liquid. A qualitative discontinuity has been generated through the medium of a quantitatively continuous change. Now, the ape-like and the man-like brains are each of them vehicles of the same pair of factors. In each there is first the interest in the perceptually present pertaining to the spatial body, and second the interest in the conceptually absent pertaining to the mind or temporal history of the individual. Let the cells of the simian cortex, in which the physical interest in the present dominates the psychical interest in the absent, increase in number and connectivity as slowly and gradually as you please through any number of generations, and there will come a time when a "boiling point" will be reached—interest in the absent will overtop interest in the present and the *man* will have emerged from the *animal.*

May I guard here against a possible misunderstanding? I do not mean to imply by the illustration just used, or by anything said before, that the sharp distinction in *essence* between the higher and lower levels of life carries with it a correspondingly sharp separation in *existence.* All that the experts may say as to the blend of plant and animal functions in creatures below man, I am, of course, ready to accept. While, as to the inextricable shifting and blending of personal and animal traits, in the individuals of the human species, not only in the days of Pithecanthropus Erectus, but in our own time and country—it is too sadly obvious to require telling. The coming of personal life is like the coming of the tide or the change from winter to spring. It consists of waves of advance and recession. The water boils, but the steam lapses back into the liquid state. Winter has days of spring warmth, and conversely. Animals at their best will sometimes manifest more truly personal living than men.

Let us note once more that an essential phase of the new type of life is the new level of *individuality* which it involves. The dominance of the memory system over the perceptual system brings with it the emancipation of the creature's *private* history from the history of his *species*. The mind and spirit which he *acquires* as an individual count for more than the organs and instincts which he *inherits* from his species. Persons will unite into families, tribes, and nations, and into all sorts of less permanent and more specialized organizations. But in each case the group will, or should, exist for the good of its members rather than the members for the sake of the group. The value of even the Beloved Community will consist, not in itself, but in its ministry to the persons who compose it and in the opportunities which it presents for individual creativeness and reciprocal affection.

In my paper, thus far, I have been mainly concerned with a schematic description of the three levels of life; and I have, in addition, already attempted something in the way of that quantitative or materialistic explanation of their successive appearance which is the goal of my inquiry. I wish now to proceed to a more definite and extended explanation of Emergent Evolution; and to that end I shall offer a hypothesis as to the nature of life and its relation to the material matrix with which it is so intimately associated.

But before presenting my own theory, I will state the three other conceptions which have been applied to the problem, and give in a few words my reasons for rejecting them.

First of all, there is the conception of the Mechanist, who holds that the peculiar behavior of living beings can be adequately explained as the outcome of a system whose laws differ only in their degree of complication from the laws obtaining in the inorganic world. I cannot accept this answer to the question, because, in agreement with Driesch, McDougall, and Bergson, I cannot conceive of any way in which a mere aggregate of material particles, no matter how complex, could provide for that preservation of the past along with the present which we directly experience in what we call *duration.* One configuration of molecules could give place to another, but it would seem impossible for the earlier and later configurations of the same particles to exist and act together at the same time.

Second, there is the conception of the Vitalist or Dualist, according to which the essence of life and mind is incommensurably and inexplicably different from matter, and at least potentially separable from it, though capable of interacting causally with it. I cannot accept this view as satisfactory, because it seems to me to leave a bigger problem than it takes away—the difficulty of understanding how an "entelechy" or "animistic factor," not spatial and not located in space, can be conceived as interacting with the brain, or even as existing concretely at all.

Third, there is the view of the Emergent Evolutionists, who agree with the Dualists as to the hopelessly inexplicable contrast in essence between life or mind on the one hand and mere matter on the other, but differ from them in that they admit that the contrasts have come about as the result of natural evolution. They say that when the arrangement of the particles of a material system attains a certain stage of complexity, new properties are manifested, and new laws of behavior emerge, which cannot be made homogeneous or commensurable with the older and simpler laws of mechanics. They plead for the autonomy of biology and psychology, and for the irreducibility and ultimacy of such categories as organicity and mentality; and they demand that we rest satisfied with this methodological pluralism and accept with "natural piety" the emergence of the new and higher levels of being. I cannot accept this theory as final, because, in spite of its advantages over Mechanism and Dualism, it seems to me to substitute a statement of the problem for its solution. The emergence of new properties and laws constitutes a question rather than an answer; and it should act as a stimulant rather than a sedative. *The history of science is the history of replacing empirically given emergence by rational etiology.*

Ice emerges into water, and motion emerges into heat, but it is the molecular theory that gives us an understanding of how in each case the transition is possible. When we pass from the intra-molar to the intra-molecular or inter-atomic, we find in the minds of all chemists the methodological ideal of explaining the emergence of the new qualities of chemical compounds in terms of the quantitative relations of the atoms composing the molecule. And when we pass from the chemical realm of the intra-molecular to the intra-atomic or inter-electronic domain of radioactive phenomena, do we not find an analogous faith in the possibility of explaining such specific properties as those of hydrogen and helium and of uranium, radium, and lead in terms of the quantitative relations of the protons and electrons composing the atoms? If there should be a step beyond this to an intra-electronic domain, we should again expect to find that the new elements (Schroedinger waves or whatever they might be) would explain through their relational structure the protons and electrons which were their emergent resultants. In short, throughout the entire hierarchy of successively larger wholes, from the lowest sub-electronic elements up to the colloidal and crystalline masses that are visible to our eyes, we can expect to find (as in large and promising measure we have already found), a series of structures each of which will possess a nature different from the parts which compose it, but explainable in terms of the relations between those parts. The successive levels of being will indeed be different, but the difference will be commensurable and intelligible, rather than ultimate and unanalyzable.

Whenever we are confronted with the emergence of a

novel form, we never rest content with an attitude of "natural piety." "Natural piety" is scientific treason, a betrayal of the faith that has generated progress and enabled us to replace the helpless acceptance of novelties as brute facts with an increasingly satisfactory understanding and mastery of their genesis.

Now, I wish to guard against an exaggeration of this doctrine of Rational Etiology, which would be fatal to its utility and even to its truth. In explaining the novelties of Emergent Evolution, we do not explain them away. The solid condition of matter remains just as different from the liquid condition after the change is explained in terms of molecular interrelationships as before that explanation was attained. There is the new kind of behavior after the fluid has frozen, and there is the new and unique quality or immediacy which we call solidity and which we contrast with the antecedent quality of liquidity. More than this we should not desire. It would, indeed, be the greatest of pities if the Helmholzian analysis of a clang into its constituent tones were to deprive us of the clang itself.

There is, moreover, a second aspect of the situation which we must not lose sight of. The analysis of a thing into its parts not only fails to destroy its immediate quality as such, it fails also to touch the attributes that pertain to it in virtue of the larger wholes of which it is itself a part. The analytic explanation of a mental state, for example, must be supplemented by its configurational or synthetic interpretation in terms of the *Gestalt* within which it is contained and from which it receives its meaning and value. On the mental and on the vital levels of being, this configurational aspect of a thing may, in fact, be of more importance than the other or analytic aspect. And even on the inorganic plane, the qualities of a phenomenon that are contributed by its context must not be neglected.

Now, if we have been right in holding that the properties of inorganic nature (within the limits just noted) can be explained analytically in terms of the parts of which the structure is composed, may we not hope that the greater gap between the inorganic on the one hand and the vital and mental on the other can, at least to some extent, be similarly explained? It is in the faith that this question should be answered affirmatively that I am proposing the hypothesis which, apart from any claim which it may have for final validity, seems to be the kind of hypothesis for which we should look.

In the beginning of our discussion we noted that the fundamental property of a living being was its possession and use of a history. Now everything, living or dead, possesses a history; but only a living thing uses its history to determine its conduct. It not only has a past, but it has a past that is present and operative.

That this is so is obvious and undeniable. *How* it is so is the great problem. To explain life would be to explain how the material structure called protoplasm can retain and operate with events that have been, but are no longer, members of the physical world.

There is one and only one physically definable situation in which a sequence of past events can be present and causally operative with their specificities undestroyed. This is the situation in which a series of motions or kinetic energies have been successively transformed into modes of stress or potential energy, and superimposed upon one and the same material system. A simple illustration of this superposition of energies is afforded by a rope which is first twisted, then folded upon itself, then twisted and folded again, and so on. A rope treated in this fashion will, when released, regurgitate more or less the same series of overt motions which were imposed upon it, thus revealing the fact that the past has been present in the present. If protoplasm were a structure capable of retaining in an intensive or potential form the energies given to it by the environment, it would possess what as a matter of fact it does possess: the capacity to respond to the present in the light of its accumulated and retained past history. Its reactions would be of the trigger-type, in which the response bears no fixed and measurable relation to the stimulus that releases it. Any system, such as a twisted rope, in which potential energy is stored up betrays "irritability" when teased. There is more to it than appears to an external observer. Its actions cannot be explained in terms of its contemporary environment (which alone is externally visible), but only in relation to its past environments, the contacts with which constitute its history.

If the reader will be kind enough to grant that my twisted rope is strikingly analogous to protoplasm in respect to the primary property of *preserving the past*, and the resultant secondary property of *irritability*, I will at once reciprocate the kindness by confessing that there the analogy ends. The case of the rope and similar cases of potential energy in the inorganic world lack the property which next to history itself is the most important characteristic of a life-system; I refer to *anabolism* and its climactic phase, which is *reproduction*.

A quality, as a pattern of any kind, may pass from one place to another in two ways: by *conduction* and by *induction*. The curse that rests upon most accumulations of potential energy in the inorganic realm is that they tend to waste themselves in motions which conduct and dissipate their accumulated energies over the environment. The Increase of Entropy or the Second Law of Thermodynamics is the name given to the one-way tendency of energy to flow from the more concentrated, differentiated, and organized conditions to the more dissipated, more uniform, and more random conditions. The intense waves caused by the stone dropped in the pool spread out over the water. The hot stove in the warm room never sucks up the warmth and grows hotter and thus more differentiated, but diffuses its heat to the cooler environment until thermal differentiation is gone and thermal equilibrium is attained. Humpty Dumpty falls from the wall and his exquisite organization is irremediably lost in the squash.

Now, if we turn from death and the ways of dead things to life and the ways of growth, we find the opposite to all this. Protoplasm presents us with concentration rather than dissipation of energies and their patterns, and with an increase of differentiation and organization and, thus, with at least temporary and local decreases of entropy. Instead of waiting for the wind to blow Humpty Dumpty from the wall, let us gently replace him in the warm nest on which the mother hen is sitting. We shall then see the fertilized germ impose its primary energy patterns upon the comparatively amorphous material of the egg. The latter, as food for the growing embryo, will gradually be transformed by a miraculous ontogenetic anabolism into the lungs and liver, wings and beak and brain of the chick. Like the acorn and elm seed planted in the same soil, the life-system amplifies and reproduces its pattern at the expense of the environing food. To describe this anabolism as "the interaction of organism and environment" is the sorriest and most mischievous of truisms, for it masks the infinite prepotency of the living member of the partnership. Vital growth is transposition of the organism's pattern to the food around and within it. And this transfer of pattern takes place by *induction* rather than by *conduction.* I would illustrate this by another analogy. Instead of the twisted rope, let us take a group of electrifiable bodies insulated from their environment except with respect to the wires through which we shall charge them with current. When charged, we leave them suspended near each other in a viscous fluid, and then "feed" them with other electrifiable particles placed among them. We shall expect to find the electrostatic force-pattern of the system imposing itself upon the new particles by inducing in them charges appropriate to their position in the field. Similarly chargeable particles added from time to time would in their turn receive charges determined by their positions and by the increasingly complex pattern of the whole. Nor would it be beyond the possibilities of arrangement to create a situation in which the entire pattern or a portion of it would by induction duplicate or "reproduce" itself. The point is that, with induction in contrast to conduction, fields of potential energy or force can be transferred from one material system to another without loss of specificity, and that the new and more complex system that results contains more rather than less organization. There is, at least locally and temporarily, the same sort of reversal of the principle of entropy that a life system seems to exhibit in the anabolism by which it builds up or synthesizes the comparatively less organized food-molecules into its own comparatively more organized tissues.

If we knew with sufficient detail the fine structure of protoplasmic units, molecules or molecule-clusters, we might expect to understand just how this quasi-induction, with the accompanying growth of the organism, takes place. To discover this would be to discover how a material system storing up a history in the form of potential energy (which is the only physically possible form in which the past can be present in the present) amplifies and reproduces that strange intensive pattern. Life, once started, would ramify and spread over the fortunate earth; its varied forms sometimes perpetuating themselves unchanged, sometimes simplifying or degenerating, and sometimes evolving into more diverse and more complex or higher types.

It seems to me that it is a great mistake to measure vital excellence by degree of adjustment to environment. If life be at all as we have described it, its business is not to adjust itself to the environment, but to adjust the environment to it, to impose its pattern upon its surroundings and increasingly inform them. It is the inorganic systems that tend toward conformity and orthodoxy and approximate in their increase of entropy more and more to undifferentiation and equilibrium, thermodynamic or otherwise, with their environment. The deader a thing is, the more stable its adaptation to its *milieu*. A block of granite, a diatom, a clam, an ape, a Socrates, embody in increasing measure an aggressive and rebellious power to impose their retrospective and impliedly prospective patterns upon a neutral or more or less hostile world. This invasive, insurgent, and heterodox temper of life does not, of course, preclude —on the contrary, it necessitates—a certain modicum of adaptation. Life must stoop to conquer; but unending conquest, not conformity, is its goal.

And now, did space permit, we could formulate again and with more precision, in terms of our theory, the main ascending steps in evolution. As it is, we shall content ourselves with a summary outline of the three successively emerging levels of Plant, Animal, and Person, interpreted materialistically in the sense already defined. That is to say, we shall endeavor to show that there are the same two factors in any pair of successive levels, and that the transition from one to the other, momentous though it be, is adequately explained by a continuous *quantitative* growth of the lower factor until the critical point is reached when it gains ascendancy over its former superior and there *emerges* a novel quality of being seemingly discontinuous with that which gave it birth.

(1) *From the Inorganic to the Organic.*—In the domain of dead matter and in the domain of life we find the same two factors: *first*, the factor of kinetic energy with its tendency to diffuse and run down by *conduction;* and

second, the factor of potential energy with its tendency to perpetuate and reproduce by polaric *induction* the past history which it invisibly embodies. But in the domain of the inorganic, the visible and primarily spatial energy of motion predominates. Energy is, to be sure, accumulated and concentrated in electric, magnetic, and gravitational fields and in the explosive combinations of atomic systems; but in the main, it tends to dissipate and diffuse into motion. It is saved only to be spent. It is not until the coming of the type of carbon-compound called *protoplasm* that we find a material system that is capable not only of storing in potential form and specific pattern the energies that impinge upon it, but also of propagating them or imposing them by a kind of induction upon new matter. This capacity of a thing for preserving *and reproducing* its past history is the definitive property of a living being. Once started, it tends to spread and inform more and more of the environment. It tends also to increase the richness of its own organization, and so to evolve new and higher types of itself. It is definitely anti-entropic, if not in physical literalness, at least in intent and significance. It is a level of being on which the temporal dominates the spatial, and history, ceasing to be external and factitious, becomes internal and causally operative as such.

(2) *From Plant Life or Mere Life to Animal Life.*—On each of these levels of the evolutionary process, we find the same two vital factors: *first*, the factor or capacity for receiving, retaining, and organizing the energies that are bound up with matter as food; and *second*, the factor or capacity for receiving, retaining, and organizing energies not bound up with matter. Thus, the plant not only anabolizes the soil that feeds it, but by its chlorophyll mechanism receives and stores up the radiant energy of light waves. And the animal, also, not only takes in food and builds it up into the specific tissues of his bodily struc-

ture, but through his nervous system (or through those diffused and less differentiated receptors which in the lowest animals are the evolutionary ancestors of the nervous system) he retains and organizes the impinging energies of light, of sound, of mechanical or molar contacts, and of those molecular contacts which when dissolved in liquid constitute taste and when in volatile or gaseous form constitute smell. But whereas the chlorophyll mechanism in the plant resembles the animal nervous system in the single point of being an energy-receptor rather than a food-receptor, the nervous system differs from the chlorophyll system in these two all-important respects: it receives and retains the impinging energies in such a way as to preserve their individual specificities; and second and relatedly, it preserves the energy-traces distinct from one another and distinct in their entirety from the growth-system of the organism. The plant uses up the free energy which it receives from the environment in its business of structural growth. The animal uses the free energies which it receives to build up a cerebral memory-system which enjoys a certain autonomy and insulation, so that it does not go into structure, but into function or behavior. And the fact that the different energy-impacts are not fused into an undifferentiated mass, but are retained with something of their incoming distinctness, gives to the animal a particularized internal record of the extra-organic objects that are relevant to his weal and woe. This internal record constitutes a secondary organism within the primary organism. It embodies a private history by which he guides his behavior. He learns by experience, which means that he reacts to the present in the light of his individual past. His life is not like that of the plant, entirely occupied with preserving and amplifying his material structure. He is a *doer* and not merely a *grower*. We are not to construe the emergence of animal life from mere life as indicating a descent of animals from plants. The chlorophyll mechanism is the brother or cousin rather than the ancestor of the nervous system. The brute and the vegetable are, as Bergson has pointed out, divergent alternative developments from the undifferentiated protista, who were the common ancestors both of the protozoa and the protophytes. But, whereas the chlorophyll receptor merely provides a new and richer means of extending that anabolism or structure-building (which is the generic character of mere life as such) by utilizing sunlight as well as food, the acquirement of a nervous system results in a new and higher level of life, on which, over and above the capacity to build a body in the ancestral form, there is the added capacity to build a private and individual history and an internal and individual replica of the objects in the outside world. This secondary organism is both the cause and the effect of the self-directive and increasingly adaptive motions by which life begins its conquest of the extra-organic environment.

(3) *From the Animal to the Person.*—In both the animal and the person there are the same two factors: *first*, the vegetal and inherited factor of body-building anabolism; *second*, the private history of the organism's own adventures with the surrounding world. And in the early part of our study we set forth with some care the manner in which the gradual increase of the second factor to the point of emancipation from the mere service of the first factor resulted in the emergence of the rational or personal type of life. We need now only to restate the conclusion, in terms of our hypothesis, as to the identity of the history embodied as an operative factor in a life-system with the pattern of energies stored up in potential form. It is when the potential energies constituting the memory-system or secondary organism become sufficiently strong to be capa-

ble of functioning autonomously and independently of the sensory solicitations of the environment that the individual becomes freed from the *here* and *now* of his body, and life becomes spirit.

(4) *From the Personal to the Divine.*—No one can discuss Emergent Evolution without having in mind the great book of S. Alexander, *Space, Time, and Deity*. And although the present essay is a protest against one aspect of that work and a plea that when confronted with the emergence of new levels of being we should put search for a rational etiology in place of the attitude of "natural piety," yet it is Alexander's treatment of Deity as the not yet achieved stage of evolution that suggests the question as to whether our own theory provides a basis for conceiving of a level that is higher, not merely in degree, but in kind, than personal life at its best.

Man, like other animals, extends his vital power of organization beyond the limits of his organism. Beehives, birds' nests, and human dwelling houses are examples of the animal ability to objectify in extra-organic material the needs for bodily shelter and procreation. It is, however, in his laboratories and churches and in such quasi-physical institutions as government and school that man objectifies his distinctively human capacities and by a kind of sublimated anabolism makes carnate in his culture the ideals of his spirit. These cultural embodiments of the human spirit are not themselves alive. They differ from the physical offspring and the body cells which are the living creatures of a living being. The latter are, however, embodiments only of the organism and not of the mind or spirit. *If man were able to give actual life to the children of his spirit and to endow them with the same independence and capacity for self-preservation and reproduction as that possessed by the fruits of his body, he would have attained the next higher level of evolution, which, following*

Alexander, we may denominate the level of Deity. We should need, in short, to be like Pygmalion and bring into existence living Galateas, who would incarnate our needs and aspirations and at the same time share with us the boon of independent and self-perpetuating existence. Then we should be as Gods. As it is, our cultural creatures are but shadows and images, transitory reflections of spirit in the flux of matter, precarious adjectives of a substance not their own. Whether we are to attain to the higher level which we can now only vaguely imagine, and whether the Macrocosm has already attained or from the beginning possessed it, we have no sure means of knowing. Deity may be only an essence, destined never to emerge into existence. Or, if it exists, it may be only as a prerogative of the universe as a whole. But there is also the possibility that even finite beings may in time achieve it.

In conclusion I would advert to the question which each writer in this volume will, I suppose, have put to himself: What relevance has the essay which he has been privileged to tender as a tribute of affection and admiration for John Dewey to the philosophy of John Dewey himself? "A materialistic theory of Emergent Evolution," even if well-founded, might at first hearing sound alien to the temper of Dewey's own work, which has so consistently expressed a distrust of old and conventional labels. I am sensitive to the defect in this respect not only of my title, but of my whole discussion. I am, however, to some extent consoled by the reflection that while the founder of Instrumentalism has protested against the older categories and captions by which philosophers have separated themselves from one another and from the reality which they sought to interpret, he has supplemented that protest by much concrete and positive insistence upon the pluralistic, the contingent, and the discontinuous phases of experience. And furthermore, he has accompanied his plea for a due recognition of the discrete with an equally positive demand that the heterogeneities and pluralities of experience be included in the one homogeneous continuum of nature.

If my paper has to any degree mitigated the conflict between the earlier concept of a continuous evolution and the more recent concept of an emergence of successive discontinuities, it will in so far forth, I hope, have been in harmony with the philosophy of "Experience and Nature."

14

VARIATION, HEREDITY, AND CONSCIOUSNESS [1]

An analysis of the mechanistic and vitalistic interpretations of variation; heredity, and consciousness, combined with an exposition and defense of the theory that these three basic aspects of life are expressions of protoplasm's capacity to accumulate within itself intensive hierarchies of potential energy. It presupposes some knowledge of biology and psychology.

Introduction: A Mechanist Answer to the Vitalist Challenge

From the days of Democritus to those of Darwin there were many attempts by materialistic philosophers to explain the seemingly purposive phenomena of life and mind in terms of the physical categories of science. The total of these efforts netted more of failure than of success. One after another of the problems of inorganic nature had been conquered by the patient application of mechanistic methods, but the outstanding characters of living matter had resisted elucidation by these methods and maintained a stubborn independence. Some of the organic processes and their material products had, to be sure, been reduced to terms of physics and chemistry, but the correlation of organs and functions in the individual, and the adaptation of the various species to one another and to the environment, remained quite unexplained. Up to the time of Dar-

[1] Reprinted from *Proceedings of the Aristotelian Society*, London, Williams and Norgate, Vol. 21, 1921, pp. 13–50.

win, the materialists were forced to rely mainly upon an appeal to faith rather than proof. Their method had succeeded in the inorganic fields of astronomy, physics, and chemistry, and should be trusted to achieve a similar triumph in the fields of biology and psychology.

Since the coming of Darwin, however, the balance against materialism has become a balance in its favor. The fact of evolution itself affords a presumption of the ultimate homogeneity of organic and inorganic laws; and the great idea of natural selection as a method by which the adaptation of organs and the evolution of species can be at least partially explained without the aid of design has put the opponents of materialism on the defensive. Biology and psychology can no longer be regarded as islands of safety in which the teleological philosophers may take refuge from the steadily rising tide of mechanistic science. And yet, despite the threatening situation in which they find themselves, the defenders of the doctrine of teleology have by no means abandoned hope. Bergson in France, McDougall in England, and Driesch in Germany have attacked mechanistic philosophy as not only inadequate to cope with the known facts of phylogeny, ontogeny, and consciousness, but as being definitely in conflict with those facts.

The present status of the controversy as I see it is this: in the first place, the anti-Mechanists—whether out-and-out idealists or mere dualists—have succeeded in demonstrating that mechanistic categories, even when strengthened by the Darwinian principle of Natural Selection, fail to explain the basic characters of vital activity. And they have shown that this failure is not due to the mere complexity of living systems, but rather to the incorrigible purposiveness which life exhibits, whether it be studied externally as in biology or internally as in psychology, and whether we consider its development in the individual or in the species.

In the second place, however, it seems to me that the success of Vitalism in the way of destructive criticism is offset by its failure to afford a constructive principle of explanation. Whether we consider the relatively definite entelechy theories of Driesch, McDougall, and Bergson or the more general appeals to a category of organicity and to a "fitness of the environment," which characterize, respectively, the idealism of Dr. Haldane and the Neo-Paleyism of Professor Henderson, we find a failure to provide principles which are homogeneous with the established truths and fruitful methods of mechanistic science. In short, we are confronted at the present time with a situation in which the teleological and psychical characters of living beings remain as aliens in the country of science. The Mechanists would have us forcibly deport these dangerous foreigners and then ignore, so far as possible, their very existence. In other words, they would reduce teleology to an illusion and consciousness to an epiphenomenon. On the other hand, the Vitalists would permit teleological processes and psychic agencies to run amuck throughout the whole domain of science, introducing destruction and paralysis, and generally disorganizing the peaceful industry of producing a material cause for every material effect. Each of these plans is dangerous, and in the end fruitless. The real remedy is to assimilate or naturalize the alien entities of teleology and consciousness and give them citizenship in the society of the mechanistic sciences. Until they are thus naturalized, they will continue a menace to the experimental study of nature.

The present paper is an attempt to point out one way in which the process of naturalization can be brought about. Variation, Heredity, and Consciousness are the three aspects of life which give most trouble to the advocates of a mechanistic world view. And the fact that the comments which I wish to offer upon these three sets of problems have a certain unity of principle is my only excuse for dealing in a single paper with such vast and diversified fields of knowledge. Aside from the pretentiousness of its title, there is another and more serious defect of my essay for which I ask forgiveness. I have been obliged to use old-fashioned and more or less discredited categories in order to express my thought. In the writings of Hume, Mill, and Comte, of Mach and Pearson, and now of Professor Whitehead and Mr. Russell, there has been a steady development of the methodological standpoint of positivism or descriptionism. A notable aspect of this development of descriptionism is the tendency to abandon the old conception of Force, as a mere unjustifiable hypostatization of our feelings of effort and muscular strain. In the face of this formidable consensus of experts, I have talked in my paper about forces and still more questionable entities such as "super-forces." I would plead in defense that the experiences of pressure and effort have as good a claim to objective validity as have visual qualities of extension and shape; and no one of the advantages of the latter for purposes of description is incompatible with according an objective status to qualities like force and effort, which are methodologically less useful. For example, the assumption of the *methodological* Behaviorist that mind can best be described in terms of its manifestation in bodily movement does not imply the conclusion of the *metaphysical* Behaviorist that mind itself is therefore unreal. And it seems to me that in quite the same way we could hold that the methodological advantage of describing *force* in terms of its overt and measurable manifestation in change of motion need not imply the metaphysical conclusion that force itself is therefore unreal. And, in addition to the above excuse, I would urge that, as it has proved possible in many branches of physics to translate, without serious change of meaning, the older dynamic terminology of explanation into the modern language of kinematic description, so it might also be possible for a friendly scientific critic to translate into the language of today the old-fashioned concepts which my ignorance compels me to use.

Finally, as to the actual errors which I may have committed quite irrespective of terminology, I can only hope that they are not so grave or so numerous as to render the paper altogether worthless, and that among the experts here present there may be some who, after demonstrating the errors, will be willing to undertake the more difficult business of explaining to what extent if at all my hypotheses can be amended to fit the facts as they know them.

And now, without further preamble, I proceed to the consideration, in turn, of the three distinct yet related aspects of vital activity which appear to offer most resistance to mechanistic explanation. It will be my aim to show that, as regards each of the three sets of problems, it is possible to point out a solution which is statable in mechanistic terms, but which at the same time provides full satisfaction to the demand of the Vitalist or anti-Mechanist that the purposive and psychic characters of life be not reduced to an epiphenomenal status of dependence upon blind processes but be recognized as genuinely operative factors in the economy of nature.

I. Variation

The analogy of the germinal telogenesis of congenital variation to the psycho-cerebral telogenesis of creative imagination, and the mechanistic explanation of each as the resultant of a system of biological vectors.

Phylogenetic evolution consists in the progressive realization in the species of organs which are fitted to cope with the environment. Each of these organs of adaptation is a *telos* or purposive structure, and once granted the origin of variations in sufficient number and of a sufficient degree of utility, the teleological process by which they are actualized in the species can be mechanistically explained by Darwin's principle of Natural Selection. But before a telos can be actualized in the organism, it must have originated in the germ. Teleology must be preceded by *Telogenesis*.

Since the abandonment of Lamarck's conception of the transmission of acquired characters, the most vulnerable point in the mechanistic theory of evolution, and the point against which the Vitalists have aimed some of their strongest attacks, is the notion that the useful variations on which Natural Selection must work are accidental or non-purposeful in origin. In matters of purely quantitative variation, such as size and weight, we might well admit that good or plus variations and bad or minus variations in the germinal determinants of any organ are equally probable; and a perfectly "blind" or mechanistic conception of their origin would suffice. But the development through a succession of minute variations of such organs as eyes and lungs is a very different matter. The number of meaningful combinations of letters is infinitely smaller than the number of meaningless juxtapositions; and similarly, the number of useful combinations of cells and cell-elements such as would be required to constitute an organ like an eye is infinitely smaller, and their occurrence is therefore infinitely less probable, than the number of useless or harmful arrangements. That the molecules and atoms of a fertilized germ cell should group themselves by mere chance, that is, by merely physical or blind forces, in such a way as to initiate or advance the formation of a useful bodily organ would seem to be enormously improbable. Such general considerations, combined with the more special objection that the earlier stages in the development of useful organs have no survival value on which Natural Selection can work, have led the vitalists to believe in what is called "orthogenesis," that is, an intrinsic tendency of the germ plasm to vary in one of the comparatively few directions that make for progress rather than in any of the virtually infinite number of ways that would be useless.

The remedies proposed by the Vitalists are, however, worse than the disease which they are designed to cure. We must grant the existence of something like orthogenesis; but to explain it by abandoning mechanistic categories and invoking an *anima ex machina* as first aid to the physiologist when in trouble is bad hypothetical methodology and hurtful to scientific progress. The activities of a Drieschian *entelechy* or a Bergsonian *élan vital* are at best hopelessly incommensurable with the known modes of bodily activity.

The first and most natural way out of the difficulty would consist in a revival of the Lamarckian belief in the ability of the soma plasm to impart to the germ plasm which it contains the specific adaptive improvements in eyes or lungs which had been acquired by the animal through functional adjustment to the light and air of its environment. But lack of empirical evidence for the inheritance of such acquirements, combined with the absence of any known mechanism by which specific somatic improvements could be transmitted to the reproductive cells, suffice to convince the great majority of biologists that this way out is fruitless. Moreover, even if Lamarckianism were acceptable, it would scarcely apply to some of the most striking of the congenitally useful characters, such as those of the worker bees, in which there has been little chance for the parents to have acquired the advantageous capacities which appear in their offspring.

A second way out of the difficulty might seem to be

furnished by the mutation theory of De Vries; but this innovation upon Darwinism meets the difficulty to which the parent theory was subject in the matter of explaining how Natural Selection could act on those organs which in their incipient stages possessed no survival value, only at the price of increasing to a preposterous degree the overdrafts on the theory of probability. For, if it is difficult to see how merely physical or chemical disturbances in the germ plasm could suffice to produce even the minutely favorable variations which Darwin himself believed in, it is proportionately more difficult to believe that "mutations" or large variations could be the product of blind or mechanical causes. It is hard enough to believe that handfuls of letters thrown into the air would fall into place as intelligible words; it is infinitely harder to believe that they would so fall as to make whole sentences. In short, any advantages of the De Vriesian mutations (as substitutes for the minute variations of the Darwinians) are fully offset by the greater improbability of such mutations arising mechanistically.

In difficulties of this character it is often possible to derive help from analogies; suppose, then, that we turn aside for a moment from the problem of the origin of useful variations in the germ to that other problem (too much neglected by psychologists) as to the origin of useful variations in conscious life. It is so natural for us to consider the teleological phase of mental activity in which purposes are deliberately realized in conduct or in art, that we are apt to forget that earlier and more spontaneous telogenetic phase in which the ideal or purpose originates. Yet this earlier telogenesis is at least as important as the later teleology; and it is most certainly its necessary condition. Before an ideal can be actualized, it must have originated.

Telogenesis is the heart of what Bergson calls "creative evolution"; and that great philosopher has clearly demonstrated that creative evolution depends upon the cumulative preservation of the past. Because of this preservation of the past, every product of a telogenetic process must have two basic characteristics: first, the characteristic of *pertinence* and, second, the characteristic of *novelty*. Since a telos arises from the past, it must be pertinent or relevant to it; it must carry on or carry out the tendencies which generate it, and make explicit what was implicit. But that which is a function of the whole past cannot be a mere repetition of a part of the past; hence, the telos that arises will not merely be *pertinent*, it will also be *novel*. Real duration of the old is the condition and cause of a real creation of the new.

The theory that evolution is the working out of a divine plan—a repetition in time of what pre-existed in eternity—is criticized by Bergson on the ground that such an explanation does not solve the problem of design in the cosmos, but merely shifts it from the relatively accessible domain of the evolution of species in nature to the relatively inaccessible domain of the genetic psychology of the Deity. The question of how purposes can originate in the world is not answered by saying that they originated at a previous time in a divine or absolute mind.

Let us now consider some of the ways in which the two characteristics of *pertinence* and *novelty* are expressed in the telogenetic processes of consciousness.

(1) In cognitive experience, the formation of a hypothesis which harmonizes and explains a mass of data is a typical case of telogenesis. The hypothesis flashes up in the creative imagination of the scientist. It is *novel* in that it differs from each of the remembered facts which contributed to generate it; and at the same time it is *pertinent* in that it explains them all. It reconciles their hitherto conflicting or unrelated tendencies, and carries them out and through to a victorious peace.

(2) In the conative sphere, telogenesis is virtually identical with external adjustment or *adaptation*. When in

action, our problems are solved not by carrying out in detail a premeditated plan, but rather by novel and pertinent adaptation to the exigencies of the environment. This power to make unpurposed yet purposeful adjustments is sagacity.

(3) In the domain of affective experience, telogenesis is exemplified in almost any case of artistic creation or expression. Humor, in particular, because of the suddenness and spontaneity which is of its essence, is a perfect case of telogenetic activity. The flash of wit or pat remark, when at its best, is the acme of both pertinence and novelty. It is fresh, sudden, original, yet it expresses the quintessence of a prior situation with more accuracy than could be attained by the most laborious copying. I think we may say that, in general, it is only second-rate art that is either romantic or realistic. For it is only when art is second-rate that it will have to secure novelty at the expense of accuracy, or accuracy at the expense of novelty. In first-rate art the best of the one will be the best of the other. The most pertinent illumination of nature will be also the most novel and original.

(4) One of the best examples of telogenesis, and one in which the cognitive, conative, and affective interests are equally involved, is afforded by the activity of speech or talk. In talking, a man does not and cannot plan out his words in advance. His sentences are not duplicates of what pre-existed; they do not repeat his thoughts: they express them. It is only in giving a speech that has been committed to memory that one's talk is teleological rather than telogenetic. In unpremeditated talk, the meanings demanded by the topic under discussion are held by the mind in solution, and the words spoken are the crystals precipitated from the solution. Now, there are some psychologists who are so biased in favor of teleology that they would explain these cases of telogenesis by assuming that

the novel and pertinent creations of consciousness are always pre-existent in a subconsciousness. Even if this were true, the problem of accounting for these useful variations would only be shifted to another and less manageable domain. We should immediately have to inquire as to how the words and sentences pre-existent in the subconscious had themselves originated. In short, the telogenetic process in which variations arise that are at once pertinent and novel, purposeful yet unpurposed, is an ultimate fact and can in no way be reduced to mere teleology.

It will be recalled that we digressed from our primary problem as to the origin of useful variations in the germ plasm in order to see if the better-known but analogous cases of telogenesis in conscious activity would afford any suggestion for a mechanistic solution. In what follows, I shall try to show that the foundation for such a mechanistic solution is afforded by the principle of *biological vectors*, and that that principle is applicable not only to congenital variation but to the types of telogenesis exhibited by vital systems and by creative imagination.

A vector is a quantity having both magnitude and direction. It may be symbolized by a straight line of definite length and definite direction. The sum of two vectors is given by the diagonal of a parallelogram whose two adjacent sides are the vectors to be added. Vectors or directed lines can represent not only velocities and accelerations or forces, but also the higher spatio-temporal derivatives such as accelerations of accelerations, or "super-forces," which will be explained in the second part of the paper. The result of combining or fusing two or more of such forces or "super-forces" will always be expressed by a resultant vector which is got by the process of geometrical addition just mentioned. A very simple case of the combination of vectors will serve as an illustration of the general law. A body acted upon by a westward force and a northward force, simultaneously, will move or tend to move in a northwesterly direction. If the magnitude and direction of the westward force is represented by a three-inch line pointing west, and the magnitude and direction of the northward force is represented by a four-inch line pointing north and making a second side of a rectangle, then the magnitude and direction of the resulting motion or tendency to move will be represented by the diagonal of the rectangle, that is, by a line five inches long and having a direction slightly north of northwest. In this case, as in others, the resultant of a combination of vectors will be a vector having the qualities of *pertinence* and *novelty*. For the northwesterly force is pertinent in that it carries out the westerly and northerly characters of its components, while its novelty is manifest in its differing from each of those characters. It is like orange light, which differs from the red and yellow from which it arises and at the same time, in its own new and richer hue, carries out and expresses the simpler and more primitive characters of its constituents.

Now, without committing ourselves to a strict psychophysical parallelism, we can accept the theory that mental states are somehow correlated with physical states. And these physical correlates of mental states can only be conceived as of the nature of velocities, accelerations, or forces in the cerebrum—in other words, as vectors and groups of vectors. The unity and continuity of the cerebral system will provide for a constant interaction and combination of these cerebral vectors, with the consequence that new vectors will be produced as resultants or summations. Each of these resultants will have the characters of *pertinence* and *novelty* in relation to the constituents by which it was generated. It will, in short, have precisely the qualities which we found to be exemplified in the telogenetic products of psychic adaptation and creative imagination.

In this connection it is important for us to realize that, while Mechanists are not agreed on any metaphysical theory of the nature of the relation of a mental state to its physical concomitant, they are agreed that the concomitance itself is a fact. Hence, any fusion or combination of the cerebral correlates of mental states must be accompanied by a corresponding fusion or combination of the mental states themselves. And since the combination of cerebral factors is of necessity a vector addition whose sum must express in a new tendency the harmonious fulfilment and unification of the pre-existing tendencies, so on the mental side there would with equal necessity result those same unpurposed yet purposeful syntheses which were given as illustrations of telogenesis in the field of conscious activity.

How will our principle of biological vectors apply to the problem of the origin of useful variations in the germ plasm?

The fertilized germ of an animal is like the human brain in that it is the bearer of a mass of tendencies representing the past. In the brain these traces of the past constitute the memories from the synthesis of which arise the felicitous telogenetic novelties of *creative imagination.* In the case of the germ, the traces of the past constitute not memories but the hereditary determinants from whose orthogenetic synthesis arise the useful variations or telogenetic novelties of *creative evolution.*

If the millions of ancestral qualities which must be embodied as determinants in the chromatin of the germ plasm are conceived as we conceived the physical correlates of the brain's memories, namely, as of the nature of velocities, accelerations, or forces, they will together constitute a vector system, constantly giving rise to other vectors, which will be not only novel but pertinent. Like the flashes of inspiration, these resultant vectors will express in new ways the combined tendencies from which they arose; and without having abandoned the categories of Mechanism, we shall have justified orthogenesis.

In short, creative evolution and creative imagination are diverse in media, but identical in activity. Nature is not stone blind like the atoms of the older Materialism, nor, on the other hand, is she as depicted in the older Theism, a moral agent endowed with prevision and engaged in the realization of pre-existent plans. She is an artist who works as she goes, giving spontaneous inspiration rather than deliberate edification, and beauty rather than goodness.

II. Heredity

The preservation of the past in the present, and the teleology of assimilation, reproduction, and ontogeny mechanistically explained by the conception of life as a system of super-forces.

There are two facts about heredity on which the Vitalists base their protest against Mechanism. In the first place, there is the capacity of life to preserve in the germ the infinitely rich manifold of hereditary determinants embodying the past ancestry of the plant or animal; and in the second place, there is the teleological capacity of life to actualize this heredity-manifold progressively in the stages of embryonic growth.

I shall try to show that if we conceive of the germ as a hierarchical system of what I will call "*super-forces*," it will be possible to explain both of these aspects of heredity in terms of mechanistic categories.

The basic concepts of physical science are Mass, Space, and Time. The other conceptions are derived by combining these notions.

Thus, the velocity of a moving body is expressed by dividing the space through which the body moves by the time during which it moves; and the velocity of the body at any instant can be expressed by the limit approached by the fraction as *s* and *t* approach zero. Acceleration is the rate at which a velocity is changing. Force is the product of the mass and the acceleration. Momentum can be expressed as the product of the mass and the velocity. Energy can be expressed as one-half the product of the mass and the square of the velocity. According to Professor Karl Pearson, while these conceptions are sufficient for the ordinary purposes of mechanics, we could form concepts of higher orders of acceleration which would conform to the same laws of geometrical representation and combination as apply to simple accelerations and to velocities. Thus, the rate at which an acceleration was changing or tending to change would be the first of the higher orders of acceleration, and the rate at which this rate itself was changing or tending to change would be the second of the higher orders of acceleration. Each of these successive orders of acceleration is derived from the preceding order by dividing by the time factor and taking the limiting value which the resulting fraction approaches as the numerator and denominator approach zero. This process is known as differentiation; and the series of higher orders of acceleration which result from the process constitute what are called the higher derivatives of space with regard to time. Inasmuch as force is defined as the product of the mass and the simple acceleration to which the mass is subject, we can use the term "super-force" to denote the product of a mass factor and any higher order of acceleration which it may embody or to which it may be subject.

So much for the meaning of super-forces: I wish now to call attention to some of their characteristics which have a bearing upon the problem of the nature of the germ plasm. In the first place, they can exist as physical realities without being visible or externally observable. Even velocity itself, the first of the derivatives of space with regard to time, is only visible through a series of instants and not at a single instant. And when the velocity is zero, and the body appears to be quietly resting, it may possess any degree of acceleration or of super-acceleration without exhibiting any sign of such potentialities. A single particle may be the bearer, at one and the same instant, of any number of successively higher super-forces. That is to say, it may have an acceleration, and a tendency to change that acceleration positively or negatively, and a tendency to change that rate of change positively or negatively; and so on without limit. And, as we have said, these successive degrees of super-force are accurately expressible in terms of the successive derivatives of space with regard to time. From this there follows the important consequence that a very meager system of molecules could be the bearer of an indefinitely rich manifold of super-forces, not existing side by side or extensively and visibly, but superposed on one another intensively and invisibly. Now, despite our ignorance of the intimate molecular and inter-molecular structure of the germ plasm, there are two things about it in this connection which we know: (1) that the number of hereditary tendencies stored up in it from past generations is indefinitely rich; and (2) that, if by some impossibly perfect microscope we observed all that there was to observe in such a germ, we should see nothing but the chemical atoms with their constituent electrons grouped together in molecular and inter-molecular systems. The masses, sizes, and shapes of these atoms, their relative positions and velocities, would be observable, and they would certainly seem to constitute a system rich enough to be an adequate causal ground for the somatic structures that are to issue from them. And yet, despite this seeming richness of the theoretically observable manifold of atoms in the germ plasm, a moment's reflection will reveal the pitiful inadequacy of the merely spatial and kinematic aspect of the germ to afford a sufficient causal ground for the somatic effects that are to follow. For many, if not all, of the resulting soma cells will as individuals be as complex in structure as the original germ cell; hence, all the causal determinations of the germ will be needed to explain them. Yet this is only the beginning; for there is the whole incredibly complex and adaptive arrangement of these cells in the tissues and organs of the soma at any one stage of its development to be accounted for by the nature of the germ. Nor is even this all; for any one of these last-named somatic complexes is but one of the long series of diverse forms which evolve in a temporal series through all the stages of embryonic and post-embryonic growth. And this series shows in its temporal structure the same degree of purposeful complexity as is found spatially in any one of its stages. Nor can the environment help us here. For, while it is, of course, an absolutely necessary condition for the development of the germ and is in perpetual interaction with it, yet its role is relatively passive so far as concerns the specific hereditary characters which were all determined by what the germ contained, and which are preserved intact through all the interactions of the germ and its environing food. Indeed, as a final consideration showing the impossibility of accounting for the spatial and temporal richness of the soma in terms merely of the theoretically observable distribution of the atoms in the germ plasm, we may note that if that distribution were all there was to the germ, its specificity, such as it was, would be completely washed out and lost in the interaction with the environment; for the arrangement of the atoms of the system after the first contact with the environment would be as much characteristic of the latter as of the germ itself; so that as the interaction continued, the living being would lose more and more of the highly specific nature of its germinal origin and would take on more and more of the relatively unspecific character of its environment. And at the end of such a give-and-take process, the germ cells of the next generation would have almost none of the characters of the species. Instead of this fading out of the complex of germinal characters through successive admixtures with the environment, we find, as we have just said, precisely the opposite state of affairs. The individual somehow preserves all its hereditary specificity quite intact throughout the long and complicated processes of its growth to maturity. If, then, it is impossible for these reasons to identify the hereditary characters with the positions and velocities of the atoms of the germ plasm, no matter how numerous or complex, with what physical aspects of the latter can they be identified? With none, say the vitalists, who thereupon proceed to bring in their nonphysical entelechies, psychoids, and so forth.

According to the hypothesis here defended, self-perpetuating *complexes of hereditary characters can be and must be identified with the super-forces of the germ plasm.* For, while these super-forces are strictly physical in nature and capable of mathematical formulation as the higher derivatives of velocities, it is they and they alone which can constitute an indefinitely rich intensive manifold of separate specific tendencies such as we know the germ to contain; and it is also they and they alone which are able to preserve their own systemic structure intact through all the vicissitudes of interaction with environing systems. That this last claim is justified can be seen by considering that even acceleration, not to mention super-acceleration, is not affected directly by a change of position. Thus, when a falling body is stopped in its fall and brought to rest, its gravitative acceleration continues as before. The value of a derivative is not altered by an alteration in the value of the derivatives of lower order than itself, and consequently the super-accelerations or super-forces in the germ plasm which are represented by these higher derivatives can preserve their pattern unchanged throughout the morphological changes of embryonic growth.

And now that we have seen the striking correspondences that obtain between the rich intensive manifold of self-perpetuating hereditary characteristics in the germ plasm and the equally rich intensive manifold of self-perpetuating super-forces which we are suggesting as a mechanistic explanation of this germinal specificity, let us consider the second of the basic characters of the germ plasm, namely, the sequential teleology of the embryonic process in which are progressively unfolded the series of hereditary forms.

The process by which the fertilized cell divides into two cells, each possessing the life-pattern of the parent, involves the transposition of the complex of hereditary characteristics from the system of atoms which originally possesses it to the system of atoms which up to that time has not possessed it, but which as relatively simple food material has been stored in the cell. The initial mystery of growth is this mystery of assimilative anabolism by means of which one system of atoms within a cell conveys its life-pattern to another system. The actual division of the cells is only the climactic stage of the process of transference of a life-pattern of hereditary characteristics from the primary constituents of a cell to its secondary or food-constituents. Now, it has long been noted that such phenomena as the splitting up of the chromosomes and the formation of duplicate centrosomes bear a *prima facie* resemblance to processes of magnetic and electrostatic induction in which a force-pattern is transferred from one body to another; but, so far as I am informed, the resemblance of electrical induction to what happens in the cell is so vitiated by the multitude of differences between the complex protoplasmic substance and the relatively simple media of electrical and magnetic induction that the analogy has not led to any fruitful results. Now, if our hypothesis of the identity of the life-pattern of a cell with the hierarchical system of super-forces of which its atoms may be the bearer is correct, the analogy between biological and physical induction might be rescued.

And just as the electric or magnetic field constituting a pattern of relatively simple stresses can induce in suitable material near by a corresponding pattern of stresses, so we should expect a cellular complex of super-forces to induce a corresponding pattern of super-forces in the suitable material near by. And just as iron particles in the neighborhood of a given magnet conform to the lines of force of that particular magnet, so would food particles within the field of a given cell conform themselves to the biological pattern of that particular cell, becoming nerve tissue, muscle tissue, or bone tissue, as the case might be.

Anabolism is thus the transmission of the chemical form of the substance that eats to the substance eaten. In this way living matter renews and increases its own substance at the expense of other matter.

When a cell has in this way increased its own substance to a certain point, then either with or without the stimulus of another cell, that is, either sexually or asexually, it reproduces itself in new cells. The daughter cells exhibit more or less of the pattern and chemical structure of the parent cell, and so in unicellular reproduction no less than in assimilation, the essence of the process is the transmission of a form or pattern from one body of matter to another.

Now the ontogenesis or embryonic development of a multicellular organism might appear to be of a nature quite different from the processes of assimilation and unicellular reproduction which we have just considered. For here we have a group of cells which in their growth and reproduction result not only in new types of cell-pattern, but also in a whole series of cell-groupings. New tissues and new organs are progressively differentiated from the seemingly simple and homogeneous germ cell. But here, too, we can regard the process as only another example of the capacity of living matter to impose and transmit its own form. For the cells of each new generation will have their natures determined not merely by the individual parent cells, but by the group of parent cells acting collectively. The pattern of the new cell will thus be a compound, one set of characteristics a direct inheritance or reproduction of its own parent cell, and the rest of its characteristics determined by the structure of the group and its position in that structure. We should thus expect a unified system of developing cells to exhibit a progressive differentiation of form. To symbolize the process, let us denote the original fertilized cell from which a complex organism is to develop by A, and the two daughter cells into which it divides by A_1 and A_2. Now, when one of these daughter cells, say A_1, proceeds in its turn to divide, the resulting cells should be determined in their pattern not merely by A_1, but by A_1 modified by A_2. The compound pattern thus resulting in the second generation we could symbolize by B. The B cells will in their turn give rise to new cells whose pattern will be a compound of the B characteristics modified by the pattern imposed by the cell group. This third type of cell we could symbolize by C, and so on. These familiar facts are generalized in the statement that the character of any part of an organism is determined partly by its immediate cell parents and partly by its relation to the entire organism. Now certain experiments, described by Driesch, which have been performed upon the embryos of frogs, throw an interesting light on the connection of the two features. If a part of the embryo of a frog be properly separated from the rest, it will develop; but sometimes it develops into an entire tadpole of reduced size and sometimes into a specific part of a tadpole. These divergent results would seem to indicate that the two sets of characteristics which constitute the cell-pattern of each cell in a multicellular organism are relatively distinct, and that sometimes one set and sometimes another dominates in its descendants. In the case in which a separated part of the embryo develops into an entire animal, the original characters of the parent cells have proved more potent than the characters superimposed by the general group. The germ plasm, as we might say, triumphs over the soma plasm, and the cells act like germinal or reproductive cells. But in the case in which the fragments of the embryo develop only into specific parts of the animal, such as special tissues and organs, why here it is the soma plasm characters that triumph over the germ plasm characters. That is to say, the differential characters in each cell which have been superimposed upon it not by its parents, but by the whole group of cells in virtue of its position in that group, determine a continuance of its development into the special tissues and organs demanded by the group as a whole.

Now, in the light of such facts, it is possible to understand in general, although the details are hidden from us, how certain of the cells of a complex organism might, and probably would, always retain as their dominant characteristics the pattern inherited from the parent cells rather than the differentiating pattern which would be due to their relation to the group. Such cells would be the germinal or reproductive cells whose function it is to reproduce the new organism as a whole rather than some special organ or tissue. So, though each cell in a complex organism might be regarded as theoretically capable of reproducing, under proper conditions, the organism as a whole, yet only those cells which were not forced by the demands of the group as a whole to develop some special instrument of service would actually serve as the seeds of a new generation.

Now, all this is, of course, merely descriptive and not explanatory. But in view of the general theory I am arguing for, I have thought it worth while to indicate how the distinctively vital processes of growth and reproduction can all be regarded as the different manifestations of a single principle—the principle in accordance with which living substance imposes its characteristic form or nature upon new matter. And it is here that the concept of each cell as a complex of super-forces appears to me to be helpful. We know that it is a characteristic of a system of forces or potential energies not only to pass into motion and to result from motion, but also to superimpose its form upon its environment. Every stress implies a counterstress of the same character as itself. A magnet not only tends to produce motion in the iron filings that come into its field, but it imposes upon them its own stress pattern. An electric charge not only attracts or repels into motion another charge, but it induces a counter-charge on neighboring bodies. If any part of a living cell is the bearer of a complex system of stresses or potential energies, we should expect to have those stresses imposed upon and duplicated in any matter that was suited to take them. The process by which food substance is assimilated to the tissue of the cell would be, as we have said before, analogous to the process by which iron filings arrange themselves in accordance with the field of force of a magnet. In protoplasm, however, the stress patterns that are transmitted are primarily of a chemical rather than a physical order, and manifest themselves in the grouping of atoms into new molecules. It is apparently only in carbon compounds of the kind that compose protoplasm that there is sufficient flexibility of molecular structure to allow of any very noticeable or continued propagation and variation of stress patterns from one molecule to another. Crystallization, which has always been recognized as more or less remotely analogous to life, may be identically the same in principle but with the single all-important difference that in crystallization it is only a stress pattern between molecules that is reproduced, whereas in protoplasm, thanks to the peculiar structure of carbon, instead of the meager variations of intermolecular or physical stress patterns, it is possible to transmit by a process analogous to electrostatic inductions those intramolecular systems which we have termed "super-forces."

The hierarchical systems of super-forces of which protoplasm is the bearer, are, however, not only incomparably more varied than the simple stress-systems of crystals, but in their chemical manifestations they seem to furnish an exclusive instance of an object definable in purely physical terms and at the same time embodying a system of invisible and intensive magnitudes. So far as I can see, there is no limit in theory to the number of strains which might be superposed in series upon a single material field. Each of these imposed strains would be the trace of a past event and the promise of a future event. The system would, in short, consist of a temporal series of past and future events compressed into a series of intensive magnitudes symbolized by the successively higher derivatives of space with regard to time, and actually though invisibly present in their totality at every instant. We may assist our imagination to appreciate the nature of such a system if we think of a rope upon which there has been imposed in succession a long series of twists on twists. As long as such a rope is held tight, it will embody at each single instant the whole series of successive strains to which it has been subjected, in an invisible intensive hierarchy; and if there were a medium suited for the purpose, it might convey to that medium by a kind of induction its own pattern of super-forces. When the rope is released, however, it will unfold or twist, and yield back in the form of a visible temporal series something like the series imposed upon it, but with the order of terms reversed.

If for the gross and meager plasticity of the rope we substitute the infinitely varied plasticity of protoplasm, and if for the brief series of crude twists given to the rope and returned by it we substitute the incredibly extended succession of specific energies which have been received by the cell and infinitesimal traces of which have been retained, then we shall have something like a mechanistic explanation of the two outstanding mysteries of heredity. These, it will be remembered, were (1) the mystery of how a minute germ can contain and maintain in all integrity the determinants of a million generations of past life; and (2) the mystery of how that same germ with admirable teleology can actualize in unicellular reproduction and multicellular ontogeny the complex of potentialities with which it is invisibly pregnant.

It remains to us now, in the concluding section of our discussion, to meet the last and most formidable of the three challenges of Vitalism—the challenge to explain in mechanistic terms the general characters of conscious thought and activity, and the peculiar characters of the qualitative and durational elements of psychic existence.

III. Consciousness

The points at issue between mechanistic parallelism and vitalistic interactionism. The general and special characters of conscious life. The mechanistic explanation of the former by the conception of cerebral super-forces or potential energies, and of the latter by the conception of sensations as modes of "anergy."

The general controversy between mechanism and vitalism, when applied to psychology, becomes the more specialized controversy between psychophysical parallelism and interactionism.

Parallelism, which on all practical issues is indistinguishable from epiphenomenalism, insists (1) that you cannot conceive of a non-spatial state of consciousness in a causal interaction with a physical body; and (2) that even if you could, the law of the conservation of energy would be violated unless every effect in the brain were produced by a physical cause. Consequently, consciousness must be regarded as a non-intervening or "parallel" aspect of brain processes. As against this theory, the interactionists contend (1) that consciousness is of such a character that you cannot conceive of it as a mere concomitant of the blind or mechanical motions in the brain; and (2) that even if you could so conceive it, its existence as an epiphenomenon would be opposed to the biological law that vital functions tend to be developed and preserved on account of the useful effects which they produce. Thus, each party to the controversy is supported by the inconceivability of its rival and by the apparent demands of physics on the one hand and of biology on the other.

The psychophysical dispute between Mechanist-parallelism and Vitalist-interactionism is not mitigated but only confused by mixing it with the epistemological dispute between realism and idealism. The problem is just as clear-cut and perplexing when translated into the language of idealism or of phenomenalism as when left in the simpler and more primitive language of realism. To describe the motions in your brain as streams of actual or possible perceptions of an external observer, or as abstractions from an organic whole of experiences, does not make it any easier to conceive them as causally related to the private and personal unity of thoughts and purposes which constitute your mind.

The characters of mind or consciousness on which the Vitalist bases his challenge to the Mechanist fall into two groups, which we will call the general and the special.

The general characters are those common to all vital systems; the special are those that are or that seem to be peculiar to consciousness, notably the baffling specificity or qualitativeness of its elements. Let us consider them in turn.

Under the general characters may be enumerated the following: (1) *Telogenesis*, or the capacity to initiate useful or purposive variations; (2) *Teleology*, or the capacity to reproduce or actualize a form or pattern by transmitting it through a kind of induction from one body to another; (3) *Extension in time*, or the capacity of living matter to sum up at each present moment of its existence a long series of past events in the form of an invisible hierarchy of intensive magnitudes.

In the first section of this paper, in which Telogenesis was the topic considered, we endeavored to show that between the activity of the germ, giving rise to useful and inheritable variations, and the activity of the brain, giving rise to novel and pertinent ideals, there was not only a vague analogy but a profound identity. By conceiving of germ and brain as systems of forces and super-forces, each element of which could be treated as a vector, we were able to interpret both kinds of telogenesis as a process of vector addition. The germ and the brain are as closely connected in their teleology as in their telogenesis. The process by which the stress-pattern of hereditary determinants is transmitted in assimilation and reproduction from the original germ cell to the food particles within it is identical in principle with the process by which the stress-pattern of a purpose based upon memories stored up in the cerebrum is transmitted to or actualized in a moral action or an artistic creation. For example, a man having as his purposes the artistic telos of painting a beggar and the moral telos of giving alms to the beggar actualizes those ideals on his canvas and by his conduct. And the capacity to transmit from the brain to the outside world of canvas and conduct these pre-existent patterns is essentially identical with the capacity of the germ cell to transmit its pattern of chemical forms to the food contained in it and to other cells. To conceive of the pre-existent pattern as part of a system of super-forces and of its transmission as a kind of induction affords a basis for interpreting both germinal and cerebral teleology in mechanistic terms.

So much for telogenesis and teleology. The third of the general characters in which the conscious action of the brain resembles the ontogenetic activity of the germ is the capacity to extend in time and embody at each present instant in an invisible system of intensive magnitudes a long series of past events. Here, again, the arguments for identifying this present past with a hierarchy of super-forces or forms of potential energy superimposed one upon another apply equally to the system of acquired memories stored up in the brain and to the system of inherited determinants stored up in the germ. Neither brain nor germ would exhibit to an external observer the essentially private history of the past contained in it. Mere positions and velocities of the atoms, if adequately disclosed by a perfect microscope, could show nothing but what was present. A hierarchy of superimposed stresses is the only physical analogue of life's power to extend in time.

Despite the resemblances of conscious life to life in general with respect to telogenesis, teleology, and temporal extension, there are certain differences between the two systems that should be kept in mind. The central nervous system exhibits in a new way the vital capacity for retaining and expressing specific potentialities. Instead of assimilating energy joined with matter in the form of food particles, the brain takes its energy "neat" and assimilates it as it comes in the form of sensory impulses. And by storing up traces of the specific forms of vibration that proceed from extra-organic objects and traverse the afferent nerves, it builds up a "psychic organism," a life within a life, composed not of differentiated forms of matter, but of differentiated forms of energy. These cerebral energy-forms are the instruments of memory, and they implicate or reveal a world outside themselves both in time and space. It is by virtue of the self-transcending implications of cerebral traces that we are enabled to experience duration and to act teleologically, that is, to act at each moment with reference to events of the past and future.

There are several other curious analogies which hold between the field of consciousness and a field of superforces or potential energies. There is, for example, the polarity of subject and object, which has its analogue in the universal opposition of forces to one another, every tendency to action engendering an equal and opposite tendency to reaction. There is also the primary unity of a field of force (as distinguished from the essential plurality of a mere aggregate of material particles) and the perfect and instantaneous rapport between its components; these characters correspond, respectively, to the unity of consciousness and to the organic and reciprocal interaction of its contents.

Aside from these various analogies, the hypothesis here defended is greatly strengthened by the fact that sensations seem to arise at the very times when the sensory neural currents are being redirected at the cerebral synapses into motor currents of discharge. And as no form of motion can be changed in direction without some of its energy passing through a latent or potential phase, it seems highly probable that the not-externally-observable potentialities into which neural energies are transformed are identical with the not-externally-observable psychic states which then and only then come into existence. Moreover, when the neural stress is intense, the sensation is also intense;

while the smoother and more automatic the neural current, the less vivid is the consciousness that is synchronous with it.

But let us turn from these general and structural characters which (with some variation) are shared in common by conscious life and by the life of cells, to those other and more special characters which are peculiar to the contents of consciousness and definable in psychical terms. These exclusively psychological characters are (1) the pure qualitativeness of sensations; and (2) the duration, or specious presentness, of all former consciousness.

Not even Mechanists attempt to reduce these characters to physical terms; they content themselves with the view that mental states, as such, are epiphenomenal concomitants of cerebral motions and, thus, subject, vicariously as it were, to the mechanistic laws of the motions with which they are concomitant.

I believe that it is possible to interpret in physical terms the very sensations themselves; and furthermore, I believe that this ultra-materialism can be seen to satisfy the legitimate demand of the Vitalists that mind be regarded as a really efficient determiner of bodily motions rather than as the epiphenomenal concomitant of them. But if the hypothesis which I am about to propose is to convey any meaning, it will be necessary to bear with my attempt to express what, so far as I know, is a new category.[2]

Our customary modes of thought recognize mere rest as

[2] Some years ago, after I had published a rough preliminary formulation of the conception that I am now about to present, my attention was called to an earlier book, to which I cannot now get access, in which *feeling* was interpreted as a sort of negative correlate to *force*. There was, as I remember it, no attempt to define it in terms of space and time, and no attempt to conceive of the forms or traces which it might leave after the stimulus inducing it had ceased to act. But in its general character it was like what I shall refer to as "anergy." The title of the book was something like *Mind and Force*, and the author's name was, as I recall it, Duncan.

the only alternative to motion; and while there can be many degrees of motion, there can only be one degree of rest. I want to suggest that there can be many degrees of rest, or, rather, that there are modes of existence on the other side of mere rest. Just as zero is the boundary between the decreasing series of positive numbers and an equally rich increasing series of negative numbers, so the resting condition of a body may be the boundary between the decreasing series of its positive velocities and an equally rich increasing series of its negatives of velocity. By these negatives of velocity, I do not, of course, mean what are ordinarily called negative velocities or negative motions, that is, mere movements in an opposite or negative direction. It is not the direction that is to be negatived, but the motion itself. Now, energy may be roughly defined as the quantity of actual or potential motion, the quantity being measured for certain reasons in a certain way, to wit, by the product of a mass factor and the integral of the velocity, that is, the square of the velocity divided by two. Energy then is, as it were, the tendency to change spatial position. Now, the negative of energy would be a tendency to cling to or endure in one position. It would, perhaps, be related to velocity as inertia is related to acceleration. Let us combine the root of the word *energy* with alpha privative, and coin the word *anergy* as the name for this new condition. This anergy or duration will increase as the velocity decreases: and if we use the ratio s/t to denote velocity, we can use the ratio t/s to denote slowness or duration. As we decrease the fraction s/t denoting the fastness of the change, we shall increase the reciprocal fraction t/s. In other words, the less the speed, the more the slowness. Suppose, now, that the speed becomes zero; then the slowness will become infinite. When slowness becomes infinite, it ceases to be a mere negative *adjective* and becomes a true *substantive*, that is, a thing existing in its own right. As long as a body is actually moving at all, its duration is merely potential. When it stops and its motion becomes potential, its duration becomes actual. That which was a *traversing of space* has become an extension in time, a "chunk" or lump of *durational being.*

When a vibration-wave proceeding over a sensory nerve is gradually brought to a stop by the resistance of the synapse, its energy is transformed from a visible and kinetic form to an invisible and potential form. As its velocity passes through the zero-phase, its slowness passes through an infinity-phase. I ask you to entertain the suggestion that this *infinity-phase of slowness* is the common stuff of all sensations and that the critical points of zero and infinity through which the motion and the slowness, respectively, pass afford the basis for that qualitative absoluteness and discontinuity that differentiate sensations from mere rates of change. If we accept this suggestion and admit provisionally that ($t/s = \infty$) is a kind of definition in terms of *quantity* of the general *quality* of mere durational being common to all sensations, we shall find as a reward for our faith a very striking corroboration of Fechner's interpretation of Weber's Law. For, when the wave of neural motion encounters resistance at the synapse, each of its cross sections in continuous series will be transformed successively into cross sections of durational being. And the intensive quantity of durational being thus produced will be the result of a continuous summation or integration. Thus, the intensity of the sensation t/s will increase to its maximum through the time that the velocity of the wave decreases to zero; and, consequently, it can be measured by the product of a mass factor (which is large for sound and small for light and which I will not here discuss) and the integral of the reciprocal of the velocity with regard to the velocity, that is,

$$\int_{V_n \frac{ds}{dt}}^{V_0} \frac{dt}{ds} = \log \frac{ds}{dt}.$$

In other words, if the being of a sensation is as I have described it, the intensity of a sensation will tend to increase with the logarithm of the stimulus, rather than with the stimulus directly. This deduction of Fechner's Law permits us to understand the curious analogy to that law which determines our appreciation of the intervals of pitch. The vibration-numbers which cause sensations of successively higher octaves form a *geometric* series, 128, 256, 512, and so forth. But our sensations of the successive octaval increments of pitch constitute an *arithmetic* series having equal differences between its terms, and as such proportioned to the logarithms of the series of stimuli. Now, if the velocity of each wave when reduced to zero is transformed by integration into a durational quality determined in its nature by the reciprocal of the velocity and in its degree by the logarithm of the velocity, then the frequency of the waves themselves or the velocity of their succession will be analogously transformed by integration into a specific quality of being or duration, measured in its degree by the logarithm of the frequency and modifying, or *inhering in*, the original quality.

There are several other peculiar characters of sensations and sensation-differences which could be interpreted in terms of our hypothesis that they are modes of anergy or durational being which make their appearance whenever energy is transformed from a kinetic to a potential phase. For example, whether a sensory quality will appear as primarily spatial like color, or as primarily temporal like sound, should be determined not, as in the case of intensity, by the velocity of the stimulus wave multiplied by a mass factor, but by the length of time which was necessary to absorb the wave. This is very long in the case of sound and very short in the case of light; hence, the former appears as an essentially temporal thing and the latter as essentially spatial or extended.

The modes of anergy which are produced by the modes of energy of the stimuli will have two sets of properties, the one set relative, continuous, and quantitative, the other absolute, discontinuous, and qualitative. The first set will be determined directly by the relations of the stimuli to one another and to the system as a whole, and only indirectly by the character of each stimulus. These will be the so-called "primary" qualities of size, shape, and position, and of date and duration. The other set of characters will be determined directly by the intrinsic character of each stimulus, and only indirectly by the relations of the stimuli to one another. These will be the so-called "secondary" qualities, the specific and incommensurable modalities of touch, sight, hearing, taste, and smell. Each neural stimulus has what may be called an intrinsic form or pattern constituted by the interrelations of its velocity, its duration, and its acceleration. Where this complex of measurable properties of an energy or motion is transformed into anergy or duration, it ceases to be a quantitative complex and becomes a single unanalyzable, incommensurable specificity. The primarily extensive quantity of motion has become a primarily intensive quality of being. This change from energy into anergy is a change of the spatio-temporal into the temporo-spatial. If a motion were infinitely fast, it would fill many places at a single instant and could be called "matter." If a sensation were infinitely enduring, it would fill many moments of time at a single point, and could be called "substance." As it is, motion has only specious extension, and sensations have only specious duration or specious presentness. Thus, motion and sensation are partly substantive and partly adjectival. Each can be treated as a self-identical magnitude capable of being conserved and discriminated; but each needs something more substantive than itself in which to inhere. There could be no motion that was not the motion of an extended object, and no sensation that was not the sensation of an enduring subject.

Now, just as the form of a motion is, as such, independent of the amount of its mass factor, so the form of a sensation is, as such, independent of its intensity factor. The kinetic energy of the nerve current that passes into a potential form when a sensation is produced begins at once to pass back into the kinetic energy of the motor nerve currents of reaction; and as it thus passes out and away, the intensity of the sensation dependent upon it fades toward zero, leaving the anergy form as a clear sensory trace. The clearness of these sensory traces is independent of the infinitesimal and ever diminishing intensities which they retain as the correlates of the infinitesimal and ever diminishing remnants of the potential energies of the stimuli correlated with them. These anergy forms are, of course, our memory images. They sum up at each present instant a succession of past happenings, and constitute an organic system of modifications of whatever it is in the cerebrum that is susceptible of bearing an intensive hierarchy of superimposed stresses and strains.

If consciousness is identical with the forms of anergy and their correlated traces of potential energy stored up in the brain, why is it that the brain is not conscious during sleep? And why is it that we are only conscious when kinetic nerve currents are flowing over the sensorimotor arc? It would seem that if consciousness is to be identified with anything in the brain, it should be identified with the active rather than the quiescent cerebral condition. I should attempt to meet this seeming difficulty in the following way.

There may exist many systems of potential energy, or of forces and super-forces, in one material body; and these systems may be relatively insulated from one another. The system of traces of potential energy that controls the action of the body during waking life includes only so many of the stored-up anergy traces in the brain as happen to be associated with the sensorimotor currents more intimately than with the rest of the brain traces. Therefore, the consciousness of our waking life at any instant includes only those of our memories which are associated more intimately with present sensations than with the rest of our memories. We can think of the totality of the brain's energy forms as divided into two fields or realms. One set of traces will be tending to discharge toward the sensorimotor arc. The rest will be tending to discharge more toward one another than toward the sensorimotor arc. What I call "my consciousness" at any one moment will be the equivalent of the more intense of these two systems. Now, the potential energy produced by the redirection of a present afferent nerve current will usually be stronger than the energies that form the residual potentials of past nerve currents. Hence, "my consciousness," or the dominant psychic condition of my brain, will usually if not always consist of those ideas which are grouped around a nucleus of present sensation. And set over against it will be the broader and fainter system, the affinity of whose elements for one another is stronger than their affinity for the elements of the first system. *The latter system would constitute the subconscious.* Let me try to make this clearer by a hydraulic analogy. Consider a lake formed by damming a stream. The stream is flowing into the lake, and there is a leak, in the middle of the dam almost but not quite large enough to let out as much water as flows in, with the result that the lake grows slowly larger. Now, to these natural conditions let us add a circumstance somewhat artificial: let us suppose that there is a certain strong force of attraction between the water of the lake and the containing shores. Then, in such a situation we should find the particles of the water tending to divide into two rival systems. The water in the immediate neighborhood of the stream flowing through the lake would have a bias or tendency to flow with it through the outlet, while the water in the immediate vicinity of the shores would have by supposition a bias or tendency toward the shores that was stronger than the suction tendency of the stream. Where the line between the two fields fell would, of course, depend upon the relative strength of the suction force of the stream and the counter attraction of the shores. Each field of stress would have a unity of its own. Now, for the water of the lake substitute the sensorially accumulated energy in the brain; for the stream flowing through the lake substitute the sensorimotor stream of neural currents that flows through the brain during waking moments; and for the attraction of the shores of the lake substitute the attraction of the anergy forms for one another (the nature of which is expressed in the psychological laws of association), and we shall have a fair picture of that characteristic of our cerebral apparatus that is responsible for the fact that in waking life the dominant or controlling consciousness will contain in its unified field of attention only a certain small part of the wealth of the psychic reality which the brain contains. In our analogy, sleep would be represented by a partial, and trance or swoon by a total, closure of the gates of ingress and egress of the lake. In that situation the self would cease to be divided into a conscious and a subconscious system, and there would ensue a single super-sensory experience over whose mighty array of objects the lines of attention (which have their correlates in the lines of stress) would be uniformly dispersed. But the little rill of sensory waking consciousness which is all of the mind that any of us knows directly would (except perhaps in the case of the mystics) be completely amnesic with respect to any such subliminal revelation.

In concluding this last section of our discussion, I should like to say just a word as to the bearing of our hypothesis upon the three great questions of traditional philosophy—the Freedom of the Will, the Immortality of the Soul, and the Existence of God. Is a definitely negative answer to each of these questions implied by the ultra-materialistic conception of consciousness as anergy which we have defended? I believe that this is by no means the case. It seems to me rather that, while the theory in question does not in itself commit us either to an affirmative or a negative position with respect to these problems, it does make it possible to formulate them with rather more definiteness than is customary.

Whether the will is free becomes the question as to whether that in the brain which is the bearer of the modes of actual anergy and of potential energy possesses in itself a power of spontaneous and indeterminate activity.

Whether the soul is immortal becomes the question as to whether the system of psychic traces or super-forces can continue to exist, perhaps as a specific deformation or individualized field of strain in the ether, apart from the matrix of material particles which have conditioned its origin and growth.

Whether there exists a God or a cosmic mind becomes the question as to whether the total system of physical energies and forces making up the universe possesses the kind of unity which when found in the human brain expresses an individual consciousness.

While the theory itself, in spite of its radical materialism, permits, as we have said, either an affirmative or negative answer to all three of these questions, I personally believe, for reasons not stated in this paper, that the affirmative answers are in each case correct. For it seems to me improbable that there could be a continuous and determinate interchange of energies by secondary causality throughout the world unless each real element of the world possessed a spark of primary causality, that is, of free and spontaneous activity. And it seems equally improbable that the curious intensive hierarchy of super-forces which embody the present traces of the past, and which constitute vital systems, could be entirely dependent upon the groups of atoms which encase them; and finally, it seems to me improbable, in view of the omnipresence of uniform laws, that the universe as a whole should lack the degree of unity which we discover in those parts of it that are embodied in protoplasm.

Conclusion

In the first section of this paper we considered the Vitalist challenge to the Mechanists to explain in physical terms the origin of those useful variations which arise in the germ plasm with a greater frequency than could be expected if they were the product of the blind or merely mechanical agencies recognized in physics and chemistry. We attempted to meet the challenge by means of the conception of biological vectors, according to which all of the unpurposed yet purposeful products of telogenesis, not only in the germ plasm but in the brain when occupied with creative imagination, can be explained as the result of a system of protoplasmic stresses, and, as such, felicitously expressive in their novelty and pertinence of the whole from which they originate.

In the second section of the paper we dealt with the Vitalist challenge to the Mechanist to explain without the aid of extra-physical categories how the minute germ cell could be the bearer of a manifold of hereditary determinants involving thousands or millions of ancestral generations in the past, and capable of teleological development into a duplicate of the organism from which it came. We attempted to meet the challenge by conceiving of the germ as a system of super-forces or superimposed stresses definable in mechanical terms yet embodying a manifold of invisible intensive determinants equal in richness to the serial events of its ancestral past and capable of unfolding and reproducing its own pattern by a kind of induction through the serial stages of embryonic growth.

Last, in the third section of our discussion, we have endeavored to meet the Vitalist challenge to explain mind in physical terms by the suggestion that the structure of conscious life is analogous to the structure of life in general and capable of being explained in the same way, except that the system of cerebral super-forces in which the past is stored up in the present is composed of traces of potential energy acquired by the brain through the transformation of the kinetic energies of sensory nerve currents. And, as a basis for a physical interpretation of the essentially specific and qualitative nature of mental elements, we suggested the new category of "anergy" as a form of durational being inevitably produced whenever the energy of motion was transformed into the invisible phase which we call potential.

Our theory agreed with Vitalism and interactionism in recognizing the genuine efficacy in nature of telogenesis, teleology, and consciousness; but it agreed also with Mechanism and parallelism in refusing to admit the existence of any factor not definable in physical terms. Consciousness is not, as Santayana puts it, "a lyric cry"; nor is it an otiose and epiphenomenal spectator of bodily doings. Our minds are imbedded in the matter of our brains, and they play a real part in the economy of nature. It is just because of the physical reality of our minds that we can transcend the mechanical contacts of the *here* and *now*, and, through memory and imagination, adjust our behavior not only to an environment extending indefinitely in space and time, but also to that Platonic realm of logical and ethical ideals which are independent of the vicissitudes of time and existence.

15

* CONSCIOUSNESS A FORM OF ENERGY[1]

A systematic account of the analogies between a field of consciousness as experienced from within and a field of potential energies as experienced from without, followed by a demonstration of the probable identity of the two fields. It presupposes some knowledge of psychology.

I. Introduction

FROM THE TIME of Plato and Democritus to the present day, there have been two opposite views concerning the nature of mind. The Right Wing followers of Plato have regarded mental states as the expression of an immaterial entity or soul, while the Left Wing followers of Democritus have regarded the same states as aspects or correlates of bodily motions. Both parties have, of course, their various factions, but those internal differences are relatively unimportant and are quite overshadowed by the essential unity of each school and its essential opposition to the other.

We may conceive of the soul in the manner of Plato himself or in the manner of St. Thomas Aquinas or after the fashion of Descartes or of Berkeley or even of Kant and his successors. To philosophers, the differences will undoubtedly seem great, but for psychologists there will be

[1] In part from *Essays Philosophical and Psychological in Honor of William James*, New York, Longmans, Green and Company, 1908, pages 105–134, and from a paper read at the Eleventh International Congress of Psychology, Paris, 1937.

little to choose between one form of immaterial entity and another. They will be all of them equally objectionable. And with regard to the several sects of the Left Wing, the situation is analogous. For, consider Hobbes, Hartley, Hume, LaMettrie, Condillac, and the many others of the long line of associationists, some avowedly materialists, others more cautious and inclining to positivism or phenomenalism. Are they not all using essentially the same method and aiming at essentially the same goal? Even the contemporary American Behaviorists who would identify the mental with the extra-cerebral responses of the organism, and particularly with the mechanism of speech, are in line with their forebears in a Left Wing attempt to reduce conscious states and processes to a form or aspect of the motion of matter.

Midway between the monistic materialism of Democritus and the dualistic spiritualism of Plato there have ever been the Aristotelian compromisers. From Aristotle himself to the "configurationists" or Gestaltists of present-day Germany, who, whether they admit it or not, are veritable Aristotelians or neo-Aristotelians, there has existed a school of vigorous conscientious psychologists who have been transported by the *aperçu* that mind is an "organic unity," the "form" of the body, and that consciousness is a "configuration" in which the structure of the whole dominates and determines the behavior of the parts. This group have always felt their superiority to the mechanists of the Left and to the spiritualists of the Right, and they have added much to our knowledge of the facts of mental life. What they have forgotten is that the statement of a problem is not the same as its solution. Their guilt is the guilt of the platitudinarian who mistakes the elaboration of a situation for its explanation. They see that the categories of Formal Cause and Organicity apply to the mind, but they fail to see that through the centuries from Aristotle to Descartes and

Galileo these same categories were tried and found wanting, not because they were false, but because they were sterile.

The hypothesis that I am about to present differs from the three that I have just outlined, though it takes account of the measure of truth embodied in each of them. In its methodology it is essentially materialistic, I might almost say ultra-materialistic. But instead of following the belief of the classical materialists that states of mind are the inner aspects or correlates of cerebral motions, I shall argue that they are the reciprocals of those motions or, more precisely, the integrals of those reciprocals. In short, while sensations are as truly types of physical energy as are motions themselves, it is my theory that they are the *non-kinetic* forms of energy into which motions disappear and from which they reappear.

II. Statement of the Problem

The most perplexing and perhaps the most central philosophical problem is that of the nature of consciousness and the manner of its relation to the world which it reveals but in which it also abides. A physical influence of some sort, a fact accessible to the external perception of more than one observer, is propagated along a nerve fiber, and at a certain period in its progress there occurs a fact of an entirely different nature, to wit, a psychical fact which is accessible to the internal perception of only one observer. Nature, in her transmutations of energy, affords many instances of disparateness between the antecedent and consequent stages of a process, but in none of them is the consequent a member of a different order of being from that of the antecedent. Between the consciousness of an object or of a quality and the neural process which antecedes and perhaps accompanies that consciousness, there is a difference far transcending all differences of quality, magnitude, time, and place with which physics is conversant. The system of physical objects seems to be a closed system, complete in itself, in which no room can be found for the individual's consciousness of those objects. And yet the consciousness of objects is an undeniable consequence of certain processes in those objects. Now, it is at once the aim and the duty of science to reveal everywhere the hidden continuity that must underlie the most seemingly discontinuous of changes. And the greatness of the change from stimulus to sensation may in no wise excuse a neglect of the puzzle presented therein.

The clear-thinking Cartesians were the first to realize the crucial nature of the psychophysical problem, and the first to make a sustained and serious attempt at its solution. They failed; and those who came after inherited from them not their fine passion for the problem itself, but only that false antithesis of consciousness and extension which had made failure inevitable. Since then there have been several attempts to explain away the problem by means of a general idealistic metaphysic, or to restate in it such a way that the difference between physical and psychical should appear as a purely functional or methodological distinction. But, for the most part, both science and philosophy have resigned themselves to the acceptance of an inexplicable concomitance or "parallelism" between the physical and psychical series of events, a working hypothesis that is relatively independent of ultimate theories concerning the primacy of one or the other of these series. Quite recently, however, there has grown up both here and abroad a new interest in the nature of consciousness and a new kind of protest against the epistemology of idealism. These currents, which attempt to revive realism by combining with it a direct or presentative theory of knowledge (the "New

Realism") and correlatively to define consciousness as a relation between objects rather than as a substance in which they inhere, promise much of interest and value. But I believe these trends will fall short of their own ideal, should they persist in separating the problem of the nature of consciousness from the problem of its genesis. A definition of consciousness either as a relation of implicativeness which under certain conditions subsists between objects (Woodbridge), or as a diaphanous medium through which on occasion objects are united (G. E. Moore), seems to me to require supplementation. For such definitions, however apt in their estimates of the properties of an experience revealed in introspection, are not designed to throw light upon the physical and physiological origin of the experience. Nor can the psychophysical problem which so perplexed the Cartesians be brusquely dismissed as a question pertaining exclusively to the mechanisms of the body and its reactions. If evolution has taught us anything in scientific method, it has taught us that a sound definition will throw light on the genesis of that which is defined. Now, it is by no accident that the mind has a body; and the fact that sensations follow upon stimuli is not irrelevant to the nature of sensations. The problem of the nature of consciousness is, in short, irremediably involved in the problem of its mechanism; and the latter problem is dual, including as it does the question of how conscious elements are related to neural currents, and the broader question of the relation of consciousness as a whole to the living organism, without which as a matrix the mind could neither begin nor, so far as we yet know, continue to exist.

In the following investigation of the nature of the psychical, I propose to examine consciousness (1) from the standpoint of introspection; (2) from the external standpoint of its relation to stimuli. Lack of space precludes consideration of the third and still larger problem which concerns the relation of consciousness to the general life process of the individual.[2]

III. Consciousness from Within: Psychosis and Hylosis [3]

When we examine introspectively (or retrospectively) a direct perceptual experience, it appears to contain (1) elements which, while they momentarily belong to our experience, seem in no sense to be its peculiar property. We regard these elements as mere sojourners and transients in our consciousness, entering or leaving it at pleasure, belonging at the same time to other experiences than ours and capable of existing in their own right apart from any of these experiences. Such objects are the chairs, stones, stars, animals, and so forth, that we call *physical*. We find (2) a quite different set of elements, such as feelings, desires, volitions, and so forth, which seem to stand in no such loose and dissoluble relations to our experience. We can conceive of them neither as parts of another experience nor as capable of subsisting in their own right apart from any experience or consciousness of them. These elements are called *psychical*. We find (3) a certain relational form or structure applicable to the experience as a whole, and also to the psychical parts of it, but not applicable to the first-named or physical elements. The physical elements are, then, distinguished from the psychical not only by their capacity to exist in many experiences or in none, but also by their possessing a form or structure that is in some respects the antithesis of the psychical structure, which latter is also the structure of the experience as a whole; and it is

[2] This "larger problem" is touched upon in Essays 6, 11, 13, and 14.

[3] The word *psychosis* is used in this paper not in its more recent sense as designating an insane condition of mind, but as a name for any experience or phase of consciousness at a given moment. *Hylosis* designates the material states and processes concomitant with a *psychosis*.

in their contrast of structure, rather than in their contrast of content, that the most promising basis for a clear distinction between physical and psychical is to be found.

The problem of further defining the psychical is, indeed, complicated at the outset by the consideration that, while the physical is capable of becoming a part of the psychical system, from which it is to be distinguished, yet from another point of view the physical world may be regarded as itself containing the totality of the very experiences which reveal and contain it. We might compare the situation to a lake in which there were a number of whirlpools, through each one of which all the water flowed or could flow. The water (physical objects) could then be said to be contained in the whirlpools (consciousness), while at the same time the whirlpools themselves would be in their turn contained in the water of the lake. Let us seek to formulate the differences in structure of these two curiously interpenetrating systems.

The physical world and every portion of that world is a system in which the plurality of the elements is primary and the unity of the system is secondary. Every material object is conceived as being susceptible of indefinite division and subdivision into parts. Whatever is physical is essentially plural; such unity as pertains to it is factitious or external. This essential divisibility or compositeness of material objects is the real justification for formulating their behavior in terms of atomistic and mechanistic analysis. We never rest satisfied with the view of one object influencing another by means of its nature or quality, for we know that nature or quality is dependent upon the parts of the thing and upon their relations. And the reduction of quality to quantity in the physical world rests on the fact that qualities act only vicariously; never in their own right, but always as the correlates of spatio-temporal relations. The static aspect of this truth is evidenced in our appreciation of the impossibility of a quality or universal having physical existence apart from matter. It must inhere in the latter as its state or accident. In the material world, a thing must *be* before it can be *somewhat*.

Let us turn, now, to a consideration of the structure of a *psychosis*, by which term is meant an individual's consciousness-of-objects or total experience at any given moment. Like a material system (which, for convenience, we may name a *hylosis*), every psychosis possesses both unity and variety. But the plurality of elements in a psychical system is always secondary and subordinate to its unity as a whole. My experience of ten inches is by no means composed of ten one-inch experiences. I cannot possibly imagine that experience divided up into separate parts. And, as in the material system we found the compositeness of the whole reflected in the compositeness of each of its parts, so in the psychosis we find the unity and indivisibility of the whole repeated in the similar unity and indivisibility of each psychical element. My consciousness of the room, for example, includes my consciousness of the table. The consciousness of the table includes the consciousness of the table's legs. But it would be as impossible to separate my consciousness of the table legs from the consciousness of the other parts of the table, as to separate my consciousness of the table from my consciousness of the room. Unity or indivisibility is as fundamental a property of the experiencing manifold as plurality or divisibility is of the experienced manifold. We must not interpret this to mean that the physical world lacks quality and unity or that the psychical lacks quantity and plurality. Each order contains as much of both quantity and quality as does the other; only in the physical world it is the qualities that are secondary and factitious, while in the psychical the reverse is true. But let us see to what extent this abstract formulation of the differentia of the psychical can serve to explain certain of its other and more familiar properties.

The first of these subsidiary characteristics to which I would call attention is the psychical status of class-concepts, universals, or attributes in their relation to the particular things in which they inhere. It often happens in my own experience, and I presume in that of others, that the quality of a sensation is perceived before the local sign or particular place to which that quality will be referred. A sound or even a color is appreciated as such, and only later is it viewed as an attribute *inhering* along with other attributes in a particular object. And as, in direct experience, the only meaning we can give to a "thing" in distinction from its "states" is the definite position in the spatio-temporal system in which those states or qualities are exemplified, I interpret this felt priority of a quality to its local sign as justifying in the sphere of a psychosis the Platonic contention of the primacy of *class-forms* or natures to the *class-members* which embody them. And if this primacy be questioned in the case of sense experience, I feel sure it will be accepted as holding true of the more conceptual phases of our mental life. We have to know the meaning of a general term before we can apply it to particular objects. The members of a class are, for thought, primarily only the more or less accidental embodiments of a certain nature or meaning. And a general term may be analyzed and discussed in complete disregard of whether or not it happens to be actualized here, there, or anywhere. Professor Woodworth's discovery of the imageless or non-sensorial elements of many clearly defined topics of thought and plans of action gives striking emphasis to the truth in question; though, even without appeal to these non-sensory elements, it seems to me, as I have said, easy to imagine a specific nature without also imagining it as existing at a particular place, that is, as a particular object. I can certainly think of making a journey to San Francisco without considering whether I shall go by way of Chicago or by way of St. Louis, this week or next week or never. What the British nominalists thought they had proved was the impossibility of conceiving universals or abstractions. What they really did prove was the impossibility of conceiving universals or abstractions *as particular physical objects.* The same innocent and irrelevant truism had been triumphantly established, some centuries before, by Aristotle against Plato in his "tritos anthropos" argument. In a psychical system, the universal is primary and the particular secondary for the same reason that in a physical system the reverse is true—that reason being that the quantity and plurality of a physical system underlie its quality and unity, while in the psychical system it is the unity and quality that are fundamental. That the mind is the place of forms is one of the well-known criteria for distinguishing it from matter, and is directly deducible from the differentia that we have adopted.

A second and even more familiar characteristic of the psychosis is its capacity for past and future events, for memory images, and for ideals. In the physical world, the present *is* real; the past was and the future will be real, but only the present is. It is, then, a distinguishing feature of the psychical that in each present moment of its flow the past not only was but *is* present, as remembered, and the future not only will be but *is* present, as imagined. We might put it this way: at or in each moment of physical time only that one moment is present, while within the unity of each moment of psychical time, many other moments both past and future are present. This curious capacity of the psychical to *extend in time*, although it has been made the basis for the timeless egos of subjective idealism, is in no wise incompatible with the mind's presence in time. It is this extra dimension which more than any one thing gives to the conscious being his supreme advantage in competing with beings not conscious, enabling him, as it does, to respond to the impulse of the moment in the light of past knowledge and future goods. And yet this temporal unity of specious past and future in each actual present is but another aspect of the unity of my perception of one part of the spatial field with my perception of the other parts of the field.

A third of these subsidiary marks of the psychical, and one closely consequent upon the second, is the purposive or teleological character of mental causality as contrasted with the "blind" or mechanical causality of the physical world. The goal of a conscious process is present from the beginning and takes an active part in selecting the links that lead up to its realization. This would be an impossible paradox in a purely material system, for the future, as such, has no physical existence except at the moment when it ceases to be future; and all causes act on the instant, *ab extra* or mechanically, the telos of the process playing no part in its own actualization. In a psychosis, the individual elements, instead of being self-existent constituents of an aggregate, are each of them subordinate both in their being and in their behavior to the structure or form of their system. If the tendency of the system as a whole be identical with the tendency of one of its elements, then in the ensuing process that element will have a very peculiar prominence. Though not necessarily strong in its own right, it will act catalytically as a kind of center about which the other elements will gradually be distributed. A possibility-element in a psychosis differs from a fact-element in not being able to maintain itself except by the aid of other elements. When we experience a future ideal in process of gradually attaining to what we call "actualization," we note its passage from a parasitic or dependent position in our psychosis to a status of self-dependence and self-existence. And when the process is voluntary, we perceive the other elements contributing to this change of status in response to the demands of the system as a whole. Factuality, indeed, differs from possibility not merely as present and past differ from future, but as the fixed and must-be-admitted differ from the dismissible-at-pleasure. Facts are. They are also stubborn. Ideals are unborn things of the future; they dwell dimly in the conceptual fringe of our consciousness and clamor or plead, according to their natures, for us to incarnate them in its perceptual nucleus of fact. Teleological causation is not, then, the mere influence of a conceived future element upon other elements of the psychosis. Self-active and self-directive, it is a movement of crystallization on the part of the psychosis as a whole toward and around one of its own members—a movement in which the factual elements are, despite their individual tendencies, made to adapt themselves to the reception into their own order of the element which, though present with them, is nevertheless future and so of a different order.

Thus, inadequately, I have attempted to depict the three traditional marks by which consciousness is contrasted with the real though passing show of its physical objects. These marks of mind were (1) its capacity for forms or universals; (2) its capacity for non-actual things of the past and future; and (3) its capacity for self-directed and teleological causality: psychical realism versus physical nominalism; psychical time-extension versus physical flux; psychical finalism versus physical mechanism. I have tried, further, to show that these three capacities are merely three different expressions of that general character of the psychical which I accepted as the basis of its definition, namely, its essential unity and indivisibility as based upon the primacy of the structure or form of the system considered collectively as a whole over the plurality of its elements considered distributively as an aggregate. We have now to take the second step in our problem and to investigate the process in which the events of a psychosis are consequent upon physical events in the brain.

IV. Consciousness from Without: Intensive Sensation and Kinetic Stimulus

We are at the outset confronted with a certain postulate or assumption adopted by the Cartesians and by almost all later philosophers. The assumption was as natural and excusable as it was false and mischievous; unless it can be refuted, any attempt to solve the psychophysical problem must appear futile. This momentous postulate is the expression of a twofold exaggeration of that distinction between psychical and physical which has been described above. Direct experience, together with profound insight into scientific method, convinced Descartes that matter was fundamentally quantitative or spatial, infinitely divisible, and controlled by mechanical law; and that mind, on the other hand, was teleological, indivisible, and qualitative. In the first flush of enthusiasm over this true discovery, it was falsely inferred to mean that matter was *nothing but* quantitative and that mind was *nothing but* qualitative. The result was a dual denudation of the physical and psychical orders. *All true or non-quantitative qualities, that is, all "secondary" qualities, were removed from the material world and dumped bodily into the mind, that mind being at the same time and from a similar motive deprived of all real extension and real presence in the physical world of its objects.* And in place of two contrasting relational nexuses, exhibiting contrasting types of behavior, there ensued the extraordinary conception of two separate *realms* of events: a physical realm pre-empting all real space, and over against this a psychical realm which, not being in space, was nowhere at all, though, of course, quite "real."

The appalling dualism thus begotten speedily led all who could clearly realize its implications to abandon any conception of a causal relation between the two sundered halves of the universe. All true causality involves a transfer of influence or energy from the causal agent to the patient on which the effect is produced. But energy cannot be transferred from somewhere to nowhere and back again from the nowhere of the mind to the space of the brain and the physical world. Such a "transfer," if it could mean anything, would mean that energy was annihilated in sensation and created in volition. It was the recognition of this implication that led quite properly to the doctrine of the conservation of energy being invoked as an additional argument against any interaction of physical and psychical. Nothing was left but to describe the synchronous and thoroughly correlated occurrences in the two realms as a mysterious relation of "parallelism." And, in spite of the growing demands of Darwinian biology on the one hand and of common sense and direct experience on the other, psychophysical parallelism, which when properly interpreted means automatism or the epiphenomenality of consciousness, stands today as the scandalous but irrefutable consequence of postulating a material world without qualities and a world of minds that lack spatiality and exist—*nowhere.*

As I have elsewhere [4] argued in detail against this postulate, I may confine myself here to a very summary statement of what seem to me to be its invalidities:

1. Each man feels his mind to be located in his body. This immediate revelation in experience of the spatiality of consciousness is not and is not felt to be in the least incompatible with its intensive unity and indivisibility.

2. The fact that each consciousness feels itself to be

[4] *The Monist,* January, 1908, "Are Mental Processes in Space?"

in space is not felt to be incompatible with the intuitive conviction that that consciousness could never be visible or in any way accessible to the external perception of another observer. To the eye of such an external observer, the space occupied by consciousness would always appear filled with the purely physical objects of matter and motion.

Suppose, now, that we are freed from the paradoxical antithesis of consciousness and space—how does the psychophysical problem present itself? A physical influence or stimulus which, though not lacking quality, is primarily quantitative and accessible to the external sense of many observers is transmitted along a sensory nerve and appears to give rise to a sensation or psychical state which, though not lacking in quantity and spatiality, is accessible to the internal perception of only one observer. *That* this happens is an obvious fact easily verifiable in any experience and not to be got rid of by any metaphysical or methodological theory whatsoever. But can we conceive *how* it happens? A clue to the answer is, I believe, to be found in a certain type of occurrence in the physical world. When an elastic body collides with a fixed barrier, the motion of the body gradually decreases to zero and then begins to increase again in an opposite direction up to almost its original amount. At the moment prior to the rebound, there is no motion in any direction; for, before a reflected motion southward can begin, the incident northward motion must wholly cease. The motion in the world is not conserved in the sense of being the same in amount at every moment of existence. But energy is supposed to be conserved in just this sense. Hence, energy is of two kinds, of which visible motion is one; and it is only the sum of the two phases that is constant. The energy which is not motion but into which and from which motion passes is called "potential." Naturally, the nature of this invisible type of energy is a question of some interest. There are, I understand, three theories of its nature: (1) There is the theory that it is some sort of invisible motion (other than heat) of the particles of a body into which the molar motion is transformed. This appears untenable for the reason that precisely the same problem will necessarily recur in connection with these particles, no matter how tiny they are made or how often we subdivide them. Two particles collide, lose their motions, and regain them in opposite directions. What becomes of the energy of these little motions during the moment of their redirection? (2) There is the theory that the kinetic energy of elastic bodies prior to collision passes at the moment of collision into nothing and comes out again from nothing quite fresh and unchanged in form or quantity. This is the view of potential energy that seems most in favor at present. According to it, potential energy is really nothing but potential. It is in no sense actual, but is just the sheer possibility of a certain quantity of motion. In favor of this conception it might be said, I suppose, that potential energy is not and from its very nature cannot be perceptible to external observers; that it is consequently not actual in any intelligible sense. And, again, that to consider it as actual would be, if not absurd, at least useless, for it is only measurable indirectly, in terms of the motion of which it is the promise. (3) There is finally the older view that potential energy is stress or force; that, as such, it is just as actual as the motion from which it has come and into which it will pass; that it is "potential" only with respect to motion; and that motion itself might with equal propriety be called "potential energy of stress." In favor of this third view it might be said: (*a*) That it has never been empirically refuted, is still held by some physicists, and has in the past been held by men of the insight of Faraday. (*b*) That potential energy, though not visible or externally perceptible, is nevertheless definitely and directly perceivable internally or by *participation* in it through what is ineptly called the "muscular sense"; and that it is absurd to speak of the stress quality revealed by this internal or muscular sense as being less real or more anthropomorphic than the motion quality revealed by the visual sense. (*c*) That energy in the form of stress, while most easily measurable in terms of the motion which it will yield, is nevertheless capable of as precise mathematical formulation as that motion itself, to wit, as $m \cdot a \cdot s$, or the product of the *mass*, the *acceleration*, and the *space* through which that acceleration obtains. In short, the third view, according to which force is a real phase of energy, is, first, logically necessary in order to avoid the unthinkable paradox of a real motion passing into and issuing from nonentity; it is, second, a direct revelation of experience; it is, third, capable in its own right of mathematical symbolization.

When we formulate kinetic or motion energy as $\frac{1}{2} mv^2$, we recognize it to be the product of the mass and the integral (with respect to velocity) of the velocity. In the same way, potential energy formulated as $m \cdot a \cdot s$ may be recognized as the product of the mass and the derivative (with respect to time) of the velocity. Acceleration is the derivative of the same function of which $\frac{1}{2} v^2$ is the integral, the function $v = \frac{ds}{dt}$.[5]

If one places his hand between a fixed spring and a body moving uniformly into collision with it, he can get as clear

[5] Of course, equal quantities of the potential energy denoted by $m \cdot a \cdot s$ may differ in kind according to the relative values of the three factors, (m), (a), and (s). And leaving aside variations in the mass factor, we should have two types of potential energy: one would be of the type instanced by a system of widely separated bodies attracting one another by the force of gravity, and the other of the type presented by a compressed spring. In the former type, a relatively small acceleration (a) extends through a relatively great space (s); while in the latter, a relatively great acceleration (a) acts through the relatively small space (s) occupied by the spring; the product ($a \cdot s$), however, is the same in both cases.

and direct a perception of this continuous transfer of motion into a stress which is felt to be homogeneous, though not identical with it, as he can of any other phenomenon whatever. The same experiment also gives an idea of the mathematical homogeneity of motion and stress. What is the a priori warrant for believing that reality can contain only integrals of velocities and not their derivatives? Of course, stress, from its very nature, can never be revealed to the visual sense, while motion can. But is it not an over-enthusiasm for the instrumental excellence of the retina to regard it as having a monopoly in revealing the qualities of the actual? To be consistent in carrying out the apotheosis of the retinal and the condemnation of the muscular sense, we should have to define the inertia and the gravitational property of mass itself in terms of the motion with which they can undoubtedly be correlated. But I cannot see how such a reduction of mechanics to a geometry of the motion of shadows or visible forms would possess any exclusive ontological validity, even if Professor Karl Pearson be right as to its superior methodological elegance.[6] Let us assume, then, that potential energy or stress is as real as kinetic energy, and that consequently we should speak of an *intensive* rather than of a *potential* phase of energy. The two forms of energy are successive and alternating phases rather than simultaneous and coexistent aspects. Of course, any physical system can exemplify—and, as a matter of fact, does exemplify—both kinds of energy; yet the same bit of energy cannot be both kinetic and potential at the same time: to the extent that it becomes potential, it ceases to be kinetic, and vice versa.

Though interchangeable and equivalent in quantity, the two forms of energy are contrasting in quality. There are,

[6] Cf. *The Grammar of Science*, especially Chapters VI and VIII, in which the reality of force is attacked as an exploded superstition, and even mass is defined exclusively in terms of motion.

indeed, several of these contrasting characteristics of which I shall speak later, but the chief contrast is with respect to observability: kinetic energy can be externally perceived in its present actuality, while potential energy can only be inferred as a result of a motion that is past and as a promise or possibility of a motion that is to come. This is the reason and the only reason for calling the latter form of energy by the somewhat derogatory name "potential." But what is this potentiality of future motion? There is no such thing as a bare or empty potentiality. The potentiality of a chicken is the actuality of an egg; and, in general, the possibility or potentiality of anything is always in itself the actuality of something else.

But if potential energy is something more than a bare potentiality of future motion, what can that something be? It has been suggested (as I said above and here repeat) that it is a motion of small particles—that the potential energy of a mass is the kinetic or actual motion of its invisible molecules or atoms. But (as we have seen) that suggestion is futile, for those particles, whatever their ultimate nature, will have each its own motion which, whenever changed in direction, must in its turn pass through a latent or potential phase.

If potential energy is by its very nature not observable from without, is it perhaps observable from within? Let us see. A stimulus passes over a sensory nerve as a form of motion. Somewhere in the synapses of the cerebrum, that current of kinetic energy is checked and then redirected along other neural pathways, and finally it passes out along the efferent or motor nerves as a motor reaction, that is, an observable motion. These motions along the nerves, like any other motions, must pass into a potential or invisible phase at their moment of redirection; and as nearly as we can tell, it is just at those moments when motions cease or are checked that sensations begin. Now, if the internally observable phenomena that we call sensations occur at the very times when the externally observable motions which are their causes pass from the kinetic to the potential form of energy, *is it not overwhelmingly probable that the two simultaneous phenomena are identical, and that the potential energy into which the motion of a neural stimulus is transformed is in itself the actual entity which we call a "sensation"?* In the case of sensations, at least, our question as to what is the actual nature of energy when in its latent or potential form seems to have been answered. But if the nonkinetic form of energy is as actual and positive a reality as motion itself, why has it been condemned to a half-real or twilight status signified by the derogatory word *potential?* The reason is obvious. Physical science is interested in the externally observable, and is rightly suspicious of anything that cannot be so regarded. Yet, unfortunately, the domain of the externally observable is not logically continuous or self-explanatory. It is filled with holes, abysses, and discontinuities which cannot be altogether neglected. It is at this point that the blessed word *potential* comes to the rescue. A good empirically observable motion of a man's fingers winding his watch reaches an end and disappears from view. But during the next 24 hours or so the exact equivalent of that motion comes dribbling back into the observable world in the form of orderly motions of the hands of the watch around the dial. What to do with the energy during the period when it was hidden? Call it *potential* (stored up in the mainspring of the watch)—not an actuality, but a *possibility*, a hybrid mixture of something and nothing. The situation is analogous to that in the field of number prior to Argand. The square root of minus one ($\sqrt{-1}$), and its multiples, were merely "imaginary" numbers—potentialities of the real numbers produced by the operation of squaring. Then came Argand and demonstrated that these imaginary or half-real numbers could be given a perfectly good geometrical status by representing them on a vertical line perpendicular to the horizontal line whose points depict the numbers called "real." Now, humbly and with all apologies, I am seeking to render a service to "potential" energy analogous to the service that Argand rendered to the imaginary (and complex) numbers. For my theory suggests that the entity which from the point of view of an external observer or physicist we call "potential energy" is in itself and for itself (from the point of view of the internal observer who has it or *is* it) nothing but *sensation*—the simplest form of a conscious state. It follows that, while sensations are the potentialities of motions, motions are equally the potentialities of sensations. The potentiality of the physical is the actuality of the psychical, and the potentiality of the psychical is the actuality of the physical. In short, the two phases of energy, the intensive and the extensive, are equally real in themselves despite the fact that each is the potentiality of the other.

If my theory is valid, it not only removes potential energy from the limbo of semi-nonentity, but at the same time it removes sensations and the higher mental states derived from them from the limbo of epiphenomenality. Even the staunchest of materialists must feel guilty of a certain impiety in denying causal efficacy to mind and its processes. If I am right, sensations will no longer be mysterious and embarrassing superfluities, *de trop* in the mechanistic world, but rather will they be integral members of that world, true causal links in the chain of material motions.

V. Correspondences Between a Field of Potential Energy and a Field of Consciousness

Perhaps the most striking resemblance between consciousness and potential energy is the essential invisibility or privacy which characterizes both energy in its intensive phase and also the nonphysical objects of consciousness. Leibniz reminds us that the most powerful microscope could not, if applied to the brain of a fellow-man, disclose anything of his thoughts and feelings. We may remind ourselves that the most powerful microscope, if applied to a compressed spring or to the space of a magnetic or a gravitational field, would be equally unable to disclose the stresses therein. As objects of external or visual perception, potential energy and the psychical are *both* of them nonexistent. We can feel stress only by participating in it, just as we could feel our neighbor's toothache only by participating in it through some such inter-organic, nerve-grafting device as Professor Pearson has suggested. From the external point of view, potential energy and my neighbor's toothache are objects which I must postulate in order to explain the otherwise inexplicable hiatuses in the series of visual perceptions which originate from and terminate in them.

Second, both consciousness and intensive energy seem to pervade the space of the things they influence, and in this both resemble matter. But in thus extending in space, they each of them seem to forfeit thereby no whit of their peculiar unity and indivisibility; and in this both of them differ from matter. You cannot imagine your consciousness, although it pervades the space of its perceptual objects, being divided into pieces or composed of them. No more can you imagine dividing into separate pieces that elastic stress that pervades the planetary system.

Third, we pointed out, in the first section of this paper,

how from the essential primacy of unity over divisibility in a psychical system there followed that curious conformity in the behavior of its elements to the structural form of the system as a whole which was manifested in the teleological nature of psychical processes. Now consider the behavior of a swarm of moving iron filings when they come within the field of a magnet. Prior to their advent in the field, each is in its existence relatively autonomous as respects the others, though subservient to the impulses received in actual impact with them (mechanism). Once within the magnetic field, however, the filings forget, as it were, their individual strifes, and each, in relative indifference to the bumps of its fellows, assumes the position demanded of it by the structure of the field into which it has come. The formless chaos of filings gives place to the ordered system which so surprisingly incarnates, or bodies forth to the eye, the invisible and indivisible Faraday lines of magnetic stress.

Fourth, *the conditions under which a stimulus is followed by a sensation happen also to be conditions under which energy passes from a kinetic into an intensive phase.* Perceptions are presumed to arise synchronously with the redirection in the central nervous system of afferent currents into efferent channels. When this process of redirection is prolonged by reason of the many conflicts with the cerebral association currents induced by the afferent intruders, then the consciousness is prolonged, keen, and complex. When, on the other hand, by reason either of innate adjustments or of long practice, the journey through the central labyrinth is quick, smooth, and direct, then the consciousness, if present at all, is simple, faint, and brief. Note that the condition for motion passing into stress is always that it meet with some obstacle by which it is redirected, and that the proportion of the energy that becomes potential depends on the degree of change in the motion's direction. If a ball be thrown perpendicularly against a wall, the whole of the incident motion must disappear before the reflected motion can ensue. But if it be thrown obliquely, then only so much of the motion can pass into stress as is equal to that imaginary component of the motion which is normal to the wall. Several observers might conceivably follow with their eyes the nerve current as it traversed the circuit from sensory origin to motor terminus and at the very moments when the whole or some part of its kinetic energy did, by reason of a change in its direction due to the interference of rival currents of cerebral origin, disappear into an intensive or potential phase: at those same moments there would be *reported* a psychical fact accessible only to the observation of the one person through whose brain the stimulus was passing.

"When a thing looks like a frog and acts like a frog and croaks like a frog, we call it a frog." And on the strength of the four fundamental resemblances described above, I propose as a possible solution of the psychophysical problem the following theory: *What I, from within, would call my sensations are neither more nor less than what you, from without, would describe as the forms of potential energy to which the kinetic energies of neural stimuli would necessarily give rise in passing through my brain.*

We do not as yet know enough about the nature of the neural stimulus or "current" to form a satisfactory conception of the manner of its transformation into the potential phase. If it be some form of vibration or ordinary wave motion, then the change is of the same sort as that undergone by a stream of sound waves in changing from the incident to the reflected path. If, on the other hand, the nerve "current" be electrical in its nature, resembling, as has recently been suggested, the relatively slow progress of energy along a telegraphic cable, then its transformation into potential energy might perhaps be likened to that wrought by an electromagnet in which a portion of the energy of the electric current is drained off into the potential form of a magnetic stress in the surrounding field.

I hasten, however, to answer an objection which is obvious and which might appear crushing. We know, it may be said, what force is—at least, if we choose, as I have done, to give that name to the quality revealed by the muscular sense. And we know what a sensation in general is. They are plainly different, and to identify one with the other is sheer silliness. It is like saying with the materialist that a sensation *is* a mode of motion. To identify odor with color, or pain with sound, would be futilities of the same kind.

To this objection two answers may be made. First, it will be remembered that when we abandoned the modern dualistic postulate of a non-spatial consciousness, we abandoned also its equally vicious correlate—the postulate of an abstract physical world made up of mere quantitative relations and lacking all the specific natures or secondary qualities that are correlated with those relations. Now, if we return to the older view of common sense, according to which every physical thing and every motion or stimulus proceeding from it has correlated with it a specific nature —not a "substantial form," but rather a form inhering in the motion that carries it—then the change of the kinetic energy of the stimulus into the potential energy of the sensation will not be a mysterious change of sheer quantity into sheer quality, but only the change into a qualitative form of stress of a similarly qualitative form of motion. So what we perceive as mere undifferentiated stress is simply the general "substance" of sensations, that is, the basic and generic quality common to them all, the different degrees of which are felt as the differences of intensity to which every sensation is alike susceptible. Stress as physical substance would thus be related to particular sensations precisely as extended matter is related to particular objects. All physical objects are experienced as having the general quality of materiality in addition to the specific qualities by which they differ.

But, second, it may also be said in explanation of the difference between mere stress and the rich variety of our feelings and sensations that what we have so far been considering as potential energy and formulating as *m.a.s.* is only one, and that the simplest and lowest, of the intensive phases into which kinetic energy may pass and from which it may come. Acceleration is only the first derivative of velocity with respect to time; and if an energy quantum can pass from the extensive phase represented by the integral of a velocity ($\frac{1}{2}\, v^2$) into the intensive one represented by its first derivative $\left(\frac{dv}{dt}\right)$, it would seem that it might on occasion pass equally well into any or all of the infinity of higher phases of intensive energy symbolized by the series of velocity derivatives of higher order than the first: $\left(\frac{d^2v}{dt^2}, \frac{d^3v}{dt^3}, \frac{d^4v}{dt^4} \ldots\right)$. The qualities denoted by these higher derivatives would have no place or meaning in the physical world except as higher orders of the potentiality of motion, but they could well exist as actualities in the intensive sphere of the psychical. They would constitute those tertiary contents of consciousness which even the most realistic of Realists can hardly imagine to exist apart from some awareness of them. I refer to such things as love, envy, fear, and hate, and the whole inexhaustible host of the finer forms and nuances of these.

And here, then, in the answer to what might have seemed a fatal objection, we find a fifth fundamental resemblance between the psychical and the intensive phase of energy with which our theory seeks to identify it. Any given psychosis contains only a tiny fraction of the totality of physical events; but the psychical in general has the capacity not only for all perceptible physical objects, but also for the whole assemblage of thoughts and feelings about those objects. This consideration alone would be sufficient to disprove a parallelism of the "double-aspect" type. The assemblage of possible psychical elements or forms of intensive energy denoted by the higher derivatives is to the assemblage of possible physical events or kinetic energies denoted merely by the first order of integrals, as a multi-dimensional manifold is to the uni-dimensional manifold that forms the lowest and limiting of its "cross sections." Or, to express the same thing in another way, we can say that the physical world of public objects is the indefinitely extending and ever-present surface of contact from which originate and in which terminate the series of intensive or psychical events, the latter being private and insulated from one another except in so far as they participate in the common physical order. Or, finally, we might liken the relation between physical and psychical to that obtaining between the one kind of wealth embodied in money and the totality of objects of wealth which are being constantly interchanged and mutually evaluated through the agency of that money as a universal medium of circulation.

VI. Conclusion: *Res Cogitans* and *Res Extensa*

If our hypothesis is valid, the mind of man or of any animal is an organism within an organism—an attenuated organism of potential energies embodying the past and built up within the ever-present cerebral organism which is its matrix. What sort of causal relations will obtain between the memory system or mind and the material body from whose soil it has grown?

I believe that René Descartes has given the key to the solution of this great problem of psychophysical causality in his theory that, while the mind *cannot add* to the energies of the physical world, it *can control the direction* of those energies. I gratefully accept this Cartesian thought, but I must qualify my acceptance by pointing out what has often been pointed out by others, including Descartes himself, that it is difficult to imagine how a completely non-spatial entity like his *res cogitans* could have any causal relation to a *res extensa* with which it had no point in common. Suppose, however, that *res cogitans*, instead of being hopelessly alien to the material world, were what I believe it to be—a field of potential energies within the world? Then, no matter how faint or attenuated such a field might be, it would be not only possible but necessary that any and all energies traversing it should be in some degree causally modified by it. A mind thus conceived, in spite of or rather, let me say, because of its thoroughly materialistic nature, would be capable of guiding by its memories the organism in which it was set; and through that guidance it could impose upon the blind and mechanistic forces of environing nature more and more of its own forms and purposes. Though physical in its constitution, it would function as a spiritual substance—a veritable *res cogitans* within the larger *res extensa.* I do not know whether Descartes would forgive me for modifying one part of his theory in order to make the other part work; and I do not know either whether M. Bergson could forgive me for a corresponding translation into physical terms of the famous *durée réelle*, which I gratefully accept from him as constituting the essential nature of the psyche. But while I must remain in doubt as to whether my hypothesis would be more pleasing or more displeasing to the two French philosophers to whom I owe most, I have introduced their views into this discussion because I wished to show the extent to which the form of psychological theory which I am defending could provide for the elements of metaphysical truth in Cartesian and Bergsonian Dualism without departing from the well-established validity and fruitfulness of a completely "materialistic" methodology.

Note

My theory that the mind is a hierarchical system of potential or intensive energies accumulated in the brain may be on the verge of an experimental demonstration. Professor Burr of the Department of Physiology and Professor Northrop of the Department of Philosophy at Yale, working together with an apparatus designed by Professor Burr and his colleagues in Physics, have discovered that a living organism is pervaded by a faint but unmistakable field of electric force which may perhaps serve as an agency, not mechanistic in the narrower sense, but definable in physical terms, that controls and unifies the purposive processes of ontogenetic or embryonic development. Up to the present they have not found and measured any secondary and differentiated cerebral field. But that there is in the brain itself such a field is evidenced by the electromagnetic waves which proceed from the cerebrum and which in their character and pattern indicate the mental condition (sleeping or waking, normal or abnormal) of the subject. If Burr and Northrop should succeed in discovering by their delicate apparatus the direct presence of this cerebral field of force, it would be a step toward an experimental confirmation of my hypothesis that the mind with its memories consists of a system of potential energies—a physical but indivisible soul within the divisible and material body.

Section VI—Theology

16

* THE PROMETHEAN CHALLENGE TO RELIGION [1]

A plea for a new orientation in religion in which the life-affirming and rationalistic attitudes of the anticlerical opponents of the church can be combined with a belief in God and in the possibility of a mystic communion with Him.

THE LEGEND of Prometheus is the golden legend of Greece, and in it is expressed in the form of a local myth the quintessence of human idealism.

Prometheus has stolen from heaven the secret of fire, symbol of creative intelligence, and given it to men to be for them a basis of the useful arts and a means of perpetual progress. Zeus, the omnipotent, punishes this defiance of his will by dooming the rebel to imprisonment and torture. Pinioned to a great rock, an eagle continuously eating at his vitals, Prometheus, a god in rebellion against God, endures through the ages with conscience clear and will unbroken.

Unlike the patient Job, he does not yield his ideal of right to the force of might; and unlike proud Lucifer, he seeks power not for himself, but for men—through the emancipation of their reason and the utilization of their intelligence. So it is that the name Prometheus has come

[1] Reprinted from *The New Republic*, August 6, 1924, Vol. 39, No. 505, pp. 289–295.

to stand as a symbol of the highest faith that the heart can hold—the faith that unshackled intellect is the friend, not the enemy, of conscience, and that no might, not even the might of heaven itself, can increase or decrease or in any way alter the validity of what is morally right.

The challenge which the mythical Prometheus hurled at a mythical Zeus has a profound significance for the actual institutions of an actual world; for it is the eternally inspiring challenge to revise and if necessary to destroy without pity any institution that is opposed to the demands of an evolving humanity.

Now it is upon the institution of religion that the Promethean challenge bears most directly; for religion combines with its supernatural hope an anti-rational authoritarianism, and combines with its super-rational vision of a life of service an anti-natural asceticism. To meet the Promethean challenge, religion would have to do two things: it would have to purge its supernaturalism of the authoritarian opposition to free inquiry; and it would have to remove from its gospel of altruism the ascetic opposition to the needs and satisfactions of earthly life.

Religion is man's belief in a power greater than he and vitally related to him. This greater power may be conceived as one or many, personal or impersonal, within the world or apart from it. As man develops a clear consciousness of values and virtues, he ascribes them to the objects of his worship. The gods are made the repositories of human ideals and come thereby to be conceived as not only physically stronger, but also spiritually higher than their human creators. Religion thus develops into a combination of two sets of beliefs: physical beliefs as to the origin and control of nature, and ethical beliefs as to the destiny and duty of human life. The climax of this development is the unification of the two kinds of belief in the faith that supernatural power and superhuman goodness are jointly embodied and co-present in a single divine being. Now, in order to appreciate the ethical significance of religion, we must understand something of the way in which man first develops those moral values with which he later endows his gods.

Like all animals, man possesses needs, impulses, and desires, the satisfaction of which constitutes his good. And, like all the higher animals, man modifies his direct momentary and individual impulses by three kinds of indirect control: memory, sympathy, and suggestibility.

Consider, for example, the dog. She first controls her present impulse to take the meat from her master's plate by the memory of past whippings. Second, the same dog can control her natural impulse to flee from abuse by a sympathetic sense of the needs of her offspring. And third, our dog may break training altogether and against her own interest yield to the suggestion of barking or running with the pack of which she is a member.

The human conscience contains the same three types of mediate control which are found in the higher animals, but in man these factors of memory, sympathy, and suggestibility are not only immensely more extensive, but they are consciously recognized as agencies distinct from and often opposed to the immediate impulses which they control. Animal training which is based on the memory of punishments and rewards becomes a twofold human "prospectiveness" which includes courage—the capacity to face pain—and temperance—the capacity to forego pleasure; animal sympathy becomes human justice and love; and animal suggestibility becomes human loyalty to group customs and to a leader's commands. Unconscious modification of behavior gives place to conscious self-direction of conduct, and a spiritual or moral sense of values is added to the physical senses of sight and hearing.

The evolution of conscience is paralleled in almost every

respect by the evolution of reason. Sensations, like impulses, are common to all animals; and in all higher animals sensations, like impulses, are modified and reinterpreted in the light of a past that is remembered, an objective world that is inferred, and a testimony that is accepted. And as in the field of conduct, so also in the field of cognition, the threefold system of secondary controls develops into a clear consciousness of truth and reality as distinguished from sensation and appearance; in short, animal intelligence evolves into human reason. And as conscience revaluates each primary satisfaction of impulse in the light of its relation to what is morally approved as good, so reason reinterprets each primary experience of sense in the light of its relation to what is logically verified as true. Reason is conscience in the field of thinking and conscience is reason in the field of action.

Now, there is one aspect of the evolution of human conscience that is most unfortunate. The factor of suggestibility which makes man tend to accept and believe what is told to him merely because it is told to him is the least valuable and at the same time the most influential of the three elements of which conscience is compounded. Long before self-control and justice attained the level of consciously recognized virtues, conformity to the folkways of the human pack and obedience to customs, laws, and commands grew to be the larger portion of acknowledged duty. Language testifies to this truth in that the words *moral* and *ethical* both meant originally "the customary." This predominantly authoritarian character of primitive morality is not without its useful side. The customs of a group are often the best means for the preservation and development of its members. But along with what is useful there is much that is purely arbitrary and wasteful. And even those rules which at a given period and in a given situation were of benefit become in other situations positively harmful. "Taboo" is the name given to a rule that is considered morally binding regardless of its consequences. And the observance of taboos is at once the largest and the poorest part of human morals.

We have said that man ascribes his moral values to the gods that he worships and thus transforms his religion from something very like magic into an innocent and happy trust in the goodness of the powers operating in nature. If this were all, religion would have nothing to its discredit. But, unfortunately, in endowing the gods with moral excellence, man also reinterprets the natural ideals of his group as supernatural commands. The authoritarian character of primitive morality is thus intensified and perpetuated in religion. And the dangers and wastes of accepting customs as in themselves good are enormously increased by the belief that those customs are the unchangeable will of heaven. So long as a moral code is based only on the will of society, it can be changed as the society changes and improves. But when once a code of practice is viewed as divinely commanded, it becomes unamendable and sacrosanct. To question it or reform it is a sacrilege that must be suppressed at any cost. And what religion does with primitive ideals of virtue it does also with primitive ideas of truth. For in primitive physics no less than in primitive ethics, almost all beliefs are accepted on authority, and our ancestors' guesses as to the origin of the world and the laws of nature get reinterpreted as revelations of divine wisdom which must never be questioned or revised.

The result of this process of sanctification is to subject later generations to the dead hand of the past. Progress in science and in morals is made all but impossible, for, no matter how many new facts are discovered and no matter how many new rules of conduct are required by changed situations, the earlier and less adequate beliefs cannot be revised without treason to the gods of our fathers. The consequences of this situation, as so far exhibited in human history, are fairly uniform. Conscience and reason are not wholly authoritarian; and as a society develops its culture, the new and growing mass of unorthodox knowledge increasingly presses against the old body of orthodox beliefs until a crisis is reached. Reason breaks through the shell of faith and a religious revolution is on.

When the old order goes, much that was good goes with it; and when the new order comes, it often brings new evils. In the past these revolutions have been led by individual prophets who have believed themselves to be divinely inspired. The new regime is therefore as religious and as authoritarian in spirit as the old, even though it incorporates in its dogmas a less inadequate body of scientific and ethical theories. Despite the general uniformity of these successive revolutions, there is in them a certain clearly defined principle of progress which is, I believe, destined soon to produce a result which, if not disastrous, will be at any rate momentous.

Each time that one authority is overthrown by another, the authoritarian principle itself is shaken and weakened. Moreover, with each successive revolution it is increasingly difficult to incorporate the new secular knowledge into the new system of dogma. And finally, the spirit of secularization itself grows steadily stronger and its devotees grow more and more indifferent and even hostile not only to the authoritarianism of religion, but also to its supernatural hope and spiritual devotion. While the monarchs fight with one another, the faith in monarchy as a principle grows steadily weaker. I believe that a period is now rapidly approaching in which for the first time in history religion will be confronted, not with a palace revolution, replacing one prophet by another, but with a popular and secular revolution directed against all gods and all prophets. The forces of this threatened revolution are not composed of small bands of intellectuals or of temporary political leaders like those of France in 1790 or Russia in 1920. The new revolutionary army consists of the growing multitude of moderately educated men and women who find increasing difficulty in reconciling not only the facts but the spirit of evolutionary science and modern social ethics with supernatural religion as we have known it.

We often hear the question as to whether a new religion is likely to appear. It seems to me improbable that any new religion, in the sense in which the old religions were new, will ever again come to our planet. For while the new facts of science and the new needs of ethics could doubtless be incorporated in the form of a new religious revelation, the spirit of secular independence and freedom of thought which has become an essential part of modern culture could not by its very nature be reduced to any authoritarian scheme of dogma, no matter how adequate or how generous its provisions.

If no new revelation is to be looked for and if the rising tide of secularism is threatening to sweep away the good as well as the evil of the traditional religions, it seems to me that it may be worth while to examine our inherited faith in the light of the Promethean challenge. For that challenge was directed against Zeus as the embodiment of unreasoning authority; and the modern hostility to the church, while seemingly directed to the mysticism and supernaturalism of its theories, is in reality directed to the authoritarianism of its spirit. Christianity, like every other religion, consists of two main parts, physical or metaphysical beliefs about nature, and ethical or spiritual beliefs about human duty. It is the ethics rather than the physics that I wish to discuss; and therefore it will be sufficient to remind ourselves that the Christian conception of the world of physical nature when considered as a philosophy is a form of theistic idealism, differentiated from other forms by its adherence to the Hebraic account of the creation of the world, the fall of Adam, and the punishment, instruction, and protection given by God to Adam's descendants and especially to the children of Israel. To this supernatural cosmogony and supernatural history contained in the Jewish scriptures Christianity adds the new doctrine of the incarnation, in which Christ figures as savior and exemplar and teacher of men on earth and finally as judge and arbiter of their eternal destiny.

Interwoven with this metaphysics is a system of ethics in which we can perceive three fairly distinct doctrines concerning man's duty. The first and greatest of these is the ideal of charity or service, which is conceived as the supreme principle of righteous living. This cardinal virtue of altruism is to be carried to the point of forgiveness of sin and love of enemies.

The second of the main trends in Christian ethics is asceticism. The premise of the ascetics' attitude is the conviction that the natural goods of the body are incompatible with the ultimate goods of the spirit, and the conclusion from this premise is the belief that virtue consists primarily in a repudiation of the world and the flesh.

The third member of the Christian trinity of virtues is obedience to divine authority. Not only in our moral practice, but in our theoretical beliefs, we are bidden to accept with humble, unquestioning faith the words of the Bible.

The organization formed for the furtherance of these ethical and metaphysical doctrines is the Christian church; and all Christians agree that the church's dual office is to teach the faith and to administer its saving benefits to whomsoever will accept them. The history of Occidental morals during the Christian era is centered in the history of the Christian church: its conquest of paganism, its various attainments of temporal and political power, its internal schisms and heresies, and its external conflicts with such tendencies in science and in ethics as have been in appearance or reality opposed to its teaching.

Throughout this great and many-sided story one may see in operation the three basic trends of Christian ethics: altruism, asceticism, and authoritarianism—sometimes fused indistinguishably with one another and with the body of metaphysical dogma, and at other times clear and distinct from one another and from their metaphysical associates. Let us consider them from the standpoint of their relative importance and their bearing not upon past history, but upon that present and impending secular revolution of which we have spoken.

Asceticism is, of course, not peculiar to Christianity; it is the natural and illegitimate daughter of every form of human morality. Morality is the resistance to the lesser needs of the moment as a means of satisfying the greater and more enduring needs of others and of oneself at other times. This control of, and resistance to, natural impulses, only justifiable as a means, comes to be regarded as an end in itself; and conscience, arising as an aid to more happiness, degenerates into an obstacle to any happiness. The ascetic habit of mind is prolific in devising theories to justify its own perversity. The spontaneous impulses of our nature, because they are to be resisted, must be hated, and because they are hated, they must be bad. The flesh and the devil are identical. And as not even the ascetic can subsist entirely on negations, it becomes necessary to excuse the hatred of natural values by the claim that it is the only means to the attainment of supernatural values. The supposedly real good of another world is the inverse of the supposedly illusory good of this world. The spirit thrives when the flesh is mortified. This inversion of moral values with which asceticism justifies itself has appealed to many brave souls. The work of conquering oneself, of eating out one's very heart, calls for all and more than all that the strongest spirit has to give. It is the courage and endurance of the ascetics that have masked from us the ugliness and moral madness of their practice. We need not trace the various forms which Christian asceticism has taken, or compare Catholic monasticism, in which asceticism is intense and concentrated in select groups, with Protestant puritanism, in which asceticism is less intense but diffused over the entire body.

The modern secular conscience revolts against every variety of asceticism, partly because of its cruelty and ugliness, but more because of its individual futility, and most of all because of the terrible social waste of spiritual energy which it involves. It has long been known that too much preoccupation with one's natural impulses tends to increase them. The fighter needs his foe and the ascetic needs the flesh which he is pledged to oppose. The continuous searching of oneself for sin creates the very thing one would destroy. To this ancient knowledge must be added the teaching of the newer psychology according to which nature's impulses suppressed from conscious life wreak their revenge in the unconscious, and like hidden ulcers distribute their poison not only to the moral but even to the mental and physical organism. So much for the dangers of asceticism to the ascetics themselves.

As for the waste to society of these ascetic practices, we need only to picture to ourselves what glorious consequences to earthly life would have resulted if the spiritual energies that men have devoted to fasting, celibacy, and voluntary poverty had been directed to alleviating hunger, making sex love more beautiful, and distributing wealth more equitably. What perfectly enormous losses and wastes have been involved in the long fight to decrease and destroy the very natural goods which should be created more abundantly and distributed more broadly and justly!

If we turn from Christian asceticism to Christian authoritarianism, we find a somewhat similar situation. Authoritarianism, like asceticism, is not peculiar to Christianity; every religion tends to make its God the authority for its good, to interpret ideals of natural excellence as commands of supernatural power. This subordination of right to might and of ethics to religion has borne many hideous fruits. Let me attempt to enumerate what seem to me to be the most important. I group them under three heads: (1) the menace to ethical ideas, (2) the menace to religious faith, (3) the menace to social progress.

1. The authoritarian element in our present Christianity is a menace to our ethical ideals first of all because it exalts monarchical power above democratic leadership. The conception of God as a great king whose mere will is our law is, as Professor Overstreet has pointed out, a vestige of a pre-democratic age, and it therefore gives to religion a note that is subtly but unmistakably discordant with the highest social aspirations of the present day. Then, too, when God is thus made the source and sanction of moral laws, He becomes, like other monarchs, immune to the duties prescribed for his subjects. His ways are not our ways. He can visit the sins of the fathers upon the children. He can create and permit to function a nature whose earthquakes and storms make no distinction between the just and the unjust. As creator and Lord of all it is He who creates Satan and permits him to work evil. Finally—and this is the most extraordinary anomaly of all—He is not only above that justice which He makes binding upon his creatures, but He is endowed with that will to vengeance which is depicted as the cardinal sin for man. The Christ ideal of universal love and forgiveness is directly and shamelessly contradicted by the conception of a God who condemns to a hell of eternal torture the vast majority of his children. Here clearly is a double standard of

morals: the higher standard for man and the lower one for God. Vengeance is mine, saith the Lord, charity and forgiveness are for you to practice. The consequences of a double standard are ethically disastrous. The ideals of the higher standard tend to sink to the level of the lower. If God allows nature to create injustice, then for us to go counter to nature and to interfere with her laws savors of sacrilege. And if the Almighty is to torture freethinkers and sinners in hell, why should not we with our inquisitions and prisons do likewise on earth? And if God visits upon the children the sins of the fathers, why should not we visit upon the so-called illegitimate children the sins that are attributed to their fathers?

In a thousand other ugly ways like these does the principle of authority in religion degrade the ideals of morality. But even this is not all. For in teaching children the morality of commands rather than the morality of ideals, we inoculate them with the poisonous idea that the moral sense derives its ultimate sanction from the power of an almighty God. And too often it happens that these children when older come to doubt some part of the supernaturalistic metaphysics in which they have been trained. The result is not that tragic and often noble sadness which is the necessary and sufficient concomitant of atheism, but rather a complete disintegration of the moral tissues. If goodness depends on God and if there is no God, then there can be no goodness. If the moral void is to be filled at all by those who have lost faith in religion, it must be filled with a worship of nature. Ethics, they have been taught, depends on authority, and there is no authority left but nature. Now nature is a harlot. All things to all men. Orderly and capricious, beautiful and ugly, but above all—brute force, sheer power. Even the worst of the gods embodies something of the goodness of his human creators. Not so, nature, red with tooth and claw, rewarding always the strong and the cunning. Through the whole radical movement today there runs the new nature-worship with its cynical so-called realism that sneers at every ideal as mere ideology or camouflage for the selfish interest of some group or class. And this authoritarian naturalism of the radicals of today is the direct heritage of the authoritarian supernaturalism of the conservatives of yesterday. The generations that make right depend on heavenly might will sooner or later be followed by a generation who will gratify their morbid inherited craving for an external power on which to base their ideals by looking for that power in the mud beneath their feet. Let us turn now from this survey of the menace of authoritarianism to ethics and consider the menace of that principle to religion itself.

2. The chief dangers here have already been touched upon. When the religious consciousness interprets rules of conduct as divine commands, it fastens upon later generations a code of life that can never be amended. No matter how sound the system of moral and scientific beliefs may have been, no matter even if they actually possessed the divinely revealed truth which they claim, when once they are made sacrosanct and immune from criticism or change, they defeat their own purpose. Life is growth; new discoveries require new theories, new situations call for new practices. We advance by inquiry and experiment. In so far as religion refuses to submit its authoritarian dogmas to free and fearless examination, it arrays itself against the entire drive of the ascending human spirit. It declares war on all that is most honest, brave, and free. It deprives its own best teachings of the possibility of vindication in the open court of reason. What unconscious and damning irony there is in the authoritarian habit of coupling freethinker and atheist together! Free thought is thought that is free, free from bias, free from subsidies and from all secret greeds and terrors. How humiliating

to an honest theist to find the church confessing that to think freely would lead to atheism, that Christian truth is so poor and weak a thing that it must be shielded from the light of reason and guarded from its critics by the base weapons of censorship and inquisition!

3. The last of the three kinds of menace embodied in authoritarianism is its menace to social efficiency on account of the enormous waste of human energy which it involves. In this matter of moral waste the authoritarian and the ascetic are similar, and many of the worst features of religious morality are expressions of their united influence. Both separately and in conjunction these mistaken zealots encumber the moral world with mere rules and laws, most of them suppressive and prohibitory, all of them to be observed as ends in themselves regardless of their consequences, and none of them to be changed or questioned. Under such a reign of law there is little place for ideals of happiness and beauty. Intelligent pursuit of the good is tied down in the tangle of ethical red tape, and man's fund of spiritual energy, so pitifully small at best, is wasted in perpetual legalistic disputes. Not only is authoritarian religion at war with secular science and ethics; it is at war with itself. Each faction regards itself as orthodox and the others as heterodox. Now, under a morality of taboos, such as that of authoritarianism, to be orthodox or correct in belief is not a piece of good fortune that makes a man humbly grateful and extra eager to extend his light to those less favored; it is in itself a virtue of which he is proud. And heterodoxy or honest error is not viewed as a misfortune calling for charity, but rather as a sin to be punished. It is to this aspect of authoritarian religion that we are indebted for the terrible religious wars and the far more terrible persecutions practiced by the different sects upon one another and by each and all of

them upon those men, brave and free, who refused to submit to intellectual and moral enslavement.

There is, as I see it, only one cure for the sickness and weakness of our religion today: to heed the Promethean challenge hurled so bravely and so long ago at the god-king Zeus. That challenge to God was at the same time a clear call to man to use his intelligence to increase happiness, beauty, and goodness on earth. To understand how the Promethean ideal might be realized, we need only turn to that third element of the Christian moral system, the virtue of charity. Like asceticism and authoritarianism, this phase of morality is not confined to Christianity. We find it present to some extent in the most primitive moral cults, while in Hebraism and Zoroastrianism, Stoicism and Confucianism, and most of all in Buddhism, the duty of justice and sympathy is variously and explicitly recognized.

Yet in Christianity there is a new emphasis upon the altruistic principle which is revolutionary and unique in history. Charity or love is not secondary but primary, not limited to one's own group or nation, but universal, not negative but positive. Even in Buddhism service to others is tainted by the pessimistic conception that the ultimate purpose of giving is not the enhancement of life in others but the negation of life and of the will to life in oneself.

The teaching of Christ is that love to the uttermost limit is the supreme concern of human living. And this teaching was given a terrible concreteness and actuality by its embodiment in the life and death of the teacher. It was given also a mystical and cosmical significance by the religious doctrine of the incarnation. The old god of power died and the new god of love was born. Jehovah had been redeemed by Christ, and for the first time in the long history of heaven the evil which Prometheus had challenged was laid. The Son of Man was to be a comrade, a brother, and a leader by moral right, rather than a monarch ruling by irresponsible might. So far, the new supernaturalism was innocent of intellectual offense and infinitely beautiful. God was love. The one perfect thing in life was the thing most real in the universe. To gain the friendship of the new God and to share his everlasting life, nothing was necessary but an open heart and the will to pity and to help. The sacred learning in the Hebrew law, the pride of skill in Greek philosophy, the patrician descent from the valorous leaders of Rome, were useless or worse. The new way of eternal life was so straight and clear that the dullest peasant, the humblest slave, the weakest child, and even the most abandoned criminal could find and take it if he would. The saving grace precious beyond all price was free to be had for the asking.

The wonder is not that the leader of this revolt was finally crucified, but that the various social, spiritual, and intellectual tyrants whose rule he overthrew allowed him to live at all. Certainly since his death they have done what they could to make up for that initial error.

The moral ideal of Christian love is like a pillar of flaming light extending from earth to heaven, but the supernatural religion of freedom, solace, and joy that should have evolved from it was choked and poisoned. The successors of Christ, from St. Paul down to the censors, obscurantists, and tyrants of today have done their conscientious worst to hide the light from men. The long series of authoritarians and ascetics have changed the clear into the obscure, the beautiful into the ugly, and with what was most gentle and generous they have associated what was most cruel and mean. They have debauched a religion of liberty, service, tolerance, and progress to their own base ends of persecution, reaction, and gloom.

Through all the world today there is an ominous muttering. Not only the small though growing army of scientists who view the efforts of religious fanatics to check the teachings of science with a contempt so deep and cold that they can hardly be brought to express it, and not only the men of letters and liberal authors who show a more voluble contempt for the spirit of censorious puritanism which is growing beyond the stage of an ugly American joke are significant; but far more meaningful than these is the sullen rage of the multitude of workers throughout the world who for the first time are really coming to hate the Christian scheme.

If religion is to be saved from destruction from without, it must be revolutionized from within. And it is a Promethean revolution that is needed: no new prophet as substitute for Christ, but a great purging and cleansing of Christianity and of all religion as it exists today.

What would a Prometheanized religion be like? Would there be left of Christianity, for example, anything more than a vague and worldly humanitarianism, a platitudinous philanthropy touched with inarticulate emotion? Many liberal and well-meaning people so believe, and, though aware of the anomalies of orthodoxy and of the growing dangers to the whole structure of religion, they fear that any breach in the ranks of authority would be more dangerous still. I think such fears are completely ungrounded, and by way of conclusion I will attempt to outline some of the principal characteristics of a religion transfigured by a Promethean revolution.

First of all, there would be the welcome and luminous absence of sacrosanct authority. Such dogmas as remained, and they would be many, would be transformed into hypotheses. The most fantastic theory of the supernatural, if held as a hypothesis, is honorable, and belief in it is honest and to be respected. There would be no lack of propaganda and missionary zeal. Those who had faith in a theory would be proud to have it vindicated by criticism. For the irreligious freethinking would be optional, but for religionists it would be compulsory. A church member who refused to allow his belief to be tested in the light of reason would be expelled as one of little faith. The various schools and sects would not persecute one another, for why should one seeker for truth hate another? Why should he not rather co-operate with him the better to realize their common end? If a theory is not true, no one would wish it to survive; if it is true, it will survive. How senseless and perverse not to test it!

Not only would theists cease to hate one another—they would cease to hate atheists. They would love and respect them. For if you are walking comfortably in the light of a supernatural faith that the universe is on your side, why should you not love and respect the man who walks in darkness, crippled by the fear that the things we care for most are at the mercy of blind force—deprived of your hope of God and another world, yet fighting bravely by your side for the same ideals for which you fight? A strange inversion of Christian charity to hate such a one.

And in this Promethean religion, heaven would be no less free than earth of that hateful spirit of monarchical authority. We should not love goodness because it is commanded by God, but should love God because He is good. We should base our religion on our ethics; not as now, our ethics on a supernatural physics. And there would be no longer that curious double standard, according to which the same God who commands us to forgive our enemies no matter how many times they offend, reserves for Himself the right to wreak infinite vengeance on His enemies after one trial life on earth. That nightmare monster of authoritarian religion, veritable anti-Christ, would have been consigned to his own hell, the single one of all imagined beings who would really deserve it.

As in our religion, so in our ethics. The principle of authority would be gone, and with it the great clutter of prohibitions and taboos—rules taken as ends in themselves rather than as means to happiness. The one supreme and single purpose of morality would be the making of life more abundant, which means the developing to a maximum the potentialities of every creature. Love and work by all for the maximum well-being of all. All moral rules—the oldest and most revered, like those established for marriage and property, no less than the newest and queerest proposals—would be appraised without prejudice and in the cold light of intelligence, to be accepted or rejected only according to their efficiency in promoting the ideal of freer and more abundant living.

The banishment of asceticism and authoritarianism would for the first time in history bring human ethics into active partnership with human science. Once clear away the morality of taboos, and all the forces of intelligence could be mobilized in the service of progress, and the vast energies of thought and will that have been wasted in religious wars could be utilized for moral and religious work.

Would there be in such a Promethean religion a place for piety and the reverent study of the teachers of the past? Just as the undeniable courage and enthusiasm of the ascetics is their one real claim on human gratitude, so the one point for which authoritarians are to be praised is their loyal guardianship of the treasures of the past. Yet even here they have, as it were, stood in their own light, for by defending with force the inspired words of the prophets and protecting them from free inquiry, they have brought into disrepute the very doctrines that they love.

There would be piety in a Promethean world, but it would be an anarchistic piety. We should no longer mock and insult the great revolutionists of the past by making their revolutionary doctrines the basis of a new tyranny which is often as unsuited to our day as the doctrines which they overthrew were to theirs.

Promethean piety would be devotion to the spirit of freedom that animated the innovators of old, while for the literal content of their teaching there would be no more than a sympathetic and affectionate interest. Moreover, the most inspired truth will be dimmed and brought under suspicion if guarded by censors from free criticism. The deepest and truest piety with which we can honor the teachings of the past, be they the teachings of sages or prophets or even of God Himself, is not to seal them up in cans, thought-tight and sacrosanct, but to expose them to the sun and air and let their truth win an honorable victory over our minds.

That is piety in the Promethean sense. Its practice would do away with the mutual fear and distrust which now sunders those who know and love the spiritual insights of the prophets from those who know and respect the intellectual discoveries of the scientists.

Whether such a revolution as I have attempted to depict can come about, I am not sure. Perhaps it is too late. Perhaps the defilers have done their work so well that the new age of reason will have no place for religion, its good or its bad. But on the other hand, perhaps there may still be time for a great experiment, a really new adventure in the life of the spirit. It would consist of a union of the old supernatural hope for God and immortality with the modern secular demand for the emancipation of creative intelligence. Such an adventure would be the Promethean religion.

17

THE TRINITY—A SPECULATION [1]

An exposition and defense of a trinitarian theory of the world-ground, somewhat similar to the Christian theory, but providing for a different conception of the origin of evil. An attempt to reconcile the idea of a God limited in power with the idea of a God infinite and all-embracing. It presupposes some knowledge of philosophy and theology.

To REINTERPRET the categories of one age in the light of another is probably a bad business; certainly it is a business which has been much overdone during the past hundred years, in which "modernism" after "modernism," refusing to abandon the ancient concepts of religion, has yet striven to adapt them to the new presuppositions which, in some cases, are in direct contradiction to those from which the beloved concepts originated.

The doctrine of the Trinity is one of these ancient notions, and the sort of reinterpretation which I have in mind to attempt might well appear more than ordinarily sterile; first, because most of those calling themselves liberals today find it sufficiently difficult to believe in even the vaguest theistic ground for the universe, not to mention one that is in an essential sense triune; and second, because when once the strictly orthodox idea of the Trinity is departed from, we are beset by a mass of analogies, as loose as they are trite, which the number three has suggested and which have

[1] Reprinted from *Religious Realism*, ed. by D. C. Macintosh, New York, The Macmillan Company, 1932, No. 15, pp. 495–502.

been tediously exploited by philosophers from Plotinus and Porphyry to Hegel and Freud. And the prospect of a further addition to these analogies would seem peculiarly uninviting.

In the face of such objections, I am nevertheless impelled to suggest a new conception of trinitarian theism, and for the following reasons:

The world of things as they are is not self-explanatory; it bears the earmarks, if not of a manufactured product, at least of a thing that has been derived from something other than itself. Now, I am well aware that this indictment of reality on the ground of its rationalistic insufficiency has been answered by angry demurrers, in which we are told that causality is a category whose application is at best interphenomenal and intramundane, and that to extend it by a kind of transcendental extrapolation and make it apply to a supposed relation between the world and something else is an outrageous abuse of logical procedure. All creationists have, of course, been in some measure guilty of this act of extrapolation, but Anselm, and later Fichte and Hegel, committed the crime, if crime it be, on a grand scale. Not content with explaining natural existence by supernatural existence, they propounded the conception of existence as itself derived from purely logical being or essence. We remember the bitterness with which Schopenhauer attacked this notion of *causa sui*, particularly in its Fichtean form, and also the devastating criticism to which Kant subjected the Anselmian argument. As to the Empiricists, they have since the days of Hume objected to the category of causality even as applied to intramundane phenomena, and any suggestion that it be extrapolated and used to explain the origin of the world from a supernatural existent or, still worse, from a more logical essence appears to them the height of absurdity. Whether the world seems to us self-explanatory or the opposite is an accident of our own mental constitution, they will tell us, and in neither case are we justified in going beyond the realm of experiential data. To attempt it will only make a bad matter worse.

Despite this momentous opposition, I feel, as I have already confessed, an urgent need of going beyond the world to explain the world, and I refuse to recognize the validity of any a priori limitation or censorship of our use of explanatory categories. Whether we gain or lose by extrapolating a concept such as causality is a question that can be answered only pragmatically, by trying and seeing.

The world of things as they are comprises the realm of subsistence or essence and the realm of existence or spatio-temporal particulars. The domain of existing things seems to consist of protons and electrons, the unit masses of positive and negative electricity. Recent physics in its wave mechanics suggests that the protonic and electronic units may themselves be composed of units still smaller and wavelike in character; and that in any event the mass factor which they embody is reducible to and interchangeable with the more fundamental factor of *energy*. But whether the ultimate elements of the material world are the hard little atoms of old, the protons and electrons of the Bohr atoms of yesterday, the Schroedinger waves of today, or their as yet unguessed successors of tomorrow, the outstanding fact about them is their diffusion over all space and their amazing similarity. And we are moved to ask: *What is the probability that such a situation of widespread diffusion of homogeneous units could exist unless those units had originated from a single source?* Such a probability would, it seems to me, be very small, and the greater the number of primary elements (that is, elements underived from one another), the smaller it would be and, consequently, the greater would be the counterprobability that they had been derived from a single cause. In short, the principle of *one ground for similars,* if not an axiom, has about it a strongly axiomatic flavor.

When we pass to the further question as to whether any element of consciousness or personality can be ascribed to an originating or First Cause of the primary existential elements, I can see no ground for answering in the affirmative. It seems rather that the thing or principle responsible for the origin of nature as we find it was a power of fecundity, self-repetition, or increase, and that the only hope of ascribing to it *mind* or *life* would depend on showing that those categories are interpretable as later phases, "emergent" yet inevitable developments of the principle of development itself. Following upon the increase of being by mere number and extent, there would be an increase of the second order, consisting in the harmonization of the earlier elements of being. This secondary growth would be intensive rather than extensive, and would consist in the removal of interferences or negations exerted by the units of being upon one another.

If, then, we take the principle of growth as Hegel took his principle of *Negativität* and study its "dialectic," we find it involving at first a phase of mere multiplication and conservation of sheer being. And then, if further growth is to be realized, organized existence and an intensive increase of being through harmonization will supervene upon the earlier extensive phase. And this harmonization would at its maximum involve life, consciousness, and finally personality. Such would seem to constitute the "immanent dialectic" of the concept of increase or growth, a *That* whose *What* consists of *being ever more than itself.* Of all our concepts, this notion seems to me best suited for a first principle or absolute *Prius.*

Now, if we turn from existence to subsistence and survey that Realm of Essence which has been discovered by Plato, carefully explored by Husserl, and gloriously proclaimed in all its dimensions by Santayana, we find, I think, traces of the same principle of fecundity, self-increase, or growth to a maximum which we postulated at the core of the naturally existing world of matter. That the realm of essence contains all that is possible is a truth that is three-quarters a truism. This maximum totality of forms or natures is a level of being that is logical and timeless, and so by its very nature immune to genesis in any ordinary or temporal sense. Now, in that little section of the domain of subsistence consisting of the number series, the higher integers do not attain their timeless being at any later moments than the integers one and two; yet the being of those higher integers presupposes the being of the lower, as logically though not temporally prior to their own. Could we but see as only God can see the expanse of subsistence in its entirety, and with the same clarity with which we see the island of number that is contained within it, I believe that we should see also a single thread of dialectical genesis which would constitute its structure a logical hierarchy. And that arch-essence would then, I believe, be found to be not the principle of *Negativität* which Hegel used so bravely, but something more like that ideal of the Good held to by Plato, Anselm, and Leibniz. This ideal I should wish to formulate as a principle of growth or increase to a maximum. And as before on the existential level, so now on this level of essential being, the first phase of dialectical development would be sheer wealth of qualitative variation resulting in the totality of possibles, while the second dialectical phase would be the integration or harmonization of this All in its collective aspect into a single organic unity of maximum compossibility equivalent to a complete subsistential personality.

Let us now make a bold quasi-Leibnizian and quasi-Herbartian postulate, and assume that any possibility tends to be compossible or actual, and fails only to the extent that it is inhibited by others, so that the world of existence is a sort of vector resultant of the tendencies to exist of all the essences. From this it would follow that the totality of essences in its collective unity and integrated personality would (as Anselm believed) entail its own incarnation in existence.

We should have, then, as the outcome of a cosmic *Prius* consisting of the principle of unlimited increase or growth: first, "God the Father," a preconscious and prepersonal power expressing itself in the production of mere existential and subsistential *being* in maximum abundance. Taken in their distributive plurality, these beings would constitute the World; second, there would be that same existential and subsistential totality of things, but now taken collectively in its integrated and personal unity; this would be the Logos or "God the Son." Now, if the *Prius* of "maximum increase" is to be true to itself, there would be a third phase of its "immanent dialectic" which would consist not of an *entity* but of an unending *activity* by which the independent and self-willed constituents of the world had their several natures increased or enhanced by being brought more and more into harmony with one another and with the personality of the totality. This Third Phase of the creative power would be "God the Holy Ghost," expressing itself in what we recognize as "evolution," but evolution interpreted as the working of God in that World which is within him—the spirit of the Whole fructifying and organizing its own independent and self-existing parts.

This last phase of Deity is inferable from reasons less abstract and dialectical than those invoked to prove the two phases preceding it. For our world exhibits not only (1) things evil and nonpurposeful and (2) things good and purposeful, but (3) a mighty *trend*, slow yet unmistakable, from the nonpurposeful to the purposeful. And these three aspects of the world would seem to indicate that the world-ground is correlatively threefold: first, a transcendent originating cause, second a concretely actualized person, and third, an immanent and progressively more pervasive partner in the company of its own effects.

If I may use a simile to make my meaning clearer, it is as if there were in the beginning a seed from which grew a stalk with an abundant welter of boughs, branches, and twigs, each self-existent and endowed with something of the primary causality and sheer spontaneity of the originating seed. From the central stalk there then came as a second creation a blossom and a fruit which was the actualized perfection of what was, in the seed, potential only. Following upon these primary and secondary epochs of creation, there came a third, in which the boughs and branches, partly of themselves and partly aided by the central life of the stalk, began in their own right to develop blossoms, each after its kind.

By way of conclusion, I wish briefly to point out in what respect my speculation as to the triune world-ground differs from what I understand to be the orthodox conception of the Trinity.

My First Phase differs from "God the Father" in being not personal but impersonal or prepersonal; for, as I tried to make plain, the first phase in the dialectical development of a principle of increase would be mere multiplication of entities, existential or quantitative and subsistential or qualitative. Personal or integrated being emerges from the impersonal as its Second Phase, the continuance of growth on a higher dimensional level. Thus, God does not consciously create the world with its disorder and evil, he creates himself and *awakens* to his own existence to find a world within him as an earlier product of that primordial ontological gestation of which his own conscious personality or Logos was the climactic phase. "In the beginning" were Chaos and Old Night, but upon that Chaos, Cosmos supervened. God looked upon the world within him and saw not that "it was good," but that *it was to be made good;* and as personality had supervened upon mere life, so the *evolution* of the world in its distributive plurality supervenes upon the personalized perfection of its unified totality.

This conception of the world-ground resembles the Plotinian rather than the Christian Trinity, in making the First Phase nonpersonal. But it differs from the scheme of Plotinus in not regarding the First Phase or the One as ineffably *higher* but rather as *lower* than the Logos and the World-Soul. Hence, Nature and Life are not to be thought of as a descent or falling away from God, with the implication that the goal of life is escape from the world and reabsorption in the One or Brahma or Nirvana. On the contrary, the goal of life for us, as for God, is endless increase and enhancement and furtherance of a more and more individuated worldly existence.

As to the Second Person of the Trinity, there is little difference, metaphysically speaking, between the conception of Plotinus and that of the Church. Historically and concretely, there is, of course, the immense difference in the emphasis upon the earthly life of Jesus of Nazareth. All I can say on this subject is that, just as an author might put himself into his book as one of its characters, so there would be nothing absurd or impossible in the belief that the Soul of the World had literally embodied itself in one of its own members; and the fact that the utterances ascribed to Jesus and his life as told in the Story (even when freed from conventional and distastefully improbable claims of a lack of any earthly imperfections) contain elements of supreme and infinite beauty would make it possible to believe that he was an incarnation of God in some less figurative sense than another man could be, even if he were equally good. But while such a supposition seems to me conceivable, I think that it is more probable, and perhaps more in accord with the spirit of Christ and the meaning which he attached to his own mission, to think of his divinity as consisting in what he made of his life by his own efforts as a mortal man, rather than to impute to him the physical and metaphysical advantages of a miraculously inherited nature.

Finally, with regard to the Third Phase of the world-ground, I believe that Nature as revealed by science gives broad and clear evidences of an upbuilding or synthesizing agency which expresses itself not only in the genesis and ascent of life upon our planet, but in the far more widespread evolution of inorganic compounds from their simpler elements. How can we accept the intolerably arbitrary conception (recently advocated in high quarters) of a God who created the world some quadrillions of years ago, all wound up with a maximum of complex organization and a minimum of entropy, and then left it to run down and dissipate its substance in a sea of insignificant and impotent waves of radiant energy? Is it not more plausible to believe that the world's failure to have run down by this time is due, not to the accident of its youth, but to a factor as yet undiscovered by astronomy and mechanics but continuously operative in all nature and indirectly manifested in the development of living individuals and in the evolution of their species? Such a factor would be the steady foe of entropy or decay. And this *anti-entropic* agency which builds the atoms and their inorganic compounds, and the still stranger protoplasmic organisms, might also, as the immanent God or Holy Ghost, build up and strengthen with grace the hearts of men.

⋙ 18 ⋘

* THE TWO IMMORTALITIES [1]

A brief argument in support of personal immortality and an appeal for a more effective commemoration of the less known members of universities and other great social organizations.

EACH NEW DEATH opens afresh the half-forgotten wound in Life's side and brings to us a clear and sorrowful consciousness of the transiency of all existence. Before forgetfulness sets in again we strive to heal the wound, and in two quite different ways. We hope against hope that death may not be really death; and second, we make a high resolve that at least in our own hearts and deeds the dead shall live vicariously on, their values cherished and conserved. Against the fact of death we pit these immortalities: the one of hope, the other of resolution. And on an occasion like the present, when a university meets to commemorate and mourn its dead, it would seem appropriate to follow the familiar custom and take account once more not only of the prospect of direct and personal immortality, but also of the manner in which, quite irrespective of that prospect, an institution such as ours can in its own enduring corporate life give something of vicarious immortality to the individuals who were once its servants and its parts.

[1] Address delivered at the Annual Commemoration Service, St. Paul's Chapel, Columbia University, 8 January, 1933. Reprinted from the Columbia University Quarterly, March, 1933, Vol. XXV, No. 1, pp. 1–8, by permission of Columbia University Press.

I

The belief that a person survives the death of his body is perhaps as old as the human race itself. To the primitive mind it is axiomatic; to the followers of the great religions it is all but axiomatic; to small minorities of the sophisticated in centuries past it has seemed an incredible superstition. To an increasing number of ordinary and thoughtful folk it has during the last fifty years become a hypothesis open to the gravest doubt. There probably is today a larger proportion of educated people than ever before who have definitely abandoned the belief.

The contemporary reasons for disbelief are the same in kind as in the time of Lucretius. The mind of a man varies with the variation of his body. It is therefore an adjective of his body and incapable of existing apart from it. So runs the ancient argument. But while this reasoning has not changed in kind, it has grown enormously in extent and in impressive detail. In place of the vague and general recognition of a certain dependence of the mind and its states upon the condition of the body, we now have the multitudinous discoveries of biology, physiology, and physiological psychology, all tending to show that between the parts and processes of the nervous system on the one hand, and the forms and functions of the mind on the other, there is a correlation that is verifiable, predictable, and in large measure controllable. The various effects of drugs and glandular extracts, of operative surgery and of changed conditions of environment, combine to give momentous proof of this dependence of the individual mind upon the individual body. Then, too, the facts of paleontology and of comparative anatomy and physiology give overwhelming testimony to the kinship of all animals to one another and to man, and indicate a long development of higher forms from lower. Phylogeny thus corroborates ontogeny, and in the evolution of the species no less than in the growth of the individual the thing called mind seems more and more revealed as being an aspect or inseparable adjective of matter and its motions.

This is, however, only half the story, for while the sciences of life and mind have been piling up the evidence for a complete dependence of the mental upon the physical, the sciences of *inorganic* nature, such as chemistry and physics, have developed in the meantime a conception of the constitution of bodies which makes it more and more difficult to regard the material as the all-sufficient ground of the vital and the psychical. The small, hard particles of ancient metaphysical speculation and of nineteenth-century physical science have been found divisible, so that the old word *atom* as used by chemists has become a misnomer. Each of the so-called atoms is composed, in varying number and proportion, of units of positive and negative electricity; and these in turn perhaps may be conceived as energy in the form of waves. But while the new physics with its two great theories of Relativity and Quanta is vastly more complicated than the old, in one fundamental respect it is the same. Neither the atoms of the nineteenth century nor the novel elemental units of today, whether they are thought of as particles, as waves, or from a different standpoint as "events" in "space-time," afford us any clue as to why they are organized and how they come to be organized as they are in a living being. The more the physicist discovers about matter, the more difficult it becomes to understand how the myriads of material elements, each connected with every other by simple quantitative relations analogous to attraction and repulsion, can possibly attain and maintain the increasingly elaborate unities of organization that are characteristic of living bodies and of the cerebral structures on which mental activity depends.

Very different from the physicist's view of the organism

is the view revealed to the biologist. He sees it not as an aggregate of whirling particles but as a unified system, or system of systems; and so great and so richly mysterious is the complexity of its material that he can easily believe that the intricacies of its structure are an adequate ground for the mental life that accompanies its processes. And, again, for the physiologist who sees the organism and its nervous system as consisting of hundreds of reflex arcs and similar reactive mechanisms, it is still comparatively easy to believe that those structures could themselves, if they were but fully known, account for their own hierarchical unities. But when physiology gives place to chemistry, the pluralities increase and it ceases to be at all easy to conceive of the unity of the organism in terms of the multitude of chemical reactions that are discovered in its parts. Biology, physiology, chemistry, and physics present a series of more and more accurate pictures of material aggregates; and as the pictures become more and more adequate from the standpoint of mechanistic science, they become less and less adequate to explain the unities of life and mind.

Perhaps this accounts for a curious anomaly in the world of present-day science: that those who know least about matter think most of it while those who know most of it think least of it as an all-sufficient explanation of existence—as though distance lent enchantment and familiarity bred contempt. We are acquainted with the names of Eddington and Jeans, of Compton and Millikan, great physicists who have seen matter, if not face to face, then as nearly so as is possible today. It is these masters of material science who confess their lack of faith in materialism as an explanation of the world as they know it. And there is something faintly resembling the humorous in the courteous magnanimity with which our social scientists apologize to the public for each lapse from atheistic grace on the part of their colleagues in the exact sciences. Physicists and astronomers are, so we are told, excellent fellows, but they have sentimental leanings toward religion which are due to childhood memories and to ignorance of the hard facts on which modern disillusionment is founded. Now, not to be outdone in magnanimity, we may venture the hypothesis that the religious and mystical sympathies frequently expressed by those who know matter and its laws at first hand may possibly be due to their knowledge rather than to their ignorance. Stripped of the gloss of sensory perception and of the slipshod and provisional categories which the students of mind and life are compelled to employ, the material structures of a living organism lose much of their explanatory power. And when the macroscopic perspective of biology gives place to the intimate close-up of physics, the myriads of mechanically related particles composing an organism reveal their impotence to account for the strangely purposeful unities which indubitably characterize its behavior.

The point need not be pressed, but it should be pondered. That increasing portion of the public who with confident finality reject the possibility of personal survival are convinced that their disillusionment is grounded in science. They are rightly impressed with the scientific evidences for the control of mental manifestations by matter. But they fail to consider the evidence at least equally scientific for the inability of that same matter to explain the conscious and rational beings which are rooted in it. Mind grows in the body as a plant grows in the soil, but the body hardly more explains the mind than the soil explains the plant.

The ancient questions as to whether a personality or any other form of mind can survive the material matrix by which it is so definitely conditioned, and if so in what form or mode of being such survival is to be conceived, remain today, as in times gone by, questions that are beyond the power of science to answer. If answered at all, they will be answered by mystical faith or by metaphysical speculation, not by anything that is proved or even implied by the ascertained facts of either psychology or physics.

Before leaving the subject, there is one aspect of it that should be well and seriously considered both by those who still hope and by those from whom hope has gone. However desperate the chance for individual survival may be, the chance for collective survival in the sense of an endless material continuance of our race and its culture is more desperate by far. The probability is overwhelming that our planet, our solar system, and even our galaxy will at some time in the future cease to contain any of the life that now exists. If not in a million then in a billion or a trillion years, the works of man will have utterly vanished and it will be as though they had never been. The vast mausoleums of enduring stone, even the Pyramids themselves, are more assuredly mortal than the beings whose bodies they enshrine. Many of those today who have quite cheerfully abandoned the belief in immortality thoughtlessly transfer their faith in permanence from the souls of individuals to the material life of the species. Now, the latter will undoubtedly last for a very long time. And there are many to whom grief over the certainty of a world annihilation that is to come only in the remote future seems academic and absurd. Yet a world that dies after a trillion years will be just as dead and its mortality as tragic and as final as if it died tomorrow. If it is racial immortality rather than the mere postponement of racial death that is to take the place of the lost hope, then there is for such immortality simply no chance at all. Even at the cost of additional disillusionment, this truth should be acknowledged. For there is a humiliation bordering upon shame in changing from a faith that is at worst only improbable to one that is at best assuredly false. If the existence of all that we hold dear is at the mercy of senseless mechanical agencies and is doomed in the course of their permutations to suffer utter annihilation, it behooves us to admit that awful fact and frankly face the shadow of its presence.

It is important to realize this momentous bearing of the disbelief in survival not only upon our own individual happiness but upon any hope that the world as it is resembles the world as we would have it. But there is a point far more important than this, and of more fundamental significance than the issue of immortality itself. The truth referred to is the great truth that eternity matters more than duration, that the quality of a life matters more than its length of days, and that the spirit of man can suffer no deeper indignity than to make the ideals of goodness and beauty and the sense of moral obligation depend for their validity upon the vicissitudes of mere existence.

Whether death is but a prelude and whether at the heart of things there is something somehow good are dreadful questions, and in their answers fraught with doubt we hear the echoes of human hope and fear. Philosophy cannot resolve these questions that religion meets by faith. There is, however, one high certainty that is quite philosophy's own: *Ideals are eternal things*, and the life that incarnates them attains an absolute value that time alone could not create and that death is powerless to destroy.

II

Whether the dead live on in their own right is beyond our power to know, and their destiny, whatever it may be, is something that we in no way can affect. But whether they shall live vicariously here on earth in our own minds and hearts depends entirely upon ourselves. And the question now confronts us as to how we can conserve their personalities and deeds, and let sorrow for their death give place to joy that they have lived.

For an institution to confer such immortality upon its departed friends is in some ways more easy than for an individual. It has a larger and more enduring memory in which its past can dwell. But this advantage of the social over the individual organism is more than balanced by the difficulty of doing justice to the multitude of claimants for its piety, the thousands of those who knew the institution but whom the institution did not know or knew too casually and transiently to remember. It is easy for Columbia to mourn its more famous dead: the woman of gracious heart and mind, the wise and kindly clergyman, the great engineer and soldier, who as Trustees participated in its government; the scholars of distinction who as teachers contributed so richly to its intellectual life. *But how shall the University commemorate its hosts of lesser dead?*

In a perfectly organized society, were it even as large as the whole world, every individual would have some special function in which he could excel. No matter how humble his position, he would be given the opportunity to make his service and his life in some degree superlative. Though not known to all or even to many, he would be known to the other individuals of the little group with whom he worked. That group would constitute a cell, and of such cells in hierarchy upon hierarchy the social organism would be composed. Now, Columbia is far removed from such a close-knit organism. Our age is mastered by machines, and individuals must be flattened out and reduced to uniformity if the machines are to run smoothly. Like the great city itself, the University contains numbers of unattached and lonely souls, some of them lacking even the ties of family or of friends. They come and go with none but the barest and most formal recognition of their presence. Yet they are members of the University, and at least to some degree their lives are identified with it. Columbia should make provision not only for their intellectual needs while alive, but for their mourning and commemoration when they die. To do this for each individual as such and with any measure of adequacy is manifestly impossible; but collectively it might be done and done significantly.

It was an inspired thought that led the nations to establish a memorial to the Unknown Soldier, for by that means they rendered collective honor to those whom they could not honor individually. To the tomb of the Unknown Soldier all parents may go with the realization that here at last their own son's life, however obscure, is commemorated enduringly. So enduringly, so fitly, and so beautifully that it is in that place above all other places that the nation and the nation's guests do homage to the dead. All great institutions should follow this example and thus conserve the lesser and less known of former members' lives. There should be not, of course, a tomb in any literal sense, but a building, a room, or some appropriate shrine established by the University as sacred to the memory of its unknown scholars. In this way we could in some degree atone to each and every member of our own society whose identity for one reason or another we had failed to recognize during life. Though cold in death, he could be rescued from complete oblivion and his life conserved in ours symbolically but none the less effectively.

It is the birthright of every human being to be cherished by his fellows and to be recognized as a person, a spirit, irreplaceable, precious, and sacred, the embodiment, at least potentially, of those transcendent values which pertain to personality and to personality alone. And yet, in spite of this essential right, persons today are trampled by the mass, and, through pressure of their own sheer numbers, their individualities are lost.

As Columbia grows in age, its glorious dead increase. Its past becomes more great and its actual present life, of which that past is part, gains in power and in depth. In cherishing the heritage of our dead, let us resolve to cherish it in its entirety, and in some form preserve the lives of *all* our members, not only those whose claim is obvious by reason of their fame but those other lesser ones whose need is yet more poignant and compelling.

19

* THE TRUE, THE GOOD, AND THE BEAUTIFUL FROM A PRAGMATIC STANDPOINT[1]

Truth, goodness, and beauty are depicted as sharply contrasting species of one and the same genus.

BY THE "PRAGMATIC STANDPOINT" I shall here mean the disposition to reinterpret the logical, ethical, and esthetic values of experience in the light of their relation to the life processes of the organism. From this standpoint, human experience may be viewed as a series of efforts to bring about a harmonious adjustment or vital equilibrium between the private experience of the individual and the incomparably broader experience of an environing nature. Every experience, whether it be predominantly cognitive, conative, or affective, involves in some way this demand of the organism for an adjustment of internal to external relations. To offer a defense of this viewpoint would be superfluous. The new life which has come into psychology by the adoption of the functional or biological method of investigation is a sufficient vindication of that method. I wish rather to call attention to the fact that this

[1] Read before the American Philosophical Association, December, 1908. Reprinted from *The Journal of Philosophy, Psychology and Scientific Methods*, Vol. VI, No. 9, April 29, 1909, pages 233–238.

new pragmatic method does not justify some of those who call themselves pragmatists in identifying together or confounding the types of value which we call the true, the good, and the beautiful; but that, on the contrary, it provides a new and firmer basis for distinguishing sharply between these values. In other words, granting the right of the pragmatist to regard truth and beauty no less than goodness as forms of organic adjustment or equilibrium, I would deny the conclusion that truth and beauty are therefore mere forms of goodness.

By way of preliminary justification of this position, we may observe that there are obviously three ways in which an individual element and its environing context may attain to harmony or equilibrium. First, the element may undergo whatever alteration of its nature is demanded by the context, the context itself remaining unaltered; or second, the context may undergo whatever alteration is demanded by the element, the latter remaining unaltered; or third, the element and its context may each of them spontaneously, and without compulsion from one another, attain to harmony or equilibrium.

Let us first consider which of these three kinds of equilibrium may be interpreted to constitute cognitive value or truth. Truth is a quality belonging primarily to judgments, and whatever our views as to its ultimate nature, I think we might all agree that a judgment is true when and only when it states a fact. What a judgment states may be called the judgment-content in distinction from the mere act of making the judgment. For example, in the judgment *A* is *B*, the judgment-content is the complex idea "*A*-a-case-of-*B*" or "A-standing-in-the-subsumptive-relation-to-B." Truth applies to a judgment only in respect to the judgment-content, not in respect to the judgment-act. If the content of the judgment is a fact, then the judgment is called true; if its content is not a fact, it is called false. When we say that truth is the agreement of a judgment with fact, we mean no more than this: that the relation which the judgment asserts shall have the status of fact. The problem of defining truth, then, reduces to the problem of defining fact. Now, most of us, I suppose, would be willing to admit, first, that the only facts that we can know anything about are those that are either perceptually or conceptually experienced, and, second, that we distinguish a fact from an appearance not by an impossible comparison of it with a standard outside of experience, but by observing whether it be consistent or inconsistent with the totality of other experience. Thus, the objects and events of a dream are called appearances rather than facts not because of any internal inconsistency, but because they are inconsistent with the broader and more inclusive experience of waking life. The crookedness of the stick partly immersed in water is regarded as mere appearance because it is incompatible with the general system of experiences which relate to the stick. May we not say, then, that a judgment is true when what it asserts is consistent with the totality of experience contents? The cognitive interest or the interest in attaining truth will then be neither more nor less than the attempt to make the contents of individual judgments consistent with the contents of other judgments previously verified, and so indirectly with the general system of the things and relations given in experience. As long as there is conflict or lack of consistency between any judgment and the general system, there is to the rational mind a condition of instability and dissatisfaction. The cognitive situation demands that the judgment content be so altered as to make it harmonious with that general system of which it is a part; when this is done, equilibrium results and we have the experience of cognitive value or truth.

The type of equilibrium here evidenced would seem to

be the first of the three types mentioned above, for when we are testing the truth of a judgment it is essential to the success of the process that we make the judgment accord with the environing facts. This point will come out more clearly, however, if we compare judgment with desire and conation.

Now, a judgment and a desire are alike, first, in that both are elements in an individual consciousness. They are alike, second, in that the occurrence of each implies a demand for a certain end or goal. And they are alike, third, in that this end or goal is a condition of equilibrium between the element and the total context. Alike in these three respects, the judgment and the desire differ in the manner in which the common goal, that is, harmony with the environment, is to be attained. The briefest and most familiar way of stating this difference is to say that *a judgment is satisfied when its content conforms to the environment of fact, while a desire is satisfied when the environment of fact conforms to it.* In both cognition and conation, an effort is made to adjust the individual to his environment; but in cognition the adjustment is brought about by manipulating ideas in such a way as to make them conform to the environment, while in conation the adjustment is brought about in the opposite way, namely, by manipulating the environment in such a way as to make it conform to the needs and desires of the individual. And there is a second difference between judgments and desires that is bound up with this contrast in their methods of realization. They differ in origin. The judgment-content is something *given to* the individual; the desire *springs from* the individual. The environment presents its demands to the individual as facts, while the individual presents his demands to the environment as desires. When the individual conforms to the cognitive demands of the environment, he affirms them in judgments that are *true.*

When the environment conforms to or gratifies the conative demands of the individual, the resulting equilibrium is called *good;* thus, we see that, as truth, or cognitive value, corresponds to the first of the three possible types of equilibrium, so goodness or conative value corresponds to the second of these types. But cognition and conation are not merely different in method and in origin, they are different also in their temporal outlook or attitude. The conative attitude is essentially prospective; one cannot will anything except it be regarded as a possibility, and a possibility is always future. The cognitive attitude, on the other hand, is essentially retrospective, for it addresses itself to a realm of facts, and every fact is a *factum,* a *fait accompli,* something done and therefore past.

It is curious that in the face of these contrasts between the cognitive interest in truth and the conative interest in goodness, certain pragmatists, notably Dr. Schiller in his philosophy of humanism, should attempt to reduce the true to a form of the good. The reason for this error lies, I think, in the similar, though opposite, error of conventional British idealism, for Schiller's humanism is, after all, scarcely more than a very thoroughgoing inversion of Bradley's absolutism. Now, the temper of Mr. Bradley's system is essentially Spinozistic, and, except for his phraseology, there is little to remind us of Fichte and the other right-wing idealists from whom he is descended. Spinozistic absolutism is, of course, monistic and subordinates the individual to the environing system or absolute. Regarded merely as a mode or appearance of the latter, the individual and all the contents of his consciousness (desires as well as judgments) can achieve value or equilibrium in only one way—by conforming humbly and *in toto* to the demands of an eternal and immutable order. Because whatever is, is true, the absolutist assumes that whatever is, is right. The good is reduced to a form of the true, and the plastic and indeterminate future which is the sphere of the will is subordinated to the timeless order of truth. Absolutism may, indeed, be defined as the attempt to view reality under the fixed and immutable form of the past, and humanism is the answering attempt to view all things under the form of the plastic and changeable future.

It was inevitable that the former should call forth the latter as its appropriate reaction. The best antidote for the intellectualistic ethic of Mr. Bradley was the voluntaristic logic of Mr. Schiller. But why neglect the middle ground of common sense? Why do both absolutists and humanists overlook the fact that reality, with its past and its future, is comprehensive enough to include the fixed order of fact demanded by the truth-seeker and also the plastic realm of opportunity presupposed in all pursuit of the good? It is doubtless true that these two phases of experience never occur in complete isolation from each other. No experience is so purely conative as not to have a cognitive aspect, and none is so purely cognitive as to be free from the element of conation. But despite their inseparability, the conative and the cognitive types of value are as distinct from one another as north and south, and to seek to identify them or to reduce either to a form of the other is sheer confusion.

And now that we have seen in what way the true and the good correspond, respectively, to the first and the second of the three general types of adjustment by means of which the individual may attain to equilibrium with his environment, it remains to inquire whether there be an analogous correspondence between the remaining type of adjustment and the experience of beauty. At the outset of this final portion of our inquiry, we must take into consideration that the beautiful is not the only kind of value applicable to feeling. The pleasant is equally with the beautiful descriptive of affective value, and it is necessary before going further to adopt some conception of their relation. If we revert for a moment to the concept of cognitive value or truth, we may note that truths are of two grades, particular and universal. In a particular judgment the relation constituting the judgment-content is a transitory and not a permanent fact. The judgment, "some dogs are black" asserts that the quality of black occurs at some times, but not necessarily at all times, in coexistence with the qualities connoted by the term *dog*. But the judgment "all dogs are animals" asserts that at each and every time that we might experience the qualities connoted by the term *dog*, we should also experience in coexistence with them the qualities connoted by the term *animal*. Now, corresponding to this division of the objects of cognition into particular and universal truths is a quite similar division of the objects of conation and desire. There are the goods that satisfy our casual and temporary desires, and there is that higher grade of good which consists in the satisfaction of wants that are permanent and universal—necessary to our very existence as social and spiritual beings. The two classes of desires are often found at variance with one another, and the term *good* is sometimes used in the ethical and restricted sense to designate only things which possess the higher form of conative value: the things which, as we say, ought to be desired. Returning now to a consideration of the distinction between the beautiful and the merely pleasant, I think we shall find that it is the same sort of distinction as that between the particular and the universal truths, or as that between the merely desired and the ethically desirable or good. Writers on esthetics seem to differ sharply on this point, but their differences are, after all, more apparent than real. Compare, for example, the views of Marshall, Santayana, and Kant. The beautiful, says Dr. Marshall, is the permanently pleasant; Professor Santayana defines beauty as pleasure objectified or externalized. Now, it goes without saying that if an object is a permanent source of pleasure, the pleasantness will be localized in the object, for the same reason that sweetness is localized in sugar, or that any quality is localized in the object which regularly or permanently evokes it. And conversely, if the pleasure aroused by an object be fleeting, irregular, and variable, dependent on our passing mood rather than on the nature of the object, why then we shall not tend to localize the pleasantness in the object, but only in ourselves, and we shall regard the object as being merely pleasant, not as being beautiful. To define beauty with Marshall as the permanent in pleasure, or, with Santayana, as pleasure objectified, actually and pragmatically amounts to the same thing. For Kant, the important phase of the relation between beauty and pleasantness lies in the element of universality which distinguishes the esthetic from the merely hedonic experience. But here, again, we have a conception quite in accord with the two just considered. For if the pleasantness of anything is due primarily to the permanent nature of the object rather than to the changing mood of the conscious subject, it will normally be aroused in all similar subjects, will be, that is, a universal or public pleasure concerning which all should be able to agree. The beautiful, then, would seem to be neither more nor less than the permanently, objectively, and universally pleasurable. The further definition of beauty will thus depend upon the definition of pleasure.

Pleasure, like most of the ultimate types of experience, is difficult to define. It may be, but is not necessarily, an object of desire. It usually, though not invariably, attends the satisfaction of a desire. It resembles the objects of cognition in that it may be given to the individual without any anticipation or effort on his part, but it differs from a fact of cognition in that it is never forced upon the individual against his desire. It seems, indeed, to be somewhat between the cognitive and the conative forms of experience. In cognition it is the environment which primarily determines our experience, while in volitional activity our experience is primarily determined by ourselves. But whether we shall feel pleasure or not depends neither on the nature of the environment nor on the nature of the individual, but solely on the particular relation at the moment of one to the other. When the environment happens to accord with the organism, or with any part of it, in such a way as to accelerate or facilitate its processes, then, and only then, does pleasure result. Thus, the essential feature of affective value, distinguishing it from the values of cognition and conation, is that it is neither enforced nor achieved, but simply happens. Indeed, much that Kant says of the freedom and spontaneity characterizing the experience of beauty might, it seems to me, with even more obvious truth, be applied to the experience of mere pleasure.

The type of equilibrium or adjustment between organism and environment that is demanded for the realization of esthetic and hedonic values is one in which individual and environment each independently or spontaneously accords with the other.

To conclude: I have tried to show that corresponding to the three great types of human value which are called the true, the good, and the beautiful, there are three processes of adjustment through which the human organism may attain to equilibrium with its environment: these are, first, the adapting of the individual perceptions and judgments to the facts of the environment, which gives the cognitive value of truth; second, the adapting of the facts of the environment to the desires of the individual, which gives the conative value of good; and, third, the spontaneous and unenforced adaptation of individual needs and environing facts to one another, which gives the affective values of beauty or of pleasure. The pragmatic method as thus applied to the analysis of values by no means confirms the conclusion adopted by the humanistic pragmatists that cognition and feeling are reducible to conation, but seems rather to provide additional reasons for regarding these three types of experience as severally distinct and irreducible.

20

* BEAUTY IS NOT ALL: AN APPEAL FOR ESTHETIC PLURALISM[1]

An appeal to artists to supplement their creations of beauty or objectified joy with creations in which any emotion, even the most painful and terrible, is objectified, to the end that art may cease to be a sophisticated affair of the studios and become once more a power in the life of the people.

BEAUTY is defined by Santayana as pleasure objectified, and by Kant as the power of an object to cause pleasure by its intrinsic essence rather than by its existential relation to an observer. The two definitions can be shown to mean the same thing because pleasure is only externalized in an object when it is derived from its essence.

Beauty is generally regarded as the sole aim of most art. But an art which in its content or subject matter objectifies only joyous emotion is sentimental and boring. The justifiable revolt against it takes three principal forms: (1) Moralism, (2) Realism, (3) "Unrealism."

Moralism reduces art to a servile status, making it a means to some ethical or sociological end. In this process the truly esthetic values are in danger of being warped or destroyed.

Realism seeks to imitate nature and to arouse in the spectator the pleasure of recognizing and identifying what is

[1] From *Deuxième Congrès International D'Esthétique et de Science De L'Art,* Paris, Félix Alcan, 1937, Tome I, pp. 142–145.

familiar. This pleasure is pardonable and even innocent, but is not esthetic, though it is often thought to be. Realism is, moreover, too eager to be contrasted with "idealism," and consequently tends to emphasize the disagreeable and trivial aspects of existence.

When challenged for their esthetic irrelevancies, both realists and moralists are apt to defend their claim to be regarded as artists by appealing to the adequacy or effectiveness of their performance. If what is done is not beautiful, it is at least beautifully done.

"Unrealism" is concerned with neither edification nor imitation. It aims directly at beauty of form. And as attention to form must compete with attention to content, the significance of the one requires the insignificance of the other. To achieve this goal of *form at any price,* the subject matter should at least be trivial, and wherever possible it should be altogether meaningless. Unrealism is not confined to painting and sculpture. It has made its way a little into music, a great deal into recent poetry, and in one notable instance even into prose. It is capable of blending to some extent with realism and moralism as they are capable of blending with each other. I suppose that surrealism is but a whimsical and highly piquant blend of realism and unrealism.

Without denying for one moment either the beauty of pure form or the esthetic value of the strange technique by which unrealism seeks to bring it forth, one may be permitted to regret a certain preciosity and exclusiveness that narrows the appeal of the movement and confines it mainly to the studios. Art for art's sake is good, but art for the sake of artists is not so good. It is unfair and a little selfish that those endowed with power to enrich and illuminate the lives of their less fortunate brethren should hug their gifts to themselves and revel in a collectivistic narcissism. Yet so long as purely formal beauty is the one end to be achieved, a considerable degree of such exclusiveness is inevitable.

Without going back to an optimistic sentimentalism, there is a way for art to recapture that significant *content* which, and which only, in contrast to significant *form*, can warm the hearts of the esthetic proletarians who, alas, make up the majority of mankind. This is the way of Esthetic Pluralism.

Let us return to the definitions of beauty given by Kant and Santayana and subject them to a simple but momentous extension.

Instead of restricting the realm of the esthetic to objectified *pleasure*, why not broaden it to include objectified *emotion*—and by "emotion" I mean feeling of any kind—the sad, the terrible, and even the horrible? This does not mean that all emotion, still less all expression of any kind, is to be accorded esthetic value. As beauty was not mere pleasure but rather objectified pleasure, so esthetic values are not mere emotions but only such emotions as are objectified. And neither pleasure nor any other feeling is objectified, that is, localized or vested in an object rather than in the conscious subject himself, unless the emotion is, in the Kantian sense, regarded as due to the intrinsic form of the thing and not to its spatio-temporal relations to the percipient. This is what I mean by "Esthetic Pluralism." Beauty is objectified joy, and as such the highest and loveliest of esthetic values. But Beauty is not all—she is a queen, a constitutional sovereign, but not a dictator. And just as hero and heroine shine all the brighter when not the sole persons in the tale, so would the objectified pleasures, if set off and enhanced by objectifications of other emotions, lose the saccharinity and banality that led to the modernistic movements of revolt.

Drama and fiction have, of course, taken this road quite spontaneously without waiting for the sanction of estheticians. If the masters of painting and sculpture would do it also and abandon their fixation on beauty either of form or of content as the sole thing that was worth their while, they could make of their galleries macrocosms of the human heart and the totality of its passions. And from these macrocosms not only the aristocracy of connoisseurs and sophisticates but the vast multitude of common men could nourish and enrich their lives. An art thus broadened and freed from its ivory tower might regain, in our own sad days, all and more than all of the power and the glory which pertained to it in the great days of Greece.

Section VIII—Ethics

21

* THE PHILOSOPHY OF FRIEDRICH NIETZSCHE[1]

A comparison of the strong and weak points in the philosophy of Nietzsche with the strong and weak points of the Christian philosophy.

Biographical Note

Friedrich Nietzsche was born at Röchen in the Prussian province of Saxony on October 15, 1844. He became insane in January, 1889, and from then to the day of his death, August 25, 1900, he remained a hopeless mental invalid. His father and both of his grandfathers were clergymen.

Nietzsche received his early education in the schools of Naumburg. At fourteen he was given a scholarship in the famous Landesschule, Pforta, where he remained for six years. After studying philology and theology at the University of Bonn for six months, he went to Leipzig, where he studied philology for two years. He left the university for a brief period of voluntary military service which was terminated by a fall from his horse and a severe illness. In 1868 he was honored by an appointment to the Professorship of Classical Philology at the University of Bâle; and Leipzig, in recognition of this distinction, conferred upon him the doctor's degree without further examination. At

[1] *Warner Library*, 1918, Vol. 18, pp. 10664A–10666M.

the outbreak of the Franco-Prussian War, he obtained leave of absence to serve with the Prussian army as a hospital attendent. He contracted dysentery, and his health became permanently undermined. In 1879 he was forced by his poor health to resign his professorship. The University gave him a pension, which, added to a small private income, enabled him to live comfortably during the ten years preceding his final illness. Much of this last period of his active life was spent in Italy.

Despite Nietzsche's high position in academic circles, his books were not favorably received and he was obliged to publish many of them at his own expense. It was not until 1888 that Taine in Paris and Brandes in Copenhagen proclaimed to the learned world their belief in the greatness of his philosophy.

There was in Nietzsche's life much of loneliness and disappointment as well as ill-health. He was devoted to his sister Elizabeth, who nursed him during his last years and who has given us his biography, but her marriage displeased him and brought about an estrangement. His warm friendship with Wagner ended in a permanent quarrel.

His philosophy was for a long time received either with indifference, misunderstanding, or actual hostility. These causes combined with his invalidism to increase the harshness and bitterness of his attitude toward the accepted standards of society. It would, however, be a pious and foolish mistake to seek for the key of his teaching in the unhappy circumstances of his life and temperament or to view his doctrines as in any way a precursor of the insanity with which his life ended, for the philosophy of Nietzsche, like all philosophy that is truly great, possesses an intrinsic significance which far transcends the biographical and social conditions under which it originated.

Nietzsche's principal works are as follows: *The Birth of Tragedy* (1872); *Thoughts Out of Season* (1873–6);

Human, All-too-Human (1878); *Dawn of Day* (1881); *The Joyful Wisdom* (1882); *Thus Spake Zarathustra* (1883–4); *Beyond Good and Evil* (1886); *The Genealogy of Morals* (1887); *The Twilight of the Idols* (1889); *The Will to Power* (published posthumously in 1901).

There is an edition of Nietzsche's complete works in English by Oscar Levy. The standard biography is by his sister, Frau Elizabeth Forste Nietzsche. It has been translated into English and is entitled *The Lonely Nietzsche.*

An enormous number of books and articles have been written on Nietzsche and his philosophy. A brief but very illuminating exposition of his teaching is entitled *Nietzsche, his Life and Works,* by Anthony M. Ludovici.

The Philosophy of Nietzsche

Nietzsche's philosophy is, in the main, an elaborate, sustained, and passionate attack upon the two great ideals of the present day—the moral ideal of Christianity and the social ideal of democracy. This attempt to overthrow all accepted standards, or, in Nietzsche's own phrase, to "transvaluate all values," is, however, based more or less directly upon a general metaphysical theory of the nature of evolution and of the origin of human morality. Hence, before treating of Nietzsche's more specific criticism of modern ethical ideals, we must consider the broad foundation of his philosophical system.

I. The Will to Power as the Mainspring of Nature and the Ground of All Values

Our philosopher, like his great predecessor Schopenhauer, holds that the driving force of all nature is identical with what in our own life we call "will." According to Schopenhauer, however, the world-will aimed at life and aimed also at contentment and peace. As life is essentially active and restless, it is incompatible with the ideal of peace, and therefore we must recognize the truth of "pessimism," which is the belief that life is evil and that a denial of life and of the will to live is the only way to attain the good.

Nietzsche, starting from the same premises as Schopenhauer, arrives at an opposite conclusion. The world-will is not merely a *will to live*, it is a *will to power;* and it is in power that it finds its good, and not at all in peace and contentment. Thus, the same spectacle that makes of Schopenhauer a pessimist makes Nietzsche an optimist. The spectacle of life as a perpetual war fills Schopenhauer with despair, because he loves peace. The same spectacle fills Nietzsche with courage and happiness, because he loves power rather than peace.

The Nietzschean theory of evolution as a progressive realization of the will to power brings him into a certain conflict with the Darwinian conception of evolution as a struggle for existence. If life is a struggle for existence, it will find its essence and goal in what Herbert Spencer described as the "adjustment of internal to external relations"; and the fitness, value, or success of a living organism will be measured by the extent to which it is adapted to its environment. But for Nietzsche, the basic instinct of life is not self-preservation but self-aggrandizement, and the measure of value is not the extent to which life adapts itself to the environment, but the extent to which it conquers the environment and adapts it to its own needs. Had Nietzsche possessed a greater knowledge of natural science, or had his main interest been directed to biological problems, he might have developed his theory that life is an aggressive rather than a defensive tendency into a vitalistic theory of evolution very similar to that set forth by the great French philosopher, Henri Bergson. As it was, he used the theory only as a general basis for his doctrine of the nature and origin of moral values.

The genealogy of morals is explained by Nietzsche in

terms of the will to power somewhat as follows: Power being the primary end of every life, whatever serves as a means to that end will possess value. "Good" is a eulogistic name by which any class of individuals denominates the instrumentalities and rules of conduct which favor its own interests. If a class were to appeal to all individuals to follow those rules which it frankly declared to be in its own interest, no one outside the class would feel any impulse to accede to the appeal. It is, then, of the highest importance that the selfish motive of class interest which underlies all moral codes be disguised. And the usual way of accomplishing the disguise is to use words like *goodness*, *righteousness*, and *justice*, which have a deceptive flavor of objective validity and universal obligation. In an analogous way and for analogous reasons, it has proved expedient for any class seeking to achieve or to preserve power to use such words as *evil*, *criminal*, *unjust*, and *immoral* to denominate actions or ideas which are opposed to its own interest. When once we recognize the truth of the foregoing account of the genealogy of morals, we are forced to adopt a standpoint that is "beyond good and evil"; for inasmuch as the interests of different groups conflict with one another, there can be no such thing as an objective and universal good obligatory upon everyone to pursue. One man's meat is another man's poison, and what is "morally good" from the standpoint of one class may be "morally evil" from the standpoint of another. There is no morality; there are only moralities.

This doctrine of ethical relativism was by no means original with Nietzsche. We find it clearly recognized in the days of ancient Greece; Plato imputes it to his contemporary, the sophist Thrasymachus, when he makes him declare that "Justice is the interest of the stronger." The long line of modern moralists, from Hobbes to those of the present, who hold that every man does, must, and should aim only at his own greatest happiness, have naturally tended to view any system of morality as merely a means to this end and as objectively binding only in so far as the state may in its own interest prescribe it for the citizens.

The same thought will be expressed differently by different groups: To the devout royalist, "The King can do no wrong"; the ardent patriot will say, "My country, right or wrong"; the socialist will speak of "bourgeois morals and working-class morals." These are all just different forms of the doctrine that "might makes right."

Nietzsche, however, expressed the underlying thought of ethical relativism with more force and clearness than any of its other adherents. For in most of them there was a vague feeling that the interest of the individual could be made to coincide with the interest of society, or that what was for the good of one's own class or country would ultimately be for the good of all. Nietzsche alone proclaimed the conflict of interests which takes the form of a conflict of moralities to be *irreconcilable.* For to Nietzsche it was power rather than prosperity or contentment which was the aim of life; and power cannot be universalized. It can be obtained by one class only at the expense of the defeat of another. Were there no conquered, there could be no conquerors; without slaves there would be no masters.

That there is a disconcerting amount of truth in this Nietzschean doctrine of ethical relativism cannot be denied. Of course, we all take our own morality with the greatest seriousness, and yet we frequently discover in our friends a foolish habit of investing with moral dignity a course of action which has nothing to commend it except that it works to their advantage. There is no conscious hypocrisy in this, but rather an unconscious aversion to seeing ourselves spiritually naked, and a consequent universal tendency to clothe our subjective interests in the respectable garb of an "objective morality." So much for the strength of ethical egoism and relativism; their weakness appears as soon as we raise the question, from an outsider's standpoint, as to the relative merits of the different moral codes and the different types of ego which are open to us to follow. Let us suppose that we have each of us decided that the highest moral good means *my* highest self-interest; what kind of self shall I become? Shall I make my ego the sort of ego which finds its attainment of power or life-fulfillment in narrow or physical happiness, or in broad spiritual happiness? In domination over others, or in co-operation with others? Admitting that the pig at the trough and the martyr at the stake are each actuated by self-interest, which of these self-interests shall I prefer and strive to attain? It is no answer to say, "Whichever is to my greatest interest," for that is like saying, "It is to my interest to seek what is to my interest." What is required is a criterion or principle for deciding which kind of self-interest is the best. In order to get such a criterion, I must put aside the relativistic or egoistic standpoint as being irrelevant or tautologous, and go back to the old problem of traditional ethics and consider which of the various and more or less conflicting ideals of life possesses the greatest amount of objective value or goodness.

It is quite amusing to observe how Nietzsche, with a sublime unconsciousness of what he is doing, goes through this circle of reasoning exactly as all the other defenders of egoism have done before.

Having discredited to his own satisfaction all moral codes and all uses of the terms *good* and *evil* as merely relative and expressive only of the self-interest of some individual or group of individuals, and having thus brought himself to the lofty standpoint of "beyond good and evil," we find him suddenly indulging in such terms as *noble* and *base*, *heroic*, and *contemptible*, *beautiful*, and *ugly*. And he uses these words to characterize rules of conduct and types of character which he regards as intrinsically worthy and unworthy, respectively. He is a man of deeply moral nature, and his moral preferences are far too profound and too passionate to permit him from mere self-consistency to retain an attitude of cynical indifference to the struggle of ideals. But he is naïve enough to suppose that, by substituting esthetic names like *noble* and *beautiful* for the conventional ethical names *good* and *virtuous*, he has got beyond the moral standpoint altogether. What he grandiosely describes as the "transvaluation of all values" is nothing more nor less than a defense of certain values which appear to Nietzsche as supremely and objectively righteous. But though our philosopher reveals himself as after all only a moralist, he is none the less a very original and important moralist. The main significance of his moral code can best be studied by contrasting it, as he himself does, with the current ideals of Christianity and democracy; but before entering upon that undertaking, there are two principles that serve Nietzsche as the metaphysical foundation of his ethics and which consequently should be mentioned in this introductory section of our exposition.

The first of these metaphysical principles is one that we have already spoken of in connection with the conception of ethical relativism. It expresses Nietzsche's conviction that Nature's Will to Power, which is the ground of all existence, as well as of all value, is a *pluralistic* will that manifests itself in conflicting tendencies, the realization of some of which would be incompatible with the realization of others. The life-need of the lion cannot be fulfilled save at the expense of the lamb. The needs of the higher men are often in outright opposition to those of the lower. Hence, the greatest good cannot be a universal good. The attainment of the best must entail the frustration, or partial frustration, of certain aims which would otherwise be desirable and justifiable. This principle which generates Nietzsche's ethical relativism remains with him throughout and is largely responsible for some of the harsher features of his constructive teaching. Its measure of truth depends upon the meaning which is given to the ideal of "power," toward which all life must strive. If "power" is taken in the narrow or material sense of forcible dominance by one group over another group—then Nietzsche is right, and the attainment of life's ideal by all would be impossible. If, however, "power" is interpreted more broadly (and Nietzsche himself sometimes so interprets it) as the fulfillment of all one's capacities, an Aristotelian self-realization, there would be no necessary or permanent obstacle to its universal attainment.

The second basic principle of Nietzschean morality concerns the goal of the will to power, when conceived as a process of biological evolution. From every past species has evolved a higher species. Man must realize this trend of the life-force, and put himself in harmony with it. He should ever treat himself as a bridge or transition between man and a being higher than man, a "beyond-man" or "superman" into which man may evolve. It is this superman which in Nietzsche's system takes the place of God as the supreme object of devotion. Our dealings with our fellow men, and our own self-fulfillment, are to be ruled in the light of this "being that is yet to be." Most of the traditional religious values are associated with an attitude of looking backward in time and upward. In the Nietzschean substitute for religion, they appear in a reversed perspective. The superman, whom we are to reverence, is our creature, to whom we are to give being, not our creator, from whom we derive being. We are to look forward into the future for our inspiration rather than backward into the past. In place of the semi-religious emotion of patriotism, which is loyalty for our "fatherland," we must cultivate a new emotion for which there is as yet no name—a loyalty to our "children's-land." Marriage should possess a new significance; it should be treated as a eugenic sacrament, not to be entered into from motives of passion or friendship, but in the conviction that it may be the means of producing lives that are higher than ours, and that will, then, contribute to the evolution of the superman.

As Nietzsche's attack on all morality developed into a new form of morals, so his attack upon religion develops into a new form of religious piety. He is fond of telling us that "God is dead," but, descended as he is from long lines of parsons, he cannot be satisfied with any ordinary kind of atheism. God's death leaves in his deeply religious nature an emotional void which must be filled by the futuristic apotheosis of our superhuman posterity. Nietzsche's "Zarathustra" is the prophet of the superman; and, underneath the gay and blustering aphorisms of the new prophet, it is easy to detect the grim earnestness of old-time religion.

The very originality of this doctrine baffles the attempt to evaluate it. Always, in the past, theology has been preceded by religion. Religious ceremonies and their attendant emotions have attained to a considerable development before there has been felt any need for their attempted rationalization as theology. We are now asked to reverse the process. A new kind of theology, that of the superman, is presented to us, and we are expected to develop an emotional reaction. We can hardly achieve it. Our religious pieties have been so steeped in retrospection that we cannot easily make them prospective and face the future with a worshipful attitude. The Nietzschean demand that we substitute the strange thought of a Divine Posterity for the familiar thought of a Divine Father appeals to us as empty and bizarre. No new technique of religious feeling for dealing with it has as yet been developed, though it may come in time. And as to the truth or falsity of the superman theory, science affords no more determinate answer. There is no evidence that human nature has undergone any intrinsic evolution during the period of recorded history. Our progress has been cultural, not biological. We see more than our ancestors only because we can stand upon their shoulders and profit by their mistakes, not because we are ourselves higher or greater than they were. We may indulge a well-founded hope that this cultural progress will continue, and there is a possibility that it may be supplemented by a mutation of a more intrinsic or biological character. But that the degree of such future progress will be comparable to our past progress from the simian to the human, and so justify the expectation of a new race of supermen, has hardly anything to support it except the blind religious faith of Friedrich Nietzsche.

II. The Anti-Christianity of Nietzsche

The men of the present day, so far as their moral ideals are concerned, are divided by Nietzsche into three classes: (1) There are the orthodox Christians who believe both in the theology of the Church and in her ethical teachings. These are the simple folk, numerous but unimportant. They have not even heard that God is dead, and hence their doctrine of life is consistent, though entirely false. They do not greatly matter. (2) There are the majority of educated people, who have lost all the supernatural beliefs taught by the Church, but who inconsistently retain the whole system of Christian ideals. They flatter themselves with being "emancipated," "anti-clerical," "secularized," "humanitarian," but they are black Christians at heart for all their boasting and differ from the first class only in their possession of superficial culture. (3) There are those few who are really emancipated and disillusioned, who have discarded the morals as well as the theology of the Church, but who have found nothing positive to take the place of what they have lost. They alternate between a despairing attitude of universal denial, which is nihilism or pessimism, and the feverish pursuit of frivolous and more or less degenerate doctrinal fads.

As a cure for all this mental and moral sickness, Nietzsche proffers his new gospel of Zarathustra as Anti-Christ. He begins by laying bare the origin of those Christian ideals which, whether they are reluctantly retained or reluctantly abandoned, are in either case the main source of the confusion and distress of the modern age.

The multitude of moral codes, each one of which has arisen as a disguised expression of the self-interest of some individual or group of individuals, can in the main be reduced to two generically opposed types: master-morality and slave-morality. Master-morality expresses the interests and ideals of great and successful men, the leaders of the race. It is summed up in two principles: (1) It is a life-affirming doctrine. All that makes for the fulfillment of impulse, appetite, ambition, and power is good. (2) The power of the great man is incompatible with the power of lesser men; hence, hardness, pride, sternness, and pitilessness are good.

Slave-morality, of which Christianity is the most perfect example, is in both respects the opposite of master-morality. It is (1) a life-denying doctrine. All that makes for the fulfillment of impulse, appetite, ambition, and power is evil. The obedient, the humble, the poor in spirit, the long suffering, those who turn the other cheek when unjustly smitten and who fight only against their own appetites of hunger and sex and their own desires for fame and wealth, are blessed. (2) The denial of one's self is associated with the service of others; hence, love, gentleness, pity, and devotion to all our fellows and particularly to the weak and suffering are also blessed. Christianity, in short, is life-denying and altruistic, while master-morality is life-affirming and egoistic.

To Nietzsche, the set of values embodied in the slave-morality of the Christians is the absolute inversion of the true or natural values embodied in master-morality. The reason why these negative ideals have come to be generally accepted can be understood only by discovering the manner in which they originated, which is briefly as follows: The weak and unsuccessful man will make a virtue of necessity and imitate the fox in the fable of the sour grapes by eulogizing the irremediable conditions of his failure. What can't be cured can be praised as a good, and what men call good they will end by believing to be good. Moreover, slaves that enjoy their servitude and regard obedience and non-resistance as virtues will be pleasing in the eyes of their masters. For a slave to cringe is good, but to praise and enjoy cringing is still better. In Nietzsche's view, it is the Christian who says, "Evil, be thou my good," and if the saying pleases his Master, assures his own safety, and even gains an illusion of self-respect that is a very real though unearthly consolation. It was for this reason that the Christian inversion of moral values made such a tremendous appeal to the weak and downtrodden masses to whom it was preached. Every slave, however, has in him something of the master's nature; hence, the inversion of values would, if taken all by itself, be a little too much of a *tour de force.* To meet this residual longing for real values, the Christian supplements his praise of earthly failure with a belief in another world, a paradise or heaven in which he will enjoy the kind of satisfaction that the unregenerate masters enjoy in this world. Thus, the meek are blessed because of the intrinsic beauty of their meekness, and also because they will some day inherit the earth.

It is small wonder that with this double appeal the Christian religion has carried all before it.

As for the second principle of Christianity—its ideal of service or love—it is explained by Nietzsche as a natural development of weakness. Weak individuals can defend themselves only by banding together into a herd as do cattle when attacked by a lion. The sympathy and loyalty which Christians enjoin are the necessary manifestations of that spirit of co-operation which is essential to the success of the herd. Slave-morality is thus also herd-morality. Great and strong natures are capable of standing alone, and have neither the need nor the obligation of sympathy and co-operation.

Now, if this were the whole story, all would be well. Christianity is a fit and wholesome doctrine for the lower classes, for it keeps them contented and orderly. Unfortunately, however, the diseases of slaves are sometimes caught by their owners; and Christianity has proved diabolically contagious in that it has spread through all ranks of society, so that many of the masters and natural leaders of men have been poisoned by its sophistry and become self-enslaved. This weakening of the masters, combined with the undue increase in the numbers and cohesiveness of the herd, threatens humanity with ruin. Great men and their positive ideals are in danger of being absorbed by the crowd of small men and negative ideals. It is to avert this danger to humanity and to the superhumanity that is to come that Nietzsche sends Zarathustra to preach the gospel of Anti-Christ. And Zarathustra is to preach not to all men (for that would be both dangerous and futile), but to the few great men, who are exhorted to rouse themselves from their slumberous subserviency to the morals and conventions of the herd, and to cast aside Christian law and humanitarian sentiment whenever those ideals operate to restrain the affirmation and development of their will to power. The positive morality of a life-affirming egoism is, thus, to replace among the masters the negative or Christian morality of a life-denying altruism, which is fit only for the slave-like herd who constitute the majority of mankind.

We can but indicate the line of thought by which Nietzsche's grave and bitter arraignment of Christian ethics might be met. Of the two essentially Christian ideals, life-denial and altruism, the former deserves most of the condemnation which our philosopher pours out upon it. "Other-worldly" asceticism should have no place in the modern Occidental world, in which evolutionary progress here on earth is both an established fact and a living faith. The notion that self-abasement, poverty, and bodily misery are either good in themselves or good as preparation for a remote future life, while it has doubtless brought consolation to many downtrodden individuals, has, nevertheless, proved itself a reactionary force of the worst sort and a persistent obstacle to all forms of social progress. It has prevented the oppressed from protesting, and has given moral sanction to the cruel indifference and complacence of the oppressors. The inverted ideal of repression and denial should be replaced by Zarathustra's call to a life of affirmation and fulfillment. Whatever makes for the furtherance of life and the attainment of desire is in so far good. The only time an excuse may be given for denying any of the impulses of nature is when their fulfillment would result in the thwarting of stronger or more numerous impulses on the part of ourselves or others. Moral evil is only the preference of a lesser to a greater good.

With the second of the Christian principles, namely, the ideal of altruism or love, the case is the reverse. If life-fulfillment is good, it is irrational and absurd to limit it to any one person or group, even if the person be oneself and the group be one's own class. The greatest, as well as the most accessible, form of self-realization consists in co-operating with others and helping wherever help is needed. To follow Nietzsche and banish Christian charity by limiting one's ideal of power or life-enhancement to a harsh and narrow dominance over others would not only be irrational, it would deprive the one thus acting of that broadest and most enduring form of happiness which consists in sympathy with all and more especially with the weak, whose need is most urgent. *The problem of modern ethics is to purge Christian altruism of its taint of asceticism, and to purge the life-affirming ideals of Nietzsche of their taint of cruelty and selfishness, and then combine the two ideals into a single system.*

III. The Anti-Democracy of Nietzsche

Democracy is applied Christianity, and for that reason Nietzsche hates it. The Christians would exalt the commonplace Demos and reduce to the dead level of mediocrity all men of superior strength and ability. Democracy may call itself anti-clerical and humanitarian and boast of its emancipation from theological superstition, but it retains, nevertheless, the essential error of the religion from which it sprang. Political democracy is the enthronement of herd-morality and herd-mentality in the realm of government. It is bad enough, but the economic democracy or socialism which is the goal of democratic evolution is far worse. For in socialism we have herd-morality supreme not only in government, but in property and industry, and hence in all domains of human affairs.

The strength of this Nietzschean criticism of democracy can be illustrated as follows: Imagine all the individuals of a community to be arranged in a series according to their abilities. Assume that the series runs from zero per cent at its lowest to 100 per cent at its highest. If such a community is democratically operated, each member will possess an equal share in directing its affairs and receiving its benefits, with the result that the efficiency of management will be exactly 50 per cent, or just one-half what it would be under the aristocratic plan in which the best members, or those ranking 100 per cent in ability, are the rulers. Why should we tolerate government by the average when we might have government by the best? In organizing any private enterprise we should, as a matter of course, secure our directors from the expert minority of ability. Why should we make a wasteful exception to the rule of reason in the great enterprise of political and economic government?

Nietzsche's theory of aristocracy differs in two respects from the traditional conception. (1) He does not identify his ideal aristocracy with any of the actually established aristocracies, not even that of his own country. He is not a nationalist, and he would not base the claim to aristocratic privilege on the inheritance of wealth or title. Not the Junkers of Prussia, but the best men of Europe, should have the power to rule; and they would constitute an aristocracy *de jure* and not merely *de facto*. (2) The second point in which Nietzsche differs from the ordinary Tory is in the thoroughgoingness of his advocacy of aristocracy. The democratic slogan is "Government of the people, for the people, and by the people"; the traditional aristocrat replies: "Government of the people for the benefit of all, but conducted by the few." Nietzsche, however, would have government of the people, conducted by the few and for the benefit of the few. In other words, he has no patience with the Tory pretense of *noblesse oblige*, or the claim that an aristocracy is really in the interest of the majority. The herd will, to be sure, get certain incidental benefits from the rule of great men, just as cattle benefit from the shade of a great tree. But the tree exists for its own sake and not for the sake of the cattle, and analogously your true aristocrats will use and should use the power which they seize for their own welfare, rather than for the welfare of the people. For, to Nietzsche, true goodness or power is intensive rather than extensive, and the real value of any group or race is measured by the greatness of its greatest members and not by the uniformly distributed greatness of its average. A community of groveling slaves which contained a single Napoleon or Shakespeare would be preferable to a community composed entirely of prosperous and fairly intelligent Philistines.

To what extent and in what manner can we answer Nietzsche's attack upon the ideals of democracy? I believe that we can answer it to the same extent and in the same manner that we answered his attack upon the ideals of Christianity. For Nietzsche is right in maintaining that democracy, despite all of its secular formulations, is nothing but Christianity applied to the field of government. In each case it is an affair of the dominance of herd-morality over master-morality. It will be remembered that we found the Christian ethics to be summed up in two ideals: (1) asceticism or a denial of one's own will to life; (2) altruism or love of other lives, while Nietzsche's anti-Christianity was similarly reducible to the two principles opposed to the above, namely, (1) the will to power, or the right and duty of affirming one's own life-impulses; (2) egoism or the disregard of other lives. We suggested that the conflict could be solved by a doctrine of life-affirming altruism, which would combine the second of the Christian principles with the first of those of Nietzsche. Now, the democratic philosophy of government, like Christianity itself, can be shown to embody two main principles, one of which is false and subject to the objection brought against it by Nietzsche, while the other is true and capable of being harmonized with what is best in the Nietzschean ideals of aristocracy. These principles are as follows: (1) All men are equal in the sense that they have equal and uniform abilities. Whatever varies from the average should be crushed by the herd and made to conform. (2) All men are equal in the sense that they merit equal opportunities to develop their various and unequal abilities. Freedom to vary from the average is a universal right and the chief source of progress; it should be encouraged by the herd rather than suppressed.

Against the first of these doctrines, Nietzsche's argument is unanswerable; but when we come to the second principle of democracy, in which the equality of all men is interpreted as equality of opportunity, the situation is reversed. The same moral sense which approves your own right to develop your capacities carries with it a recognition of the equal right of your neighbor to develop his capacities. The ground for giving the great man a chance to make himself great is also a ground for giving the little man a chance to make himself as great as he can. The right of each is the right of all; and as long as we are possessed of reason and a social sense, we cannot regard the right to a fair start in the race for life as other than universal. Moreover, social expediency and efficiency reinforce individual justice, for the only way to discover the fastest runners is to allow all to run. So far from being opposed to aristocracy, democracy in the true sense is the least fallible method of finding the genuine aristocrats and conferring power upon them. Only by an artificially imposed equality of opportunity can we disclose natural inequalities of merit.

If we were to follow Nietzsche in opposing this second principle of democracy, and deny the right to equality of opportunity, we should secure not the superior members of his *de jure* aristocracy, but only such artificially and accidentally privileged persons as constitute the *de facto* aristocracies of the present day. And, finally, the same considerations that would dictate the choice of aristocrats by a democracy of equal rights would operate to prevent the aristocrats when once chosen from ruling exclusively in their own interests, as Nietzsche would have them, rather than in the interest of all. For the only way to retain either their power or their right to power would be to preserve the fair play for the many, on which the discovery of the truly great must depend. In short, Nietzsche was wrong in believing that there is any necessary incompatibility between the intensive excellence and efficiency embodied in great leaders and the extensive excellence or justice embodied in the welfare and prosperity of the entire community. Those who ruled by force over an oppressed people could never be so great as those who owed their rise to victory in honorable competition. In general, the fairest race produces as its winners the fastest runners.

Our analysis of Nietzsche's anti-democracy has led us to conclude that the half of his theory of aristocracy in which he emphasizes the importance of providing for the inequalities of men and for the freedom of the great from the tyranny of the majority is true, and that the form of democracy opposed to it is false; while the second half of his theory, in which he proclaims the right of the few to tyrannize in their own interest over the many, we find to be false, and the opposing principle of democracy as equality of opportunity we find to be not only true in itself but actually implied as a corollary of what is justifiable in his own theory of aristocracy. In short, Nietzsche's aristocratic philosophy of politics can supplement our traditional theory of democracy in the same way and to the same extent that his life-affirming philosophy of morals can supplement our traditional theory of Christianity.

Nietzsche's work will endure, for its appeal is to the deepest instincts of human nature, both those of good and those of evil.

THE MISSING LINK IN THE CASE FOR UTILITARIANISM[1]

An attempt to provide a basis for the higher and lower qualities of pleasure, recognized by John Stuart Mill, without departing from the conception essential to utilitarianism that all differences in value are quantitative.

I. An Analysis of the Two Minor Objections and of the One Major Objection to Utilitarianism

Utilitarianism is beset by three objections which come, as it were, from the Left, the Center, and the Right. The objection from the Left is primarily logical; that from the Center is primarily psychological; while the third objection, which proceeds from the Right, is primarily and properly ethical. It is with this last objection that my paper is mainly concerned; but before proceeding to a discussion of the problems which it raises, I desire to comment briefly upon the arguments of those who find fault, respectively, with the altruistic logic and with the hedonistic psychology of Utilitarianism.

1. *The egoist's objection to the altruistic logic of Utilitarianism.* It has been charged that John Stuart Mill and the other Utilitarians have failed to show any logical justification for adding to the self-evident reasonableness of each seeking his own good an alleged obligation of each

[1] Reprinted from *Studies in the History of Ideas,* Vol. II, pages 275–290, by permission of Columbia University Press.

to seek the good of all. This objection of the egoists has been answered by three more or less interconnected arguments, any one of which seems to me adequate to refute it.

In the first place, the egoist may be reminded that the same principle of reason that would make us admit that facts when experienced by others are as much facts as when experienced by oneself should also make us admit that values are as much values when experienced by others as when experienced by oneself. To recognize a thing as true is to feel a logical obligation to assent to it. To recognize a thing as good is to feel a moral obligation to strive for it whenever possible. Hence, if the egoist would deny his obligation to seek the good of others, he must deny the existence of the good of others and maintain that no pleasure or other admittedly good thing can exist except inside his own skin.

Second, as Sidgwick and others have pointed out, the egoist, in admitting the validity of a value when it is to occur in his future self, uses the same principle of reason that the altruist uses in recognizing the validity of a value when it is to occur in another self. From the standpoint of the mere feeling of the moment, one's future self is another self, and the obligation of *prudence* that would bid us consider the welfare of what is temporally another self is no better justified than the obligation of *sympathy* that would bid us consider the welfare of what is spatially another self.

Third, as my colleague Professor Lord has suggested, if despite the two answers just given, the egoist still persists in his ethical solipsism, he may be invited to consider the criterion by which he will evaluate the various kinds of self which he has it in him to become. For, granting his claim that it is only his own ego that he must serve, the question will at once arise as to which of his many potential egos he will try to realize. Will he best serve his egoistic ideal by becoming a saint or a swine? He cannot decide except by reintroducing the diverse theories of the nature of the truly good, which he supposed he had banished by limiting the domain of values to the circle of his own consciousness. In short, the egoist or solipsist in ethics is in the same plight as the ordinary solipsist. When he has been exempted from the many objections to his theory and allowed to identify the universe with his ego, he finds in the new universe all the problems of facts and values that he found in the old universe. To locate the universe within oneself is always a sterile conceit, and it is no more enlightening when it is the universe of values than when it is the universe of facts.

2. *The Behaviorist's objection to the hedonistic psychology of Utilitarianism.* The hedonistic tradition in terms of which Utilitarianism was formulated by Bentham and Mill has an element of subjectivistic psychology which is offensive to the objectivistic pragmatists and behaviorists of the present day.

When men attain what they have sought for, there usually occurs in their experience a peculiar and unanalyzable state of feeling to which we give the name "pleasure." Because pleasure in some form accompanies the attainment of any and every valued object, and also because it stands out as a clear and simple datum of introspective psychology, it was natural to assume that it was itself the essence of all value. The theory that the feeling of attaining the good is, itself, the only good which we should seek to attain is Hedonism; and the artificiality of the theory has been recognized not only by pragmatists and behaviorists, but by the long line of objectively minded philosophers from Aristotle down. As a matter of fact, when thirsty men drink water or lonely men seek companions, it is water and companions that are desired rather than the states of pleasurable feeling which will probably result from the attainment of those desires. The valuing attitude is always directed at least primarily to objects rather than to pleasure. And even when the value attached to an object is revised in the light of the pleasure that it brings, there remains an element of artificiality in substituting the feeling which measures the good for the good itself.

A second inadequacy of hedonistic psychology (or perhaps it is the same inadequacy expressed in a different way) consists in its restriction of the valuing attitude to the present as distinguished from the past and the future. Future values are *desired*, past values are *appreciated*, and it is only present values that are *enjoyed*. All will admit that these temporally distinct forms of valuing can vary independently and differ from one another in degree even when applied to the same object. The enjoyment of an object may be more or less intense than the desire for it. And it is equally common for the appreciation of an object or its valuation in retrospect to differ in degree both from its prospective and from its contemporaneous valuation. It is not easy to decide which of the three temporal perspectives in which values are apprehended is the most reliable. In favor of measuring value in terms of the pleasure we derive from it, it may be urged that we are closest to a good when we are possessing or enjoying it, and that its real value is therefore more correctly known when it is present than when it is past or future. But on the other hand, it might be maintained that pleasure is not self-explanatory, but is a resultant of fulfilling an organic need or tendency, and that it is the need of the individual for some increment or complement of his nature that constitutes the objective basis of a value or a good. This conception of the good as *fulfillment of tendency* or *increment of psychic being* is best represented in consciousness by the experience of *desire*. In other words, we know better what we need when we need it than when we have it.

And finally, the partisan of "appreciation" could make out a case for the superiority of the retrospective method of estimating value by appealing to the fact that it was only after the distracting excitements of desire and enjoyment had both passed away that the mind was sufficiently cool to form a judgment as to the real value of what it had desired and enjoyed.

If the hedonist replies to his two rivals by insisting that desire is only pleasure in prospect and that appreciation is nothing but pleasure in retrospect, he does but beg the question at issue. It could with equal justice be replied, first, that pleasure was merely the completion of desire, or, second, that it was the potentiality of appreciation.

It is not our purpose to attempt a solution of the problem as to which of the three temporal perspectives is least distortive of value. Whether or not the hedonist has the best of the triangular controversy, it is possible to restate the theory of Utilitarianism without committing ourselves on what is, after all, more a matter of psychological interpretation than of ethics proper.

Let us use the word *happiness* to denote the attainment of any object that is either desired in prospect, enjoyed in the present, or appreciated in retrospect. Using *happiness* in the sense just stated, the conventional formulation of Utilitarianism as the theory that the *summum bonum* consists in the greatest happiness of the greatest number has a meaning that is true to its essential ethical tradition but free from the objections that have been brought against the hedonistic psychology. For to identify value with happiness is to identify it not with the subjective feeling of pleasure, but with any and all experiences the attainment of which is desired, enjoyed, or appreciated.

And now, having to the best of our ability disposed of the objections to Utilitarianism which are chiefly logical and psychological in character, we are prepared to consider what is by far the most serious of the attacks that have been made upon the theory.

3. *The Intuitionist's objection to the ethics of Utilitarianism.* Everybody will admit that, in addition to the *natural* valuation of desire, enjoyment, and appreciation, there is a distinctively *moral* valuation of "*approval.*" We do sometimes give this judgment of moral approval to things which neither in themselves nor in their consequences are objects of desire, enjoyment, or appreciation. Courage, justice, and obedience to God's will are examples of things which, irrespective of their consequences for happiness, may elicit moral approval. Now, it is the contention of Utilitarians that such judgments of moral approval are merely *de facto* and not *de jure*, and that they can be and should be reduced to the natural valuations of desire, appreciation, and enjoyment which constitute happiness. Anti-Utilitarians, or Intuitionists, on the other hand, contend that the distinctively moral judgments of approval are *de jure* as well as *de facto*, and that they cannot be and should not be reduced to the natural values constituting happiness.

The chief argument in support of the Utilitarian claim is that analysis will show that in many cases the distinctively moral valuations have arisen and been maintained on account of their supposed efficacy for happiness, and that they are thus cases of the transfer of an original natural valuation to something associated with it, while as for those cases of moral approval which can be shown by analysis to have no bearing upon anyone's happiness, the Utilitarian claims that when once this lack of relation to happiness is clearly perceived, the human conscience will cease to feel any reason for retaining its attitude of approval. In short, for the Utilitarian, *all seemingly non-eudaemonistic valuations exist by reason of a neglected but tacit assumption of their derivation from valuations that are eudaemonistic.*

The principal argument in support of the Intuitionist position is the claim that no amount of analysis can reduce the qualitative hierarchy of moral valuations to the quantitative hierarchy of degrees of happiness. We feel, for example, that the happiness of a Socrates is morally higher than the happiness of a pig. If this moral difference were reducible to mere difference in the quantities of happiness involved, it should be possible by increasing the number of pigs, together with the intensity and duration of their happiness, to get a quantity of moral value equal to that embodied in a Socrates. Merely to state the case is sufficient to reveal its impossibility. No amount of pig-happiness, however great, could equal Socratic happiness, however small. But, if the greater quantity of goodness in the case of Socrates is not a greater quantity of happiness, then goodness must be something other than happiness. And it is by partaking of this *quality other than happiness* that all values, including happiness itself, are ultimately evaluated. The anti-Utilitarians may differ among themselves as to the nature of the final and non-eudaemonistic value in which they all believe. Some will define it, as Kant did, in terms of an absolute reasonableness or self-consistency; others will agree with Martineau in regarding it as a self-evident and not further analyzable sentiment of *preference* which reveals a clear-cut hierarchy of the virtues, no one of which is reducible to any other. Still others will hold that conformity to God's will is the supreme and self-evident principle of value.

It seems to me that the positive arguments of the Utilitarians fail to meet the chief point that is raised by the Intuitionists. We must admit, I believe, that such arguments as those contained in Mill's analysis of justice suffice to prove that all cases of distinctively moral valuation can be shown either to have a connection with eudaemonistic valuation or else to be no true values at all. But granted that a reference to happiness must be admitted as an essential part of valuation, it still remains for the Utilitarian to convince us that it is the whole of value. It is this that has not been proved. The happiness of a Socrates is adjudged superior to any quantity of happiness on the part of a pig, and the Intuitionist argues that this *incommensurability* of the two quantities of happiness implies a principle of goodness other than that of happiness itself.

It is the failure to meet this argument that constitutes the real weakness or gap in the long chain of evidence by which the ethics of "greatest happiness" is established. I think it may properly be called "the missing link in the case for utilitarianism."

The difficulty was recognized by John Stuart Mill himself. In a well-known passage occurring on pages 7 and 8 of his *Utilitarianism*, Mill writes on the subject as follows:

"It is quite compatible with the principle of utility to recognize the fact that some *kinds* of pleasure are more desirable and more valuable than others. It would be absurd that while, in estimating all other things, quality is considered as well as quantity, the estimation of pleasures should be supposed to depend on quantity alone.

"If I am asked what I mean by difference of quality in pleasure, or what makes one pleasure more valuable than another, merely as pleasure, except its being greater in amount, there is but one possible answer. Of two pleasures, if there be one to which all or almost all who have experience of both give a decided preference, irrespective of any feeling of moral obligation to prefer it, that is the more desirable pleasure. If one of the two is, by those who are competently acquainted with both, placed so far above the other that they prefer it, even though knowing it to be attended with a greater amount of discontent, and would not resign it for any quantity of the other pleasure which their nature is capable of, we are justified in ascribing to the preferred enjoyment a superiority in quality, so far outweighing quantity as to render it, in comparison, of small account."

The doctrine here set forth by Mill has been regarded by many as a surrender to the Intuitionist. In a previous passage Mill has explicitly defined "happiness" as "pleasure and the absence of pain"; and in the passage quoted he admits the necessity of recognizing a quality by the possession of which a quantitatively smaller pleasure is and should be preferred to a quantitatively larger pleasure. This is exactly what Intuitionists like Martineau would claim. And when Mill declares that the qualitative principle can only be described as an intrinsic and unanalyzable *preference* of one pleasure to another that would be felt by an individual who had experienced both, he is in a slightly more empirical fashion expressing the particular species of intuitionism which Martineau defends. If pleasures are to be preferred on any other principle than their own intrinsic quantity, then it is in that principle as well as in pleasure itself that true and ultimate value must be sought. And whether with Mill and Martineau we regard the new principle as an indefinable preferability or superiority, or whether with Kant and others we attempt to analyze it further, the fact remains that we have abandoned the attempt to reduce all values to happiness alone.

Now, I believe that it is possible to admit that some kinds of happiness are incommensurably higher than other kinds without invoking a principle of qualitative superiority which would deliver us into the hands of the Intuitionists. And in the second section of my paper I shall try to explain and justify the use of the categories of *potentiality* and *dimensionality* as adequate to this purpose.

II. A Possible Answer to the Major Objection to Utilitarianism

Man can be considered as a producer of happiness in others and as a consumer of happiness in himself. Viewed in either capacity, his rational or spiritual character bears to his sensory or physical nature a relation analogous (1) to the relation of a permanent potentiality to its successive actualizations; and (2) to the relation of a being of higher dimensionality to a being of lower dimensionality. My thesis will be that both as a producer and as a consumer of happiness, the spiritual value or virtue emphasized by Intuitionists is the *volume* of which the natural value or pleasure emphasized by Utilitarians is the *surface*.

1. *Man as a Producer of Happiness.* When Mill defined matter as the permanent possibility of sensation or of sensory perception, he offered a conception which gave to the prevailing positivism or phenomenalism of his day precisely the corrective that was most needed. It is difficult for even the staunchest of positivists to believe that the full reality of an existent body such as a table can be adequately exhausted by any number of merely actual perceptions of it. At the same time, his well-grounded aversion to admitting non-experienceable entities makes him loath to supplement the fleeting appearances by anything with a definite nature of its own such as atoms or souls. Now, Mill's conception of a body as a permanent possibility of perception permits our positivist to harmonize his natural human craving for something *substantial* with his acquired philosophic aversion to anything *not phenomenal.* To Mill the table in itself is nothing alien *to* experience, but it is infinitely rich in its potentialities *of* experience. It is like a sphere which, while not alien in nature to the circles which constitute its cross-sections, is nevertheless incapable of being exhausted by those circles, no matter how great their number.

Suppose, now, that we use an analogy drawn from Mill's physical philosophy to fill in the apparent gap in his moral philosophy. Let us define *virtue* as the *permanent potentiality of happiness.* Habits of character, such as courage and charity, will then appear neither as things mysteriously alien to happiness nor, on the other hand, as merely instrumental or transient causes of happiness. They will bear to happiness the same relation that Mill believed bodies to bear to our experience of them. They will be the substantive rather than transient causes of happiness. And the happiness of which a virtue is the permanent potentiality will be related to that virtue as a surface is related to the volume of which it is the cross-section. The tender and courageous character will be a potentially infinite producer of happiness. And in this infinity of the cause lies hidden the secret of its superiority to any and all of its effects. Conscience revolts against any form of utilitarianism that would make happiness equal in value to virtue. But this by no means justifies the Intuitionist's assuming that the value of virtue is alien in kind to the value of happiness. Its incommensurable superiority is due to its higher dimensionality. The volume is incommensurate with the surface, but its superiority is one of infinite quantity rather than of sheer quality. To suppose that virtue has a principle of value other than the value of happiness is to violate our ethical reason, while to suppose that the value of happiness is commensurable with the value of virtue is to violate our moral sentiment. To reconcile the qualitative homogeneity of happiness and virtue with their quantitative incommensurability is to harmonize Utilitarian theory with human conscience. It is my contention that the conception of virtue as the permanent potentiality of happiness, and therefore a substantive cause of higher dimensionality than its transitory effects, brings about the harmony in question.

2. *Man as a Consumer of Happiness.* When we considered man as a producer of happiness, we considered his virtues in relation to their effects upon others. Suppose, now, that we consider the character of man not as a producer, but as a consumer of value. Or, to put the matter in words that may appear less strained: we are to turn from the inquiry into the relation between happiness and the virtue that causes it and consider the relation between sensory happiness and the incommensurably superior happiness that we may call spiritual or rational.

Reason is not opposed to the senses; it is, rather, their harmonizer. And sensations are harmonized not by any external power, but by an internal reference of each actual sensation to the totality of possible sensations. Reason, whether theoretical or practical, whether concerned with perceptions or with desires, is nothing other than the capacity to estimate the part in the light of the whole.

Rational beings differ from merely sensuous beings not in the possession of some unanalyzable quality, but in the infinitely and therefore incommensurably greater volume of their needs. The needs of the sensuous nature are for *this and that, here and now.* The rational nature, on the other hand, apprehends the past and the future as well as the present, the distant as well as the near, and therein possesses needs and capacities which, without being alien in quality, are infinitely richer in quantity than the needs and capacities of the senses. The rational or spiritual being is, in short, of a higher dimensionality than the merely sensory being. Now, if happiness is the possession of whatever is desired, enjoyed, or appreciated; and if a rational being is of higher dimensionality than a merely sensory being, then the fulfillment of the needs of the rational being will constitute an incommensurably greater happiness than the fulfillment of any sensory needs no matter how great their number or their intensity. Man is a producer of happiness in others insofar as he possesses virtues; he is a consumer of spiritual happiness in himself insofar as he possesses an infinite system of capacities in which the virtues are included.

It is the conception of spirit as having a higher dimensionality than sense that enables us to agree with Mill that no amount of pig-happiness could equal the happiness of Socrates, and to maintain at the same time that the difference between the two kinds of happiness is quantitative rather than qualitative. *The concept of dimensionality thus affords a means of providing for the incommensurability of kinds of happiness without going outside the principle of happiness itself in determining the nature of the good.*

III. Conclusion

I have attempted to fill a gap in the logic of Utilitarianism by showing how it is possible to concede the incommensurable superiority of spiritual satisfaction to sensory happiness without appealing to any quality of value other than happiness itself; and I have used the category of spatial dimensionality to illustrate this combination of homogeneity of quality with incommensurability of quantity.

Some readers will feel that my introduction of dimensionality into the realm of value is no more than an analogy, and one that is artificial and unenlightening. To them I would appeal to entertain the argument even while discarding the terms in which I have couched it. Quite apart from the concept of dimensionality, is it not possible in general to regard one thing as infinitely or incommensurably greater than another without conceding a difference in quality? If this is possible in general, may it not be actually exemplified in the relation between the two kinds of satisfaction which are termed moral and sensory? If such is the case, the Utilitarian ethics is on the one hand freed from the *inconsistency* which resulted from Mill's appeal to a quality other than pleasure for evaluating pleasures; while on the other hand it is freed from the *inadequacy* which results if to escape the inconsistency of Mill we admit that the satisfactions of a pig are commensurable with those of a human being.

The question under discussion involves issues far more important than the dialectical consistency or adequacy of a particular theory of ethics. In all ethical theory and in all moral practice there is implicit the same dilemma as that which becomes technically explicit in the logic of Utilitarianism. The problem in this larger setting may be stated as follows: The term *good* in its primary and intrinsic meaning is applied to two classes of things: the happy satisfactions of desire and the virtuous satisfactions of conscience. Happiness and virtue are each of them ultimately and irreducibly "good"; but since they often appear incompatible, there arises as the ground-problem, alike of moral conduct and of ethical theory, the question of their mutual adjustment. For this problem there are two general types of solution, each of them with many special forms. The one type of solution takes the natural satisfactions of desire as constituting the essential good; the other takes the spiritual satisfactions of conscience as constituting the essential good. Each of these rival schools has yielded on occasion to the temptation to postpone and obscure the main problem in three ways: (1) by a transcendental theology according to which God harmonizes happiness with virtue; or (2) by a transcendental cosmology according to which some law of Karma automatically accomplishes the same result; or (3) by a transcendental psychology according to which conscience is declared, despite evidence to the contrary, to be a source of extreme pleasure to those who follow it. Sooner or later, however, the exigency of the ethical problem itself forces it out from these metaphysical shades into the light of explicit attention. And there then develops an apparently incurable weakness in each of the alternative theories between which we seem forced to choose.

These weaknesses are, respectively, the weakness of *worldliness* and the weakness of *other-worldliness*. The "happiness-ethics" suffers from "worldliness" because it can find no legitimate way, in terms of mere happiness, of according to the satisfactions of conscience the dignity which experience demands for them. The "conscience-ethics" suffers from "other-worldliness" because it can find no legitimate way, in terms of mere conscience, of according to the satisfactions of desire the value which experience demands for them. The one way is broad but shallow, the other deep but narrow.

John Stuart Mill saw the necessity of an ultimate reduction of the content of the good to happiness, but he also saw the impossibility of reducing the dignity of conscience and of spiritual satisfactions to any quantity of sensory satisfactions. Hence his attempt to combine Hedonism with a non-Hedonic principle of evaluation.

I believe that Mill's solution of this ground-problem of ethics can be made self-consistent (1) by conceiving of human nature as possessing an undeniable element of spirituality which should be sacrificed to nothing; but (2) by conceiving of this spiritual nature expressed in conscience as not qualitatively alien to sensory desires, but infinitely or incommensurably greater in magnitude than they are. Spirit is to be thought of as the permanent potentiality of desire; and sensory satisfaction as the temporary actualization of spiritual need. The one is to the other as the sphere is to the circle.

Dialectical compromises can often be made to display their hollowness by applying the pragmatic test. How would a defender of such a compromise as I am proposing apply his theory to concrete problems—as an Intuitionist, or as a Utilitarian? Lacking space really to meet this just pragmatic query, I can only roughly indicate the line of answer. The *subjective* motives of the Intuitionist would be respected and praised, while the *objective* purpose of the Utilitarians would be preached and enforced. When a misguided and traditional conscience conflicted with a liberal and enlightened happiness, it would be the duty of the individual to follow his conscience and the duty of society to control and educate him. Such a policy would result in many conflicts, but it would make possible the scientific clarification of ethics which is desired by the Utilitarians and would at the same time conserve those spiritual dignities and enthusiasms which are cherished by Intuitionists.

* THE GEOMETRY OF THE GOOD LIFE[1]

The account of a new law of values—the "law of increasing returns"—in accordance with which values are strengthened by concentration and weakened by diffusion, resulting in an "ethical dualism" calling for one tactic for enhancing good and an opposite tactic for diminishing evil.

HUMAN LIFE, like space itself, is possessed of length and breadth and depth, and the possible patterns of life no less than the possible solids in space have shape and structure to which geometry is applicable in something more than an idly metaphorical sense. The good life differs from the life that is mean or wasteful; and that difference is significantly analogous to a difference in geometrical structure.

All life is growth, and growth is the making actual of what is potential, the incarnation in material form and external behavior of inner and hidden possibilities. The good life is the more abundant life, the life in which the potentialities of an individual or of a society are made as rich and as numerous as possible and then realized with maximum effectiveness. The problem of ethics is not, as tradition conceives it, a problem of how to conform to taboos and commandments, be they natural or social or

1 Address delivered at the Opening Exercises of the 179th academic year of Columbia University in McMillin Academic Theatre, 28 September, 1932. Reprinted from the *Columbia University Quarterly*, December, 1932, Vol. XXIV, No. 4, pages 383–391, by permission of Columbia University Press.

even divine. It is simply the problem of *how to make the most of one's life*. Whatever the abilities or disabilities with which nature has endowed us at birth; and whatever the opportunities or limitations which environment may chance to impose, it is within the free power of each of us to make the most or the least of what his destiny offers.

Now, it goes without saying that the larger the self is in respect to the breadth of its interests, the more abundant will be its life. It is, therefore, imperative that the seeker for the good life should expand his narrower ego by including within it the interests of others. A life thus enriched through vicarious identification with other lives attains an infinite increase in its spiritual substance, and therefore possesses an infinitely greater capacity for happiness than a life from which love and service are absent and all interests restricted to the narrow confines of the material self.

Even more obvious than the duty of enlarging one's self through sympathetic inclusion of other selves is the second duty of inhibiting and repressing all interests the fulfillment of which would be incompatible with other interests more intense or more enduring. Evil is the thwarting of an interest, the defeat of an aspiration, a plan, or a bodily need. Having no appeal of its own, it derives power by associating itself with some lesser good. Temptation to evil is temptation to prefer the lesser to the greater good, and to choose the smaller gratification of the present rather than the larger gratification of the future. The false perspective of the senses makes whatever is near seem large and important. Conscience, like intelligence, corrects these distortions of sensuous propinquity and reveals facts and values in their true proportions. The search for the good life is, thus, a twofold search, partly positive and partly negative. Not merely a quest for happiness, it is also a fight against misery.

Now, it is in connection with this double aspect of the good life—its positive and its negative sides—that we are confronted with a strange law entailing consequences that are stranger still. This law is, I believe, not generally recognized; and in the remainder of my address I shall endeavor to explain it and to illustrate its curious bearings upon what I have called the "Geometry of the Good Life."

The new law to which I call your attention is the opposite of the well-known economic Law of Diminishing Returns in accordance with which increasing concentration of effort brings a decreasing proportion of material reward. In the realm of spiritual values the situation is just the reverse. Increasing concentration upon a value brings an increase in its intensity which is out of all proportion to the factors involved in its production. A great beauty is worth more than many pretties. The spiritual energies concentrated in a great devotion bring a value incomparably greater than that which the same energy would yield if scattered or dissipated in a number of small attachments. A major poet is worth more than his own weight in minor poets. And no community would be willing to exchange the genius of a Shakespeare, a Newton, or a Beethoven for even a vast number of men endowed with second- and third-rate talent. Nor should we care to substitute for a sublime monument of architecture a whole swarm of nice and comfortable buildings. This curious law in accordance with which values gain by concentration we shall call the "Law of Increasing Returns."

It is important to realize that this rule or law holds for values that are negative as well as for those that are positive. A supreme misery or agony, a crushing defeat or shame, the destruction of the central purpose of a life or of that life itself cannot be equalled in its evil by any number of small and bearable discomforts.

From this fact that our law works uniformly for good and for evil it follows that we must pursue one tactic in seeking for the goods of life and the reverse tactic in fighting against evil.

Of course, if our powers were unlimited, the maximum good life would be one in which every person had at every moment an ecstasy of happiness and in which evil of every kind was completely absent. To dream of such a theoretical maximum is, however, idle and unprofitable, a sheer waste of imagination. The world we live in is no fairyland, but the realm of a nature that is harshly unconcerned with individual happiness. And our powers of mind and heart are not unlimited, but pitifully small to cope with the environment that hems us in. The amount of unavoidable evil will always be great, and the amount of attainable good will always be small when compared with an abstract maximum. Not that maximum possible to imagination, but rather the optimum possible of attainment by good will and intelligence, should be the goal and guide of our efforts.

Given a certain quantity of potential or prospective good, and given also a certain quantity of potential or prospective evil, how can we distribute these quantities over the individual moments of a single life or over the individual members of a society in such a way as to make the evil most endurable and the good most enjoyable? In the light of our Law of Increasing Returns, the answer should be obvious and has, indeed, already been indicated. The evils of life should be scattered as broadly as possible and the goods should be concentrated and heightened. Below the zero line of indifference, evil will be spread out in a multitude of comparatively harmless ripples, each moment bearing its little share and as many individuals as possible suffering as little as possible. Above the line of neutral value the picture will be the reverse. Great ecstasies and extremes of good fortune scattered here and there with comparative inequality and discontinuity. Mountainous peaks of good above the level of neutrality, but below that level a series of uniformly widespread and therefore very slight depressions. In short, when viewed geometrically, the figure of the good life or life of optimum value is profoundly asymmetrical.

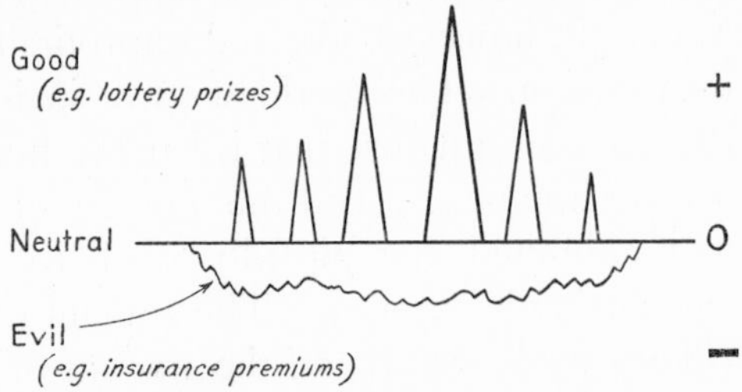

FIG. 4. THE GEOMETRY OF THE GOOD LIFE, SHOWING THE ASYMMETRY OF POSITIVE AND NEGATIVE VALUES AS BASED UPON THE LAW OF INCREASING RETURNS.

There are two social institutions that illustrate instructively this asymmetry, one very familiar and respectable, the other not so familiar and not at all respectable. I refer to the institution of Insurance and to the institution of the Lottery.

Insurance is the wise device by which we substitute for a single great pain a lot of little pains. The burning down of one's house, for example, would entail a great loss. In place of that misery or as offset to it, we substitute a whole series of small miseries, the long-drawn-out payment of our insurance premiums. The gain is obvious and great. The unbearable is replaced by the bearable. And as it is for the individual, so also is it for society. No community can be regarded as ethically mature until its catastrophic tragedies are guarded against by compulsory insurance, all of us carrying small burdens in order that none of us may be hopelessly crushed.

Now, the obverse of Insurance is the Lottery, which increases good by substituting one or a few great goods that are really worth while for many little goods so small that they hardly count. Ten million people each presented with ten cents are not thereby made particularly happy. Suppose that our philanthropist, instead of weakening his million-dollar benefaction by pulverizing it into inconsequentiality, had chosen to distribute it into a not inconsiderable number of large lumps varying in size from a hundred to a hundred thousand dollars each; you can easily see how much greater would be the volume of happiness that would ensue. Now, every community can be its own philanthropist, and by a judicious conformity to the geometry of the good life can not only minimize its suffering by insurance, but also maximize its joys through the analogous institution of the lottery. Not that the lottery is as important as insurance. For evil is usually more evil than good is good; therefore, insurance should come first. A community should make certain that misery is minimized before going in for joy. But when the many have been insured against any lack of necessities, the community may then with a clean conscience and light heart attend to the business of making the most of its luxuries by great though necessarily unequally distributed concentrations such as pertain to the lottery.

If the taxpayers of the nation realized the conditions of an optimum disbursement of their taxes, they would make a plan both wise and gay in accordance with which one-quarter of the national income would be made to suffice for the ordinary expenses of government, and one-half for universal insurance against the economic disabilities of childhood and old age, of accident, illness, and unemployment. The remaining quarter could then be expended on an annual lottery in which delightful prizes would rain down like meteors from the sky, bringing joyous excitement to all, and luxury and even wealth to their fortunate recipients. As for the many who did not win, they would have as consolation the knowledge that with comparatively little pain to themselves, they had produced comparatively great pleasure for their neighbors. And under such conditions only those very mean in spirit would begrudge to the winners the joy of their winning.

But, alas, the vital asymmetry of the geometry of values as exemplified in the twin principles of lottery and insurance is usually overlooked, and most of the maxims of traditional morality both social and personal are based on the assumption that the tactics to be employed in furthering good are the same as those to be used in hindering evil.

Consider the exhortations to be temperate, to choose the golden mean, "nothing too much" and "safety first." Here are dangerous half-truths. Temperance is well enough in the realm of negative values, the lower realm of sin and sorrow. There indeed we should walk warily, and where we cannot altogether avoid the pitfalls, we should have many small woes and peccadilloes rather than a few of great magnitude. But in the domain of positive values, the domain of joy and virtue, this golden mean is but leaden folly. The lover who tempers his love with safety and moderation, the friend or parent who tempers his loyalty and affection with canny and calculating caution, the scientists and artists who refuse to let themselves go the whole way in the quest for truth and beauty, are all foredoomed to lose the prizes of significant living.

Many of you here today are about to begin your college course, and there is no department of the good life in which the Law of Increasing Returns applies with greater accuracy than to the student life of an American college. A great number of subjects are open to your choice, all of them potential sources of delight. If you find them dull, it will be because you bring dullness with you. The danger that confronts you is not the danger of bad subjects, but the more insidious danger of too many good subjects which by their diverse attractions distract the mind and prevent significant attainment in any single line. In our collegiate and in our general cultural life, no less than in the domain of economics, we are suffering from an overproduction of good things—an overproduction that is combined with an inability to distribute to the consumers the goods that they need.

The curriculum teems with good courses; the newspapers are crowded with news of importance; the magazines of each month contain at least one article so good that if it were written in terms of the life of some ancient city in whose long buried ruins an archeologist had discovered it, it would be hailed as a classic worthy of study by generations of schoolboys. We suffer, in short, from an embarrassment of riches. The modern American college is too often a failure because it does not impart to the student anything that will stick to the ribs of his memory and retain real significance ten years after graduation. This failure is becoming more noticeable each year, and we pedagogues are accustomed to explain it by picking upon some one of the so-called extracurricular activities of students such as football or ping-pong or parties or whatever one of the lesser joys we may happen at the moment to dislike. As I see it, our failure is due, not to the diabolism of the modern youth, but rather to a simple and innocent mistake. We try to give him and he tries to take too many good things from the intellectual banquet that the college offers. The result is a potpourri, a melange, a goulash of diversified information impossible to be assimilated and therefore impossible to be remembered.

If you will but disregard all well-meaning advice to disperse your study over a wide field, and if you will take instead something like the highly unified course of study prescribed for students in the honors course at Oxford or Cambridge, then you will realize, if in no other way, the truth of the Law of Increasing Returns. And years after graduation you will find that you will know more of what you studied in college than when you were studying it. For whatever your chosen field may be, geology or German literature or mathematics or economics or any other of the many departments that are open to you, there will come a time, a magical moment in your scholastic life, when you will feel the body of concentrated, unified, and painfully acquired knowledge within you become suddenly quick and alive in its own right. From that moment your interest will lure you and tempt you to its further pursuit. You will have acquired an enthusiasm that will grow by what it feeds upon and be to you an ever mounting joy. Around that central interest as a nucleus, other interests will organize themselves, and the distractions of the college and the city, be they good or bad, will take their natural and subordinate place in the background of your life.

If, on the other hand, you pursue that will-o'-the-wisp of two generations ago, the all-round liberal education supposedly befitting a gentleman and consisting of a polite acquaintance with a dozen varied subjects, you will find after ten years that none of these acquaintances have become friends, and that most of them will have slipped altogether from your mind. Knowledge is not a continuous affair. It is discontinuous, and consists of two distinct levels. There is a lower level in which you know only enough of a subject to know whether you wish to know more of it. This lower level can be attained by listening to a few lectures or reading a few books. And in the first year of your college course you will do well to sample in this cursory fashion as many new fields as possible. Then, on the basis of that sampling, you can choose the field most congenial to your intellectual tastes and abilities, and by concentrated study in that single field you can attain the second and higher level of knowledge, where an enduring and increasing grasp of your material will draw you on without boredom or effort. Any degree of knowledge that lies in between these two levels is sheer waste. It will be more than is necessary to make an intelligent election, and less than sufficient to make the subject a significant possession of your life after graduation.

And now before closing, there is one more application of the Law of Increasing Returns to which I must call your attention. Society today stands at the crossroads, and the coming generation will probably decide for many following generations which course humanity will follow. The alternatives confronting us are clear and familiar: Capitalism and Communism. Capitalism provides the opportunity for individual initiative, variation, and experiment with tremendous rewards for success and equally tremendous punishment for failure. Communism would ensure security for all at the cost of suppressing with an iron hand individual initiative, self-interest, and responsibility.

Yet, however unattractive this alternative to capitalism may appear, some change from the present system is assuredly necessary. For, with the development of machinery, fewer and fewer workers produce more and more goods. And the fewer the workers, the fewer the buyers, for the workers are the buyers. It follows that as our production becomes more efficient, our distribution becomes less efficient, owing to the steady increase in the number of those who by reason of being unemployed are unable to buy what they need. Hence, unless something is done, we shall find the crises of overproduction with their attendant unemployment becoming ever more tragically acute.

Now, if our conception of the geometry of the good life as based on the Law of Increasing Returns is a valid conception, the way out of our present predicament is clear: not communism itself nor any uniformly applied blend of communism and individualism, but a sharp division of the economic sphere into positive and negative zones. For the negative zone of poverty and misery we shall require a thoroughgoing collectivism, but in the positive zone of prosperity and power we can retain and intensify the economics of individualism. By such benignly contrasting procedures we shall minimize the poverty of the many without restricting the riches of the few. For values gain by concentration and lose by diffusion, and to attain the optimum life for a society, as for an individual, we must minimize the evils by uniformly distributing them and maximize the good by allowing for great and unequal concentrations. No cake for anybody until there is bread for everybody. But when the majority is once securely provided with the necessities of life, the minority should be permitted whatever luxuries it may be able to achieve, whether through intrinsic merit or sheer luck.

This will mean that in evaluating proposals for the collective control of economic activity we ought carefully to distinguish between those whose intent is the control of riches and those whose intent is the control of poverty. These types of control are not, as is usually assumed, equal in value and bound up together. On the contrary, they are often separable and always contrasted, the one being desirable and the other the reverse. The control of evil is always good, while the control of good is always evil. The great society of the future will communize its poverty and capitalize its wealth. It will be radically asymmetrical, for it will conform to the geometry of the good life, in which evils are minimized by being uniformly dispersed while goods are maximized by being unequally concentrated.

I wish that you would consider carefully this idea that I have expressed awkwardly. For I believe that the Law of Increasing Returns, if faithfully obeyed, will yield the optimum of happiness, not only for us as individuals, but for that new and better community in the building of which you will participate.

24

* DEMOCRACY AT THE CROSSROADS [1]

An analysis of Liberalism, Parliamentarianism, and Capitalism as the three components of Democracy, in the light of the challenge of Totalitarianism, followed by a plan of ECONOMIC DUALISM, *by means of which the essentials of democracy could be saved.*

INTRODUCTION

OLD FAITHS are weakening today, and ideals that have long been regarded as axiomatic are rudely and confidently and effectively challenged. One of these faiths that is weakening is the faith in democracy. And the challenge to its ideals is more rather than less menacing in that it comes simultaneously from the Right and from the Left.

The democracy that is under attack and whose fate swings in the balance is not merely a form of government, but something far broader and deeper. The right of the people to rule themselves, which is the primary and literal meaning of *democracy*, has its premise in an ideal of ethics and its conclusion in a system of economics. And along with the political regime in which a parliament elected by all citizens makes laws that apply to all citizens, democracy

[1] An address delivered at the Eighth International Congress of Philosophy in Prague, September 6, 1934. Reprinted from *The International Journal of Ethics,* Vol. XLV, No. 2, January, 1935, pp. 138–169, by permission of the University of Chicago Press.

as a category comprehends the liberalism from which it was born and the capitalism into which it has grown. Both the defenders of democracy and those who attack it are, for the most part, agreed that the three phases of the concept are bound up in one another, and that parliamentarianism, liberalism, and capitalism must stand or fall together. Believing, as I do, that the enemies of democracy are growing both in number and in power, and that the arguments exposing the ineptitudes, hypocrisies, and cruelties of parliamentarianism, liberalism, and capitalism as they actually exist today are becoming clearer and stronger, I deem it no exaggeration to say that we are approaching a veritable crisis in which the democratic civilization of the Western world stands at the crossroads and must choose between radical reconstruction and total annihilation.

As to the nature of this crisis and the nature of the reconstruction that is called for, there are certain ideas which I have deeply at heart. And because they pertain to the role that philosophy can play in the situation confronting us, I venture to present them for your consideration.

1. Democracy as Parliamentarianism: Its Inefficiency and Corruption

If a nation as a whole is to enjoy independence rather than external control, and if its individual citizens are to enjoy equality of rights and opportunities, it would seem obvious that its governing body should be a parliament in which the diverse interests and beliefs of the population should be represented by delegates freely elected by the votes of all normal adult inhabitants. And it would seem equally obvious that the laws enacted by such a parliament would be an adequate expression of the national will. In such a democracy there would be no individual who could complain that his own preferences had been denied expression, and there would be no group or faction that would not be directly represented by its delegate in the parliament.

The ancient objections to this type of polity were based upon a denial of the premise of equality of rights and the universal suffrage which is the correlate of that equality. The *contemporary* opponents of democracy, however, accept for the most part and in theory the democratic ideal of an equality of rights for all citizens. But they hold that a parliament elected by the votes of the nation is misrepresentative of the will of the nation, and that its enactments, instead of expressing the fusion and fulfillment of all interests, will embody either a confusion and frustration of all, or a sly and surreptitious triumph of the more crafty and powerful at the expense of the others.

With flaming indignation at these ineptitudes and corruptions of the democratic parliament, the modern advocates of dictatorship urge the abandonment of universal suffrage and the establishment of the totalitarian state, in which a single party subject to a single leader seizes all power, and, disdaining the confusions of a popular election, rules openly and boldly by right of strength. Whether the economic object of the dictatorship is a fascistic preservation and regulation of capitalistic enterprise in the interest of a mystical *nationalism*, or whether, on the other hand, it is a communistic abolition of individual capital in the interest of a mystical *proletarianism*—there is an essential identity of political form underlying the rival philosophies of dictatorship.

As to the validity of this indictment of parliamentarianism, and as to the justice of the substitute that is proposed, any reasonably adequate discussion of the issue here would be, of course, impossible. Instead of attempting it, I shall offer only a simple confession of faith.

Men are obviously unequal in ability and in virtue; and, in the face of these undeniable differences, to grant to each an equal voice in determining the affairs of all appears to be an absurdity. Why should a nation be governed by its mediocre average rather than by its best? Why, indeed? But this objection to democracy, so clearly expressed by Plato and so deeply believed by the defenders of aristocracy in every age, has ceased to be an effective menace to parliamentary government. And the reason that it has ceased is that there is no clear and generally acceptable way of discovering the true *aristoi*, the superior minority to whom the powers of leadership should obviously be intrusted. In default of a better, or less arbitrary, criterion of the right to power, the criterion of popularity as attested at the polls has forced its way to acceptance. The actual and practicable alternative to government by a majority is not government by the admittedly best, but government by a minority which would merely claim to be the best, in the face of opinion to the contrary by most of us.

Loving democracy as I do and believing firmly in its ultimate validity, I nevertheless feel that the indictment brought against the present type of democratic parliament possesses so many elements of logical and ethical strength that we are faced with the choice between complete surrender to the totalitarians and fundamental reconstruction of our own system. To attain the reconstruction that appears to me both necessary and possible, we should begin by admitting humbly and frankly that diffusion of power means diffusion of responsibility, and that diffusion of political responsibility in a capitalistic world has for its all but inevitable consequence either a paralyzing inefficiency or a creeping corruption—or, indeed, both of these together.

If a group of explorers in the wilderness were to be of two minds as to whether a bottomless chasm confronting them could or could not be crossed by each man leaping with all his strength, and if by a democratic parliamentary method the group should decide on a compromise to consist of each leaping mildly or with half his strength, the result would be sufficiently tragic and ludicrous. But often there is almost as much of the ludicrous or tragic in the gray and compromising decisions with which a modern parliament decides issues in which a "yes" or a "no," a black or a white, are the only significant alternatives. Parliamentary diffusion of responsibility and power can be avoided only by concentrating power and responsibility in a single leader or in a comparatively small group whose decisions shall be final. To this extent we should, indeed, have a dictatorship rather than a democratic parliament acting for the nation. There is, however, a second principle of the philosophy of dictatorship which both by its friends and its enemies is all too often assumed to follow as a corollary from the first. This alleged corollary of a concentration of governmental power is that such power shall be virtually unlimited, both in its *extent* and in its *duration.*

Now, in my opinion it is just by refusing to grant to any dictator this second dimension of power, and by retaining in the hands of the people or their representatives in parliament the right to decide upon the general character of the issues and the particular length of time during which its leader shall act, that a nation can preserve its essential democracy and at the same time enjoy without danger the admitted advantages of an effective dictatorship.

It is my contention that any nation can meet successfully the grave indictment brought against the institution of parliamentary democracy by the proponents of the totalitarian state by thus delegating dictatorial powers strictly limited in duration and in extent to an elected leader.

The sort of dual regime which I am proposing is, of course, familiar enough in the emergency of war. For when the crisis confronting a nation is sufficiently acute, the most democratic of parliaments will realize the necessity of delegating its powers temporarily to a smaller and more unified body than itself.

In my own country, suffering from an economic depression of unprecedented severity, the federal Congress, though quite as jealous as any other parliament of its constitutional prerogatives, has not hesitated to delegate to its democratically elected leader, President Roosevelt, many of its own powers. To the extent to which this has been done we have gained the effective unity of direction and centralized responsibility of a dictatorship, without in any way surrendering the hard-won rights of a free people.

I believe that this new mode of incarnating the will of the country as a whole in a single leader and his chosen advisors should be adopted more and more, not merely as the exceptional but as the normal method of all genuinely democratic governments. The kind of dictatorship thus ensuing would be a loan rather than a gift, and a supplement to parliament rather than a substitute for it. Indeed, so far from suffering an eclipse and becoming a mere appendage to the will of a tyrant, a parliament which should delegate many of its powers to a leader of its choice would become more important than the kind of parliament now existing. For, however often the loan was renewed, it would still be a loan, and its continuance would be subject to the good behavior of the leader as judged by the people and their representatives. Under such an elective dictatorship it goes without saying that instead of censorship and suppression of the organs of public opinion, there would be an absolute necessity for their complete and unrestricted freedom. For by such freedom and by it alone could the nation be assured that its own will was truly expressed in the will of its leader.

II. Democracy as Liberalism: Its Hypocrisy and Futility

"Justice is the interest of the stronger," exclaims Thrasymachus. And in that ancient utterance the case against liberalism is epitomized. For liberalism is a dual faith: faith, on the one hand, in the power of the human mind to discover by trial and error, and by individual reason and experiment, ideals that are universally valid; and faith, on the other hand, in the power of the human heart and will to respond to those ideals with disinterested devotion.

If justice in a society is always and merely the interest of stronger individuals or of a stronger class, then its claim to be an ideal discovered by disinterested inquiry and responded to with disinterested devotion is made invalid. If there is no right except might, we must resign ourselves to the cynical belief that so-called ideals are merely disguises in which the interests of one part of a community are masked in order to triumph more effectively over the interests of the others.

From Protagoras and Thrasymachus to Machiavelli, and from Machiavelli to Marx and Pareto, the attacks upon liberalism have been many and bitter. And from Socrates to Mazzini and John Stuart Mill, and from these in turn to the three great presidents of our own day, Wilson, Franklin Roosevelt, and Masaryk, the faith in ideals and their efficacy has been stoutly defended.

At present it would seem that the forces of attack were in the ascendant, and that liberals were losing their faith and accepting, however reluctantly, the doctrine of *Real-Politik.*

There are many who will feel that there is a certain propriety in the present trend, and that at the worst it is an inevitable consequence of the dialectic of history. Must not philosophy follow theology into the limbo of things outgrown? And should not the "twilight of the gods" be succeeded by a *twilight of ideals?* There is, however, a great difference between the two passings. For when faith in the gods was lost, however tragic that loss may have been, there was at least left the faith in man. But if man is to lose faith in himself and in the integrity of his own mind and will, then there is nothing of real value to remain. The whole enterprise of human culture is reduced to the level of a blind and beastlike struggle of force against force.

What is the reason for this waning of hope in the possibility of disinterested action? And by what method, if any, is it possible to prevent the imminent death of what is called liberalism?

The answers to both questions are as easy and clear as their applications are difficult and obscure. Liberals are losing ground because they have not practiced what they preached. And the cure for the sickness is in the removal of its cause. Ideals that are more honored in the breach than in the observance cease to be assets and become liabilities. Imagine the spectacle of liberal philosophers marching complacently in front of the bread lines of a starving world and praising in chorus the eternal truths of "liberty," "equality," and "fraternity"! Their words would be a shame and a hissing, not because they were false, but because they were true. For truths of an ethical nature demand actualization. And the greater their truth, the greater and sterner is the demand for such actualization. The right to praise an ideal is a right that should be earned. To see the better and follow the worse is *sin*—and that is a person's own business. But to boast of the better and sanction the worse is *insolence*—and should be publicly resented. If liberalism is to die, it will die at the hands of the very liberals who praise it in words at the same time that they betray it in deeds.

It was a favorite teaching of William James that one should never indulge in the luxury of a high and generous emotion without paying some price, however small, in the form of an actual good deed. Without such a price, the fine sentiment will become a mechanism of escape from duty, a drug for conscience, and an anodyne for the wholesome pain of pity. Whether or not it be true that "religion is the opium of the people," it is assuredly true that the lip service to ideals of social justice in which so many of us liberal philosophers delight to indulge is opium for our spirit and certain to bring doom to our guild and death and oblivion to that high tradition which we, as descendants, however unworthy, of Socrates and of Plato, are sworn to uphold.

To warn of the danger to the individual soul of indulging in empty idealism was, as we have said, the work of William James. If we turn from that leader of the past to the leader of American philosophy today, we find in the work of John Dewey an application of the same thought, but directed to the social rather than to the individual function of ethical idealism. Impressed by the divorce of abstract ideals from concrete practice so tragically attested by history, Dewey has devoted his life to the integration of these two sides of experience. And in many different connections he has urged the necessity of reinterpreting our *aspirations* in the light of our *applications*.

Ideals that cannot be implemented cannot endure. *And the challenge of today to the philosophy of today is to supplement reason with intelligence and abstract enthusiasm with concrete achievement.* If this task proves too difficult for the powers of liberals, then liberalism itself will "pass in music out of sight" and be replaced by the harsh and disillusioned struggle for power which we call by the name of *Real-Politik*.

Ideals must be implemented or die, but in what domain of cultural life is the demand for that implementation most urgent? Without any doubt it is in the domain of economics. There, more than anywhere else, has our civilization failed to make real its boasted ideals of liberty and equality for all. Let us turn, then, to the third phase of our subject and consider the system of capitalism in which democracy has attained a melancholy and momentous culmination.

III. Democracy as Capitalism: The Three Stages of the Industrial Revolution

In its abstract essence, capitalism is the system in which all members of a community have equal rights and equal opportunities to do what they will with the property that they own. It is self-rule or democracy in the field of economics, and the liberty which it seems to provide for individual initiative and variation should guarantee to every man the fruit of his labor and ability. Moreover, not only individual justice but social progress should ensue. For in a system of economic Darwinism the free competitive struggle for existence between various industrial ideals and undertakings might well be expected to bring a survival of the fittest and a consequent evolution of human happiness through human control over nature.

When we turn from this conception of capitalism in the abstract to a consideration of capitalism in the concrete, the contrast between the two pictures is painful.

What is called the Industrial Revolution is the outcome of applying material science to the satisfaction of human needs; and it consists in the substitution of machines for hand tools. The machines are vastly more productive than the hand tools which they replace; and by reason of their size and cost they can be owned and controlled only by the capitalists who have used their savings to build them, and not by the laborers who work at them. The owners of the machines divide the product into wages paid to the workers and profits retained for themselves, as compensation for the capital which they have risked.

This Industrial Revolution and the capitalistic system in which it is embodied and expressed exhibit three successive, but overlapping, stages. The first stage is a sort of golden age in which all classes in the community benefit. An enterprise is started with somebody's savings. Those who are employed in it get more as wages than they were previously making by working for themselves, otherwise they would not have accepted the employment. The profits received by the employer justly compensate him for his foresight and his skill and for the risk which he underwent. These profits are proportional to the satisfaction of the public with the goods produced, and thus furnish an automatic and objective measure of the value of the enterprise. Nobody has lost and everyone has gained.

Upon this first stage of capitalism there supervenes a second stage that is by no means so pleasant. The vast increase in wealth resulting from the substitution of machinery for hand tools results in an even greater increase in the population. And while the rich become richer and many of the poor become rich, there exists in ever increasing numbers a surplus of workers who must bid against one another for the means of life. The freedom of the laborer to sell his labor to an employer for more than he could make by working for himself degenerates into a tragic compulsion to seek a master. For in a developed capitalism and a thoroughly industrialized society, those who control the machines have absolute mastery of those who must find work at the machines or starve.

It is, of course, true that as the number of workers increases, the number of new enterprises to absorb their labor increases also. But the tragedy consists in the fact that the latter increase is less rapid than the former. If there were ten jobs to every nine applicants, the workers could more or less dictate their terms; but when, as is almost always the case, there are ten applicants for every nine jobs, the workers must take whatever they can get, and fight with one another even for that. In this situation the only hope for the laborers lies in banding together in unions and so creating artificially a partial monopoly of their labor which enables them to bargain collectively and on something like equal terms with their employers.

In lieu of a natural scarcity of labor caused by war, famine, pestilence, or a quite utopian degree of birth control, the artificial monopoly produced by the trade union is in general the workers' only alternative to virtual slavery. And it is this system of a capitalism ameliorated and complicated by trade-unionism which during the past hundred years has spread over a large part of the world. Having a thousand varied forms, it is in essence everywhere the same. Tremendously effective in the production of material comforts, many of which are available for everybody, it is also productive of the most obscene contrasts in human living: vulgar riches and irresponsible power for the few, with grinding poverty and degrading dependence for the many. And through it all we find an ominously growing sense of class antagonism and prospective social revolution.

This is the system under which we live, and it is too familiar to us to call for further comment.

Less familiar, and hence more interesting, is that third stage of the Industrial Revolution, which is now supervening upon the second as the second supervened on the first. These superventions, as we remarked before, are not substitutions but supplementations. The first stage of capitalism continues after the second has come; and both the second and the first continue along with the third stage which we are now entering. In this new stage a new variable begins to dominate the situation. It is the *increase in technical efficiency of production.* Though present and operating from the very beginning of the machine age, it has until recently been relatively unimportant because, as the methods of manufacture improved, the markets expanded rapidly enough to absorb the new goods. When some new invention made it possible for an employer to produce an equal or even a greater quantity of goods with only half the number of workers, the men no longer wanted were turned off, and they were the only ones to suffer, for sooner or later the fortunate capitalist would use his increased profits to start a new enterprise in which more workers could find jobs, and so what is called technological unemployment could cure itself with no loss to the community other than the suffering of the old workers who had been turned off by reason of the new invention.

Recently, however, the improvements in machinery have been increasing more rapidly than the increase of new markets, with the result that vast quantities of goods accumulate in the warehouses. These goods, however much they are needed, cannot be sold because the only ones who could buy them are the workers who are employed in producing them. And as the proportion of workers grows less, the proportion of buyers grows less, for *the workers are the buyers*—and without employment and the money it brings, they cannot buy the goods that are produced in such tragic abundance. But this is not all. For when the laborers, by reason of unemployment, are unable to make purchases, the manufacturers are unable to make sales, so that not only the proletariat but the middle classes and finally even the rich and the very rich are brought to the verge of ruin.

As the production of goods grows more efficient, the distribution and consumption of goods grow less efficient.

This is the new and terrible law of a capitalist economy in an age of machinery, and by it other laws are quite overshadowed. It is responsible for the well-known and universally recognized spectacle of *starvation in the midst of plenty*—not merely tragedy, but unnecessary tragedy—tragedy combined with absurdity.

Now, theoretically or in the abstract, there are two perfectly good remedies for the crisis. First: an expansion of markets, both external and internal, by means of which the surplus of workers would be put to work at new enterprises and thus get money to buy the surplus of goods. And, second, a shortening of working hours which would spread employment over a larger number of workers. The trouble with the first of these remedies is just the fact that improvements in efficiency of production seem to increase faster and increasingly faster than the expansion of markets. The trouble with the second remedy is that there is an all but irresistible reluctance on the part both of the employers and of the more ambitious of their employees to forego, by a shortening of hours and a sharing of jobs, the greater profits and higher wages that in any single industry are made possible by improved methods of making goods.

The result is the above-mentioned "starvation in the midst of plenty"—an economic paradox which is as absurd as it is tragic, and as inevitable as it is widespread and familiar.

The first stage of the Industrial Revolution is the stage in which both the workers and the capitalists derive benefit. The second stage is one in which the capitalists benefit and the workers lose. In the third stage not only the workers but even the capitalists themselves tend to lose. And the system as a whole appears doomed by its intrinsic nature to a complete collapse.

In the democratic countries today the majority of both

laymen and experts probably still believe that the depression from which we are suffering is only a transitory phase of the business cycle, a crisis from which the world will emerge successfully.

But there are others, and their numbers are growing, who believe as I do that technological unemployment is destined to increase at a rate too fast for new enterprises to absorb it, and that this depression, so far from being a transitory crisis, may turn out to be a chronic condition that is incurable by the operation of purely economic factors.

Those of us who feel in this way look naturally to some kind of governmental action as the only means of escape.

IV. Fascism and Socialism as Alternatives

If *laissez faire* is to be abandoned and government is to intervene, there are two forms which the intervention may take, socialistic and fascistic. Under socialism private capital is abolished; under fascism, it is regulated. Each form of governmental intervention has a democratic and an anti-democratic variety. Democratic or Fabian socialism would possess and administer the nation's property by orderly parliamentary methods. Bolshevistic or anti-democratic socialism would achieve this economic revolution by direct action and dictatorship. Now, regardless of whether one's feelings toward communism are strongly sympathetic or violently hostile, I think it must be admitted that, both as to its tactic and as to its goal, it is gaining over its more democratic rival. If self-interest and desire for private profit are to be given up as the primary incentives to economic life, then force and a more or less militaristic compulsion must take their place. *Some of the people all of the time and all of the people some of the time* are capable of rising to heights of unselfish service, and of doing even harder work for the love of comrades than for the love of self. *But most of the people most of the time*, pursuing their dull routine jobs and no longer lifted out of themselves by the heroic enthusiasm of war or revolution, tend to lapse into an indifference that is wasteful and perhaps corrupt. This comparative inefficiency of bureaucratic enterprise will be admitted even by socialists. Now, I believe that what is true of socialism is true also of fascism. The gentler and more democratic form must either fail or evolve into the sterner and admittedly undemocratic. The governmental regulation of capital, which is fascism, no less than the governmental ownership of capital, which is socialism, cannot succeed by halfway measures. In either case there must be regimentation and tyrannous control of individual rights and liberties; in short, dictatorship. I say this the more regretfully because the present policy of my own country, the "New Deal" as we term it, would seem to be a kind of "Fabian fascism" in which by democratic methods and in a spirit of good will the government through various bureaucratic agencies attempts gently to regulate those wages and prices in industry which when left to themselves had brought us to the verge of ruin.

But despite the high courage and vision of our leader, we are facing a situation disconcertingly similar to the prohibition policy which we have recently abandoned. It is a situation in which the less scrupulous industrialists refuse to conform to the codes that are established in the interest of all. And we may well be compelled in the near future to decide whether to abandon the new controls or to stiffen and enforce them by an army of spies and inquisitors. The latter alternative would take us perilously close to that fascism which our sincerely democratic President would desire at any cost to avoid.

The seemingly obvious cure for such a situation, and the unemployment entailed by it, is to enforce shorter and shorter hours to the end that the number of workers should be increased. But, as we have already seen, this creates the situation in which the more ambitious workers would be strongly tempted to conspire with the employer to work, let us say, six hours a day rather than four; they to get more wages, he to get more profits, and only the feeble force of democratically chosen bureaucrats to restrain for the good of the whole this strong and steady drive of self-interest by parts of the whole. In all such conflicts between economic self-interest and political restraint, the former is bound to win and the latter is bound to be corrupted and defeated, unless, indeed, it consents to abandon its democratic form and becomes a thoroughgoing fascistic dictatorship.

If our diagnosis is correct and if capitalism is doomed to die from the self-contradiction which grows and gnaws like a cancer within its body, we would seem to be faced with the necessity of abandoning the democracy which we love and choosing either the dictatorship that is fascism or the dictatorship that is communism. For capitalism, with all its evils, is the embodiment of democracy in economic form, and if the rights and liberties of private property are to be abolished in favor of bureaucratic ownership or bureaucratic regulation by the state, then those other rights and liberties which constitute the essence of human personality and without which the human individual would be degraded to the status of a bee in a hive or a cog in a machine, must be abolished also.

V. Economic Dualism: The Way of Escape

Permit me to suggest to you a way of escape, a plan which, if wholeheartedly adopted, would not only lead us out of the present depression and keep us from similar depressions in the future, but would preserve the essential features of our political, cultural, and economic democracy.

This plan is, in the first place, a substitute for the plans of all those who favor revolution, be they communists or be they fascists. It is, in the second place, a substitute for the halfway revolution of those who favor the so-called "planned economy" in which business and industry are to be half controlled and half uncontrolled by governmental interference. And, finally, the plan I have in mind, in spite of its far-flung implications, is, I believe, comparatively simple and practicable, capable of being understood by everyone and worked for by everyone, regardless of ultimate differences in economic or political creed.

Let us begin with a question: Why should private charity or public doles ever be given to enable the unemployed to live in idleness, when it is work rather than idleness they desire? It seems a pity to go to great expense to give people something that they do not really want. The public should support the unemployed in idleness only if there appears to be no other way of helping them. Now, ordinarily, when a man works, he works either for himself or for a capitalist who profits by hiring him. In an age of machinery and of specialized industry there are few individuals other than farmers who can work for themselves; and as for the second alternative of working for an employer, the essence of a depression is just that there are no employers who can profit by hiring the men who are unemployed. There is, however, a third way in which men can work. If no one will hire them to work, and if as individuals they cannot work for themselves, *why not have them working for one another?* This third way of working will, to be sure, bring no profits to anybody in money. For the unemployed have nothing to pay to one another—nothing, that is, except the goods that they can by mutual aid succeed in producing. But that kind of nothing is a very great deal. For what men really need is not money, but the goods that money will buy. And when these goods can be attained without money, the money itself becomes superfluous.

If this very simple analysis is sound, it would seem obvious that the way to cure unemployment in a capitalistic society is to provide means and opportunity for the superfluous workers to support one another. There are many ways in which this can be done.

In England there are village communities under the management of those ubiquitous doers of wise and kindly deeds, the Quakers; and in these communities the means and instruments of small-scale production are put at the disposal of unemployed workers. And in my country during the years of the depression there have sprung up a great many organizations of unemployed men and women who exchange with one another their services and the goods produced by those services. Some of these organizations are completely self-sustaining, others are helped by private agencies, still others—and their number is fortunately increasing—are initiated and managed by the government.

In spite of the great service which these associations have rendered during the last few years, there is about all of them an inevitable looseness and diffusion of responsible direction that would work against their becoming adequate to care for the very large numbers of those who may be expected to remain unemployed even when the present depression has passed.

To what extent the present number of unemployed can be reduced by developing new markets, both foreign and domestic, and by the movement for shorter hours and sharing jobs, or, on the other hand, to what extent it may be increased by the remorseless advance in technology with its replacement of men by machines, the future alone will decide. But whether the number of the permanently unemployed be greater or less than it is now, it will in any event be far too large to be dealt with adequately by the loose and temporary associations for self-support that have ameliorated the distress of our recent emergency.

The only permanently adequate means by which mutual self-support on a large scale could be achieved would be by organizing communities under the management of paid experts. In such communities all who desired could enlist, as in the army, for a minimum period of service, at the end of which they would have the option of re-enlisting or of seeking employment in private industry. To be really successful, these communities, instituted and managed at the expense of the government, would need to be conducted in accordance with three basic principles—at least two of which would differentiate them sharply from the multitudes of co-operative communities, both those purely commercial and those organized for some idealistic or utopian purpose which have been tried in the past and which (with the exception of certain strictly religious and monastic societies) have always failed or dissolved for one reason or another.

These three principles for our proposed communities are the principles (1) of economic insulation, (2) of communistic or egalitarian sharing of material goods, and (3) of dictatorship or direction by experts in whom power and responsibility would be vested. Let us consider these principles in turn.

1. *Economic insulation.*—Whenever it is proposed that the taxpayer's money be used by the government to put the unemployed to work producing goods, there are protests by the private manufacturers, farmers, and merchants who object to the government as a competitor, especially at a time like the present when the market is glutted with a surplus of unsalable goods.

One has only to consider the tragic plight of American agriculture to realize how preposterous it would be to organize government farms to produce crops of which there are already too great an abundance. And to other kinds of production by the government of goods for sale there would be the same kind of objection.

The second group who look with suspicion on schemes for putting the unemployed to work with government money are the labor unions. For here we are confronted with a dilemma: Either the wages to be paid would bankrupt the government or they would be less than the union standard. In the latter case, the hard-won wage level will be in danger of being permanently lowered. It was only by overriding the protests of responsible leaders of the American Federation of Labor that the otherwise beneficial plan of President Roosevelt for organizing the unemployed in an industrial army for afforestation and other similar work was passed by Congress.

It is because of this reasonable opposition from business and labor that it would be necessary to apply our first principle of economic insulation to the plan for organizing the unemployed for permanent large-scale production. This would mean that the goods made by the unemployed would be consumed by the unemployed and not permitted to be sold in the open market. There would, thus, be no profits accruing to the government at the expense of private business. And as there would be no profit, so also there would be no wage—either at the union level or at any lower level. In lieu of wages there would be rations given to the workers from the goods that they themselves produced. The communities would, thus, be as nearly as possible self-contained and autonomous, resulting in no demoralization either of wages or of prices. This complete insulation of goods would not necessitate a corresponding insulation of the community workers from the general society surrounding them. Like members of the army, they would be lodged and fed by themselves, but in their leisure time they would be free to interchange visits with their friends outside.

2. *Communism or Egalitarianism.*—The proposed communities should be communes in which the goods produced should be distributed equally, or in proportion to the needs rather than to the abilities of all members in good standing. In the outside world of capitalistic enterprise, the dominant motive is the desire for private profit. *To each according to his abilities and his luck; and from each according to his need for the job.* There is much to be said in favor of that system and much to be said against it. For better or for worse, it is the system to which all capitalistic countries are committed. Now, the proposed communities for the unemployed are to be islands of refuge from that world of competition. They will contain those who, for one reason or for another, have turned out to be unsuited or who feel themselves to be unsuited to the environment of business enterprise. There would be no point in duplicating that environment within the communities. The workers there are to receive goods rather than money, and it would be out of keeping with the spirit of the new community life to penalize the weaker members by giving them less in the way of the necessities of food, shelter, and clothing than those who physically or mentally were more fortunately endowed. As long as the workers did the best they could, they should be entitled to share equally in the collective product.

If the motive of private profit is to be eliminated from the communes, its place must be taken by those other motives stressed by socialists of all ages. The love of work for its own sake, the desire for the esteem of one's comrades and the fear of their disesteem, the ambition to excel and to receive the greater responsibility and power that recognized excellence will bring: these incentives will go far to call out the best efforts of which men are capable. With the finer characters, they would probably be even more effective than the incentive of private profit. With the baser sort of person, however, they would be far less potent and would need to be supplemented by definite disciplinary organization and control.

3. *Dictatorship.*—Centralized control from above would be a fundamental requisite in the communes not only for the reason just mentioned, but because of the very nature of modern industry. Machines require the direction of experts. A great power house with its highly technical complexities is no more suited to the democratic methods of town meeting or parliament than is a ship in a storm or an army in a battle. If the communes are to be managed at all, they must be managed by experts, by men who understand the mechanisms of industry and the manner of their direction and operation. And not only would the management of the separate industrial enterprises be a job for technicians or engineers, but the co-ordinating and uniting of them into a single industrial organism would also be a job for engineers, or at least for men of the engineering type of mind. It would, in any event, be an absurdity to intrust that sort of power to the workers themselves—the more so when we remember that the latter will consist of men and women who, whatever their intrinsic talent, will hardly be likely to possess on the average any great degree of managerial ability.

The fact that the communes were managed by experts and were to that extent dictatorships rather than democracies would not, of course, preclude the worker's viewpoint from being represented by councils chosen by the workers themselves. There would, moreover, be plenty of opportunity for the more able and responsible workers to rise to positions of power and to participate in the management of affairs to whatever extent the official controllers might regard as appropriate. It would be the prospect of this greater power and responsibility, rather than the prospect of larger material reward, that would operate as an incentive and make a strong appeal to the self-interest of the members of the communes. But the material rewards themselves, though shared in common and not depending on competition, would be a very tangible inducement to the workers to do their best. The knowledge that no one outside the communes would profit from their labor, and that they themselves would receive the entire product, would lend a continuing zest to the work and effectively differentiate it both from the productive work performed for the benefit of the private employer or even for the government, and from the unproductive work of an army training camp.

The simplest type of commune, and the one involving the least expense to the government, would be a farm on which the unemployed would be given clothing, shelter, and the opportunity to produce their food. This simple agricultural commune could easily be expanded to include on a moderate scale various essential industries so that most of the necessities and some of the comforts of life could be produced by the members of each commune for themselves. But while the communes could be started in this simple manner, we might hope that something quite different and far superior would soon replace the small self-supporting unit.

Modern industry is machine industry, and its extraordinary efficiency involves specialization and mass production. If our proposed system of communal production is to enjoy the advantages of modern technology, the communes must be *interdependent* rather than *autonomous*, and each must specialize and operate on a large scale some one of the basic industries to the end that the specialized products of each commune can be exchanged for those of the others. In this way, and in this way only, would it be possible to build within a capitalistic society a chain of communes dependent upon one another and sufficing for one another. We should then have a dual economy—two completely independent economic systems, a *fascistic communism* within a *democratic capitalism.* Each system would be economically and industrially insulated from the other, but there would be no social or physical barriers, and all citizens would be free to choose whichever system they thought would suit them and at stated periods to change from one to the other.

There is, so far as I can see, but one grave objection to the economic dualism here proposed. It is an objection, not logical, but psychological, consisting in the all but universal prejudice in favor of monism rather than dualism. It does not occur to people that it is not necessary to choose either all black or all white or all of some compromise gray. Or if there does occur the thought of a twofold system, the black for those who need black and white for those who want white, that thought is rejected as unworthy of serious consideration. Those who desire the entire social system to be capitalistic will dispute with those who desire it to be communistic. And, though in violent opposition to each other, they will agree in thinking that society must choose between their views or accept some uniformly applied compromise in which the weak points of each extreme would be blended.

Yet such attitudes, despite their almost universal prevalence, are wrong. And the reason they are wrong is that the surplus of goods enjoyed by the rich and the deficit of goods suffered by the poor are not simple mathematical opposites, but qualitatively different conditions requiring qualitatively different treatments. Friends gambling with their surplus of money can have a pleasant party. Those same friends gambling for one another's vital necessities make as ugly a spectacle as can be imagined. A regime that is appropriate to an economy of surplus is tragically inappropriate to an economy of deficit. To make unemployed and starving men wait upon the fluctuations of capitalistic business is shameful. They should be cared for and their necessities assured by any society that claims to be civilized. Especially is this true today, when not even the most conservative economist will deny that with our modern industrial technique we could produce more than enough to give every human being alive a decent minimum of subsistence. The trouble is, as we have said, that under capitalism the adequacy of distribution falls increasingly behind the adequacy of production, with the result that more and more is given to those that already have, while from those that have not is taken away even that which they had. For these less fortunate ones, communism is the only means by which their bitter need can be satisfied. But it does not at all follow from this that communism should be made universal. Capitalism, with all its manifest advantages, can be perfectly well retained for the benefit of the fortunate minority and for the progress of society as a whole. In short, what the situation demands is not a single economic system, capitalistic or communistic, but an economic dualism in which capitalism for those who can afford it is accompanied by communism for those who need it.

How would the standard of living in the communes compare with the standards of the capitalistic world? Only the experiment itself can answer the question definitely; but, prior to the actual test, we can be reasonably certain of the lower and the upper limits between which the results would lie.

At the worst, the standard of living in the communes would be no lower than in military barracks. There would be the bare necessities of life and a minimum of education and recreation. And even at that low level, the communes might be a considerable strain on the taxpayers. Yet even this most pessimistic prospect would be an improvement upon what we have now. For it would be less of an evil to have the unemployed working inefficiently and under clumsy and expensive supervision than for them to be, as at present, supported in idleness and by a combination of private and public charity. No matter how badly they were managed, the communes could not fail to be partly self-supporting; and partial self-support is less demoralizing, even if not less expensive, than the enforced parasitism of life on the dole.

If we turn from the lowest level of what might be hoped for to the highest level and the most optimistic prospect, we find ourselves confronted with the roseate pictures painted by the advocates of technocracy. According to those utopian engineers, we are assured that in an industrial society under a dictatorship of technicians, with every adult compelled to do exactly the work that the chief engineer and his general staff decided to be best for the general welfare, the material prosperity would be so extraordinary that each inhabitant would enjoy a standard of living equal to what now requires $20,000 a year to attain. And we are further informed that this luxury could be obtained by an annual output of only 660 hours of work by each of the adult workers. Thus, for something like four hours a day, four days in the week, ten months in the year, a person would be a cog in the industrial machine with no more freedom than a robot; but for the remaining nine-tenths of his time, he would be as free as air and could devote himself to science, art, philosophy, religion, or sheer play and sheer idleness, according to his fancy.

Life in the chain of communes that we are proposing would be somewhere in between this technocratic paradise and the dreary barracks that would define the communes at their worst. There is, as we have said, no way of deciding, in advance of the actual trial, just how near to the one or the other of these extremes the truth would be found.

The technocrats are enthusiasts, and though they claim to speak with the authority of engineers and on the basis of data carefully gathered and scientifically analyzed, yet there can be little doubt that their claims are wildly exaggerated. Shall we say that they have magnified the practical possibilities of efficiency in a system of directed industrial production to double or treble or even to ten times what might reasonably be expected? Let us go to a fantastic extreme of safety and assume that they have been guilty of a fortyfold exaggeration, and have overstated their case by 4,000 per cent; and that, instead of $20,000 worth of wealth to be enjoyed during the year by each member working 16 hours a week for ten months, there would be only one-fortieth of that amount. In that case the workers in the communes would get the equivalent, in the goods they had produced, of only $500 a year. To allow for such a fortyfold exaggeration on the part of the technocrats is to employ a larger *coefficient of mendacity* than the sternest reactionary has ever felt it necessary to use in discounting the claims of the wildest radical. Yet, even with this absurd underestimate, we can see what incredible improvement would come to any country if all of its inhabitants who were unemployed could be assured of the equivalent of $500 a year by enlisting in a commune and working obediently for only 16 hours a week under the direction of the experts in control.

Let us keep in mind that in return for the discipline to be undergone by the members of the communes there would be several most important compensations. In addition to the absence of poverty, there would be an absence of the fear of poverty—and to many if not all human beings the fear of suffering is more disrupting than the suffering itself. There would, to be sure, be an absence of riches as well as of poverty, but that would bring with it a freedom from the preoccupation with wealth which is often as disruptive of character as the fear of poverty is disruptive of peace.

With but 16 working hours to the week, there would be much more leisure for recreation and for the pursuit of one's favorite avocation than is usually available in the hurly-burly of the capitalistic world.

Family life could go on in the communes quite as well and far more securely than in our present society. There would be provision for education—compulsory for children and optional for adults. And, finally, for the zest of competition between individuals for wealth, there would be substituted what the Russians call "socialistic competition"—the unmalicious rivalry of the communes with one another, each striving to excel in the co-operative enterprise of producing for the common good.

What would be the effect of the communes upon the capitalistic world within which they would exist as islands of refuge in a stormy sea? Would capitalistic production and distribution be interfered with by the presence in the same country of communist production and communist distribution? Of one part of the answer we can be sure. If the two systems of economy were economically insulated the one from the other, there need be no interference. Each society would carry on for itself, producing and distributing in its own way. Private manufacturers and merchants would have no cause to complain that the government supported by their taxes was competing with them in business. This much I think is clear; but in one very important respect the new capitalism would differ from that which we have today. It would have to function *without the whip of hunger*. Workers would no longer, as at present, be confronted with the alternatives of accepting whatever wage was offered or else sinking into the abyss of jobless poverty. There would always be open to them the opportunity of enlisting in the communes. Hence, the capitalist employer, if he wanted men to work for him, would have to offer them enough to make it worth their while. He could exploit the ambition of his workers and even their greed, but he could not exploit their terror or their misery. Perhaps the capitalist system could not survive without the threat of starvation for its workers. In that case, it does not deserve to survive. But if, on the other hand, it can survive in a society from which poverty and insecurity have been banished, then it does deserve to survive. In either case, what ought to be would be.

I myself believe that capitalism, even when deprived of its poisonous power to injure and oppress, would be able to continue. We are so overwhelmed today by the evils of capitalism as it is that we tend to forget the advantages of capitalism as it might be. Let us remember, then, that in its ideal intent the capitalist system is the system in which every individual is free to do his own stuff and take his own risk, his failure or success to be determined automatically by the worth of his enterprise, that worth to be empirically proved by the demand for his goods rather than estimated a priori by a body of officials.

Who of us is not glad that the two obscure mechanics, Wilbur and Orville Wright, were able to save their pennies and build their weird machine and then try it out at Kitty Hawk and so give the world that gift of flight for which it had waited vainly from the mythical days of Daedalus? Suppose that instead of what did happen under capitalism, it had been necessary for those brothers to go, caps in hand, before a body of bureaucratic officials, even the best you can imagine, and say to them: "So please you, Comrade Commissars, we pray you to grant us out of the communal resources the means to build a flying machine." To such a plea we can hear the reply of our competent and conscientious technocratic commissars. "Go back, dear boys, to the repairing of bicycles, for which you have shown yourselves fitted, and do not ask us to waste the sacred collective resources of the comrades in trying out the experiments of those who are without training or reputation in science."

Admiration for the communistic philosophy must not make us forget that the basic law of progress is opportunity to vary, to change, to experiment with new things. Throughout the human world and throughout the vast subhuman world from which humanity emerged, every upward step a group has made began with some individual variation. No orthodoxy is so broad but that it started as a heterodoxy whose starter or founder was in a minority of one. The variation may be a new tooth or claw in an animal, or it may be a new article of commerce tried out by some ambitious huckster. Or it may be a new religion, a new scientific hypothesis or invention—one success to a thousand failures, but that one destined perhaps to initiate a new epoch. It is a priceless thing, this freedom, and in the economic field it is the system of *laissez faire* that seeks to provide it. Capitalistic enterprise, granting all its raucous din and waste and all the deep vulgarity of its high-pressure salesmanship and advertising, to say nothing of the cheating and chicanery that must forever accompany a production of goods for profit rather than for use—granting all this and more, the system still claims one intrinsic value, and that is *liberty*. Liberty as an ideal? Perhaps. But as a reality, hardly. For, as society exists today, there are a hundred economic slaves for each free entrepreneur. Yet could we once remove from society the threat of poverty, the new capitalism that would ensue could furnish in fact and for all its participants that liberty of which the old capitalism has boasted but which it has actually conferred upon only a fortunate minority. Capitalism, thus purified and held in check by the rival way of production offered by the communes, might gain a new lease of life; and for the first time the system of individual enterprise would be forced to pay its own way unsubsidized by the misery and fear of men who have nowhere else to turn. Then, too, a momentous experiment would have been set going, a continuing test in the great laboratory of a nation's life of two alternative ways of production. Now we live in a scientific age, an age in which theories are verified, not by force but by experiment. Surely, as citizens of our time, it should be a manifest duty to test the all-important rival theories about society by the same methods that are used to test the theories about physical nature.

What would be the cost to the taxpayers of this experiment of communism within capitalism? That would, of course, all depend upon how elaborate was the scale on which we desired to begin. By spending comparatively little we could accomplish quite a little—and by spending more, a great deal could be accomplished. Even if the initial costs of equipping the communes and managing them for the first few years were very high, we must bear in mind three great compensations. First, from the moment the communes were started, all genuine poverty would be abolished and the mountainous expenses of public and private charities would be reduced to almost nothing. Second, as time went on, the expense to the taxpayers of maintaining the communes would become less because the communes themselves would become more and more nearly self-supporting in that they would produce not only goods for consumption but also the means and instruments for the production of such goods.

And along with the steady lowering of expense for the taxpayers would be the steady rise in the standards of living for the people who would be members of the communes.

Restricted at first to bare necessities, they would gradually attain for themselves more and more of the comforts of life. If the experiment had any considerable measure of success, if communal production could really be made to work when carried on under the direction of expert technicians who would be untrammeled by the exigencies and distractions of making monetary profits for financiers, there would be no reason why life in the communes should not, in the course of years, come to equal or even surpass, in its luxuries and amenities, the life in the surrounding capitalistic world.

There is one great institution in our present society that might be used as a most important instrument in establishing and managing the communes. I refer to the army. Here is an organization with a high and long-standing tradition of public service. Pacifists regard soldiers as killers of their fellow-men, and that, of course, is what the soldiers are. But when the army leaves for the front, the patriots who weep and cheer do not think of the soldiers as men going out to kill, but as men going out to die and to risk dying, and not for their own profit, but for the defense and protection of others. And this conception of the soldier is no less valid than that other conception held by the pacifists. The soldier is indeed two men in one: a man who goes forth to kill and a man who goes forth to die. If only we could find a way to preserve the heroism of the fighting man and at the same time give that heroism some less wasteful and dreadful objective than the killing of his fellows, we should have solved one of the gravest problems that confronts humanity. As William James so clearly realized, pacifism merely in and of itself is a negative ideal. To make it thrill and gain a real appeal, some means must be devised by which peace can be "waged" even as war is "waged." And to that end militarism must be *sublimated* rather than *suppressed*.

Can we imagine a finer way of sublimating militarism—not only its fighting spirit and tradition of discipline, but its immense material resources—than to offer to our armies the chance for a great adventure in building under expert direction communes of refuge, and thus waging a victorious war against the universal public enemies, insecurity, poverty, and misery?

Now, it may be objected that the experimental communes here proposed would embody all the evils of that fascism to which they purport to be an alternative. To any such objection I answer that if the opportunity for production under a dictatorship of experts can be called fascism, it is in the first place a fascism that is optional rather than compulsory, leaving the individual free to enlist at intervals of one to three years, and to get out of the system if he does not like it; that in the second place it is a fascism that applies its disciplinary control only to a man's work and only during his working hours, leaving the cultural part of his life and his hours of leisure quite free from regimentation; that in the third place it is a fascism to be used not as a weapon against communistic equality and in favor of a society of classes and castes, but, on the contrary, as a means of securing the effectiveness of a thoroughgoing egalitarian communism by bringing to its aid all the resources of technical science administered by technical experts.

I have argued that the world is confronted today with a crisis that is political, cultural, and economic. The democracy that we have been brought up to regard as axiomatic in its validity is being definitely challenged by more than one country. Its parliamentarianism and liberalism are held to be both clumsy and hypocritical. And its capitalism is charged with being cruel and sordid, unsuited to the age of machine industry because incapable of *distributing* with any degree of equity the goods that are so efficiently *produced.* The new Italy is a spiritual challenge to our democratic system, so also perhaps is the new Germany. But the greatest challenge of all is the New Russia. For there, in the Union of Soviet Socialist Republics, we see a nation of a hundred and sixty million peasants and laborers, possessing only the most meager equipment of the machinery which we have in such abundance, and endowed with only a fraction of the skill possessed by us. Yet it is this same nation which under the appallingly ruthless leadership of a relatively small band of Marxian doctrinaires is changing the face of two continents and creating or trying to create a new type of civilization. If the Russians do succeed, working under enormous handicaps and armed only with a fighting faith, an atheistic religion as intense and as fiercely intolerant as that of the early Christians, it will be imperative that we, citizens of the capitalistic democracies, should either give place to them and their system or else *prove by our deeds* that we have the will to purge our economic life of unemployment and misery and transmute the ideals which as liberals we cherish from the hollow mockery which they have become into the actuality which they demand and deserve.

The economic dualism that I have proposed would not only offer to all men a continuing choice between the two great ways of life, the way of economic liberty at the price of economic risk and the way of economic security at the price of economic discipline, but also it would offer to the men of science in an age of science an experiment by means of which the strong and weak points of each regime could be scientifically established, without either the tyranny or the bloodshed that has attended the fascist and communist revolutions in Europe. Though a bloodless alternative to revolution, the experiment would be of revolutionary significance to every free country in which it was tried. For it would preserve and apply to the needs of our own tragic time the institutions which our ancestors have fought through the centuries to attain. Certain it is that, unless some very radical adaptation of the ideals of democracy to an age of machinery can be right speedily made, a cultural inheritance that is of irreplaceable value will be utterly and irretrievably lost.

POSTSCRIPT

CONFESSIONS OF AN ANIMISTIC MATERIALIST[1]

One of a series of intellectual autobiographies in which American teachers of philosophy were asked to explain for the benefit of their students how they arrived at their conclusions.

THE FIRST QUESTION of a philosophic kind that I can remember considering concerned the nature of the soul and its relation to the body. Having been informed by my mother that the soul was that which made you laugh and cry and think and move, I asked if you could get it out by boring very carefully up through the foot and leg until you reached it somewhere in the chest. To this question my mother was giving a hesitant and somewhat puzzled negative, when my father broke in impatiently with the warning that I must never think of the soul in that way, that it was not at all the kind of thing that had a place inside the body from which it could be fished out.

I mention this little incident of early childhood because the question I asked then is the kind of question I have been asking ever since, and the reproof for it administered by my father is the same reproof that I have received many times from my teachers and colleagues in philosophy.

[1] Reprinted from Adams, G. P., and Montague, W. P., eds., *Contemporary American Philosophy*, London, Allen and Unwin; New York, The Macmillan Company, 1930, pages 135–159.

I feel myself to be a thing in a world of things. And the thing that I am does not seem to me to be the thing that my body is. The two are alike in being substantive rather than adjectival. They are alike also in being agents and patients in space and time, but they are contrasted with respect to the laws and processes pertaining to them. The intimate union in existence of these entities so disparate in essence has become to me ever more mysterious. All my thinking has been oriented with regard to the psychophysical problem. And blessed or cursed by this "animistic complex," and goaded on by it, I have sought continuously for an intellectual theory that will bridge a dualism imposed upon me by feeling or intuition and increasingly confirmed by the evidences of experience.

Next to the metaphysical question of mind and body there came, and continued, the religious problem. Church services in the early morning with my mother gave me a poignant sense of the beauty of the Christian doctrine. Sunday School and the atmosphere of a small New England community gave me an equally poignant sense of the falsity and incredible ugliness of the authoritarian and ascetic aspects of that same doctrine. Cool, condescending appoval or an equally cool and tolerant contempt, which are the usual alternative attitudes toward Christianity that are prescribed by the "genteel tradition" in American philosophy, have never done justice to its baffling mixture of what is best with what is worst. Love and enthusiasm for one half of the church, righteous hate and contempt for the other, are sternly called for.

Somewhere between twelve and fifteen I read Bellamy's *Looking Backward*, Abbott's *Flatland*, and articles on theosophy by Blavatsky and others. Bellamy, in addition to making me a socialist, made me realize that the business of the good life was an institutional as well as an individual affair. *Flatland* and the theosophy stimulated and made more explicit what might be called my metaphysical interests. The characteristically theosophic attempt to explain the mind and its doings in terms of material or pseudo-material categories appealed to my animistic attitude, and seemed to me then, as indeed it does now, to be the most delightful of pastimes.

It was not until the middle of my sophomore year that my formal education took on significance. I suddenly found myself suspended from college, and very miserably I made visits to my various professors to get instructions for the enforced period of home work. Josiah Royce, whose course in the history of philosophy I had been taking with some real interest, received me kindly, and inquired what I planned to fit myself for. I replied that I didn't know, but supposed that I should have to be a lawyer. Whereupon he asked me encouragingly if I had ever thought of the academic career. I never had, and I hardly knew the meaning of the phrase; but the fact that here was a great man showing me sympathy and faith in my dark hour stirred me unforgettably. By hard, eager study I passed well the final examination in his course. It had opened a new world to me. Everything was changed, and I was happy. In my junior and senior years in college, and in the three years in the graduate school that followed, I gave my whole time, so far as I was allowed, to philosophy. The classes suddenly ceased to be tedious interludes between parties, and became themselves the most exciting of parties.

Everyone knows the extraordinary company who dispensed philosophy at Harvard in the late 'nineties: Palmer, James and Royce, Munsterberg and Santayana. Each of them had a distinctive philosophy, and each of them preached it with the force of conviction. Their methods of teaching were almost as different as their viewpoints. Palmer's lectures were incomparably the most finished, as to both content and form, of all that I have ever heard; and whether because of or in spite of their literary perfection, their pedagogical effectiveness was extraordinary. I had the good luck to be his assistant or reader, and so had an opportunity to see the progress in philosophic comprehension made by the large group of undergraduates in his course, each of whom was required to submit four papers during the year. Quite apart from this ideal of pedagogical technique, and in addition to many specific illuminations, I owe to Palmer the realization that a naturalistic relativism, as regards the varying *content* of the good, is quite compatible with a Kantian rigorism as regards the invariant *form* of right or duty.

The classroom lectures of James were in striking contrast to those of Palmer, and, indeed, to the polish of his own formal papers. He would utter his thoughts spontaneously, just as they came. As a result, his talks were most uneven in quality. The roughness and irregularity were, however, more than balanced by the simplicity and directness of his conversational manner. It was an inspiration to see and hear a great man work out his own thoughts in the presence of his students. The informal and colloquial speech coming from a scholar and a genius possessed a peculiar piquancy. I have seen him stop in the middle of a sentence with some such remark as: "By George, Mr. Smith, perhaps you were right, after all, in what you said a few minutes ago; I had never really thought of that." Mr. Smith, thus honored, would, of course, become the envy of all of us and the devoted slave of his master. Nor would he realize that James, with characteristic and unconscious generosity, had probably read into his comment a richness and meaning of which Smith himself had been quite innocent.

The part of James's philosophy that concerned his Pragmatism and Radical Empiricism left me uninterested or actually repelled, but to the more mystical and less explicitly developed phases of his thought I owe much. His conception of the subconscious and hidden energies of men, his Transmission hypothesis, his defense of indeterminism and of a finite God, I greedily accepted. Taken in connection with the Tychism of his friend, Charles Peirce, they furnished me with a large part of my philosophic faith. For Peirce himself I had a kind of worship. While his intellect was cold and clear, his metaphysical imagination was capricious, scintillating, and unbridled, and his whole personality was so rich and mysterious that he seemed a being apart, a superman. I would rather have been like him than like anyone else I ever met. And on the two or three occasions in which he carefully criticized and then praised some of my student writing, I was transported with happiness.

It is to Santayana [2] especially that I owe my realization of Plato's truth. I took his course at about the same time that I read Huxley's *Evolution and Ethics* and Stevenson's *Pulvis et Umbra.* In all three the teaching was to the effect that value did not depend on existence, nor right on might, nor ethics on religion. An atheistic nature, red with tooth and claw, could in no sense absolve man from his obligation to actualize ideals of beauty and goodness; nor could it deprive him of the consolation of knowing that those ideals were always and eternally there, be the world what it might. The fact that I did not share the pessimism of Huxley and Santayana as to the existing world in no way lessened my debt of gratitude.

Another thing I got from Santayana's courses was support and confirmation of my temperamental belief in a world of substances. Hegel's hideous slogan, "Not sub-

[2] My first philosophic article, "A Plea for Soul Substance" (*Psychological Review*, November 1899), was written with his kind advice and encouragement.

stance, but sub*ject*," so fertile in sterilities of every kind, had been pretty generally adopted by professional philosophers, and it was a relief to hear Santayana, who had gone through that epistemological hell with his common sense unscathed, talk delightfully and quietly about the various substances of which the world might conceivably be composed.

It was, however, to Josiah Royce that my debt was greatest, though in another sense it was also least. He taught me almost all that I know about the world's great philosophers, and yet in his own philosophy there was hardly anything that seemed to me true. His lectures on the history of metaphysics were glorious affairs. He not only made the various systems clear in themselves, but he portrayed their interrelations so luminously and with such originality and depth of insight that the whole course of speculative thought was presented in a series of magnificent vistas and then given the unity of a single great picture of the human mind objectified. He had an unexampled power of making abstract ideas concrete and almost sensuously vivid. It was the ideas themselves rather than the biographical details or even the identities of their authors that he emphasized; and I think all his students were impressed with the fact that, however it may be in other history, in the history of philosophy, at least, it is not the *who's who* but the *what's what* that really matters. I not only got from Royce my knowledge and appreciation of philosophy, but I got from him the kindest and most painstaking assistance in working out my own philosophic problems. He gave me this technical help through my five years of advanced study, and he accompanied it with continuous personal interest and affectionate counsel. He had, moreover, started me going and trusted me when I was down and out. I owed everything to him, and it seemed mean and disloyal for me not to become his disciple. He was my dear teacher, and I longed to call him master, but I couldn't because his idealistic premises seemed to me false. Despite this I felt the tug of the will to believe wherever I could find elements within my teacher's philosophy that did not seem definitely false. And in a system so rich there were, of course, many such elements. I remember particularly the hypothesis about the varying time-spans in nature put forward in the second volume of *The World and the Individual*, and how I jumped at it with almost tearful gratitude not only as a clear and great thought but one that might even be true. For it was a new and challenging contribution to the great pan-psychist tradition. It could be studied and appraised on its own merits in the light of what was known and guessed about the world. And it did not in the least depend upon the monstrous premise on which the rest of the book was based, that that great nature in which we are such recent and humble participants is itself the product of our social consciousness and of the funny little techniques of communication which we have developed.

My doctor's thesis, formidably entitled *An Introduction to the Ontological Implicates of Practical Reason*, was suggested by Kant's *Critique* and by Hegel's *Phenomenology*. Sheldon and I worked a great deal together, and we each felt that the principle of *negativität* was inadequate to the great enterprise of categorial deduction which, translated into modern terms, meant the search for a principle of hierarchical organization in the domain of subsistence or essence. We were cheerfully confident of being able to remedy the defect. Sheldon took the principle of the *Self-Repeater* and I took the principle of growth or increase, perhaps suggested by Bergson's *durée*, to which James had introduced us. Royce christened my principle the *Pleon*, and helped me with his customary generous kindness to lick the thing into shape. I supplemented my revision of the Hegelian deduction of the categories with an adaptation of Kant's treatment of the sense of duty as revealing a reality more ultimate than anything contained in the world of sense perception, and attempted to show that in the experience of moral obligation the Pleon revealed itself in its true colors as the principle of reality itself. The thesis was long and must have been pretty awful as judged by contemporary standards; but it was fun to write, and it got me the degree.

The following year I got my first regular job under Professor Howison in the University of California. Howison, like Royce, had a variant of post-Kantian idealism, but it was more original than Royce's, though not nearly so well organized and supported. It was a sort of Fichtean monadism in which God was no Absolute, but merely *primus inter pares*, and the world was the phenomenal manifestation of the society of eternal persons who, by timelessly recognizing one another and one another's recognitions of one another, and so forth, *à la* Leibniz, created the time process and generally kept things going. The pluralism was in refreshing contrast to the anthropophagous absolutes of Royce and Bradley; and to its author, at any rate, it had come as a genuine *aperçu*. He preached it with fiery and unflagging earnestness, and so great was the force of his personality that people all over the Pacific Coast began and have continued to study the philosophy of German Idealism. The spirit at Berkeley was very different from that at Harvard. Under Howison, philosophy was not a fencing-match in which friendly gentlemen exchanged playful thrusts and courteously applauded their adversaries. It was a grim thing of life and death for the soul, a veritable religion in which either you were orthodox (Howisonian), or you were damned. I, with my realism, was mostly damned, and would have been completely had it not been that Howison was really two persons—a grand inquisitor who would burn your body to save your soul, and also one of the kindest men alive. I was lucky enough to win his affection, and not only his professional condemnation; so for four years he kept me on, scolding me angrily for my rotten views and even warning his students against my courses, and then, together with dear Mrs. Howison, showering me and my family with every sort of friendly kindness and material help.

It was for me a strange, hard-working time, and in striking contrast to the dreaming and brooding years at Cambridge. I learned to teach, and found I could do it all right, which was a great relief, because both I and my Harvard teachers had had grave doubts about my being able to. I formed a friendship with Overstreet, who was at that time devoted to the study of Plotinus and in high favor with Howison, and that helped me, as it has ever since. I took two interesting courses, one with Professor Slate in physics and one with Professor Stringham in mathematics. The course with Slate was a splendid one, and started me reading hard such books on science as I could understand. Stringham's course had an even stronger effect. He was a man much like Peirce. He had a Pythagorean sense for the things that really count, and a Lewis Carroll humor. I had no ear for music, but I think I got from his functions and series the kind of experience that musicians must get from their music. The numbers had always had for me an almost pathological fascination and an almost tangible objectivity. To regard the number 37, for example, as the product of a human mind, a result of the counting activity by which we reached it, seemed not only false but idiotic. The numbers stand in vast and infinite array with all their still more multitudinous interrelations full of unending and delightful surprises. They are what they are, and must through all time be what they have been, more steadfast than the stars and more clear and beautiful than existing things can ever hope to be. It would be easier and less absurd to suppose that Baedeker had by his descriptions created the Jungfrau at which I am now looking than to suppose that the ephemeral mathematicians of this planet create by their technique of procedure the timeless truths which they discover.

Stringham's course revived all my old interest in mathematics, and the result was disastrous, for I became an addict and began to neglect my philosophy in order to play amateurishly with the new problems. Cardan's solution of the Cubic seemed intolerably complicated, and I got the feeling that the ease with which equational knots of any degree could be tied must mean that an equally general formula for untieing them must exist. On that presumably hopeless quest I spent days and nights undissuaded by the kindly warning of my mathematical colleagues that the general equations of even the fifth degree had been actually proved to be insoluble by the ordinary methods which I was using. Then, also, there were the several simple-seeming series for the summation of which no formula had yet been found; and always, and best of all, there was the ancient lure of the primes. I suppose it was vanity or laziness or an unacknowledged distrust of my own competency to master the real stuff I needed that prevented me from fitting myself by serious study for this new game. I preferred instead to wait until the house was quiet, and then like a secret drinker unlock my cupboard and take out with guilty joy, not the good little black bottle, but the nice blank book in which I kept my scribblings, and hold high revel with myself through the night, exploring the lovely grottoes in which the roots of my equations lurked, bound by mysterious threads to combinations of the known and visible coefficients on the surface up above. In the more than twenty-five years in which I have indulged this vice, I have discovered—at least, I think I have discovered—a few odd and pretty things, though certainly not enough as yet to justify the hours filched from philosophy.

In spite of this disastrous by-product of my work with Stringham, and perhaps partly because of it, but still more because of the course with Slate and the reading which grew out of it, I began to take realism with a new seriousness. Science was discovering most exciting things. With the atoms being not only arranged in families, but actually caught and counted, it seemed a piece of pedantic insolence for philosophers who knew nothing of the new work, and cared nothing for it, to label the atoms and their electronic constituents "vicious abstractions from the organic unity of experience" or similar barren nonsense. If philosophy was to play its historic role, it must acquaint itself with the new truths and exploit whatever speculative possibilities they contained. Idealism began to seem to me not just a falsity to be neglected, but a positive menace debauching the minds of the youths who studied it. There was need for a definite campaign to deliver philosophy from the fog of confusion that threatened to obliterate it. This feeling as to the increasing importance of getting the epistemological situation properly cleared up, not as an end in itself, but as an indispensable prerequisite to a worthwhile philosophy, made me glad to accept the call to Columbia in 1903.

The new place was quite different in atmosphere from either Harvard or Berkeley, and wonderfully stimulating. Sheldon was there, and we could resume both our golf and our duets in ultimate romantic metaphysics. Woodbridge was as realistic as I was myself—perhaps more realistic—at least as concerned the world of concrete existence. And it was almost disconcerting to find that what had for so long been my daring and dangerous heresy was now taken by the head of my department as a mere matter of course.

And yet there were moments even in those early days when I had misgivings that the new realistic accord was itself not so close as it appeared and as I wanted it to be. For Woodbridge seemed to have nothing of that inner veil of sensation through which we all must pass to reach the outer world. When a distant star would hit him in the eye with its light, his body would bow or gesture in the direction from which the light had come; and he would say in effect: "*That* is my perception of the star—*voilà tout!*" What could it mean to identify the publicly observable bodily antecedents and consequents of an experience with the experience itself, the latter being obviously private and not observable by others?

It was the first case of acute behaviorism that I had seen, and the first, I believe, that existed. To believe in the outer world was indeed very good, but to purchase that belief at the cost of denying the inner world was too high a price even for realism. The baby had been emptied out with the bath. But, even though the theory were as queer as it seemed, it was original and never put forward before. And in philosophy, at least, we should do everything once. So I was not very much troubled if my friend, for some unaccountable reason, chose to make believe that his own sensations were nonexistent. Moreover, Descartes had tried this theory on the animals, and it was a sporting thing for a man to be willing to try it out on himself.

Under the stimulus of this new and, to me, delightful association, I changed from the representative or dualistic theory of perception to a presentative or monistic theory. Not that I ever doubted the existence of my own mental states and their location inside my skull, but I got to believe that the objects immediately present in perception were not those states, but their meanings or implicates, which as such could coincide (though they need not) not only in essence, but in position and date, with the things and events in the extracranial world. The states that do this revealing are not themselves revealed. They are not motions, but they are describable in physical terms. What kind of event it is that can reveal events at other places and times than its own is one phase of the psychophysical problem. That intracerebral states can and do reveal without creating such events is sufficient for epistemology.

Beginning about 1910 there came the association with Perry, Holt, and the others, which resulted in the publication of *The New Realism.* We set out with high hope of success, confident in one another and of the sympathy of our big brothers in Europe—Russell, Moore, and Meinong. We wanted, first of all, to introduce into philosophy the two methods that had been so profitably employed in science: the method of co-operative work, and the method of isolating problems and tackling them one by one. And in addition to these methodological policies we had (at least, so I thought) several epistemological theses which we all believed to be true and which we intended to establish.

To me, at least, these theses committed us to no decision as to the more properly metaphysical issues concerning the ultimate nature of the world, or even of the nature of mind and its functions. On the latter questions I was pretty sure that I was not in agreement with my confreres, except possibly with Pitkin. Our realism was thus not a philosophy; it was rather a prolegomenon to philosophy and a declaration of independence that would make it possible to investigate the nature of things on their own merits without dragging in the tedious and usually irrelevant fact that they could be experienced by us.

But even within the domain of epistemology, or closely connected with it, there were incipient differences that were destined soon to loom large. The cognitive function was interpreted by Perry and Holt, as by Woodbridge and Watson, to be nothing more than a "specific response," that is, a motion of the organism, or some part of it, elicited by a stimulus. For reasons already stated, this seemed to me preposterously false. Magnify the importance of bodily movements as much as we please, they can never be other than north or south, east or west, up or down, or in directions intermediate to these. But the peculiar rapport between an individual and the objects of which he is aware extends to past and future and to the realm of the abstract. And it is impossible for the body to move in the "direction" of such entities. But what is perhaps an even more serious difference between my neo-realist colleagues and myself has developed in recent years. The objects which appear in distorted illusory and hallucinatory experience, which were always for me not existential, but merely subsistential complexes of essences that could not on reflection be believed to be in real space, however vividly they might appear there at the moment of perception, have been given an existential status by most of those calling themselves neo-realists. The result is to make of the space in which we live and move a dumping-ground for all the contents of dreams and illusions, actual and possible. Any space would crack under such a strain, and of course "neo-realist" space has cracked and broken up into a series of "private spaces" and a "public space" as a construct of each individual. Are there as many public spaces as there are individuals who construct them? Do they interpenetrate completely or partly? Or are they mutually external and side by side in a super-public space which is not a construct? These last questions must also be asked about the private spaces. And *where* were the individuals who constructed public space before they did their constructing, that is, when they were babies or embryos? I would rather be an idealist, at least a Kantian idealist, than swallow any such mess. For Kantian space, even when reduced to an a priori form of perception, could still keep up, though in straitened circumstances, a semblance of Euclidean respectability and enjoy a dignified priority to its own contents.

It seems to me to be a certainty that the things of which the existing world consists must at each instant have ultimately univocal positions, regardless of all of the conflicting perspectives in which they may appear. And if we make temporal cross sections of these things, as we always can, and thus treat them as histories or continuous series of events, and accept in addition the Special Theory of Relativity, the situation is not essentially altered; for, though in that case space and time will have become interdependent aspects of the single four-dimensional continuum of "space-time," yet even so each event will enjoy a univocal "date-locus" or absolute "position" in the new continuum. How otherwise could the events be unambiguously interrelated by the Eddington "intervals," which are to remain invariant regardless of the perspectives which vary with the motions of the systems from which they are taken? Nor do the spaces and times of even these varying perspectives include places for hallucinatory contents. Relativity to the photographic plates on moving systems is not relativity to the apperception-masses of the men suffering from nightmares or delirium.

If neo-realism is to mean an ontological equalitarianism in which existential status is to be accorded to every content of perceptual experience, whether veridical or illusory, then such a theory is not *realism* at all. We may give new names, such as "sense data" or "sensa" or "sensibilia," to the rabble of experiential contents, and insist piously on calling them "physical" in every sentence; but they are not properly physical, for they are not properly things at all. They are not agents and patients; they cannot go under their own power; and, worst of all, they are totally incapable of orderly arrangement in a single *milieu*, whether a space or a time or the space-time of Relativity. They are, in fact, nothing but the well-known adjectival sense impressions of Hume and Mill and Mach and Pearson masquerading under fancy appellations. And in treating them as the sole constituents of the world of existence, the New Realism has surrendered unconditionally to the old phenomenalism.

These sad trends toward behaviorism and positivism, which have taken place in the last ten years and which I have attempted to describe, spoiled my interest in the movement from which I had hoped so much good would result; and once more, as in the old days at Harvard and at Berkeley, I am left without a party.

My general ethical theory had developed smoothly into an articulate conception of what I had always vaguely longed for. The good life was the most abundant life. Happiness was increment of psychic substance—fulfillment of tendencies and capacities. We should seek a maximum of it and a minimum of its opposite for all. Courage and sympathy were the means to that end. They were the intensive and extensive coefficients of righteousness and the only primary virtues.

As to the religious question which had from the beginning been my second philosophic interest, I felt that my views were crystallizing into a fairly coherent structure. And this structure was based upon two postulates:

1. The Problem of Good is insoluble in terms of the traditional Atheism.

2. The Problem of Evil is insoluble in terms of the traditional Theism.

There seemed to be too much of goodness and purposivness in the world to be the outcome of blindly or mechanistically determined particles, but also too much evil and inconsequentiality to be compatible with any power at once omnipotent and benign. There must be a God, a force or trend upward, to account for the more than casual amount of goodness in existence, and there must be a tremendous limitation in such a power to account for the evil. The finite Deity of Mill and James was thus indicated, on grounds both of metaphysical plausibility and of ethical satisfaction.

When, however, we consider, not the processes of the Universe, but its structure, we must recognize that the only chance for the existence of anything worthy the appellation of Deity must turn on the possibility that the cosmos has a life and a mind of its own over and above the lesser things included within it. In the old and unattractive words, we may ask: Is there any likelihood that the world is an animal? Can the sprawling galaxies conceivably possess that degree of integration and organicity which would constitute them an adequate vehicle or external manifestation of a unitary and personal experience? To this question I could give an affirmative answer. Not with certainty, but yet with high probability, we may believe that the enduring unity of the whole is more rather than less than the transitory unities of its parts. Such a Being would, like other beings, possess an "environment," which would, however, be internal rather than external, and would consist of its own confused and recalcitrant constituents: "that in God which is not God." Encompassing this unitary totality of existence there would abide the eternal Logos, or totality of subsistent possibles, of which the actual world is itself but an infinitesimal fraction—an indeterminate and ever-changing precipitate of compossibility; the resultant, so to speak, of a struggle for existence on the part of the essences. The will to good, or the tendency toward harmony, would be but one essence among many; but its intent to inform the stubborn and warring parts of the universe with the harmony and unity of the Logos would give it an advantage over all other less eirenic tendencies. And the epic of cosmic evolution would consist in the uncertain, imperfect, and interrupted, but generally progressive, leavening of an infinite chaos by the element in it of divine love and good. This little yet perfect thing working in the heart of all things we can symbolize as Prometheus or as Christ, the finite will of a God whose essence and substance are all-comprehending and infinite.

I am painfully aware, not only of the inadequacy of my language to express this Leibnizo-Peircian theory, but of what will appear to my colleagues as the antiquated and fantastic character of the theory itself. And I am equally well aware that no such theological system of hazardous and far-flung speculation, were it a thousand times more skillful and more plausible, could constitute more than the intellectual husk of religious experience itself. The feelings of loneliness, insufficiency, and terror are the real drives that generate religion. The ancient and pathetic hope that the world is somehow kin to us, and that the things for which we care most are not ultimately at the mercy of blind and indifferent forces, impels the search for God. And when this hope is reinforced by a mystic sense of being sustained by something sweet and quick, not of us but very close to us, we have enough to justify the attempt to reconcile the need of our heart with the cold and meager knowledge of the facts of existence.

Of far greater importance to me than the beliefs on epistemology, ethics, and religion, the nature and genesis of which I have been describing, was a certain conception of the nature of the mind and its relation to the body which came to me in a curious way and which has seemed to me to constitute the solution of the problem which of all problems had interested me most. I have tried in four or five articles to present and defend the hypothesis in question, but my failure to convey to my friends my own conviction of its truth and importance warns me that I shall probably fail also in this new and necessarily brief account of the nature of the theory and the manner of its genesis.

In my second year of teaching at Berkeley, I had been using as textbooks Höffding's *Psychology*, Pearson's *Grammar of Science*, and the *Critique of Pure Reason.* In Höffding I had come across a reference to Lotze's comment on Herbart's doctrine of degrees of intensity in mental states. I do not remember the exact point of the matter, but it had been haunting my mind, and I had commented upon it to my class. In Pearson I had been struck with a statement to the effect that whether the analogy between sense impressions and forms of strain was anything more than a mere analogy he would leave undetermined. In my course on Kant we had been dealing with the "Analogies of Experience," particularly the one concerned with intensive quantity. At the close of a morning in which the discussion in the Kant class had been especially lively and profitable, I was walking home to lunch in fine spirits and full of satisfaction with the students and with the work that we were doing together. Suddenly I had the strangest experience; and if in my attempt to describe it I make it seem silly or even meaningless, I can only ask the reader's patience on the ground that, however preposterous he may find it, it has meant more to me than anything else that has happened in my life. The feeling came as I was crossing a little brook; and it was as if I could look into and down through each point of space and perceive a kind of well of infinite depth. The new realm was like a fourth dimension in that it was perpendicular to the three dimensions of space, and yet as contained within each point it seemed to be a lesser thing than a spatial dimension. I described it to myself as a "hypo-space," a realm of negative dimensionality or essential fractions of the punctiform units of an extensive manifold. It seemed to be the domain of intensity and density, so that if I thought of a continuous solid being diminished in its extent until it had shrunk to a point, that would not be a zero of mass magnitude, for each point of a solid must be as different from a point of empty space as a finite sphere of solid is from the same sphere of empty space. After you reduced matter to points, each of those solid points would have to *wane or fade down* in density or intensity in order to reach the true zero of mass. The first implication or application of my *aperçu*, if I may dignify to that extent my novel experience, was the realization that there was room inside a point for a whole microcosmic intensive replica, though in a curious inverted form, of the extended macrocosm outside; and that the elements of that intensive replica would have, on the one hand, a privacy and invisibility, and on the other hand, a unity and organicity which, while preserving the plurality of specificities, would permit of their being superposed upon one another rather than placed side by side as in extensive pluralities. The different elements would occupy the same place, just as a shape and its color, or a tone-magnitude and its pitch. The second reflection it occurred to me to make on the new conception was that whenever a motion or stream of kinetic energy was checked and transformed into a potential state of strain or stress, the place of that strain and of an indefinite number of further strains that could be successively superposed upon it was the new dimension that stretched in and "down" through each point of space. It was because of this beautiful and unsuspected hiding place for energies that they were enabled to pass into the seeming nothingness of mere potentiality and emerge again with all their specificities unscathed. And then, as I put these two sets of reflections together, it came over me suddenly that I had discovered the real nature of the psychical and the manner of its relation to the cerebral matrix in which it was so elusively located. I had found the way in which sensations were produced at the points in the brain where the neural currents were transformed into potential energy prior to their reissuance as motor responses. I had found the place where an indefinitely rich system of memories could be piled up as traces left by the sensory currents during the potential stage of their journey. I had found how it was that a sequence of successive moments, mutually exclusive in the physical order, could nevertheless be felt as a solid chunk of duration extending back and down into the past, the "specious present" or *durée réelle* of Bergson, which more than anything else differentiates the mental from the moment-to-moment reality of a physical system. I had, in short, discovered the soul in its hiding place, and not indirectly through dialectical inference, but concretely through an intuition. I walked off the little bridge on which I had stopped when the thing came on me, and went home in a daze of ecstasy.

The ideas initiated by the strange experience that I had undergone have persisted up to the present, and, despite the epistemological, sociological, and religious interests to which I have referred, my dominant philosophic purpose has been to make clear to myself and others the full meaning of what had been revealed in my intuition while crossing the brook. To the fulfillment of this purpose there have been obstacles—in particular, my own self-distrust. I knew that I had the taint of the circle-squarer deep in me, and that fantastic analogies were apt to seize on my mind and gain an importance and a fascination far beyond their logical value. Perhaps it was because of my weakness and tolerance for the fantastic that the various pseudophilosophic cranks, who are always appealing to universities for academic endorsement of their wild schemes, were usually referred to me by my colleagues in philosophy and psychology. I recall one poor lady who had accepted as a commonplace and established fact the crazy notion that every name had a "vibration rate" which, by a sort of sympathetic magic, controlled the object named. Her own original addition to this nonsense was the great theory that the word *vibration* must itself have a vibration rate which, could it only be discovered, would be a potent control over the whole universe. I proceeded, as in less acute cases, to disillusionize her gently but firmly as to any hope of academic encouragement for her theory. As at last she turned to go, I noticed the stricken look begin to fade from her face and the horrible secret smile of the paranoiac gradually triumph over the hurt. I felt an eerie goose-flesh shudder on my own part, and suddenly the memory of John Bunyan came to my mind, and I thought, "There, but for the Grace of God, go I"—and perhaps there I do go anyway. Was it not terribly possible that my own gorgeous intuition might turn out to be of the same pitiful tinsel stuff as that of the vibration-lady whose idea I had just sentenced to a well-deserved death?

In the more than twenty-five years that have elapsed, my theory has developed through four successive stages, psychological, epistemological, biological, and cosmological. I will try to set down briefly and in turn the principal conclusions in each of these fields.

1. *Psychological.* Sensations are the modes of intensive or potential energy into which the afferent currents of motion or kinetic energy are transformed at those points in the nervous system (presumably the synapses) in which they are redirected into efferent currents of muscular and other responses. When and where the energy of the stimulus ceases to be externally observable as motion, there and then the new kind of energy, purely private and internally observable as sensation, comes into existence. What from the standpoint of the physicist is mere potentiality of future motion, is in and for itself the actuality of feeling and sensation. These intensive energy-forms fade out rapidly, though never completely, into their appropri-

ate motor responses; but their traces, in all their specificity, are retained, accumulated, and superposed on one another after the fashion of the successive twists imposed upon a rope or spring. They constitute the memory system of the individual; and, like a faint but pervasive field of force, they modify in accordance with their structure and pattern the responses to later stimuli. There thus grows up an organism within the organism, an enduring and ever-present register of the succession of past sensations, not externally observable yet causally effective upon the visible cerebral matrix. Unless we are to assume that a complex system of motions could pass at their moments of redirection into complete nothingness and emerge unscathed in magnitude and in form, we must believe that those energies in their latent or so-called potential phase possess, though invisible, all the richness and definiteness of structure that characterize their visible antecedents and consequents. The character of such a field of potential energy, as indirectly inferred from without, possesses all the essential characters of the mind as directly experienced from within. Looked at from either standpoint, we find privacy, unity, "extension in time," or duration of the past in the present, and variety of content without divisibility or side-by-sideness. In any extensive aggregate of particles in motion, the unity is factitious and secondary, and the behavior is the sum of behaviors of the separate elements. The forms and relations of the system are not, as such, primarily effective. But a field of force is like a mind in that the organic unity and pattern of the whole dominates the behavior of the constituents, which are thus distinct phases rather than separate parts. And the forms and relations or *gestalten* within such an intensive aggregate become primary and effective determiners.

These, in briefest summary, are some of the reasons in support of the theory that the potentiality of external motion is the actuality of internal experience. Furthermore, such a theory has what seems to me a very important methodological advantage over other theories of the relation of mind to body. It enables us, in the first place, to accept as true the various points which psychophysical dualists, from Descartes to Bergson, have urged so effectively as revealing the impossibility of the kind of structure which we know as mind being a mere concomitant or inseparable aspect of the very different and essentially contrasting kind of structure which we know as brain. But, in the second place, the theory enables us to express these truths of dualism without departing from the physical categories which constitute the strength and fruitfulness of the mechanistic conception. To treat mind as a field of potential energy is to do justice both to its uniqueness of structure and to its homogeneity with the material world of which it is an integral part.

2. *Epistemological.* Turning from the psychophysical problem of the relation of mind to brain to that quite other, though related, problem of the relation of the individual as knower (whatever else he may be) to the object as known (whatever else it may be), we find an extraordinary situation—a situation in which an organism or system of events is in a curious and unique rapport with other events whose loci and dates are different from its own. Consciousness may, indeed, be defined as a situation in which certain events (the objects) enjoy a vicarious efficacy in spaces and times other than their own—namely, those of the brain that knows them. For when my conduct is controlled by my awareness of spatio-temporally distant objects, to that extent those objects are causally efficacious in positions other than their proper ones. And, again, from the side of the knower or subject, the internal states by means of which he apprehends are controlled by their external and objective meanings rather than by their sensory content.

The psychophysical theory that the mind is a system of potential energies enables us to understand how and why its objects are other than itself. For potential energy has a double, self-transcending reference. As the determiner of future motions, it is an agent and faces futureward; but as the "determinee" of past motions, it faces pastward and is a patient. It is this retrospective reference of potentialities to their causes that constitutes the curious cognitive function. We live forward, but we experience backward. Facts are what we apprehend, and every fact is a *factum*, something done, a *fait accompli*. This explains the curious relativity of objects known to the subject that knows them, a relativity that is "selective" but never constitutive, like the relativity of historical events to the words that describe them. *Which things* we shall know at any moment depends on our internal states at that moment, but *the things* thus known are independent both in essence and existence of the states that reveal them. And as a potentiality viewed as a forward-facing tendency may be counteracted and fail to produce its characteristic effect, so may that same potentiality, in its backward-facing or cognitive reference, fail to reveal its true cause. This is the explanation of error. Our cognitive states reveal their normal or most probable implicates, which may be, but need not be, identical with existing objects.

3. *Biological*. The outstanding mystery of organic life is the peculiar capacity of a fertilized germ to embody in its own material structure—apart from the truth or falsity of the Lamarckian theory—the structures of its myriad of ancestors. These present embodiments of an enormous past certainly do not exist side by side or within one another, as the "encasement" theory would have it, nor can they be accounted for in terms of the number of possible combinations and permutations of their atoms. These various possible arrangements would, of course, be

more than sufficient numerically, but they would not persist in any definite order through the intercourse with the environment. Their definiteness of arrangement would be washed out through successive interactions. In order to account for the persistence of the heredity-structure through all the vicissitudes of ontogeny and later growth, it is necessary to allow to the germ tremendous causal prepotency over its environment. The latter is only a releasing and sustaining condition, and by no means an equal partner in the interactions. Now, if the ancestral past of a germ is present in it as a system of potential energies superposed to any degree upon one another in an intensive hierarchy, then we have an adequate system of causal determiners of the process that ensues, and the reason for its persistence with unaltered specificity is plain. Preformation becomes reconciled with epigenesis. For the constellation of atoms in the material structure of the chromosomes can be meager and without resemblance to the structures that are to ensue (epigenesis), while at the same time the hierarchy of intensive energy forms may embody in their own invisible and temporally ordered structure an infinitely rich system of all, and more than all, of the forms of past ancestry and of possible future posterity. This is a sort of preformationism, but it is "energic" rather than materialistic.

4. *Cosmological.* The Einstein Theory of Relativity might appear at first sight to have no relevant bearings upon my hypothesis as to the nature of mind and life, and yet it has seemed increasingly to be congruent with it. The Einstein-Minkowski world is a four-dimensional continuum of space-time. As usually conceived, that world is in a queer sense static. The time aspect of it is like time that is past. The present flowing of time, what Whitehead calls the fact of *Passage*, is not provided for. It is a world whose objects, when temporally considered, are

histories; but, as in the world of Spinoza, they are histories that *sub specie aeternitatis* have been always completed. Now, if we amend this world to provide for its life as well as its shadowgraph, we may fancy it is a space-time hypersphere, not static, but growing or expanding cumulatively and (if the Special Theory of Relativity is true) non-Euclideanly—in a direction perpendicular to its "surface." The three-dimensional "surface" of this growing hypersphere is the spatial or material world. The electrons and protons may be thought of as the hills and hollows, or pimples and dimples, which are opposite and unequal fourth-dimensional displacements in the three-dimensional "surface" of our space. They would be produced by equal and opposite corkscrew "twist-thrusts." If the "surface" were *not* expanding, the equal and opposite "twist-thrusts" would give protuberances and depressions that also were respectively equal. But in an *expanding* spherical surface, equal *twists* would be correlated with unequal *thrusts* or displacements in the direction of the perpendicular. If these displacements represent the mass of the hill or hollow and the twists represent the electric charge, then we could understand how the degree of a depression (protonic mass) could be greater (1,845 times greater) than the degree of an elevation (electronic mass), though their degrees of twist or electric charge were equal.

If material particles can be thought of (following Clifford) as the permanent four-dimensional departures from the three-dimensional surface of the ether on which they float, then the associated vital and psychical systems of potential energy, registering the actual past and so foreshadowing the probable future of the bodies with which they are connected, can be conceived as the temporary and more tenuous four-dimensional extensions (or durations) that are the invisible appendages of their visible matrices. Thus, I believe that the mind, as a system of potential energies in the cerebrum, is a real soul, thick or deep in the direction of the past from which the world has moved. The world is a true "pleon," a self-increaser, and the vital and mental structures contained in it are moving all together with a cumulative growth-motion in a fourth-dimensional direction. That motion we perceive, not as such, but as the *passage of time.* The inner part of the world-hypersphere constitutes its definite and still enduring past, while the as yet unoccupied space outside, into which it will grow, constitutes its indefinite future, filled only with the possibilities which are the shadows thrown forward by what already is. The world-soul, like the souls of men, hangs down in time, extends into the past. Its material existence and ours at each present instant is but the three-dimensional cross section, the fighting-front of a four-dimensional spiritual reality.

I have made a desperate attempt to express in a few paragraphs the broader implications or applications of my theory of the character of mind and organic life. My philosophic speculations have brought me to the goal of a cosmological spiritualism, but a spiritualism that in a sense can be expressed in physical categories. And so, with equal propriety, it may be termed a spiritualistic or animistic materialism. The hopes and fears of one's heart exert such hidden and potent influences on one's intellect that it is hard for anyone to be sure whether his conclusions in matters of life-and-death importance are intellectually honest. At times I feel a sort of shame and self-mistrust that I should have come out with a philosophy so optimistic. That the world is a spirit, and that we are; and that perhaps we share even the immortality of a Life that contains and sustains us, is a creed almost too happy and too good to be true. And yet I do believe that if not true, it is something very like the truth.

APPENDIX

QUESTIONS ON PART I

Foreword

1. What is philosophy?
2. State the similarities and differences between philosophy and religion.
3. What is the relation between philosophy and art?
4. Compare philosophy with science.
5. Name the divisions of philosophy. Which are elementary and which are composite? Subdivide the primary topics of philosophy.
6. With what is logic concerned? Distinguish between Formal Logic and Material Logic.
7. Describe what the author calls "The Wheel of Knowledge."
8. What is the function of metaphysics? Can its function be exhausted by science? Defend your answer.
9. Differentiate ontology from cosmology.
10. What is value? Distinguish between Esthetics and Ethics. Why does the author prefer the term *Kalology* to others?
11. Define epistemology. Trace how the distinction between appearance and reality is derived from our experience.
12. What is theology?

Chapter I

1. Analyze the two assumptions of Aristotle's logic.
2. With what is the preliminary part of logic concerned?
3. Define inductive logic. What is the great philosophical problem involved in it?
4. Analyze the components of a syllogism.
5. Illustrate and symbolize some possible syllogisms.

6. Explain and illustrate how a syllogism is identified by figure and mood.

7. What are the axioms of the figures of the syllogism?

8. What kind of conclusions can each of the figures prove?

9. How many valid syllogisms are there? How can the valid syllogisms be derived? How can the total number of formally possible syllogisms be found?

10. List the syllogistic rules which determine the validity of a syllogism.

11. What modification of Aristotle's logic was advocated by George Boole?

12. Explain the charge that the Aristotelian syllogism begs the question. What arguments are used by the author to vindicate the syllogism against that charge? What do you think of his arguments?

13. Discuss the objection of artificiality brought against the syllogism as traditionally formulated. What, according to the author, was Aristotle's mistake in formulating the syllogism? What is the author's plan for removing the above objection? Appraise his plan.

Chapter II

1. Name and illustrate the sources of our beliefs.

2. What schools of Material Logic can be derived from the sources of our beliefs?

3. How does the author approach Authoritarianism? What is your reaction to that approach?

4. Appraise intuition as a criterion of truth.

5. Compare briefly Rationalism and Empiricism.

6. How and where is the strength of Pragmatism realized?

7. What is the function of Skepticism?

8. What synthesis of the methods of Material Logic does the author suggest? To what extent is such a synthesis a solution of the problem of Material Logic?

Chapter III

1. How does the author revise the usual approach to the problem of epistemology?

2. What defense of Epistemological Objectivism does the author offer? Evaluate his analysis.

3. Discuss Epistemological Subjectivism. Show how the author criticizes it by his concept of "re-creation." Is his criticism convincing? Defend your answer.

4. What is Epistemological Dualism? When, according to the author, is a copy more than a copy in conception? Do you agree with his answer? Why?

5. How does perception differ from conception? Does sense perception ever deceive us?

6. Explain the two kinds of apprehension that are neither conception nor sense perception.

7. What are the four answers to the question as to the status of secondary qualities? Which answer, if any, do you consider cogent? What experiment does the author suggest for solving this problem?

8. Compare the respective locations and dates of perceived objects and real objects. When, according to the author, is a copy more than a copy in perception? Appraise his answer.

9. Discuss Relativism. What, for the author, is right and wrong with it? Do you agree with his conclusions? Why?

10. What is the author's "Epistemological Eirenicon"? What, in your opinion, is its value?

Chapter IV

1. What the the two primary problems of metaphysics?

2. To what type of metaphysical theory does the primitive duality of human experience lead?

3. Discuss the three types of metaphysical theory which arise as a reaction to Dualism.

4. Appraise the metaphor of the compass, used by the author.

5. What, according to the author, are the strong points and weak points of Dualism? Of Positivism? Of Idealism? Of Materialism? Evaluate his analysis.

Chapter V

1. Explain how the four possible answers to metaphysics become contracted into two possible answers.

2. What are the strong and weak points of Materialism when applied to the individual or microcosm? Do you believe that Materialism has more strength than weakness? Defend your answer.

3. Discuss the author's approach to the problem of Materialism versus Dualism as applied to the individual. To what extent do you believe his analysis should be taken as a basis for the solution of the problem?

4. Why is mass regarded as a form of energy?

5. What are the various kinds of energy mentioned in the conclusion to this chapter?

6. What is the distinctive characteristic of the transmission of energy in the growth of protoplasm?

7. What does the author mean by his suggestion that the complex of hereditary characters is an intensive hierarchy of potential energies?

8. What arguments can be given in support of the author's hypothesis that the sensations and memories of which mind consists are forms of potential energy?

9. How would that hypothesis, if true, bridge the gap between spiritualistic dualism and monistic materialism?

Chapter VI

1. Compare briefly religion and theology.

2. Name and describe the four possible solutions to the basic problem of theology.

3. Why are Pantheism and Polytheism comparatively unimportant for the author? Do you agree? Defend your answer.

4. Discuss Theism in relation to the "Problem of Evil." What dilemma does the problem involve?

5. Describe the attempts of Theism to reconcile the existence of evil with divine omnipotence by modifying our conception of divine goodness. What objections are raised by the author against this attempt? What do you consider the value of these objections?

6. Describe the attempts of Theism to reconcile the existence of evil with divine goodness by limiting divine power. What objections may be offered against the attempt? Does the author's theory of a God infinite in mind and substance but finite in *will* solve the Problem of Evil?

7. How does the author analyze and criticize atheism? What is the "Problem of Good"? Is the author right in his claim against pantheism that the infinity of God as coextensive with the universe is not incompatible with His being a Person?

8. Sum up the author's solutions of the basic problems of theology and state your agreements and disagreements with those solutions.

Chapter VII

1. What two kinds of value does esthetic experience involve? What theories of esthetics are derived from them?
2. Describe and illustrate the rhythm of reason.
3. Evaluate the author's remarks on the relation between music and mathematics.
4. Compare the objectivistic theory of esthetics with the subjectivistic theory. How does the author reconcile the conflict between the two theories? What is the value of his criterion?
5. What kinds of beauty characterize classicism and romanticism?
6. Indicate the esthetic relevance of classifying hedonic satisfactions according to the extensive-intensive series.
7. What are the two opposite aspects of esthetic experience? Appraise the author's definition of esthetic experience as "emotive perception."
8. Discuss Kant's theory of esthetics in connection with the two aspects of beauty. How does the author criticize the Kantian analysis? What do you think of his criticism?
9. Compare the sublime with the beautiful.
10. Discuss the nature of the comic with its corollaries.
11. What is the relation between esthetic values and the function of art? Appraise the author's conclusion.

Chapter VIII

1. What is wrong with the extreme subjective theory of ethical value?
2. Explain the three components of conscience. Evaluate their significance.
3. What is asceticism? What objections may be raised against it?
4. Appraise authoritarianism in ethics.
5. What are the other forms of "Rightism" in ethics besides asceticism and authoritarianism?
6. Is duty exclusively social? Defend your answer.

7. How does the author describe the change from an intuitionist conception of moral value to a utilitarian conception?

8. What are the strong and weak points in utilitarianism?

9. How does the author attempt to reconcile the ethics of the Right with the ethics of the Good? What do you think of his "Perfectionism"?

10. What alternative divisions of the field of ethics are possible?

11. What reasons are given by the author for making the opposition between egoism and altruism relatively unimportant? Are these reasons valid?

12. State the relation between individual and social ethics.

13. Define the ethical problems of government, the family, education, religion, group relations.

14. Examine the problem of property and its three principal solutions. What are the author's comments on these solutions? What is the theory of "Economic Dualism" which he offers as a solution to the problem? What is its value? How is it related to the broader dualism derived from his "Law of Increasing Returns"?

QUESTIONS ON PART II

I. On the Nature of Induction

1. Describe and criticize the usual conception of induction as a mode of direct inference.

2. Show how Mill's canons embody implicitly the eliminative principle.

3. Examine the two advantages resulting from the author's identification of induction with the indirect type of argument.

II. A Defense of Causality

1. Describe the two kinds of concurrence within the world of actual and possible data.

2. What two reasons does the author give for postulating a transcendent causal power? Do you believe they are valid?

3. What objection may be raised against the argument from probability in defense of causality? How does the author answer this objection?

4. What is the crucial assumption upon which the author's hypothesis is based?

III. The Antinomy and Its Implications for Logical Theory

1. How are the types of logical theory derived? Illustrate the kind of belief that each can best validate.

2. What is meant by *antinomy?* Distinguish between major and minor antinomies.

3. What are the three extreme methods used in dealing with a major antinomy? Examine the author's comments on these methods. Which method, if any, is convincing to you?

4. Compare the three compromise theories used in dealing

with a major antinomy. Why does the author defend the "double-aspect" theory? Do you agree with his position? Is there any solution for the antinomic situation other than those mentioned by the author?

IV. The Rainbow Series and the Logarithm of Aleph Null

1. In what respects can the arguments of this paper be regarded as illustrations of the methods of Formal and Material Logic?

2. Compare "Mathematical Induction" as exemplified at the end of the first section with ordinary induction. Give two or three other examples of Mathematical Induction.

3. Is the analogy of the new series as expressed in the second section with the rainbow sufficiently close to justify calling it the "rainbow series"?

4. Is the one-to-one correspondence between transfinites of a kind to destroy what Cantor regarded as their distinctive relations to one another?

V. The Story of American Realism

1. Trace the insurgency in the American philosophy of the present century.

2. What are the fundamental postulates which the New Realists shared in common? Examine their arguments in support of these postulates.

3. Show how the epistemological controversy in contemporary American philosophy was triangular.

4. Explain what the author considers the two major fallacies of the New Realism. Do you admit that they are fallacies?

5. Discuss the epistemology of Critical Realism. Does the author see anything novel in it? Is he correct in his judgment?

6. Examine the influence of American Realism on American philosophy.

VI. Truth Subsistential and Existential

1. What are the various names by which the domain of abstract substantives may be called?

2. Discuss the formal problem of truth. How does the author reconcile the theory of coherence with the theory of correspondence?

3. How does the author's hypothesis concerning the union of subsistence with existence differ from the Aristotelian theory? Which of the two do you consider better, and why? Is there a third alternative?

4. What evidence is there that the whole of subsistence contains a structure? What effect, if any, does the world of subsistence exert upon the world of existence?

5. What are the practical implications of the doctrine of subsistence?

VII. Substance, Potentiality, and Cause

1. State the case for Rationalism and for Positivism. Which is more cogent?

2. Show how the author's theory is a compromise between Rationalism and Positivism. What is the value of this compromise?

3. What evidence is there that the essence of all substance is *durée réelle?*

4. How does the author differ from Descartes and from Bergson?

VIII. A Theory of Time Perception

1. Distinguish the specious present from the metaphysical present.

2. On what, according to the author, does the solution of the problem of the specious present depend? Is his analysis convincing?

3. How are duration and succession, "time dragging" and "time flying," explained?

4. Discuss the rhythmic character of consciousness in relation to the specious present.

5. Differentiate memory proper from the consciousness of the just past.

6. How does the feeling of familiarity differ from memory?

7. What are the conditions under which time perception originates?

IX. Beyond Physics

1. Indicate how and why contemporary physics is regarded by some as a new handmaid to theology.

2. Compare the nineteenth-century universe with the twentieth-century universe.

3. Why is the Quantum Theory a more devastating revolution than the Relativity Theory?

4. What theological conclusions, if any, may be drawn from the Relativity and Quantum Theories?

5. Do you think that "Pan-psychism" is a strong bridge to span the gap between science and religion? Defend your answer.

X. The Einstein Theory and a Possible Alternative

1. What are the three reasons for the author's choice of the topic of this paper?

2. Mention the five main characteristics of Einstein's Special Theory of Relativity.

3. Show the connection between the premises of the Special Theory of Relativity and the Michelson-Morley experiment.

4. Elaborate the three possibly fatal paradoxes to which the Special Theory of Relativity leads. Are these paradoxes unavoidable if Einstein's Theory is accepted?

5. What is the crucial assumption contained in the premises of the Special Theory of Relativity? What experiment does the author design to test it? Enumerate the possible objections to the experiment suggested.

6. What are the possible alternatives to the crucial assumption? Elaborate and evaluate the author's alternative.

7. Compare the Special Theory with the General Theory of Relativity.

XI. A Possible Interpretation of the Quantum

1. Discuss the essential features of Planck's Quantum Theory.

2. How does the author answer the question as to why the short waves of radiation have more energy than the long waves? What are your comments on this possible solution?

3. What are the author's objections to Eddington's Sweepstake Theory? How does he reconcile the undulatory and corpuscular aspects of radiation? Appraise his analysis.

4. What is the author's hypothesis as to the structure of atoms? What, in your opinion, are its advantages or disadvantages?

XII. Time and the Fourth Dimension

1. Do you agree with the author that philosophy is primarily vision rather than proof?
2. What are the possible relations of space and time to the subjects that know them and to the objects that fill them?
3. Discuss the problem of the relation of space and time to each other. What are the similarities and differences between time and a spatial dimension?
4. What, if anything, is wrong with Minkowski's picture of the world?
5. What hypothesis concerning the time problem is advanced by the author? Do you believe the objections to it are fatal? Defend your answer.
6. Examine critically the author's picture of the cosmos.

XIII. Consciousness a Form of Energy

1. How, in essence, does the author's hypothesis differ from the Platonic, Democritean, and Aristotelian conceptions of mind?
2. Analyze the nature of the psychophysical problem.
3. Distinguish the structure of a psychical system from the structure of a physical system.
4. What is the basic assumption upon which Descartes's conception of the psychophysical problem depends? What are the author's objections to that assumption? Are these objections valid?
5. What are the three theories as to the nature of potential energy? Why does the author accept the view that potential energy is stress?
6. What is the chief contrast between kinetic and potential energy?
7. Enumerate the resemblances between a field of potential energy and a field of consciousness. Do you believe the author is justified in identifying the two fields? Defend your answer.
8. What is the relation between the author's view and the views of Descartes and Bergson?

9. Indicate the significance of the author's theory of consciousness. What are the possibilities, if any, for an experimental test of its truth?

XIV. Variation, Heredity, and Consciousness

1. Describe the present status of the controversy between mechanists and vitalists. How, in general, does the author meet this controversy?

2. Discuss the theories which attempt to explain the origin of useful variations in the germ plasm. What theory does the author propose? What analogy does he employ? Illustrate by examples "telogenesis" in the psychological field and in the biological field. What is the value of the principle of "biological vectors"?

3. What are the two facts about heredity on which the vitalists base their protest against mechanism? Show how the author attempts to explain both of these facts by the conception of life as a system of "super-forces." Do you accept his solution? Defend your answer.

4. What are the points at issue between mechanistic parallelism and vitalistic interactionism? What are the general and special characters of conscious life? Analyze and appraise the author's conception of conscious life as consisting of modes of "anergy." What is the bearing of this conception upon the three great questions of traditional philosophy?

XV. A Materialistic Theory of Emergent Evolution

1. What are the general characteristics common to all forms of life? Distinguish the three specific types of life revealed in our experience.

2. How can a quantitatively continuous process give rise to qualitatively discontinuous types of life? Illustrate the answer by applying it to the main ascending steps in evolution.

3. State the three conceptions applied to the problem of Emergent Evolution, and the reasons why the author rejects them. Do you agree with his criticisms? Defend your answer.

4. Describe the hypothesis which the author proposes to solve the problem of Emergent Evolution. What is its significance?

5. What are the practical consequences of the author's measure of vital excellence?

6. What conception can you form of a level of evolution higher than the human? Is there any reason to believe that such a level will be reached?

XVI. The Promethean Challenge to Religion

1. What is religion? How does human conscience evolve?

2. What kind of revolution is confronting religion today? How does the author propose to meet it?

3. What are the three basic trends of Christian ethics? What position does the author take toward each of them? Do you agree with his conclusions? Defend your answer.

4. Outline and evaluate the principal characteristics of a Prometheanized religion.

XVII. The Two Immortalities

1. What are the two immortalities? Which is more believable, and why?

2. What are the contemporary reasons for disbelief in personal immortality? What bearing does the curious anomaly in contemporary science have upon this question?

3. Do you agree with the author that the problem of personal survival is at present beyond the power of science to solve? Defend your answer.

4. Is the chance for collective survival more desperate than the chance for individual survival?

5. Why is eternity more important than immortality?

XVIII. The Trinity: A Speculation

1. What reasons does the author present for his conception of Trinitarian Theism? Are they valid? Defend your answer.

2. What, according to the author, is responsible for the origin of nature?

3. How does the author apply the principle of growth to the Trinity?

4. In what respects does the author's view differ from the orthodox conception of the Trinity? How does it compare with the Plotinian Trinity? Which view do you prefer, and why?

XIX. The True, the Good, and the Beautiful from a Pragmatic Standpoint

1. What is meant by the pragmatic standpoint? How does the author criticize it? Do you agree with his criticism? Defend your answer.
2. Analyze the three kinds of equilibrium between the individual and the environment. What type of experience does each define?
3. State the similarities and differences between a judgment and a desire.
4. Is the true a form of the good? Defend your answer.
5. What is the distinction between the beautiful and the merely pleasant?

XX. Beauty Is Not All: An Appeal for Esthetic Pluralism

1. Is the contemporary revolt against beauty of *content* and the emphasis on beauty of *form* justifiable? What are the three chief forms of this revolt?
2. Do you agree with the author's criticism of "unrealism"? Defend your answer.
3. Discuss and evaluate the author's theory of Esthetic Pluralism.

XXI. The Missing Link in the Case for Utilitarianism

1. Analyze the three objections to Utilitarianism. How would you answer these objections? Which objection is the most serious, and why?
2. Compare the ethics of Utilitarianism with the ethics of Intuitionism. Why do the positive arguments of the Utilitarians fail to meet the chief point raised by the Intuitionists?
3. What is the author's answer to the Intuitionist's objection to Utilitarianism? Do you believe his thesis fills the gap in the logic of Utilitarianism? Defend your answer.
4. Show how in all ethical theory there is implicit the same dilemma as that which becomes explicit in the logic of Utilitarianism.

XXII. The Philosophy of Friedrich Nietzsche

1. What is the relation between Nietzsche's life and thought?
2. Outline Nietzsche's metaphysics. Show how his metaphysics serves for the foundation of his genealogy of morals.
3. State and estimate the two principles which Nietzsche employs as a metaphysical foundation for his ethics.
4. Discuss the anti-Christianity of Nietzsche. What is your reaction to it? How does the author criticize it?
5. Discuss the anti-democracy of Nietzsche. How does the author answer his attack on the ideals of democracy? What additional arguments would you urge?

XXIII. The Geometry of the Good Life

1. In what terms does the author define the good life? Appraise his approach.
2. Describe the "Law of Increasing Returns." What are the two kinds of tactic demanded by this law? Which should be applied to the goods and which to the evils of life? What social institutions illustrate this law?
3. Show how the asymmetrical character of the good life is neglected by the maxims of traditional morality.
4. Apply the "Law of Increasing Returns" to education and to our present economic crisis.

XXIV. Democracy at the Crossroads

1. What is the indictment brought against parliamentarianism by the philosophy of dictatorship? Is the indictment valid? Defend your answer.
2. Indicate the hypocrisy and futility of liberalism in practice.
3. Discuss democracy as capitalism. What are the three stages of the Industrial Revolution? Why does the third stage seem to require a reconstruction of capitalism?
4. What are the alternatives to the present crisis? What way of escape does the author suggest? What, in your opinion, is the value of "economic dualism"?

INDEXES

INDEX OF NAMES

A

Abbott, E., 649
Adams, G. P., 232, 267
Aikins, 174, 180
Alcott, B., 231
Alexander, S., 438, 439
Anaxagoras, 274
Anselm, St., 532, 535
Aquinas, St. Thomas, 79, 216, 482
Archimedes, 43, 217, 292
Argand, J. R., 501, 502
Aristotelian, 29, 35, 262, 273, 483, 572
Aristotle, 18, 26, 33, 35, 129, 272, 483, 491
Avenarius, R., 248

B

Bacon, F., 43
Bakewell, C. M., 231
Barrett, C., 232
Bellamy, E., 649
Bentham, J., 586
Bergson, H., 66, 98, 106, 136, 212, 213, 221, 222, 224, 254, 404, 408, 412, 413, 414, 426, 437, 442, 448, 449, 509, 567, 654, 668, 671
Bergsonian, 129, 219, 417, 447
Berkeley, G., 83, 240, 384, 482
Blanshard, B., 232
Blavatsky, H. P., 649
Boehme, J., 122
Bohr, N., 292, 293, 533
Boodin, J. E., 233
Boole, G., 28, 29
Booth, E., 119
Bowne, B., 231, 232
Bradley, F. H., 95, 209, 211, 240, 554, 555, 655
Bragg, Sir W., 340, 346
Brightman, E., 231
Buddha, 150
Buddhism, 129, 208, 210, 230, 525
Bunyan, J., 669
Burr, H. S., 510
Butler, N. M., 231

C

Calkins, M., 231
Cantor, G., 194, 201
Cantorian, 189
Cardan, J., 657
Carrel, A., 99
Carroll, L., 656
Cartesian, 65, 79, 112, 485, 486, 494, 509, 510
Carus, P., 230
Case, T., 230
Cattell, J. McK., x
Christ, 150, 518, 521, 525 *ff.*, 538, 539, 665
Clifford, W. K., 289, 293, 324, 325, 401, 402, 674
Cohen, M., 234
Columbus, C., 243
Compton, A., 543
Comte, A., 8, 85, 295, 444
Condillac, E. B., 483
Confucianism, 525
Creighton, J. E., 231
Cunningham, G. W., 232

D

Damien, Father, 118
Darwin, C., 441, 442, 446, 448
Darwinian, 129, 215, 216, 281, 282, 495, 567

Davidson, T., 231, 232
Davis, B., 316
De Broglie, L., 89, 414
Democritus, 90, 296, 441, 482, 483
Descartes, R., 65, 66 *f*., 79, 82, 235, 239, 254, 255, 259, 289, 296, 326, 384, 408, 411, 413, 414, 482, 483, 494, 509, 659, 671
De Sitter, W., 318, 342
De Vries, H., 448
Dewey, J., 33, 81, 232, 233, 439, 620
Drake, D., 253, 256
Driesch, H., 426, 442, 461
Ducasse, C. J., 138
Duncan (?), 470
Duncan, 231

E

Eddington, Sir A. S., 282, 289 *f*., 292 *ff*., 310, 311, 332, 342, 344, 349, 543, 662
Eddy, M. B., 95
Einstein, A., 43, 90, 285, 287, 289, 298 *ff*., 324, 325, 342, 382, 390, 415, 419, 673
Einsteinian, 314, 323, 342, 400
Emerson, R. W., 231
Epicurus, 293
Euclid, 217
Euclidian, 276, 283, 289, 293, 325, 326, 390, 397, 398, 401 *f*., 662
Euler, L., 200
Everett, W. G., 231

F

Faraday, M., 497, 504
Fechner, G. T., 112, 293, 369, 472, 473
Fibonacci, L., 125
Fichte, J. G., 231, 532, 554, 655
Fitzgerald, G. F., 301, 306, 309
Flewelling, R., 231
Freud, S., 532
Fullerton, G., 231, 232

G

Galileo, G., 65, 413, 484
Galton, F., 43
Gandhi, M., 119
Gapon, Father, 118
Ginsberg, J., ix
Gorgias, 206
Greene, T. M., 231

H

Haldane, Viscount, 443
Hamilton, Sir W., 207, 230
Harris, W. T., 231
Hartley, D., 483
Hegel, G. W. F., 532, 534, 535, 652, 654
Heisenberg, W., 90
Helmholz, H. L. F. von, 429
Henderson, L. J., 443
Heraclitus, 215, 216, 217, 414
Herbart, J. F., 413, 666
Herbartian, 273, 365, 535
Hobbes, T., 82, 83, 137, 254, 255, 483, 568
Hobhouse, L. T., 174
Hocking, W. E., 231
Höffding, H., 666
Hollingworth, H. L., 134
Holt, E. B., 233, 245, 246, 660
Howison, 382, 383, 655
Hume, D., 83, 85, 95, 185, 248, 259, 312, 324, 412, 444, 483, 532, 663
Husserl, E., 534
Hyslop, J. H., 230

J

James, W., 6, 62, 81, 95, 134, 149, 212, 232, 252, 620, 644, 650, 651, 654, 664
Jeans, Sir J., 543
Jevons, S., 179, 180
Job, 115
Jones, A. L., 20
Juarez, J., 66

K

Kant, I., 64, 125, 132 *ff*., 143, 208, 209, 221, 296, 384, 482, 532,

Kant (*Cont.*):
556, 557, 558, 560, 562, 590, 592, 654, 655, 661
Kantian, 137, 145, 147, 651, 661
Kasner, E., ix
Keyser, C., ix
King, L., 349

L

Ladd, G. T., 231
Laird, J., 155
Lamarck, J. B., 446, 447, 672
La Mettrie, J. O., 483
Leibniz, G. W., 83, 216, 231, 275, 293, 296, 384, 503, 535
Leibnizian, 83, 274
Leighton, J. A., 231
Leucippus, 90
Locke, J., 235, 239, 254, 255, 259
Loeb, J., 370
Loewenberg, J., 234, 264
Lord, H. G., 156, 585
Lorentz, H. A., 301, 305, 309
Lorentzian, 306, 310, 314
Lotze, H., 666
Lovejoy, A. O., 247, 253, 256
Lucretius, 118, 541
Ludovici, A. M., 566

M

Mach, E., 304, 324, 444, 663
Machiavelli, N., 618
Macintosh, D. C., 234
Marshall, H. R., 556, 557
Martineau, J., 590, 592
Marvin, W. T., 233, 245
Marx, K., 118, 618
Masaryk, T. G., 618
Maxwell, C., 354
McCosh, J., 230
McDougall, W., 426, 442
McGilvary, E. B., 233
Meinong, A., 263, 660
Michelson-Morley, 283, 284, 299 *f.*
Mill, J. S., 21, 22, 85, 174, 179, 212, 248, 444, 584, 586, 590, 591 *ff.*, 618, 663, 664
Millikan, R. A., 543
Minkowski, H., 389, 391, 405
Moore, G. E., 237, 486, 660
Muensterberg, H., 231, 232, 650
Muirhead, J. H., 264

N

Newton, I., 90, 243, 298, 304, 392, 413, 419
Newtonian, 314, 323, 324, 342
Nietzsche, F., 564 *ff.*
Northrop, F. S. C., 510

O

Ormond, J., 231
Overstreet, H. A., 521, 656

P

Palmer, G. H., 231, 650, 651
Pareto, B., 618
Parkhurst, H. H., 130
Parmenides, 208, 211
Pascal, B., 41
Paul, St., 526
Pearson, K., 444, 455, 499, 663, 666
Peirce, C. S., 230, 275, 652
Perry, R. B., 233, 236, 245, 246, 660
Pitkin, W. B., 67, 233, 235, 245, 660
Planck, M., 291, 327, 328, 338, 355
Plato, 116, 216, 262, 271, 272, 280, 296, 482, 483, 491, 534, 535, 568, 615, 620, 652
Platonic, 82, 171, 172, 230, 254, 257, 258, 262, 273, 279, 481, 490
Plotinus, 532, 538, 656
Porphyry, 532
Pratt, J. B., 253
Prichard, 148
Promethean, 517, 525, 527
Prometheus, 115, 280, 511, 665
Protagoras, 618
Pythagoras, 217, 243, 656

R

Reid, 235
Rich, G. V., ix
Rieber, C. H., 231
Riemann, G. F. B., 324, 325, 326, 397, 400, 401

Riemannian, 276, 283
Ritz, 341, 342
Rogers, A. K., 253
Romanelli, P., ix
Roosevelt, F., 617, 618, 632
Rosmini, 231
Ross, Sir W. D., 148
Royce, J., 231, 232, 234, 260, 276, 650, 653, 654, 655
Russell, B., 29, 223, 224, 256, 384, 444, 660
Rutherford-Bohr, 360

S

Sabine, 232
Santayana, G., 126, 133, 138, 253, 254, 257, 258, 263, 275, 480, 535, 556, 557, 560, 562, 650, 652, 653
Schiller, F. C. S., 554, 555
Schopenhauer, A., 129, 293, 532, 566, 567
Schroedinger, E., 293, 414, 428, 533
Sellars, R. W., 253
Sheldon, W. H., 100 *f.*, 654, 658
Sidgwick, H., 155, 585
Slate, F., 656, 658
Smart, H. R., 232
Smith, T. V., 153
Socrates, 618, 620
Socratic, 154
Spaulding, E. G., 233, 245
Spencer, H., 207, 230, 281, 295, 567
Spinoza, B., 111, 254, 255, 275, 293, 674
Spinozistic, 232, 554
Stace, W. T., 231
Stebbing, L. S., 33
Sterling, H., 281
Stevenson, R. L., 652
Stringham, I., 398, 656, 657, 658
Strong, C. A., 253
Sumner, F. B., 67
Swabey, M. and W. C., 232

T

Tagore, R., 119
Thales, 383
Thomas, N., 165
Thomistic, 79, 230
Thrasymachus, 172, 568, 618

U

Urban, W., 231

W

Watson, J. B., 281, 660
Weber, E. H., 379, 472
Weierstrass, K., 223
Wenley, 231
Weyl, H., 310
Whitehead, A. N., 4, 29, 256, 444, 673
Whyburn, W. M., 200, 201
Woodbridge, F. J. E., 233, 486, 658 *f.*, 660
Woodworth, R. S., 490
Wright, W. and O., 641

Z

Zarathustra, 573, 575, 577
Zeno, 203, 207 *ff.*, 211, 220 *f.*, 224
Zenonian, 210, 218
Zoroastrianism, 573, 575, 577

INDEX OF SUBJECTS

A

Absolute:
  anthropophagous, 655
  light as an, 299, 321
  Lilliputian, 291
  mind, 74, 86 *f.*
  motion, 310, 319, 320, 341, 342, 395, 396, 397
  rotation, 304, 305
  Self, 94
  space, 319, 320
  time, 372
  value, 546
Absolutism, 240, 554 *f.*
Abstractions, reality of, 22
  and see Essences, Universals, *and* Subsistence
Action:
  and thought, 43
  in physics, 331
Agnosticism, *see* Skepticism
Aleph null, 193 *ff.*
Algebra:
  of geometry, 189, 326
  of logic, 28
Altruism, 141, 512, 518, 578, 579, 581
Anabolism, 105, 120, 121, 431, 432, 433, 437, 459, 460
Anergy, 465, 470, 471 *f.*, 474, 475, 477, 478, 480
Animistic materialism, 649, 675
Anti-intellectualism, 212
Antinomies:
  major, 206
  minor, 204 *f.*
  of the specious present, 363
  Zeno's, 220 *ff.*
Appearances:
  for relativism, 73
  perceptual, 69
Appearances (*Cont.*):
  relative to perception, 270
Aristocracy, 159, 580, 582 *f.*, 615
Art, 4, 124 *ff.*, 450, 560 *f.*
Asceticism, 145 *f.*, 512, 518, 519 *f.*, 529, 578, 579
Assumptions:
  of Aristotle, 18, 19
  of Einstein, 311
  of induction, 22
Atheism, 111, 117, 119, 522, 524, 528, 663
Atoms, 89, 98, 103 *f.*, 121, 292 *f.*, 343 *ff.*, 349 *ff.*, 415, 428, 456, 458, 459, 460
Authoritarianism, 40 *f.*, 45, 113, 127, 142, 143, 146, 205, 218, 269, 512, 515, 516, 517, 519, 521 *f.*, 529
Axiom of idealism, 237
Axioms:
  of deductive logic, 25, 35
  of religion, 87

B

Beauty, 124, 126, 127, 129, 131, 132, 155, 538, 555 *f.*, 560
Behaviorism, 246, 252, 253, 444, 483, 586, 659, 663
Being:
  of all thinkable objects, 54
  of subsistent possibles, 664
  timeless, 535
  ways of, 6, 8, 77 *f.*, 93 *f.*
Beliefs:
  grounds of, 7 *f.*, 38 *f.*, 203
  unrelated, 31
  versus truth, 267
Biology, 9, 213, 282, 418, 427, 441, 442, 466, 541, 543, 544

Body:
and death, 94, 541
and mind, 79, 95 *f.*, 99, 406, 486, 541 *f.*, 544, 665
Bolshevism, 280
Botany, 43
Brain, 55, 56, 66, 68, 106 *f.*, 239, 293, 404, 423, 425, 427, 452, 453, 466, 468, 475, 476, 477, 480, 484, 503, 671

C

Capitalism, 163, 165, 609, 613, 621 *f.*, 628, 637
benefits, 641 *ff.*
first stage, 622, 628
second stage, 622
third stage, 623
Categorical:
imperative, 143 *f.*, 148
obligation, 145, 146
Categories, 11, 274, 326, 401, 409, 411, 412, 427, 441, 442, 454, 480, 483, 544, 592, 675
Causality and Cause, 20, 56, 78, 87, 176, 182, 183 *f.*, 254, 258, 284, 408, 409, 410, 411, 412, 479, 483, 492, 495, 502, 509, 532 *ff.*
Chemistry, 9, 441, 442, 542, 543
Chlorophyl, 436, 437
Christianity, 517 *ff.*, 566, 571, 575
Christian Science, 208, 210
Coherence theory, 265 *f.*
Collectivism, 165, 610
Comic, 135 *f.*
Communes of economic dualism, 631 *ff.*
Communism, 164, 165, 609, 626, 637
Compossibility, 266, 267, 275, 536, 664
Conception versus perception, 62, 220
Conscience, 141, 142, 143, 144, 148, 149, 151, 152, 154, 513 *f.*, 519, 594
Consciousness, 56, 108 *f.*, 112, 237, 246, 369, 371, 441, 465 *ff.*, 475, 480
as mode of potential energy, 102, 108 *f.*, 469, 482 *ff.*, 484, 503 *ff.*
Conservation of energy, 120, 466, 495, 496
Constant, Planck's, 328, 338, 355
Constants of physics, 326
Continuum, 225, 384, 386, 388, 391, 440
four-dimensional, 673
Copy theory, 57, 59, 69, 82, 238
Correspondence theory, 265 *f.*
Cosmology, 12, 13, 235, 296, 297
and see Metaphysics, Materialism, Idealism, Dualism, *and* Positivism
Cosmos, *see* Universe
Creative:
evolution, 448, 453, 454
God, 78, 521, 537
imagination, 449, 453, 454, 479
power, 536
Cumulativeness, 395, 396, 406

D

Death, 92, 94, 405, 541
Deduction, 20, 22, 25, 35, 47
categorial, 274, 654, 655
Deity, 438, 536, 664
and see God
Democracy, 127, 159, 162, 164, 566, 571, 579 *ff.*, 581 *f.*
as capitalism, 621, 628
as liberalism, 618 *ff.*
as parliamentarianism, 613 *ff.*
under fire, 645
Derivatives, higher, 459, 464, 499, 507
Dictatorship:
fascistic and communistic, 628
limited, 616 *f.*
Dimension:
fourth, 287, 298, 382 *ff.*, 390, 392
of the self, 153
Dimensionality, 592, 594, 596
negative, 666
Disproof, 32, 33, 173
Dissipation of energy, 119
and see Law of Thermodynamics
Distribution, 162 *f.*
under capitalism, 624
under dual economy, 640
Doppler effect, 341, 342

Dreams, 88, 249, 424
Dualism:
 economic, 165, 628 *ff.*
 educational, 606 *ff.*
 epistemological, 57 *f.*, 75, 81, 82, 239, 254, 272, 298, 413
 ethical, 166
 metaphysical, 79, 80, 82 *f.*, 93, 96 *f.*, 427, 442, 495, 506
Duration:
 and eternity, 546
 and growth, 395
Durée réelle, 98, 106, 122, 412, 413, 414, 416, 509, 668

E

Education, 160
 two levels of, 606 *ff.*
Ego, large or small, 156, 601
 and see Self
Egocentric predicament, 236, 238, 243
Egoism, 584 *f.*
Eirenicon, epistemological, 76
Élan vital, 447
Electrodynamics, 325
Electrons:
 as four-dimensional displacements, 325, 402 *f.*, 674
 in squirm theory, 350 *ff.*
Emotion:
 cosmic, 112
 esthetic, 131, 138
 objectified in art, 562
Empiricism, 42 *f.*, 48, 205, 218, 269
 radical, 651
 ultra-, 211 *f.*, 218 *f.*
Encasement theory, 672
Energy:
 and sensation, 404 *f.*, 502, 505, 669
 concentration of, 432, 435 *f.*
 conservation of, 120, 466, 495, 496
 dissipation of, 119
 forms, 107
 kinetic, 56, 103, 106, 404, 416, 430, 434, 497, 498, 499, 667
 life as mode of, 673
 mind as form of, 102, 108 *f.*, 473 *f.*, 482 *ff.*, 503 *ff.*, 675
 patterns, 67, 105, 436
Energy (*Cont.*):
 potential or intensive, 56, 102, 104, 106, 107, 109, 122, 406, 415, 416, 430, 431, 463, 466, 468, 484, 496 *f.*, 498, 499 *ff.*, 503 *ff.*, 667, 673
 radiant, 291, 327, 339
 system, 106
 transformation of, 473, 475, 480, 484, 505
 types of, 104
Entelechy, 101, 427, 443
Entropy, 120, 294, 431, 432, 433, 539
Epigenesis, 673
Epiphenomenalism, 244, 466, 495, 502
Epistemology, 15
 four types of, 52 *ff.*
 relation to metaphysics, 81 *f.*, 83
 and see Dualism, Realism, Relativism, *and* Subjectivism
Erg, 291
Error, 252, 266, 270, 672
 problem of, 249 *ff.*
Essences, 238, 254, 263, 272 *f.*, 275, 439, 533, 534, 535, 664
 and see Universals
Esthetic:
 emotion, 138
 experience, 124, 131
 value, 127
 versus hedonic, 132, 133
Esthetics, 14
 theories of, 126
Eternal:
 ideals, 546
 order, 554
Ether, 205, 283, 285, 301, 302, 310, 312, 402, 406
Ethics:
 and democracy, 612
 applied, 166
 Christian, 517 *f.*, 575, 578, 581
 for pragmatism, 244
 individual, 140 *ff.*
 Nietzschean, 576 *f.*, 581
 of greatest happiness, 591, 596
 of the good, 148 *f.*, 154 *f.*
 of the right, 145, 154 *f.*

Ethics (*Cont.*):
problem of, 600
Promethean, 529
social, 157 *ff.*
solipsistic, 585 *f.*
versus religion, 652
Evil:
as illusion, 114
as thwarted self-interest, 568, 575, 601
intensity of, 605
problem of, 113 *f.*, 663
reduction of, 166, 604
Evolution, 121, 123, 129, 424, 445, 486, 538, 567, 572
cosmic, 415, 665
creative, 448, 453, 454
emergent, 415, 418, 425, 426, 427, 429
of conscience, 513 *f.*
of happiness, 621
Existence:
and subsistence, 54, 238, 272 *ff.*, 278, 439, 533
and value, 652
for logic, 36
for mathematics, 195
mental, 82
of God, 478
struggle for, 621
struggle for, of essences, 664
Experience:
as perception, 84
esthetic, 124, 128
permanent possibility of, 86, 593

F

Faith:
animal, 258
of religion, 171
Fascism, 280
Fabian, 165, 280, 627
optional, 645
Finite:
age of universe, 121
being, 112
God, 117
space, 288, 400
universe, 288, 326
Force, 304, 313, 325, 326, 444, 453, 455, 469, 497 *f.*, 506
centrifugal, 317, 321
field of, 313, 319, 321, 469, 670, 673
magnetic, 350 *ff.*, 402
Freedom:
achievement of, 642
under elective dictatorship, 617

G

Geometry:
algebra of, 326
analytic, 289
and physics, 324
Lobachewskian, 298
non-Euclidian, 289
of four dimensions, 398
of mechanics, 326
of the Good Life, 600 *ff.*
Riemannian, 283, 325
Germ plasm, 447, 448, 451, 453, 454 *f.*, 456 *f.*, 458, 462, 479
Gestalt, 429, 483
God:
Christian, 526
creative, 78, 521
Father and Son, 536
finite, 117, 123, 652, 664, 665
good, 113 *f.*, 115, 280
immanent, 535
mystic's, 146
not absolute, 655
omnipotent, 113 *ff.*, 280, 521 *f.*
omniscient, 535
self-creative, 537
Golden Mean, 129, 606
Good:
as fulfillment, 587
as greatest happiness, 151, 152
as self-interest, 568
concentration of, 166 *f.*, 604, 605 *f.*
degrees of, 601
ethics of, 148 *f.*
life, 600 *ff.*, 663
multiplication of, 166
of happiness, 597
pleasure as, 153
problem of, 119, 663

Good (*Cont.*):
  versus truth, 48, 245, 554 *f.*, 585
  and see Value
Growth:
  and duration, 395
  life as, 600
  principle of, 534, 654

H

Happiness:
  and conscience, 519
  and virtue, 593 *f.*
  as an end, 529
  as fulfillment, 663
  good of, 597
  grades of, 152 *f.*, 590, 595 *f.*
  greatest, 151, 588
  permanent possibility of, 154, 594
Hedonism and Hedonic, 129, 134, 155, 584, 586 *f.*, 588, 598
Heredity, 441, 454 *ff.*
Hierarchy:
  logical, 535
  of growth, 534
  of life, 419 *ff.*, 434 *ff.*
  of intensive or potential energies, 673
  of substances, 415 *f.*
  of super-forces, 460, 464, 479
  of virtues, 590
Humanism, 554 *f.*
Hylosis, 487 *f.*, 489
Hypersphere, 287, 289, 320, 400, 406, 407, 674
Hypo-space, 666

I

Idealism:
  ethical, 620
  metaphysical, 80, 81, 86 *f.*, 94 *f.*, 231, 236, 237, 240, 244, 256, 407, 466, 485, 491, 554, 655, 658
Ideals, 279, 491, 492, 493, 523, 546, 566, 586
  actualization of, 619 *ff.*, 646
  efficacy of, 618
  Platonic, 481
Ideas:
  Platonic, 272
  and see Essences *and* Universals
Imagination, 33, 42, 88 *f.*, 132, 213, 449, 451, 452, 481
  creative, 449, 453, 454, 479
Immortality, 405 f., 540 *ff.*, 675
  racial, 545
  vicarious, 546 *f.*
Imperative:
  categorical, 143 *f.*, 148
  hypothetical, 143 *f.*, 148
Individualism, 162, 610
Induction, 17, 20, 173 *ff.*
  imperfect, 175 *f.*
  perfect, 174, 175
Infinite:
  aggregate, 193
  beauty, 538
  God, 117, 123
  mass, 322
  plurality, 220
  series, 208
  series of dates, 385
  slowness, 471, 474
  speed, 474
  time, 287
  value, 117
Instrumentalism, 232, 233, 439
Insurance, for distributing evil, 604
Intensive energies, *see* Energy, potential
Intuitionism, 41 *f.*, 45 *f.*, 145, 147, 148, 151, 153, 205, 589, 591, 592, 599

J

Judgment:
  and desire, 553
  and truth, 263 *ff.*, 551
  esthetic, 128
  possible, 265
  two aspects of, 264
  and see Error *and* Truth

K

Kalology, 13
Katabolism, 120, 121, 422

Knowledge:
- about, 62, 63
- and ways of knowing, 7
- by acquaintance, 62, 63, 183
- conceptual, 52 *ff*., 69, 70
- copy theory of, 57, 59, 69, 82, 238
- correspondence theory, 265 *ff*., 269
- disjunctive, 186
- higher level of, 609
- monistic theories of, 58, 71, 404, 406, 416, 444
- of possibility, 186
- perceptual, 62 *ff*., 70
- presentative theory of, 485
- problem of, 7 *f*., 15, 235
- sources of, 38 *ff*.
- utilizable, 411
- verifiable, 86
- wheel of, 8 *ff*.
- *and see* Epistemology, Dualism, Realism, Relativism, Subjectivism, Truth, *and* Objects

Kratocracy, 159

L

Laws:
- abstract, 218, 219
- Fechner's, 473
- kinds of, 79
- Newtonian, 324
- of association, 477
- of atoms, 90
- of capitalist economy, 625
- of classical physics, 291
- of diminishing returns, 602
- of increasing returns, 166, 600, 602, 603, 606, 608, 609, 610, 611
- of nature, 49, 78, 95
- of physical science, 9
- of relativity, 365
- of space and number, 217
- of Thermodynamics, 120, 284, 431
- of vectors, 451 *f*.
- uniform, 479
- versus chance, 293
- Weber's, 379, 472

Liberalism, 618, 619, 620

Life:
- and environment, 433 *f*.
- and mind, 48
- animal, 420 *f*., 423, 435
- as growth, 600
- evolution of, 105 *f*.
- good, 600 *ff*., 663
- human, 423, 457 *f*.
- levels of, 419
- mystery of, 672
- plant, 420, 423, 435
- versus matter, 427

Light:
- as an absolute, 299, 321
- corpuscular theory of, 313, 341, 348
- intensity of, 328
- relativity theory of, 298 *ff*., 390
- squirm theory of, 347 *f*.
- undulatory theory of, 349
- velocity of, 286, 288, 298 *f*., 302, 342
  - independent of observer, 302
  - independent of velocity of source, 299, 312, 313

Logic:
- altruistic, 584
- deductive, 20, 22, 25
- formal, 8, 18 *ff*.
- inductive, 20 *f*., 31, 173 *ff*.
- material, 8, 38 *ff*., 203
- symbolic, 29
- voluntaristic, 555

Logos, 216, 536, 537, 538, 664

Lottery for concentrating of good, 604, 605 *f*.

M

Macrocosm, 439
- and microcosm, 667
- dualistic theory of, 82 *f*.
- idealistic theory of, 86 *f*.
- materialistic theory of, 89 *f*.
- positivistic theory of, 83 *f*.
- *and see* Universe

Mass, 102, 106, 108, 353, 454, 499

Materialism and Mechanism, 66, 80, 89 *ff*., 93, 95 *f*., 100, 101, 117, 119, 406, 419, 426, 427, 465, 479, 483, 484, 543

Materialism and Mechanism (*Cont.*)
  animistic, 675
Mathematics, 8, 47, 124, 278
  and see Algebra, Geometry, *and* Number
Matter:
  as four-dimensional extensions, 402 *f.*, 674
  ultimate particles of, 102, 349 *ff.*, 533, 542
  versus God, 117
  versus mind, 79, 109, 414
Mechanics, 455
  geometry of, 326
Mechanistic, 78, 106
  and see Materialism
Memory, 67, 107, 122, 213, 371 *ff.*, 397, 415, 416, 421 *f.*, 423, 424, 426, 468, 469, 475, 481, 491, 513, 668, 670
Metaphysics, 8, 10
  dualistic, 78, 80, 82 *f.*, 93, 96 *f.*, 427, 442, 495, 506
  first problem of, 77, 102
  idealistic, 86 *f.* (*and see* Idealism)
  materialistic, 89 *f.*, 95 *f.* (*and see* Materialism)
  of the macrocosm, 82 *f.*, 86 *f.*, 89 *f.*
  of the microcosm, 95 *f.*
  positivistic, 81, 83 *f.* (*and see* Positivism)
  relation to epistemology, 81 *f.*, 83
Methods:
  of disproof, 32
  of induction, 177 *ff.*, 236
  of philosophy, 5
Microcosm:
  and macrocosm, 667
  dualistic theory of, 96
  materialistic theory of, 95
Might versus right, 161, 280, 511, 521, 522, 528, 652
Militarism sublimated, 644 *f.*
Mind:
  and anabolism, 122
  and body, 79, 95 *f.*, 99, 406, 486, 541 *f.*, 544, 665
  and brain, 293, 671
  and death, 94
Mind (*Cont.*):
  and life, 106, 480
  and matter, 79, 109, 414
  as form of energy, 102, 108 *f.*, 404 *f.*, 482 *ff.*, 503 *ff.*, 669 *f.*, 673 *ff.*
  cosmic, 122, 478, 664
  hallmarks of, 107
  nature of, 482
  social, 157
Monads, 83, 274
Monism:
  epistemological, 58, 71, 298, 404, 406, 416, 444
  materialistic, 483
  prejudice in favor of, 636
  and see Materialism *and* Idealism
Monotheism, 112
Morality, master and slave, 575
Motion:
  absolute, 310, 319, 341, 342, 395, 396, 397
  actual and potential, 419
  duration as, 395, 397
  for relativity theory, 287, 288, 289, 306 *ff.*, 309 *ff.*
  in time, 393
  intra-relative, 319, 320, 322, 395
  negative, 471
  of space system, 399
  and see Velocity
Mutations, 448
Mysticism, 41 *f.*, 45 *f.*, 205, 211, 212, 270, 545

N

Naturalism:
  as materialism, 90
  of Dewey, 81
Natural selection, 442
Nature:
  and the Ways of Being, 77 *ff.*
  in relation to value, 17, 110
  knowledge in relation to, 52 *ff.*
  uniformity of, 22, 186, 188
Negative:
  curvature, 298
  dimensionality, 666
  motion, 471
  premises and conclusions, 27 *f.*

Negative (*Cont.*):
propositions in induction, 178
results of Michelson-Morley experiment, 301, 312, 313
values, 138, 166, 602, 606
Negativität, 534, 535, 654
Nominalism, 491, 493
Non-being, 208 *f.*, 218
Numbers:
complex, 502
imaginary, 501 *f.*
objectivity of, 656
ordinal and cardinal, 396
prime, 656, 657
subsistence of, 535
transfinite, 189

O

Objectivism:
epistemological, 54, 75
in esthetics, 124, 131
relativistic, 247 *f.*, 256
and see Realism
Objects:
abstract, 222
as experiences, 84, 240
as history of events, 391
conceptual, 52 *ff.*, 235, 238, 279
illusory, 245, 247 *ff.*, 661
imaginary, 36
independent of experience, 57, 236 *ff.*
knowable, 44
of desire, 556, 557
of dreams, 552
perceptual, 236 *f.*, 239, 243, 248, 250, 255, 270
real, 53, 249 *f.*
sensory, 408
thinkable, 54
unreal, 16, 54, 74, 249 *f.*, 265
Ontology, 11, 13, 235
Orthogenesis, 447, 454

P

Paleontology, 541
Pan-psychism, 293, 654
Pantheism, 111 *f.*, 115, 232
Paradox:
of quantum theory, 340 *ff.*
of relativity, 307 *f.*
of starvation, 163
Perfectionism, 155
Personalism, 231, 232
Pessimism, 567, 652
Petitio principii, 29
Phenomenalism, 324, 397, 483, 663
and see Positivism
Philosophy:
and art, 4 *f.*
and religion, 3 *f.*, 171, 546
and science, 5 *f.*, 50, 234, 295, 296, 658
and skepticism, 50
and theology, 618
and vision, 382
divisions of, 6 *f.*
traditional, 478
Physics, 9, 281, 295, 327, 441, 442, 466, 542, 543, 544
and geometry, 324
new, 283 *ff.*
Physiology, 67, 541, 543
Piety, anarchistic, 529 *f.*
Pleasure:
and beauty, 127, 133, 556 *f.*
as good, 153, 585, 586
grades of, 591
objectified, 138, 557, 560
permanent possibility of, 126, 557
Pleon, 654 *f.*, 675
Pluralism, 232, 244, 427, 562, 571, 655
Plutocracy, 159
Polytheism, 111, 116
Positivism, 71 *f.*, 80, 83 *ff.*, 94, 183, 397, 408, 410, 411, 444, 593, 663
Possibilities:
knowledge of, 186
of pleasure, 126
permanent, of experience, 86, 593
permanent, of happiness, 154, 594
permanent, of pleasure, 126, 557
Possible:
and actual, 275
and compossible, 267
cosmos, 383

Possibles, subsistent, 664
Potential, *see* Energy
Potentiality, 408, 409, 411, 412, 592, 593
Pragmatism, 43 *f.*, 48 *f.*, 205, 232, 233, 241, 244, 260, 270, 550 *f.*, 586, 651
Predicament, egocentric, 236, 237, 238, 243
Preformation, 673
Probability, 184 *ff.*, 410, 432
  principle of, 186
Problem:
  in deduction, 28, 29
  in induction, 22, 31
  of error, 249 *ff.*
  of ethics, 600
  of evil, 113 *f.*, 663
  of good, 119, 663
  of knowledge, 7 *f.*, 15, 235
  of metaphysics, 77, 102
  of theology, 123
Production, 164
  under Capitalism, 624
  under dual economy, 640
Proof:
  and vision, 382
  theory of, 34
  two sorts of, 20, 173
Protons:
  as four-dimensional displacements, 325, 402 *f.*, 674
  in squirm theory, 350 *ff.*
Protoplasm, 9, 105, 430, 432, 435, 441, 463, 465, 479
Prudence, 141, 148 *f.*, 150
Psychodynamics, 413
Psychology, 10, 427, 441, 442, 465, 541
Psychophysical, 95, 255
  parallelism, 452, 465, 480, 485, 495, 508
  problem, 485, 486, 494, 496, 505, 649, 671
Psychosis, 482 *f.*, 489, 492, 493

Q

Qualities:
  and quantity, 488, 494, 596
  and relations, 59
Qualities (*Cont.*):
  of life, 546
  primary, 65, 474
  secondary, 65, 66, 474, 494, 506
  tertiary, 507
Quantum theory, 284, 290 *ff.*, 327 *ff.*, 359, 542

R

Rainbow Series, 192 *f.*, 197
Rationalism, 42 *f.*, 47 *f.*, 124, 205, 269, 408, 410
  ultra-, 206 *f.*, 218 *f.*
Realism:
  and idealism, 240, 244
  and pragmatism, 241, 244
  critical, 233, 248, 252 *ff.*
  dualistic, 257, 259, 659
  existential, 235 *f.*
  naïve, 65
  new, 233 *ff.*, 485, 660
  presentative, 235, 659
  Scottish, 230
  subsistential, 235, 275 *f.*, 279
  Thomistic, 230
  and see Objectivism
Reality:
  and appearance, 15 *f.*, 71
  and truth, 58, 74, 265
  as experiences, 74, 83
  of abstractions, 222
  of perceived objects, 236 *f.*, 243, 248, 250, 255, 270
  of substance, 408, 409, 411, 412, 414 *f.*, 653
  spiritual, 654
  ultimate, 87
Reason:
  and proof, 19, 34
  and sense, 206, 220 *ff.*, 595
  evolution of, 513 *f.*
  and see Rationalism
Reciprocals of motion, 484
Re-creation:
  of causes, 56
  of the past, 55
Reductio ad absurdum, 174, 180, 305
Relations:
  and qualities, 59
  between classes, 18

Relations (*Cont.*):
between experiences, 85
cognitive, 235, 244
external, 60, 91
internal, 240
mathematical, 326
temporal and spatial, 419
Relativism, 71 *f.*, 75, 81, 83, 241, 568 *f.*
objective, 247 *ff.*
Relativity:
law of, 365
of motion, 302
of space and time, 286 *f.*, 297, 384, 390
selective, 672
theory, 284, 542, 673
general theory, 324 *ff.*
special theory, 286, 297 *ff.*, 342, 390, 400, 662, 674
Religion:
and philosophy, 3 *f.*, 171, 546
and theology, 573
as an institution, 160
atheistic, 646
definition of, 512
drives to, 665
Nietzschean, 572
Promethean, 511 *ff.*, 529
theistic, 81
versus ethics, 652
vision of, 3
Rest, degrees of, 471
Revolution:
in art, 127
industrial, 162, 621 *ff.*
in physics, 284 *f.*, 314
in religion, 527, 530
Right:
ethics of, 145 *f.*, 154
versus might, 161, 280, 511, 521, 522, 528, 652
Rigorism, 145, 651

S

Science:
and deduction, 47
and materialism, 101
and philosophy, 5 *f.*, 295, 296
mature and immature, 43
Science (*Cont.*):
mechanistic, 543
modern, 91
social, 543
and see Biology, Botany, Chemistry, Physics, Physiology, *and* Relativity theory
Selection, natural, 442, 446, 447, 448
Selective relativity, 672
Self:
Absolute, 94
future, 585
kinds of, 570
larger, 585, 601
of the moment, 157
and see Ego
Self-determination, 106, 109
Sense and reason, 206, 220 *ff.*, 595
Senses, higher and lower, 134 *ff.*
Series:
arithmetic, 473
geometric, 473
Rainbow, 192 *f.*, 197
unsummed, 657
Skepticism, 44, 49 *f.*, 206 *f.*, 256, 258
Socialism, 579
Bolshevistic, 626
Fabian, 165, 626
national, 164
Sociology, 10, 213
Solipsism, 585
Soul, 407, 415, 482, 668, 675
world, 538
Sources of knowledge or belief, 38, 203
Space:
absolute, 319, 320
as basic concept, 454
awareness of, 64
compared with time, 384, 385 *ff.*, 388, 393, 399, 406, 414
constitution of, 225
curved, 402
divisions of, 221
Euclidean, 283
finite, 287, 400
four-dimensional, 298, 325, 382 *ff.*
hypo-, 666
in Einstein theory, 287 *ff.*, 297 *f.*, 309 *f.*, 325

Space (*Cont.*):
in relation to life, 106
in relation to mind, 414, 495 *f.*, 503
Kantian, 661
Lobachewskian, 298
nature of, 221 *ff.*
of perception, 239, 251
private and public, 661
relativity of, 287, 384
Riemannian, 276, 283
Specious past and future, 492
Specious present, 246, 363, 367, 370, 372, 376, 378, 379, 381, 396, 668
Stoicism, 145, 147, 148, 525
Subconscious, 476
Subjectivism, 54 *f.*, 75, 81, 86, 126 *f.*, 140, 240, 586
Subsistence, 254, 271, 533, 535
and existence, 54, 238, 272 *ff.*, 278, 439, 533
components of, 271
of the possible, 664
relation to ethics, 279
structure of, 275 *f.*
and see Essences *and* Universals
Substance:
mental and material, 83 *f.*
psychic, 153, 255, 663
reality of, 408, 409, 411, 412, 414 *f.*, 653
spiritual, 601
Sufficient Reason, Principle of, 275
Suggestibility, 141, 513
Super-forces, 444, 451, 454 *ff.*, 458, 460, 463, 467
Superman, 572
Sweepstake Theory, 342 *f.*
Syllogisms:
archetypal, 176
Aristotelian, 23
disjunctive, 173
four kinds of, 24
rules of, 27 *f.*
valid, 26
Symbolic logic, 29
Sympathy, 141, 149 *ff.*, 513, 585
Systems:
energy, 106, 476
Systems (*Cont.*):
hierarchy of, 103
mechanistic, 78
of memories, 108
vector, 453
vital, 106

T

Taboos, 515, 524, 529, 600
Teleology, 78, 80, 91, 92, 106, 107, 443, 446 *ff.*, 450, 467, 468, 480, 492, 493, 494, 504
Telogenesis, 446, 448, 449, 450, 453, 467, 468, 480
Temporalism, 253
Theism, 81, 110, 111, 113, 115, 116, 261, 454, 663
Theology, 17, 50, 110 *f.*, 123, 292, 293, 573, 618
Thermodynamics, laws of, 120, 284, 431
Time:
and space, 385 *ff.*, 393, 399, 406, 414
as basic concept, 454
as fourth dimension, 298, 392, 415
as movement in higher dimension, 393, 399
compared with space, 384 *f.*
constitution of, 225
divisions of, 221
extension in, 467, 468, 472, 491, 493, 670
infinite, 287
in relation to mind, 414
in relativity theory, 287 *ff.*, 297, 303 *f.*, 309 *f.*
of awareness, 64
of conception, 55
of perception, 239, 363 *ff.*
passage, 368, 391, 673, 675
perception, 363 *ff.*
relativity of, 287, 384
two problems of, 394
Timocracy, 159
Transfinites:
Cantorian, 189, 194
logarithmic, 193
Trinity, 531 *ff.*, 537

Truth:
  and judgment, 263 *ff.*, 551
  and reality, 58, 74, 265
  as coherence, 265 *ff.*, 269
  as correspondence, 265 *ff.*, 269
  criteria of, 203
  for pragmatism, 241
  for religion, 3
  for science, 6
  meaning of, 264
  objective, 242
  subsistential and existential, 263 *ff.*
  versus value, 48, 245, 553, 585
Truths of ethics, 619
Tychism, 652

U

Ugly, 127
Uniformity of nature, 22, 186, 188
Universals, 235, 238, 262 *f.*, 271, 272, 489, 490, 491
  and see Essences *and* Subsistence
Universe, 120, 122, 274, 286 *ff.*, 308, 311
  block, 232
  finite, 276, 283, 288, 325, 326, 400,
  of discourse, 36
  possible, 383 *ff.*
  and see Macrocosm
Unreal objects, 16, 54, 74, 249 *f.*, 265
Utilitarianism, 148 *f.*, 151 *ff.*, 584, 586, 588 *ff.*

V

Value:
  absolute, 546
  and existence, 652
  as power, 567
  as relative, 245
  as what is liked, 13, 140
  Christian, 576
  concentration and diffusion of, 166, 610
  esthetic, 112, 127, 135, 560
Value (*Cont.*):
  infinite, 117
  in relation to life, 550
  in relation to nature, 17, 110
  intrinsic and instrumental, 13
  moral, 153, 513 *ff.*
  negative, 138, 166, 602, 606
  past, present, and future, 587
  Platonic, 171
  primary and secondary, 152, 158
  realization of, 558
  sensory and non-sensory, 14
  theory of, 14
  transvaluation of, 566
  versus truth, 48, 245, 553, 585
  and see Good
Variation, 441, 447 *ff.*, 479
Vectors, 451 *f.*, 453
Velocity:
  derivatives of, 499, 507
  infinite, 474
  internal, 334, 338, 347, 348, 356
  negative, 471
  of fields of force, 313
  of light, 286, 298 *f.*, 302, 342
  of moving bodies, 300 *f.*, 307, 313, 454
  through ether, 284 *f.*
Virtue, 145
  and happiness, 593 *f.*
Vision, 36, 42, 171 *f.*, 382
Vitalism, 96, 427, 442, 443, 445, 446, 454, 465, 466, 479

W

Ways:
  of being, 6, 8, 77 *f.*, 93 *f.*
  of knowing, 6, 7, 18 *f.*, 38 *f.*
  of liking, 6, 13, 124 *f.*, 140 *f.*
Wheel of Knowledge, 8 *ff.*
Will:
  freedom of, 478
  to power, 566, 567, 571
Workers:
  the buyers, 609, 624
  under dual economy, 640 *f.*